A SOCIAL SCIENCE BIBLIOGRAPHY OF NORTHERN IRELAND 1945-1983

Material published since 1945

relating to Northern Ireland since 1921

COMPILED BY:

BILL ROLSTON
MIKE TOMLINSON
LIAM O'DOWD
BOB MILLER
JIM SMYTH

The Queen's University, Belfast
1983

British Library Cataloguing in Publication data:

A Social science bibliography of Northern Ireland
    1945-1983.
    1. Social sciences - Northern Ireland -
Bibliography
I. Rolston, Bill
    016.3   Z7161.A15

    ISBN   0-85389-228-8
    ISBN   0-85389-229-6   Pbk

First Published 1983

Printed in Northern Ireland by the Print Workshop

Enquiries concerning omissions, errors and any other aspect
of this project should be addressed to:

Bill Rolston   Mike Tomlinson
Dept of Sociology and   Dept of Social Studies
Social Policy   OR   Queen's University
Ulster Polytechnic   Belfast BT7 1NN
Jordanstown
Co. Antrim BT37 0QB

The Bibliography may be ordered from the Distributor:

            THE UNIVERSITY BOOKSHOP
            UNIVERSITY ROAD
            BELFAST
            NORTHERN IRELAND

A SOCIAL SCIENCE BIBLIOGRAPHY OF NORTHERN IRELAND 1945-1983

TABLE OF CONTENTS

TABLE OF CONTENTS (continued)

PREFACE

We would like to thank Queen's University, Belfast, for financially supporting the publication of this bibliography and the Committee for Social Science Research in Ireland for grant-aid in the early stages of the project.

The computerisation owes much to the help and the inspiration of Lawrence Asquith and other staff in Computer Services at the Ulster Polytechnic. Thanks are also due to Jim McClean and other staff of Queen's University Computer Centre. Professor John Whyte gave us considerable support and made many useful suggestions. Mr Michael Henry and Mr Gordon Wheeler of Queen's University Library, staff at the Linenhall Library and the Irish section of Belfast Central Library, Paddy Brannigan, Professor Alfred McClung Lee and Professor Roy Wallis provided help and/or information at various stages. Finally, we are very grateful to all our colleagues in the Social Science departments of Queen's University, the Ulster Polytechnic and elsewhere who supplied citations and/or commented on drafts of the bibliography.

Mike Tomlinson
Liam O'Dowd
Bob Miller
Jim Smyth
Department of Social Studies
Queen's University
Belfast

Bill Rolston
Department of Sociology
and Social Policy
Ulster Polytechnic
Jordanstown

Belfast, July 1983.

ERRATA

Delete the following duplicates:
2263, 2784, 2980, 3308, 3349, 5190

In entry 2252, the author should read "Mitchel,N C"

The following entries have been coded under the wrong topic.
The correct topics are listed below:
1239-1240: Specific Economic Analysis; 2157: Specific Political
Analysis; 2413: Religion; 2480: Political Parties; 2536:
General Political Analysis; 2629: Labour/Employment; 5419-5420:
General Histories; 5492: Bibliographies.

The following entries should be included under (Edited) Books:

BRIDGES,G; BLUNT,R (EDS)
SILVER LININGS
LAWRENCE AND WISHART
LONDON
1981

ROLING,B (ED)
STUDIES IN PEACE RESEARCH (1)
ROYAL VAN GORCUM
ASSEN
1968

STUCHLIK,M (ED)
THE QUEEN'S UNIVERSITY PAPERS IN SOCIAL
ANTHROPOLOGY: VOL. 2 - GOALS AND
BEHAVIOUR
QUEEN'S UNIVERSITY
BELFAST
1977

INTRODUCTION

The amount of political and social commentary on Northern
Ireland - NI- has now assumed vast proportions. Much of this
literature is scattered throughout a large number of
international publications, making it relatively inaccessible
to students and researchers. Existing bibliographies tend to be
either specialised or related exclusively to the recent
"troubles". This bibliography attempts to go beyond existing
work, both in terms of scale and range of subjects covered.
It includes material published since 1945 which deals with the
period since 1921.

Entitled a "Social Science" Bibliography, social science has
been defined very broadly to include the following disciplines:
politics, sociology, economics, geography, education,
psychology, medico-social research, socio-legal studies, social
administration, demography, anthropology, urban (rural) studies,
and general history. A wide range of unpublished material
is included, notably social science dissertations and theses on
NI and a variety of conference and seminar papers.

Much of the material included falls outside a strictly academic
definition, although it is likely to be of interest to academic
researchers. A wide selection of government publications,
political pamphlets, other pamphlets and occasional papers, and
substantial journalistic articles (excluding newspaper
articles) is included. Creative literature has been excluded,
although a small number of social scientific analyses of
literature is included. Archaeology, folklore, local studies,
and planning in a purely technical sense are not covered,
except where these subjects seem to have broad interest to
social scientists.

No bibliography which seeks to bridge the gap between general
and specialised interests can claim to be fully comprehensive
or error-free. Furthermore, the ever-increasing pace of
publication of new material renders bibliographic exercises
quickly out of date. To help alleviate these problems, this
bibliography has been computerised using the FAMULUS programme,
which is specially designed for the compilation and management
of bibliographies. The main advantages of computerisation are,
firstly, the ease of management of a large data base (including
search facilities) and, secondly, the assistance provided in
periodic and systematic up-dating of the data. It will be
possible, therefore, to produce supplements to this
bibliography which can include not only new publications,
but also omissions in the present publication and
corrections to any inaccurate entries that may have escaped our
notice. Perhaps the scale of the up-dating problem can be
gauged from the fact that we have included circa three hundred
items published between January and June 1983. Even so, we do
not claim the same degree of comprehensiveness for the first
half of 1983 as we do for the previous period.

Organisation and Presentation

Entries are numbered consecutively, but are arranged
alphabetically (1) under twenty seven different headings. Each
entry takes the following form:

> Author(s)
> Title
> Publisher/Source (Source may refer to a journal or
>   edited book, for example)
> City of Publication (In the case of lesser known
>   journals, city is indicated where available)
> Date of Publication/Troubles-related code/Form of
>   Publication code

The single digit (Troubles-related) code after the date of
publication ranges from 1 to 3, as follows:

> 1. directly related to the "troubles" (that is, the NI
>   conflict since 1968)
> 2. not directly related to the "troubles"
> 3. unknown.

The second (double digit) code refers to form of publication,
as follows:

> 01   Journal article (includes magazine articles)
> 02   Book
> 03   Government publication
> 04   Thesis/Dissertation
> 05   Bibliography and/or discussion of a bibliography
> 06   Chronology
> 07   Article, section or chapter of a book (generally
>   an edited book)
> 08   Unpublished paper
> 09   Political pamphlet
> 10   Other pamphlet and other forms of publication
>   (excluding conference papers)
> 11   Conference papers
> 99   Unknown

---

1. The alphabetising conventions used in the bibliography are
   those of the FAMULUS bibliographical programme and differ
   significantly from conventional library practice. For
   example, "Mc" and "Mac" are alphabetised literally and "O'"
   precedes "O" followed by any other letter. Thus, "O'Riordan"
   precedes "Oakley". The subject index does follow
   conventional library usage, however.

Journal or Magazine Articles

Only articles of two pages or more are included. There is a
bias towards including American magazines due to the use of the
DIALOG bibliographical system (see below), which was one of the
major bases of the bibliography. Despite their obvious
importance, local and national newspapers, and the independent
Belfast magazine Fortnight, are excluded for reasons of
manageability and the existing ease of access to these sources.
The major opinion polls undertaken by Fortnight have been
included.

Government Publications

This category includes the following:
>   a. Belfast HMSO Command Papers on socially relevant
>   topics
>   b. Similar London HMSO Command Papers relating to NI
>   c. Reports of Government agencies, advisory bodies and
>   departments.

In the case of (c) emphasis was placed on reports produced for
public readership rather than on internal publications. Annual
reports, Census publications, Digests of Statistics and the
Ulster Yearbook are excluded.

Dissertations/Theses

Postgraduate (at the Master's level and above) dissertations/
theses are included. Work completed (outside North America) in
partial fulfillment of degree requirements is largely excluded.

Political/Other Pamphlets

We do not claim comprehensive coverage of the large numbers of
political pamphlets produced in NI, especially since 1968. We
have drawn, however, on the most complete collections of these
publications in NI. The major political parties and most of the
minor political groupings are represented. We have also
included the occasional papers of a wide variety of pressure
groups and institutions such as the Churches and voluntary
organisations. Here again, however, we do not claim
comprehensive coverage.

Unpublished Papers

Unpublished papers such as conference papers and mimeoed
articles of limited circulation have been included, where
possible giving the institution in which the author is
employed. A range of author-published material is also included.

Chapters in (Edited) Books

In many instances we have entered and separately coded each
chapter of an edited book, where it is possible and relevant to

do so. We have also included under this heading chapters or sections from non-edited books, where the latter do not deal exclusively with NI.

Topics and Other Headings: Definitions

The basic organisation of the bibliography is by topic. The topics chosen reflect, in part, our own research interests, but the author, subject and geographical indexes will allow alternative modes of access to the material. In some cases the same entry will appear under two (but no more than two) topic headings. Definitions are as follows:

Bibliographies of NI (entries 1-89):
a list of general bibliographies, as well as those dealing with specific topics and disciplines, which include material on NI (see footnote 2).

General Histories of Ireland, including NI (entries 90-202):
a selection of histories, published since 1945, which treat NI in a general way since 1921 and which cover a substantial time period.

General Political Analyses (entries 203-1043):
analysis of, or commentary on, the broad political situation past or present.

Specific Political Commentary (entries 1044-1278):
includes biographies and autobiographies of political figures, commentary on, or reporting of, personalities, social movements and specific events not covered under any other topic.

Political System (entries 1279-1658):
includes discussion of the design and working of the civil service, local government, the electoral process (including elections), the constitution (in the sense of NI's position within the United Kingdom) and other political and administrative institutions.

Political Parties (entries 1659-1723):
discussions of the history, policies and composition of specific political parties.

2. The Centre for the Study of Conflict in the New University of Ulster in Coleraine produces surveys of research in progress and some published material at intervals. The Economic and Social Research Institute in Dublin produces annual registers of research in progress in Ireland, North and South. Of somewhat less direct relevance to the present bibliography are periodic bibliographies of published material, theses and research in progress, published in Irish Historical Studies. Occasionally relevant items appear also in History Thesis Abstracts (volumes 1 to 3) published by the Irish Committee of Historical Sciences and in the annual Irish Economic and Social History Review.

General Economic Analyses (entries 1724-2091):
analyses of the NI economy and its main sectors, that is,
agriculture, manufacturing, services and the financial system.
General discussions of the cost of living, inflation, taxation,
energy policy, regional development and economic planning are
also included.

Specific Economic Analyses (entries 2092-2347):
discussions, analyses and histories of specific firms and
industries (excluding the sectors listed in "General Economic
Analyses" above). Also included are the economies of specific
localities within NI, the retail trade and cooperatives.

Labour/Employment (entries 2348-2552):
includes trades unions, industrial relations, labour law,
labour markets and unemployment

Population (entries 2553-2643):
general demographic analyses, statistical profiles of the
population, census analysis, migration, social mobility and
occupational structure.

Urban Studies, Physical Planning and the Environment (entries
        2644-2859):
area plans, transportation planning and social aspects of the
environment (especially the built environment) in both urban
and rural areas.

Housing (entries 2860-2986):
the finances, provision, management and legislation of housing.

Poverty and Deprivation (entries 2987-3069):
refers mainly to the various forms and consequences of income
inequality.

Health and Social Welfare (entries 3070-3490):
covers analyses of legislation, social provision, and the
social distribution of sickness and disease. Also included are
general analyses of social policy, community development and
social work.

Gender and Women's Studies (entries 3491-3566):
any analysis which takes sexuality, male-female relationships,
or women alone, as its primary concern.

Children and Young People (entries 3567-3736):
discussions and analyses of childhood and adolescence (for
example, the social psychological aspects of childhood).
Entries are double-coded in the case of youth unemployment with
"Labour/Employment", and of juvenile delinquency with "Criminal
Justice System". Schools and schooling are excluded from this
category and are included under "Education" instead.

Education (entries 3737-4177):
the management, social role and consequences of the formal
education system.

Religion (entries 4178-4321):
discussions of formal religious practices, beliefs and
institutions, notably the Churches.

Protestant/Catholic Division and Sectarianism (entries 4322-4555):
discussions of the specificity of Protestant/Catholic division
in NI, notably the way in which ethnicity, nationality and
religion are intertwined to form a basic cleavage in social
identity. Also included is sectarianism, that is, the
particular representation of Protestant/Catholic division which
involves attaching negative values or prejudice to the practices
and beliefs of either side.

Insurgency/Counter-Insurgency (entries 4556-4912):
accounts or analyses of illegal, armed or violent groups or
organisations in revolt against the status quo. Also included
are analyses and discussions of the control or elimination of
illegal, armed or violent threats (for example, riots,
terrorism or rebellion) which challenge the status quo.

Criminal Justice System (entries 4913-5202):
the design and actual working of the judicial and penal system,
that is, the police, courts and prisons.

Mass Media (entries 5203-5277):
analyses of the operation and content of television, radio,
newspapers and popular magazines vis a vis Northern Ireland.

Culture and the Arts (entries 5278-5411):
social anthropological material (for example, community
studies), some folklore and social scientific analyses of
literature and the arts.

Any Other General Topic (entries 5412-5494):
includes material on a general, not easily classifiable topic,
which is not included under any of the above headings.

Any Other Specific Topic (entries 5495-5616):
includes items with a specific subject matter not included
under any other topic.

Unknown (entries 5616-5620):
a residual category with few entries, where the subject is
completely unknown to the compilers.

(Edited) Books (entries 5621-5842):
this section includes:
        a. edited books with chapter(s) on Northern Ireland,
        b. non-edited books with individual chapters or
           sections on Northern Ireland.
In the case of (a) and (b), topic, form or "troubles" codes are
not assigned. Individual chapter(s) are entered separately
under the appropriate topic and coded fully (see Guide to Use
below). In some instances, edited books are coded when they
deal exclusively with a single Northern Ireland theme and/or
where individual chapters are not listed. These books are
classified under the main topics rather than under "(Edited)
Books".

Journal Abbreviations/Index:
an alphabetical listing of all journals and journal
abbreviations which appear in the bibliography. Abbreviated
journals are defined in full, where appropriate.

Other Abbreviations:
includes an alphabetical listing of all other abbreviations

used and the full listing of the names of the organisations,
political parties, government agencies, etc. to which they
correspond. "Northern Ireland" is abbreviated to "NI"
throughout the bibliography.

Author Index:
alphabetical listing of all authors, followed by the number of
each entry in which that author's name occurs. Numbers in
brackets refer to authors cited in the "Publisher" field.

Subject Index:
this is constructed SOLELY using words or phrases found in the
"Title" field, excluding words which are found in the topic
headings, such as "Education", "Housing", "Labour/Employment".
Words occurring very frequently, such as "Northern Ireland",
"Ulster", "Belfast", "UK", "(Great) Britain", "England",
"regional development", "planning", "Catholic" and "Protestant"
are also excluded. Numbers in brackets refer to dates.

Geographical Index:
includes terms occurring in the "Title" field. Again, it
excludes "Ulster", "NI", "Belfast", "UK", "(Great) Britain"
and "England".

Sources

1. The major existing bibliographies on NI were cross checked.

2. Irish social science journals published since 1945 were
   manually checked for articles on NI.

3. Major social science journals outside Ireland were checked
   manually for relevant entries.

4. Computerised reference sources were searched for social
   science entries on NI, using keywords. These included
   BLAISE, developed in Britain, which contains entries on all
   books indexed by the British National Bibliography and the
   U.S. Library of Congress since the mid-1960s (over one and a
   half million titles). DIALOG, an American system, was also
   searched. It contains entries of all journal articles held in
   the Social Science Citation Index, Sociological Abstracts
   Index, the Education Resources Information Centre,
   Comprehensive Dissertation Abstracts, PAIS International,
   U.S. Political Science Documents, Psychological Abstracts,
   Magazine Index, Population Bibliography and Historical
   Abstracts.

5. All Irish university libraries, including those of the
   Ulster Polytechnic and the National Institute of Higher
   Education were checked for social science theses/
   dissertations relevant to NI to complement those culled from
   the International Dissertation Abstracts.

6. A number of library sources were manually checked for
   relevant entries. These included the Irish Collections in
   the Belfast Linenhall Library, Belfast Central Library,

Queen's University, Belfast and the Ulster Polytechnic. The British Humanities Index and the Irish Publication Record were also checked.

7. The bibliographies of a variety of academic books on NI were searched, as were the contents of our personal research bibliographies and collections of conference papers. Colleagues in a wide variety of disciplines in Queen's University and elsewhere were consulted.

Guide to Using the Bibliography

Example 1:

>
> Jahoda,G; Harrison,S
> Belfast Children: Some Effects of a Conflict Environment
> Ir J Psychol 3(1)
> 1975 1 01

For full journal name, see list of journal abbreviations. Here the reference is to the Irish Journal of Psychology, volume 3, number 1. The last line of the entry includes the date of publication (1975), the single-digit "troubles-related" code (in this case, 1, which means that the article is troubles-related), and the form of publication code (in this case, 01, which designates a journal article).

Example 2:

>
> Scope
> Social Policies and the Political Parties
> Scope 18
> Belfast
> 1978 2 01

This entry refers to an unsigned article (01) in the journal Scope, volume 18, published in Belfast in 1978. The article is not directly related to the "troubles" (hence, 2).

Example 3:

>
> NIEC
> Economic Assessment: April 1983
> NIEC
> Belfast
> 1983 2 03

For full author name check the list of Other Abbreviations. In this case, NIEC refers to the Northern Ireland Economic Council, which is also the publisher. Date of publication is 1983, the entry is not directly related to the "troubles" (2) and the form of publication (03) designates a government publication, as NIEC is a government agency.

Example 4:

        Whyte,J H
        How Much Discrimination Was There Under the
        Unionist Regime, 1921-1968?
        in Gallagher,T; O'Connell,J (Eds)
        Manchester
        1983 2 07

This entry refers to a chapter in an edited book (07),
published in Manchester. For full details of the source, look
for "Gallagher,T; O'Connell,J (Eds)" in the "(Edited) Books"
section at the end of the bibliography. The full reference is:

        Gallagher,T; O'Connell,J (Eds)
        Contemporary Irish Studies
        Manchester U P
        1983

"U P" refers to "University Press" (see list of Other
Abbreviations). Note that in this instance the source is not
fully coded.

Example 5:

        Schlesinger,P
        Reporting NI
        in Schlesinger,P
        London
        1977 1 07

This entry refers to a chapter on NI in a non-edited book not
exclusively concerned with NI. For the full source reference,
see "(Edited) Books" at the end of the bibliography. It is:

        Schlesinger,P
        Putting Reality Together: BBC News
        Constable
        London
        1977

1 ALLEN, K ET AL (EDS)
REGIONAL PROBLEMS AND POLICIES IN THE
EUROPEAN COMMUNITIES: A BIBLIOGRAPHY
SAXON HOUSE
FARNBOROUGH
1979

2 ANTRIM COUNTY LIBRARY
SUBJECT CATALOGUE OF BOOKS AND SOME
OTHER MATERIAL RELATING TO COUNTY ANTRIM
ANTRIM COUNTY LIBRARY
BALLYMENA
1969

3 BELFAST LIBRARY AND SOCIETY FOR
PROMOTING KNOWLEDGE
NI POLITICAL LITERATURE, 1968-72
IRISH U P
DUBLIN
1973

4 BELFAST LIBRARY AND SOCIETY FOR
PROMOTING KNOWLEDGE
NI POLITICAL LITERATURE, 1973-75
IRISH MICROFILMS
DUBLIN
1976

5 BELFAST PUBLIC LIBRARIES
NI 1920-50: A SELECTED LIST OF BOOKS AND
PAMPHLETS IN THE BELFAST PUBLIC
LIBRARIES
BELFAST PUBLIC LIBRARIES
BELFAST
1950

6 BLAXTER, L
IRISH RURAL SOCIETY: A SELECTED
BIBLIOGRAPHY 1920-1972
QUB
BELFAST
1973

7 BOTTOMLEY, P
THE ULSTER TEXTILE INDUSTRY: A CATALOGUE
OF BUSINESS RECORDS IN PRONI
HMSO
BELFAST
1979

8 BRUNT, R M
BIBLIOGRAPHY OF NI POLITICS
QUB
BELFAST
1974

9 BURRIDGE, K; REID, P
THE NORTH COAST, ANTRIM AND LONDONDERRY:
A BIBLIOGRAPHY
LONDONDERRY COUNTY LIBRARY
COLERAINE
1973

10 CAMPBELL, B M S
REGISTER OF RESEARCH IN
PROGRESS...RELATING TO HISTORICAL
GEOGRAPHY IN IRELAND
DEPT GEOG QUB
BELFAST
1978

11 CARSON, W R H
A BIBLIOGRAPHY OF PRINTED MATERIAL
RELATING TO THE COUNTY AND COUNTY
BOROUGH OF LONDONDERRY
LIBRARY ASSOCIATION
LONDON
1968

12 COLLETT, R J
NI STATISTICS: A GUIDE TO THE PRINCIPAL
SOURCES
QUB
BELFAST
1979

13 COOLAHAN, J ET AL
REGISTER OF THESES ON EDUCATIONAL TOPICS
IN UNIVERSITIES IN IRELAND
OFFICINA TYPOGRAPHICA
GALWAY
1980

14 CORNOG, D
UNCONVENTIONAL WARFARE: A BIBLIOGRAPHY
OF BIBLIOGRAPHIES
GOVERNMENT PRINTING OFFICE
WASHINGTON
1964

15 COSYNS-VERHAEGEN, R
ACTUALITE DU TERROREME: SELECTION
BIBLIOGRAPHIQUE
BRUSSELS
1973

16 CULTURAL RELATIONS COMMITTEE OF IRELAND
BOOKS ON IRELAND
NATIONAL LIBRARY OF IRELAND/SIGN OF THE
THREE CANDLES
DUBLIN
1953

17 DARBY, J
REGISTER OF RESEARCH INTO THE IRISH
CONFLICT
NICRC
BELFAST
1972

18 DARBY, J; DODGE, N; HEPBURN, A C
REGISTER OF RESEARCH INTO THE IRISH
CONFLICT, 1981
CENTRE FOR THE STUDY OF CONFLICT, NUU
COLERAINE
1981

19 DAVIES, K
BIBLIOGRAPHY OF MR T W FREEMAN'S
CONTRIBUTIONS TO THE GEOGRAPHY OF
IRELAND
IR GEOG 6(5)
1973

20 DEUTSCH, R
NI, 1921-1974: A SELECT BIBLIOGRAPHY
GARLAND
NEW YORK
1975

21 EAGER, A
A GUIDE TO IRISH BIBLIOGRAPHICAL
MATERIAL: A BIBLIOGRAPHY OF
BIBLIOGRAPHIES
LIBRARY ASSOCIATION
LONDON
1964

22 ELLIOT, J
NI: A READER'S GUIDE
LIBRARY ASSOCIATION
LONDON
1980

23 EUSTACE, J G
IRELAND: A BIBLIOGRAPHY
IN ALLEN, K ET AL (EDS)
FARNBOROUGH
1978

24 EVANS, E
THESES ON SUBJECTS RELATING TO IRELAND
PRESENTED FOR HIGHER DEGREES ...
INST IRISH STUD QUB
BELFAST
1968

25 AN FORAS FORBARTHA
URBAN AND REGIONAL RESEARCH PROJECTS IN
IRELAND: AN ANNOTATED LIST
AN FORAS FORBARTHA
DUBLIN
1974

26 FORD, V G R
NI: A SHORT BIBLIOGRAPHY OF JOURNALS,
BOOKS AND PAPERS ON GEOGRAPHICAL AND
ALLIED TOPICS
DEPT GEOG QUB
BELFAST
1966

27 FRANCIS, J P E
NI LOCAL STUDIES NO. 1
BALLYMENA AREA LIBRARY
BALLYMENA
1981

28 FRANCIS, J P E
NI LOCAL STUDIES NO. 2
BALLYMENA AREA LIBRARY
BALLYMENA
1982

29 GREER, D S (ED)
INDEX TO CASES DECIDED IN THE COURTS OF
NI 1921-70
INCORP CO LAW REPORTING
BELFAST
1975

30 GRIFFIN, W D
IRELAND, 6000 B.C. TO 1972: A CHRONOLOGY
AND FACT BOOK
OCEANA
DOBBS FERRY, NY
1973

31 HARLAND AND WOLFF, LTD.
BOOKLETS AND PAMPHLETS ON THE HISTORY
AND DEVELOPMENT OF THE COMPANY
HARLAND AND WOLFF, LTD.
BELFAST
1952

32 HAYES, R J
MANUSCRIPT SOURCES FOR THE HISTORY OF
IRISH CIVILIZATION (11 VOLUMES)
G.K. HALL
BOSTON
1965-1979

33 HEPPLE, B A; NEESON, J M; O'HIGGINS, P
A BIBLIOGRAPHY OF THE LITERATURE ON
BRITISH AND IRISH LABOUR LAW
MANSELL
LONDON
1975

34 HOBART, A E L
A LIST OF PERIODICAL REFERENCES RELATING
TO NI 1921-59
AUTHOR
1959

35 HUGHES, N
NI: PLANNING AND DEVELOPMENT
AN FORAS FORBARTHA
DUBLIN
1973

36 HUMPHREYS, A L
A HANDBOOK TO COUNTY BIBLIOGRAPHY, BEING
A BIBLIOGRAPHY OF BIBLIOGRAPHIES. . . .
DAWSONS
LONDON
1974

37 INTERNATIONAL REVIEW OF ADMINISTRATIVE
SCIENCES
ARTICLES ON PUBLIC ADMINISTRATION IN
IRELAND
INT R 34(1)
1968

38 JOANNON, P
CINQUANTE LIVRES RECANTS SUR L'IRLANDE
DU NORD
ET IRL 2
1973

39 JOANNON, P
LISTES OUVRAGES CONSACRES A L'HISTOIRE,
POLITIQUE, INSTITUTIONS... 1974-75
ET IRL 4
1975

40 JOHNSON, S
POVERTY AND INEQUALITY IN NI: A
PRELIMINARY BIBLIOGRAPHY
POLICY STUDIES INSTITUTE
LONDON
1980

41 JOHNSTON, M
IAN PAISLEY: A BIBLIOGRAPHY
COLLEGE OF LIBRARIANSHIP
ABERYSTWYTH
1977

42 JONES, J B
REGISTER OF RESEARCH INTO UNITED KINGDOM
POLITICS
STUD PUBL POL 23
GLASGOW
1978

43 MAGUIRE, M
A BIBLIOGRAPHY OF PUBLISHED WORKS ON
IRISH FOREIGN RELATIONS 1921-1978
ROYAL IRISH ACADEMY
DUBLIN
1981

44 MARTIN, G H; MCINTYRE, S
A BIBLIOGRAPHY OF BRITISH AND IRISH
MUNICIPAL HISTORY
LEICESTER U P
LEICESTER
1972

45 MCFETRIDGE, L
NI LOCAL STUDIES NO.3
BALLYMENA AREA LIBRARY
BALLYMENA
1982

46 MCKEE, J
LONDONDERRY: A BIBLIOGRAPHY
AUTHOR
1959

47 MEGAN, A K
UNION LIST OF CURRENT PERIODICALS AND
SERIALS IN NI
PUBLIC LIBRARIES
BELFAST
1966

48 MICKOLUS, E
THE LITERATURE OF TERRORISM: A
SELECTIVELY ANNOTATED BIBLIOGRAPHY
GREENWOOD PRESS
WESTPORT
1980

49 MULVEY, H
MODERN IRISH HISTORY SINCE 1940: A
BIBLIOGRAPHICAL SURVEY
IN FURBER, E C (ED)
CAMBRIDGE, MASS
1966

50 MULVEY, H
THIRTY YEARS WORK IN IRISH HISTORY:
TWENTIETH CENTURY IRELAND, 1914-70
IR HIST STUD 17
1971

Bibliographies/

51 NATIONAL BUILDING AGENCY
UNION LIST OF CURRENT PERIODICALS AND
SERIALS RELATING TO NI HOUSING EXECUTIVE
INTERESTS
NATIONAL BUILDING AGENCY
LONDON
1973

52 NATIONAL LIBRARY OF IRELAND
SELECT LIST OF BOOKS ON IRELAND
NATIONAL LIBRARY OF IRELAND
DUBLIN
1978

53 NI LIBRARY ADVISORY COUNCIL
LIST OF CURRENT PERIODICALS AND SERIALS
IN NI LIBRARIES
NI LIBRARY ADVISORY COUNCIL
BELFAST
1957

54 NIC GHIOLLA PHADRAIG,M
BIBLIOGRAPHY OF DEMOGRAPHY, HUMAN
GEOGRAPHY, MIGRATION, RURAL AND URBAN
SOCIOLOGY IN IRELAND
SOC STUD 1
MAYNOOTH
1972

55 NIC GHIOLLA PHADRAIG,M
BIBLIOGRAPHY OF SOCIO-ECONOMIC STUDIES
IN IRELAND
SOC STUD 1
MAYNOOTH
1972

56 NIC GHIOLLA PHADRAIG,M
BIBLIOGRAPHY OF SOCIOLOGY OF EDUCATION
IN IRELAND
SOC STUD 1
MAYNOOTH
1972

57 NIC GHIOLLA PHADRAIG,M
BIBLIOGRAPHY OF THE SOCIAL ASPECTS OF
THE LEGAL SYSTEM, POLITICS,
ADMINISTRATION IN IRELAND
SOC STUD 1
MAYNOOTH
1972

58 NIC GHIOLLA PHADRAIG,M
BIBLIOGRAPHY OF THE SOCIAL SCIENCES IN
IRELAND
SOC STUD 2
MAYNOOTH
1973

59 NIC GHIOLLA PHADRAIG,M
SELECT BIBLIOGRAPHY OF SOCIAL PROBLEMS
AND SOCIAL SERVICES IN IRELAND
SOC STUD 1
MAYNOOTH
1972

60 NICER
REGISTER OF RESEARCH IN EDUCATION VOL 2
: 1970-72
NICER
BELFAST
1973

61 NICER
REGISTER OF RESEARCH IN EDUCATION VOL 4:
1975-78
NICER
BELFAST
1979

62 NICER
REGISTER OF RESEARCH IN EDUCATION, VOL
1: 1945-70
NICER
BELFAST
1971

63 NICER
REGISTER OF RESEARCH IN EDUCATION, VOL
3: 1972-75
NICER
BELFAST
1976

64 NICRC
REGISTER OF RESEARCH INTO THE IRISH
CONFLICT
NICRC
BELFAST
1972

65 O'BRIEN,K (ED)
DIGEST OF IRISH AFFAIRS 1969-78
ACADEMY PRESS
DUBLIN
1980

66 O'HIGGINS,P
A BIBLIOGRAPHY OF PERIODICAL LITERATURE
RELATIVE TO IRISH LAW: FIRST SUPPLEMENT
BANBRIDGE CHRONICLE PRESS/NI LEG QUART
BELFAST
1973

67 O'NEILL,T P
SOURCES OF IRISH LOCAL HISTORY
LIBRARY ASSOCIATION OF IRELAND
BELFAST
1958

68 PARTINGTON,J
BIBLIOGRAPHY OF NI POLITICS 1969 TO
APRIL 1973
DEPT POLIT SCI QUB
BELFAST
1977

69 POLLOCK,L; MCALLISTER,I
BIBLIOGRAPHY OF UNITED KINGDOM POLITICS:
SCOTLAND, WALES, AND NI
CSPP
GLASGOW
1980

70 PRONI
NI IN THE SECOND WORLD WAR: A GUIDE TO
OFFICIAL DOCUMENTS ON PRONI
PRONI
BELFAST
1976

71 PRONI
NI TOWN PLANS 1828-1966: A CATALOGUE
PRONI/ORDNANCE SURVEY OF NI
BELFAST
1981

72 PRONI
SOURCES FOR THE STUDY OF LOCAL HISTORY
IN NI
PRONI
BELFAST
1968

73 RAMSEY,P
BIBLIOGRAPHY ON POLITICS IN NI 1922-45
DEPT POLIT SCI QUB
BELFAST
1973

74 ROSE,R
ULSTER POLITICS: A SELECT BIBLIOGRAPHY
OF POLITICAL DISCORD
POLIT STUD (OXFORD) 20
1972

75 RUDDOCK,A
LIST OF BOOKS AND ARTICLES ON ECONOMIC
HISTORY OF GB AND NI
ECON HISTORY R 1(2)
LONDON
1949

76 RUSSELL, H
HOUSING IN NI: A SELECT READING LIST
BELFAST PUBLIC LIBRARIES
BELFAST
1982

77 RUSSELL, H
NI LOCAL HISTORY: A CHECKLIST OF BOOKS
AND ARTICLES ON NI - VOL. 1
BELFAST PUBLIC LIBRARIES
BELFAST
1970

78 RUSSELL, H
NI LOCAL HISTORY: A CHECKLIST OF BOOKS
AND ARTICLES ON NI - VOL. 2, NO. 1
BELFAST PUBLIC LIBRARIES
BELFAST
1971

79 RUSSELL, H
NI LOCAL HISTORY: A CHECKLIST OF BOOKS
AND ARTICLES ON NI - VOL.2, NO.2
BELFAST PUBLIC LIBRARIES
BELFAST
1971

80 RUSSELL, H
NI LOCAL HISTORY: A CHECKLIST OF BOOKS
AND ARTICLES ON NI - VOL.3, NO.1
BELFAST PUBLIC LIBRARIES
BELFAST
1972

81 SCOTT, D
SURVEY RESEARCH IN NI
DEPT POLIT SCI STRATHCLYDE
GLASGOW
1969

82 SHANNON, M O
MODERN IRELAND: A BIBLIOGRAPHY ON
POLITICS, PLANNING, RESEARCH AND
DEVELOPMENT
LIBRARY ASSOCIATION
LONDON
1981

83 SHARKIE, B R
A BIBLIOGRAPHY OF PRINTED MATERIAL
RELATING TO COUNTY ANTRIM
LIBRARY ASSOCIATION
LONDON
1972

84 TREW, K
REGISTER OF RESEARCH IN EDUCATION - NI:
VOLUME ONE 1945-70
NICER
BELFAST
1970

85 TREW, K
REGISTER OF RESEARCH IN EDUCATION - NI:
VOLUME THREE 1972-75
NICER
BELFAST
1976

86 TREW, K
REGISTER OF RESEARCH IN EDUCATION - NI:
VOLUME TWO 1970-72
NICER
BELFAST
1973

87 WHELAN, M
REGISTER OF RESEARCH PROJECTS IN THE
SOCIAL SCIENCES IN PROGRESS IN IRELAND
ESRI
DUBLIN
1977

88 WILSON, J A
REGISTER OF RESEARCH IN EDUCATION - NI:
VOLUME FOUR 1975-78
NICER
BELFAST
1979

89 WRIGHT, J E
BIBLIOGRAPHY OF ARTICLES ON THE HISTORY
OF ECONOMIC THOUGHT IN IRISH PERIODICALS
HIST OF ECONOMIC THOUGHT NEWSLETTER 18
1977

Bibliographies

90 AKENSON, D H
   THE UNITED STATES AND IRELAND
   HARVARD U P
   CAMBRIDGE, MASSACHUSETTS
   1973 2 02

91 BECKETT, J C
   THE ANGLO-IRISH TRADITION
   FABER
   LONDON
   1976 2 01

92 BECKETT, J C
   COMMENT ON CHAPTER BY MANSERGH
   IN WATT, D (ED)
   LONDON
   1981 2 07

93 BECKETT, J C
   CONFRONTATIONS: STUDIES IN IRISH HISTORY
   FABER
   LONDON
   1972 2 02

94 BECKETT, J C
   MAKING OF MODERN IRELAND
   FABER
   LONDON
   1966 2 02

95 BECKETT, J C
   NI
   IN CROZIER, B; MOSS, R (EDS)
   LONDON
   1972 1 01

96 BECKETT, J C
   NI
   J CONTEMP HIST 6(1)
   1971 1 01

97 BECKETT, J C
   A SHORT HISTORY OF IRELAND
   HUTCHINSON
   LONDON
   1979 2 02

98 BEW, P; GIBBON, P; PATTERSON, H
   THE STATE IN NI, 1921-1972: POLITICAL
   CLASS FORCES AND SOCIAL CLASS
   MANCHESTER U P
   MANCHESTER
   1979 2 02

99 BIGGS-DAVISON, J
   THE HAND IS RED
   JOHNSON
   LONDON
   1974 2 02

100 BLAKE, J W
    NI IN THE SECOND WORLD WAR
    HMSO
    BELFAST
    1956 2 02

101 BOTTIGHEIMER, K S
    IRELAND AND THE IRISH: A SHORT HISTORY
    COLUMBIA U P
    NEW YORK
    1982 1 02

102 BOWMAN, J
    DE VALERA AND THE ULSTER QUESTION
    CLARENDON PRESS
    OXFORD
    1982 2 02

103 BOWMAN, J
    DE VALERA AND THE ULSTER QUESTION
    TCD PHD
    DUBLIN
    1980 2 04

104 BROAD, R ET AL
    THE TROUBLES: THE BACKGROUND TO THE
    QUESTION OF NI
    THAMES TELEVISION/MACDONALD FUTURA
    1980 1 02

105 BUCKLAND, P
    FACTORY OF GRIEVANCES: DEVOLVED
    GOVERNMENT IN NI
    GILL AND MACMILLAN
    DUBLIN
    1979 2 02

106 BUCKLAND, P
    A HISTORY OF NI
    GILL AND MACMILLAN
    DUBLIN
    1981 1 02

107 BUCKLAND, P
    IRISH UNIONISM
    HISTORICAL ASSOCIATION
    LONDON
    1973 2 10

108 BUCKLAND, P
    IRISH UNIONISM, 1885-1923: A DOCUMENTARY
    HISTORY
    HMSO
    BELFAST
    1973 2 03

109 BUCKLAND, P
    IRISH UNIONISM: SELECT DOCUMENTS
    HMSO
    BELFAST
    1972 2 02

110 CAMPBELL, J J
    BETWEEN THE WARS
    IN BECKETT, J C; GLASSCOCK, R E (EDS)
    BELFAST
    1967 2 07

111 CARROLL, F M
    AMERICAN OPINION AND THE IRISH QUESTION
    GILL AND MACMILLAN
    DUBLIN
    1978 1 02

112 CARROLL, J T
    IRELAND IN THE WAR YEARS, 1939-1945
    DAVID AND CHARLES
    NEWTON ABBOTT
    1975 2 02

113 CLARK, D
    IRISH BLOOD: NI AND THE AMERICAN
    CONSCIENCE
    KENNIKAT
    NEW YORK
    1977 1 02

114 CLARKSON, L A
    WRITING OF IRISH ECONOMIC AND SOCIAL
    HISTORY SINCE 1968
    ECON HISTORY R FEB
    1980 2 01

115 COLLINS, M E
    IRELAND 1800-1970
    LONGMANS
    LONDON
    1976 2 02

116 COOGAN, T P
    IRELAND SINCE THE RISING
    PALL MALL
    LONDON
    1966 2 02

117 COOKE,A B; ELLIOTT,S; HEPBURN,A C
NI: THE FORMATIVE YEARS, 1921-1929
HANOVER
BRIGHTON
        2 02

118 CRONIN,S
IRELAND SINCE THE TREATY
IRISH FREEDOM PRESS
DUBLIN
1971 2 02

119 CRONIN,S
IRISH NATIONALISM: A HISTORY OF ITS
ROOTS AND DEVELOPMENT
ACADEMY PRESS
DUBLIN
1980 1 02

120 CURTIS,L P
COERCION AND CONCILIATION IN IRELAND
PRINCETON U P
PRINCETON
1963 2 02

121 DE PAOR,L
DIVIDED ULSTER
PENGUIN
LONDON
1970 1 02

122 DOYLE,D N; EDWARDS,O D
AMERICA AND IRELAND 1776-1976: THE
AMERICAN IDENTITY AND THE IRISH
CONNECTION
GREENWOOD PRESS
LONDON
1980 2 02

123 EDWARDS,O D
IRELAND
IN EDWARDS,O D ET AL
1968 2 07

124 EDWARDS,O D
SINS OF OUR FATHERS: ROOTS OF CONFLICT
IN NI
GILL AND MACMILLAN
DUBLIN
1970 1 02

125 EDWARDS,R D
ATLAS OF IRISH HISTORY
GILL AND MACMILLAN
DUBLIN
1973 2 02

126 EDWARDS,R D
IRELAND'S STORY
CONSTABLE
LONDON
1967 2 02

127 EDWARDS,R D
NEW HISTORY OF IRELAND
GILL AND MACMILLAN
DUBLIN
1972 2 02

128 FALLS,C
BIRTH OF ULSTER
METHUEN
LONDON
1973 2 02

129 FARRELL,M
NI: THE ORANGE STATE
PLUTO
LONDON
1980 1 02

130 FINNEGAN,R B
IRELAND: A NATION IN THE CURRENTS OF
CHANGE
WESTVIEW PRESS
BOULDER, COLORADO
1983 1 02

131 FISK,R
IN TIME OF WAR: IRELAND, ULSTER AND THE
PRICE OF NEUTRALITY, 1939-45
DEUTSCH
LONDON
1983 2 02

132 FITZGIBBON,C
RED HAND: THE ULSTER COLONY
DOUBLEDAY
GARDEN CITY, NY
1972 2 02

133 FRANCE LIBRE
ULSTER DURING THE WAR
FRANCE LIBRE JULY
1946 2 99

134 GIBBON,P
THE ORIGINS OF ULSTER UNIONISM
MANCHESTER U P
MANCHESTER
1975 2 02

135 GRAY,T
THE IRISH ANSWER: AN ANATOMY OF IRELAND
HEINEMANN
LONDON
1966 1 02

136 HAMILTON,A J
MODERN IRISH HISTORY: THE SEVERAL
IRELANDS
STUD IN HISTORY AND SOCIETY 5(1)
1973 2 01

137 HARKNESS,D W
ENGLAND'S IRISH QUESTION
IN PEELE,G; COOKE,C (EDS)
LONDON
1975 2 07

138 HARKNESS,D W
HISTORY AND THE IRISH
QUB
BELFAST
1976 2 10

139 HARKNESS,D W
IRELAND SINCE 1921
IN LEE,J (ED)
CORK
1981 2 07

140 HASLETT,E
SOCIAL HISTORY OF NI
NORTHERN PUBLISHING OFFICE
BELFAST
1960 2 02

141 HEPBURN,A C
THE CONFLICT OF NATIONALITY IN MODERN
IRELAND
ARNOLD
LONDON
1980 1 02

142 HEWITT,J
TALKING ABOUT NI
WEYLAND
HOVE, EAST SUSSEX
1980 1 02

143 HINDSLEY,W R
THE ULSTER QUESTION: THE ESTABLISHMENT
OF THE GOVERNMENT OF NI, 1918-1925
QUB PHD
BELFAST
1974 2 04

144 HOBSON,B
IRELAND YESTERDAY AND TOMORROW
ANVIL
TRALEE
1968 2 02

145 INGLIS,B
STORY OF IRELAND
FABER
LONDON
1970 2 02

General Histories/

146 JOANNON, P
    HISTOIRE DE L'IRLANDE
    PLON
    PARIS
    1973 2 02

147 JOHNSON, P
    IRELAND: A CONCISE HISTORY FROM THE
    TWELFTH CENTURY TO THE PRESENT DAY
    GRANADA
    LONDON
    1980 1 02

148 KEE, R
    GREEN FLAG: A HISTORY OF IRISH
    NATIONALISM
    WEIDENFELD AND NICOLSON
    LONDON
    1972 2 02

149 KEE, R
    IRELAND: A HISTORY
    WEIDENFELD AND NICOLSON
    LONDON
    1980 1 02

150 KENNEDY, D
    ULSTER DURING THE WAR AND AFTER
    IN NOWLAN, K D; WILLIAMS, T (EDS)
    DUBLIN
    1969 2 07

151 KOLPAKOV, A D; BOCHKAREVA, I G
    ANGLO-IRISH HISTORIOGRAPHY OF THE ULSTER
    CRISIS
    NOVAIA I NOVEISHAIA ISTORIIA 1
    USSR
    1976 1 01

152 KOLPAKOV, A D; POLIAKOVA, E
    HISTORIOGRAPHY OF THE PARTITIONING OF
    IRELAND
    VOPROSY ISTORII 9
    MOSCOW
    1974 2 01

153 LYONS, F S L
    IRELAND SINCE THE FAMINE
    FONTANA
    LONDON
    1979 2 02

154 LYSAGHT, D R O'C
    REPUBLIC OF IRELAND
    MERCIER
    CORK
    1970 2 02

155 MACAULAY, A
    CATHOLICS IN THE NORTH 1870-1970
    NEWMAN R 2(1)
    1970 1 01

156 MANSELL, D
    THE ULSTER CONFLICT: FROM THE ULSTER
    CONVENTION TO THE PRESENT
    INTERROGATIONS 11
    1977 1 01

157 MANSERGH, N
    THE INFLUENCE OF THE PAST
    IN WATT, D (ED)
    LONDON
    1981 2 07

158 MANSERGH, N
    IRISH QUESTION 1840-1921
    ALLEN AND UNWIN
    LONDON
    1965 2 02

159 MANSERGH, N
    NI: ITS PAST AND ITS FUTURE
    RACE 14(1)
    1972 1 01

160 MCCAFFREY, L
    THE CATHOLIC MINORITY IN THE NORTH
    IN O'BRIEN, F (ED)
    ROCKFORD, ILLINOIS
    1971 1 07

161 MCCAFFREY, L
    IRELAND, FROM COLONY TO NATION STATE
    PRENTICE-HALL
    ENGLEWOOD CLIFFS
    1979 2 02

162 MCCAFFREY, L
    IRISH NATIONALISM AND IRISH CATHOLICISM:
    A STUDY IN CULTURAL IDENTITY
    CHURCH HISTORY 42(4)
    CHICAGO
    1973 2 01

163 MCCAFFREY, L
    IRISH NATIONALISM AND IRISH CATHOLICISM:
    A STUDY IN CULTURAL IDENTITY
    IN MCCAFFREY, L (ED)
    NEW YORK
    1976 2 07

164 MCCRACKEN, J
    NI: 1921-1966
    IN MOODY, T W; MARTIN, F X (EDS)
    CORK
    1967 2 07

165 MCDONACH, O
    IRELAND
    PRENTICE-HALL
    NEW JERSEY ENGLEWOOD CLIFFS
    1968 2 02

166 MCGUIRE, J I
    INDEX TO BULLETIN OF THE IRISH COMMITTEE
    OF HISTORICAL SCIENCES, 1939-74
    IN LEE, J (ED)
    CORK
    1981 2 07

167 MILLER, D W
    QUEENS REBELS
    GILL AND MACMILLAN
    DUBLIN
    1978 2 02

168 MOODY, T W
    THE FIRST FORTY YEARS
    IR HIST STUD 20(80)
    1977 2 01

169 MOODY, T W
    A GENERAL SURVEY
    IN MOODY, T W; BECKETT, J C (EDS)
    LONDON
    1957 2 07

170 MOODY, T W
    THIRTY FIVE YEARS OF IRISH
    HISTORIOGRAPHY
    IN MOODY, T W (ED)
    DUBLIN
    1971 2 07

171 MOODY, T W
    THE ULSTER QUESTION, 1603-1973
    MERCIER
    CORK
    1974 2 02

172 MULVEY, H
    TWENTIETH CENTURY IRELAND 1914-70
    IN MOODY, T W (ED)
    DUBLIN
    1971 2 07

173 MURPHY, J A
    IRELAND IN THE TWENTIETH CENTURY
    GILL AND MACMILLAN
    DUBLIN
    1975 2 02

174 NEILL, K
    OUR CHANGING TIMES: IRELAND, EUROPE AND
    THE MODERN WORLD SINCE 1890
    GILL AND MACMILLAN
    DUBLIN
    1975 2 02

175 O'FARRELL, P
    ENGLAND AND IRELAND SINCE 1800
    OUP
    LONDON
    1975 2 02

176 O'FARRELL, P
    IRELAND'S ENGLISH QUESTION
    BATSFORD
    LONDON
    1971 2 02

177 O'MAHONY, T P
    THE POLITICS OF DISHONOUR: IRELAND
    1916-1977
    TALBOT PRESS
    DUBLIN
    1977 2 01

178 O'TUATHAIGH, M A G
    IRELAND, 1800-1921
    IN LEE, J (ED)
    CORK
    1981 2 07

179 PAKENHAM, F
    FORTY YEARS OF ANGLO-IRISH RELATIONS
    CORK U P
    CORK
    1957 2 02

180 PALMSTROM, A J M
    NI: THE HISTORICAL BACKGROUND
    SAMTIDEN 83(4)
    NORWAY
    1974 1 01

181 POLIAKOVA, E
    RECENT BRITISH AND IRISH BOURGEOIS
    HISTORIOGRAPHY OF THE PARTITION OF
    IRELAND
    VOPROSY ISTORII 8
    MOSCOW
    1980 2 01

182 PROBERT, B
    BEYOND ORANGE AND GREEN: THE POLITICAL
    ECONOMY OF THE NI CRISIS
    ZED PRESS/ACADEMY PRESS
    LONDON/DUBLIN
    1978 1 02

183 SAVORY, D
    CONTEMPORARY HISTORY OF IRELAND
    UUP
    BELFAST
    1958 2 29

184 SCOTT, R D
    REVOLUTION IN NI: A HISTORIOGRAPHY
    LAKEHEAD UNIV R 4(2)
    1971 1 01

185 SHEARMAN, H
    MODERN IRELAND
    HARRAP
    LONDON
    1952 2 02

186 SHEARMAN, H
    NI
    HMSO
    BELFAST
    1968 2 02

187 SHEARMAN, H
    NI 1921-1971
    HMSO
    BELFAST
    1971 2 02

188 SHEARMAN, H
    NI: ITS HISTORY, RESOURCES AND PEOPLE
    HMSO
    BELFAST
    1946 2 02

189 SHEARMAN, H
    ULSTER
    HALE
    LONDON
    1949 2 02

190 STERRING, I
    HISTORY OF IRELAND
    MULLAN
    BELFAST
    1947 2 01

191 STEVENS, P
    GOD SAVE IRELAND: THE IRISH CONFLICT IN
    THE 20TH CENTURY
    MACMILLAN
    NEW YORK
    1974 2 02

192 STEWART, A T Q
    THE NARROW GROUND: ASPECTS OF ULSTER
    1609-1969
    FABER
    LONDON
    1977 2 02

193 SWAN, H
    HIGHLIGHTS OF IRELAND'S STORY
    DUNDALGAN PRESS
    DUNDALK
    1969 2 02

194 SYLVESTER, D ET AL
    THE IRISH QUESTION
    HOLMES MCDOUGALL
    EDINBURGH
    1980 1 02

195 VAN DER STRAETEN, S; DAUFOUY, P
    THE COUNTER-REVOLUTION IN IRELAND
    BLACK AND RED
    DETROIT
    1974 1 09

196 VAN DER STRAETEN, S; DAUFOUY, P
    LA CONTRE REVOLUTION IRLANDAISE
    LES TEMPS MODERNES 311
    PARIS
    1972 1 09

197 WALLACE, M
    DRUMS AND GUNS: REVOLUTION IN ULSTER
    CHAPMAN
    LONDON
    1970 1 02

198 WALLACE, M
    NI
    IN HAWTHORNE, J (ED)
    1966 2 07

199 WALLACE, M
    NI: 50 YEARS OF SELF-GOVERNMENT
    DAVID AND CHARLES
    NEWTON ABBOT
    1971 2 02

200 WHITE, T DE VERE
    THE ANGLO-IRISH
    1972 2 02

201 WOODWARD, J W O
    DIVIDED ISLAND: IRELAND 1910-1949
    HEINEMANN
    AUCKLAND
    1976 2 02

202 YOUNGER, C
    A STATE OF DISUNION
    FONTANA
    LONDON
    1974 2 02

203 ABERG, A
IRLAND-INSEL DES UNFRIEDENS:
HINTERGRUNDE UND ZUSAMMENHANGE DER
HEUTIGEN SITUATION
SCHRODER
HAMBURG
1972 1 02

204 ADAMS, G
PEACE IN IRELAND
REPUBLICAN PRESS CENTRE
BELFAST
1976 1 09

205 AGNEW, P
THE BLUE SKIES OF ULSTER
MAGILL 5(2)
DUBLIN
1981 1 01

206 ALBREKTSEN, B
ASPEKTER VED KONFLICTEN 1 NORD-IRLAND
INT POLIT (BERGEN) 3
1972 1 01

207 ALCOCK, A E
SOME LESSONS FROM THE DEVELOPMENT OF THE
SOUTH TYROL QUESTION OF RELEVANCE TO THE
SITUATION IN NI
INST IRISH STUD QUB 18 MAY
BELFAST
1983 2 11

208 ALEXANDER, J M
AN ANALYSIS OF CONFLICT IN NI
PENNSYLVANIA UNIV PHD
1976 1 04

209 ALEXANDER, J M
FORWARD AND BACKWARD PROCESSES OF
CONFLICT ANALYSIS
BEHAV SCI 22(2)
1977 1 01

210 ALEXANDER, J M
A METAGAME ANALYSIS OF THE CONFLICT IN
NI
PEACE SCIENCE SOCIETY 3RD ANNUAL
CONFERENCE
OTTAWA
1975 1 11

211 ALEXANDER, J M
NI: AN OPERATIONS APPROACH TO CONFLICT
RESOLUTION
SEMINAR ON CONFLICT ANALYSIS, STATE DEPT
WASHINGTON, D C
1975 1 11

212 ALEXANDER, J M
AN OPERATIONAL ANALYSIS OF CONFLICT IN
NI: AN AMERICAN PERSPECTIVE
IMMACULATA COLLEGE, PENNSYLVANIA
1975 1 08

213 ALEXANDER, J M
A STUDY OF CONFLICT IN NI: AN
APPLICATION OF METAGAME THEORY
J PEACE SCI 2(1)
1976 1 01

214 ALEXANDER, J M; SAATY, T L
STABILITY ANALYSIS OF THE
FORWARD-BACKWARD PROCESS: NI CASE STUDY
BEHAV SCI 22(6)
1977 1 01

215 ALLISTER, J H
IRISH UNIFICATION ANATHEMA: THE REASONS
WHY NI REJECTS UNIFICATION WITH THE
REPUBLIC OF IRELAND
CROWN PUBLICATIONS
BELFAST
1981 1 09

216 ALLUM, P
THE IRISH QUESTION
CRANE BAG 4(2)
DUBLIN
1980 1 01

217 ALLUM, P
SUR LA QUESTION IRLANDAISE
PLURIEL 20
PARIS
1979 1 01

218 ALTER, P
IRISCHE NATIONAL BEWEGUNG ZWISCHEN
PARLAMENT UND REVOLUTION
VIENNA
1971 2 02

219 ALVAREZ, G
APUNTES PARA UN ESTUDIAS DE LAS
INSTITUTIONES POLITICAS DE IRLANDA DEL
NORTE
R ESTUD POLIT 189-190
1973 3 01

220 ANDERSON, J
REGIONS AND RELIGIONS IN IRELAND: A
SHORT CRITIQUE OF 'TWO NATIONS' THEORY
ANTIPODE 11(2)
WORCESTER, MASS
1980 1 01

221 ARBLASTER, A
BRITAIN IN IRELAND, IRELAND IN BRITAIN
SOCIALIST REGISTER
LONDON
1977 1 01

222 ARCHER, J R
THE UNIONIST TRADITION IN IRELAND
EIRE-IRELAND 15(2)
ST PAULS, MINNESOTA
1980 3 01

223 ARGAL, A
ULSTER SENZA SPERANZE DI PACIFICAZIONE
CIVITAS 25
ROME
1974 1 01

224 ARNOLD, B
BIPARTISANSHIP AND THE CONSTITUTION
STUDIES 66
1977 1 01

225 ARNOLD, B
POLITICAL CONSTRAINTS: DUBLIN
IN WATT, D (ED)
LONDON
1981 1 07

226 ARNOLD, B
THE TWO IRELANDS: A SPECIAL REPORT
BRITANNICA BOOK OF THE YEAR 1971
LONDON
1971 3 07

227 ARTHUR, P
ANGLO-IRISH RELATIONS SINCE 1968: A
'FEVER CHART' INTERPRETATION
GVT AND OPPOSITION 18(2)
LONDON
1983 2 01

228 ARTHUR, P
GOVERNMENT AND POLITICS OF NI
LONGMANS
LONDON
1980 1 02

229 ARTHUR, P
INDEPENDENCE
IN REA, D (ED)
DUBLIN
1982 1 07

230 ASHLEY, L R
PEASANTS, PLACES, PATRIOTS AND POLITICS:
THE ONOMASTICS OF IRISH INDEPENDENCE
ET IRL 2
1977 3 01

231 ATKINS, H
NI
VITAL SPEECHES 46
1979 1 01

232 ATLANTIC INFORMATION CENTRE FOR TEACHERS
CRISIS PAPER NO. 6 - NI: AN INTRODUCTION
TO EVENTS AND ACTIONS UP TO OCTOBER 1969
ATL INFOR CENT TEACHERS
LONDON
1970 1 10

233 BABY, N
LA MENACE D'UNE CRISE SOCIALE ALOUNDIT
LE CLIMAT D'INCERTITUDE
LE MONDE DIPLOMATIQUE
1977 1 01

234 BAILEY, A
ACTS OF UNION: REPORTS ON IRELAND,
1973-79
FABER
LONDON
1980 3 02

235 BAIN, H; HOWARD, N; SAATY, T L
USING THE ANALYSIS OF OPTIONS TECHNIQUE
TO ANALYZE A COMMUNITY CONFLICT
J CONFLICT RESOL 15(2)
1971 1 01

236 BALTHROP, V W
"BRITISH THUGS...FENIAN BASTARDS": A
RHETORICAL ANALYSIS OF THE CRISIS IN NI
KANSAS UNIV PHD
1978 1 04

237 BANNOV, B G
ULSTER TRAGEDY
NOVOSTI PRESS AGENCY
MOSCOW
1973 1 10

238 BARKER, A J
BLOODY ULSTER
BALLANTINE BOOKS
NEW YORK
1973 1 02

239 BARLEY, C
LES IRLANDAIS VOUS PARLENT
PARIS
1975 3 02

240 BARON, V O
JOURNAL FROM NI PART 1
CHRISTIAN CENTURY 94
1977 1 01

241 BARON, V O
JOURNAL FROM NI PART 2
CHRISTIAN CENTURY 94
1977 1 01

242 BARRINGTON, D
AFTER SUNNINGDALE
ADMIN (DUB) 24(2)
DUBLIN
1976 1 01

243 BARRINGTON, D
UNITING IRELAND
TUAIRIM
DUBLIN
1958 2 09

244 BARRITT, D P
CURRENT SCENE IN NI
QUARTERLY 3
1969 1 01

245 BARRITT, D P
NI: A PROBLEM TO EVERY SOLUTION
NORTHERN FRIENDS PEACE BOARD
LEEDS
1982 1 02

246 BARRITT, D P
NI: THE PROBLEM OF A DIVIDED COMMUNITY
MANCHESTER STATISTICAL SOCIETY
MANCHESTER
1972 1 11

247 BARRITT, D P
1961-1971: PROGRESS OR RETROGRESSION?
COMM FORUM 1(2)
1971 1 01

248 BARRITT, D P; BOOTH, A
ORANGE AND GREEN: A QUAKER STUDY OF
COMMUNITY RELATIONS IN NI
NORTHERN FRIENDS PEACE BOARD
SEDBURGH, YORKSHIRE
1969 1 10

249 BARRITT, D P; CARTER, C F
NI PROBLEM
OUP
1972 2 02

250 BARRY, B
REFLECTIONS ON CONFLICT
SOCIOLOGY 6(3)
LONDON
1972 1 01

251 BAXTER, R
SECOND ULSTER CRISIS
IN BENEWICK, R; SMITH, T (EDS)
LONDON
1972 1 07

252 BAYLEY, J; BOEHRINGER, K
STRUGGLE IN IRELAND 1968-73: IRISH CLASS
FORCES AND BRITISH IMPERIALISM
NORTH ONE PRESS
LONDON
1976 1 01

253 BEACH, S W
RELIGION AND POLITICAL CHANGE IN NI
SOCIOL ANALYSIS 38(1)
1977 1 01

254 BEATTIE, G W
THE 'TROUBLES' IN NI
B BRIT PSYCHOL SOC 32
1979 1 01

255 BEATTY, J
THE TROUBLES TODAY
NEW REPUBLIC NOV 15
1980 1 01

256 BEDARIDA, C
L'ANGLETERRE EN FACE DE L'AUTONOMIE DE
L'IRLANDE
R FRANC SCI POLIT 8(2)
1958 2 01

257 BEESON, T
NI'S ORDEAL: NO EASY SOLUTION
CHRISTIAN CENTURY JUN 3
1981 1 01

258 BELFAST LIBERTARIAN GROUP
IRELAND, DEAD OR ALIVE? AN ANALYSIS OF
IRISH POLITICS
BELFAST LIBERTARIAN GROUP
BELFAST
       1 09

259 BELFAST TELEGRAPH
SURVEY CONDUCTED BY NATIONAL OPINION
POLLS
BELFAST TELEGRAPH
BELFAST
1967 2 10

260 BELL,G
BRITISH LABOUR AND IRELAND 1969-1979
OTHER PRESS
LONDON
1979 1 09

261 BELL,G
THE PROTESTANT WORKING CLASS: STILL NO
SURRENDER
IRL SOCIALIST R 7
1980 1 01

262 BELL,G
PROTESTANTS OF ULSTER
PLUTO
LONDON
1976 1 02

263 BELL,G
TROUBLESOME BUSINESS: THE LABOUR PARTY
AND THE IRISH QUESTION
PLUTO
LONDON
1982 1 02

264 BELL,J B
THE CHRONICLERS OF VIOLENCE IN NI
R POLITICS 34
LONDON
1972 1 01

265 BELL,J B
CHRONICLERS OF VIOLENCE IN NI REVISITED:
THE ANALYSIS OF TRAGEDY
R POLITICS 36(4)
1974 1 01

266 BELL,J B
THE CHRONICLERS OF VIOLENCE IN NI: A
TRAGEDY IN ENDLESS ACTS
R POLITICS 38(4)
1976 1 01

267 BELL,J B
CHRONICLERS OF VIOLENCE: THE TROUBLES IN
NI INTERPRETED
EIRE-IRELAND 1
1972 1 01

268 BELL,J B
IRISH TEMPLATE
IN BELL,J B (ED)
1976 1 07

269 BELOFF,H
A PLACE NOT SO FAR APART: CONCLUSIONS OF
AN OUTSIDER
IN HARBISON,J; HARBISON,J (EDS)
1980 1 07

270 BENNETT,F
IRISH PROBLEM: A NEW APPROACH - (1)
ANAMOLIES UNLIMITED
CONTEMP R 220(1276)
1972 1 01

271 BENNETT,F
IRISH PROBLEM: A NEW APPROACH - (2) FEAR
IS THE KEY
CONTEMP R 221(1278)
1972 1 01

272 BENNETT,J
INTRODUCTION
IN CRONIN,S; ROCHE,R (EDS)
TRALEE
1977 1 10

273 BENNETT,J
THE NI CONFLICT AND BRITISH POWER
PONTE 30(1)
FIRENZE
1974 1 01

274 BENNETT,J
NORTHERN CONFLICT AND BRITISH POWER
ATLANTIS 5
1973 1 01

275 BEW,P
PROBLEMS OF IRISH UNIONISM
ECON AND SOCIETY 6(1)
1977 2 01

276 BEW,P; GIBBON,P; PATTERSON,H
ASPECTS OF NATIONALISM AND SOCIALISM IN
IRELAND 1968-78
IN MORGAN,A; PURDIE,B (EDS)
LONDON
1980 1 07

277 BEW,P; PATTERSON,H
THE PROTESTANT-CATHOLIC CONFLICT IN
ULSTER
J INT AFF 36(2)
NEW YORK
1982 1 01

278 BICO
AGAINST ULSTER NATIONALISM
ATHOL BOOKS
BELFAST
1975 2 09

279 BICO
BIRTH OF ULSTER UNIONISM
ATHOL BOOKS
BELFAST
1972 2 09

280 BICO
ECONOMICS OF PARTITION
ATHOL BOOKS
BELFAST
1972 2 09

281 BICO
IMPERIALISM
ATHOL BOOKS
BELFAST
1975 2 09

282 BICO
IRISH ACTION: NATIONALIST POLITICS IN NI
IN THE STORMONT PERIOD
ATHOL BOOKS
BELFAST
1980 2 09

283 BICO
LABOUR IN ULSTER
ATHOL BOOKS
BELFAST
1979 2 09

284 BICO
ON THE DEMOCRATIC VALIDITY OF THE NI
STATE
ATHOL BOOKS
BELFAST
1971 2 09

285 BICO
ON THE HISTORIC IRISH NATION
ATHOL BOOKS
BELFAST
1972 2 09

286 BICO
TWO IRISH NATIONS
ATHOL BOOKS
BELFAST
1975 2 09

287 BICO
ULSTER AS IT IS: CATHOLIC/PROTESTANT
CONFLICT SINCE CATHOLIC EMANCIPATION
ATHOL BOOKS
BELFAST
1973 2 09

288 BIG FLAME
IRELAND: RISING IN THE NORTH
BIG FLAME PUBLICATIONS
BIRMINGHAM
1975 1 09

289 BIGGS-DAVISON,J
CATHOLICS AND THE UNION
UNIONIST RESEARCH DEPT
BELFAST
1972 2 09

290 BIGGS-DAVISON,J
HOME RULE FOR NI
BLACKWOOD'S MAG 311(1880)
1972 2 01

291 BIGGS-DAVISON,J
THOUGHTS ON THE ULSTER DISCONTENTS
CONTEMP R 233
1978 1 01

292 BIGGS-DAVISON,J
UNITED IRELAND? NO! UNITED ISLANDS? YES!
CONTEMP R 239
LONDON
1981 1 01

293 BIGGS-DAVISON,J
WHOSE 'OTHER ISLAND'?
THE REMINDER 1
UPMINSTER
1971 1 01

294 BINCHEY,M
THE CONTINUING TRAGEDY OF IRELAND
CENTER MAG JULY-AUG
1981 1 01

295 BINDER,F J
THE PROBLEM OF THE PARTITION OF IRELAND:
A SIMPLE EXPLANATION
ULSTER UNIONIST COUNCIL
BELFAST
1961 2 09

296 BING,G H C
JOHN BULL'S OTHER ISLAND
TRIBUNE PAMPHLET
LONDON
1950 2 09

297 BIRCH,A H
MINORITY NATIONALIST MOVEMENTS AND
THEORIES OF POLITICAL INTEGRATION
WLD POLITICS 30(3)
1978 2 01

298 BIRCH,A H
POLITICAL INTEGRATION AND DISINTEGRATION
IN THE BRITISH ISLES
ALLEN AND UNWIN
LONDON
1977 2 02

299 BIRRELL,W D
NI: THE OBSTACLES TO POWER SHARING
POLIT QUART 52(2)
1981 1 01

300 BLACKWOOD'S MAGAZINE
ULSTER IN THE SHADOWS
BLACKWOOD'S MAG 311
1972 1 01

301 BLADES,M; SCOTT,D
WHAT PRICE NI?
FABIAN SOCIETY
LONDON
1970 1 09

302 BLAKE,N
CIVIL LIBERTIES AND SOCIALISM IN NI
NIASL
BELFAST
1983 1 10

303 BLANSHARD,P
NI AND PARTITION
IN BLANSHARD,P
BOSTON
1953 2 07

304 BLEAKLEY,D
CRISIS IN IRELAND
FABIAN RES SERIES 318
LONDON
1974 1 09

305 BLEAKLEY,D
IRELAND AND BRITAIN 1690-1990: A SEARCH
FOR PEACE
FELLOWSHIP OF RECONCILIATION
1982 1 10

306 BLEAKLEY,D
PEACE IN ULSTER
MOWBRAYS
LONDON
1972 1 02

307 BLYTHE,E
BRISEADH NA TEORANN
DUBLIN
1955 2 10

308 BLYTHE,E
NEED FOR A NEW DEPARTURE IN NORTHERN
POLICY
DUBLIN
1959 2 10

309 BLYTHE,E
NEW DEPARTURE IN NORTHERN POLICY: APPEAL
TO THE LEADERS OF NATIONALIST OPINION
CLANCY
DUBLIN
1956 2 02

310 BLYTHE,E
WHAT HAPPENED TO THE NORTH?
EVERYMAN
1970 1 01

311 BOAL,F W
TWO NATIONS IN IRELAND
ANTIPODE 11(2)
WORCESTER, MASS
1980 1 01

312 BOAL,F W; BUCHANAN,R H
CONFLICT IN NI
GEOGR MAG 41(5)
1969 1 01

313 BOAL,F W; DOUGLAS,J N H
OVERVIEW
IN BOAL,F W; DOUGLAS,J N H (EDS)
LONDON
1982 2 07

314 BOLAND,K
WE WON'T STAND IDLY BY
KELLY
DUBLIN
1972 1 02

315 BONIECKI,Z
IS THIS THE LAST CHAPTER OF THE IRISH
QUESTION?
NOWE DROGI 279
WARSAW
1972 1 01

316 BONNET,C
L'ORDRE D'ORANGE ET LA VIE POLITIQUE EN
IRLANDE DU NORD
ET IRL 2
1977 1 01

317 BONNET,C
ORANGE ORDER
PARIS UNIV PHD
PARIS
1972 2 04

318 BOSERUP,A
CONTRADICTIONS AND STRUGGLES IN NI
SOCIALIST REGISTER
1972 1 01

319 BOSERUP,A
POLITICS OF PROTRACTED CONFLICT
TRANSACTION 7(5)
1970   1   01

320 BOSERUP,A
POWER IN A POST-COLONIAL SETTING: THE
WHY AND WHITHER OF RELIGIOUS
CONFRONTATION
INT PEACE RES SOC PAP 18
1970   1   01

321 BOSERUP,A
RANK ANALYSIS OF A POLARISED COMMUNITY:
A CASE STUDY FROM NI
INT PEACE RES SOC PAP 8
1967   1   01

322 BOSERUP,A
REVOLUTION AND COUNTER-REVOLUTION IN NI
VARDPOLITIKENS DAGSFRAGOR
1971   1   01

323 BOSERUP,A
WHO IS THE PRINCIPAL ENEMY?
INDEPENDENT LABOUR PARTY
LONDON
1972   1   09

324 BOWMAN,D J
WHAT TO THINK ABOUT NI
COMMONWEAL JUN 19
1981   1   01

325 BOYCE,D G
ENGLISHMEN AND IRISH TROUBLES: BRITISH
PUBLIC OPINION
J CAPA
1972   2   02

326 BOYD,A
GUILTY MEN OF ULSTER
EVERYMAN
1970   1   01

327 BOYD,A
HOLY WAR IN BELFAST
ANVIL
TRALEE
1969   2   02

328 BOYD,A
NI: EXTENDING THE QUESTION
LEFT PERSPECTIVES 1(2)
1980   1   01

329 BOYD,A
ORANGEMAN AND HIS ENEMIES
AQUARIUS
BENBURB
1971   1   01

330 BOYD,A
PARTITION OF IRELAND
ANVIL
DUBLIN
1979   2   02

331 BOYD,A
TWO IRELANDS
FABIAN RES SERIES 269
LONDON
1968   1   09

332 BOYD,A; IRELAND,J
NEW PARTITION OF IRELAND
AUTHORS
BELFAST
1968   1   09

333 BOYLE,J F; JACKSON,J A; MILLER,R L;
ROCHE,S
ATTITUDES IN IRELAND - NATIONAL
IDENTITY, ATTITUDES AND POLITICAL
BEHAVIOUR
DEPT SOCIOL   TCD
DUBLIN
1976   2   10

334 BOYLE,J F; JACKSON,J A; MILLER,R L;
ROCHE,S
INITIAL FACTOR ANALYSIS OF THE NI
ATTITUDE DATA
DEPT SOC STUD QUB
BELFAST
1976   2   08

335 BOYLE,J F; JACKSON,J A; MILLER,R L;
ROCHE,S
NATIONAL IDENTITY AND POLITICAL
ALLEGIANCE IN NI
DEPT SOC STUD QUB
BELFAST
1976   1   08

336 BOYLE,J F; JACKSON,J A; MILLER,R L;
ROCHE,S
RESPONDENTS' PERCEPTIONS OF THE CAUSES
OF THE NI CONFLICT
DEPT SOC STUD QUB
BELFAST
1976   1   08

337 BOYLE,J F; JACKSON,J A; MILLER,R L;
ROCHE,S
SUMMARY TABLES OF ATTITUDES IN NI
DEPT SOC STUD QUB
BELFAST
1976   2   08

338 BOYLE,K
NI: DISMANTLING THE PROTESTANT STATE
NEW BLACKFRIARS 52
1971   1   01

339 BOYLE,K; HADDEN,T; HILLYARD,P
LAW AND STATE: THE CASE OF NI
MARTIN ROBERTSON
LONDON
1975   1   02

340 BOYLE,K; HADDEN,T; HILLYARD,P
TEN YEARS ON IN NI
COBDEN TRUST
LONDON
1981   1   02

341 BOYLE,P
ULSTER REVISITED
IN O'CONNOR,U (ED)
1974   1   07

342 BRADFORD,R
FOUNDATIONS FOR PROGRESS
ADMIN (DUB) 20(4)
1972   1   01

343 BRADY,J
IRELAND AS PREDICAMENT
MONTH 233(1259)
1972   2   01

344 BRADY,J
MEANING AND RELEVANCE OF PLURALISM IN NI
STUDIES
1979   1   01

345 BRADY,J
NATIONAL IDENTITY AND THE IRISH QUESTION
MONTH 235(1285)
1974   1   01

346 BRADY,J
PLURALISM AND NI
STUDIES 67
1978   1   01

347 BRADY,S
ARMS AND THE MEN
WICKLOW
1971   1   02

348 BREWER,J; SMYTH,J
THE PARAMETERS OF A PUZZLE: CONFLICT
MANAGEMENT IN NI AND SOUTH AFRICA
ECPR
ESSEX
1983   1   11

349 BROOKEBOROUGH, B
AS I SEE IT
SOLON 1(2)
1970 2 01

350 BROWN, D
WHO IS CAESAR?
SOLON 1(2)
1970 2 01

351 BROWNE, V
HAVE GOOD CHEER, NO POPE HERE
MAGILL 2(11)
DUBLIN
1979 1 01

352 BRUCE, A
TWO IRELANDS: A SPECIAL REPORT
IN UNKNOWN
1971 2 07

353 BUDGE, I; O'LEARY, C
BELFAST: APPROACH TO CRISIS. A STUDY OF
BELFAST POLITICS 1613-1970
MACMILLAN
LONDON
1973 1 01

354 BUICK, A
THE IRISH QUESTION: A SOCIALIST ANALYSIS
WERELDSOCIALISME
BRUSSELS
1977 1 09

355 BUNDRED, S
THE BRITISH LABOUR PARTY AND THE
REPUBLICAN STRUGGLE
IRIS 5
DUBLIN
1983 1 01

356 BURKETT, T
GROSSBRITANNIENS GESELLSCHAFTLICHES
DILEMMA: EVOLUTION UND VERFALL
EUROPA ARCHIV 31(5)
BONN
1976 1 01

357 BURTON, F
POLITICS OF LEGITIMACY: STRUGGLES IN A
BELFAST COMMUNITY
RKP
LONDON
1978 1 02

358 BUTLER, H
"WE ARE THE PEOPLE OF BURKE" - IRISH
PROTESTANTS' ATTITUDES TO REUNION
TWENTIETH CENTURY STUD NOVEMBER
1954 2 01

359 BUTTERWECK, H
GROSSBRITANNIENS IRISHER BELFAST
ARBEIT UND WIRT 28
1974 1 01

360 BYRNE, D
NI AND THE CRISIS: SOME POLITICAL
IMPLICATIONS
DEPT SOCIOL AND SOC POLICY ULSTER
COLLEGE
BELFAST
1980 2 08

361 BYRNE, D
THEORISING NI
DEPT SOC ADMIN DURHAM UNIV
DURHAM
1980 2 08

362 CAGIANELLI, G
L'EUROPA FINISCE A BELFAST
EDITRICE A.V.E
ROME
1971 1 02

363 CAHILL, K M
HEALING HANDS
FOREIGN POLICY 37
NEW YORK
1980 1 01

364 CAHILL, K M
IRISH ESSAYS
JOHN JAY PRESS
NEW YORK
1980 1 02

365 CALLAGHAN, J
HOUSE DIVIDED
COLLINS
LONDON
1973 1 02

366 CALVERT, H
NI PROBLEM
UNITED NATIONS ASSOC
LONDON
1972 1 10

367 CALVERT, J
BACKGROUND TO THE POLITICAL, SOCIAL AND
ECONOMIC PROBLEMS OF NI
AUSTRAL FOR AFF REC 48
CANBERRA
1977 2 01

368 CAMBRIDGE REVIEW
IRISH ISSUE
CAMBRIDGE R 94(2213)
1973 1 10

369 CARASSO, J P
LA RUMEUR IRLANDAISE
DUNOEL
PARIS
1970 1 02

370 CARLETON, W
QUESTION OF IRISH PARTITION
YALE R
1951 2 01

371 CARLOW, P
UNION JACK OR TRICOLOUR?
WLD R
1949 2 01

372 CARNDUFF, T
THE ORANGE SOCIETY
THE BELL 17(4)
DUBLIN
1951 2 01

373 CARSANIGA, G
NI: SLAVES AND UNDERSLAVES
PONTE 28(3)
FIRENZE
1972 1 01

374 CASTERAN, C
GUERRE CIVILE EN IRLANDE
MERCURE DE FRANCE
PARIS
1970 1 02

375 CATHERWOOD, F
POSSIBLE SETTLEMENT OF THE NI PROBLEM
IN CROZIER, B; MOSS, R (EDS)
LONDON
1972 1 07

376 CATTELAIN, J P
IRELANDE, NATURE ET VIOLENCE
BESANCON
1977 1 02

377 CHALK, P
CLASS UNITY, NATIONALISM AND IRISH TRADE
UNIONS
IRL SOCIALIST R 2
LONDON
1978 2 01

General Political Analyses/

378 CHERIOUX,J; BERNARD,D; GUILLAUME,M
ETUDES POLITIQUES ANGLO-SAXONNES: IRLAND
DU NORD, CONNECTICUT, NEW YORK...
COLIN
PARIS
1950 2 02

379 CHERTKOW,P S
ORANGEISM AND REPUBLICANISM, 1948-1972:
A STUDY OF TWO OPPOSED MOVEMENTS
LONDON UNIV PHD
LONDON
1974 1 04

380 CHICHESTER-CLARK,J
SPOTLIGHT ON NI
ROYAL COMMONWEALTH SOCIETY
1971 1 99

381 CHILLINGWORTH,H R
RELIGION AND THE IRISH PROBLEM
MODERN CHURCHMAN
1952 2 01

382 CHRISTOPH,H; CHRISTOPH,S
REPORTAGEN AUS D. NI BURGERKREIG
HOHMANN
TRIER
1978 1 02

383 CLARK,D
PASSION OF PROTRACTED CONFLICT
TRANSACTION 7(5)
1970 1 01

384 CLARKE,A
IRELAND AND THE GENERAL CRISIS
PAST AND PRESENT 48
1970 1 01

385 CLARKSON,A; MURPHY,P
LOYALIST WORKING CLASS
REVOLUTIONARY COMMUNIST PAPERS 7
LONDON
1981 1 01

386 CLARKSON,J D
LABOUR AND NATIONALISM IN IRELAND
AMS PRESS
NEW YORK
1970 2 02

387 CLUTTERBUCK,R
NI: IS THERE A WAY?
WASHINGTON R STRATEGIC AND INT STUD APR
WASHINGTON, D.C.
1981 1 01

388 COCATRE-ZILGIEN,A
L'IMBROGLIO IRLANDAIS, INDEPENDENCE ET
PARTITION
R EGYPT DR INT 8
1952 2 01

389 COCATRE-ZILGIEN,A
LES RAISONS DE MALAISE NORD-IRLANDAIS
R DR PUB SCI POLIT 86(1)
1970 1 01

390 COCATRE-ZILGIEN,A
REGARDS SUR L'IRLANDE ACUTELLE
R DR PUB SCI POLIT 89(6)
1973 3 01

391 COHAN,A S
RELIGIOUS VALUES AND AN END TO PARTITION
LANCASTER
1971 1 08

392 COLACRAI DE TREVISAN,M
CONFLICTO ANGLO-IRLANDES
R POLITICS INT 152
MADRID
1977 1 01

393 COLLINS,A
ULSTER UNDER HOME RULE: A CRITICISM
CHRISTUS REX 10(2)
1956 2 01

394 COMMITTEE FOR WITHDRAWAL FROM IRELAND
IRELAND: VOICES FOR WITHDRAWAL
INFORMATION ON IRELAND
LONDON
1980 1 09

395 COMMUNIST PARTY OF IRELAND
A DEMOCRATIC SOLUTION
COMMUNIST PARTY OF IRELAND
BELFAST
       1 09

396 COMMUNIST PARTY OF IRELAND
THE SITUATION IN THE NORTH
COMMUNIST PARTY OF IRELAND
BELFAST
1969 1 09

397 CONWAY,A
CONSTRUCTIVE CONFLICT: THE VIEW FROM THE
REPUBLIC
NEW HUMANIST MARCH
1973 1 01

398 CONWAY,A
THERE ARE NO EVIL MEN - A FRESH LOOK AT
THE IRISH QUESTION AND A SUGGESTED WAY
FORWARD
NEW IRELAND MOVEMENT
DUBLIN
1972 1 09

399 COOKE,R
CRISIS IN NI: A BIBLE PROTESTANT
VIEWPOINT
WORD OF TRUTH PUBLICATIONS
LOS ANGELES
1972 1 02

400 COOKE,R
THUNDER OF PAPAL PROPAGANDA
AUTHOR
PASADENA
1969 3 02

401 CORELLI,B
THE COLLAPSE OF BRITISH POWER
METHUEN
LONDON
1972 3 02

402 CORRIGAN,A
EYEWITNESSES IN NI
VOICE OF ULSTER PUBLICATIONS
DUNGANNON
1969 1 09

403 COSGRAVE,P
INSOLUBLE PROBLEM OF ULSTER
ROUND TABLE 59(235)
1969 1 01

404 COUGHLAN,A
COMMENT ON NORTH-SOUTH COMPARISONS
ADMIN (DUB) 20(4)
1972 2 01

405 COUGHLAN,A
NORTHERN CRISIS
SOLIDARITY PUBLICATIONS
DUBLIN
1969 1 09

406 COUGHLAN,A
WAY TO PEACE IN IRELAND: THE NECESSITY
FOR BRITISH COMMITMENT TO END THE UNION
DUBLIN
1974 1 09

407 COX,H
ESTABLISHING NI: SOME FEATURES OF THE
PERIOD 1912-25
LANCASTER UNIV
LANCASTER
1971 2 99

408 COX,H
ULSTER: DRAWING THE LINE SOMEWHERE
DEPT POLITICS LIVERPOOL UNIV
LIVERPOOL
       1 08

409 CRAIG,W
FUTURE OF NI
STYLETYPE PRINTING
BELFAST
1973 1 09

410 CRANSTON,D
ENDLESSLY MARCHING MEN: THE ULSTER
PROTESTANT CONFUSED
CAMBRIDGE R
1973 1 01

411 CRICK,B
COMMENTARY: TEN YEARS IN ULSTER
POLIT QUART 50(1)
1979 1 01

412 CRICK,B
THE SOVEREIGNTY OF PARLIAMENT AND THE
IRISH QUESTION
IN REA,D (ED)
DUBLIN
1982 1 07

413 CRITCHLEY,J
IRELAND: A NEW PARTITION
BOW PUBLICATIONS
LONDON
1972 1 09

414 CRONIN,S
THE RIGHTS OF MAN IN IRELAND
REPUBLICAN PUBLICATIONS
DUBLIN
1970 1 09

415 CROSSBOW
NI
CROSSBOW 15(58)
1972 3 01

416 CURRAN,J
SEPARATISM AND NI
IN HALL,R (ED)
1979 3 07

417 CURRAN,J
ULSTER REPARTITION: A POSSIBLE ANSWER
AMERICA JAN 31
1976 1 01

418 DALY,C B
PEACE - THE WORK OF JUSTICE: ADDRESSES
ON THE NORTHERN TRAGEDY, 1973-79
VERITAS
DUBLIN
1979 1 02

419 DALY,C B
VIOLENCE DESTROYS THE WORK OF JUSTICE:
COOPERATION AND POLITICAL PARTNERSHIP. .
. .
VITAL SPEECHES APR 1
1980 1 01

420 DALY,C B
VIOLENCE IN IRELAND
VERITAS
DUBLIN
1973 1 02

421 DANIEL,T K
MYTH AND THE MILITANTS: A NEW LOOK AT
THE ULSTER LOYALISTS
POLIT STUD (OXFORD) 24(4)
OXFORD
1976 1 01

422 DARBY,J
CONFLICT AND CONCILIATION IN NI
NEW COMM 4(1-2)
1976 1 01

423 DARBY,J
CONFLICT IN NI: THE DEVELOPMENT OF A
POLARIZED COMMUNITY
GILL AND MACMILLAN
DUBLIN
1976 1 02

424 DARBY,J
IDEOLOGY AND THE ANALYSIS OF CONFLICT IN
NI
NEW COMM 9(2)
LONDON
1981 1 01

425 DARBY,J
REPORT FROM NI
NEW COMM 3(3)
1974 1 01

426 DAVIES,C
IRELAND AND DECOLONISATION
IRL SOCIALIST R
LONDON
1977 1 01

427 DAVIES,C
NI: BEYOND BRITISH NATIONHOOD, BEYOND
BRITISH REFORM
IRL SOCIALIST R 2
LONDON
1978 1 01

428 DAVIS,E E; SINNOTT,R
ATTITUDES IN THE REPUBLIC OF IRELAND
RELEVANT TO THE NI PROBLEM
ESRI
DUBLIN
1979 1 10

429 DAVISON,M
NI: EXPORTING THE PROBLEM
LEFT PERSPECTIVES 1(2)
DUBLIN
1980 1 01

430 DE PAOR,L
IRELAND'S IDENTITIES
CRANE BAG 3(1)
DUBLIN
1979 1 01

431 DEEDES,W
IRISH LESSONS
INT R 4
1975 1 01

432 DELANOE,N
LES PROTESTANTS
TEMPS MODERNES 311
PARIS
1972 1 01

433 DERWIN,D; GOODWILLIE,J; KERRIGAN,G;
TRENCH,B
IRELAND: A SPECIAL SURVEY
INT SOCIALISM 92
1976 1 01

434 DEVLIN,P
THE POLITICS OF CLASS
LEFT PERSPECTIVES 1(3)
1981 1 01

435 DEWAR,M
THE JUNIOR ORANGEMAN'S CATECHISM
REID AND WRIGHT
BELFAST
1966 2 09

436 DEWAR,M
WHY ORANGEISM?
GRAND ORANGE LODGE OF IRELAND
BELFAST
1959 2 09

437 DEWAR,M; BROWN,J; LONG,S E
ORANGEISM, A NEW HISTORICAL APPRECIATION
GRAND ORANGE LODGE OF IRELAND
BELFAST
1967 2 99

438 DICKIE-CLARK,H
STUDY OF CONFLICT IN SOUTH AFRICA AND NI
SOC DYNAMICS 2(1)
1976 1 01

General Political Analyses/ 16

439 DOGGETT,A; HICKMAN,M
WOMEN AND NATIONALISM
IRL SOCIALIST R 8
LONDON
1981 1   01

440 DOHERTY,P
A CATHOLIC LOOKS AT THE NORTHERN STATE
IN SOCIAL STUDY CONFERENCE
DUBLIN
1974 1   07

441 DORLAND,A G
THE REUNIFICATION OF IRELAND
DALHOUSIE R 40
1960 2   01

442 DORN,R
IRISH NATIONALISM AND BRITISH
IMPERIALISM
REVOLUTIONARY MARXIST GROUP
DUBLIN
1973 1   09

443 DOUGLAS,J N H
GEOGRAPHY AND POLITICAL PROBLEMS
IN BOWEN,E; CARTER,H; TAYLOR,J (EDS)
ABERYSTWYTH
1968 2   07

444 DOUGLAS,J N H
IRRECONCILABLE BORDER
GEOGR MAG 49(3)
1976 1   01

445 DOUGLAS,J N H
POLITICS
IN DAWSON,J; DOORNKAMP,J (EDS)
LONDON
1973 3   07

446 DOUGLAS,J N H; BOAL,F W
THE NI PROBLEM
IN BOAL,F W; DOUGLAS,J N H (EDS)
LONDON
1982 1   07

447 DOUGLAS,J N H; OSBORNE,R D
INTRANSIGENT QUEST FOR PEACE
GEOGR MAG 49
1973 1   01

448 DOUGLAS,W
IMPOSSIBILITY OF IRISH UNION, THE AUTHOR
BEING SECRETARY OF THE ULSTER UNIONIST
ASSOCIATION
THE BELL 14(1)
1947 2   01

449 DOWNING,J D
NI: BEYOND RELIGION AND HISTORY
IN DOWNING,J D; SMYTH,J; ROLSTON,B
LONDON
1977 1   10

450 DRAUGHTSMAN'S AND ALLIED TECHNICIANS
ASSOCIATION, NUMBER 3 DIVISIONAL COUNCIL
TRADE UNIONISTS AND THE 'IRISH QUESTION'
THE DRAUGHTSMAN AUG
RICHMOND, SURREY
1964 2   01

451 DUDA,G
IRLAND IM SPANNUNGSFELD: UBERSTAATLICHER
MACHTPOLITIK
PAHL VERLAG
BEBENBURG
1978 1   02

452 DUGGAN,G
NI - SUCCESS OR FAILURE?
IRISH TIMES
DUBLIN
1950 2   10

453 DUGGAN,G
UNITED IRELAND
IRISH TIMES
DUBLIN
1954 2   10

454 DUNNE,G
THE IRISH SEA OF TROUBLES
AMERICA 126
1972 1   01

455 DUTTER,L E
NI AND THEORIES OF ETHNIC POLITICS
J CONFLICT RESOL 24(4)
LONDON
1980 1   01

456 ECCLESTONE,G; ELLIOTT,E
THE IRISH PROBLEM AND OURSELVES
GENERAL SYNOD BOARD
LONDON
1977 1   10

457 EDWARDS,O D
SCOTLAND: LESSONS FROM IRELAND
IN BROWN,G (ED)
EDINBURGH
1975 2   07

458 EDWARDS,R D
IRISH ATTITUDES TO THE NORTH
ADMIN (DUB) 28(1)
DUBLIN
1980 1   01

459 EILBERG,J; FISH,H
NI: A ROLE FOR THE UNITED STATES?
US HOUSE COMMITTEE ON THE JUDICIARY,
SUBCOMMITTEE ON IMMIGRATION,
WASHINGTON, D.C.
1979 1   03

460 ELLIOT,E
POINT DE VUE D'UN PROTESTANT MODERE
TEMPS MODERNES 311
1972 1   01

461 ELLIOTT,R S; HICKIE,J
ULSTER: SOCIAL BACKGROUND OF THE
CONFLICT
IN BUTTERWORTH,E; WEIR,D (EDS)
LONDON
1972 1   01

462 ELLIS,P B
HISTORY OF THE IRISH WORKING CLASS
GOLLANCZ
LONDON
1972 2   02

463 EVGENYEV,F
THE TRAGEDY OF ULSTER
INT AFF 5
LONDON
1972 1   01

464 FAIRWEATHER,E
DON'T YOU KNOW THERE'S A WAR GOING ON?
SPARE RIB 78
1979 1   10

465 FARRELL,M
BATTLE FOR ALGERIA
PD
BELFAST
1973 1   09

466 FARRELL,M
NI: AN ANTI-IMPERIALIST STRUGGLE
SOCIALIST REGISTER
LONDON
1977 1   01

467 FARRELL,M
NI: LOVELY LAND, BUT 'SOMETHING HERE IS
SEPTIC'
NATIONAL CATHOLIC REPORTER SEPT 11
1981 1   01

468 FARRELL,M
STRUGGLE IN THE NORTH
PD
BELFAST
1972 1   09

469 FARREN,S
A DILEMMA FOR SOCIALISTS
LEFT PERSPECTIVES 1(3)
DUBLIN
1981 1 01

470 FAULKNER,B
IRELAND TODAY
AQUARIUS
1971 2 01

471 FAULKNER,J R
AN OPERATIONAL RESEARCHER LOOKS AT THE
SITUATION IN ULSTER
SUSSEX UNIV MSC
BRIGHTON
1976 1 04

472 FELDMAN,E J
TALE OF FOUR CITIES: THE CRISIS OF
FRENCH ALGERIA AND BRITISH IRELAND
JOHNS HOPKINS UNIV
BALTIMORE
        3 99

473 FENNELL,D
CHANGING FACE OF CATHOLIC IRELAND
CHAPMAN
LONDON
1968 2 02

474 FENNELL,D
FAILURE OF THE IRISH REVOLUTION AND ITS
SUCCESS
CAPUCHIN ANNUAL
DUBLIN
1964 1 01

475 FENNELL,D
THE NORTHERN CATHOLIC
IRISH TIMES
DUBLIN
1959 2 10

476 FIELDS,R
SOCIETY ON THE RUN: A PSYCHOLOGY OF NI
PENGUIN
HARMONDSWORTH
1973 1 02

477 FIELDS,R
SOCIETY UNDER SIEGE: A PSYCHOLOGY OF NI
TEMPLE U P
PHILADELPHIA
1977 1 02

478 FINE GAEL
IRELAND: OUR FUTURE TOGETHER
FINE GAEL
DUBLIN
1979 1 09

479 FITZGERALD,G
IRELAND'S IDENTITY PROBLEMS
ET IRL 1
1976 1 01

480 FITZGERALD,G
IRISH IDENTITIES: THE DIMBLEBY LECTURE
BBC
LONDON
1982 1 10

481 FITZGERALD,G
IRLANDE: UNE LUEUR D'ESPOIR?
PREUVES 16
1973 3 01

482 FITZGERALD,G
THE PROBLEM OF NI
BULL DEPT FOREIGN AFFAIRS
DUBLIN
1977 1 03

483 FITZGERALD,G
SCENARIOS OF DISASTER AND HOPE - NI
WORLDVIEW 17(11)
1974 1 01

484 FITZGERALD,G
TOWARDS A NATIONAL PURPOSE
STUDIES 53
1964 2 01

485 FITZGERALD,G
TOWARDS A NEW IRELAND
GILL AND MACMILLAN
DUBLIN
1972   02

486 FLYNN,D
LABOUR AND IRELAND: WHICH WAY TO
WITHDRAWAL?
CHARTIST COLLECTIVE
LONDON
1983 1 09

487 FLYNN,P J
NI: A CASE STUDY IN INTERNAL WAR
CATHOLIC UNIV OF AMERICA PHD
WASHINGTON, D C
1977 1 04

488 FONSECA,E
IRLANDA: QUEM TEM RAZAO?
J PORT ECON E FINS 19
1971 1 01

489 FONSECA,E
A TRAGEDIA IRLANDESA
J PORT ECON E FINS 19
1972 1 01

490 FORSYTHE,J I
ULSTER QUESTION
LINK MAGAZINE DEC
BELFAST
1969 1 10

491 FORTNIGHT
FORTNIGHT OPINION POLL
FORTNIGHT 178
BELFAST
1980 1 01

492 FORTNIGHT
FORTNIGHT OPINION POLL
FORTNIGHT 44
BELFAST
1972 1 01

493 FORTNIGHT
FORTNIGHT OPINION POLL
FORTNIGHT 62
BELFAST
1973 1 01

494 FRASER,G
L'ANACRONIQUE IRLANDE
ANNEE POLIT ET ECON 45(225)
1972 1 01

495 FRASER,H
CIVIL RIGHTS,YES! CIVIL WAR, NO!
SALTCOATS (AYRSHIRE)
1969 1 99

496 FRASER,H
IRELAND 1971: IS CIVIL WAR INEVITABLE?
SALTCOATS (AYRSHIRE)
1971 1 99

497 FREEMAN,M
IRELAND'S VICTORY MEANS BRITAIN'S DEFEAT
REVOLUTIONARY COMMUNIST TENDENCY
LONDON
1980 1 09

498 FROMM,J
A CIVIL WAR NOBODY IS WINNING
U.S. NEWS AND WORLD REPORT 20 MARCH
1972 1 01

499 FULTON,J
IS THE IRISH CONFLICT RELIGIOUS?
SOC STUD 5(3-4)
        1 01

500 GAGEBY, D
NI
IN EDWARDS, O D (ED)
LONDON
1969 2 07

501 GALE, G
THE ORANGE AND THE GREEN
SPECTATOR MAY 15
LONDON
1971 1 01

502 GALE, J
OPPRESSION AND REVOLT IN IRELAND
WORKERS REVOLUTIONARY PARTY
LONDON
1975 1 09

503 GALLAGHER, T
SCOTLAND, BRITAIN AND CONFLICT IN
IRELAND
IN ALEXANDER, Y; O'DAY, A (EDS)
LONDON
1983 1 07

504 GARDNER, L
RESURGENCE OF THE MAJORITY
ULSTER VANGUARD
BELFAST
1971 1 09

505 GARVIN, S
IRELAND: THE TROUBLED TIMES THEN AND NOW
RUSI J 121(2)
LONDON
1976 1 01

506 GARVIN, S
NI: A QUESTION OF IDENTITY
RUSI J 117(1)
LONDON
1972 1 01

507 GARVIN, S
ULSTER AND IRELAND
RUSI J 118(1)
LONDON
1973 1 01

508 GEARY, R C
THE ONENESS OF IRELAND
STUDIES SPRING
DUBLIN
1981 1 01

509 GIBBON, P
THE DIALECTIC OF RELIGION AND CLASS IN
ULSTER
NEW LEFT R 55
1969 1 01

510 GIBBON, P
SOME BASIC PROBLEMS OF THE CONTEMPORARY
SITUATION
SOCIALIST REGISTER
LONDON
1977 1 01

511 GIBBONS, J
QUE SE PASSE-T-IL EN IRELANDE DU NORD?
NOUV R INT 1213
1969 1 01

512 GIBSON, N J
THE NORTHERN PROBLEM: RELIGIOUS OR
ECONOMIC OR WHAT?
COMM FORUM 1(1)
BELFAST
1971 1 01

513 GIBSON, N J
PARTITION TODAY: A NORTHERN VIEWPOINT
TUAIRIM 2
DUBLIN
1958 2 10

514 GILLIES, D
IN PLACE OF TRUTH
UNIONIST PUBLICITY DEPT
BELFAST
1973 1 09

515 GILMORE, G
THE RELEVANCE OF JAMES CONNOLLY IN
IRELAND TODAY
DOCHAS
DUBLIN
        2 09

516 GODIN, H
INTRODUCTION A L'ULSTER
BRITISH COUNCIL
LONDON
1945 2 10

517 GOLDRING, M
L'IRLANDE EN QUESTION
PENSEE 167
PARIS
1973 1 01

518 GOLDRING, M
L'IRLANDE: IDEOLOGIE D'UNE REVOLUTION
NATIONALE
EDITIONS SOCIALES
PARIS
1975 1 02

519 GOLDRING, M
LE DRAME DE L'IRELANDE
BORDAS
PARIS
1972 1 02

520 GOLDRING, M
UNE ALTERNATIVE DEMOCRATIQUE POUR
L'IRLANDE
CAH COMMUNISME 48
1972 1 01

521 GORMAN, S F
A COLONIAL HANGOVER
SENIOR SCHOLASTIC 112
1979 1 01

522 GRAHAM, A
NI: THE UNSOLVED PROBLEM
INDEPENDENT LABOUR PARTY
LONDON
        1 09

523 GRANT, H J
A STUDY OF THE PERSPECTIVES OF MODERATE
OPINION LEADERS IN THE NI SOCIAL
CONFLICT, 1968-1975
US INT UNIV PHD
LOS ANGELES
1976 1 04

524 GRATTAN, J
THE REALITIES OF BELFAST
NEW SOCIETY 16(431)
LONDON
1970 1 01

525 GRAY, T
BESIEGED, BETRAYED...AND BEWILDERED
NEW HUMANIST 88(11)
1973 1 01

526 GRAY, T
THE ORANGE ORDER
BODLEY HEAD
1972 2 02

527 GREAVES, C D
EPILOGUE
IN JACKSON, T A
LONDON
1971 1 07

528 GREAVES, C D
HOW TO END PARTITION
CONNOLLY ASSOCIATION
LONDON
1949 2 09

529 GREAVES, C D
THE IRISH CASE AGAINST PARTITION: FULL
FACTS AND PROGRAMME OF ACTION
CONNOLLY ASSOCIATION
LONDON
1956 2 09

530 GREAVES, C D
THE IRISH CRISIS
LAWRENCE AND WISHART
LONDON
1972 1 02

531 GREAVES, C D
THE IRISH QUESTION AND THE BRITISH
PEOPLE: A PLEA FOR A NEW APPROACH
CONNOLLY PUBLICATIONS
LONDON
1963 2 09

532 GREAVES, C D
NI: CIVIL RIGHTS AND POLITICAL WRONGS
COMMUNIST PARTY GB
LONDON
1969 1 09

533 GREER, H
ULSTER - IN THE EMPTY HOUSE OF THE STARE
COMMENTARY 73(1)
NEW YORK
1982 1 01

534 GREER, H
ULSTER - REPLY
COMMENTARY 73(4)
NEW YORK
1982 1 01

535 GRIBBON, S
THE SOCIAL ORIGINS OF ULSTER UNIONISM
IR ECON AND SOC HISTORY 4
DUNDALK
1977 2 01

536 GRIGG, J
THE IRISH QUESTION
WLD SURVEY 40
1972 1 01

537 GROULART, C
ULSTER, L'IRLANDE DES FOUS DE DIEU
ROSSEL
BRUSSELS
1976 1 10

538 GRUSZKA, W
NI AND ITS THIRD YEAR OF CRISIS
SPRAWY MIEDZYNARODOWE 24(11)
WARSAW
1971 1 01

539 GRUSZKA, W
ULSTER BURZY SIE (ULSTER IN TURMOIL)
MINISTERSTWA OBORONY
WARSAW
1972 1 01

540 GUELKE, A
THE AMERICAN CONNECTION TO THE NI
CONFLICT
ANNUAL CONF UK POLITICS WORKING GROUP,
POLITICAL STUDIES ASSOCIATION SEPT
BELFAST
1982 1 11

541 HACHEY, T E
ONE PEOPLE OR TWO: ORIGINS OF PARTITION
AND PROSPECTS FOR UNIFICATION IN IRELAND
J INT AFFAIRS 27(2)
NEW YORK
1973 1 01

542 HACHEY, T E
PROBLEM OF PARTITION: PERIL TO WORLD
PEACE
RAND MCNALLY
CHICAGO
1972 3 02

543 HADDEN, P
NI: FOR WORKER'S UNITY AND SOCIALISM
INQUABA YA BASEBENZI 5
LONDON
1982 1 01

544 HADDEN, P
NI: TORY CUTS - COMMON MISERY, COMMON
STRUGGLE
LABOUR AND TRADE UNION CO-ORDINATING
GROUP
BELFAST
1980 2 09

545 HADDEN, T
RECRUITING FOR THE IRA
NEW HUMANIST 89(2)
1973 1 01

546 HADDEN, T; HILLYARD, P; BOYLE, K
'TROOPS OUT' IS NO ANSWER
NEW SOCIETY 20 NOV
LONDON
1980 1 01

547 HADDEN, T; HILLYARD, P; BOYLE, K
NI: THE COMMUNAL ROOTS OF VIOLENCE
NEW SOCIETY 6 NOV
LONDON
1980 1 01

548 HAEGER, R A
IN ULSTER, VIOLENCE TURNS HOPE TO
DESPAIR
US NEWS AND WORLD REPORT 90 FEBRUARY 2
1981 1 01

549 HAEGER, R A
IS THE PEACE IN NI BECOMING POSSIBLE AT
LAST?
US NEWS AND WORLD REPORT OCT 24
1977 1 01

550 HAEGER, R A
ON THE SCENE: ULSTER'S DIRTY WAR DRAGS
ON
US NEWS AND WORLD REPORT NOV 12
1979 1 01

551 HAINSWORTH, P
NI: A EUROPEAN ROLE?
J COMMON MARKET STUD 20(1)
OXFORD
1981 2 01

552 HAMILL, J
BELFAST '79: AFTER TEN YEARS OF CIVIL
WAR...
ROLLING STONE 29 NOV
1979 1 01

553 HAMILL, P
IRELAND: THE SHADOW OF THE GUN
IN O'CONNOR, U (ED)
1974 1 07

554 HAMILTON, I
FROM LIBERALISM TO EXTREMISM
CONFLICT STUD 17
LONDON
1971 1 01

555 HAMILTON, I
IRISH TANGLE
CONFLICT STUD 16
1970 1 01

556 HAMILTON, I; MOSS, R
SPREADING IRISH CONFLICT
CONFLICT STUD 17
LONDON
1971 1 01

557 HANCOCK, G
IN THE FRONT LINE: NI
NEW INTERNATIONALIST 47
1977 1 01

558 HAND, G J
LAST FIFTY YEARS: WHAT DID DUBLIN
GOVERNMENTS DO?
SOC STUD 1(3)
1972 2 01

559 HANLY, J
IRELAND CALLING: A PLAN FOR
THE...RECOVERY OF IRELAND BASED ON
CHRISTIAN SOCIAL PRINCIPLES. . . .
PARKSIDE PRESS
DUBLIN
1958 2 02

560 HANNA, F
POLITICS IN NI
CHRISTUS REX 12(2)
DUBLIN
1958 2 01

561 HANSON, R
POLITICS AND THE PULPIT
COMM FORUM 13(3)
BELFAST
1973 3 01

562 HARKIN, B
POLITICAL POSSIBILITIES FOR THE PEOPLE
OF NI
ADMIN (DUB) 20(4)
DUBLIN
1972 1 01

563 HARMAN, C
THE STRUGGLE IN IRELAND
INT SOCIALIST
LONDON
1974 1 09

564 HARRIS, H
THE ULSTER QUESTION
ARMY QUART APRIL
1970 1 01

565 HARRISON, P
DERRY: FROM CONFLICT TO CO-EXISTENCE
NEW SOCIETY 31(642)
LONDON
1975 1 01

566 HARWOOD, J; GUINNESS, J; BIGGS-DAVISON, J
IRELAND - OUR CUBA?
MONDAY CLUB
LONDON
1970 1 09

567 HAUGHEY, C
NI: A NEW APPROACH
ET IRL 5
1980 1 01

568 HAUSER, R
A SOCIAL OPTION: SUGGESTIONS FOR AN
OVERALL COMMUNITY PLANNING APPROACH TO
THE PROBLEM OF NI
INSTITUTE FOR SOCIAL RESEARCH
LONDON
1975 1 10

569 HEALY, J
IRELAND - A DOUBLE DILEMMA
AQUARIUS
BENBURB
1972 1 01

570 HEALY, J
NEW IRELAND IN THE MAKING: AN ANALYSIS
OF THE NI PROBLEM
SOC STUD 2(1)
1973 1 01

571 HEATLEY, F
DIRECT RULE: CIVIL RIGHTS OR CIVIL WAR
NICRA
BELFAST
1972 1 09

572 HECHTER, M
GROUP FORMATION AND THE CULTURAL
DIVISION OF LABOR
AMER J SOCIOL 84(2)
CHICAGO
1978 2 01

573 HECHTER, M
INDUSTRIALISATION AND NATIONAL
DEVELOPMENT IN THE BRITISH ISLES
J DEV STUD 8(3)
LONDON
1972 2 01

574 HECHTER, M
INTERNAL COLONIALISM: THE CELTIC FRINGE
IN BRITISH NATIONAL DEVELOPMENT,
1536-1966
RKP
LONDON
1975 2 02

575 HECHTER, M
PERSISTANCE OF REGIONALISM IN THE
BRITISH ISLES: 1865-1966
AMER J SOCIOL 79(2)
CHICAGO
1973 2 01

576 HECHTER, M
POLITICAL ECONOMY OF ETHNIC CHANGE
AMER J SOCIOL 79(5)
CHICAGO
1974 2 01

577 HECHTER, M
REGIONAL INEQUALITY AND NATIONAL
INTEGRATION: THE CASE OF THE BRITISH
ISLES
J SOC HIST 5(1)
1971 2 01

578 HECHTER, M
TOWARDS A THEORY OF ETHNIC CHANGE
POLITICS AND SOC 2(1)
WASHINGTON, D C
1971 2 01

579 HEISLER, M O
ETHNIC CONFLICT IN THE WORLD TODAY
A AMER ACAD POLIT SOC SCI 433
PHILADELPHIA
1977 1 01

580 HEISLER, M O; PETERS, B G
IMPLICATIONS OF SCARCITY FOR MANAGEMENT
OF CONFLICT IN MULTICULTURAL SOCIETIES
STUD PUBL POL 20
GLASGOW
1978 2 10

581 HEMEL HEMPSTEAD CONSTITUENCY LABOUR
PARTY
IRELAND: AN ALTERNATIVE
HEMEL HEMPSTEAD CONSTITUENCY LABOUR
PARTY
LONDON
1979 1 09

582 HERMLE, R
DER KONFLIKT IN NORDIRLAND...1963-1972
KAISER MAINZ GRUNEWALD
MUNICH
1979 1 02

583 HESKIN, K
NI: A PSYCHOLOGICAL ANALYSIS
GILL AND MACMILLAN
DUBLIN
1980 2 02

584 HESKIN, K
SOCIETAL DISINTEGRATION IN NI: FACT OR
FICTION
ECON AND SOC R 12(2)
DUBLIN
1981 2 01

585 HEUSAFF, A
THE SITUATION IN IRELAND
EUROPA ETHNICA 29(3)
AUSTRIA
1972 1 01

586 HITCHENS, C
IRELAND'S BRITISH PROBLEM
NEW STATESMAN 27 APRIL
LONDON
1979 2 01

587 HOFFMAN, J
THE DIALECTIC BETWEEN DEMOCRACY AND
SOCIALISM IN THE IRISH NATIONAL QUESTION
IN MORGAN, A; PURDIE, B (EDS)
LONDON
1980 1 07

588 HOGBERG, G H
THE TRUTH ABOUT IRELAND
THE PLAIN TRUTH JUN
1972 1 01

589 HOLLAND, J
NI SINCE 68: THE BLOODSHED AND BOBBY
MYTH
NATION 227(14)
1978 1 01

590 HOLLAND, J
NI UNDER THATCHER
TIME 11 JUNE
NEW YORK
1979 2 01

591 HOLLAND, J
TOO LONG A SACRIFICE: LIFE AND DEATH IN
NI
DODD MEAD
NEW YORK
1981 1 02

592 HOLLAND, J
TOWN WITHOUT PITY - LETTERS FROM A
BELFAST GHETTO
NATION 228(11)
1979 1 01

593 HOLLAND, M
DYING MEN WHO STIR THE BOILING POT
NEW STATESMAN 5 DEC
LONDON
1980 1 01

594 HOLMES, E
POLITICAL POSSIBILITIES FOR THE PEOPLE
OF NI
ADMIN (DUB) 20(4)
DUBLIN
1972 2 01

595 HOLMES, R F G
IRISH PRESBYTERIANISM AND MODERN IRISH
NATIONALISM
IN BAKER, D; MEWS, S (EDS)
OXFORD
1981 2 07

596 HOPKINS, S
THE TWO IRELANDS: ON 'RACISM' AND
'IRISHMEN FOR EXPORT'
FREEDOM AT ISSUE 20
1973 1 01

597 HUGHES, C G
THE CATHOLIC CHURCH AND THE CRISIS IN
ULSTER
PENNSYLVANIA STATE UNIV PHD
1976 1 04

598 HUGHES, C G
NI: A STALLED REVOLUTION
SOUTH WESTERN SOCIOLOGICAL ASSOC
PUEBLO, COLORADO
1978 1 11

599 HULL, C
CONSTRUCTIVE CONFLICT: THE VIEW OF
ULSTER
NEW HUMANIST 88(11)
1973 1 01

600 HULL, R H
THE IRISH TRIANGLE: A STUDY OF THE
CONFLICT IN NI
VIRGINIA UNIV
1974 1 04

601 HULL, R H
THE IRISH TRIANGLE: CONFLICT IN NI
PRINCETON U P
PRINCETON, N J
1976 1 02

602 HUMANIST
ULSTER: SPECIAL ISSUE
HUMANIST 87(1)
LONDON
1972 1 10

603 HUME, J
THE IRISH QUESTION: A BRITISH PROBLEM
FOREIGN AFFAIRS
1980 1 01

604 HUNTER, J
AN ANALYSIS OF THE CONFLICT IN NI
IN REA, D (ED)
DUBLIN
1982 1 07

605 ICTU
POLITICAL POLICY IN NI
GAILFOYLE PRINTING
DUBLIN
        2 10

606 ICTU
PROGRAMME FOR PEACE AND PROGRESS IN NI
ICTU
BELFAST
1969 1 09

607 INK
IRELAND RESISTS AGGRESSION
INK 28
1972 1 01

608 INSIDE STORY
NI
INSIDE STORY
LONDON
1972 1 01

609 INSTITUTE FOR THE STUDY OF CONFLICT
NI: PROBLEMS AND PERSPECTIVES
CONFLICT STUD 135
LONDON
1982 1 01

610 INT SOCIALISM
ISSUE ON IRELAND
INT SOCIALISM 51
1972 1 01

611 IRELAND, D
SIX COUNTIES IN SEARCH OF A NATION:
ESSAYS AND LETTERS ON PARTITION.
1942-1946
IRISH NEWS
BELFAST
1947 2 02

612 IRISH COMMUNIST ORGANISATION
SITUATION IN THE NORTH
IR COMMUNIST ORGAN
CORK
1969 1 09

613 IRISH COUNCIL OF CHURCHES
VIOLENCE IN IRELAND
CHRISTIAN J AND VERITAS
BELFAST AND DUBLIN
1976 1 02

614 IRISH FREEDOM MOVEMENT
AN ANTI-IMPERIALIST'S GUIDE TO THE IRISH
WAR
JUNIUS PUBLICATIONS
LONDON
1983 1 02

615 JACKSON, H
TWO IRELANDS: A DUAL STUDY OF
INTER-GROUP TENSIONS
MINORITY RIGHTS GROUP
LONDON
1971 1 10

616 JACKSON, J A; ROCHE, S
NATIONAL IDENTITY IN NI
ESRI
DUBLIN
1976 1 08

617 JAMES, M
FAILURE OF BRITAIN'S IRISH POLICY
AUSTRAL QUART 47(1)
1975 1 01

618 JANKE, P; PRICE, D L
ULSTER: CONSENSUS AND COERCION
CONFLICT STUD 50
LONDON
1974 1 01

619 JENKINS, G; BAMBERY, C
SOCIALISM OR NATIONALISM
SOCIALIST R APR
LONDON
1983 2 01

620 JOANNON, P
HISTOIRE, POLITIQUE, INSTITUTIONS
IRLANDAISES 1976-77
ET IRL 2
1977 1 01

621 JOANNON, P
L'IRELANDE DU NORD: DU CONCENSUS
INTROUVABLE A L'AUTODETERMINATION
IMPOSSIBLE
IN UNKNOWN
PARIS AND NICE
1980 1 07

622 JOANNON, P
REFLEXIONS SUR LE REVISIONNISME
ET IRL 2
LILLE
1977 1 01

623 JOANNON, P; DEUTSCH, R
HISTOIRE, POLITIQUE, INSTITUTIONS
IRLANDAISES 1975-76
ET IRL 1
1976 1 01

624 JOANNON, P; DEUTSCH, R
HISTOIRE, POLITIQUE, INSTITUTIONS
IRLANDAISES: 1977-8
ET IRL 3
LILLE
1978 1 01

625 JOHNSON, J H
POLITICAL DISTINCTIVENESS OF NI
GEOGR R 51(1)
NEW YORK
1962 2 01

626 JOHNSON, R W
IRELAND AND THE RUNCIBLE MEN
NEW SOCIETY 25 JUN
LONDON
1981 2 01

627 KANE, J J
CIVIL RIGHTS IN NI
R POLITICS 33(1)
NOTRE DAME, INDIANA
1971 1 01

628 KARCH, C
NI - DEVELOPMENT OF A PRE-REVOLUTIONARY
SOCIETY
CALIFORNIA U P
DAVIS
1971 1 04

629 KELLEHER, D
IRISH UNITY THROUGH EUROPEAN UNITY
GAZ INCORP LAW SOC IR 66
1972 1 01

630 KELLEHER, D
ON TO THE REPUBLIC
RIPENING OF TIME
DUBLIN
1982 1 09

631 KELLEHER, D
REPUBLICANISM, CHRISTIANITY AND MARXISM
REPSOL
DROGHEDA
1970 1 09

632 KELLEHER, J V
CAN IRELAND UNITE?
ATLANTIC MONTHLY 193
1954 2 01

633 KELLY, H
NI: BEGINNING OR END?
EIRE-IRELAND 7(1)
ST. PAUL, MINNESOTA, USA
1972 1 01

634 KELLY, H
NI: SO FAR
EIRE-IRELAND 6(4)
ST. PAUL, MINNESOTA
1971 1 01

635 KELLY, H
THE PROSPECTS FOR PEACE
EUROP R 23(1)
1973 1 01

636 KENNEDY, C
LABOUR AND IRELAND
IRL SOCIALIST R 1
1978 2 01

637 KENNEDY, C
LABOUR, DEMOCRACY AND IRELAND
IRL SOCIALIST R 4
1979 2 01

638 KENNEDY, D
WHITHER NORTHERN NATIONALISM?
CHRISTUS REX 13(4)
1959 2 01

639 KENNEDY, E M
ULSTER IS AN INTERNATIONAL ISSUE
FOREIGN POLICY 11
NEW YORK
1973 1 01

640 KIELY, B
COUNTIES OF CONTENTION: A STUDY OF THE
ORIGINS AND IMPLICATIONS OF PARTITION OF
IRELAND
MERCIER
CORK
1945 2 02

641 KIESEL, F
FOR AN ISSUE TO THE DRAMA IN NI
SYNTHESES 27(309/310)
BELGIUM
1972 1 01

642 KIND, C
A REPORT ON IRELAND: NI AND EIRE
SWISS R WLD AFFAIRS 18
1969 1 01

643 KING, C
ON IRELAND
JONATHAN CAPE
LONDON
1971 2 02

644 KING, C
THE ORANGE AND THE GREEN
MACDONALD
LONDON
1965 2 02

645 KNOX, R
ULSTER: IRELAND'S BLIND EYE:
DIFFICULTIES IN THE WAY OF BORDER
COOPERATION
ROUND TABLE 276
LONDON
1979 1 01

646 KOHL, J
IRLAND: RELIGIOUSKRIEG ODER KLASSENKAMPF
KOLNER Z SOZ SZ-PSY 24(2)
KOLN-OPLADEN
1972 1 01

647 KOLPAKOV, A D
IRLANDIYA-OSTROV MYATEZHNYI
"NAUKA"
MOSCOW
1965 2 02

648 KOUCHNER, B
LES JOURS DE CETTE GUERRE
TEMPS MODERNES 311
1973 1 01

649 KRLOV, L S
ENGLAND AGAINST THE PEOPLE OF NI
VOPROSY ISTORII 12
MOSCOW
1978 1 01

650 KYLE, K
PANORAMA SURVEY OF IRISH OPINION
POLIT QUART 50(1)
LONDON
1979 1 01

651 LACOSTE, R
L'INSOLUBLE PROBLEME DE L'IRLANDE DU
NORD
ESCRITS DE PARIS 341
PARIS
1974 1 01

652 LAVIN, D
POLITICS IN ULSTER
WLD TODAY 24
LONDON
1968 2 01

653 LEACH, R H
THATCHER'S BRITAIN
CURRENT HISTORY MAY
1981 1 01

654 LEBOW, R N
CIVIL WAR IN IRELAND: A TRAGEDY IN
ENDLESS ACTS?
J INT AFFAIRS 27(2)
NEW YORK
1973 1 01

655 LEBOW, R N
IRELAND
IN HENDERSON, G; LEBOW, R N; STOESSINGER, J
(EDS)
NEW YORK
1972 1 07

656 LEE, G; TAYLOR, R
ULSTER
ECONOMIST
1971 1 01

657 LENNON, B
TOWARDS CO-RESPONSIBILITY IN NI
MONTH APR
LONDON
1983 1 01

658 LEON, G
POLITICS OF CIVIL RIGHTS IN NI: SOME
VIEWS AND OBSERVATIONS
CITHERA 10(1)
1970 1 01

659 LERUEZ, J
CRISE NORD-IRLANDAISE
R FRAN SCI POLIT 26(3)
1976 1 01

660 LERUEZ, J
Y A-T-IL UNE ISSUE EN IRLANDE DU NORD?
R DEFENSE NATIONALE
1972 1 01

661 LIJPHART, A
DEMOCRACY IN PLURAL SOCIETIES
YALE U P
NEW HAVEN, CONN
1977 2 02

662 LIJPHART, A
NI PROBLEM: CASES, THEORIES, AND
SOLUTIONS
BRIT J POLIT SCI 5(1)
LONDON
1975 1 01

663 LINDSAY, K
DOMINION OF ULSTER
ULSTER VANGUARD
BELFAST
1972 1 09

664 LIPSEY, D
WHAT SHOULD WE DO ABOUT NI?
NEW SOCIETY 57(984)
LONDON
1981 1 01

665 LONGFORD, LORD; MCHARDY, A
ULSTER
WEIDENFELD AND NICOLSON
LONDON
1981 1 02

666 LYNCH, J
ANGLO-IRISH PROBLEM
FOREIGN AFFAIRS 50(4)
NEW YORK
1972 1 01

667 LYNCH, J
HAVE WE BETRAYED THE MEN OF 1916?
ET IRL 2
1977 1 01

668 LYNCH, J
SPEECHES AND STATEMENTS 8/69-10/71:
IRISH UNITY, NI, ANGLO-IRISH RELATIONS
GOVERNMENT INFORMATION BUREAU
DUBLIN
1971 1 03

669 LYNN, R
THE SOCIOBIOLOGY OF NATIONALISM
NEW SOCIETY JULY 1
LONDON
1976 1 01

670 LYSAGHT, D R O'C
BRITISH IMPERIALISM IN IRELAND
IN MORGAN, A; PURDIE, B (EDS)
LONDON
1980 1 07

671 LYSAGHT, D R O'C
MAKING OF NI... AND THE BASIS OF ITS
UNDOING
CITIZENS' COMMITTEE
DUBLIN
1969 1 09

672 MACAULAY, A
BRITAIN'S NEW IRISH STATE: BASED ON
ILLEGALITY AND TREASON
CAPUCHIN ANNUAL
DUBLIN
1972 1 01

673 MACBRIDE, S
ANGLO-IRISH RELATIONS
INT AFF (LONDON) APRIL
1949 2 01

674 MACBRIDE, S
ANGLO-IRISH RELATIONSHIPS: THE
OVERWHELMING MAJORITY OF PEOPLE WANT A
UNITED IRELAND
VITAL SPEECHES NOV 1
1981 1 01

675 MACDONAGH, O
TIME'S REVENGE AND REVENGE'S TIME: A
VIEW OF ANGLO-IRISH RELATIONS
ANGLO-IRISH STUD 4
1979 1 01

676 MACEOIN, G
NI: CAPTIVE OF HISTORY
HOLT, RINEHART AND WINSTON
NEW YORK
1974 1 02

677 MACGIOLLA, T
NI: A REPUBLICAN VIEW
NEW BLACKFRIARS 57
1976 1 01

678 MACGIOLLA, T
THE STRUGGLE FOR DEMOCRACY, PEACE AND
FREEDOM
REPSOL
DUBLIN
1976 1 09

679 MAFFIA, E
ULSTER: UN CASO DI COLONIALISMO IN
GRANTI GIALLI
CRIT SOCIOL (ROMA) 19
1971 1 01

680 MAGEE, J
NI, CRISIS AND CONFLICT
RKP
LONDON
1974 1 02

681 MAGILL
NATIONAL OPINION POLL REPORT
MAGILL 1(1)
1977 1 01

682 MAHON, V
NOVEL APPROACHES TO NI VIOLENCE
J CONFLICT RES SOC 1(3)
1978 1 01

683 MAHONY, P
THE IRISH TANGLE
J SOC AND POLIT STUD 3(1)
1978 1 01

684 MALLALIEU, E L; SAVORY, D L
THE PARTITION OF IRELAND: FEELING IN
EIRE AND ULSTER'S REJOINDER
NAT R MARCH
1949 2 01

685 MANO, D K
ERIN GO BLAH
NATIONAL R NOV 28
1980 1 01

686 MARLOWE, T; PALMER, S
IRELAND: IMPERIALISM IN CRISIS 1968-78
REVOLUTIONARY COMMUNIST(8)
1978 1 01

687 MARLOWE, T; WHITTAKER, P
THE COMMUNIST PARTY OF GREAT BRITAIN AND
IRELAND: THE BRITISH ROAD TO SOCIAL
IMPERIALISM
REVOLUTIONARY COMMUNIST (7)
1977 1 01

688 MARTIN, J
THE CONFLICT IN NI: MARXIST
INTERPRETATIONS
CAPITAL AND CLASS 18
LONDON
1982 1 01

689 MASTERS, M
WORKERS AGAINST IMPERIALISM: THE BRITISH
LABOUR MOVEMENT AND IRELAND
REVOLUTIONARY COMMUNIST PAMPHLETS 5
BRIGHTON
1979 1 09

690 MASTERS, M; MURPHY, P
BRITISH IMPERIALISM AND THE IRISH CRISIS
REVOLUTIONARY COMMUNIST PAPERS 2
LONDON
1978 1 09

691 MAUTHNER, G
EXTREMISTEN, REVOLUTIONARE UND
FEINDLICHE BRUDER
WELTWOCHE 36(1826)
ZURICH
1968 1 01

692 MAWHINNEY, B; WELLS, R
CONFLICT AND CHRISTIANITY IN NI
LION
BECKHAMPSTEAD
1975 1 02

693 MCALLISTER, I
CHANGING ATTITUDES TO NI
STUD PUBL POL 11
GLASGOW
1977 1 10

694 MCALLISTER, I
UK NATIONALISM; ONE NATIONALISM OR THREE
IN MADGWICK, P; ROSE, R (EDS)
LONDON
1981 2 07

695 MCANULTY, J
A PEOPLE UNDEFEATED: TEN YEARS OF
STRUGGLE IN THE NORTH OF IRELAND
PD
BELFAST
1979 1 09

696 MCATEER, E
IRISH ACTION: NEW THOUGHTS ON AN OLD
SUBJECT
DONEGAL DEMOCRAT
BALLYSHANNON
1948 2 09

697 MCCAFFERTY, N
THE 1950'S AND 1960'S IN DERRY
IN GMELCH, S (ED)
1979 2 07

698 MCCANN, E
TEN YEARS IN THE NORTH OF IRELAND
SOCIALIST R OCT
1978 1 01

699 MCCANN, E
WAR AND AN IRISH TOWN
PENGUIN
HARMONDSWORTH
1979 1 02

700 MCCARTHY, C; BLEASE, W J
CROSS-BORDER INDUSTRIAL COOPERATION:
LIMITS AND POSSIBILITIES
ADMIN (DUB) 26(3)
1978 1 01

701 MCCARTHY,J P
THE VIEW FROM DUBLIN: PEACE PROSPECTS IN
NI
NEW LEADER 26 SEPT
1977 1 01

702 MCCLUNG LEE,A
CHANGING IMPERIAL RELATIONS IN IRELAND
ASA ANNUAL MEETING
1972 1 11

703 MCCLUNG LEE,A
IMPERIALISM, CLASS AND NI'S CIVIL WAR
CRIME AND SOCIAL JUSTICE 8
BERKLEY, CALIFORNIA
1977 1 01

704 MCCLUNG LEE,A
IS ULSTER'S CONFLICT RELIGIOUS?
CHURCH AND STATE 29
1976 1 01

705 MCCLUNG LEE,A
NONVIOLENT AGENCIES IN THE NI STRUGGLE
1968-1979
SOCIOL SOC WELFARE 7
1980 1 01

706 MCCLUNG LEE,A
SOCIAL CLASS DIFFERENCES IN NONVIOLENT
CONFRONTATIONS: THE NI CASE
AMER HISTORICAL SOCIETY
1978 1 11

707 MCCLUNG LEE,A
TO WHAT IS IRELAND'S CIVIL WAR RELEVANT?
HOLY CROSS QUART 6(1-4)
1974 1 01

708 MCCRACKEN,J
THE POLITICAL SCENE IN NI 1926-27
IN MACMANUS,F (ED)
DUBLIN
1967 2 07

709 MCDONALD,F
NI: THE UNSINKABLE MYTHS
NATIONAL R SEPT 25
1981 1 01

710 MCDOWELL,M
IRISH UNITY: A PROTESTANT'S VIEW
NATION FEB 16
1980 1 01

711 MCDOWELL,M
REMOVING THE BRITISH GUARANTEE: A POLICY
BASED ON RIGOUR OR RHETORIC?
CRANE BAG 4(2)
DUBLIN
1980 1 01

712 MCEVOY,J
CATHOLIC HOPES AND PROTESTANT FEARS
IRISH ASSOCIATION
DUBLIN
1983 2 11

713 MCKEOWN,C
THE PATH OF PEACE
PEACE PEOPLE
BELFAST
1979 1 10

714 MCKEOWN,C
THE PERSON OF PEACE
PEACE PEOPLE
BELFAST
1980 1 99

715 MCKEOWN,C
THE PRICE OF PEACE
PEACE PEOPLE PUBLICATIONS
BELFAST
1976 1 10

716 MCKEOWN,M
IRISH DIMENSIONS: FOUR ESSAYS ON ASPECTS
OF VIOLENCE IN NI
AUTHOR
BELFAST
1977 1 08

717 MCKITTRICK,D
THE CLASS STRUCTURE OF UNIONISM
CRANE BAG 4(2)
DUBLIN
1980 1 01

718 MCKITTRICK,D
THE IRISH CONNECTION
ATLAS 29
1979 1 01

719 MCLAUGHLIN,J
INDUSTRIAL CAPITALISM, ULSTER UNIONISM
AND ORANGEISM: AN HISTORICAL APPRAISAL
ANTIPODE 11(2)
WORCESTER, MASS
1980 2 01

720 MCLEAN,I
POLITICS OF NATIONALISM AND DEVOLUTION
POLIT STUD(OXFORD) 25(3)
1977 3 01

721 MCLENNAN,G
BRITAIN AND THE IRISH CRISIS
COMMUNIST PARTY
LONDON
1973 1 09

722 MCMANUS,F
ULSTER: THE FUTURE
AUTHOR
CAVAN
1972 1 09

723 MCSORLEY,R T
TRYING TO TAME THE FIGHTING IRISH
US CATHOLIC 42
1977 1 01

724 MCWHIRTER,L
INTRODUCTION TO THE SYMPOSIUM: NI - MYTH
AND REALITY
B BRIT PSYCHOL SOC MAY
1980 1 01

725 MCWHIRTER,L
NI: VISIONS OF THE FUTURE
ANNUAL CONF NI BRANCH BRIT PSYCHOL
SOCIETY
ROSAPENNA
1983 2 11

726 MENENDEZ,A J
THE BITTER HARVEST: CHURCH AND STATE IN
NI
ROBERT B LUCE
NEW YORK
1973 1 02

727 MILLER,D W
CHURCH, STATE AND NATION IN IRELAND
GILL AND MACMILLAN
DUBLIN
1973 2 02

728 MILLER,D W
PRESBYTERIANISM AND MODERNIZATION IN
ULSTER
PAST AND PRESENT 80
1978 2 01

729 MILNOR,A
POLITICS, VIOLENCE AND SOCIAL CHANGE IN
NI
WESTERN SOCIETIES PROGRAMME OCCASIONAL
PAPER
ITHACA, NEW YORK
1976 1 10

730 MITCHEL,N C
IRELAND: DIVIDED ISLAND
GEOFORUM 8
1971 1 01

General Political Analyses/

731 MITCHEL,N C; DOUGLAS,J N H
DEVOLUTION IN THE UK: NI PARADOX
GEOGR MAG 51(2)
LONDON
1978 3 01

732 MITCHELL,I; MILLER,N
THESES ON NI
SOLIDARITY 7(1)
1972 1 01

733 MITCHELL,J K
SOCIAL VIOLENCE IN NI
GEOGR R 69(2)
1979 1 01

734 MITCHELL,R
ONE ISLAND, TWO NATIONS
WORKERS' ASSOCIATION FOR A DEMOCRATIC
SETTLEMENT OF THE NATIONAL CONFLICT IN
IRELAND
DUBLIN
1973 1 09

735 MOHN,A H
TRAGEDIEN NORD-IRLAND
GYLDENDAL
OSLO
1972 1 02

736 MOHRING,H
NORDIRLAND, AUTONOMIE HANGT AM SEIDENEN
FADEN DIE HINTERGRUNDE EINER TRAGODIE
DIE ZEIT 24(43)
HAMBURG
1969 1 02

737 MOIR,P
RED HAND OF ULSTER
WORLDVIEW 19(12)
1976 1 01

738 MONDAY,M
A SUMMER OF SUNSHINE: INTERVIEWS IN NI
DAVIDSON
PHOENIX
1976 1 02

739 MOODIE,M; BRAY,F T J
BRITISH POLICY OPTIONS IN NI:
'ALTERNATIVE ROUTES TO THE CEMETERY?'
FLETCHER FORUM 1
1976 1 01

740 MOORE,R
PLURAL SOCIETIES
RACE 14(1)
1972 3 01

741 MORGAN,A
POLITICS, THE LABOUR MOVEMENT AND THE
WORKING CLASS IN BELFAST 1905-1923
QUB PHD
BELFAST
1978 2 04

742 MORGAN,A
SOCIALISM IN IRELAND: RED, GREEN AND
ORANGE
IN MORGAN,A; PURDIE,B (EDS)
1980 1 07

743 MORRISSEY,M
THE BRITISH LEFT AND THE CRISIS IN NI:
WHAT STRATEGY?
IN BRIDGES,G; BLUNT,R (EDS)
LONDON
1981 1 01

744 MORRISSEY,M
ECONOMIC CHANGE AND POLITICAL STRATEGY
IN NI
ECON BULL 8
LONDON
1981 1 01

745 MOSKIN,J R
IRISH TROUBLES
WLD PRESS R JULY
1980 2 01

746 MOSS,R
THE ULSTER DEBATE
IN CROZIER,B (ED)
LONDON
1973 1 07

747 MOXON-BROWNE,E
CURRENT POLITICAL ATTITUDES IN NI
IN CSPP 1, STRATHCLYDE UNIV
GLASGOW
1977 1 10

748 MOXON-BROWNE,E
CURRENT POLITICAL ATTITUDES IN NI
DEPT POLIT SCI QUB
BELFAST
1978 1 08

749 MOXON-BROWNE,E
IRELAND: AN EAGER CONSUMMATION
IN HERMAN,V; HAGGER,M (EDS)
FARNBOROUGH
1980 2 07

750 MOXON-BROWNE,E
NATION, CLASS AND CREED
GOWER
ALDERSHOT
1983 1 02

751 MOXON-BROWNE,E
NI
IN KOLINSKY,M (ED)
MANCHESTER
1978 2 07

752 MOXON-BROWNE,E
NI AND THE POLITICAL SCIENTIST
DEPT POLIT SCI QUB
BELFAST
1978 2 08

753 MULLEN,M
IRELAND'S RIGHT TO UNITY
BRITISH PEACE COMMITTEE
LONDON
1975 1 09

754 MULVIHILL,R F
ATTITUDES TOWARD POLITICAL VIOLENCE: A
SURVEY OF CATHOLICS AND PROTESTANTS
PHILADELPHIA UNIV
PHILADELPHIA
1979 1 04

755 MUNCK,R
CLASSE OUVRIERE ET QUESTION NATIONALE EN
IRLANDE
PLURIEL 29
1982 1 01

756 MUNCK,R
A DIVIDED WORKING CLASS: PROTESTANT AND
CATHOLIC WORKERS IN NI
LABOUR, CAPITAL AND SOCIETY 13(1)
MONTREAL
1980 1 01

757 MUNCK,R
LABOUR AND THE NATIONAL QUESTION IN
IRELAND
DEPT SOCIOL AND SOC POLICY ULSTER
COLLEGE
BELFAST
1979 1 08

758 MUNCK,R
MARXISM AND NI
R RADICAL POLIT ECON 13(3)
1981 1 01

759 MUNRO,H
THE NI IDENTITY
CONTEMP R 229(1331)
1976 1 01

760 MUNRO,H
NI: A BACKGROUND TO CRISIS
CONTEMP R 226(1313)
1975 1 01

761 MUNRO,H
NI: IS THERE A SOLUTION?
CONTEMP R 227(1314)
1975 1 01

762 MUNRO,H
THE REPUBLIC OF IRELAND: ECONOMIC
TURMOIL AND CONSTITUTIONAL QUESTIONING
CONTEMP R 239
LONDON
1981 2 01

763 MURPHY,J A
FURTHER REFLECTIONS ON NATIONALISM
CRANE BAG 2
DUBLIN
1978 2 01

764 MURPHY,J A
RELIGIOUS MAJORITIES AND MINORITIES THEN
AND NOW
CRANE BAG 5(1)
DUBLIN
1981 2 01

765 MURPHY,M
NINETEENTH AND TWENTIETH CENTURY
PATTERNS OF VIOLENT BEHAVIOUR IN IRISH
LIFE
IN SULLIVAN,E ET AL (EDS)
GAINESVILLE, FLORIDA
1976 Z 07

766 MURRAY,S
ROBINSON CRUSOE POLITICS: BEING AN ESSAY
ON NORTH OF IRELAND POLITICS
THE BELL 12(6)
1946 2 01

767 NAIRN,T
THE BREAK-UP OF BRITAIN: CRISIS AND
NEO-NATIONALISM
NEW LEFT BOOKS
LONDON
1977 2 02

768 NAIRN,T
IRELAND: REARGUARD OR VANGUARD?
LIBERATION 20(1)
1976 1 01

769 NATIONAL OPINION POLLS MARKET RESEARCH
LTD
POLITICAL OPINION IN NI
NATIONAL OPINION POLLS MARKET RESEARCH
LTD
LONDON
1974 1 10

770 NELSON,S
PROTESTANT IDEOLOGY CONSIDERED
IN CREWE,I (ED)
LONDON
1975 1 07

771 NELSON,S
PROTESTANT WORKING CLASS POLITICS
SOC STUD 5(3-4)
1976 1 01

772 NEW OUTLOOK
ULSTER: SPECIAL ISSUE
NEW OUTLOOK 1
LONDON
1972 1 01

773 NEW REVIEW
MODEST PROPOSAL TO INSTITUTIONALISE THE
WAR IN NI AND TO MAKE IT BENEFICIAL
NEW R 4(48)
1978 1 01

774 NEW SOCIETY
WHAT THE PEOPLE OF ULSTER THINK
NEW SOCIETY 6 SEPT
LONDON
1979 1 01

775 NEW ULSTER POLITICAL RESEARCH GROUP
(UDA)
BEYOND THE RELIGIOUS DIVIDE
NUPRG
BELFAST
1979 1 09

776 NEWE,G B
THE CATHOLIC IN THE NI COMMUNITY
CHRISTUS REX 18(1)
1964 2 01

777 NEWE,G B
WHITHER IRELAND NOW?
AQUARIUS
BENBURB
1974 1 01

778 NEWMAN,J
STATE OF IRELAND
FOUR COURTS PRESS
DUBLIN
1977 1 02

779 NI GOVERNMENT
RECORD OF CONSTRUCTIVE CHANGE
HMSO CMD 558
BELFAST
1971 1 03

780 NI GOVERNMENT
WHY THE BORDER MUST BE - STATEMENT BY
BROOKEBOROUGH AND OTHERS
BAIRD
BELFAST
1956 2 09

781 NI OFFICE
GOVERNMENT OF NI: A SOCIETY DIVIDED
HMSO
LONDON
1975 1 01

782 NICRA
PROPOSALS FOR PEACE
NICRA
BELFAST
1973 1 10

783 NICRA
TRUE FACTS
NICRA
BELFAST
1974 1 09

784 NILP
SIGNPOSTS TO THE NEW ULSTER
NILP
BELFAST
1964 2 09

785 NOSSITER,B
WOUND IN ULSTER
IN NOSSITER,B (ED)
1978 1 07

786 NOWLAN,K B
COMMENT ON CHAPTER BY STEWART
IN WATT,D (ED)
LONDON
1981 1 07

787 NUM
A CHALLENGE TO STATESMANSHIP: PAPER
PRESENTED TO NI CONVENTION
SPECTATOR NEWSPAPERS
BANGOR
1974 1 10

788 NUM
A COMMENTARY ON THE PROGRAMME OF REFORMS
FOR NI
NUM
BELFAST
1971 1 10

789 NUM
NI AND THE COMMON MARKET
NUM
BELFAST
1972 2 10

790 NUM
TWO IRELANDS OR ONE?
NUM
BELFAST
1972 1 10

791 NUM
VIOLENCE AND NI
NUM
BELFAST
1972 1 10

792 NUM
THE WAY FORWARD
NUM
BELFAST
1971 1 10

793 NUSIGHT
CRISIS IN THE NORTH
NUSIGHT SEPT
1969 1 01

794 O'BRADAIGH,R
OUR PEOPLE, OUR FUTURE
SINN FEIN
DUBLIN
1973 2 09

795 O'BRIEN,C C
COMMENT ON CHAPTERS BY ARNOLD, JENKINS
AND WHITE
IN WATT,D (ED)
LONDON
1981 1 07

796 O'BRIEN,C C
THE EMBERS OF EASTER 1916-66
NEW LEFT R 37
1966 2 01

797 O'BRIEN,C C
HANDS OFF
FOREIGN POLICY 37
NEW YORK
1979 1 01

798 O'BRIEN,C C
HOLY WAR IN IRELAND
NEW YORK R BOOKS 13(8)
1969 1 01

799 O'BRIEN,C C
IRELAND AND MINORITY RIGHTS
HUMANIST 88(11)
1973 1 01

800 O'BRIEN,C C
IRELAND WILL NOT HAVE PEACE: THE ROMANCE
OF FAILURE PRESUPPOSES THE NECESSITY FOR
CONTINUING BLOODSHED
HARPER'S MAG DEC
1976 1 01

801 O'BRIEN,C C
NATIONALISM AND THE RECONQUEST OF
IRELAND
CRANE BAG 1(2)
DUBLIN
1977 1 01

802 O'BRIEN,C C
NEIGHBOURS: EWART-BIGGS MEMORIAL
LECTURES, 1978-79
FABER
LONDON
1980 1 02

803 O'BRIEN,C C
NI: ITS PAST AND ITS FUTURE: THE FUTURE
RACE 14(1)
1972 1 01

804 O'BRIEN,C C
THE PROTESTANT MINORITY: WITHIN AND
WITHOUT
CRANE BAG 5(1)
DUBLIN
1981 1 01

805 O'BRIEN,C C
STATES OF IRELAND
HUTCHINSON
LONDON
1972 1 02

806 O'BRIEN,C C
VIOLENCE IN IRELAND: ANOTHER ALGERIA?
NEW YORK R BOOKS 17
1971 1 01

807 O'BRIEN,C C
WE IRISH
ET IRL 4
1975 3 01

808 O'BRIEN,C C
WHAT RIGHTS SHOULD MINORITIES HAVE?
NEW COMM 2(2)
1973 1 01

809 O'CONNOR,J F
DISTURBANCES IN NI: AN INTERNATIONAL
PROBLEM AND AN INTERNATIONAL SOLUTION
INT RELAT (LONDON) 3(12)
1971 1 01

810 O'DAY,A
THE ENGLISH FACE OF IRISH NATIONALISM
GILL AND MACMILLAN
DUBLIN
1977 2 02

811 O'DONNELL,P
THE ORANGEMAN
THE BELL 19(1)
DUBLIN
1953 2 01

812 O'DONNELL,P
UP STORMONT WAY
THE BELL 19(2)
DUBLIN
1954 2 01

813 O'DONNELL,P
WHEN A MINORITY SULKS
THE BELL 16(4)
DUBLIN
1951 2 01

814 O'DOWD,L
SHAPING AND RESHAPING THE ORANGE STATE:
AN INTRODUCTORY ANALYSIS
IN O'DOWD,L; ROLSTON,B; TOMLINSON,M
LONDON
1980 1 07

815 O'DOWD,L; ROLSTON,B; TOMLINSON,M
CLASS, SECTARIANISM AND REFORM IN NI
IN PROC CSE ANN CONF
LONDON
1979 1 11

816 O'DOWD,L; ROLSTON,B; TOMLINSON,M
FROM LABOUR TO THE TORIES: THE IDEOLOGY
OF CONTAINMENT IN NI
CAPITAL AND CLASS 18
LONDON
1982 1 01

817 O'HEARN,D
ACCUMULATION AND THE IRISH CRISIS
MONTHLY R 32(10)
1981 2 01

818 O'LEARY,C
THE CATHOLIC IN POLITICS
CHRISTUS REX 17(4)
1963 2 01

819 O'LEARY,C
CELTIC NATIONALISM: A STUDY OF ETHNIC
MOVEMENTS IN THE BRITISH ISLES
JERUSALEM J INT RELAT 2(2)
1977 2 01

820 O'LEARY,C
THE NI CRISIS AND ITS OBSERVERS
POLIT QUART 42(3)
1971 1 01

821 O'LEARY,C
NI: THE POLITICS OF ILLUSION
POLIT QUART 40(3)
LONDON
1969 1 01

822 O'MAHONY,D
IRELAND: ONE COUNTRY, TWO STATES
BRITISH SURVEY
LONDON
1966 2 02

823 O'NEILL,D
THE PARTITION OF IRELAND
GILL
DUBLIN
1949 2 02

824 O'NEILL,T
ULSTER AT THE CROSSROADS
FABER
LONDON
1969 2 02

825 OBERSCHALL,A
CONFLICT AND CONFLICT RESOLUTION IN NI
DEPT SOCIOLOGY, VANDERBILT UNIV
NASHVILLE TENNESEE
1973 1 08

826 OLIVER,J
ULSTER TODAY AND TOMORROW
PEP 574
LONDON
1978 1 10

827 OPINION RESEARCH CENTRE
WHAT THE PEOPLE OF ULSTER THINK
NEW SOCIETY 6 SEP
LONDON
1979 1 01

828 ORR,L
THE ORANGE ORDER
SOLON 1(2)
1970 2 01

829 ORRIDGE,A W
EXPLANATIONS OF IRISH NATIONALISM: A
REVIEW AND SOME SUGGESTIONS
BIRMINGHAM UNIV
BIRMINGHAM
1977 1 08

830 ORRIDGE,A W
PERIPHERAL NATIONALISM
UNIV OF BIRMINGHAM ENGLAND
1977 1 08

831 ORRIDGE,A W
UNEVEN DEVELOPMENT AND NATIONALISM
UNIV OF BIRMINGHAM
BIRMINGHAM
1978 1 08

832 OVERY,B
A PACIFIST PERSPECTIVE ON THE CIVIL
RIGHTS MOVEMENT
LANCASTER UNIV
LANCASTER
1971 1 10

833 PAGE,E
MICHAEL HECHTER'S INTERNAL COLONIAL
THESIS: SOME THEORETICAL AND
METHODOLOGICAL PROBLEMS
EUROP J POLIT RES 6(3)
AMSTERDAM
1978 2 01

834 PAISLEY,I R K
DAGGER OF TREACHERY STRIKES AT THE HEART
OF ULSTER
MARTYRS MEMORIAL PUBLICATIONS
BELFAST
1972 1 09

835 PAISLEY,I R K
NI - WHAT IS THE REAL SITUATION?
BOB JONES U P
GREENVILLE, SOUTH CAROLINA
1970 1 09

836 PAISLEY,I R K
UNITED IRELAND - NEVER!
PURITAN PRINTING
BELFAST
1972 1 09

837 PAKENHAM,F
PEACE BY ORDEAL: THE ANGLO-IRISH TREATY,
1921
SIDGWICK AND JACKSON
LONDON
1972 2 02

838 PAKENHAM,F
THE TREATY NEGOTIATIONS
IN WILLIAMS,T D (ED)
1966 2 07

839 PALME DUTT,R
IRELAND: BATTLEFRONT FOR DEMOCRACY
NEW BOOKS PUBLICATIONS
DUBLIN
1974 1 09

840 PARKER,S; DRIVER,C
CAPITALISM IN IRELAND
B CONF SOCIALIST ECON 4(2)
1975 1 01

841 PARKES,J P
IRELAND AFTER ENGLAND LEAVES
AMERICA 17 MAR
1979 1 01

842 PARKES,J P
WAR WITHOUT END, AMEN
AMERICA 19 AUG
1978 1 01

843 PARSON,D
POLITICS BEYOND THE POINT OF PRODUCTION:
CLASS STRUGGLE AND REGIONAL
UNDERDEVELOPMENT
AUTHOR
LOS ANGELES
1981 1 08

844 PATERSON,W E
NATIONALISMUS UND EUROPAISCHE
INTEGRATION: NATIONALISTISCHEN
BEWEGUNGEN IN SCHOTTLAND, WALES, IRLAND
AND BELGIEN
EUROPA ARCHIV 28(18)
BONN
1973 2 01

845 PATTERSON,H
CLASS, CONFLICT AND SECTARIANISM
BLACKSTAFF
BELFAST
1981 2 02

846 PATTERSON,H
CONSERVATIVE POLITICS AND CLASS CONFLICT
IN BELFAST
SAOTHAR 2
1976 2 01

847 PATTERSON, H
REFINING THE DEBATE ON UNIONISM
POLIT STUD (OXFORD) 24(1)
1976   2   01

848 PAWLIKOWSKI, J T
SOME MODEST PROPOSALS FOR NI
CHRISTIAN CENTURY NOV 25
1981   1   01

849 PD
FASCISM AND THE SIX COUNTIES
BELFAST
1973   1   09

850 PD
REAL ULSTER '71
BELFAST
1971   1   09

851 PD/REVOLUTIONARY STRUGGLE
FASCISM, THE THREAT IN THE NORTH OF
IRELAND
PD/REVOLUTIONARY STRUGGLE
BELFAST
1975   1   09

852 PEDERSEN, F S
CLASSES AND NATIONALISM IN THE FORMATION
OF THE IRISH STATES
AUTHOR
AARHUS, DENMARK
1979   2   02

853 PERRAUDEAU, M
IRLANDE, LE PAYS DES NEGRES ROUX
SABLES D'OLONNE
1974   1   02

854 PERRONS, D
DIALECTIC OF REGION AND CLASS IN IRELAND
URB AND REGION STUD, SUSSEX UNIV -
WORKING PAPER 8
BRIGHTON
1978   2   08

855 PERRONS, D
IRELAND AND THE BREAK-UP OF BRITAIN
ANTIPODE 11(2)
WORCESTER, MASS
1980   1   01

856 PHILLIPS, C
AN ANALYSIS OF POLITICAL OPINIONS IN NI
CONGRESSIONAL RESEARCH SERVICE
WASHINGTON, D.C.
1978   1   03

857 PHILLIPS, C
DEVELOPMENTS IN NI 1968-1979
CONGRESSIONAL RESEARCH SERVICE
WASHINGTON, D.C.
1979   1   03

858 PICKVANCE, T J
PEACE THROUGH EQUITY: PROPOSALS FOR A
PERMANENT SETTLEMENT OF THE NI CONFLICT
BIRMINGHAM
1974   1   09

859 PINTER, F
EXCLUDED SOCIETY: A CASE STUDY OF NI AND
OTHER DIVIDED SOCIETIES
LONDON UNIV PHD
LONDON
1974   1   04

860 POLITICAL QUARTERLY
IRELAND
POLIT QUART 43(2)
LONDON
1972   1   01

861 POLITICAL QUARTERLY
TEN YEARS IN ULSTER
POLIT QUART 50
LONDON
1979   1   01

862 PONTE
IRELAND CONTINUES
PONTE 30(1)
FIRENZE
1974   1   01

863 POPPE-JENSEN, J
THE CONFLICT IN NI AND ITS HISTORICAL
BACKGROUND
NORSK MILITAERT TIDSSKRIFT 143(1)
1973   1   01

864 POWER, P F
BRITISH POLICY TOWARDS THE NI CONFLICT
CINCINATTI UNIV
CINCINATTI, OHIO
1977   1   08

865 POWER, P F
CIVIL PROTEST AS AN ALTERNATIVE TO
VIOLENCE
IN SULLIVAN, E ET AL (EDS)
GAINESVILLE, FLORIDA
1976   1   07

866 POWER, P F
CIVIL PROTEST IN NI
J PEACE RES 9(3)
OSLO
1972   1   01

867 POWER, P F
CONFLICT AND INNOVATION IN ULSTER
IN BELL, W; FREEMAN, W (EDS)
LONDON
1974   1   07

868 POWER, P F
POLITICS AND THE TWO IRELANDS
WORLDVIEW 24
1981   1   01

869 POWER, P F
VIOLENCE, CONSENT AND THE NI PROBLEM
J COMMONWEALTH COMP POLIT 14(2)
LEICESTER, ENGLAND
1976   1   01

870 PRESBYTERIAN CHURCH
LOYALISM IN IRELAND
PRESBYTERIAN CHURCH
1977   1   10

871 PRESBYTERIAN CHURCH
NI SITUATION
PRESBYTERIAN CHURCH
BELFAST
1973   1   10

872 PRESBYTERIAN CHURCH
PLURALISM IN IRELAND
PRESBYTERIAN CHURCH
BELFAST
1977   1   10

873 PRESBYTERIAN CHURCH
REPUBLICANISM
PRESBYTERIAN CHURCH
BELFAST
1975   1   10

874 PRINGLE, D G
MARXISM, THE NATIONAL QUESTION AND THE
CONFLICT IN NI: A RESPONSE TO BLAUT
ANTIPODE 14(2)
NEW YORK
1983   2   01

875 PRINGLE, D G
NI CONFLICT: A FRAMEWORK FOR DISCUSSION
ANTIPODE 11(2)
WORCESTER, MASS
1980   1   01

876 PROBERT, B; TURNER, M; WALSH, F
BRITISH IMPERIALISM, IRISH NATIONALISM
AND ULSTER UNIONISM
MONTHLY R 31(9)
1980   1   01

877 PURDIE,B
THE FRIENDS OF IRELAND: BRITISH LABOUR
AND IRISH NATIONALISM, 1945-49
IN GALLAGHER,T; O'CONNELL,J (EDS)
MANCHESTER
1983 2 07

878 PURDIE,B
IRELAND UNFREE
INT MARXIST GROUP
LONDON
1972 1 09

879 PURDIE,B
RECONSIDERATIONS ON REPUBLICANISM AND
SOCIALISM
IN MORGAN,A; PURDIE,B (EDS)
LONDON
1980 1 07

880 QUIGLEY,J
COMMON MARKET: COMMON ENEMY
PD
BELFAST
1971 2 09

881 QUIGLEY,J
LA GAUCHE REVOLUTIONNAIRE EN IRLANDE
TEMPS MODERNES 311
PARIS
1972 1 01

882 RAFTERY,A
BRITAIN AND IRELAND IN THE COMMON MARKET
MARXISM TODAY 17(6)
LONDON
1973 2 01

883 RAFTERY,A
THE EXPLOITED ISLAND: ECONOMIC AND
SOCIAL BACKGROUND TO IRELAND'S CRISIS
COMMUNIST PARTY OF IRELAND
DUBLIN
1972 1 09

884 RANDOLPH,V P
THE WHYS OF VIOLENCE IN NI
FOREIGN SERVICE J 49(4)
1972 1 01

885 RAVEN,J
POLITICAL CULTURE IN IRELAND: THE VIEWS
OF TWO GENERATIONS
IPA
DUBLIN
1976 1 10

886 REDMOND,T
THE FORCES IN THE IRISH NATIONAL
LIBERATION STRUGGLE
MARXISM TODAY 17(6)
LONDON
1973 1 01

887 REES,M
THE FUTURE OF NI
CONTEMP R 223(1290)
LONDON
1973 1 01

888 REIK,M
IRELAND - RELIGIOUS WAR OR CLASS
STRUGGLE?
SATURDAY R 18 MARCH
1972 1 01

889 REVOLUTIONARY COMMUNIST GROUP
BRITAIN AND THE IRISH REVOLUTION
REVOLUTIONARY COMMUNIST 2
LONDON
1975 1 01

890 REVOLUTIONARY COMMUNIST GROUP
IRELAND: BRITISH LABOUR AND BRITISH
IMPERIALISM
REVOLUTIONARY COMMUNIST GROUP
LONDON
1976 1 09

891 REVOLUTIONARY MARXIST GROUP
BRITISH STRATEGY IN NI
PLOUGH BOOKS
DUBLIN
1975 1 09

892 REVOLUTIONARY MARXIST GROUP
IRISH NATIONALISM AND BRITISH
IMPERIALISM
PLOUGH BOOKS
DUBLIN
1973 1 09

893 REVOLUTIONARY STRUGGLE
HANDS OFF IRELAND
REVOLUTIONARY STUGGLE
DUBLIN
1977 2 09

894 REVOLUTIONARY STRUGGLE
IRELAND: THE CLASS WAR AND OUR TASKS
REVOLUTIONARY STRUGGLE
DUBLIN
1977 1 09

895 RIDDELL,P
FIRE OVER ULSTER
HAMISH HAMILTON
LONDON
1970 2 02

896 ROBB,J
CONFUSION, CONCILIATION OR CONVENTION
NEW IRELAND MOVEMENT
LURGAN
1970 1 09

897 ROBB,J
NEW IRELAND - SELLOUT OR OPPORTUNITY?
AUTHOR
BELFAST
1972 1 09

898 ROBB,J
WESTMINSTER WITHDRAWAL
NEW IRELAND MOVEMENT
BELFAST
1976 1 09

899 ROBERTS,D
ORANGE ORDER IN IRELAND: A RELIGIOUS
INSTITUTION
BRIT J SOCIOL 22(3)
1971 2 01

900 ROBINSON,D P
THE NORTH ANSWERS BACK
BELFAST
1970 1 09

901 ROBINSON,E
ULSTER: ITS RIGHTS AND RESPONSIBILITIES
AUTHOR
NEWTOWNARDS
1983 1 09

902 ROCHE,S; JACKSON,J A; MILLER,R L;
BOYLE,J F
PERCEPTIONS OF THE CAUSES OF THE NI
CONFLICT
DEPT SOCIOL TCD
DUBLIN
1976 1 08

903 ROSE,P
THE NI FIASCO
IN ROSE,P
LONDON
1981 1 07

904 ROSE,P
THE NI PROBLEM PART 1
CONTEMP R 219(1270)
LONDON
1971 1 01

905 ROSE,P
THE NI PROBLEM PART 2
CONTEMP R
LONDON
1971 1 01

906 ROSE, P
THE NI PROBLEM PART 3
CONTEMP R 220(12/72)
LONDON
1972 1   01

907 ROSE, R
DISCORD IN ULSTER
NEW COMM 1(2)
LONDON
1972 1   01

908 ROSE, R
GOVERNING WITHOUT CONSENSUS: AN IRISH
PERSPECTIVE
FABER
LONDON
1971 1   02

909 ROSE, R
ON THE PRIORITIES OF CITIZENSHIP IN THE
DEEP SOUTH AND NI
J POLIT 38(2)
1976 1   01

910 ROSE, R; MCALLISTER, I; MAIR, P
IS THERE A CONCURRING MAJORITY ABOUT NI?
CSPP 22
GLASGOW
1978 1   10

911 ROSENHEIM, A
IRELAND, BLOODY IRELAND
POLITICS TODAY 6
1979 1   01

912 ROUAT, J
DOSSIER IRLANDE DU NORD
QUIMPIER
PARIS
1974 1   02

913 RULLI, G
IRLANDA DEL NORD: CRISI INSUPERABILE?
CIVILTA CATTOLICA 2983
1974 1   01

914 RUMPF, E; HEPBURN, A C
NATIONALISM AND SOCIALISM IN
TWENTIETH-CENTURY IRELAND
LIVERPOOL U P
LIVERPOOL
1977 2   02

915 RUSSELL, J
THE CRISIS OF CONFLICT IN NI
NEW ERA JANUARY
1971 1   99

916 RUTAN, G
LABOUR IN ULSTER: OPPOSITION BY CARTEL
R POLITICS 29(4)
1967 2   01

917 RUTHERFORD, W
OPTIONS FOR ULSTER
WLD TODAY 36 AUGUST 25
LONDON
1980 1   01

918 RYAN, E
EVOLUTION TOWARDS UNITY
ADMIN (DUB) 20(4)
DUBLIN
1972 1   01

919 SAVORY, D
FROM THE HAVEN INTO THE STORM
AUTHOR
BELFAST
1967 2   09

920 SCHELLENBERG, J A
THE NI CONFLICT AND SOCIOLOGICAL THEORY
NCSA, INDIANA STATE UNIV
TERRE HAUTE
1978 1   99

921 SCHMITT, D
VIOLENCE IN NI: ETHNIC CONFLICT AND
RADICALISATION IN AN INTERNATIONAL
SETTING
GENERAL LEARNING PRESS
NEW JERSEY
1974 1   02

922 SCHUTZ, B; SCOTT, D
NATIVES AND SETTLERS: COMPARATIVE
ANALYSIS OF NI AND RHODESIA
SERIES WORLD AFFAIRS 12
DENVER
1975 1   01

923 SCOTT, F E
PERSUASION IN THE NI CIVIL RIGHTS
MOVEMENT 1964-70
LAFAYETTE UNIV PHD
INDIANA
1972 1   04

924 SCOTT, M D
CONFLICT REGULATION VERSUS MOBILIZATION:
THE DILEMMA OF NI
COLUMBIA UNIVERSITY
NEW YORK
1975 1   04

925 SCOTT, R D
NI THE POLITICS OF DISINTEGRATION
AUSTRAL OUTLOOK 27(1)
MELBOURNE
1973 3   01

926 SCOTT, R D
NI: THE POLITICS OF VIOLENCE
CANB SER ADMIN STUD 2
1977 1   01

927 SCOTT, R D
ULSTER IN PERSPECTIVE: THE RELEVANCE OF
NON-EUROPEAN EXPERIENCE
AUSTRAL OUTLOOK 23(3)
1969 1   01

928 SEE, K O'S
TOWARD A THEORY OF ETHNIC NATIONALISM: A
COMPARISON OF NI AND QUEBEC
MICHIGAN UNIV PHD
1979 1   04

929 SEE, K O'S
THE SOCIAL ORIGINS OF ETHNIC-NATIONAL
MOVEMENTS IN IRELAND AND CANADA
IN DOFNY, J; AKIWOWO, A (EDS)
LONDON
1980 2   07

930 SHEANE, M
ULSTER AND ITS FUTURE AFTER THE TROUBLES
HIGHFIELD PRESS
CHESHIRE
1977 1   02

931 SHEARMAN, H
CONFLICT IN NI
UUP
BELFAST
1972 1   09

932 SHEARMAN, H
CONFLICT IN NI
YEARBOOK WORLD AFFAIRS
1970 1   01

933 SHEARMAN, H
27 MYTHS ABOUT ULSTER
UUP
BELFAST
1972 1   09

934 SHEEHY, M
DIVIDED WE STAND: A STUDY OF PARTITION
FABER
LONDON
1955 2   02

General Political Analyses/

935 SIBBETT,R
ORANGEISM IN IRELAND AND THROUGHOUT THE
EMPIRE
BELFAST
1964 2 02

936 SIMMS,J
REMEMBERING 1690
STUDIES 25
DUBLIN
1974 2 01

937 SINCLAIR,B
BEHIND THE CRISIS IN NI
WLD MARXIST R 17(8)
CANADA
1978 1 01

938 SINN FEIN
IRELAND TODAY
SINN FEIN
DUBLIN
1969 1 09

939 SINN FEIN (OFFICIAL)
IRELAND: BACKGROUND TO WHAT IS HAPPENING
TODAY
SINN FEIN (OFFICIAL)
DUBLIN
1972 1 09

940 SINN FEIN (OFFICIAL)
REPUBLICANISM PARTS 1 AND 2
REPSOL
DUBLIN
1972 1 09

941 SINN FEIN (OFFICIAL)
TOWARDS THE SOCIALIST REPUBLIC
DUBLIN
        1 09

942 SINN FEIN (PROVISIONAL)
EIRE NUA
DUBLIN
1971 1 09

943 SINN FEIN (PROVISIONAL)
IRELAND: THE FACTS
SINN FEIN (PROVISIONAL)
DUBLIN
1971 1 09

944 SINN FEIN (PROVISIONAL)
THE QUALITY OF LIFE IN THE NEW IRELAND
DUBLIN
1973 1 09

945 SMITH,G
RECENT DISTURBANCES IN NI: SOME
DOCUMENTARY SOURCES
LIBRARIANSHIP 2(3)
1970 1 01

946 SMOOHA,S
CONTROL OF MINORITIES IN ISRAEL AND NI
COMP STUD SOC HIST 22(2)
CAMBRIDGE
1980 1 01

947 SMYTH,C
POLITICS OF DECEPTION
PURITAN PRINTING
BELFAST
1971 1 09

948 SMYTH,C
ROME: OUR ENEMY
BELFAST
1974 1 02

949 SMYTH,C
TO BE OR NOT TO BE: THAT IS THE QUESTION
FOR ULSTER
WEST ULSTER UNIONIST COUNCIL
ENISKILLEN
1970 1 09

950 SMYTH,C
ULSTER ASSAILED
UUP
BELFAST
1970 1 09

951 SMYTH,J
CHANGING FACE OF IMPERIALISM IN IRELAND
B CONF SOCIALIST ECON
LONDON
1974 1 01

952 SMYTH,J
CONFLICT WITHOUT CLASS?
IN MORGAN,A; PURDIE,B (EDS)
LONDON
1980 1 07

953 SMYTH,J
DEPENDENT INTERDEPENDENCE: IRELAND AND
BRITISH IMPERIALISM
IN DOWNING,J D; ROLSTON,B; SMYTH,J
LONDON
1977 1 07

954 SMYTH,J
DIE AUSEINANDERSETZUNG IN NORDIRLAND
APO PRESSE 18
HAMBURG
1969 1 01

955 SMYTH,J
NORDIRLAND: RELIGIONSKREIG ORDER
KLASSENKAMPF?
ROTE SKIZZE 16
KIEL
1970 1 01

956 SMYTH,J
THE WELFARE STATE IN NI: DYSFUNCTIONAL
REFORM?
ECPR
ESSEX
1983 1 11

957 SMYTH,M
THE BATTLE FOR NI
ORANGE LODGE
BELFAST
1972 1 09

958 SMYTH,M
IN DEFENCE OF ULSTER
ORANGE LODGE
BELFAST
1969 1 09

959 SMYTH,M
STAND FAST
NORTHERN WHIG
BELFAST
1974 1 09

960 SMYTH,S
FIGHT COMPROMISE OR FADE AWAY - YOUR
CHOICE
AUTHOR
BELFAST
1973 1 09

961 SNODDY,O
FROM THE BRIDGE TO THE ABYSS
CAPUCHIN ANNUAL 39
DUBLIN
1972 1 01

962 SOCIALIST PARTY OF GREAT BRITAIN AND
WORLD SOCIALIST PARTY OF IRELAND
IRELAND: PAST, PRESENT AND FUTURE
SOCIALIST PARTY OF GREAT BRITAIN AND
WORLD SOCIALIST PARTY OF IRELAND
LONDON/BELFAST
1983 1 09

963 SPARE RIB
REPUBLICANISM: WHAT OUR IRISH SISTERS
THINK
SPARE RIB 99
LONDON
1980 1 01

964 STACK,C M
UNITY, THE REPUBLIC AND THE CHURCH OF
IRELAND
THE BELL 16(4)
1951 2 01

965 STADLER,K
NORDIRLAND: ANALYSE EINEN BURGERKRIGES
FINK VERLAG
MUNICH
1979 1 02

966 STALLARD,J
NI
LABOUR MONTHLY 61(9)
1979 1 01

967 STEWART,A T Q
THE MIND OF PROTESTANT ULSTER
IN WATT,D (ED)
LONDON
1981 1 07

968 STEWART,J
CIVIL RIGHTS IN ULSTER
HUMANIST 87(1)
LONDON
1972 1 01

969 STEWART,J
NI: THE CRISIS DRAGS ON
WLD MARXIST R 16(9)
CANADA
1973 1 01

970 STEWART,J
THE ROOTS OF SOCIALISM IN IRELAND
MARXISM TODAY 17(6)
LONDON
1973 2 01

971 STEWART,J
THE SITUATION AND STRUGGLE IN NI
MARXISM TODAY AUG
LONDON
1971 1 01

972 STEWART,J
THE STRUGGLE IN THE NORTH
COMMUNIST PARTY OF IRELAND
BELFAST
1979 1 09

973 STEWART,J
ULSTER DV
CASTLE PRESS
BELFAST
1972 1 09

974 STRAUSS,E
IRISH NATIONALISM AND BRITISH DEMOCRACY
GREENWOOD PRESS
WESTPORT, CONNECTICUT
1975 2 02

975 STUART,J
IRLANDE DU NORD: C'EST TOUJOURS LA CRISE
NOUV CRITIQUE DECEMBER
1973 1 01

976 STUART,J
IRLANDE DU NORD: C'EST TOUJOURS LA CRISE
NOUV R INT OCTOBER
PARIS
1977 1 01

977 SUNDAY TIMES INSIGHT TEAM
ULSTER
PENGUIN
LONDON
1972 1 02

978 SWEETMAN,R
ON OUR KNEES
PAN BOOKS
LONDON
1972 1 02

979 TARA
IRELAND FOREVER
TARA
BELFAST
1977 1 09

980 TARGETT,G
UNHOLY SMOKE
HODDER AND STOUGHTON
LONDON
1969 1 02

981 TAYLOR,P
BRITAIN'S IRISH PROBLEM
CRANE BAG 4(2)
DUBLIN
1980 1 01

982 TERCHEK,R
CONFLICT AND CLEAVAGE IN NI
A AMER ACAD POLIT SOC SCI 433
MARYLAND
1977 1 01

983 THATCHER,M
IN MEMORY OF AIREY NEAVE: IRELAND AND
THE PROBLEMS FACING OUR SOCIETY
ET IRL 5
LILLE
1980 1 01

984 THOMPSON,J L P
DUAL INCORPORATION IN NI: A THEORY OF
SOCIAL AND POLITICAL STRUCTURE
CALIFORNIA UNIV
LOS ANGELES
1979 1 04

985 TRAILL,K A
THE DILEMMA OF NI
VESTA PRESS
CORNWALL, ONTARIO
1980 1 02

986 TREW,K
A SENSE OF NATIONAL IDENTITY
PSYCHOL SOCIETY OF IRELAND ANNUAL CONF
SLIGO
1982 2 11

987 TREW,K; MCWHIRTER,L
CONFLICT IN NI: A RESEARCH PERSPECTIVE
IN STRINGER,P (ED)
1982 1 07

988 TROOST,W
THE NORTHERN IRISH PROBLEM
SPIEGEL HIST 8(10)
1973 1 01

989 TURNER,A C
BRITAIN AND IRELAND: DILEMMAS IN THE
BRITISH BALKANS
CURRENT HISTORY 66(391)
PHILADELPHIA
1974 1 01

990 TURNER,M
SOCIAL DEMOCRATS AND NI 1964-1970
MONTHLY R 30(2)
NEW YORK
1978 1 01

991 TURNER,P
CLASS AND NATIONALISM IN IRELAND
IRL SOCIALIST R 1
LONDON
1978 1 01

992 ULSTER SPECIAL CONSTABULARY ASSOCIATION
WHY?
ULSTER SPECIAL CONSTABULARY ASSOCIATION
BELFAST
1980 1 10

993 ULSTER UNIONIST COUNCIL
FORWARD ULSTER TO TARGET 1970
UUC
BELFAST
1965 2 09

994 ULSTER UNIONIST PARTY
NI: FACT AND FALSEHOOD
UUP
BELFAST
1969 1 09

995 ULSTER UNIONIST PARTY
ULSTER - THE FACTS: THE BULLET AND THE
BOMB VERSUS THE BETTER LIFE
UUP
BELFAST
1970 1 09

996 ULSTER UNIONIST PARTY
ULSTER - THE FACTS: THIS IS THE REAL
ULSTER... NOT THIS
UUP
BELFAST
1969 1 09

997 UNIONIST RESEARCH DEPARTMENT
NI: THE HIDDEN TRUTH
UUP
BELFAST
1972 1 09

998 UTLEY, T
LESSONS OF ULSTER
DENT
LONDON
1975 1 02

999 UTLEY, T
ULSTER: A SHORT BACKGROUND ANALYSIS
UUP
BELFAST
1972 1 02

1000 VAN VORIS, W
VIOLENCE IN ULSTER: AN ORAL DOCUMENTARY
MASSACHUSETTS U P
BOSTON
1975 1 02

1001 VANGUARD UNIONIST PROGRESSIVE PARTY
COMMUNITY OF THE BRITISH ISLES
ULSTER VANGUARD
BELFAST
1973 1 09

1002 VANGUARD UNIONIST PROGRESSIVE PARTY
ULSTER A NATION
ULSTER VANGUARD
BELFAST
1972 1 09

1003 VERRIERE, J
VIRULENCE DU CHOMAGE EN IRLANDE DU NORD
NOROIS 64
PARIS
1969 1 01

1004 VOGT, H
KONFESSIONKRIEG IN NORDIRLAND
CALWER VERLAG/KOSEL-VERL
STUTTGART
1973 1 02

1005 VOGT, H
NORDIRLAND
EVANG MISSIONSVERLAG
STUTTGART
1972 1 02

1006 WALKER, J
IRELAND'S HISTORY OF REPRESSION
INTERNATIONAL SOCIALISTS
LONDON
1972 1 09

1007 WALLACE, M
DISINTEGRATING UNIONISM
EIRE-IRELAND 5(2)
ST PAUL
1970 1 01

1008 WALLACE, M
TOWARDS A TOLERANT COMMUNITY
EVERYMAN 1
1968 1 01

1009 WALLACE, M
WHAT OF THE NORTH?
EIRE-IRELAND 4(3)
ST PAUL
1969 1 01

1010 WALLACE, M; MCGONAGLE, S
DISUNITY: NI
CHRISTUS REX 19(2)
MAYNOOTH
1965 2 01

1011 WALMSLEY, A
NI: ITS POLICIES AND RECORD
UUC
BELFAST
1959 2 09

1012 WALSH, D
CRISIS IN IRELAND (GEARCHEIM IN EIRINN)
FOILSEACHAIN NAISIUNTA TEO
DUBLIN
1970 1 02

1013 WALSH, D
FROM BATTLE FRONT TO PEACE LINE
NEW HUMANIST MARCH
LONDON
1973 1 01

1014 WATT, D
SUMMARY OF THE DISCUSSION
IN WATT, D (ED)
LONDON
1981 1 07

1015 WELTGESHEHEN
FORTGANG DER EREIGNISSE BIS ZUR VORLAGE
DES ENTWURFS EINES VERFASSUNGSGETETZES
FUER NORDIRLAND DURCH GROSSBRITANNIEN IM
MAERZ
WELTGESCHEHEN JAN/MAR
1973 3 01

1016 WEST ULSTER UNIONIST COUNCIL
IT MATTERS TO YOU
WEST ULSTER UNIONIST COUNCIL
ENNISKILLEN
1970 1 09

1017 WHALE, J
THE TORIES AND NI
MAGILL 2(8)
DUBLIN
1979 1 01

1018 WHITE, J
PARTITION
MONTH 17
DUBLIN
1957 2 01

1019 WHYTE, J H
CHURCH AND STATE IN MODERN IRELAND
1923-1979
GILL AND MACMILLAN
DUBLIN
1980 2 02

1020 WHYTE, J H
A COMPARISON OF DIVIDED SOCIETIES
INST IRISH STUD QUB 18 MAY
BELFAST
1983 2 11

1021 WHYTE,J H
     INTERPRETATIONS OF THE NI CONFLICT
     EUROPEAN CONSORTIUM FOR POLITICAL
     RESEARCH
     LOUVAIN
     1976 1 11

1022 WHYTE,J H
     INTERPRETATIONS OF THE NI PROBLEM
     ECON AND SOC R 9(4)
     1978 1 01

1023 WHYTE,J H
     IRELAND: POLITICS WITHOUT SOCIAL BASES
     IN ROSE,R (ED)
     GLENCOE
     1974 1 07

1024 WHYTE,J H
     RECENT WRITING ON NI
     AMER POLIT SCI R 70
     1976 1 01

1025 WHYTE,J H
     WHY IS THE NI PROBLEM SO INTRACTABLE?
     PARL AFFAIRS 34(4)
     1981 1 01

1026 WHYTE,J H ET AL
     GOVERNING WITHOUT CONSENSUS: A CRITIQUE
     NICRC
     BELFAST
     1972 1 10

1027 WILLIAMSON,A P
     NI: PROTESTANTS UNDER SIEGE?
     CHRISTIANITY TODAY APRIL 23
     1982 1 01

1028 WILSON,D
     THE NI SITUATION
     NEWMAN R 1(2)
     LONDON
     1969 1 01

1029 WILSON,D
     THE SIXTIES: THE YEARS OF OPPORTUNITY
     AQUARIUS
     BENBURB
     1973 1 01

1030 WILSON,H
     FINAL TERM: THE LABOUR GOVERNMENT,
     1974-1976
     WEIDENFELD AND NICOLSON
     LONDON
     1980 2 02

1031 WILSON,H
     THE LABOUR GOVERNMENT 1964-1970
     WEIDENFELD AND NICOLSON
     LONDON
     1971 2 02

1032 WILSON,R
     THE LONG ORDEAL OF NI
     CHRISTIAN HERALD MAR
     1982 1 01

1033 WILSON,T
     ULSTER AND EIRE
     IN ROBSON,W (ED)
     LONDON
     1971 1 07

1034 WORKERS' ASSOCIATION
     ONE ISLAND, TWO NATIONS
     WORKERS' ASSOCIATION
     BELFAST
     1973 1 09

1035 WORKERS' ASSOCIATION
     THE WORKING CLASS SOLUTION TO THE
     NATIONAL CONFLICT IN IRELAND
     WORKERS' ASSOCIATION
     BELFAST
     1974 1 09

1036 WORKERS' RESEARCH UNIT
     DERRY TEN YEARS AFTER
     WRU BULLETIN 4
     BELFAST
     1978 1 09

1037 WORKERS' RESEARCH UNIT
     THE QUEEN COMES TO BELFAST
     WRU BULLETIN 1
     BELFAST
     1977 1 09

1038 WORLD SURVEY
     THE IRISH QUESTION
     WLD SURVEY APRIL
     LONDON
     1972 1 01

1039 WRIGHT,F
     PROTESTANT IDEOLOGY AND POLITICS IN
     ULSTER
     EUROP J SOCIOL 14
     1974 2 01

1040 WRIGHT,F
     THE ULSTER SPECTRUM
     IN CARLTON,D; SCHAERF,C (EDS)
     LONDON
     1982 1 07

1041 WRIGHT,S
     A MULTIVARIATE TIME SERIES ANALYSIS OF
     THE NORTHERN IRISH CONFLICT
     IN ALEXANDER,Y; GLEASON,J (EDS)
     OXFORD
     1981 1 07

1042 WRIGHT,S
     A MULTIVARIATE TIME-SERIES ANALYSIS OF
     THE NORTHERN IRISH CONFLICT 1969-1978
     PAP PEACE SCI SOC INT 29
     1979 1 01

1043 WRIGHT,S
     A TIME SERIES ANALYSIS OF THE NI
     CONFLICT 1969-78
     LANCASTER UNIV PHD
     LANCASTER
     1980 1 08

1044 AJEMIAN, R
READY TO DIE IN THE MAZE
TIME AUG 17
1981 1 01

1045 ALBERT, T
HOW BIRMINGHAM BOMBS BLASTED THE IRISH
COMMUNITY
COMM CARE 37
1974 1 01

1046 ARDEN, J
A CHERUB THAT SEES THEM
NEW STATESMAN MAR 14
LONDON
1980 1 01

1047 BEATTY, J
OUT OF THE MAZE
NEW REPUBLIC MAY 9
1981 1 01

1048 BENSON, D; DREW, P
'WAS THERE FIRING IN SANDY ROW THAT
NIGHT?': SOME FEATURES OF THE
ORGANISATION OF DISPUTES ABOUT RECORDED
FACTS
SOCIOL INQUIRY 48(2)
1978 1 01

1049 BERRIGAN, D
BOBBY SANDS: SUICIDE OR SACRIFICE? SHORT
LIFE, LONG DYING - FOR WHAT?
NATIONAL CATHOLIC REPORTER MAY 29
1981 1 01

1050 BEW, P; NORTON, C
UNIONIST STATE AND THE OUTDOOR RIOTS OF
1932
ECON AND SOC R 10(3)
1979 2 01

1051 BLEAKLEY, D
BRIAN FAULKNER
MOWBRAYS
LONDON
1972 2 02

1052 BLEAKLEY, D
SAIDIE PATTERSON: IRISH PEACEMAKER
BLACKSTAFF
BELFAST
1980 1 02

1053 BOYD, A
BRIAN FAULKNER AND THE CRISIS OF ULSTER
UNIONISM
ANVIL
TRALEE
1973 1 02

1054 BRESLIN, J
LEFT FOR DEAD BY AN EXECUTION SQUAD,
BERNADETTE DEVLIN REBOUNDS AS A
POLITICAL FORCE IN ULSTER
PEOPLE APRIL 27
1981 1 01

1055 BROWNE, V
THE ARMS CRISIS 1970
MAGILL 3(8)
DUBLIN
1980 1 01

1056 BROWNE, V
ARMS CRISIS 1970: QUESTIONS FOR THE DAIL
DEBATE
MAGILL 4(2)
DUBLIN
1980 1 01

1057 BROWNE, V
THE ARTFUL AMBIGUITIES OF JACK LYNCH
MAGILL 1(1)
DUBLIN
1977 1 01

1058 BROWNE, V
BERNADETTE AND PAISLEY STIR THE HUSTINGS
MAGILL 2(9)
DUBLIN
1979 1 01

1059 BROWNE, V
THE BERRY FILE
MAGILL 3(9)
DUBLIN
1980 1 01

1060 BROWNE, V
THE MISCONDUCT OF THE ARMS TRIAL
MAGILL 3(10)
DUBLIN
1980 1 01

1061 BROWNE, V
SIMPLE SILE HELPS HONEST JACK
MAGILL 3(1)
DUBLIN
1979 1 01

1062 BUCKLAND, P
JAMES CRAIG
GILL AND MACMILLAN
DUBLIN
1980 2 02

1063 BUCKMAN, P
INTERVIEW WITH BERNADETTE DEVLIN
RAMPARTS JULY
1969 1 01

1064 BUTLER, D
IRELAND'S BLOODY MONDAY
NEWSWEEK 10 SEPT
1979 1 01

1065 CARNDUFF, T
BELFAST IS AN IRISH CITY
THE BELL 23(1)
DUBLIN
1952 2 01

1066 CARTER, J
PRESIDENT CARTER STATES POLICY ON NI
DEPT OF STATE BULL 77
WASHINGTON D.C.
1977 1 03

1067 CATHOLIC TRUTH SOCIETY
PEACE IN NI: THE STORY OF THE PEACE
PEOPLE
CATHOLIC TRUTH SOCIETY
LONDON
1977 1 10

1068 CHISHOLM, A
A YEAR OF BERNADETTE
NEW STATESMAN APR 24
LONDON
1970 1 01

1069 CLIFFORD, G
IN BOBBY SANDS, THE IRA FINDS A MARTYR -
AND HIS FAMILY FINDS A HERO
PEOPLE MAY 18
1981 1 01

1070 CLUTTERBUCK, R
IRELAND'S AMERICAN ENEMIES
NEW REPUBLIC 181
1979 1 01

1071 COHAN, A S
QUESTION OF A UNITED IRELAND:
PERSPECTIVES OF THE IRISH POLITICAL
ELITE
INT AFF 53
1977 1 01

1072 COMMON, R
COMMUNITY UNDER SIEGE 1970-77
RENEWAL PRINT
BELFAST
1980 1 99

1073 COMMON, R
IRISH TROUBLES (DUNMURRY, NI)
TOWN COUNTRY PLANN 38(8)
1970 1 01

1074 CONNOR, C
REPORT ON THE TRADE UNION CAMPAIGN
AGAINST REPRESSION (TUCAR)
IRL SOCIALIST R 3
LONDON
1978 1 01

1075 CRAIG, W
SPEECH AT ULSTER VANGUARD FIRST
ANNIVERSARY RALLY, 12 FEBRUARY 1973
ULSTER VANGUARD
BELFAST
1973 1 09

1076 CREMIN, C
NI AT THE UNITED NATIONS
AUGUST/SEPTEMBER 1969
IR STUD INT AFF 1(2)
DUBLIN
1980 1 01

1077 CRICK, B
THE PALE GREEN INTERNATIONALISTS
NEW STATESMAN 98(2542)
LONDON
1979 1 01

1078 CURRENT BIOGRAPHY
MAIREAD CORRIGAN
CURRENT BIOGRAPHY 39
1978 2 01

1079 DAVIDSON, S
BERNADETTE DEVLIN: AN IRISH
REVOLUTIONARY IN IRISH AMERICA
HARPER'S MAG 240(1436)
NEW YORK
1970 1 01

1080 DEES, D
BERNADETTE DEVLIN'S MAIDEN SPEECH: A
RHETORIC OF SACRIFICE
SOUTHERN SPEECH COMMUNICATION J 38(4)
1973 1 01

1081 DER SPIEGEL
NORDIRLAND: DIESES GAUZE LAND IST
VERRUCKT
DER SPIEGEL JAN/FEB
1972 1 01

1082 DERRY LABOUR PARTY
LABOUR AND THE CIVIL RIGHTS CAMPAIGN IN
DERRY: AN OUTLINE SURVEY OF THE PROGRESS
OF THE CIVIL RIGHTS CAMPAIGN IN DERRY
DERRY LABOUR PARTY
DERRY
1968 1 09

1083 DEUTSCH, R
INTERVIEW WITH WILLIAM CRAIG (JUNE 1976)
ET IRL 1
1976 1 01

1084 DEUTSCH, R
L'ELECTION ET LA MORT DE ROBERT SANDS
ET IRL 6
LILLE
1981 1 01

1085 DEUTSCH, R
LA PAIX PAR LES FEMMES
PIERRE FAVRE
LAUSANNE
1977 1 02

1086 DEUTSCH, R
LE LANDAU ECRASE: IRLANDE, DEUX FEMMES
POUR LA PAIX
EDITIONS DE DAUPHIN
PARIS
1977 1 02

1087 DEUTSCH, R
MAIREAD CORRIGAN AND BETTY WILLIAMS: TWO
PEOPLE WHO IGNORED DANGER
BARRONS
NEW YORK
1977 1 02

1088 DEVLIN, B
BERNADETTE AND BURNTOLLET
IN O'CONNOR, U (ED)
1974 1 07

1089 DEVLIN, B
PRICE OF MY SOUL
PAN BOOKS
LONDON
1969 1 02

1090 DEVLIN, P
FALL OF THE NI EXECUTIVE
AUTHOR
BELFAST
1975 1 02

1091 DONAGHY, B
NORTH-SOUTH DIALOGUE
MAGILL 4(1)
DUBLIN
1980 1 02

1092 DONOGHUE, D
THE HUNGER STRIKERS
NEW YORK R OF BOOKS OCT 22
NEW YORK
1981 1 01

1093 DOOLEY CLARKE, D
THE HUNGER STRIKE IN NI: MEDICAL ETHICS
AND POLITICAL PROTEST
HASTINGS CENTER REPORT 11(6)
1981 1 01

1094 DUFFY, J
THE NEW IRELAND - POLITICAL
POSSIBILITIES: AN INTERVIEW WITH SEAMUS
DEANE
ATLANTIS 5
1970 1 01

1095 DWYER, T
EAMONN DE VALERA
GILL AND MACMILLAN
DUBLIN
1980 2 02

1096 ECKLEY, G
BERNADETTE DEVLIN AND EDNA O'BRIEN:
POLITICAL AND PERSONAL VIOLENCE
IN SULLIVAN, E ET AL (EDS)
GAINESVILLE, FLORIDA
1976 1 07

1097 EDWARDS, O D
A LOOK AT REVEREND IAN PAISLEY
NUSIGHT MAY
DUBLIN
1970 1 10

1098 EGAN, B; MCCORMACK, V
BURNTOLLET
LRS PUBLISHERS
LONDON
1969 1 99

1099 ERVINE, ST J
CRAIGAVON: ULSTERMAN
ALLEN AND UNWIN
LONDON
1949 2 02

1100 ESLER, G
AUNT ANNIE'S BOMB FACTORY
NEW STATESMAN 21 MAR
LONDON
1980 1 01

1101 EVASON, E
NI'S PEACE MOVEMENT: SOME EARLY
REACTIONS
COMM DEV J 12(2)
1977 1 01

1102 FARRELL, M
NOEL BROWNE AND REPUBLICANISM
MAGILL 1(10)
DUBLIN
1978 1 01

1103 FARRELL, M
WHY CHURCHILL WOULD DENOUNCE THATCHER'S
IRISH POLICY
NEW STATESMAN AUG 28
LONDON
1981 1 01

1104 FAULKNER, B
MEMOIRS OF A STATESMAN
WEIDENFELD AND NICOLSON
LONDON
1978 1 02

1105 FEEHAN, J
BOBBY SANDS AND THE TRAGEDY OF NI
MERCIER
CORK
1983 1 02

1106 FEENEY, V E
CIVIL RIGHTS MOVEMENT IN NI
EIRE-IRELAND 9(2)
1974 1 01

1107 FEENEY, V E
FROM REFORM TO RESISTANCE: A HISTORY OF
THE CIVIL RIGHTS MOVEMENT
UNIV OF WASHINGTON PHD
ST. LOUIS
1974 1 04

1108 FEENEY, V E
WESTMINSTER AND THE EARLY CIVIL RIGHTS
STRUGGLE IN NI
EIRE-IRELAND 11(4)
1976 1 01

1109 FISHER, D
A SPEAKER ON IRELAND
COMMONWEAL 8 JUNE
1979 1 01

1110 FITZPATRICK, B
INTERVIEW WITH ANDY TYRIE
CRANE BAG 4(2)
DUBLIN
1980 1 01

1111 FLACKES, W
ENDURING PREMIER
BELFAST TELEGRAPH
BELFAST
1962 2 10

1112 FOLEY, G
BERNADETTE AND THE POLITICS OF H-BLOCK
MAGILL 4(7)
DUBLIN
1981 1 01

1113 FOSTER, R
GARRETT'S CRUSADE
LONDON R OF BOOKS 4(1)
LONDON
1981 1 01

1114 FOY, T
THE ANCIENT ORDER OF HIBERNIANS: AN
IRISH POLITICAL-RELIGIOUS PRESSURE
GROUP, 1884-1975
QUB MA
BELFAST
1976 2 04

1115 GERARD, W
MONDAY, BLOODY MONDAY: KILLING OF EARL
MOUNTBATTEN
MACLEANS 92 SEPT 10
1979 1 01

1116 GILMORE, G
THE IRISH REPUBLICAN CONGRESS
CORK WORKERS CLUB (REPRINT)
CORK
1974 2 09

1117 GIVNAT, M
UNDERSTANDING THE HUNGER STRIKE
NEW SOCIETY 21 OCT
LONDON
1982 1 01

1118 GREY, W R
FIFTY YEARS AFTER
FOCUS NOV
1962 2 01

1119 GREY, W R
REMEMBERING THE ORANGEMEN MARCHING
THE BELL 17(9)
DUBLIN
1951 2 01

1120 HAND, G J
EOIN MACNEILL AND THE BOUNDARY
COMMISSION
IN MARTIN, F X; BYRNE, F J (EDS)
SHANNON
1973 2 07

1121 HARBINSON, R
NO SURRENDER: AN ULSTER CHILDHOOD
FABER
LONDON
1966 2 02

1122 HASTINGS, M
BARRICADES IN NI: THE FIGHT FOR CIVIL
RIGHTS IN NI
TAPLINGER
NEW YORK
1970 1 02

1123 HASTINGS, M
ULSTER 1969: THE FIGHT FOR CIVIL RIGHTS
IN NI
GOLLANCZ
1970 1 02

1124 HAUPTFUHRER, F
A MOTHER'S DEATH IN ULSTER IS A GRIM
REMINDER OF HER FRIENDS' SEARCH FOR
ELUSIVE PEACE
PEOPLE FEB 11
1980 1 01

1125 HERDER CORRESPONDENCE
THE FRUITS OF INSECURITY
HERDER CORRESPONDENCE 6(11)
1969 1 01

1126 HIBERNIAN J
ANCIENT ORDER OF HIBERNIANS: ITS
ORIGINS AND RECORD
HIBERNIAN J
1967 2 01

1127 HILLERY, P J
ADDRESS TO THE SECURITY COUNCIL OF THE
UNITED NATIONS ON 20TH AUGUST 1969
DEPT OF EXTERNAL AFFAIRS
DUBLIN
1969 1 03

Specific Political Commentary/

1128 HINCKLE, W
IRELAND AGONISTES
ROLLING STONE JUN 25
1981 1 01

1129 HITCHENS, C
DR. O'BRIEN AND MR. HYDE
NEW STATESMAN 98(2540)
LONDON
1979 1 01

1130 HOLLAND, J
"WHAT D'YA MEAN? WE'RE NOT IRISH!"
COMMONWEAL 31 AUG
1979 1 01

1131 HOLLAND, J
AFTER THE KILLINGS
COMMONWEAL 106 SEPT 14
1979 1 01

1132 HOLLAND, J
THE MEN ON THE BLANKET
COMMONWEAL NOV 21
1980 1 01

1133 HOLLAND, J
POLITICAL BLARNEY
NATION 228 MAR 17
1979 2 01

1134 HOLLAND, M
CARTER, KENNEDY AND IRELAND
MAGILL 1(1)
1977 1 01

1135 HOLLAND, M
DR PAISLEY'S REVERSE
NEW STATESMAN 13 MAY
LONDON
1977 1 01

1136 HOLLAND, M
THE GROWING DESPERATION OF THE BRITISH
ARMY
MAGILL 3(3)
1979 1 01

1137 HOLLAND, M
INTIMATIONS OF NORMALITY
NEW STATESMAN 6 JAN
LONDON
1978 1 01

1138 HOLLAND, M
JIM CALLAGHAN'S OTHER ALLIES
NEW STATESMAN 14 OCT
LONDON
1977 2 01

1139 HOLLAND, M
KENNEDY'S NEW IRISH POLICY
NEW STATESMAN 11 MAY
LONDON
1979 1 01

1140 HOLLAND, M
MR. ULSTER'S CHALLENGE
NEW STATESMAN 20 FEB
LONDON
1981 1 01

1141 HOLLAND, M
NO END TO NEW 'BLOODY SUNDAY'
NEW STATESMAN MAY 29
LONDON
1981 1 01

1142 HOLLAND, M
SOUTH OF THE BORDER: THATCHER AND
CREASEY WON'T CONVINCE LYNCH
NEW STATESMAN 98(2529)
LONDON
1979 1 01

1143 HOLLAND, M
THATCHER'S 'INITIATIVE' BECALMED
NEW STATESMAN NOV 30
LONDON
1979 1 01

1144 HOSENBALL, M
IRISH BURLESQUE
NEW REPUBLIC MAR 3
1982 1 01

1145 HUME, J
JOHN HUME'S DERRY
EVERYMAN
BENBURB
1970 1 10

1146 HYDE, H M
LIFE OF LORD CARSON
CONSTABLE
LONDON
1974 2 02

1147 IRELAND, D
FROM THE JUNGLE OF BELFAST: FOOTNOTES TO
HISTORY, 1904-1972
BLACKSTAFF
BELFAST
1973 2 02

1148 IRELAND, D
A REAL BELFAST HELL
IN O'CONNOR, U (ED)
NEW YORK
1974 1 07

1149 IRIS
THE DRIFT TO PAISLEYISM
IRIS 3
DUBLIN
1982 1 01

1150 IRIS
HUNGER STRIKE OPENS UP ELECTION FRONT
IRIS 1(2)
DUBLIN
1981 1 01

1151 JACOBSEN, J K
STALEMATE IN NI
DISSENT 29(3)
NEW YORK
1982 1 01

1152 JAMES, T
YEAR OF TURMOIL IN NI
POLICY JAN
1970 1 01

1153 JOHNSON, D S
THE BELFAST BOYCOTT 1920-22
IN GOLDSTROM, J M; CLARKSON, L A (EDS)
OXFORD
1981 2 07

1154 JOHNSON, D S
NI AS A PROBLEM IN THE ECONOMIC WAR
1932-38
IR HIST STUD 22
1980 2 01

1155 JONES, A
BELFAST, PLAGUED BY CIVIL WAR, 'IS THE
WEST'
NATIONAL CATHOLIC REPORTER OCT 24
1980 1 01

1156 JONES, A
NEW VIOLENCE REKINDLES OLD IRE IN NI
NATIONAL CATHOLIC REPORTER MAY 8
1981 1 01

1157 JONES, M W
THE END IS NOT YET
NEW STATESMAN 23 SEPT
LONDON
1977 2 01

1158 KEATINGE, P
THE FOREIGN POLICY OF THE IRISH
COALITION GOVERNMENT
WLD TODAY 29(8)
LONDON
1973 1 01

1159 KEENAN, B
DUBLIN, LONDON MAY TREMBLE YET
MACLEANS MAY 18
1981 1 01

1160 KEENAN, B
HUNGER THAT HURTS WHERE IT COUNTS
MACLEANS NOV 17
1980 1 01

1161 KEENAN, B
TIME RUNS OUT FOR BOBBY, AND ULSTER
MACLEANS MAY 4
1981 1 01

1162 KEENAN, B
WHEN IRISH EYES ARE FROWNING
MACLEANS DEC 29
1980 1 01

1163 KELLY, H
HOW STORMONT FELL
GILL AND MACMILLAN
DUBLIN
1972 1 02

1164 KELLY, J
GENESIS OF REVOLUTION
KELLY KANE
DUBLIN
1976 1 02

1165 KELLY, J
ORDERS FOR THE CAPTAIN?
AUTHOR
DUBLIN
1971 1 02

1166 KELLY, J
ORDERS FOR THE CAPTAIN?
IN O'CONNOR, U (ED)
1974 1 07

1167 KENNEDY, C
AN EERIE CASE OF DEJA VU
MACLEANS MAR 2
1981 1 01

1168 KENNEDY, C
MAKING OF A MARTYR: THE IRA TIGHTENS THE
TENSION AND REAPS THE REWARD
MACLEANS MAY 18
1981 1 01

1169 KENNEDY, C
THE TRIBUNAL ON BRITAIN'S PRESENCE: A
HISTORICAL PERSPECTIVE
IRL SOCIALIST R 2
1978 1 01

1170 KENNEDY, C
ULSTER'S DAYS OF RAGE
MACLEANS NOV 30
1981 1 01

1171 KENNEDY, H S
RIOT AT LANCASTER STREET
AQUARIUS
BENBURB
1972 2 01

1172 KENNEDY, R S; KLOTZ-CHAMBERLIN, P
NI'S 'GUERRILLAS OF PEACE'
CHRISTIAN CENTURY 94
1977 1 01

1173 KERRIGAN, G
PAISLEY'S WALK ON THE WILD SIDE
MAGILL 5(3)
DUBLIN
1981 1 01

1174 KETTLE, M
TALE OF TWO CITIES: PEOPLE OF DIVIDED
DERRY
NEW SOCIETY 49(875)
LONDON
1979 1 01

1175 KING, C
CECIL KING DIARY 1970-74
JONATHAN CAPE
LONDON
1975 2 02

1176 LLOYD-JONES, D
ENOCH POWELL'S ULSTER RHETORIC
NEW SOCIETY 35(696)
LONDON
1976 1 01

1177 LONG, S E
ORANGE REALITY
COUNTY GRAND ORANGE LODGE OF BELFAST
1971 2 09

1178 LONG, S E
ORANGEISM IN NI
SLIEVE CROOB PRESS
DROMARA
1970 1 10

1179 LOUSDEN, M
PEACE BY PEACE? SOCIOECONOMIC STRUCTURES
AND THE ROLE OF THE PEACE PEOPLE IN NI
CURRENT RESEARCH ON PEACE AND VIOLENCE
1(1)
OSLO
1978 1 01

1180 MACINTYRE, T
THROUGH THE BRIDEWELL GATE
FABER
LONDON
1971 1 02

1181 MACKEN, J
LETTRE OUVERTE AUX AMERICAINS D'ORIGINE
IRLANDAIS
TEMPS MODERNES 311
1972 1 01

1182 MACLEANS
A COUNTRYMAN'S LAMENT (INTERVIEW WITH
TIM PAT COOGAN)
MACLEANS APR 20
1981 1 01

1183 MALCOLMSON, A P W
PAPERS OF SIR DOUGLAS SAVORY M.P.
PRONI
BELFAST
1980 2 10

1184 MANNING, M
DAY AT THE SEA, EVENING AT THE RIOT
COMM CARE 42
1975 1 01

1185 MARRINAN, P
PAISLEY - MAN OF WRATH
ANVIL
TRALEE
1973 1 02

1186 MCCAFFERTY, N
THE PEACE PEOPLE AT WAR
MAGILL 3(11)
DUBLIN
1980 1 01

1187 MCCANN, E
THE QUEEN OVER THE WATER
NEW STATESMAN 5 AUG
LONDON
1977 2 01

1188 MCCARTHY, J P
A WAY OUT IN ULSTER: AFTER THE HUNGER
STRIKE
NEW LEADER OCT 5
1981 1 01

1189 MCCLUNG LEE, A
PEACE PEOPLE OF NI
THE CHURCHMAN
1980 1 01

Specific Political Commentary/

1190 MCCULLOUGH, D
THE EVENTS IN BELFAST
CAPUCHIN ANNUAL
DUBLIN
1966 2 01

1191 MCDONAGH, E
QUESTIONS BEYOND HUNGER STRIKE
NATIONAL CATHOLIC REPORTER MAY 29
1981 1 01

1192 MCDOWELL, M
POST-NOBEL DECLINE: PEACE PEOPLE FALL ON
HARD TIMES
COMMONWEAL MAR 28
1980 1 01

1193 MCELROY, A H
ULSTER TORIES RESPONSIBLE FOR IAN
PAISLEY
NEW OUTLOOK 56
1966 2 01

1194 MCGOVERN, G S
IRELAND IN 1977
US GOVERNMENT PRINTING OFFICE
WASHINGTON D.C.
1977 1 03

1195 MCGUIGAN, B MCK
AFTER CALLAGHAN
NEWMAN R 1(2)
1969 1 01

1196 MCHARDY, A
PAISLEY'S TRIUMPH
MAGILL 2(10)
DUBLIN
1979 1 01

1197 MICKLEY, A
THE NI PEACE MOVEMENT AND ITS EXTERNAL
EFFECTS
INST IRISH STUD QUB
BELFAST
1977 1 08

1198 MILLER, R; LUNDIN, J; FARLEY, R
BELFAST: A REPORT ON THE CURRENT
DISTURBANCES
RADIO TIMES DEC 4-10
LONDON
1971 1 01

1199 MOLONEY, E
HOW THATCHER IS HELPING THE IRA
NEW STATESMAN 29 FEB
LONDON
1980 1 01

1200 MOLONEY, E
PAISLEY
CRANE BAG 4(2)
DUBLIN
1980 1 01

1201 MOUNT, F
THE IRA AND THE BAR ROOMS OF AMERICA
AMERICAN SPECTATOR JAN
1980 1 01

1202 MULLEN, L
AN EVENING ON RAVENHILL ROAD
AMERICA 1 OCT
1977 2 01

1203 MURRAY, H T
THE GREEN AND THE RED UNBLENDING: THE
NATIONAL ASSOCIATION FOR IRISH FREEDOM
1972-1975
J ETHNIC STUD 3(2)
1975 1 01

1204 MYERS, K
THE SHORT STRAND
MAGILL 1(3)
DUBLIN
1977 1 01

1205 NEW YORKER
REPORTER AT LARGE: MATTHEW AND MARIE
NEW YORKER 8 MAY
NEW YORK
1978 2 01

1206 NEWSWEEK
ULSTER'S DAYS OF RAGE
NEWSWEEK MAY 11
1981 1 01

1207 NICRA
WE SHALL OVERCOME: THE HISTORY OF THE
STRUGGLE FOR CIVIL RIGHTS IN NI
NICRA
BELFAST
         1 09

1208 NUSIGHT
THE PHENOMENON OF PAISLEYISM
NUSIGHT OCT
1969 1 01

1209 NUSIGHT
A PROFILE OF REVEREND IAN PAISLEY
NUSIGHT OCT
1969 1 01

1210 O'BRIEN, C C
THE FOUR HORSEMEN
HARPERS DEC
1981 1 01

1211 O'CALLAGHAN, J
INSIDE THE DERRY GHETTO
NEW STATESMAN JAN 21
LONDON
1972 1 01

1212 O'DONNELL, D
THE PEACE PEOPLE OF NI
WIDESCOPE
CAMBERWELL, VICTORIA AUSTRALIA
1977 1 99

1213 O'FIGGUS, C
MAN OF THE PEOPLE: THE PARLIAMENTARY
SPEECHES OF JOHN MCQUADE ESQ
AUTHOR
BELFAST
1968 2 10

1214 O'GLAISNE, R
C C O'BRIEN AGUS AN LIOBRALACHAS
CLODHANNA TEO
DUBLIN
1974 2 10

1215 O'GLAISNE, R
IAN PAISLEY AGUS TUAISCEART EIREANN
CLO MORAINN
DUBLIN
1971 1 10

1216 O'MAHONY, T P
IRELAND'S EPIDEMIC OF VIOLENCE
AMERICA OCT 24
1981 1 01

1217 O'NEILL, T
AUTOBIOGRAPHY
HART-DAVIS
LONDON
1972 2 02

1218 O'REGAN, E D
A NORTHERNER'S DAY OUT
THE BELL 11(4)
DUBLIN
1946 2 01

1219 OAKLEY, R; ROSE, P
NI
IN OAKLEY, R; ROSE, P
LONDON
1971 1 07

1220 PAISLEY, I R K
MESSAGES FROM THE PRISON CELL
BELFAST
1968 2 09

1221 PATTERSON, H
PAISLEY AND PROTESTANT POLITICS
MARXISM TODAY 26(1)
LONDON
1982 1 01

1222 PATTERSON, M
GANDHI SPEAKS TO ULSTER
AUTHOR
BELFAST
1973 1 10

1223 PELL, C
SOME THOUGHTS ON THE SITUATION IN NI
US SENATE COMMITTEE ON FOREIGN RELATIONS
WASHINGTON D.C.
1981 1 03

1224 PHILLIPS, C
NI AND U.S. INTERESTS
CONGRESSIONAL RESEARCH SERVICE
WASHINGTON, D.C.
1982 1 03

1225 POGANY, I
COULD THE UN KEEP THE PEACE IN NI?
WLD TODAY 37
LONDON
1981 1 01

1226 POLLAK, A
KINCORAGATE PUTS PAISLEY ON THE SPOT
NEW STATESMAN FEB 12
LONDON
1982 2 01

1227 POWELL, S
FOR ULSTER, DESPAIR SHROUDS THE FUTURE
US NEWS MAY 18
1981 1 01

1228 POWELL, S
IN IRELAND, A BATTLE OF HEART VS. HEAD
US NEWS AND WORLD REPORT 90 JUNE 29
1981 1 01

1229 POWER, J
CAN THE PEACE PEOPLE BRING AN IRISH
PEACE?
ENCOUNTER 48
LONDON
1977 1 01

1230 POWER, J
PEACE PEOPLE: A REPORT FROM IRELAND
ENCOUNTER 48(3)
LONDON
1977 1 01

1231 POWER, P F
THE POPE AND NI
WORLDVIEW 1
1980 2 01

1232 RAFTERY, A
LENIN ON IRELAND
NEW BOOKS
DUBLIN
1970 2 02

1233 RAGG, N
SURVEY OF INTERNEES' FAMILIES
NICRA
BELFAST
1972 1 09

1234 RAYMOND, R J
IRISH AMERICA AND NI: AN END TO
ROMANTICISM
WLD TODAY MAR
LONDON
1983 1 01

1235 REED, D
NI'S AGONY WITHOUT END
READER'S DIGEST JAN
1982 1 01

1236 REES, M
NI 1974
CONTEMP R 224(1297)
LONDON
1974 1 01

1237 RICE, R
THE NORTH IN THE SIXTIES - A PERSONAL
REPORT
NUSIGHT DEC
DUBLIN
1969 1 10

1238 ROBERTS, A
PASSIVE RESISTANCE IN ULSTER
NEW SOCIETY 6 JUN
1974 1 10

1239 ROBERTS, G A
THE LINEN INDUSTRY OF NI
BANKER 75
1945 2 01

1240 ROBERTS, G A
THE LINEN INDUSTRY SINCE DEVALUATION
BANKER 95
1950 2 01

1241 ROBERTSON, J
RELUCTANT JUDAS: THE LIFE AND DEATH OF
KENNETH LENNON
LONDON
1976 1 02

1242 ROBINSON, P
ULSTER IN PERIL: AN EXPOSURE OF THE
DUBLIN SUMMIT
DEMOCRATIC UNIONIST PARTY
BELFAST
1981 1 09

1243 ROTH, A
MARCHING TO DIFFERENT DRUMMERS: THE
PASSION FOR PARADES IN NI
HARPERS MAG 244(1463)
1972 1 01

1244 ROUND TABLE
BELFAST, LONDON AND DUBLIN: A FRAGILE
CONGRUENCE OF POLICY
ROUND TABLE 241
LONDON
1971 1 01

1245 RUSSELL, G
DEATHWATCH IN H BLOCK
TIME MAY 4
1981 1 01

1246 RUSSELL, G
SHADOW OF GUNMAN
TIME MAY 18
1981 1 01

1247 SANDS, B
THE WRITING OF BOBBY SANDS
SINN FEIN POW DEPARTMENT
DUBLIN
1981 1 09

1248 SAYERS, J E
THE LEGACY OF O'NEILL: ULSTER UNIONISM
ON A NEW COURSE
ROUND TABLE 59(235)
BELFAST
1969 1 01

1249 SAYERS, J E
A SETBACK FOR LIBERAL HOPES: MR PAISLEY
RUNS O'NEILL CLOSE
ROUND TABLE 59(234)
BELFAST
1969 1 01

Specific Political Commentary/

1250 SAYERS, J E
VIOLENCE AND UNREASON IN CONTROL:
CONTINUING DISTRUST OF UNIONIST RULE
ROUND TABLE 59(236)
BELFAST
1969 1 01

1251 SCHWARTZ, M
REFUGEE FROM H BLOCK
AMERICA NOV 22
1980 1 01

1252 SEAMUS COSTELLO MEMORIAL COMMITTEE
SEAMUS COSTELLO 1939-1977: IRISH
REPUBLICAN SOCIALIST
SEAMUS COSTELLO MEMORIAL COMMITTEE
DUBLIN
1982 1 09

1253 SHANN, R
THE ANGEL OF THE FALLS ROAD
WOMAN 26 JUL
LONDON
1975 1 10

1254 SHERIDAN, R
INTERVIEW WITH SEAN MACBRIDE
CRANE BAG 2(1/2)
DUBLIN
1978 1 01

1255 SINN FEIN (OFFICIAL)
DOCUMENT ON IRISH LIBERATION SUBMITTED
TO WORLD CONGRESS OF PEACE FORCES,
MOSCOW 1973
SINN FEIN (OFFICIAL)
DUBLIN
1974 1 09

1256 SINN FEIN (OFFICIAL)
FIANNA FAIL: THE IRA CONNECTION
SINN FEIN (OFFICIAL)
DUBLIN
1973 1 09

1257 SINN FEIN (OFFICIAL)
LIAM MCMILLAN, SEPARATIST, SOCIALIST,
REPUBLICAN
REPSOL
DUBLIN
1975 1 09

1258 SMYTH, M
A PROTESTANT LOOKS AT THE REPUBLIC
IN SOCIAL STUDY CONFERENCE
DUBLIN
1974 1 07

1259 SOCIALIST STANDARD
REPORT FROM BELFAST: THE FAILURE OF
CIVIL RIGHTS IN NI
SOCIALIST STANDARD OCT
LONDON
1969 1 09

1260 SPECTATOR
ULSTER BEYOND THE TURMOIL
SPECTATOR 12 SEPT
1970 1 01

1261 STEWART, A T Q
EDWARD CARSON
GILL AND MACMILLAN
DUBLIN
1981 2 02

1262 STEWART, E
THE PRESENT SITUATION OF THE CIVIL
RIGHTS MOVEMENT
MARXISM TODAY 17(6)
LONDON
1973 1 01

1263 STOKELL, I
WHY I LEFT THE ARMY
NEW STATESMAN 26 JUN
LONDON
1981 1 01

1264 TARGETT, G
BERNADETTE: THE STORY OF BERNADETTE
DEVLIN
HODDER AND STOUGHTON
LONDON
1975 1 02

1265 THOMPSON, J
THE NI CIVIL RIGHTS MOVEMENT
QUB MA
BELFAST
1973 1 04

1266 TIME
IN THE SHADOW OF THE GUNMEN
TIME JAN 10
NEW YORK
1972 1 01

1267 TIME
A NATION MOURNS ITS LOSS
TIME 10 SEPT
NEW YORK
1979 1 01

1268 ULSTER GROUP
RECENT EVENTS IN NI IN PERSPECTIVE
ULSTER GROUP
LONDON
1972 1 09

1269 ULSTER UNIONIST COUNCIL
BERNADETTE'S MILLION
ULSTER UNIONIST COUNCIL
BELFAST
1969 1 09

1270 ULSTER UNIONIST PARTY
ULSTER - THE FACTS: YOUNG LADY WITH A
60 A WEEK JOB
UUP
BELFAST
1969 1 09

1271 US CONGRESS COMMITTEE ON FOREIGN AFFAIRS
REPORT OF CONGRESSMAN WOLFF ON TRIP TO
NI
GOVERNMENT PRINTING OFFICE
WASHINGTON
1972 1 03

1272 US HOUSE OF REPRESENTATIVES
NI SUBCOMMITTEE HEARINGS
US GOVERNMENT PRINTING OFFICE
WASHINGTON
1972 1 03

1273 WALKER, I
"I WISH IT WAS OVER, BUT..."
NEW SOCIETY 57(976)
LONDON
1981 1 01

1274 WATSON, A
LIBERAL WATERSHED
COMM FORUM 3(1)
BELFAST
1973 1 01

1275 WHEELER, M
SOVIET INTEREST IN IRELAND
SURVEY 21(3)
LONDON
1975 1 01

1276 WHIPPLE, C; BENSON, H
THE ENDLESS WAKE
LIFE OCT
1981 1 01

1277 WILSON, S
THE CARSON TRAIL
CROWN PUBLICATIONS
BELFAST
1981 1 02

1278 WINTOUR, P
JIM'S ULSTER GAMBLE
NEW STATESMAN 9 MAR
LONDON
1979 1 01

1279 ALEXANDER, A
LOCAL GOVERNMENT IN IRELAND
ADMIN (DUB) 27(1)
1979   2   01

1280 ALL-PARTY ANTI-PARTITION CONFERENCE
DISCRIMINATION: A STUDY IN INJUSTICE TO
A MINORITY
ALL-PARTY ANTI-PARTITION CONFERENCE
DUBLIN
1950   2   09

1281 ALL-PARTY ANTI-PARTITION CONFERENCE
ONE VOTE EQUALS TWO: A STUDY IN THE
PRACTICE AND PURPOSE OF BOUNDARY
MANIPULATION
ALL-PARTY ANTI-PARTITION CONFERENCE
DUBLIN
1950   2   09

1282 ALVAREZ, C
APUNTES PARA UN ESTUDIAS DE LAS
INSTITUTIONES POLITICAS DE IRLANDA DEL
NORTE
R ESTUD POLIT 189-190
1973   3   01

1283 ANDREWS, J H
PAPERS OF THE IRISH BOUNDARY COMMISSION
IR GEOG 5(5)
DUBLIN
1968   2   01

1284 ARCHER, J R
NI CONSTITUTIONAL PROPOSALS AND THE
PROBLEM OF IDENTITY
R POLITICS 40(2)
1978   1   01

1285 ARNOLD, B
BIPARTISANSHIP AND THE CONSTITUTION
STUDIES 66
1977   1   01

1286 ARTHUR, P
DEVOLUTION AS ADMINISTRATIVE CONVENIENCE
PARL AFFAIRS 30
1977   1   01

1287 ARTHUR, P
FUTURE OF THE CONSOCIATIONAL MODEL IN NI
DEPT POLITICS ULSTER COLLEGE
BELFAST
1979   1   08

1288 ARTHUR, P
GOVERNMENT AND POLITICS OF NI
LONGMANS
LONDON
1980   1   02

1289 ARTHUR, P
INDEPENDENCE
IN REA, D (ED)
DUBLIN
1982   1   07

1290 ARTHUR, P
WHAT RELEVANCE DOES CONSOCIATIONALISM
HAVE FOR THE NI PROBLEM?
INST IRISH STUD QUB 18 MAY
BELFAST
1983   1   11

1291 ATKINSON, G; PARRISS, H
REGIONAL AND COUNTY GOVERNMENT IN THE
UNITED KINGDOM OF GREAT BRITAIN AND NI
INST DE SCIENCES SOCIALES
BARCELONA
1966   2   99

1292 ATLANTIC INFORMATION CENTRE FOR TEACHERS
NI, THE WHITE PAPER
ATLANTIC EDUCATIONAL PUBLICATIONS
LONDON
1973   1   10

1293 AUNGER, E A
IN SEARCH OF POLITICAL STABILITY: A
COMPARATIVE STUDY OF NEW BRUNSWICK AND
NI
MCGILL - QUEEN'S U P
TORONTO
1981   1   02

1294 AUNGER, E A
SOCIAL FRAGMENTATION AND POLITICAL
STABILITY: COMPARATIVE STUDY OF NEW
BRUNSWICK AND NI
CALIFORNIA UNIV PHD
DAVIS, CALIFORNIA
1978   2   04

1295 BARRINGTON, D
AFTER SUNNINGDALE
ADMIN (DUB) 24(2)
DUBLIN
1976   1   01

1296 BARRINGTON, D
COUNCIL OF IRELAND IN THE CONSTITUTIONAL
CONTEXT
ADMIN (DUB) 20(4)
1972   1   01

1297 BARTON, B
THE GOVERNMENT OF NI, 1920-23
ATHOL BOOKS
BELFAST
1980   2   09

1298 BARTON, B
NI GOVERNMENT POLICY IN RELATION TO LAW
AND ORDER AND LOCAL GOVERNMENT 1920-1923
NUU MA
COLERAINE
1977   2   04

1299 BELL, J S E; MCCREADY, P E
THE REORGANISATION OF HEALTH AND
PERSONAL SOCIAL SERVICES IN NI: SECOND
REPORT
DEPT BUSINESS STUD QUB/NUFFIELD
PROVINCIAL HOSPITALS TRUST
BELFAST
1976   2   10

1300 BENN, J
COMMISSIONER FOR COMPLAINTS
COMM FORUM 2(1)
BELFAST
1972   1   01

1301 BENN, J
COMMISSIONER'S COMPLAINT
NUU
COLERAINE
1973   1   10

1302 BIRCH, A H
CELTIC FRINGE IN HISTORICAL PERSPECTIVE
PARL AFFAIRS 29(2)
1976   2   01

1303 BIRCH, A H
NOTE ON DEVOLUTION
POLIT STUD (OXFORD) 4
1956   2   01

1304 BIRCH, A H
POLITICAL INTEGRATION AND DISINTEGRATION
IN THE BRITISH ISLES
ALLEN AND UNWIN
LONDON
1977 2 02

1305 BIRRELL, W D
CENTRALISATION OF LOCAL GOVERNMENT IN
NI: AN APPRAISAL
LOC GOVT STUD 4(4)
1978 2 01

1306 BIRRELL, W D
LOCAL GOVERNMENT COUNCILLORS IN NI
CSPP
GLASGOW
1981 2 10

1307 BIRRELL, W D
LOCAL GOVERNMENT COUNCILLORS IN NI AND
THE REPUBLIC OF IRELAND: THEIR SOCIAL
BACKGROUND, MOTIVATION AND ROLE
IN GALLAGHER, T; O'CONNELL, J (EDS)
MANCHESTER
1983 2 07

1308 BIRRELL, W D
MECHANICS OF DEVOLUTION: NI EXPERIENCE
AND THE SCOTLAND AND WALES BILLS
POLIT QUART 49(3)
1978 2 01

1309 BIRRELL, W D
NI CIVIL SERVICE - FROM DEVOLUTION TO
DIRECT RULE
PUBL ADM
1978 2 01

1310 BIRRELL, W D
NI: THE OBSTACLES TO POWER SHARING
POLIT QUART 52(2)
1981 1 01

1311 BIRRELL, W D
NI'S EXPERIENCE OF DEVOLUTION: ITS
RELEVANCE TO DEVOLUTION PROPOSALS
IN CSPP
1977 2 07

1312 BIRRELL, W D
THE STORMONT-WESTMINSTER RELATIONSHIP
PARL AFFAIRS 26
1973 2 01

1313 BIRRELL, W D; MURIE, A S
POLICY AND GOVERNMENT IN NI: LESSONS OF
DEVOLUTION
GILL AND MACMILLAN
DUBLIN
1980 1 02

1314 BLACKBURN, A
NI ELECTORAL LAW 1921-1972: THE QUESTION
OF DISCRIMINATION
QUB LLM
BELFAST
1981 1 04

1315 BLOCK, G D M
LOCAL GOVERNMENT IN NI
TOWN COUNTRY PLANN 38(2)
LONDON
1970 3 01

1316 BLOMQUIST, P
THE LEISURE CENTRE BOOM
SCOPE 22
BELFAST
1979 2 01

1317 BOAL, F W; BUCHANAN, R H
1969 NI ELECTION
IR GEOG 4(1)
1969 2 01

1318 BOGDANOR, V
DEVOLUTION
OUP
LONDON
1979 2 02

1319 BOW GROUP
LOCAL GOVERNMENT IN ULSTER: A NEW
ORGANIZATION STRUCTURE
BOW GROUP
LONDON
1969 1 09

1320 BOYCE, D G
DICEY, KILBRANDON AND DEVOLUTION
POLIT QUART 46(3)
LONDON
1975 2 01

1321 BRENNAN, P
LES ELECTIONS A WESTMINSTER EN IRLANDE
DU NORD 1922-79
EDITIONS JEAN TOUZOT
PARIS
1982 2 02

1322 BRETT, C E B
MEMORANDUM OF EVIDENCE TO THE COMMISSION
ON THE CONSTITUTION
BELFAST
        1 08

1323 BUDGE, I; O'LEARY, C
ATTITUDINAL AND BACKGROUND
CROSS-CUTTING: FURTHER EVIDENCE FROM
GLASGOW AND BELFAST
MIDWEST J POLIT SCI 16(4)
1972 2 01

1324 BUDGE, I; O'LEARY, C
BELFAST: APPROACH TO CRISIS. A STUDY OF
BELFAST POLITICS 1613-1970
MACMILLAN
LONDON
1973 1 01

1325 BUDGE, I; O'LEARY, C
CROSS-CUTTING CLEAVAGES, AGREEMENT AND
COMPROMISE: AN ASSESSMENT OF THREE
LEADING HYPOTHESES AGAINST SCOTTISH & NI
SURVEY RESPONSES
MIDWEST J POLIT SCI 15(1)
1971 2 01

1326 BUGLER, J
NORTH DERRY VOTES: A MICROCOSM OF ULSTER
NEW SOCIETY 20 FEBRUARY
LONDON
1969 3 01

1327 BUNTING, R T
BLUE PRINT FOR LOCAL
GOVERNMENT...SUBMITTED...TO DOWN CO
COUNCIL
AUTHOR
1967 2 10

1328 BUSTEED, M A
GEOGRAPHY AND VOTING BEHAVIOUR
OUP
LONDON
1975 2 02

1329 BUSTEED, M A
RESHAPING BELFAST'S LOCAL GOVERNMENT
ADMIN (DUB) 18(3)
1970 2 01

1330 BUSTEED, M A; MASON, H
LOCAL GOVERNMENT REFORM IN NI
IR GEOG 4(3)
1971 2 01

1331 CAHILL, G A
THE IRISH PARLIAMENTARY TRADITION: PAST
AND PRESENT
IN SULLIVAN, E ET AL (EDS)
GAINSVILLE, FLORIDA
1976 2 07

1332 CALVERT, H
CONSTITUTIONAL LAW IN NI
STEVENS
LONDON
1968 2 02

1333 CALVERT, H
DEVOLUTION
PROFESSIONAL BOOKS
LONDON
1975 2 02

1334 CALVERT, H
NI'S STATUS: FUNDAMENTAL QUESTIONS OF
FUNDAMENTAL LAW
SOLON 1(2)
1970 2 01

1335 CAMBLIN, G
ADMINISTRATIVE STRUCTURES FOR
DEVELOPMENT IN NI
IRISH REGIONAL STUD ASSOC CONFERENCE
GALWAY
1969 2 11

1336 CAMERON COMMISSION
DISTURBANCES IN NI: REPORT OF THE
COMMISSION APPOINTED BY THE GOVERNOR OF
NI
HMSO CMD, 532
BELFAST
1969 1 03

1337 CAMPAIGN FOR SOCIAL JUSTICE IN NI
PLAIN TRUTH
CAMPAIGN FOR SOCIAL JUSTICE IN NI
DUNGANNON
1969 1 09

1338 CARTY, R K
SOCIAL CLEAVAGES AND PARTY SYSTEMS: A
RECONSIDERATION OF THE IRISH CASE
EUROP J POLIT RES 4(2)
1976 1 01

1339 CAUL, B
AN AREA BOARD REVISITED
SCOPE 35
BELFAST
1980 2 01

1340 CHALK, P
GENERAL ELECTION RESULTS IN THE SIX
COUNTIES
IRL SOCIALIST R 5
LONDON
1979 2 01

1341 CHIEF ELECTORAL OFFICER FOR NI
ANALYSIS OF REGISTER OF ELECTORS
CHIEF ELECT OFF FOR NI
BELFAST
      2 03

1342 COAKLEY, J
NATIONAL TERRITORIES AND CULTURAL
FRONTIERS: CONFLICTS OF PRINCIPLE IN THE
FORMATION OF STATES IN EUROPE
WESTERN EUROPEAN POLITICS 5(4)
1982 2 01

1343 COAKLEY, J
SPATIAL UNITS AND THE REPORTING OF IRISH
STATISTICAL DATA: REGIONAL DIVISIONS
ADMIN (DUB) 27(1)
1979 2 01

1344 COMMON, R
RESHAPING BOUNDARIES IN NI
GEOGR MAG 44(2)
1971 2 01

1345 COOPER, R G
THE WORK OF THE FAIR EMPLOYMENT AGENCY
IN HEPBURN, A C (ED)
COLERAINE
1982 2 07

1346 CRICK, B
THE SOVEREIGNTY OF PARLIAMENT AND THE
IRISH QUESTION
IN REA, D (ED)
DUBLIN
1982 1 07

1347 CURRAN, J
ULSTER REPARTITION: A POSSIBLE ANSWER
AMERICA JAN 31
1976 1 01

1348 CURRAN, J
THE ANGLO-IRISH AGREEMENT OF 1925:
HARDLY A 'DAMN GOOD BARGAIN'
HISTORIAN 40(1)
1977 2 01

1349 DALY, C B
FORWARD FROM THE GREEN PAPER
SOC STUD 2(1)
1973 1 01

1350 DARBY, J
NI: THE 1973 WHITE PAPER
NEW COMM 2(2)
1973 1 01

1351 DEMPSEY, P
THE FAIR EMPLOYMENT AGENCY: AN EMPTY
EXERCISE IN 'REFORM'
IRIS 4
DUBLIN
1982 1 01

1352 DERRYNANE
STORMONT, THE PUPPET GOVERNMENT: A STUDY
IN LEGAL CODOLOGY
CONNOLLY PUBLICATIONS
LONDON
1965 1 09

1353 DEUTSCH, R
L'ADMINISTRATION DIRECTE DE L'ULSTER PAR
WESTMINSTER
ET IRL 1
1976 1 01

1354 DHSS (NI)
CONSULTATIVE PAPER ON THE STRUCTURE AND
MANAGEMENT OF HEALTH AND PERSONAL SOCIAL
SERVICES IN NI
HMSO
LONDON
1979 2 03

1355 DITCH, J
DIRECT RULE AND NI ADMINISTRATION
ADMIN (DUB) 25(3)
DUBLIN
1977 1 01

1356 DITCH, J
NI AND THE EEC
ULSTER POLY
BELFAST
1977 2 08

1357 DITCH, J
NI IN THE EUROPEAN ECONOMIC COMMUNITY
'UNITED KINGDOM POLITICS' CONF
GLASGOW
1977 2 08

1358 DONALDSON, A
CO-OPERATION BETWEEN NI AND THE IRISH
REPUBLIC
INT COMP LAW QUART 3
1954 2 01

1359 DONALDSON, A
CONSTITUTION OF NI: ITS ORIGINS AND
DEVELOPMENT
TORONTO UNIV LAW J 11(1)
TORONTO
1955 2 01

1360 DONALDSON, A
FUNDAMENTAL RIGHTS IN THE CONSTITUTION
OF NI
CANADIAN BAR R 37
1959 2 01

1361 DONALDSON, A
SENATE OF NI
PUBL LAW
LONDON
1958 2 01

1362 DONALDSON, A
SOME COMPARATIVE ASPECTS OF IRISH LAW
DUKE U P
DURHAM, NORTH CAROLINA
1957 2 10

1363 DONNISON, D
NI CIVIL SERVICE
NEW SOCIETY 5 JULY
LONDON
1973 2 01

1364 DOUGLAS, J N H
VOTING BEHAVIOUR AND CONSTITUTIONAL
REFORM IN NI
IN EVENDEN, L; CUNNINGHAM, F (EDS)
LONDON
1974 2 07

1365 DOUGLAS, J N H; OSBORNE, R D
INCREASED REPRESENTATION FOR NI
IR GEOG 13
BELFAST
1980 1 01

1366 DOUGLAS, J N H; OSBORNE, R D
NI'S INCREASED REPRESENTATION IN THE
WESTMINSTER PARLIAMENT
IR GEOG 14
1981 2 01

1367 DOWLING, B R
SOME ECONOMIC IMPLICATIONS OF A FEDERAL
IRELAND
IN GIBSON, N J (ED)
1974 2 07

1368 DUTTER, L E
ELECTORAL COMPETITION IN PLURAL
SOCIETIES: THE CASE OF NI
ROCHESTER UNIV PHD
NEW YORK
1974 3 04

1369 DUTTER, L E
THE STRUCTURE OF VOTER PREFERENCES: THE
1921, 1925, 1973 AND 1975 NORTHERN IRISH
PARLIAMENTARY ELECTIONS
COMP POLIT STUD 14(4)
BEVERLY HILLS
1982 2 01

1370 EDWARDS, O D; HARKNESS, D W
CABINET PAPERS NORTH AND SOUTH - A
REPORT
IRISH TIMES
DUBLIN
1966 2 10

1371 ELCOCK, H
OPPORTUNITY FOR OMBUDSMAN: THE NI
COMMISSIONER FOR COMPLAINTS
PUBL ADM 50
LONDON
1972 2 01

1372 ELECTORAL REFORM SOCIETY
ELECTORAL SYSTEM OF NI
ELECTORAL REFORM SOCIETY
LONDON
1970 2 02

1373 ELLIOTT, S
ELECTORAL SYSTEM IN NI SINCE 1920
QUB PHD
BELFAST
1971 2 04

1374 ELLIOTT, S
THE FIRST ELECTION TO THE EUROPEAN
PARLIAMENT
QUB
BELFAST
1980 2 08

1375 ELLIOTT, S
NI PARLIAMENTARY ELECTION RESULTS
1921-1972
POLITICAL REFERENCE PUBLICATIONS
CHICHESTER
1973 2 02

1376 ELLIOTT, S
NI'S ELECTIONS: THE ASSEMBLY'S HERITAGE
COMM FORUM 3(3)
BELFAST
1973 2 01

1377 ELLIOTT, S; SMITH, F J
NI LOCAL GOVERNMENT ELECTIONS OF 1977
QUB
BELFAST
1977 2 10

1378 ELLIOTT, S; SMITH, F J
NI: THE DISTRICT COUNCIL ELECTIONS OF
1981
QUB
BELFAST
1981 2 10

1379 ERCMAN, S
THE PROBLEM OF DISCRIMINATION AND
MEASURES WHICH SHOULD BE TAKEN FOR ITS
ELIMINATION
ANNALES DE LA FACULTE DE DROIT
D'ISTANBUL
ISTANBUL
1970 1 01

1380 FAIR, J
THE ANGLO-IRISH TREATY OF 1921: UNIONIST
ASPECTS OF THE PEACE
J BRIT STUD 7
1972 2 01

1381 FANNING, R
THE RESPONSE OF LONDON AND BELFAST
GOVERNMENTS TO THE DECLARATION OF THE
REPUBLIC OF IRELAND 1948-49
INT AFF 58(1)
LONDON
1982 2 01

1382 FARRELL, M
THE PROVOS AT THE BALLOT BOX
MAGILL 6(9)
DUBLIN
1983 1 01

1383 FENNELL, D
IRLANDE: LA DECENTRALISATION CONTRE LE
NATIONALISME
PLURIEL 25
PARIS
1981 1 01

1384 FENNELL, D
NEW NATIONALISM FOR THE NEW IRELAND
COMHAIRLE ULADH
MONAGHAN
1972 2 09

1385 FENNELL, D
SKETCHES OF THE NEW IRELAND
AUTHOR
GALWAY
1973 1 09

1386 FERMANAGH CIVIL RIGHTS ASSOCIATION
FERMANAGH FACTS
FERMANAGH CIVIL RIGHTS ASSOCIATION
ENNISKILLEN
1969 1 09

1387 FITZGERALD, M
NI: WHERE IS LOCAL DEMOCRACY?
LOC GOVT CHRON 5817
1978 2 01

1388 FREER, L G
RECENT TENDENCIES IN NI ADMINISTRATION
IN NEWARK, F H ET AL (EDS)
LONDON
1953 2 07

1389 FURNISS, N
NI AS A CASE STUDY OF DECENTRALISATION
IN UNITARY STATES
WLD POLITICS 27(3)
1975 1 01

1390 GALLAGHER,F
ANGLO-IRISH TREATY
HUTCHINSON
LONDON
1965   2   02

1391 GALLAGHER,F
INDIVISIBLE ISLAND
GOLLANCZ
LONDON
1957   2   02

1392 GIBSON,F
SOCIAL SERVICE RE-ORGANISATION IN NI
SOC WORK TODAY 2(18)
LONDON
1971   2   01

1393 GIBSON,M W
REDRESS FOR THE CITIZEN
IN RHODES,E (ED)
DERRY
1967   2   07

1394 GIBSON,N J
"THE TOTAL INTEGRATION OPTION" IN
ULSTER: THE ECONOMIC CASE
UTV
BELFAST
1975   2   10

1395 GIBSON,N J
CONSTITUTION-BUILDING IN IRELAND
ADMIN(DUB) 20(4)
DUBLIN
1972   1   01

1396 GIBSON,N J
POLITICAL AND ECONOMIC INTEGRATION
IN REA,D (ED)
DUBLIN
1982   1   07

1397 GIBSON,N J
POLITICAL POSSIBILITIES FOR THE PEOPLE
OF NI
ADMIN (DUB) 20(4)
DUBLIN
1974   1   01

1398 GIBSON,N J
SOME ECONOMIC IMPLICATIONS OF THE
VARIOUS SOLUTIONS TO THE NI PROBLEM
IN VAIZEY,J (ED)
1975   1   07

1399 GOULD,M H
THE ADMINISTRATIVE UNITS USED FOR WATER
SUPPLY PURPOSES IN NI FROM 1828
ROYAL SOCIETY HEALTH J 101(3)
LONDON
1981   2   01

1400 GRACE,E
THE IRISH DIMENSION
ADMIN (DUB) 20(4)
DUBLIN
1972   3   01

1401 GRACE,E
RESPONSIBILITY AND CONSENT
ADMIN (DUB) 20(4)
DUBLIN
1972   3   01

1402 GRAHAM,D
NI: A STATE BEYOND REFORM
SAI ANNUAL CONF
WEXFORD
1983   1   11

1403 GREEN,A J
DEVOLUTION AND PUBLIC FINANCE: STORMONT
FROM 1921 TO 1972
CSPP 48
GLASGOW
1979   2   10

1404 GRIFFITHS,H
NICRC
NEW COMM 1(2)
1972   2   01

1405 GRIFFITHS,H
THE NICRC: A CASE STUDY IN AGENCY
CONFLICT
NUU
COLERAINE
1974   2   10

1406 GRIFFITHS,H; BLACK,R
THE FUTURE OF LOCAL GOVERNMENT
NICRC
BELFAST
1971   2   10

1407 GUELKE,A
NI DIVISIONS AND INTERNATIONAL
LEGITIMACY
INST IRISH STUD QUB 18 MAY
BELFAST
1983   2   11

1408 HADFIELD,B
COMMITTEES OF THE HOUSE OF COMMONS AND
NI AFFAIRS
NI LEG QUART 23(3)
BELFAST
1981   2   01

1409 HAINSWORTH,P
THE EUROPEAN ELECTION OF 1979 IN NI -
LINKAGE POLITICS
PARL AFFAIRS 32(4)
1979   2   01

1410 HAND,G J
REPORT OF THE IRISH BOUNDARY COMMISSION,
1925
IRISH U P
DUBLIN
1969   2   02

1411 HARKNESS,D A E
AGRICULTURAL ADMINISTRATION IN NI
IN NEWARK,F H ET AL (EDS)
LONDON
1953   2   07

1412 HARKNESS,D W
THE DIFFICULTIES OF DEVOLUTION: THE
POST-WAR DEBATE AT STORMONT
IR JURIST 12(1)
1977   2   01

1413 HAYES,M
SOME ASPECTS OF LOCAL GOVERNMENT IN NI
IN RHODES,E (ED)
DERRY
1967   2   07

1414 HEATLEY,F
CIVIL RIGHTS IN THE SIX COUNTIES
IN CELTIC LEAGUE ANNUAL
DUBLIN
1969   1   07

1415 HEWITT,C
CATHOLIC GRIEVANCES, CATHOLIC
NATIONALISM AND VIOLENCE IN NI DURING
THE CIVIL RIGHTS PERIOD - A
CONSIDERATION
BRIT J SOCIOL 32(3)
LONDON
1981   1   01

1416 HILL,D
DEVOLUTION AND LOCAL GOVERNMENT
DEPT POLITICS UNIV OF SOUTHAMPTON
SOUTHAMPTON
1977   3   08

1417 HILL,D
LOCAL GOVERNMENT AND DEVOLUTION
POLIT STUD ASSOC CONF
ABERYSTWYTH
1977   3   11

1418 HILLAN, J J
A REAL CONSTITUTION: A SUGGESTED
FRAMEWORK FOR NATIONALIST GOVERNMENT
NATIONAL DEMOCRATIC GROUP
BELFAST
1969 1 09

1419 HODSON, R
LONDONDERRY COMMISSION AS A BLUE-PRINT
FOR THE FUTURE
FINANCIAL TIMES SURVEY ON NI 22 JAN
LONDON
1973 2 10

1420 HOGWOOD, B
INTERGOVERNMENTAL STRUCTURES AND
INDUSTRIAL POLICY IN THE UNITED KINGDOM
STUD PUBL POL 2
GLASGOW
1977 2 10

1421 HOLMES, E
CENTRE PARTY COALITION GOVERNMENT
COMM FORUM 2(2)
BELFAST
1972 2 01

1422 HOLMES, E
POLITICAL POSSIBILITIES FOR THE PEOPLE
OF NI
ADMIN (DUB) 20(4)
DUBLIN
1972 2 01

1423 HOME OFFICE
DISQUALIFICATION OF CERTAIN MEMBERS OF
THE SENATE AND HOUSE OF COMMONS OF NI
HMSO CMD 9698
LONDON
1956 2 03

1424 IRIS
A RIOTOUS ASSEMBLY? A LOOK AT
DIRECT-RULER PRIOR'S PROPOSALS FOR A
SIX-COUNTY DEVOLVED ASSEMBLY
IRIS 3
DUBLIN
1982 1 01

1425 IRISH COMMUNIST ORGANISATION
STORMONT ELECTIONS: A WORKING CLASS
ANALYSIS
IR COMMUNIST ORGAN
BELFAST
1969 2 09

1426 IRISH NEWS
COMMENTARY UPON THE WHITE PAPER (CMD
558): A RECORD OF CONSTRUCTIVE CHANGE
IRISH NEWS
BELFAST
1971 1 10

1427 JAMISON, D
LOCAL GOVERNMENT IN BELFAST
LOC GOVT R 13 MAY
1972 2 01

1428 JENKINS, P
POLITICAL CONSTRAINTS: LONDON
IN WATT, D (ED)
LONDON
1981 1 07

1429 JOHNSON, J H
REORGANISATION OF LOCAL GOVERNMENT IN NI
AREA 4
1970 2 01

1430 JONES, G W
INTERGOVERNMENTAL RELATIONS IN BRITAIN
A AMER ACAD POLIT SOC SCI 416
1974 2 01

1431 KEATINGE, P
AN ODD COUPLE? OBSTACLES AND
OPPORTUNITIES IN INTER-STATE POLITICAL
CO-OPERATION BETWEEN THE REPUBLIC OF
IRELAND AND THE UK
IN REA, D (ED)
DUBLIN
1982 1 07

1432 KEATINGE, P
TRANSNATIONALISM AND AUTONOMY: THE CASE
OF IRELAND AND ANGLO-IRISH RELATIONS
TCD
DUBLIN
1978 2 08

1433 KENNEDY, D
CATHOLICS IN NI: 1926-1939
IN MACMANUS, F (ED)
DUBLIN
1967 2 07

1434 KENNEDY, H
POLITICS IN NI: A STUDY OF ONE-PARTY
DOMINATION
MICHIGAN UNIV PHD
1967 2 04

1435 KENNEDY, J A D
PARLIAMENT AND EXECUTIVE
IN RHODES, E (ED)
1967 2 07

1436 KINGSTON, W
CASE FOR A PRINCIPALITY OF ULSTER
POLIT QUART 46(3)
LONDON
1975 1 01

1437 KINGSTON, W
NI - IF REASON FAILS
POLIT QUART 44(1)
LONDON
1973 1 01

1438 KINGSTON, W
NI - THE ELEMENTS OF A SOLUTION
POLIT QUART 43(2)
LONDON
1972 1 01

1439 KNIGHT, J
ELECTION OF THE CONSTITUTIONAL
CONVENTION MAY 1975
ARTHUR MCDOUGALL FUND
LONDON
1975 2 10

1440 KNIGHT, J
NI - THE ELECTIONS OF 1973
ARTHUR MCDOUGALL FUND
LONDON
1974 2 10

1441 KNIGHT, J; BAXTER-MOORE, N
NI ELECTIONS OF THE 1920'S
ELECTORAL REFORM SOCIETY
LONDON
1971 2 10

1442 KNIGHT, J; BAXTER-MOORE, N
NI LOCAL GOVERNMENT ELECTIONS, 30TH MAY
1973
ARTHUR MCDOUGALL FUND
LONDON
1973 2 10

1443 KYLE, K
COMMENT ON CHAPTER BY PALLEY
IN WATT, D (ED)
LONDON
1981 1 07

1444 KYLE, K
SUNNINGDALE AND AFTER: BRITAIN, IRELAND
AND ULSTER
WLD TODAY 31(11)
LONDON
1975 1 01

1445 LAKEMAN, E
NI RETURNS TO STV
NEW OUTLOOK 1
1974 2 01

1446 LAKEMAN, E
PROPORTIONAL REPRESENTATION IN NI
COMM FORUM 1(2)
BELFAST
1971 2 01

1447 LAVER, M J
INTRODUCING STV AND INTERPRETING RESULTS
- THE CASE OF NI, 1973 - 1975
PARL AFFAIRS 29(2)
1976 2 01

1448 LAVER, M J
STRATEGIC CAMPAIGN BEHAVIOUR FOR
ELECTORS AND PARTIES: NI ASSEMBLY
ELECTION OF 1973
EUROP J POLIT RES 3(1)
AMSTERDAM
1975 1 01

1449 LAVER, M J
STRATEGIC CAMPAIGN BEHAVIOUR FOR
ELECTORS AND PARTIES: THE NI ASSEMBLY
ELECTION
IN BUDGE, I; CREWER, J; FARLE, D (EDS)
NEW YORK
1976 1 07

1450 LAVER, M J
THEORY AND PRACTICE OF PARTY COMPETITION
- ULSTER, 1973-75
SAGE PROFESSIONAL PAPERS IN CONTEMPORARY
SOCIOLOGY 2(601)
LONDON
1976 1 01

1451 LAVIN, D
NI ELECTIONS
WLD TODAY 21
LONDON
1965 2 01

1452 LAWRENCE, R J
DEVOLUTION RECONSIDERED
POLIT STUD (OXFORD) 4(1)
OXFORD
1956 2 01

1453 LAWRENCE, R J
DEVOLUTION: A REJOINDER
POLIT STUD (OXFORD) 5(1)
OXFORD
1957 2 01

1454 LAWRENCE, R J
GOVERNMENT OF NI: PUBLIC FINANCE AND
PUBLIC SERVICES 1921-1964
CLARENDON PRESS
OXFORD
1965 2 02

1455 LAWRENCE, R J
GOVERNMENT OF NI: PUBLIC FINANCE AND THE
ORGANISATION OF PUBLIC SERVICES
QUB PHD
BELFAST
1964 2 04

1456 LAWRENCE, R J
LOCAL GOVERNMENT IN NI: AREAS, FUNCTIONS
AND FINANCE
JSSISI
1966 2 01

1457 LAWRENCE, R J
NI
IN THORNHILL, W (ED)
LONDON
1975 2 07

1458 LAWRENCE, R J
NI AT WESTMINSTER
PARL AFFAIRS 20(1)
1967 2 01

1459 LAWRENCE, R J
POLITICS AND PUBLIC ADMINISTRATION IN NI
ADMIN (DUB) 16(2)
DUBLIN
1968 2 01

1460 LAWRENCE, R J; ELLIOTT, S
NI BORDER POLL
HMSO CMND 5875
LONDON
1975 2 03

1461 LAWRENCE, R J; ELLIOTT, S; LAVER, M J
NI GENERAL ELECTIONS OF 1973
HMSO CMND 5851
LONDON
1975 2 03

1462 LEAVY, J
POLITICAL THINKING BEHIND SUNNINGDALE
TALBOT
DUBLIN
1973 1 02

1463 LEAVY, J
POLITICS OF PROCESS AND THE IRISH
QUESTION: SOME FURTHER REFLECTIONS
STUDIES 64
DUBLIN
1975 1 01

1464 LEAVY, J
STRUCTURE OR PROCESS? NEW APPROACHES TO
THE PROBLEM OF NI
STUDIES 62
DUBLIN
1973 1 01

1465 LEE, G
CONSTITUTION AND STATE OF EMERGENCY
IR LAW STUDIES 103
1969 1 01

1466 LEITCH, W A
GOVERNMENT AND PARLIAMENT
IN RHODES, E (ED)
1967 2 07

1467 LERUEZ, J
IRLANDE DU NORD: INTEGRATION OU
SECESSION
R FRAN SCI POLIT 21(4)
1971 1 01

1468 LIEBERMAN, S M
IMPLEMENTATION OF PROCEDURAL REFORM IN
NI
DEPT POLIT SCI YALE UNIV
NEW HAVEN, CONN
1974 2 08

1469 LIEBERMAN, S M
IRISH ANALYTICAL PERSPECTIVES: THE
LIMITS OF AN OMBUDSMAN
CALIFORNIA UNIV
BERKELEY, CALIFORNIA
1973 2 08

1470 LIEBERMAN, S M
UNCERTAINTY, POWERLESSNESS, AND
POLYARCHY
DEPT POLIT SCI YALE UNIV
NEW HAVEN, CONN
1974 1 08

1471 LINDSAY, K
ULSTERMAN'S GUIDE TO THE WHITE PAPER
ULSTER VANGUARD
BELFAST
1973 1 09

1472 LLOYD-GEORGE, M
REGIONAL PARLIAMENTS
PARL AFFAIRS 8(4)
1955 2 01

1473 LOFTS, D
STRUCTURE OF LOCAL GOVERNMENT IN NI
CONFERENCE OF LOCAL AUTHORITIES IN NI
PORTRUSH
1959 2 11

Political System/

1474 LONG,M
ULSTER - THE CASE FOR REGIONALISM
UUP
BELFAST
1973 2 09

1475 LOUGHRAN,G F
PROBLEM OF LOCAL GOVERNMENT IN NI
ADMIN (DUB) 13
DUBLIN
1965 2 01

1476 LOWRY,D R
LEGISLATION IN A SOCIAL VACUUM: THE
FAILURE OF THE FAIR EMPLOYMENT (NI) ACT
NEW YORK UNIV J INT LAW AND POLITICS
9(3)
NEW YORK
1977 1 01

1477 LYNN,R J
REVENUE RAISING
IN RHODES,E (ED)
1967 2 07

1478 LYONS,F S L
ALTERNATIVES OPEN TO GOVERNMENTS
IN CROZIER,B; MOSS,R (EDS)
LONDON
1972 1 07

1479 MACAULAY,A
THE GOVERNMENT OF IRELAND ACT 1920: THE
ORIGINS OF PARTITION
CAPUCHIN ANNUAL 38
DUBLIN
1971 2 01

1480 MACIVOR,B
THE FUTURE OF NORTH-SOUTH RELATIONSHIPS
IN IRELAND (1)
INST COMMONWEALTH AFF
LONDON
1971 2 01

1481 MACKINTOSH,J P
THE DEVOLUTION OF POWER
CHATTO AND WINDUS
LONDON
1968 2 02

1482 MACKINTOSH,J P
REPORT OF THE REVIEW BODY ON LOCAL
GOVERNMENT IN NI 1970: MACRORY REPORT
PUBL ADM 49(1)
1971 2 01

1483 MACRORY REPORT
LOCAL GOVERNMENT IN NI
HMSO CMD 546
BELFAST
1970 2 03

1484 MAGUIRE,P
PARLIAMENT AND THE DIRECT RULE OF NI
IR JURIST 10(1)
1975 1 01

1485 MAIR,P
BREAKUP OF THE UK: IRISH EXPERIENCE OF
REGIME CHANGE, 1918-49
STUD PUBL POL 13
STRATHCLYDE, GLASGOW
1978 2 10

1486 MAIR,P
BREAKUP OF THE UK: IRISH EXPERIENCE OF
REGIME CHANGE, 1921-49
J COMMONWEALTH COMP POLIT 16
1978 2 01

1487 MAIR,P
THE SEIZURE OF AUTHORITY: IRISH
EXPERIENCE OF CONSTITUTIONAL CHANGE,
1918-49
IN CSPP 1
1977 2 10

1488 MALTBY,A
GOVERNMENT OF NI: A CATALOGUE AND
BREVIATE OF PARLIAMENTARY PAPERS
IRISH U P
SHANNON
1974 2 02

1489 MANNING,M
SUNNINGDALE AND THE LAW
GARDA R 2(2)
1974 1 01

1490 MANSERGH,N
GOVERNMENT OF IRELAND ACT: ITS ORIGINS
AND PURPOSES
HISTORICAL STUD 9
1974 2 07

1491 MANSFIELD,F
FOCUS ON NI
MUNICIPAL AND PUBL SERVICES J 80(18)
1972 2 01

1492 MARSHALL,W
COUNCIL OF IRELAND IN THE CONTEXT OF
EUROPE
ADMIN (DUB) 20(4)
1972 1 01

1493 MAYNARD,J ; MCREADY,P
THE REORGANISATION OF HEALTH AND
PERSONAL SOCIAL SERVICES IN NI
DEPT BUS STUD QUB
BELFAST
1974 2 10

1494 MCALLISTER,I
CENTRE-PERIPHERY WITHIN NI: A MODEL FOR
THE DEVELOPMENT OF A PARTY SYSTEM
DEPT POLIT STRATHCLYDE UNIV
GLASGOW
1979 1 08

1495 MCALLISTER,I
LEGITIMACY OF OPPOSITION: THE COLLAPSE
OF THE 1974 NI EXECUTIVE
EIRE-IRELAND 12(4)
1977 1 01

1496 MCALLISTER,I
THE MANY-SIDED CENTRIFUGALISM OF NI
GVT AND OPPOSITION 12(2)
1977 1 01

1497 MCALLISTER,I
THE MODERN DEVELOPMENT OF THE NI PARTY
SYSTEM
PARL AFFAIRS 30(2)
1979 2 01

1498 MCALLISTER,I
PARTY ORGANISATION AND MINORITY
NATIONALISM: A COMPARATIVE STUDY IN THE
UK
STUD PUBL POL 43
1979 2 10

1499 MCALLISTER,I
SOCIAL INFLUENCES ON VOTERS AND
NON-VOTERS: A NOTE ON TWO NI ELECTIONS
POLIT STUD (OXFORD) 24(4)
1976 2 01

1500 MCALLISTER,I
TERRITORIAL DIFFERENTIATION AND PARTY
DEVELOPMENT IN NI
IN GALLAGHER,T; O'CONNELL,J (EDS)
MANCHESTER
1983 2 07

1501 MCALLISTER,I
TERRITORIAL DIFFERENTIATION AND PARTY
DEVELOPMENT IN NI
STUD PUBL POL 66
GLASGOW
1980 1 10

Political System/

1502 MCALLISTER, I
1975 NI CONVENTION ELECTION
SURVEY RES CENTRE OCCASIONAL PAPER 14
GLASGOW
1975 1 10

1503 MCALLISTER, I; NELSON, S
DEVELOPMENTS IN THE NI PARTY SYSTEM
PARL AFFAIRS 32(3)
LONDON
1979 2 01

1504 MCALLISTER, I; PARRY, R; ROSE, R
UK RANKINGS: THE TERRITORIAL DIMENSION
TO SOCIAL INDICATORS
STUD PUBL POL 44
1979 2 10

1505 MCBIRNEY, R
STORMONT-WESTMINSTER RELATIONS
IN RHODES, E (ED)
LONDON
1967 2 07

1506 MCCOLGAN, J
BRITISH POLICY AND THE IRISH
ADMINISTRATION 1920-22
ALLEN AND UNWIN
LONDON
1983 2 02

1507 MCCOLGAN, J
PARTITION AND THE IRISH 1920-22
ADMIN (DUB) 28(2)
DUBLIN
1980 2 01

1508 MCCONAGHY, D
COLLAPSE OF A LOCAL GOVERNMENT
MUNICIPAL R 49(585)
1978 3 01

1509 MCCRUDDEN, J C
DISCRIMINATION AGAINST MINORITY GROUPS
IN EMPLOYMENT: A COMPARISON OF LEGAL
REMEDIES IN THE UNITED KINGDOM AND THE
UNITED STATES
OXFORD UNIV DPHIL
OXFORD
1981 2 04

1510 MCCRUDDEN, J C
THE EXPERIENCE OF THE LEGAL ENFORCEMENT
OF THE FAIR EMPLOYMENT (NI) ACT 1976
IN CORMACK, R; OSBORNE, R D (EDS)
BELFAST
1983 2 07

1511 MCDOWELL, M
THE BRITISH INITIATIVE IN ULSTER
CONFLICT QUART 1(1)
1980 1 01

1512 MCDOWELL, M
A NEW ULSTER INITIATIVE
NEW LEADER 63 MAY 5
1980 1 01

1513 MCGILL, P F
THE SENATE IN NI 1921-1962
QUB PHD
BELFAST
1965 2 04

1514 MCGURNAGHAN, M A; SIMPSON, J V
ULSTER IN EUROPE: NI AND THE EUROPEAN
PARLIAMENT
NUM
BELFAST
1979 2 09

1515 MCLAUGHLIN, J
DISCRIMINATION IN NI: HISTORICAL ROOTS
AND CONTEMPORARY PATTERNS
ST. PATRICK'S COLL MA
MAYNOOTH
1979 1 04

1516 MCLENNAN, G
BRITAIN AND THE WHITE PAPER: A COMMUNIST
VIEW OF THE WHITE PAPER
COMMUNIST PARTY
LONDON
1973 1 09

1517 MINISTRY OF DEVELOPMENT (NI)
REORGANISATION OF SERVICES
MINISTRY OF DEVELOPMENT (NI)
BELFAST
1971 2 03

1518 MINISTRY OF EDUCATION (NI)
LOCAL EDUCATION AUTHORITIES AND
VOLUNTARY SCHOOLS
HMSO CMD 513
BELFAST
1967 2 03

1519 MINISTRY OF HEALTH AND LOCAL GOVERNMENT
(NI)
THE ADMINISTRATION OF TOWN AND COUNTRY
PLANNING IN NI
HMSO CMD 465
BELFAST
1964 2 03

1520 MINISTRY OF HEALTH AND SOCIAL SERVICES
(NI)
ADMINISTRATIVE STRUCTURE OF HOSPITAL
MANAGEMENT COMMITTEES
HMSO
BELFAST
1966 2 03

1521 MINISTRY OF HEALTH AND SOCIAL SERVICES
(NI)
REPORT AND RECOMMENDATIONS OF THE
WORKING PARTY OF DISCRIMINATION IN THE
PRIVATE SECTOR OF EMPLOYMENT
HMSO
BELFAST
1973 1 03

1522 MINNS, R; THORNLEY, J
LOCAL GOVERNMENT ECONOMIC PLANNING AND
THE PROVISION OF RISK CAPITAL FOR SMALL
FIRMS
CENTRE FOR ENVIRONMENTAL STUDIES
LONDON
1978 2 11

1523 MOORE, J
EMERGENCE OF NI AS A BI-PARTISAN
QUESTION IN BRITISH PARTY POLITICS
DEPT POLIT YORK UNIV
YORK
1979 1 08

1524 MURPHY, M
LOCAL GOVERNMENT AREAS IN NI: A CASE
STUDY IN DECISION MAKING
QUB PHD
BELFAST
1979 2 04

1525 MYANT, C; WARREN, J
NO PEACE IN THE WHITE PAPER
BRITISH PEACE COMMITTEE
LONDON
1973 1 09

1526 NEALON, T
IRELAND: A PARLIAMENTARY DIRECTORY,
1973-74
INSTITUTE OF PUBLIC ADMINISTRATION
DUBLIN
1974 2 02

1527 NEILL, D C
THE ELECTION IN NI
IN BUTLER, D E (ED)
1952 2 07

1528 NEILL, D C
SOME CONSEQUENCES OF GOVERNMENT BY
DEVOLUTION IN NI
IN NEWARK, F H ET AL (EDS)
LONDON
1953 2 07

Political System/

1529 NEILL,D C
THE ULSTER EXPERIMENT
NEW SOCIETY 27 OCT
1966 2 01

1530 NELSON,S
THE ULSTER INDEPENDENCE DEBATE
INST IRISH STUD QUB
BELFAST
1977 1 11

1531 NEVIN,E
THE ECONOMICS OF DEVOLUTION
WALES U P
CARDIFF
1978 2 02

1532 NEW ULSTER POLITICAL RESEARCH GROUP
(UDA)
BEYOND THE RELIGIOUS DIVIDE
NUPRG
BELFAST
1979 1 09

1533 NEWARK,F H
THE CONSITITUTION OF NI
HMSO
BELFAST
1952 2 07

1534 NEWARK,F H
THE CONSTITUTION OF NI THE FIRST
TWENTY-FIVE YEARS
NI LEG QUART 8
1948 2 01

1535 NEWARK,F H
THE LAW AND THE CONSTITUTION
IN WILSON,T (ED)
1955 2 07

1536 NEWARK,F H
SEVERABILITY OF NI STATUTES
NI LEG QUART 9(1)
BELFAST
1950 2 01

1537 NEWLAND,R
WHY X-VOTING FAILS AND PREFERENTIAL
VOTING WORKS
ELECTORAL REFORM SOCIETY
LONDON
1972 2 10

1538 NI GOVERNMENT
A COMMENTARY...TO ACCOMPANY THE CAMERON
REPORT, INCORPORATING AN ACCOUNT OF
PROGRESS AND A PROGRAMME OF ACTION
HMSO
BELFAST
1969 1 03

1539 NI GOVERNMENT
THE FUTURE DEVELOPMENT OF THE PARLIAMENT
AND GOVERNMENT OF NI
HMSO CMD 560
BELFAST
1971 1 03

1540 NI GOVERNMENT
MICROFILM OF PARLIAMENTARY PUBLICATIONS,
1922-1972
OCEANA
DOBBS FERRY, NY
       2 10

1541 NI GOVERNMENT
POLITICAL SETTLEMENT
HMSO CMD 568
BELFAST
1972 1 03

1542 NI GOVERNMENT
RECORD OF CONSTRUCTIVE CHANGE
HMSO CMD 558
BELFAST
1971 1 03

1543 NI GOVERNMENT
RESHAPING OF LOCAL GOVERNMENT
HMSO CMD 517
BELFAST
1967 2 03

1544 NI GOVERNMENT
RESHAPING OF LOCAL GOVERNMENT: FURTHER
PROPOSALS
HMSO CMD 530
BELFAST
1967 2 03

1545 NI OFFICE
THE FUTURE OF NI
HMSO
LONDON
1972 1 03

1546 NI OFFICE
NI CONSTITUTIONAL PROPOSALS
HMSO CMND 5259
LONDON
1975 2 03

1547 NICRC
THE FUTURE OF LOCAL GOVERNMENT
NICRC
BELFAST
1971 2 10

1548 NILP
THE ULSTER CONVENTION: WHERE NILP STANDS
NILP
BELFAST
1974 1 09

1549 NUGENT REPORT
REPORT OF THE COMMITTEE ON THE FINANCES
OF LOCAL GOVERNMENT
HMSO CMD 369
BELFAST
1957 2 03

1550 NUM
THE LEGAL BASIS FOR PARTITION IN NI
NUM
BELFAST
1971 1 10

1551 NUM
A NEW CONSTITUTION FOR NI
NUM
BELFAST
1972 1 10

1552 NUM
THE REFORM OF STORMONT
NUM
BELFAST
1971 1 10

1553 NUM
WHAT PRICE INDEPENDENCE?
NUM
BELFAST
1976 1 09

1554 O'CONNELL,E
DAIL ULADH: SHAPING A NEW SOCIETY
DUBLIN
       1 99

1555 O'DONOGHUE,F
THE GENERAL ELECTION IN ULSTER
CONTEMP R 184 DEC
1953 2 01

1556 O'GADHRA,N
RE-THINKING THE PR SYSTEM
SOC STUD 6
1977 2 01

1557 O'LEARY,C
BELFAST WEST
IN BUTLER,D E; KING,A (EDS)
1966 2 07

1558 O'LEARY,C
IRELAND: NORTH AND SOUTH
IN FINER,S E (ED)
LONDON
1975 2 07

1559 O'LEARY,C
IRISH ELECTIONS, 1918-77
GILL AND MACMILLAN
DUBLIN
1979 2 02

1560 O'LEARY,C
THE NI GENERAL ELECTION (1969)
IN HERMANS,F A (ED)
1969 2 07

1561 O'LEARY,C
NI, 1945-72
IN LEE,J (ED)
DUBLIN
1979 2 07

1562 O'LEARY,C
NI: THE POLITICS OF ILLUSION
POLIT QUART 40(3)
LONDON
1969 1 01

1563 O'LEARY,C
THE POLITICAL PARTIES OF NI
IN SCOTT,H (ED)
LONDON
1976 2 07

1564 O'LEARY,C; BUDGE,I
PERMANENT SUPREMACY AND PERMANENT
OPPOSITION: THE PARLIAMENT IN NI 1921-72
IN ELDRIDGE,A R
DURHAM, N CAROLINA
1977 2 07

1565 O'RIORDAN,M
THE WHITE PAPER ON NI
MARXISM TODAY 17(6)
1973 1 01

1566 OLIVER,J
THE EVOLUTION OF CONSTITUTIONAL POLICY
IN NI OVER THE PAST FIFTEEN YEARS
IN REA,D (ED)
DUBLIN
1982 1 07

1567 OLIVER,J
THE ULSTER CONVENTION
BLACKWOOD'S MAG 320(1930)
1976 1 01

1568 OLIVER,J
WORKING AT STORMONT
IPA
DUBLIN
1978 2 02

1569 ORBIS
THE FAILURE OF POWER SHARING IN NI
ORBIS 18(2)
1974 1 01

1570 OSBORNE,R D
ELECTIONS WITH A DIFFERENCE
GEOGR MAG JULY
1975 2 01

1571 OSBORNE,R D
FAIR EMPLOYMENT IN COOKSTOWN? A NOTE ON
ANTI-DISCRIMINATION POLICY IN NI
J SOC POL 11(4)
1982 2 01

1572 OSBORNE,R D
FAIR EMPLOYMENT IN NI
NEW COMM 8(1-2)
LONDON
1980 1 01

1573 OSBORNE,R D
LOCAL GOVERNMENT ELECTORAL AREAS IN NI
IR GEOG 11
1978 2 01

1574 OSBORNE,R D
THE NI PARLIAMENTARY ELECTORAL SYSTEM:
THE 1929 REAPPORTIONMENT
IR GEOG 12
1979 2 01

1575 OSBORNE,R D
NI: REPRESENTATION AT WESTMINSTER AND
THE BOUNDARY COMMISSION
IR GEOG 9
1976 2 01

1576 OSBORNE,R D
PARLIAMENTARY SEAT REDISTRIBUTION (NI)
AREA 7(3)
1975 2 01

1577 OSBORNE,R D
THE POLITICAL SYSTEM, VOTING PATTERNS
AND VOTING BEHAVIOUR IN NI
QUB PHD
BELFAST
1977 2 04

1578 OSBORNE,R D
PROPOSALS FOR ULSTER
GEOGR MAG DEC
1975 2 01

1579 OSBORNE,R D
VOTING BEHAVIOUR IN NI 1921-1977
IN BOAL,F W; DOUGLAS,J N H (EDS)
LONDON
1982 2 07

1580 OSBORNE,R D; SINGLETON,D
POLITICAL PROCESSES AND BEHAVIOUR
IN BOAL,F W; DOUGLAS,J N H (EDS)
LONDON
1982 1 07

1581 PALLEY,C
CONSTITUTIONAL LAW AND MINORITIES
MINORITY RIGHTS GROUP
LONDON
1978 2 10

1582 PALLEY,C
CONSTITUTIONAL SOLUTIONS TO THE IRISH
PROBLEM
CURRENT LEG PROBLEMS
1980 1 01

1583 PALLEY,C
EVOLUTION, DISINTEGRATION, AND POSSIBLE
RECONSTRUCTION OF THE NI CONSTITUTION
ANGLO-AMER LAW R 1
1972 1 01

1584 PALLEY,C
WAYS FORWARD: THE CONSTITUTIONAL OPTIONS
IN WATT,D (ED)
LONDON
1981 1 07

1585 PALMER,S A
THE PARLIAMENT OF NI: A GENERAL SYSTEMS
APPROACH TO CONFLICT
OHIO STATE UNIV PHD
1976 2 04

1586 PATTEN,P
LOCAL GOVERNMENT REFORM: HEALTH AND
SOCIAL SERVICES
COMM FORUM 3(1)
BELFAST
1973 2 01

1587 PECK,J
DUBLIN FROM DOWNING STREET
GILL AND MACMILLAN
DUBLIN
1978 2 02

1588 PIVERONOUS,P J
THE ASSOCIATE STATE IDEA: A COMPROMISE
SOLUTION TO THE PROBLEM OF IRISH UNITY
IN SULLIVAN,E ET AL (EDS)
GAINESVILLE, FLORIDA
1976 1 07

1589 POOLE,K P
NI COMMISSIONER FOR COMPLAINTS
PUBL LAW
LONDON
1972 2 01

1590 POWER,P F
SUNNINGDALE STRATEGY AND NORTHERN
MAJORITY CONSENT DOCTRINE IN ANGLO-IRISH
RELATIONS
EIRE-IRELAND 12(1)
1977 1 01

1591 PRINGLE,D G
ELECTORAL SYSTEMS AND POLITICAL
MANIPULATION: A CASE STUDY OF NI IN THE
1920S
ECON AND SOC R 11(3)
DUBLIN
1980 2 01

1592 PRINGLE,D G
THE NI CONVENTION ELECTION
MILIEU 4
1978 2 01

1593 PRINGLE,D G
THE NI WESTMINSTER ELECTIONS 1979
IR GEOG 12
DUBLIN
1979 2 01

1594 QUB CONSERVATIVE AND UNIONIST
ASSOCIATION
PR AND ULSTER
QUB CONSERVATIVE AND UNIONIST
ASSOCIATION
BELFAST
1972 2 09

1595 QUECKETT,A
THE CONSTITUTION OF NI 1926-1946
HMSO
BELFAST
1946 2 03

1596 ROBINSON,M
FUTURE OF NORTH-SOUTH RELATIONSHIPS IN
IRELAND
INST COMMONWEALTH AFF
LONDON
1971 1 01

1597 ROSE,R
THE DYNAMICS OF A DIVIDED REGIME
GVT AND OPPOSITION 5(2)
LONDON
1970 1 01

1598 ROSE,R
NI: A TIME OF CHOICE
MACMILLAN
LONDON
1976 1 02

1599 ROSE,R
NORDIRLAND: DIE HEUTIGEN ALTERNATIUEN
EUROPA ARCHIV 32(16)
FRANKFURT
1977 1 01

1600 ROSE,R
ULSTER: THE PROBLEM OF DIRECT RULE
NEW SOCIETY JUN 10
LONDON
1971 1 01

1601 RUTAN,G
NI UNDER ULSTER UNIONIST RULE: THE
ANTI-MOVEMENT POLITICAL SYSTEM,
1920-1963
NORTH CAROLINA UNIV PHD
CHAPEL HILL
1964 1 04

1602 RYAN,J L
THE ROLE OF STATUTORY BODIES IN PUBLIC
ADMINISTRATION
IN RHODES,E (ED)
DERRY
1967 2 07

1603 SAVORY,D
THE ORIGIN OF AND THE CONSTITUTION OF NI
UUC
BELFAST
1963 2 09

1604 SAVORY,D
THE PARTITION OF IRELAND
CONTEMP R 193
1958 2 01

1605 SAYERS,J E
THE POLITICAL PARTIES AND THE SOCIAL
BACKGROUND
IN WILSON,T (ED)
OXFORD
1955 2 01

1606 SAYERS,J E
THE RELATIONSHIPS OF THE PRESS AND
PUBLIC ADMINISTRATION
IN RHODES,E (ED)
DERRY
1967 2 07

1607 SCHMITT,D
THE CONSEQUENCES OF ADMINISTRATIVE
EMPLOYEES IN EQUAL OPPORTUNITY
STRATEGIES: COMPARATIVE ANALYSIS OF THE
UNITED STATES AND NI
AMER POLIT SCI ASSOC ANNUAL CONF
1981 2 11

1608 SCHMITT,D
EQUAL OPPORTUNITY AS A TECHNIQUE TOWARD
THE CONTROL OF POLITICAL VIOLENCE: THE
CASE OF THE FEA
CURRENT RESEARCH PEACE AND VIOLENCE
1980 1 01

1609 SCOPE
COMMUNITY CANDIDATES: A FEW QUESTIONS
SCOPE 7
BELFAST
1976 2 01

1610 SCOPE
DISTRICT COMMITTEES: HOW WELL DO THEY
DO?
SCOPE 8
BELFAST
1977 2 01

1611 SCOPE
DISTRICT COUNCILS AND COMMUNITY WORK
SCOPE 3
BELFAST
1976 2 01

1612 SCOPE
DISTRICT COUNCILS AND COMMUNITY WORK:
TWENTY MONTHS ON
SCOPE 13
BELFAST
1977 2 01

1613 SCOTT,R D
THE BRITISH ELECTION IN NI: CALM BEFORE
THE STORM
DALHOUSIE R 50(2)
1970 1 01

1614 SCOTT,R D
THE 1970 BRITISH GENERAL ELECTION IN
ULSTER
PARL AFFAIRS 24(1)
1971 2 01

1615 SHEA, P
VOICES AND THE SOUND OF DRUMS
BLACKSTAFF
BELFAST
1981 2 02

1616 SHEARMAN, H
ANGLO IRISH RELATIONS
FABER
LONDON
1948 2 02

1617 SHEARMAN, H
CONSTITUTIONAL AND POLITICAL DEVELOPMENT
ON NI 1920-54
IN MOODY, T W; BECKETT, J C (EDS)
LONDON
1957 2 07

1618 SHEARMAN, H
HOW NI IS GOVERNED: CENTRAL AND LOCAL
GOVERNMENT IN NI
HMSO
BELFAST
1951 2 02

1619 SHEARMAN, H
RECENT DEVELOPMENTS IN ANGLO IRISH
RELATIONS
WLD AFFAIRS APR
LONDON
1949 2 02

1620 SHERIDAN, L A
CONSTITUTIONAL LAW
IN KEETON, G W; LLOYD, D (EDS)
LONDON
1955 2 07

1621 SIMPSON, J V
THE ECONOMICS OF THE NORTH'S OPTIONS
MANAGEMENT 21(9)
LONDON
1974 1 01

1622 SIMPSON, J V
LOCAL GOVERNMENT IN A DEVELOPING ECONOMY
ADMIN (DUB) 14(2)
DUBLIN
1966 1 01

1623 SIMPSON, J V
THE RESHAPING OF LOCAL GOVERNMENT IN NI
NUU
COLERAINE
1969 2 10

1624 SINNOTT, R; DAVIS, E E
POLITICAL MOBILIZATION, POLITICAL
INSTITUTIONALIZATION AND THE MAINTENANCE
OF ETHNIC CONFLICT
ETHNIC AND RACIAL STUDIES 4(4)
LONDON
1981 1 01

1625 SMYTH, S
SOME ASPECTS OF POWER SHARING AND
FEDERALISM
ULSTER RADICAL ASSOC
BELFAST
1975 1 09

1626 SPJUT, R
THE NI CONSTITUTIONAL SETTLEMENT OF 1973
AND THE LOYALIST OPPOSITION
IR JURIST 12
DUBLIN
1977 1 01

1627 TOMLINSON, M
RELEGATING LOCAL GOVERNMENT
IN O'DOWD, L; ROLSTON, B; TOMLINSON, M
LONDON
1980 1 07

1628 ULSTER INDEPENDENCE PARTY
TOWARD AN INDEPENDENT ULSTER: ECONOMIC
AND FEASIBILITY STUDY 1
ULSTER INDEPENDENCE PARTY
BELFAST
1978 1 09

1629 ULSTER LAWYER
THE ULSTER CONSTITUTION
HUMANIST 87(1)
1972 3 01

1630 ULSTER LOYALIST CENTRAL COORDINATING
COMMITTEE
YOUR FUTURE? ULSTER CAN SURVIVE
UNFETTERED
ULCCC
BELFAST
1976 1 09

1631 ULSTER UNIONIST COUNCIL
ULSTER GENERAL ELECTION 1969
UUC
BELFAST
1969 2 09

1632 ULSTER UNIONIST PARTY
THE ASSEMBLY ELECTIONS 1973 AND THE 1974
UNITED KINGDOM GENERAL ELECTIONS
UUP
BELFAST
1975 1 09

1633 ULSTER UNIONIST PARTY
THE CONVENTION ELECTIONS 1975
UUP
BELFAST
1975 1 09

1634 ULSTER UNIONIST PARTY
PR AND THE LOCAL GOVERNMENT ELECTION
72-73
UUP
BELFAST
1973 2 09

1635 UNIONIST RESEARCH DEPARTMENT
THE FUTURE OF NI: A COMMENTARY ON THE
GOVERNMENT'S GREEN PAPER
UNIONIST RESEARCH DEPT
BELFAST
1972 1 09

1636 UNIONIST RESEARCH DEPARTMENT
TOWARDS THE FUTURE: A UNIONIST
BLUE-PRINT
UNIONIST RESEARCH DEPT
BELFAST
1972 1 09

1637 UNITED KINGDOM GOVERNMENT
THE FUTURE OF NI
HMSO
LONDON
1975 1 03

1638 UNITED ULSTER UNIONIST COUNCIL
THE CONVENTION ELECTIONS 1975
BELFAST
1975 1 09

1639 UNITED ULSTER UNIONIST COUNCIL
GUIDE TO THE CONVENTION REPORT 1974
BELFAST
1974 1 09

1640 WALKLAND, S
PARLIAMENTARY CONTROL OF DELEGATED
LEGISLATION IN NI
PUBL ADM 37
LONDON
1959 2 01

1641 WALLACE, M
HOME RULE IN NI: ANOMALIES OF DEVOLUTION
NI LEG QUART 18(1)
BELFAST
1967 2 01

1642 WALLACE, M
     REFORM OF THE NORTH
     EIRE-IRELAND 5(3)
     ST PAUL
     1970 1 01

1643 WHALE, J
     ULSTER ACCEPTS LONDON DOMINATION
     ROUND TABLE 60(237)
     LONDON
     1970 1 01

1644 WHITE, B
     POLITICAL CONSTRAINTS: BELFAST
     IN WATT, D (ED)
     LONDON
     1981 1 07

1645 WHITE, B
     PUBLIC SERVICES
     IN DARBY, J; WILLIAMSON, A (EDS)
     LONDON
     1978 1 07

1646 WHITE, B
     REFORMING ULSTER
     SOLON 1(2)
     1970 1 01

1647 WHYTE, J H
     HOW MUCH DISCRIMINATION WAS THERE UNDER
     THE UNIONIST REGIME, 1921-1968?
     IN GALLAGHER, T; O'CONNELL, J (EDS)
     MANCHESTER
     1983 2 07

1648 WHYTE, J H
     INTRA-UNIONIST DISPUTES IN THE NI HOUSE
     OF COMMONS 1921-72
     ECON AND SOC R 5(1)
     DUBLIN
     1974 2 01

1649 WHYTE, J H
     PROPORTIONAL REPRESENTATION: A
     DISCUSSION
     NEWMAN R 3(1)
     1971 2 01

1650 WHYTE, J H
     THE REFORM OF STORMONT
     NUM
     BELFAST
     1971 1 10

1651 WHYTE, J H
     WHITEHALL, BELFAST AND DUBLIN: NEW LIGHT
     ON THE TREATY AND THE BORDER
     STUDIES 60
     1971 2 01

1652 WILES, P
     REPARTITIONING IRELAND
     ROUND TABLE 246
     LONDON
     1972 1 01

1653 WILSON, T
     DEVOLUTION AND PARTITION
     IN WILSON, T (ED)
     LONDON
     1955 2 07

1654 WILSON, T
     AN INDEPENDENT NI
     IN GIBSON, N J (ED)
     1974 1 07

1655 WILSON, T
     REPARTITIONING IRELAND
     ROUND TABLE 248
     LONDON
     1972 1 01

1656 WILSON, T
     THE ULSTER CRISIS: REFORMED GOVERNMENT
     WITH A NEW BORDER?
     ROUND TABLE 245
     LONDON
     1972 1 01

1657 WINDELSHAM, LORD
     MINISTERS IN ULSTER: THE MACHINERY OF
     DIRECT RULE
     PUBL ADM 51
     LONDON
     1973 2 02

1658 WINDELSHAM, LORD
     POLITICS IN PRACTICE
     CAPE
     LONDON
     1975 2 02

1659 ARTHUR,P
PEOPLE'S DEMOCRACY
BLACKSTAFF
BELFAST
1973 1 02

1660 ARTHUR,P
PEOPLE'S DEMOCRACY 1968-1970
QUB MSSC
BELFAST
1972 1 04

1661 BAXTER,L ET AL
DISCUSSION ON THE STRATEGY OF PEOPLE'S
DEMOCRACY
NEW LEFT R 55
1969 1 01

1662 BEACH,S W
SOCIAL MOVEMENT RADICALISATION: THE CASE
OF THE PEOPLE'S DEMOCRACY IN NI
SOCIOL QUART 18(3)
1977 1 01

1663 BELL,G
BRITISH LABOUR AND IRELAND 1969-1979
OTHER PRESS
LONDON
1979 1 09

1664 BELL,G
TROUBLESOME BUSINESS: THE LABOUR PARTY
AND THE IRISH QUESTION
PLUTO
LONDON
1982 1 02

1665 BICO
THE PEOPLE'S DEMOCRACY: FROM A WORKING
CLASS VIEWPOINT
BICO
CORK
1970 1 09

1666 BOYCE,D G
BRITISH CONSERVATIVE OPINION, THE ULSTER
QUESTION...
IR HIST STUD 17(65)
DUBLIN
1970 2 01

1667 BRENNAN,I
NI: A PROGRAMME FOR ACTION
COMMUNIST PARTY GB
LONDON
1975 1 09

1668 BUNDRED,S
THE BRITISH LABOUR PARTY AND THE
REPUBLICAN STRUGGLE
IRIS 5
DUBLIN
1983 1 01

1669 CALLENDER,L
THE PEOPLE'S DEMOCRACY AND THE CLASS
STRUGGLE
COMMUNIST COMMENT 10 JANUARY
1970 1 01

1670 CALLENDER,L
WHAT IS THE NEW SDLP?
COMMUNIST COMMENT 18
1970 1 01

1671 CALVERT,D
A DECADE OF THE DUP
CROWN PUBLICATIONS
BELFAST
1981 1 09

1672 CAMPAIGN FOR LABOUR REPRESENTATION IN NI
ULSTER: WHAT THE LABOUR PARTY NEEDS TO
DO
CAMPAIGN FOR LABOUR REPRESENTATION IN NI
BELFAST
1980 1 09

1673 CAMPBELL,N
THE UNIONIST PARTY AND THE PROTESTANT
WORKING CLASS, 1918-26
NUU MA
COLERAINE
1978 2 04

1674 COMERFORD,J
DYNAMICS OF A RADICAL MOVEMENT IN NI
POLITICS: THE PEOPLE'S DEMOCRACY
STRATHCLYDE UNIV MSC
GLASGOW
1972 1 04

1675 COMMUNIST PARTY OF IRELAND
THE CRISIS IN THE UNIONIST PARTY
COMMUNIST PARTY OF IRELAND
BELFAST
1969 1 09

1676 COMMUNIST PARTY OF IRELAND
OUTLINE HISTORY
NEW BOOKS
DUBLIN
1975 2 09

1677 DELANEY,S
SINN FEIN AND THE ASSEMBLY
IRIS 4
DUBLIN
1982 1 01

1678 FARRELL,M
PEOPLE'S DEMOCRACY: A DISCUSSION ON
STRATEGY
NEW LEFT R 55
1969 1 01

1679 FARRELL,M
THE PROVOS AT THE BALLOT BOX
MAGILL 6(9)
DUBLIN
1983 1 01

1680 FLYNN,D
LABOUR AND IRELAND: WHICH WAY TO
WITHDRAWAL?
CHARTIST COLLECTIVE
LONDON
1983 1 09

1681 GALLAGHER,T
RELIGION, REACTION AND REVOLT IN NI: THE
IMPACT OF PAISLEYISM IN ULSTER
J CHURCH AND STATE 23
1981 1 01

1682 GIBBON,P
IRELAND - SPLIT IN SINN FEIN
NEW LEFT R 60
1970 1 01

1683 GRAHAM,J
THE CONSENSUS FORMING STRATEGY OF THE
NILP, 1949-1968
QUB MA
BELFAST
1972 2 04

1684 GUELKE,A
THE 'BALLOT BOMB': THE NI ASSEMBLY
ELECTION AND THE PROVISIONAL IRA
ECPR
ESSEX
1983 1 11

1685 GUELKE,A
THE CHANGING POLITICS OF ULSTER'S
VIOLENT MEN
NEW SOCIETY 29 JULY
LONDON
1982 1 01

1686 HARBINSON,J F
HISTORY OF THE NILP: 1881-1949
MSC (ECON)
BELFAST
1966 2 04

1687 HARBINSON,J F
ULSTER UNIONIST PARTY 1882-1973. ITS
DEVELOPMENT AND ORGANISATION
BLACKSTAFF
BELFAST
1973 2 02

1688 HEMEL HEMPSTEAD CONSTITUENCY LABOUR
PARTY
IRELAND: AN ALTERNATIVE
HEMEL HEMPSTEAD CONSTITUENCY LABOUR
PARTY
LONDON
1979 1 09

1689 HOLLAND,M
TEN YEARS OF THE SDLP
NEW STATESMAN AUG 29
LONDON
1980 2 01

1690 IRIS
AG LABHAIRT LEIS AN UACHTARAN - RUAIRI O
BRADAIGH
IRIS 1(1)
DUBLIN
1981 1 01

1691 KENNEDY,C
LABOUR AND IRELAND
IRL SOCIALIST R 1
1978 2 01

1692 KENNEDY,C
LABOUR, DEMOCRACY AND IRELAND
IRL SOCIALIST R 4
1979 2 01

1693 KENNEDY,H
POLITICS IN NI: A STUDY OF ONE-PARTY
DOMINATION
MICHIGAN UNIV PHD
1967 2 04

1694 KINGHAN,N
UNITED WE STOOD: THE STORY OF THE ULSTER
WOMEN'S UNIONIST COUNCIL 1911-1974
APPLETREE PRESS
BELFAST
1975 2 02

1695 LEVY,J
LA PEOPLE'S DEMOCRACY
TEMPS MODERNES 311
1972 1 01

1696 MACY,C
SINN FEIN AND THE IRAS: PARTS 1 AND 2
HUMANIST 87(1)
1972 1 01

1697 MARLOWE,T; WHITTAKER,P
THE COMMUNIST PARTY OF GREAT BRITAIN AND
IRELAND: THE BRITISH ROAD TO SOCIAL
IMPERIALISM
REVOLUTIONARY COMMUNIST (7)
1977 1 01

1698 MASTERS,M
WORKERS AGAINST IMPERIALISM: THE BRITISH
LABOUR MOVEMENT AND IRELAND
REVOLUTIONARY COMMUNIST PAMPHLETS 5
BRIGHTON
1979 1 09

1699 MCALLISTER,I
NI SOCIAL DEMOCRATIC AND LABOUR PARTY
MACMILLAN
LONDON
1977 2 02

1700 MCALLISTER,I
PARTY ORGANISATION AND MINORITY
NATIONALISM: A COMPARATIVE STUDY IN THE
UK
STUD PUBL POL 43
1979 2 10

1701 MCALLISTER,I
POLITICAL OPPOSITION IN NI; THE NATIONAL
DEMOCRATIC PARTY, 1965-70
ECON AND SOC R 6(3)
1975 2 01

1702 MCALLISTER,I
POLITICAL PARTIES AND SOCIAL CHANGE IN
ULSTER: THE CASE OF THE SDLP
SOC STUD 5(1)
1976 2 01

1703 MCALLISTER,I; WILSON,B
BI-CONFESSIONALISM IN A CONFESSIONAL
PARTY SYSTEM: THE NI ALLIANCE PARTY
ECON AND SOC R 9(3)
1978 2 01

1704 MILOTTE,M
COMMUNISM IN MODERN IRELAND: THE PURSUIT
OF THE WORKERS' REPUBLIC SINCE 1916
GILL AND MACMILLAN
DUBLIN
1983 2 02

1705 MILOTTE,M
COMMUNIST POLITICS IN IRELAND, 1916-1945
QUB PHD
BELFAST
1977 2 04

1706 MUMFORD,D
IS THERE A FUTURE FOR THE NI LIBERAL
PARTY?
NEW OUTLOOK 1
1974 2 01

1707 MURNAGHAN,S
IS THERE A FUTURE FOR THE NI LIBERAL
PARTY?
NEW OUTLOOK 1
1974 2 01

1708 NOLAN,S
THE COMMUNIST PARTY OF IRELAND
MARXISM TODAY 17(6)
1973 2 01

1709 O'LEARY,C
THE POLITICAL PARTIES OF NI
IN SCOTT,H (ED)
LONDON
1976 2 07

1710 PURDIE,B
THE FRIENDS OF IRELAND: BRITISH LABOUR
AND IRISH NATIONALISM, 1945-49
IN GALLAGHER,T; O'CONNELL,J (EDS)
MANCHESTER
1983 2 07

1711 QUIGLEY,J
LA GAUCHE REVOLUTIONNAIRE EN IRLANDE
TEMPS MODERNES 311
PARIS
1972 1 01

1712 REVOLUTIONARY COMMUNIST GROUP
IRELAND: BRITISH LABOUR AND BRITISH
IMPERIALISM
REVOLUTIONARY COMMUNIST GROUP
LONDON
1976 1 09

1713 ROONEY,E
     FROM REPUBLICAN MOVEMENT TO THE WORKERS'
     PARTY: THE RESTRUCTURING OF REPUBLICAN
     IDEOLOGY
     IN CURTIN,C; KELLY,M; O'DOWD,L (EDS)
     DUBLIN
     1983 1 07

1714 SAVAGE,K
     THE SDLP'S NEW IRELAND
     IRL SOCIALIST R 7
     LONDON
     1980 1 01

1715 SAYERS,J E
     THE POLITICAL PARTIES AND THE SOCIAL
     BACKGROUND
     IN WILSON,T (ED)
     OXFORD
     1955 2 01

1716 SCOPE
     SOCIAL POLICIES AND THE POLITICAL
     PARTIES
     SCOPE 18
     BELFAST
     1978 2 01

1717 SINN FEIN (OFFICIAL)
     WAYS AND MEANS: A HANDBOOK FOR MEMBERS
     OF THE REPUBLICAN MOVEMENT
     REPSOL
     DUBLIN
     1970 1 09

1718 SINN FEIN (PROVISIONAL)
     SINN FEIN YESTERDAY AND TODAY
     SINN FEIN (PROVISIONAL)
     DUBLIN
     1971 1 09

1719 ULSTER UNIONIST COUNCIL
     PROGRESS REPORT 3 1953-55
     UUC
     BELFAST
     1958 2 09

1720 VANGUARD UNIONIST PROGRESSIVE PARTY
     SPELLING IT OUT: A BRIEF STATEMENT OF
     BASIC PRINCIPLES
     ULSTER VANGUARD
     BELFAST
     1972 1 09

1721 WHYTE,J H
     INTRA-UNIONIST DISPUTES IN THE NI HOUSE
     OF COMMONS 1921-72
     ECON AND SOC R 5(1)
     DUBLIN
     1974 2 01

1722 WILSON,B
     THE ALLIANCE PARTY OF NI
     STRATHCLYDE UNIV MSC
     GLASGOW
     1976 2 04

1723 WORKERS' ASSOCIATION
     SDLP: WHAT A CATHOLIC PARTY NEEDS TO DO
     WORKERS' ASSOCIATION
     BELFAST
     1975 1 09

1724 ADVERTISERS' WEEKLY
NI: AN INDUSTRIAL AND ECONOMIC SURVEY
ADVERTISERS' WEEKLY
1948 2 01

1725 AGNEW, N
RATING AND VALUATION IN NI
QUB PHD
BELFAST
1945 2 04

1726 ALCOCK, A E
PERIPHERAL REGIONS AND DIVIDED
COMMUNITIES IN EUROPE: THE CASE OF NI
INT INST MINORITY RIGHTS AND REGIONALISM
BOLZONO
1978 1 08

1727 ALEXANDER, D J
CHANGES IN FARM STRUCTURE
AGRIC NI 40
1965 2 01

1728 ALEXANDER, D J
FARMHAND MOBILITY AND ADJUSTMENTS IN
FARMING IN NI
JSSISI 21
1965 2 01

1729 ALLISON, D
NEW AMERICAN INVESTMENT IN NI
FORTUNE 2 JULY
1979 2 01

1730 ARLOW, B
CLEARING, INDUSTRIAL AND MERCHANT BANKS
IN NI
TRADE AND INDUSTRY IN NI 5(7)
BELFAST
1982 2 01

1731 ARMSTRONG, D L
THE ECONOMIC HISTORY OF AGRICULTURE IN
NI
QUB PHD
BELFAST
1952 2 04

1732 ARMSTRONG, J; MCCLELLAND, D; O'BRIEN, T
A POLICY FOR RURAL PROBLEM AREAS IN NI:
DISCUSSION DOCUMENT
SCHOOL OF APPLIED ECON ULSTER
POLYTECHNIC
BELFAST
1980 2 10

1733 ATTWOOD, E A
AGRICULTURAL DEVELOPMENTS IN IRELAND
NORTH AND SOUTH
JSSISI
1967 2 01

1734 AUGHEY, A
EUROPEAN COMMUNITY: REGIONAL POLICY,
JUSTICE AND THE NI CASE
ADMIN (DUB) 30(4)
DUBLIN
1982 2 01

1735 BANKER
ECONOMIC PARADOX IN ULSTER
BANKER
1951 2 01

1736 BANKERS' MAGAZINE
IRISH BANKING AND ECONOMIC REVIEW FOR
1951: NI AND EIRE
BANKERS' MAG
1952 2 01

1737 BARR, A
NI'S ECONOMIC SITUATION
LABOUR MONTHLY 60(7)
1978 2 01

1738 BARROW, G L
EMERGENCE OF THE IRISH BANKING SYSTEM
GILL AND MACMILLAN
DUBLIN
1975 2 02

1739 BATES, J
ECONOMICS, EFFICIENCY AND MANAGEMENT
QUB
BELFAST
1966 2 10

1740 BATES, J
MANAGEMENT NEEDS IN NI
INDIAN ADMINISTRATIVE AND MANAGEMENT R
3(3-4)
1971 2 01

1741 BATES, J; BELL, M
MANAGEMENT OF NI INDUSTRY
DEPT BUS STUD QUB
BELFAST
1971 2 10

1742 BATES, J; BELL, M
SMALL MANUFACTURING BUSINESS IN NI
JSSISI
1973 2 01

1743 BAYLEY, J
NI 1950-1970: THE ECONOMIC BASE
NI SOCIALIST RES INST
BELFAST
1973 1 10

1744 BDP
REDEVELOPMENT AND THE SMALL BUSINESS:
CITY OF BELFAST
BDP
BELFAST
1968 2 10

1745 BELFAST NEWSLETTER
ULSTER AND EUROPEAN FREE TRADE
BELFAST NEWSLETTER
BELFAST
1959 2 10

1746 BELL, R
INVESTMENT IN NI
JSSISI 20(2)
DUBLIN
1959 2 01

1747 BLACK, W
AGRICULTURE AND REGIONAL DEVELOPMENT IN
NI
AGRICULTURAL PROGRESS 44
1969 2 01

1748 BLACK, W
THE ECONOMY OF NI: PERFORMANCE AND
PROSPECTS
IR BANKING R
1980 2 01

1749 BLACK, W
THE EFFECTS OF THE RECESSION ON THE
ECONOMY OF NI
IR BANKING R DEC
1981 2 01

1750 BLACK, W
GROWTH TARGETS FOR NI
IR BANKING R JUN
1963 2 01

1751 BLACK, W
INDUSTRIAL CHANGE IN THE TWENTIETH
CENTURY
IN BECKETT, J C; GLASSCOCK, R E (EDS)
LONDON
1967 2 07

1752 BLACK,W
INDUSTRIAL DEVELOPMENT AND REGIONAL
POLICY
IN GIBSON,N J; SPENCER,J E (EDS)
DUBLIN
1977 2 07

1753 BLACK,W
IRISH ECONOMIES
QUB
BELFAST
1977 2 10

1754 BLACK,W
THE NI ECONOMY: PROBLEMS AND PROSPECTS
IR BANKING R JUNE
1976 2 01

1755 BLACK,W
REGIONAL INDUSTRIAL DEVELOPMENT IN NI
COLUMBIA J WLD BUS 8
1973 2 01

1756 BLACK,W
ULSTER'S INCREASING RESILIENCE
BANKER 112
LONDON
1962 2 01

1757 BLACK,W; SIMPSON,J V
GROWTH CENTRES IN IRELAND
IR BANKING R
1968 2 01

1758 BOWERS,J
ANATOMY OF REGIONAL ACTIVITY RATES
NATIONAL INSTITUTE OF ECONOMIC AND
SOCIAL RESEARCH
1970 2 01

1759 BRISTOW,J
ALL-IRELAND PERSPECTIVES
IN REA,D (ED)
DUBLIN
1982 1 07

1760 BRISTOW,J
PUBLIC FINANCE AND FISCAL POLICY
IN GIBSON,N J; SPENCER,J E (EDS)
DUBLIN
1977 2 07

1761 BRISTOW,J
THE WILSON REPORT ON NI
STUDIES 54(2)
DUBLIN
1965 1 01

1762 BROOKE,A C
ECONOMIC DEVELOPMENT OF NI
IN RHODES,E (ED)
1967 2 07

1763 BROWN,A J
FRAMEWORK OF REGIONAL ECONOMICS IN THE
UK
CUP
CAMBRIDGE
1972 2 02

1764 BUCHANAN,R H
FIVE YEAR PLAN FOR ULSTER
GEOGR MAG 42
1970 2 01

1765 BUCHANAN,R H
LAND IN NEED OF INDUSTRY
GEOGR MAG 49
1977 2 01

1766 BURNISON,G
REVIEW OF NI CONSTRUCTION INDUSTRY: PART
1
BUILDING AND CONTRACT J 7(1)
1971 2 01

1767 BURNISON,G
REVIEW OF NI CONSTRUCTION INDUSTRY: PART
2
BUILDING AND CONTRACT J 7(3)
1971 2 01

1768 BURNS,G ET AL
UNEMPLOYMENT: RECOMMENDATIONS FOR ACTION
WITHIN A STRATEGY FOR ECONOMIC
DEVELOPMENT: MAIN REPORT
ULSTER POLY
BELFAST
1982 2 10

1769 BUSINESS WEEK
NI ENTICING FOREIGN CAPITAL TO A
WAR-TORN PROVINCE
BUS WEEK JUNE 26
1978 1 01

1770 BUSTEED,M A
EXAMINATION OF SPATIAL PATTERNS CREATED
BY SOCIAL MOVEMENTS AND FUNCTIONAL
ACTIVITY
QUB MA
BELFAST
1967 2 04

1771 BUSTEED,M A
SMALL-SCALE ECONOMIC DEVELOPMENT IN NI
SCOTT GEOGR MAG 92(3)
1976 2 01

1772 BYRNE,D
THE DEINDUSTRIALIZATION OF NI
ANTIPODE 11(2)
WORCESTER, MASS
1980 2 01

1773 CAMBLIN,G
ECONOMIC PLANNING AND REGIONAL
DEVELOPMENT
CHARTERED SURVEYOR 100
LONDON
1967 2 01

1774 CAMPBELL,A D
ECONOMY OF NI
SCOTT J POLIT ECON 5
1968 2 01

1775 CARSON,W
ULSTER AND THE IRISH REPUBLIC
CLELAND
BELFAST
1957 2 02

1776 CARTER,C F
NI AS PART OF THE UK
IN GIBSON,N J (ED)
1974 2 07

1777 CARTER,C F
THE NI ECONOMY: A PERSONAL PERSPECTIVE
(2)
IN HARVEY,S; REA,D (EDS)
BELFAST
1983 2 07

1778 CARTER,C F
NI: AN ECONOMIC SURVEY - 1. THE LAST
DEPRESSED AREA
BANKER
1954 2 01

1779 CARTER,C F
SEVERE DEPRESSION: THE PROBLEM OF NI
POLICY STUD 1(4)
LONDON
1981 2 01

1780 CARTER,C F
THE WILSON REPORT: A FURTHER COMMENT
STUDIES 54(2)
DUBLIN
1965 2 01

1781 CARTER,C F; ROBSON,M
     A COMPARISON OF THE NATIONAL INCOMES AND
     SOCIAL ACCOUNTS OF NI, THE REPUBLIC OF
     IRELAND AND THE UNITED KINGDOM
     JSSISI
     DUBLIN
     1954 2 01

1782 CLARKE,P
     RELATIONSHIP BETWEEN PHYSICAL AND
     REGIONAL ECONOMIC PLANNING IN THEORY AND
     PRACTICE WITH SPECIAL REFERENCE TO NI
     LONDON UNIV COLLEGE MPHIL
     LONDON
     1971 2 04

1783 CLEWS,J
     NEW INDUSTRIES FOR NI
     NEW COMMONWEALTH 37
     1959 2 01

1784 COMMON,R
     LAND DRAINAGE AND WATER USE IN IRELAND
     IN STEPHENS,N; GLASSCOCK,R E (EDS)
     BELFAST
     1970 2 07

1785 COMMON,R
     REGIONAL DEVELOPMENT PROSPECTS IN NI
     AREA 8(1)
     1976 2 01

1786 COMMON,R
     WATER AND SOCIETY IN ULSTER
     IN HOUSE,J W (ED)
     1966 2 07

1787 CONFEDERATION OF BRITISH INDUSTRY
     EFFECTS OF BRITISH ENTRY TO THE EEC ON
     NI
     CBI
     BELFAST
     1971 2 10

1788 COOK,J
     FINANCIAL RELATIONS BETWEEN THE
     EXCHEQUERS OF THE UK AND NI
     IN NEWARK,F H ET AL (EDS)
     LONDON
     1953 2 07

1789 COOPERS AND LYBRAND ASSOCIATES
     NI ECONOMY: CURRENT ECONOMIC SITUATION
     AND PROSPECTS FOR 1980
     COOPERS AND LYBRAND ASSOCIATES
     BELFAST
     1980 2 10

1790 COOPERS AND LYBRAND ASSOCIATES
     THE NI ECONOMY: THE CURRENT ECONOMIC
     SITUATION AND PROSPECTS FOR 1982
     COOPERS AND LYBRAND ASSOCIATES
     BELFAST
     1982 2 10

1791 COOPERS AND LYBRAND ASSOCIATES
     THE NI ECONOMY: THE CURRENT ECONOMIC
     SITUATION AND SHORT TERM PROSPECTS FOR
     1981
     COOPERS AND LYBRAND ASSOCIATES
     BELFAST
     1981 2 10

1792 CORLEY,T A B
     PERSONAL SAVINGS IN NI 1950-51 TO
     1959-60
     JSSISI 115
     DUBLIN
     1962 2 01

1793 CORLEY,T A B
     PERSONAL WEALTH OF NI 1920-1960
     JSSISI
     1963 2 01

1794 COWDY,R
     THE PRICE OF PROTECTION
     TRADE AND INDUSTRY IN NI 5(9)
     BELFAST
     1982 1 01

1795 CROSSLAND,B
     SCHOOL AND INDUSTRY
     NORTH TEACH 12(3)
     BELFAST
     1977 2 01

1796 CROTTY,R
     NORTHERN DIVERGENCE
     INST DEVOPMENT STUD
     SUSSEX
     1976 2 11

1797 CULLEN,B
     NI: WANTED, ECONOMIC INITIATIVE
     LEFT PERSPECTIVES 2(2)
     DUBLIN
     1982 2 01

1798 CULLEN,L M
     ECONOMIC HISTORY OF IRELAND SINCE 1600
     BATSFORD
     LONDON
     1972 2 02

1799 CURRAN,R G
     CONFIDENCE - ULSTER'S KEY WEAPON
     GEOGR MAG 45(2)
     1972 3 01

1800 CUTHBERT,N
     DEVELOPMENT ON THE SPOT: ECONOMIC GROWTH
     IN NI
     RESEARCH 14
     1961 2 01

1801 CUTHBERT,N
     EFFECT OF DEATH DUTY ON THE LEVEL AND
     ORGANISATION OF INDUSTRY IN NI
     INST BANK IRL J
     1952 2 01

1802 CUTHBERT,N
     NI ECONOMY
     QUB
     BELFAST
     1970 2 10

1803 CUTHBERT,N
     NI'S INVESTMENT ACCOUNT
     INST BANK IRL J
     1951 2 01

1804 CUTHBERT,N
     SOME COMMENTS ON PROFESSOR GIBSON'S
     PAPER
     IN VAIZEY,J (ED)
     DUBLIN
     1975 2 01

1805 CUTHBERT,N
     TOTAL CIVILIAN INCOME IN NI
     JSSISI 104
     DUBLIN
     1950 2 01

1806 CUTHBERT,N; BLACK,W
     NI AWAITS A PLAN
     BANKER 114
     1964 2 01

1807 CUTHBERT,N; BLACK,W
     REGIONAL POLICY RE-EXAMINED
     SCOTT J POLIT ECON 11
     1964 2 01

1808 CUTHBERT,N; BLACK,W
     ULSTER'S PLAN: AN INTERIM ASSESSMENT
     BANKER 116
     1966 2 01

1809 DAVIES,C
     NI: ECONOMIC TRENDS
     IRL SOCIALIST R 5
     LONDON
     1979 1 01

1810 DAVIES,R; MCGURNAGHAN,M
NI: THE ECONOMICS OF ADVERSITY
NAT WESTMINSTER BANK QUART R
1975 1 01

1811 DAVIES,R; MCGURNAGHAN,M; SAMS,K I
NI ECONOMY: PROGRESS (1968-1975) AND
PROSPECTS
REG STUD 2(5)
1977 2 01

1812 DAVISON,B
PUBLIC AUDIT IN NI
QUB PHD
BELFAST
1980 2 04

1813 DENNISON,S R
HOW MUCH DEVELOPMENT IN ULSTER?
BANKER 110
1960 2 01

1814 DEPT OF AGRICULTURE (NI)
STATISTICAL REVIEW OF NI AGRICULTURE
1981
DEPT OF AGRICULTURE (NI)
BELFAST
1982 2 03

1815 DOWLING,B R
SOME ECONOMIC IMPLICATIONS OF A FEDERAL
IRELAND
IN GIBSON,N J (ED)
1974 2 07

1816 DRUDY,P
LAND USE IN BRITAIN AND IRELAND
ANGLO-IRISH STUD 1
1976 2 01

1817 ECONOMIST
ULSTER: A SURVEY
ECONOMIST 239(6666)
1971 2 10

1818 EDWARDS,C J W
LAND MOBILITY ON FARMS IN NI
J AGRICULTURAL ECON 33(1)
MANCHESTER
1982 2 01

1819 EDWARDS,C J W
RECENT STRUCTURAL CHANGES IN NI
AGRICULTURE
IR J AGRIC ECON AND RURAL SOCIOL 8(1)
DUBLIN
1980 2 01

1820 FERRIS,T
COMPARISONS OF PRODUCTIVITY ON LIVING
STANDARDS: IRELAND AND OTHER EEC
COUNTRIES
IR BANKING R MAR
1981 2 01

1821 FITZGERALD,G
IRISH ECONOMY NORTH AND SOUTH
STUDIES 45
1956 2 01

1822 FREEMAN,T W
AGRICULTURAL REGIONS AND RURAL
POPULATION OF IRELAND
B GEOGR SOC IRL 1(2)
1945 2 01

1823 FREEMAN,T W
FARMING IN IRISH LIFE
GEOGR J 110
1948 2 01

1824 FREEMAN,T W
FORESTRY AND LAND USE SURVEY
IR FORESTRY 7
1950 2 01

1825 FREEMAN,T W
LAND USE IN NI
GEOGR J 118
1952 2 01

1826 FREEMAN,T W
PROSPECT FOR IRISH AGRICULTURE
GEOGR J 120(3)
1954 2 01

1827 FRENCH,P
NI REDISCOVERED BY AMERICAN INVESTORS
BUS WEEK 19 NOV
1979 2 01

1828 FROST,L R
CHANGING WORLD - RECENT TRENDS IN
AGRICULTURE IN NI
GEOG 57(4)
1972 2 01

1829 FURNESS,G W
SOME FEATURES OF FARM INCOME AND
STRUCTURAL VARIATIONS IN REGIONS OF THE
UNITED KINGDOM
J AGRIC ECON 33(3)
1982 2 01

1830 GEARY,P T
EXPENDITURE AND PRICE ELASTICITIES FOR
NI, 1967 AND 1972
DEPT ECONOMICS UCD
DUBLIN
1975 2 10

1831 GEARY,P T
NI PHILLIP'S CURVE: A NOTE
DEPT ECONOMICS UCD
DUBLIN
1975 2 08

1832 GEARY,P T
WAGES, PRICES, INCOME AND WEALTH
IN GIBSON,N J; SPENCER,J E (EDS)
DUBLIN
1977 2 07

1833 GIBSON,N J
"THE TOTAL INTEGRATION OPTION" IN
ULSTER: THE ECONOMIC CASE
UTV
BELFAST
1975 2 10

1834 GIBSON,N J
BANKING IN IRELAND: AN INQUIRY AND
ASSESSMENT
QUB PHD
BELFAST
1959 2 04

1835 GIBSON,N J
THE BANKING SYSTEM
IN GIBSON,N J; SPENCER,J E (EDS)
1977 2 07

1836 GIBSON,N J
ECONOMIC CONDITIONS AND POLICY IN NI
ECON AND SOC R 4(3)
DUBLIN
1973 2 01

1837 GIBSON,N J
MERITS AND PROBLEMS OF PLANNING - NI
CHRISTUS REX 18(4)
1964 2 01

1838 GIBSON,N J
THE NI ECONOMY: A PERSONAL PERSPECTIVE
(1)
IN HARVEY,S; REA,D (EDS)
BELFAST
1983 2 07

1839 GIBSON,N J
THE NORTHERN IRISH ECONOMY: PERFORMANCE
AND PROSPECTS
SOLON 1(2)
1970 2 01

General Economic Analyses/

1840 GIBSON, N J
NOTE ON FINANCIAL RELATIONSHIPS BETWEEN
BRITAIN AND NI
ADMIN (DUB) 20(4)
DUBLIN
1972 1 01

1841 GIBSON, N J
NOTE ON GOVERNMENT ECONOMIC POLICY IN NI
WITH SPECIAL REFERENCE TO EMPLOYMENT
AUTHOR
1973 2 08

1842 GIBSON, N J
POLITICAL AND ECONOMIC INTEGRATION
IN REA, D (ED)
DUBLIN
1982 1 07

1843 GIBSON, N J
THE QUIGLEY REPORT AND THE PROSPECTS FOR
THE NI ECONOMY
IR BANKING R DEC
1977 2 01

1844 GIBSON, N J
SOME ECONOMIC IMPLICATIONS OF THE
VARIOUS SOLUTIONS TO THE NI PROBLEM
IN VAIZEY, J (ED)
1975 1 07

1845 GILLMOR, D A
FOREIGN PARTICIPATION IN IRISH
MANUFACTURING
IR GEOG 5
1965 2 01

1846 GLASS, J C
TECHNICAL CHANGE IN NI MANUFACTURING
1950-68: A COMMENT
ECON AND SOC R 6
DUBLIN
1975 2 01

1847 GLASS, J C; KIOUNTOUZIS, E
LINEAR PROGRAMMING MODELS FOR
DEVELOPMENT PLANNING IN NI
ECON AND SOC R 7(2)
DUBLIN
1976 2 01

1848 GLASS, J C; KIOUNTOUZIS, E
A STUDY OF OPTIMAL RESOURCES ALLOCATION:
MODELS FOR THE NI ECONOMY
JSSISI
1974 2 01

1849 GOODYEAR, P M; EASTWOOD, D A
REGIONAL DEVELOPMENT AND SPATIAL EQUITY
IN NI
ECON AND SOC R 10(4)
1979 2 01

1850 GOODYEAR, P M; EASTWOOD, D A
SPATIAL VARIATIONS IN LEVEL OF LIVING IN
NI
IR GEOG 11
1978 2 01

1851 GRAHAM, J
A BETTER POSITION THAN COMMONLY THOUGHT
FINANCIAL TIMES SURVEY ON NI 22 JAN
LONDON
1973 2 07

1852 GRAHAM, P
ECONOMY IN CRISIS: AN HISTORICAL
PERSPECTIVE
IRIS 4
DUBLIN
1982 2 01

1853 GREEN, A J
DEVOLUTION AND PUBLIC FINANCE: STORMONT
FROM 1921 TO 1972
CSPP 48
GLASGOW
1979 2 10

1854 GREENLEES, S
THE STRUCTURE AND DEVELOPMENT OF
AGRICULTURE IN ULSTER 1900-1939
NUU MPHIL
COLERAINE
1976 2 04

1855 HALL REPORT
REPORT OF THE JOINT WORKING PARTY ON THE
ECONOMY OF NI
HMSO CMD 446
BELFAST
1962 2 03

1856 HARKNESS, D A E
AGRICULTURAL ADMINISTRATION IN NI
IN NEWARK, F H ET AL (EDS)
LONDON
1953 2 07

1857 HARRISON, R T; ANDERSON, T J
NI: THE DEVELOPMENT OF A RANK-SIZE
DISTRIBUTION
TIJDSCHR ECON SOC GEOGR 71(4)
1980 2 01

1858 HARVEY, S; REA, D
THE NI ECONOMY WITH PARTICULAR REFERENCE
TO INDUSTRIAL DEVELOPMENT
ULSTER POLYTECHNIC INNOVATION AND
RESOURCE CENTRE
NEWTOWNABBEY
1982 2 10

1859 HARVEY, S; REA, D
SOCIO-ECONOMIC CHANGE IN NI SINCE 1961
IN HARVEY, S; REA, D (EDS)
BELFAST
1983 2 07

1860 HEADEY, B
SIMULTANEOUS STAGFLATION AND
DISINTEGRATION: THE BREAK-UP OF A
MULTINATIONAL STATE
MELBOURNE J POLIT 8
MELBOURNE
1976 1 01

1861 HECHTER, M
GROUP FORMATION AND THE CULTURAL
DIVISION OF LABOR
AMER J SOCIOL 84(2)
CHICAGO
1978 2 01

1862 HECHTER, M
INDUSTRIALISATION AND NATIONAL
DEVELOPMENT IN THE BRITISH ISLES
J DEV STUD 8(3)
LONDON
1972 2 01

1863 HECHTER, M
INTERNAL COLONIALISM: THE CELTIC FRINGE
IN BRITISH NATIONAL DEVELOPMENT,
1536-1966
RKP
LONDON
1975 2 02

1864 HECHTER, M
PERSISTANCE OF REGIONALISM IN THE
BRITISH ISLES: 1865-1966
AMER J SOCIOL 79(2)
CHICAGO
1973 2 01

1865 HECHTER, M
POLITICAL ECONOMY OF ETHNIC CHANGE
AMER J SOCIOL 79(5)
CHICAGO
1974 2 01

1866 HECHTER, M
REGIONAL INEQUALITY AND NATIONAL
INTEGRATION: THE CASE OF THE BRITISH
ISLES
J SOC HIST 5(1)
1971 2 01

1867 HECHTER, M
TOWARDS A THEORY OF ETHNIC CHANGE
POLITICS AND SOC 2(1)
WASHINGTON, D C
1971 2 01

1868 HEMMING, M F W
REGIONAL PROBLEM
NAT INST ECON R 8(63)
LONDON
1963 2 01

1869 HILL, D A
THE LAND OF ULSTER: REPORT OF THE LAND
UTILISATION SURVEY OF NI
HMSO
BELFAST
1948 2 03

1870 HILL, D A
LAND UTILISATION SURVEY OF NI
SCOTT GEOGR MAG 63(1)
1947 2 01

1871 HOARE, A G
INDUSTRIAL GEOGRAPHY OF NI
SSRC, FINAL REPORT HR 3107/1-2
LONDON
      2 10

1872 HOARE, A G
INDUSTRIAL LINKAGES AND THE DUAL
ECONOMY: THE CASE OF NI
REG STUD 12(2)
1978 2 01

1873 HOARE, A G
PROBLEM REGION AND REGIONAL PROBLEM
IN BOAL, F W; DOUGLAS, J N H (EDS)
LONDON
1982 1 07

1874 HOARE, A G
SPHERES OF INFLUENCE AND REGIONAL
POLICY: THE CASE OF NI
IR GEOG 9
1976 2 01

1875 HOARE, A G
WHY THEY GO WHERE THEY GO: THE POLITICAL
IMAGERY OF INDUSTRIAL LOCATION IN NI
TRANSACTION (NEW SERIES) INST BRIT GEOGR
6
1981 2 01

1876 HOGWOOD, B
INTERGOVERNMENTAL STRUCTURES AND
INDUSTRIAL POLICY IN THE UNITED KINGDOM
STUD PUBL POL 2
GLASGOW
1977 2 10

1877 HOUSTON, J
THE NI ECONOMY: A SPECIAL CASE?
POLITICS TODAY 16
1976 2 01

1878 HUTCHINSON, R W; SHEEHAN, J
A REVIEW OF SELECTED INDICATORS OF
ECONOMIC PERFORMANCE IN NI AND THE
REPUBLIC OF IRELAND DURING THE 1970S
COOPERATION NORTH
BELFAST AND DUBLIN
1980 2 10

1879 ICTU
JOBS: AN ACTION PROGRAMME
ICTU
BELFAST
1979 2 99

1880 ICTU
UNEMPLOYMENT: A CONSTRUCTIVE APPROACH TO
THE PROBLEM IN NI
ICTU
BELFAST
1952 2 09

1881 INSTITUTE OF BANKERS IN IRELAND
NORTHERN IRISH DEVELOPMENT PROGRAMME
1970/75
INST BANK IRL J 73
1971 2 01

1882 ISLES, K S
NI ECONOMIC SURVEY: FUNDAMENTALS OF
ULSTER'S ECONOMIC PROBLEM
BANKER 87
1948 2 01

1883 ISLES, K S
NI: AN ECONOMIC SURVEY 1920-54
IN MOODY, T W; BECKETT, J C (EDS)
LONDON
1957 2 07

1884 ISLES, K S
PUBLIC FINANCE AND EMPLOYMENT
IPA
LONDON
1949 2 11

1885 ISLES, K S; CUTHBERT, N
ECONOMIC POLICY
IN WILSON, T (ED)
OXFORD
1955 2 01

1886 ISLES, K S; CUTHBERT, N
ECONOMIC SURVEY OF NI
HMSO
BELFAST
1957 2 02

1887 ISLES, K S; CUTHBERT, N
ULSTER'S ECONOMIC STRUCTURE
IN WILSON, T (ED)
OXFORD
1955 2 01

1888 JAEGER, J
EVOLVING ECONOMIC COMMUNITY POLICIES AS
THEY AFFECT REGIONS SUCH AS NI
IN HARVEY, S; REA, D (EDS)
BELFAST
1983 2 07

1889 JEFFERSON, C W
METHOD OF ESTIMATING THE STOCK OF
CAPITAL IN NI MANUFACTURING INDUSTRY
ESRI
DUBLIN
1968 2 10

1890 JEFFERSON, C W
REGIONAL ECONOMETRIC MODEL OF THE NI
ECONOMY
SCOTT J POLIT ECON 25(3)
1978 2 01

1891 JEFFERSON, C W; FAIRCLOUGH, I
AN ECONOMETRIC SIMULATION MODEL OF THE
NI ECONOMY: ESTIMATION OF MULTIPLIERS
DEPT ECONOMICS QUB
BELFAST
1980 2 10

1892 JEFFERSON, C W; FAIRCLOUGH, I
THE NI ECONOMY 1978-84: A MEDIUM TERM
FORECAST MADE IN JUNE 1980
DEPT ECONOMICS QUB
BELFAST
1980 2 10

1893 JENKINS, R
ETHNICITY AND THE RISE OF CAPITALISM IN
ULSTER
SSRC RESEARCH UNIT ON ETHNIC RELATIONS
ASTON
1982 1 08

1894 JOHNSON, D S
ECONOMIC HISTORY OF IRELAND BETWEEN THE
WARS
IR ECON AND SOC HISTORY 1
1974 2 01

1895 JOHNSON, D S
PARTITION AND CROSS-BORDER TRADE IN THE
1920S
IN ROEBUCK, P (ED)
BELFAST
1981 2 07

1896 JOHNSTON, I S
ENERGY IN NI
GEOLOGY IN NI 6
1981 2 01

1897 JOHNSTON, J
IRISH AGRICULTURE IN TRANSITION
HODGES/FIGGIS
DUBLIN
1951 2 02

1898 JOINT WORKING PARTY ON THE ECONOMY OF NI
REPORT OF JOINT WORKING PARTY ON THE
ECONOMY OF NI
HMSO CMND 1835
LONDON
1962 2 03

1899 KAY, J; JACOBSON, A
RATING AND VALUATION IN NI
RATING AND VALUATION ASSOCIATION
LONDON
1965 2 02

1900 KEEBLE, D
INDUSTRIAL LOCATION AND PLANNING IN THE
UNITED KINGDOM
METHUEN
LONDON
1976 2 02

1901 KINAHAN, R
BANKS IN THE ULSTER SCENE
BANKERS' MAG 222
LONDON
1978 2 01

1902 KINAHAN, R
ECONOMIC DEVELOPMENT: LARGE-SCALE
INVESTMENT OR SELF-HELP PROJECTS?
COMM FORUM 2(3)
BELFAST
1972 2 01

1903 LAW, D
ECONOMIC PROBLEMS OF IRELAND, SCOTLAND
AND WALES
IN VAIZEY, J (ED)
DUBLIN
1975 2 07

1904 LAW, D
INDUSTRIAL MOVEMENT AND LOCATIONAL
ADVANTAGE
MANCHESTER SCHOOL OF ECON AND SOC STUD
32
MANCHESTER
1964 2 01

1905 LEE, C H
REGIONAL ECONOMIC GROWTH IN THE UNITED
KINGDOM SINCE THE 1880'S
MCGRAW-HILL
LONDON
1971 2 02

1906 LEE, J
IRISH ECONOMIC HISTORY SINCE 1500
IN LEE, J (ED)
CORK
1981 2 07

1907 LINDSAY, E H
TRADE BETWEEN NI AND THE REPUBLIC OF
IRELAND, 1950-1974
QUB MSC
BELFAST
1978 2 04

1908 LIVERSAGE, V
THE APPROACH TO FARM PLANNING IN NI
AGRICULTURAL PROGRESS 45
1960 2 01

1909 LUKE, A E
STRUCTURAL CHANGE IN THE NI ECONOMY
JSSISI 23(4)
1977 2 01

1910 LUKE, A E; JORDAN, R J; MCCANN, D P
INDUSTRIAL DEVELOPMENT IN NI: FACTS AND
FIGURES
MINISTRY OF COMMERCE (NI)
BELFAST
1973 2 03

1911 LYONS, P M
DISTRIBUTION OF PERSONAL WEALTH IN NI
ECON AND SOC R 3(2)
DUBLIN
1972 2 01

1912 MARQUAND, J
THE EVOLVING REGIONAL PROBLEM IN THE UK
IN HARVEY, S; REA, D (EDS)
BELFAST
1983 2 07

1913 MATHUR, M
THE FINANCIAL RELATIONSHIP BETWEEN GB
AND NI (1931-45)
QUB M COMM SC
BELFAST
1947 2 04

1914 MCALEER, W E
THE DEMAND FOR ENERGY IN NI: A SYSTEMS
APPROACH
QUB PHD
BELFAST
1981 2 04

1915 MCALEER, W E
THE DEMAND FOR ENERGY IN NI: AN ACTIVITY
ANALYSIS APPROACH
NATIONAL CONF OPERATIONAL RES SOCIETY OF
IRELAND
ATHLONE
1981 2 11

1916 MCALEESE, D
CAPITAL INFLOWS AND DIRECT FOREIGN
INVESTMENT IN IRELAND, 1952-70
JSSISI 22(4)
1972 2 01

1917 MCALEESE, D
COMMENT ON CHAPTER BY MCCLEMENTS
IN WATT, D (ED)
LONDON
1981 2 07

1918 MCALEESE, D
THE FOREIGN SECTOR
IN GIBSON, N J; SPENCER, J E (EDS)
DUBLIN
1977 2 07

1919 MCALEESE, D
INDUSTRIAL SPECIALISATION AND TRADE: NI
AND THE REPUBLIC
ECON AND SOC R 7(2)
1976 2 01

1920 MCCARTHY, C; BLEASE, W J
CROSS-BORDER INDUSTRIAL COOPERATION:
LIMITS AND POSSIBILITIES
ADMIN (DUB) 26(3)
1978 1 01

1921 MCCLEMENTS, L
ECONOMIC CONSTRAINTS
IN WATT, D (ED)
LONDON
1981 2 07

1922 MCCOMISH, W
TRADE OF NI, 1922-1939: A STUDY IN
ECONOMIC GEOGRAPHY
LONDON UNIV PHD
LONDON
1948 2 04

General Economic Analyses/

1923 MCCRONE, G
REGIONAL POLICY IN BRITAIN
ALLEN AND UNWIN
LONDON
1969   2   02

1924 MCCULLOUGH, A
EMBODIED AND DISEMBODIED TECHNICAL
CHANGE IN NI MANUFACTURING 1950-68
NUU MPHIL
COLERAINE
1972   2   04

1925 MCCULLOUGH, A
TECHNICAL CHANGE IN NI MANUFACTURING
ECON AND SOC R 5(2)
1974   2   01

1926 MCGOVERN, P D
INDUSTRIAL DISPERSAL IN NI
PEP 31
1965   2   01

1927 MCGOVERN, P D
PROBLEMS OF INDUSTRIAL DISPERSAL IN NI
LONDON UNIV PHD
LONDON
1963   2   04

1928 MCGURNAGHAN, M A; SIMPSON, J V
ULSTER IN EUROPE: NI AND THE EUROPEAN
PARLIAMENT
NUM
BELFAST
1979   2   09

1929 MCLAUGHLIN, J
INDUSTRIAL CAPITALISM, ULSTER UNIONISM
AND ORANGEISM: AN HISTORICAL APPRAISAL
ANTIPODE 11(2)
WORCESTER, MASS
1980   2   01

1930 MCMULLAN, J T; MORGAN, R; MURRAY, R B
ENERGY IN NI
TECHNOLOGY IRELAND 8(4,5)
1976   2   01

1931 MCNAMEE, P
THE APPLICATION OF GOAL PROGRAMMING TO
CAPITAL INVESTMENT UNDER CONDITIONS OF
CAPITAL RATIONING
ULSTER POLY MPHIL
BELFAST
1979   2   04

1932 MCPHILLIMY, L S
ASSESSMENT OF LAND VALUES
AGRIC NI 48(11)
1974   2   01

1933 MCVITTY, D
NI ENERGY RESOURCES
ENERGY WLD 18
1975   2   01

1934 MEENAN, J
AGRICULTURE IN NI
IR MONTHLY 76
1948   2   01

1935 MICKLEWRIGHT, M
THE GEOGRAPHY OF DEVELOPMENT IN NI
WASHINGTON UNIV PHD
WASHINGTON
1970   2   04

1936 MIDLAND BANK
GROWTH AND DEVELOPMENT IN NI
MIDLAND BANK R AUG
1967   2   01

1937 MIDLAND BANK
LATE RECOVERY IN NI
MIDLAND BANK R AUG
1960   2   01

1938 MIDLAND BANK
NI: UNDERLYING PROGRESS IN DEVELOPMENT
MIDLAND BANK R AUG
1963   2   01

1939 MIDLAND BANK
POST-WAR DEVELOPMENT AND PLANS: NI
MIDLAND BANK R AUG
1947   2   01

1940 MIDLAND BANK
PROGRESS AND PROBLEMS IN NI
MIDLAND BANK R AUG
1948   2   01

1941 MINISTRY OF AGRICULTURE (NI)
OUTLINE OF NI AGRICULTURE
HMSO
BELFAST
1974   2   03

1942 MINISTRY OF AGRICULTURE (NI)
SEVENTH REPORT ON AGRICULTURAL
STATISTICS IN NI 1952-1961
HMSO CMD 508
BELFAST
1967   2   03

1943 MINISTRY OF AGRICULTURE (NI)
SIXTH REPORT UPON THE AGRICULTURAL
STATISTICS OF NI 1930-1953
HMSO CMD 371
BELFAST
1957   2   03

1944 MINISTRY OF COMMERCE (NI)
AN ECONOMIC SURVEY OF NI
MINISTRY OF COMMERCE (NI)
BELFAST
1951   2   03

1945 MINNS, R; THORNLEY, J
LOCAL GOVERNMENT ECONOMIC PLANNING AND
THE PROVISION OF RISK CAPITAL FOR SMALL
FIRMS
CENTRE FOR ENVIRONMENTAL STUDIES
LONDON
1978   2   11

1946 MOFFETT, W
AN INPUT-OUTPUT MODEL OF THE NI ECONOMY
QUB PHD
BELFAST
1975   2   04

1947 MOORE, B; RHODES, J; TARLING, R
INDUSTRIAL POLICY AND ECONOMIC
DEVELOPMENT: THE EXPERIENCE OF NI AND
THE REPUBLIC OF IRELAND
CAMBRIDGE J ECON 2
1978   2   01

1948 MOORE, R
AGRICULTURE AND THE FUTURE
BANKER 83
1947   2   01

1949 MOORE, R
AGRICULTURE IN NI
BANKER 75
1945   2   01

1950 MOORE, R
FARMERS IN THE FIGHT FOR DOLLARS: NI
BANKER 87
1948   2   01

1951 MOORE, R
ULSTER FARMERS AND THE ECONOMIC CRISIS
BANKER 91
1949   2   01

1952 MOORE, T
CONSIDERATIONS IN LAND USE
AGRIC NI 51(6)
1976   2   01

1953 MORRISSEY,M
ECONOMIC CHANGE AND POLITICAL STRATEGY
IN NI
ECON BULL 8
LONDON
1981 1 01

1954 MORRISSEY,M; AUSTIN,J
RURAL DEVELOPMENT
COMM FORUM 4(2)
1974 2 01

1955 MORTON,R
THE ENTERPRISE OF ULSTER
HISTORY TODAY 17
1967 2 01

1956 MURIE,A S; BIRRELL,W D; HILLYARD,P;
ROCHE,D J D
A SURVEY OF INDUSTRIAL MOVEMENT IN NI:
1965-69
ECON AND SOC R 4(2)
1973 2 01

1957 MURIE,A S; BIRRELL,W D; ROCHE,D J D;
HILLYARD,P
REGIONAL PLANNING AND THE ATTRACTION OF
MANUFACTURING INDUSTRY TO NI
CENTRE FOR ENVIRONMENTAL STUDIES
LONDON
1974 2 10

1958 MUSKETT,A E; MORRISON,J
AGRICULTURE
IN BRITISH ASSOCIATION FOR THE
ADVANCEMENT OF SCIENCE
BELFAST
1952 2 07

1959 NATIONAL ASSOCIATION OF BRITISH
MANUFACTURERS
NI: BLUEPRINT FOR PROSPERITY
NATIONAL ASSOCIATION OF BRITISH
MANUFACTURERS
BELFAST
     2 10

1960 NATIONAL INSTITUTE FOR ECONOMIC AND
SOCIAL RESEARCH
REGIONAL PAPERS I
CUP
CAMBRIDGE
1970 2 02

1961 NEVIN,E
THE ECONOMICS OF DEVOLUTION
WALES U P
CARDIFF
1978 2 02

1962 NI ASSEMBLY
REPORT ON INDUSTRIAL DEVELOPMENT
INCENTIVES
HMSO NIA 45
BELFAST
1983 2 03

1963 NI ASSEMBLY AGRICULTURAL COMMITTEE
SPECIAL AID FOR NI AGRICULTURE FOR THE
YEAR 1983/84
HMSO NIA 30
BELFAST
1983 2 03

1964 NI DEVELOPMENT COUNCIL
INDUSTRIAL DEVELOPMENT IN NI
NI DEVELOPMENT COUNCIL
BELFAST
1957 2 03

1965 NI DEVELOPMENT COUNCIL
REPORT ON INDUSTRIAL DEVELOPMENT
FACILITIES IN NI
NI DEVELOPMENT COUNCIL
LONDON
1962 2 03

1966 NI GOVERNMENT
NI AND THE EUROPEAN COMMUNITY
HMSO CMD 563
BELFAST
1971 2 03

1967 NI GOVERNMENT
NI DEVELOPMENT PROGRAMME 1970-75:
GOVERNMENT STATEMENT
HMSO CMD 547
BELFAST
1970 2 03

1968 NI GOVERNMENT
REPORT OF THE JOINT REVIEW BODY OF
ECONOMIC AND SOCIAL DEVELOPMENT IN NI
HMSO CMD 564
BELFAST
1971 2 03

1969 NI GOVERNMENT
REPORTS OF THE AGRICULTURAL INQUIRY
COMMITTEE
HMSO CMD 249
BELFAST
1947 2 03

1970 NI GOVERNMENT, ECONOMIC ADVISORY OFFICE
NI ECONOMIC SURVEY
HMSO CMD 453
BELFAST
1963 2 03

1971 NI GOVERNMENT, INDUSTRIAL DEVELOPMENT
DIVISION
BLUEPRINT FOR INDUSTRY
INDUSTRIAL DEVELOPMENT DIVISION
BELFAST
     2 03

1972 NI OFFICE
FINANCE AND THE ECONOMY
HMSO
LONDON
1974 2 03

1973 NI OFFICE
INDUSTRIAL DEVELOPMENT IN NI: A
FRAMEWORK FOR ACTION
HMSO
BELFAST
1981 2 03

1974 NICSS
DEVELOPING THE NEW ULSTER: A GUIDE TO
STUDIES
NICSS
BELFAST
1968 2 10

1975 NIEC
ADVANCED TECHNOLOGY
NIEC
BELFAST
1980 2 03

1976 NIEC
AREA DEVELOPMENT IN NI
HMSO
BELFAST
1969 2 03

1977 NIEC
THE AVAILABILITY, SUPPLY AND DEVELOPMENT
OF MANAGEMENT FOR INDUSTRY AND COMMERCE
IN NI
NIEC
BELFAST
1979 2 03

1978 NIEC
ECONOMIC AND SOCIAL PROGRESS IN NI: A
RESPONSE TO THE GOVERNMENT'S DISCUSSION
PAPER
NIEC
BELFAST
1979 2 03

1979 NIEC
ECONOMIC ASSESSMENT
NIEC
BELFAST
1981   2   03

1980 NIEC
ECONOMIC ASSESSMENT: APRIL 1983
NIEC
BELFAST
1983   2   03

1981 NIEC
ECONOMIC ASSESSMENT: MARCH 1982
NIEC
BELFAST
1982   2   03

1982 NIEC
ENERGY CONSERVATION
NIEC
BELFAST
1980   2   03

1983 NIEC
THE FEASIBILITY OF STATE INDUSTRY IN NI
HMSO
BELFAST
1971   2   03

1984 NIEC
THE FINANCIAL SYSTEM IN NI
NIEC
BELFAST
1982   2   03

1985 NIEC
GOVERNMENT STRATEGY ON ENERGY POLICY IN
NI: COMMENTS BY THE ECONOMIC COUNCIL
NIEC
BELFAST
1979   2   03

1986 NIEC
INDUSTRIAL DEVELOPMENT POLICY
NIEC
BELFAST
1980   2   03

1987 NIEC
THE NI CONSTRUCTION INDUSTRY
NIEC
BELFAST
1981   2   03

1988 NIEC
PRIVATE SERVICES IN ECONOMIC DEVELOPMENT
NIEC
BELFAST
1982   2   03

1989 NIEC
PUBLIC EXPENDITURE COMPARISONS BETWEEN
NI AND GREAT BRITAIN
NIEC
BELFAST
1981   2   03

1990 NIEC
RECOMMENDATIONS ON ENERGY POLICY IN NI
NIEC
BELFAST
1978   2   03

1991 NIEC
REPRESENTATIONS TO GOVERNMENT ON SOME
PROBLEMS OF AGRICULTURE
NIEC
BELFAST
1978   2   03

1992 NIEC
RESEARCH, DEVELOPMENT AND INNOVATION IN
NI
NIEC
BELFAST
1981   2   03

1993 NUGENT,R
THE ECONOMIC FUTURE OF NI
JSSISI 19
DUBLIN
1953   2   01

1994 NUGENT,R
ENCOURAGEMENT FOR NEW INDUSTRIES
BANKER 79
1946   2   01

1995 NUGENT,R
INDUSTRIAL DEVELOPMENT IN NI
INDUSTRY JULY
1947   2   01

1996 NUGENT,R
RECONSTRUCTION IN NI
BANKER 75
1945   2   01

1997 NUGENT,R
ULSTER'S ROLE IN THE EXPORT DRIVE
BANKER 83
1947   2   01

1998 NUM
NI AND THE COMMON MARKET
NUM
BELFAST
1972   2   10

1999 O'CLERY,C
THE EFFECTS OF THE EUROPEAN MONETARY
SYSTEM ON ANGLO-IRISH RELATIONS
POLIT QUART   50(2)
1979   2   01

2000 O'DOWD,L
THE CRISIS OF REGIONAL STRATEGY:
IDEOLOGY AND THE STATE IN NI
BRIT SOCIOLOGICAL ASSOC ANNUAL CONF
CARDIFF
1983   2   11

2001 O'DOWD,L
REGIONAL POLICY
IN O'DOWD,L; ROLSTON,B; TOMLINSON,M
LONDON
1980   1   07

2002 O'DOWD,L
REGIONALISM AND SOCIAL CHANGE IN NI
IN KELLY,M; O'DOWD,L; WICKHAM,J (EDS)
DUBLIN
1982   1   07

2003 O'HEARN,D
ACCUMULATION AND THE IRISH CRISIS
MONTHLY R 32(10)
1981   2   01

2004 O'LOCHLEN,B A
PATTERNS OF PUBLIC EXPENDITURE IN NI AND
THE REPUBLIC 1954-65
JSSISI 21
1968   2   01

2005 O'NEILL,H B
REGIONAL PLANNING IN IRELAND: THE CASE
FOR CONCENTRATION
IR BANKING R SEPT
1973   2   01

2006 O'NEILL,H B
SPATIAL PLANNING IN THE SMALL ECONOMY: A
CASE STUDY OF IRELAND
PRAEGER
NEW YORK
1971   2   02

2007 O'NUALLAIN,L
A COMPARISON OF THE EXTERNAL TRADE OF
THE 26 AND 6 COUNTIES OF IRELAND
1928-1949
STUDIES MARCH
1952   2   01

2008 O'NUALLAIN,L
IRELAND: THE FINANCES OF PARTITION
CLONMORE AND REYNOLDS
DUBLIN
1952 2 02

2009 ORRIDGE,A W
UNEVEN DEVELOPMENT AND NATIONALISM
UNIV OF BIRMINGHAM
BIRMINGHAM
1978 1 08

2010 OWEN,K
ADVANCING TECHNOLOGY IN NI
SCIENTIFIC AMERICAN 240
1979 2 01

2011 OZANNE,J
ULSTER LURING NEW INDUSTRIES
J COMMERCE 288
1966 2 01

2012 PAGE,E
MICHAEL HECHTER'S INTERNAL COLONIAL
THESIS: SOME THEORETICAL AND
METHODOLOGICAL PROBLEMS
EUROP J POLIT RES 6(3)
AMSTERDAM
1978 2 01

2013 PARKER,S; DRIVER,C
CAPITALISM IN IRELAND
B CONF SOCIALIST ECON 4(2)
1975 1 01

2014 PARKINSON,J R
ECONOMIC DEVELOPMENT IN NI
NOTTINGHAM UNIV
NOTTINGHAM
1970 2 29

2015 PARKINSON,J R
INDUSTRIAL PROSPECTS
IN RHODES,E; GARMANY,J (EDS)
DERRY
1966 2 07

2016 PARSON,D
POLITICS BEYOND THE POINT OF PRODUCTION:
CLASS STRUGGLE AND REGIONAL
UNDERDEVELOPMENT
AUTHOR
LOS ANGELES
1981 1 08

2017 PARSON,D
SPATIAL DEVELOPMENT: THE STRATEGY OF
ACCUMULATION IN NI
ANTIPODE 11(2)
WORCESTER, MASS
1980 2 01

2018 PERRONS,D
DIALECTIC OF REGION AND CLASS IN IRELAND
URB AND REGION STUD, SUSSEX UNIV -
WORKING PAPER 8
BRIGHTON
1978 2 08

2019 PERRONS,D
ROLE OF IRELAND IN THE NEW INTERNATIONAL
DIVISION OF LABOUR
URB AND REGION STUD, SUSSEX UNIV -
WORKING PAPER 15
BRIGHTON
1979 2 08

2020 PERRONS,D
THE ROLE OF IRELAND IN THE NEW
INTERNATIONAL DIVISION OF LABOUR: A
PROPOSED FRAMEWORK FOR REGIONAL ANALYSIS
REG STUD 15(2)
LONDON
1981 2 01

2021 PLANT LOCATION INTERNATIONAL
COMPARATIVE ANALYSIS OF THE INCENTIVES
OFFERED TO INDUSTRY IN THE EEC...
PLANT LOCATION INTERNATIONAL
BRUSSELS
1978 2 10

2022 PRIOR,J
THE NI ECONOMY: THE RELEVANT PAST, THE
PRESENT AND PROSPECTS
IN HARVEY,S; REA,D (EDS)
BELFAST
1983 2 07

2023 PYLE,D
SOME SCOPE FOR ENTERPRISE IN NI
LEDU
BELFAST
1972 2 10

2024 QUIGLEY REPORT
ECONOMIC AND INDUSTRIAL STRATEGY FOR NI:
REPORT OF A REVIEW TEAM
HMSO
BELFAST
1976 2 03

2025 RAFTERY,A
THE EXPLOITED ISLAND: ECONOMIC AND
SOCIAL BACKGROUND TO IRELAND'S CRISIS
COMMUNIST PARTY OF IRELAND
DUBLIN
1972 1 09

2026 REGAN,C
ECONOMIC DEVELOPMENT IN IRELAND: THE
HISTORICAL DIMENSION
ANTIPODE 11(2)
WORCESTER, MASS
1980 2 01

2027 REGIONAL PLANNING AND RESEARCH TEAM
THE GROWTH OF KEY CENTRE POLICY: A
CRITICAL APPRAISAL
REGIONAL PLANNING AND RESEARCH TEAM
BELFAST
1972 2 08

2028 ROBSON,P
APPENDIX: STANDARDS OF PUBLIC
EXPENDITURE IN NI
IN WILSON,T (ED)
LONDON
1955 2 02

2029 ROBSON,P
ASPECTS OF PUBLIC EXPENDITURE IN NI
JSSISI 20
DUBLIN
1954 2 01

2030 ROBSON,P
INDUSTRIAL DEVELOPMENT IN ULSTER
BANKER
LONDON
1956 2 01

2031 ROBSON,P
NI: AN ECONOMIC SURVEY
BANKER
LONDON
1953 2 01

2032 ROBSON,P
NI: AN ECONOMIC SURVEY
BANKER 103
LONDON
1954 2 01

2033 ROBSON,P
REGIONAL DEVELOPMENT AND INDUSTRIAL
DIVERSIFICATION: SOME ASPECTS OF THE
PROBLEM IN NI
ADMIN (DUB) 4(1)
DUBLIN
1956 2 01

2034 ROCHE,D J D
AN OUTLINE OF THE REGIONAL SITUATION IN
IRELAND, BRITAIN, FRANCE, ITALY
ADMIN (DUB) 21(1)
DUBLIN
1973 2 01

General Economic Analyses/

2035 ROSENFIELD,R
NI BLUEPRINT FOR DEVELOPMENT AND OVERALL
REGIONAL STRATEGY
BUILDING TRADES J 168
1974 2 01

2036 ROWTHORN,B
NI: AN ECONOMY IN CRISIS
CAMBRIDGE J ECON 5(1)
CAMBRIDGE
1981 2 01

2037 SANDFORD,E
BRITAIN'S NEW ECONOMIC PLAYGROUND
COURIER 45(20)
1965 2 01

2038 SAYERS,J E; WILSON,T
PROBLEMS OF A VULNERABLE ECONOMY
BANKER 95
1950 2 01

2039 SCOTT,W
THE ECONOMY OF NI
IR BANKING R DEC
1964 2 01

2040 SCOTT,W
NI: THE ECONOMIC POSITION
IR BANKING R JUNE
DUBLIN
1959 2 01

2041 SIMPSON,J V
THE ANATOMY OF RECESSION
MANAGEMENT
1980 2 01

2042 SIMPSON,J V
A COMPARISON OF ECONOMIC AND SOCIAL
CONDITIONS IN NI AND THE IRISH REPUBLIC
IN GIBSON,N J (ED)
COLERAINE
1974 2 07

2043 SIMPSON,J V
THE ECONOMICS OF THE NORTH'S OPTIONS
MANAGEMENT 21(9)
LONDON
1974 1 01

2044 SIMPSON,J V
ESTIMATE OF THE PROFIT OF BANKING IN NI
JSSISI
1966 2 01

2045 SIMPSON,J V
THE FINANCE OF THE PUBLIC SECTOR IN NI
1968-78
JSSISI
1980 2 01

2046 SIMPSON,J V
INDUSTRIAL DEVELOPMENT POLICY
RECONSIDERED
MANAGEMENT
1980 2 01

2047 SIMPSON,J V
PUBLIC SECTOR REVENUE AND EXPENDITURE IN
NI
ADMIN (DUB) 25(3)
DUBLIN
1977 2 01

2048 SIMPSON,J V
REGIONAL ANALYSIS: THE NI EXPERIENCE
ECON AND SOC R JULY
DUBLIN
1971 2 01

2049 SIMPSON,J V
TOO LARGE A PUBLIC SECTOR
MANAGEMENT
1980 2 01

2050 SIMPSON,J V: CUTHBERT.N; BLACK,W
INVESTMENT INCENTIVES AND THE 1965
FINANCE ACT: REGIONAL IMPLICATIONS
SCOTT J POLIT ECON
1967 2 01

2051 SIMPSON,J V; JEFFERSON.C W
THE COST OF LIVING IN NI
NI CONSUMER COUNCIL
BELFAST
1980 2 03

2052 SINCLAIR.J M
FINANCIAL LINKS WITH GREAT BRITAIN
BANKER 83
1947 2 01

2053 SINCLAIR.J M
FINANCIAL SYSTEM AND CAPITAL PROBLEMS
BANKER 91
1949 2 01

2054 SINCLAIR.J M
NI FINANCES
BANKER 79
1946 2 01

2055 SINCLAIR.R
THE FUEL AND POWER BASE OF THE NI
MANUFACTURING INDUSTRIES: A MAJOR
ECONOMIC LINK WITH THE BRITISH MAINLAND
NORTH WESTERN UNIV PHD
CHICAGO
1955 2 04

2056 SINN FEIN (OFFICIAL)
THE IRISH INDUSTRIAL REVOLUTION
REPSOL
DUBLIN
1977 2 09

2057 SINNHUBER.K A
STRUCTURAL CHANGES IN INDUSTRY IN THE
UNITED KINGDOM OF GREAT BRITAIN AND NI
SINCE 1945
OSTERREICH IN GESCHICHTE UND LITERATUR
24(1)
1980 2 01

2058 SMILES.W
ULSTER'S ORDER BOOKS NOW
BANKER 79
1946 2 01

2059 SMITH.L P P
RECENT DEVELOPMENTS IN NI AGRICULTURE
JSSISI 102
DUBLIN
1949 2 01

2060 SOCIAL STUDY CONFERENCE
CAN IRELAND AFFORD A LIVING WAGE?
DUNDALK
1955 2 09

2061 SPENCER.J E: HARRISON,M
THE STRUCTURE AND BEHAVIOUR OF THE IRISH
ECONOMIES
IN GIBSON.N J; SPENCER.J E (EDS)
DUBLIN
1970 2 19

2062 SSEMPEBWA MUKASA.E F
ADMINISTRATIVE CONTROLS OVER STATE AID
TO INDUSTRY IN NI AND UGANDA
QUB LLM
BELFAST
1969 2 04

2063 STARK.T
THE DISTRIBUTION OF INCOME IN EIGHT
COUNTRIES
ROYAL COMM ON THE DISTRIBUTION OF INCOME
AND WEALTH BACKGROUND PAPER NO. 4
LONDON
1977 2 03

2064 STATIST
THE ECONOMY OF NI
STATIST NOV
LONDON
1954 2 01

2065 STEED,G
COMMODITY FLOWS AND INTER-INDUSTRY
LINKAGES IN NI'S MANUFACTURING INDUSTRY
TIDJSCHR ECON SOC GEOGR 59(4)
1968 2 01

2066 STEED,G
A FRAMEWORK FOR THE STUDY OF
MANUFACTURING GEOGRAPHY...
WASHINGTON UNIV PHD
1966 2 04

2067 STEED,G
LOCALISED CHANGES: A 'SHIFT AND SHARE'
ANALYSIS OF NI'S MANUFACTURING MIX.
1950-1964
TIJDSCHR ECON SOC GEOGR 58
1967 2 01

2068 STEED,G; THOMAS,M
REGIONAL INDUSTRIAL CHANGE: NI 1950-1968
ANNALS ASSOC AMER GEOG
1971 2 01

2069 STEEN,M
NI PLANS FOR ECONOMIC GROWTH
CANADIAN GEOGR J 69
OTTAWA
1964 2 01

2070 STEVENSON,J
THE ECONOMIC EFFECTS OF INDUSTRIAL
ACCIDENTS WITH SPECIAL REFERENCE TO NI
QUB MSC
BELFAST
1959 2 04

2071 STOKES KENNEDY CROWLEY AND COMPANY
CASH GRANTS: THE NI OPPORTUNITY
STOKES KENNEDY CROWLEY AND COMPANY
BELFAST
1981 2 02

2072 SYMONS,L
THE AGRICULTURAL INDUSTRY, 1921-62
IN SYMONS,L (ED)
LONDON
1963 2 07

2073 SYMONS,L
RURAL LAND UTILIZATION IN IRELAND
IN STEPHENS,N; GLASSCOCK,R E (EDS)
BELFAST
1970 2 07

2074 TARRANT,J
RECENT INDUSTRIAL DEVELOPMENT IN IRELAND
GEOG 52
1967 2 01

2075 THOMAS,M
ECONOMIC GEOGRAPHY AND THE MANUFACTURING
INDUSTRIES OF NI
ECON GEOG 32
WORCESTER, MASSACHUSETTS
1956 2 01

2076 THOMAS,M
THE ECONOMIC GEOGRAPHY OF MANUFACTURING
INDUSTRY IN NI
QUB PHD
BELFAST
1954 2 04

2077 THOMAS,M
MANUFACTURING INDUSTRY IN BELFAST
ANNALS ASSOC AMER GEOG
KANSAS
1956 2 01

2078 TIMES REVIEW
BELFAST: ULSTER'S MAGNET
TIMES R INDUSTR TECH DEC
1966 2 10

2079 TRADE AND INDUSTRY
INVESTMENT IN NI: SPECIAL REPORT
TRADE AND INDUSTRY 38 JANUARY 11
1980 2 01

2080 ULSTER INDEPENDENCE PARTY
TOWARD AN INDEPENDENT ULSTER: ECONOMIC
AND FEASIBILITY STUDY 1
ULSTER INDEPENDENCE PARTY
BELFAST
1978 1 09

2081 ULSTER TELEVISION
ULSTER: THE ECONOMIC CASE
UTV
BELFAST
1975 1 10

2082 ULSTER UNION CLUB
UNIONISM OR UNITY? A SUGGESTED NEW DEAL
FOR SIX-COUNTY INDUSTRY
ULSTER UNION CLUB
BELFAST
1948 2 09

2083 UNKNOWN
NI INDUSTRIAL HANDBOOK
CARNAGHAN AND GILDEA
BELFAST
1975 2 02

2084 VAIZEY,J
FIRST CHOOSE YOUR THEORY
IN VAIZEY,J (ED)
DUBLIN
1975 2 07

2085 VINEY,M
SEVEN SEMINARS: AN APPRAISAL OF REGIONAL
PLANNING
AN FORAS FORBARTHA AND NI MINISTRY OF
DEVELOPMENT
DUBLIN
1969 2 02

2086 WILSON REPORT
ECONOMIC DEVELOPMENT IN NI
HMSO CMD 479
BELFAST
1965 2 03

2087 WILSON,D
ECONOMIC DEVELOPMENT: LARGE SCALE
INVESTMENT OR SELF HELP PROJECTS
COMM FORUM 2(3)
BELFAST
1972 1 01

2088 WILSON,E
THE FUTURE OF BANKING IN NI
INST BANK IRL J
DUBLIN
1970 2 01

2089 WILSON,T
ECONOMIC SOVEREIGNTY
IN VAIZEY,J (ED)
DUBLIN
1975 1 07

2090 WILSON,T
AN INDEPENDENT NI
IN GIBSON,N J (ED)
1974 1 07

2091 WOODWARD,V
REGIONAL SOCIAL ACCOUNTS FOR THE UK
NATIONAL INSTITUTE OF ECONOMIC AND
SOCIAL RESEARCH(UK) REGION PAPERS 1
CAMBRIDGE
1970 2 10

General Economic Analyses

2092 ALLEN,W E D
     HISTORY OF A FAMILY FIRM
     AUTHOR
     BELFAST
     1957 2 02

2093 ARLOW,B
     FIVE HUNDRED NEW JOBS IN PROSPECT FOR
     SECURITY-MINDED BELFAST FIRM
     TRADE AND INDUSTRY IN NI FEB
     BELFAST
     1983 2 01

2094 ARMSTRONG,D L
     SOME ASPECTS OF THE MARKETING OF MILK IN
     NI
     JSSISI 112
     DUBLIN
     1959 2 01

2095 BATES,J; BUCHANAN,R E; MCGRATH,D G;
     REA,D
     MANPOWER IN THE DISTRIBUTIVE INDUSTRY IN
     NI TO 1980
     DEPT BUSINESS STUD QUB
     BELFAST
     1975 2 02

2096 BATESON,P
     COMPANY LAW, RECEIVERSHIPS AND
     LIQUIDATIONS: SOME RECENT DEVELOPMENTS
     SLS/FACULTY OF LAW QUB
     BELFAST
     1981 2 10

2097 BEATTIE,R P; HOLLOWAY,G R; BATES,P J
     RECOMMISSIONING OF THE BELFAST CENTRAL
     RAILWAY
     PROC INST CIVIL ENGINEERS 64(1)
     1978 2 01

2098 BEECHAM,A
     POST-WAR PLANNING IN THE ULSTER LINEN
     INDUSTRY
     ECON J 4(217)
     1945 2 01

2099 BELFAST HARBOUR COMMISSIONERS
     BELFAST HARBOUR COMMISSIONERS CENTENARY
     1847-1947
     BELFAST HARBOUR COMMISSIONERS
     BELFAST
     1947 2 02

2100 BELFAST HARBOUR COMMISSIONERS
     THE PORT OF BELFAST
     BELFAST HARBOUR COMMISSIONERS
     BELFAST
     1974 2 10

2101 BELFAST HARBOUR COMMISSIONERS
     THE PORT OF BELFAST - A REVIEW.
     1947-1962
     BELFAST HARBOUR COMMISSIONERS
     BELFAST
     1962 2 10

2102 BELFAST OFFICIAL INDUSTRIAL HANDBOOK
     CITY OF BELFAST
     NICHOLSON AND BASS
     BELFAST
     1971 2 02

2103 BENSON REPORT
     NI RAILWAYS
     HMSO CMD 458
     BELFAST
     1963 2 03

2104 BESSBROOK SPINNING COMPANY
     BESSBROOK: A RECORD OF INDUSTRY IN A NI
     VILLAGE COMMUNITY. 1845-1945
     BESSBROOK SPINNING COMPANY
     BELFAST
     1945 2 10

2105 BLACK,W
     VARIATIONS IN EMPLOYMENT IN THE LINEN
     INDUSTRY IN NI
     QUB PHD
     BELFAST
     1955 2 04

2106 BOAL,F W
     COUNTY DOWN
     IN SYMONS,L (ED)
     1963 2 07

2107 BOAL,F W
     LAND USES IN COUNTY DOWN: A STUDY IN
     GEOGRAPHICAL ANALYSIS
     QUB MA
     BELFAST
     1958 2 04

2108 BOAL,F W; MACAODHA,B S
     THE MILK INDUSTRY IN NI
     ECON GEOG 37
     1961 2 01

2109 BOLGER,P
     THE IRISH COOPERATIVE MOVEMENT: ITS
     HISTORY AND DEVELOPMENT
     IPA
     DUBLIN
     1977 2 02

2110 BROWN,L T
     A SURVEY OF TURF-WORKING IN COUNTY DOWN
     QUB MSC
     BELFAST
     1968 2 04

2111 BROWN,W
     WORKER PARTICIPATION: THE HARLAND &
     WOLFF EXPERIENCE
     IN POLLOCK,H M (ED)
     DUBLIN
     1981 2 07

2112 BUSINESS WEEK
     HOW DELOREAN'S DREAM WOUND UP IN BELFAST
     BUS WEEK 28 AUG
     1978 2 01

2113 CALDWELL,J H
     CULLYBACKEY: AN APPRECIATION OF SOCIAL
     AND ECONOMIC CHANGE IN AN ULSTER VILLAGE
     QUB MA
     BELFAST
     1965 2 04

2114 CAMPBELL,H M
     THE MARKETING OF CALVES AND STORE CATTLE
     IN NI
     DEPT AGRIC ECON QUB
     BELFAST
     1980 2 02

2115 CARSON,W H
     THE DAM BUILDERS: THE STORY OF THE MEN
     WHO BUILT THE SILENT VALLEY RESERVOIR
     MOURNE OBSERVER PRESS
     NEWCASTLE
     1981 2 02

2116 CARTER,W
     LINEN: THE STORY OF AN IRISH INDUSTRY
     AUTHOR
     BELFAST
     1953 2 10

2117 CARTER, W
SHORT HISTORY OF THE LINEN TRADE
AUTHOR
BELFAST
1954 2 02

2118 CASE, H J ET AL
LAND USE IN GOODLAND TOWNLAND, CO.
ANTRIM FROM NEOLITHIC TIMES UNTIL TODAY
ROYAL SOCIETY ANTIQUARIES OF IRELAND J
99(1)
1969 2 01

2119 CLARKIN, H
TIDAL POWER FOR STRANGFORD LOUGH?
TECHNOLOGY IRELAND 13(8)
DUBLIN
1982 2 01

2120 COE, W E
ENGINEERING INDUSTRY OF THE NORTH OF
IRELAND
DAVID AND CHARLES
NEWTON ABBOTT
1969 2 02

2121 CONROY, J
TRICKY BUSINESS AT THE BORDER: SMUGGLING
BETWEEN NI AND THE REPUBLIC IS ALMOST A
NATIONAL SPORT
MACLEANS OCT 5
1981 2 01

2122 COOK, M C F
CHANGES IN THE AREA AND NUMBER OF FARMS
GROWING POTATOES IN NI
AGRIC NI 53
BELFAST
1979 2 01

2123 COOK, M C F
AN EXPLORATORY ESTIMATION OF MARKET
LEVEL SUPPLY RESPONSE MODELS FOR NI
POTATOES
RECORD OF AGRICULTURAL RES (NI) 29
1981 2 01

2124 COOK, M C F
SOME CHANGES IN THE PATTERN OF POTATO
GROWING IN NI
SEED POTATO 17
1977 2 01

2125 COOK, M C F
SOME DEVELOPMENTS IN THE MARKETING OF NI
SEED POTATOES
AGRIC NI 53
BELFAST
1978 2 01

2126 COOK, M C F
SOME DEVELOPMENTS IN THE MARKETING
PATTERN OF NI MUSHROOMS 1960-1978
AGRIC NI 54(5)
BELFAST
1979 2 01

2127 COOK, M C F
SOME DIFFICULTIES ENCOUNTERED IN A
DETERMINATION OF RESPONSE RELATIONSHIPS
FOR COMMERCIAL MUSHROOM PRODUCTION IN NI
ACTA HORTICULTURAE 97
1979 2 01

2128 COOK, M C F
SOME LOCATIONAL DEVELOPMENTS OF
MUSHROOMS GROWING IN NI
ACTA HORTICULTURAE 2
1974 2 01

2129 COOK, M C F
STABILISING NI'S POTATO PRODUCTION
AGRIC NI 52
BELFAST
1978 2 01

2130 COOK, M C F; STEVENSON, W G
PRICES IN ENGLAND AND WALES AND NI FOR
FRESH MUSHROOMS PRODUCED IN ENGLAND,
WALES AND NI
IR J AGRIC ECON AND RURAL SOCIOL 8(1)
DUBLIN
1980 2 01

2131 COOKE, S
THE MAIDEN CITY AND THE WESTERN OCEAN:
HISTORY OF SHIPPING FROM DERRY
MORRIS
DUBLIN
1960 2 02

2132 CORLETT, J
AVIATION IN ULSTER
BLACKSTAFF
BELFAST
1981 2 02

2133 CORNELIUS, A
NIGHTMARE OF DE LOREAN'S DREAM CAR
ENGINEER 28 JAN
LONDON
1982 2 01

2134 COX, R
THE OIL INDUSTRY AND THE GAS INDUSTRY:
PARTNERS AND COMPETITORS
BELFAST ASSOCIATION OF ENGINEERS
BELFAST
1968 2 08

2135 CRAIG, M
EXPORTING: HOW THE IDB CAN HELP
TRADE AND INDUSTRY IN NI MAR
BELFAST
1983 2 01

2136 CRAWFORD, A G S; FURNESS, G W
OUTLOOK FOR BEEF CATTLE SUPPLIES IN NI
AGRIC NI 53
BELFAST
1978 2 01

2137 CRAWFORD, W H
DOMESTIC INDUSTRY IN IRELAND: THE
EXPERIENCE OF THE LINEN INDUSTRY
GILL AND MACMILLAN
DUBLIN
1972 2 02

2138 CROSSEY, J H
THE SHIPBUILDING INDUSTRY 'THEN' AND
'NOW' (1928-1963)
BELFAST ASSOCIATION OF ENGINEERS
BELFAST
1963 2 08

2139 CRUICKSHANK, J G; CRUICKSHANK, M M
SURVEY OF NEGLECTED AGRICULTURAL LAND IN
THE SPERRIN MOUNTAINS, NI
IR GEOG 10
1977 2 01

2140 CRUICKSHANK, J G; MCHUGH, B J
COUNTY FERMANAGH
IN SYMONS, L (ED)
1963 2 07

2141 CRYAN, M
THE CREDIT UNION MOVEMENT
CHRISTUS REX 11(1)
MAYNOOTH
1957 2 01

2142 CURRIE, J R L
THE NORTHERN COUNTIES RAILWAY, VOLUME 2
DAVID AND CHARLES
NEWTON ABBOTT
1974 2 02

2143 CUTHBERT, N
EFFECTS OF SELECTIVE EMPLOYMENT TAX ON
RETAIL TRADE IN NI
INST IRISH STUD
BELFAST
1971 2 10

2144 DAVIES,G L
THE TOWN AND COALFIELD OF BALLYCASTLE,
CO. ANTRIM
IR GEOG 3(4)
1957 2 01

2145 DAVIS,J
MARKETING MARGINS ON NI BEEF
IR J AGRIC ECON AND RURAL SOCIOL 8(1)
DUBLIN
1980 2 01

2146 DAVIS,J
THE MARKETING OF AGRICULTURAL PRODUCTS
AGRIC NI 56(6)
BELFAST
1981 2 01

2147 DAVIS,J
PROFIT RATES IN THE PRODUCTION AND
DISTRIBUTION OF NI BEEF
DEPT BUSINESS STUD QUB
BELFAST
1978 2 10

2148 DAVIS,J
THE STRUCTURE AND PERFORMANCE OF THE NI
BEEF SECTOR
IR J AGRIC ECON AND RURAL SOCIOL 8(2)
1981 2 01

2149 DAVIS,J; JOHNSTON,J
THE STRUCTURE AND PERFORMANCE OF THE NI
ROAD HAULAGE INDUSTRY
J IR BUS ADM RES 4(1)
1982 2 01

2150 DAVIS,J; MCALEER,W E
WHAT'S HOLDING BACK NI HORTICULTURE?
FARM AND FOOD RES 11(1)
1980 2 01

2151 DAVIS,K C
IRELAND: A NEW FLOWERING
PUBLISHERS WEEKLY JAN 23
1981 2 01

2152 DAWSON,J
CAPITAL EXPENDITURE IN RETAILING IN NI
IR GEOG 6(3)
1971 2 01

2153 DAWSON,J
DEVELOPMENT OF SELF-SERVICE AND
SUPERMARKET RETAILING IN IRELAND
IR GEOG 6(2)
1970 2 01

2154 DAWSON,J
RETAIL STRUCTURE IN GROUPS OF TOWNS
REG URB ECON 2(1)
1972 2 01

2155 DAWSON,J
SHOP SIZE DISTRIBUTIONS IN URBAN AREAS
CAMBRIA 2(1)
1975 2 01

2156 DAWSON,J; WATKINS,D
SMALL SHOP IN THE ULSTER RETAIL ECONOMY:
A CASE STUDY IN NI
IR GEOG 9
1976 2 01

2157 DEANE,S; FITZPATRICK,B
INTERVIEW WITH JOHN HUME
CRANE BAG 4(2)
DUBLIN
1980 1 01

2158 DEPT OF AGRICULTURE (NI)
A COMPUTER PROGRAMME FOR SIMULATION AND
BUDGETTING OF BEEF FATTENING SYSTEM
DEPT OF AGRICULTURE (NI)
BELFAST
1978 2 03

2159 DEPT OF AGRICULTURE (NI)
AN ECONOMIC ANALYSIS OF EWE FLOCK
PERFORMANCE IN NI 1975 AND 1976
DEPT OF AGRICULTURE (NI)
BELFAST
1977 2 03

2160 DEPT OF AGRICULTURE (NI)
ECONOMIC FEATURES OF BARLEY PRODUCTION
IN NI
DEPT OF AGRICULTURE (NI)
BELFAST
1979 2 03

2161 DEPT OF AGRICULTURE (NI)
FARM MANAGEMENT STANDARDS 1980-81
DEPT OF AGRICULTURE (NI)
BELFAST
1981 2 03

2162 DEPT OF AGRICULTURE (NI)
LABOUR USE IN DAIRY HERDS
DEPT OF AGRICULTURE (NI)
BELFAST
1980 2 03

2163 DEPT OF AGRICULTURE (NI)
PART-TIME FARMING IN NI
DEPT OF AGRICULTURE (NI)
BELFAST
1980 2 03

2164 DILLON,M
COALISLAND: THE EVOLUTION OF AN
INDUSTRIAL LANDSCAPE
STUDIA HIBERNIA 8
1968 2 01

2165 DITCH,J; GAFFIKIN,F; MORRISSEY,M
THE POLITICAL ECONOMY OF SOUTH-EAST
ANTRIM
ULSTER POLY
BELFAST
1980 2 10

2166 DOHRS,F
THE LINEN INDUSTRY OF NI
NORTHWESTERN UNIV PHD
CHICAGO
1951 2 04

2167 DONNELLY,D
THE LOUGH NEAGH FISHING COMMUNITY
QUB MA
BELFAST
1981 2 04

2168 DUNCAN,T
CAUTIOUS BELFAST: THE STORY OF THE FIRST
FIFTY YEARS OF HARRIS MARRIAN AND CO
LTD, 1925-1975
NICHOLSON AND BASS
BELFAST
1975 2 02

2169 ECONOMIST INTELLIGENCE UNIT
NATIONAL REPORT NO. 50: GREAT BRITAIN
AND NI
INT TOURISM QUART 1
LONDON
1979 2 01

2170 EDWARDS,C J W
FARM ENTERPRISE SYSTEMS IN EAST COUNTY
LONDONDERRY
IR GEOG 7
1974 2 01

2171 EDWARDS,C J W
SHORT-TERM CHANGES IN FARM ENTERPRISE
SYSTEMS: A CASE STUDY FROM CO
LONDONDERRY
IR J AGRIC ECON AND RURAL SOCIOL 6(2)
1976 2 01

2172 EDWARDS,C J W
SPATIAL DISTRIBUTION OF LIVESTOCK IN NI
IR GEOG 10
1977 2 01

2173 EWART,W AND SON LTD
IRISH LINEN: AN ACCOUNT OF ITS PROCESSES
OF MANUFACTURE INCORPORATING THE HISTORY
OF W EWART & SON, LTD.
BELFAST
1967 2 10

2174 FALLON,I; SRODES,J
DELOREAN: THE RISE AND FALL OF A DREAM
HAMISH HAMILTON
LONDON
1983 2 02

2175 FARRELL,M
THE GREAT EEL ROBBERY
PD
BELFAST
1970 2 09

2176 FITZGERALD,G
NORTH-SOUTH COOPERATION AND THE WEST
ULSTER REGION
IN RHODES,E; GARMANY,J (EDS)
DERRY
1966 2 07

2177 FITZPATRICK,D
AN OPTIMUM ECONOMIC REPLACEMENT POLICY
FOR CAPITAL EQUIPMENT IN A BELFAST FIRM
QUB MBA
BELFAST
1970 2 04

2178 FORBES,J
CONACRE
IN SYMONS,L (ED)
LONDON
1963 2 07

2179 FURNESS,G W
THE ECONOMIC BACKGROUND TO THE EFFICIENT
USE OF GRASS
J MILK MARKETING BOARD NI JUNE
BELFAST
1974 2 01

2180 FURNESS,G W
THE ECONOMIC SITUATION OF UPLAND AREAS
IN NI AND THE IMPACT OF CURRENT POLICY
ON THESE AREAS
IN CENTRE FOR AGRICULTURAL STRATEGY
READING
1978 2 10

2181 GAFFIKIN,F
INDUSTRIAL CHANGE IN SOUTH-EAST ANTRIM
SCOPE 34
BELFAST
1980 2 01

2182 GAILEY,A
DISAPPEARANCE OF THE HORSE FROM THE
ULSTER FARM
ULSTER FOLKLIFE 4
1966 2 01

2183 GALLAGHER LTD
GALLAGHER LTD AND SUBSIDUARY COMPANIES
1857-1956
GALLAGHER LTD
LONDON
1956 2 10

2184 GAMBLE,N E
BELFAST CENTRAL RAILWAY RE-OPENING
IR GEOG 9
1976 2 01

2185 GARNSEY,R
EXPERIENCE OF COURTAULDS IN NI
IN WILSON,T (ED)
1965 2 07

2186 GIBSON,N J
IRELAND'S EVOLVING CENTRAL BANK: AND A
PROBLEM FOR ULSTER
BANKER 110
1960 2 01

2187 GIBSON,N J
THE IRISH AND BRITISH POUNDS: OLD AND
NEW RELATIONSHIPS
THREE BANKS R 125
1980 2 01

2188 GLASS,J C
FACTOR SUBSTITUTION AND DEMAND FOR
LABOUR IN THE NI ENGINEERING INDUSTRY
JSSISI
1972 2 01

2189 GOFTON,K
THE SUCCESS STORY OF MAN-MADE FIBRES
FINANCIAL TIMES SURVEY ON NI 22 JAN
LONDON
1973 2 07

2190 HALL,F G
THE BANK OF IRELAND, 1783-1946
HODGES/FIGGIS
DUBLIN
1949 2 02

2191 HANNA,L
RATHLIN ISLAND: THE ECONOMIC UNITS IN
RELATION TO THE PHYSICAL ENVIRONMENT
QUB MSC
BELFAST
1961 2 04

2192 HARRISON,H
TRENDS IN AGRICULTURAL LAND, LABOUR,
FARMING UNITS IN NI FROM THE PRESENT
UNTIL 2000 A.D.
IR J AGRIC ECON AND RURAL SOCIOL 6
1976 2 01

2193 HENEGHAN,P
TOURIST INDUSTRY IN IRELAND, 1900-75
STUDIES 65
1977 2 01

2194 HEWITT,V N; THOM,D R
ECONOMETRIC MODEL OF BUILDING SOCIETY
BEHAVIOUR IN NI
SCOTT J POLIT ECON 25(2)
1978 2 01

2195 HILL,D A
CO. ANTRIM
IN SYMONS,L (ED)
LONDON
1963 2 07

2196 HILL,D A
LAND USE IN EAST ULSTER
IR GEOG 2(5)
1953 2 01

2197 HILL,D A
LAND UTILISATION IN THE BELFAST AREA
GEOG 32
1947 2 01

2198 HILL,D A
LAND UTILISATION SURVEY OF NI - THE LAND
OF ULSTER: THE BELFAST REGION
HMSO
BELFAST
1948 2 07

2199 HUGHES,P H
AN EXAMINATION OF THE NI SEA FISHING
INDUSTRY
JSSISI 21(6)
DUBLIN
1968 2 01

2200 HUGHES,P H
MILK INDUSTRY IN NI
QUB MA
BELFAST
1952 2 04

Specific Economic Analyses/

2201 HUGHES, P H
THE SEA FISHING INDUSTRY OF NI: AN
ECONOMIC STUDY
HMSO
BELFAST
1970 2 03

2202 HUNTER, W I
FARMING IN THE LESS FAVOURED AREAS OF NI
AGRIC NI 54
BELFAST
1979 2 01

2203 HYDE, H M
SUCCESS OF THE SMALL FARM IN ULSTER
GEOGR MAG 22(10)
1950 2 01

2204 INSTITUTE OF CONTINUING EDUCATION
PAPERS PRESENTED TO CONFERENCE ON
CO-OPERATION IN NI
NUU
COLERAINE
1978   08

2205 INSTITUTE OF MECHANICAL ENGINEERS
NI AND THE REPUBLIC OF IRELAND: SURVEY
OF ENGINEERING INDUSTRIES
ENGINEER 17
1960 2 01

2206 IRWIN, W L
THE REGISTRY OF DEEDS IN NI
NI LEG QUART 22(2)
BELFAST
1971 2 01

2207 JOHNSON, D B
FOOD SHOP-DWELLING LINKAGES IN BELFAST
AND CALGARY
QUB PHD
BELFAST
1969 2 04

2208 JOHNSON, D S
CATTLE SMUGGLING ON THE IRISH BORDER
1932-38
IR ECON AND SOC HISTORY 6
COLERAINE
1979 2 01

2209 JOHNSON, J H
THE COMMERCIAL USE OF PEAT IN NI
GEOGR J 125
LONDON
1959 2 01

2210 JOHNSTON, J
AGRICULTURAL CO-OPERATION IN NI: A
HISTORY OF THE UAOS LTD.
PLUNKETT FOUNDATION
LONDON
1965 2 10

2211 KANNER, B
WHEN YOU WISH UPON A CAR
NEW YORK FEB 22
NEW YORK
1982 2 01

2212 KENNEDY, W A
THE SPATIAL STRUCTURE OF URBAN RETAIL
BUSINESS AND CONSUMER MOVEMENT:
DISCUSSION OF THEORY WITH REFERENCE TO
EAST BELFAST
QUB MA
BELFAST
1973 2 04

2213 KNOX, W J
DECADES OF THE ULSTER BANK, 1836-1964
ULSTER BANK
BELFAST
1965 2 02

2214 KUPPER, U I; MULLER VAN ISSEN, G
NORDIRLAND: AUSWIRKUNGEN AUSSERER UND
INNERER GEGENSATZE ... RAUMSTRUKTUR
GEOFR RUNDSCHAU 9
1973 2 01

2215 LAND LAW WORKING GROUP
ESTATES AND INTERESTS AND FAMILY
DEALINGS IN LAND
HMSO
BELFAST
1981 2 03

2216 LAND LAW WORKING GROUP
GROUND RENTS AND OTHER PERIODIC PAYMENTS
HMSO
BELFAST
1980 2 03

2217 LARMOR, G
MECHANISATION AND PRODUCTIVITY IN THE
LINEN INDUSTRY
JSSISI 19 ·
DUBLIN
1955 2 01

2218 LAWRENCE, R J
RATE LIABILITY OF BODIES PROVIDING
FACILITIES FOR SPORT...AND COMMUNITY
ACTIVITIES...
HMSO
BELFAST
1978 2 03

2219 LEITCH, W A
PRESENT DAY AGRICULTURAL TENANCIES IN NI
NI LEG QUART 16(4)
BELFAST
1965 2 01

2220 LIVESTOCK MARKETING COMMISSION FOR NI
NI LIVESTOCK: FACTS AND FIGURES
LIVESTOCK MARKETING COMMISSION FOR NI
BELFAST
1981 2 03

2221 LUTTON, S C
LINEN TRADE IN CO. ARMAGH SINCE THE TURN
OF THE CENTURY
CRAIGAVON HIST SOC R 2(3)
1975 2 01

2222 MACKEL, S; MCILWAINE, T; GILBERT, K
COOPERATIVES AND INDUSTRIAL SELF-HELP IN
NI
COMM FORUM 3(1)
1973 2 01

2223 MAGEE UNIVERSITY COLLEGE
THE DEVELOPMENT OF A REGION: WEST ULSTER
MAGEE UNIV COLLEGE
DERRY
1966 2 10

2224 MAGUIRE, E D
SIROCCO STORY: THE BIRTH AND GROWTH OF
AN INDUSTRY
DAVIDSON AND CO.
BELFAST
1959 2 02

2225 MAGUIRE, M
TECHNOLOGICAL CHANGE AND CONTROL OF THE
WORKPLACE: AN EXAMINATION OF CHANGES IN
THE TELECOMMUNICATIONS INDUSTRY
SAI ANNUAL CONF
WEXFORD
1983 2 11

2226 MCBURNEY, S A
BREEDING EWE FLOCK PERFORMANCE
AGRIC NI 56(3)
BELFAST
1981 2 01

2227 MCBURNEY, S A
A CASE FOR GROWING MORE BARLEY ON NI
FARMS
AGRIC NI 52
BELFAST
1978 2 01

2228 MCBURNEY, S A
AN ECONOMIC ANALYSIS OF EWE FLOCK
PERFORMANCE IN NI, 1975 AND 1976
DEPT OF AGRICULTURE (NI)
BELFAST
1977 2 03

2229 MCBURNEY, S A
ECONOMIC FEATURES OF BARLEY PRODUCTION
DEPT OF AGRICULTURE (NI)
BELFAST
1980 2 03

2230 MCBURNEY, S A
ECONOMICS OF STORE LAMB FINISHING
DEPT OF AGRICULTURE (NI)
BELFAST
1982 2 03

2231 MCBURNEY, S A
THE ECONOMICS OF STORING GRAIN
AGRIC NI 53
BELFAST
1978 2 01

2232 MCBURNEY, S A
IMPLICATIONS OF CAPITAL TRANSFER TAX FOR
NI FARMERS
DEPT OF AGRICULTURE (NI)
BELFAST
1979 2 03

2233 MCBURNEY, S A
LEASING OF AGRICULTURAL MACHINERY
AGRIC NI 56(9)
BELFAST
1982 2 01

2234 MCBURNEY, S A
THE MARKETING CHANNELS FOR EGGS PRODUCED
IN NI
AGRIC NI 49
BELFAST
1974 2 01

2235 MCCANN, A
A COMPARISON OF THE SPATIAL ASPECTS OF
THE EGG AND MILK INDUSTRIES IN CO. DOWN
QUB MA
BELFAST
1969 2 04

2236 MCCAUGHEY, J
THE PORT OF BELFAST
BANKER 79
1946 2 01

2237 MCCRACKEN, E
THE IRISH WOODS SINCE TUDOR TIMES:
DISTRIBUTION AND EXPLOITATION
INST IRISH STUD QUB
BELFAST
1971 2 02

2238 MCCUTCHEON, W
THE COLLIERIES OF EAST TYRONE FROM THE
MID SEVENTEENTH CENTURY
QUB MA
BELFAST
1958 2 04

2239 MCGUIRE, E
A HISTORY OF THE DISTILLING INDUSTRY IN
IRELAND TO 1945
QUB PHD
BELFAST
1973 2 04

2240 MCGUIRE, E
IRISH WHISKEY
GILL AND MACMILLAN
DUBLIN
1973 2 02

2241 MCGURNAGHAN, M A; SCOTT, S
TRADE AND CO-OPERATION IN ELECTRICITY
AND GAS
CO-OPERATION NORTH
BELFAST/DUBLIN
1981 2 10

2242 MCHUGH, B J
CO. TYRONE
IN SYMONS, L (ED)
1963 2 07

2243 MCHUGH, B J
THE PATTERN OF FARMING IN TYRONE
QUB MA
BELFAST
1959 2 04

2244 MCLARNON, J; CORKEY, D
A SURVEY OF FACTS, FIGURES AND OPINIONS
RELATING TO THE ECONOMIC SITUATION IN
LONDONDERRY
NICRC
BELFAST
1971 2 10

2245 MCNEILL, A
THE RISE AND DECLINE OF THREE PORTS OF
NORTH DOWN - BANGOR, GROOMSPORT AND
DONAGHADEE
QUB MA
BELFAST
1955 2 04

2246 MESSENGER, B
'YOU WILL EASY KNOW A DOFFER': THE
FOLKLORE OF THE LINEN INDUSTRY IN NI
EIRE-IRELAND 14(1)
ST PAUL
1979 2 01

2247 MESSENGER, B
FOLKLORE OF THE NORTHERN IRISH LINEN
INDUSTRY 1900-1935
INDIANA UNIV PHD
1975 2 04

2248 MESSENGER, B
PICKING UP THE LINEN THREADS
BLACKSTAFF
BELFAST
1980 2 02

2249 METCALFE, H
THE APPLICATION OF SERVICE MARKETING TO
BANKING WITH SPECIAL REFERENCE TO THE
ASSOCIATED BANKS IN IRELAND
QUB PHD
BELFAST
1980 2 04

2250 METCALFE, J E
MINING IN NI
IN METCALFE, J E
LONDON
1960 2 07

2251 METSON, J E
A QUARTERLY ECONOMETRIC MODEL OF THE
FATSTOCK AND CARCASE MEAT INDUSTRY IN NI
NUU MPHIL
COLERAINE
1972 2 04

2252 MICHAEL, N C
THE LOWER BANN FISHERIES
ULSTER FOLKLIFE 11
1965 2 01

2253 MINISTRY OF AGRICULTURE (NI)
AGRICULTURAL COOPERATION IN NI: A REPORT
ON THE PLACE OF COOPERATION IN THE
FUTURE OF NI
HMSO CMD 484
BELFAST
1965 2 03

2254 MINISTRY OF COMMERCE (NI)
ELECTRICITY DEVELOPMENT IN NI
HMSO CMD 250
BELFAST
1947 2 03

81

2255 MINISTRY OF COMMERCE (NI)
THE TOURIST INDUSTRY IN NI: INTERIM
REPORT
HMSO CMD 234
BELFAST
1946 2 03

2256 MINISTRY OF HEALTH AND LOCAL GOVERNMENT
(NI)
ULSTER LAKELAND: A TOURIST PLAN FOR
COUNTY FERMANAGH
HMSO
BELFAST
1963 2 03

2257 MITCHEL, N C
IRISH PORTS: RECENT DEVELOPMENTS
IN STEPHENS, N; GLASSCOCK, R E (EDS)
BELFAST
1970 2 07

2258 MITCHEL, N C
THE FISHERIES OF THE LOUGH NEAGH BASIN
QUB MA
BELFAST
1949 2 04

2259 MOORE, J
MOTOR MAKING IN IRELAND
BLACKSTAFF
BELFAST
1982 2 02

2260 MOORE, J D
SOME TAX IMPLICATIONS OF MARRIAGE
BREAKDOWN
SLS/FACULTY OF LAW QUB
BELFAST
1981 2 10

2261 MORRIS, D E
DEVELOPMENTS IN THE MILK AND MILK
PRODUCTS INDUSTRY OF NI
DEPT OF AGRICULTURE (NI)
BELFAST
1978 2 03

2262 MORRISON, A M
HOW DELOREAN DASHED HIS DREAM
FORTUNE MAY 3
1982 2 01

2263 MORRISSEY, M; DITCH, J; GAFFIKIN, F
THE POLITICAL ECONOMY OF SOUTH-EAST
ANTRIM
ULSTER POLY
BELFAST
1980 2 10

2264 MOSS, J E
PART-TIME FARMING IN NI: A STUDY OF
SMALL SCALE BEEF AND SHEEP FARMS
DEPT OF AGRICULTURE (NI)
BELFAST
1980 2 03

2265 MOSS, J E; KIRKE, A
CONTRACT REARING OF DAIRY HEIFERS
AGRIC NI 56(5)
BELFAST
1981 2 01

2266 NASH, G C
ROPE
BELFAST ROPEWORK COMPANY
BELFAST
1947 2 10

2267 NEILL, D B
COASTAL PASSENGER STEAMERS AND INLAND
NAVIGATIONS IN THE NORTH OF IRELAND
MUSEUM AND ART GALLERY
BELFAST
1960 2 99

2268 NI ASSEMBLY
THE PROPOSED EXTENSION OF THE
LESS-FAVOURED AREAS IN NI
HMSO NIA 36
BELFAST
1983 2 03

2269 NI ASSEMBLY
REPORT OF CONSIDERATION ON THE
DISCUSSION PAPER ON THE DETERMINING OF
THE REGIONAL RATE IN NI
HMSO NIA 42
BELFAST
1983 2 03

2270 NI ASSEMBLY AGRICULTURAL COMMITTEE
REPORT ON THE PORTAVOGIE HARBOUR
DEVELOPMENT
HMSO NIA 57
BELFAST
1983 2 03

2271 NI ASSEMBLY AGRICULTURAL COMMITTEE
REPORT ON THE PROPOSALS OF THE MINISTER
OF STATE ON THE FUTURE ADMINISTRATION OF
THE SALMON AND INLAND FISHERIES OF NI
HMSO NIA 44
BELFAST
1983 2 03

2272 NI ASSEMBLY FINANCE AND PERSONNEL
COMMITTEE
INTERIM REPORT ON RATING LIABILITY OF
YOUNG FARMERS' CLUBS
HMSO NIA 58
BELFAST
1983 2 03

2273 NI CONSUMER COUNCIL
FUNERAL COSTS IN NI: A REPORT
NI CONSUMER COUNCIL
BELFAST
1978 2 03

2274 NI DEVELOPMENT COUNCIL
FREIGHT SERVICES TO AND FROM NI
MINISTRY OF COMMERCE (NI)
LONDON
1962 2 03

2275 NI GOVERNMENT
ELECTRICITY SUPPLY IN NI
HMSO CMD 355
BELFAST
1956 2 03

2276 NI GOVERNMENT
FORESTRY IN NI
HMSO CMD 550
BELFAST
1970 2 03

2277 NI GOVERNMENT
PUBLIC ROAD FREIGHT TRANSPORT IN NI
HMSO CMD 361
BELFAST
1956 2 03

2278 NI GOVERNMENT
REPORT OF THE COMMITTEE OF INQUIRY SET
UP TO EXAMINE THE MARKETING OF PIGS
HMSO CMD 545
BELFAST
1970 2 03

2279 NI GOVERNMENT
TEN YEAR PROGRAMME FOR ELECTRICITY
SUPPLY IN NI
HMSO CMD 478
BELFAST
1965   03

2280 NI TOURIST BOARD
TOURISM IN NI 1980
NI TOURIST BOARD
BELFAST
1981 2 03

Specific Economic Analyses/

2281 NICSS
    INCREASING EMPLOYMENT IN RURAL AREAS IN
    NI: A REPORT ON THE PAST, PRESENT AND
    FUTURE USE OF PEAT LANDS
    NICSS
    BELFAST
    1964 2 10

2282 NIEC
    THE CLOTHING INDUSTRY IN NI
    NIEC
    BELFAST
    1979 2 03

2283 NIEC
    THE DEVELOPMENT OF HORTICULTURE IN NI:
    SOME COMMENTS BY THE ECONOMIC COUNCIL
    NIEC
    BELFAST
    1979 2 03

2284 NIEC
    FURTHER STUDY OF GAS PIPELINE
    NIEC
    BELFAST
    1980 2 03

2285 NIEC
    A NI MANAGEMENT CENTRE
    NIEC
    BELFAST
    1983 2 03

2286 NIEC
    STATEMENT OF VIEWS ON AIR PASSENGER
    SERVICES
    NIEC
    BELFAST
    1979 2 03

2287 NIEC
    STATEMENT OF VIEWS ON SEA FERRY SERVICES
    NIEC
    BELFAST
    1979 2 03

2288 NIEC
    STRANGFORD LOUGH TIDAL ENERGY
    NIEC
    BELFAST
    1981 2 03

2289 NOVY, H J
    ENGINEERING GROWTH: NI
    ENGINEERING 15
    1960 2 01

2290 O'BRIEN, J T
    ASPECTS OF FARMING IN NI
    CHARTERED SURVEYOR 100
    1967 2 01

2291 O'BRIEN, J T
    WEST ULSTER: TRENDS IN AGRICULTURE
    IN RHODES, E; GARMANY, J (EDS)
    DERRY
    1966 2 07

2292 O'DOWD, L; ROLSTON, B
    BRINGING HONG KONG TO BELFAST? THE CASE
    OF AN ENTERPRISE ZONE
    SAI ANNUAL CONF
    WEXFORD
    1983 2 11

2293 O'FARRELL, P N; POOLE, M A
    RETAIL GROCERY PRICE VARIATION IN NI
    REG STUD 6(1)
    1972 2 01

2294 O'KANE, M C
    SURVEY OF SOME ORGANISATIONAL
    CHARACTERISTICS OF CIVIL ENGINEERING
    FIRMS IN NI
    QUB MBA
    BELFAST
    1969 2 04

2295 O'KANE, P C; MCCLEAN, P
    AMBULANCE MAINTENANCE POLICY: DESIGN OF
    A MANAGEMENT INFORMATION SYSTEM
    HEALTH AND SOCIAL SERVICES MANAGEMENT
    RESEARCH UNIT QUB
    BELFAST
    1980 2 10

2296 PARKIN, K F
    ASPECTS OF FORESTRY IN NI
    SCOTTISH FORESTRY 23
    1969 2 01

2297 PROUDFOOT, V B
    CHANGES IN POPULATION AND FARM HOLDINGS
    IN NI
    IR GEOG 5(4)
    1967 2 01

2298 REA, D
    A COMPARATIVE FINANCIAL ANALYSIS OF
    TWENTY-SIX NI PUBLIC COMPANIES
    QUB MSC
    BELFAST
    1969 2 04

2299 REDMOND, J
    CHURCH, STATE, INDUSTRY IN EAST BELFAST
    1827-1929
    AUTHOR
    BELFAST
    1961 2 02

2300 RINGLAND, J
    A BRIEF HISTORY OF ELECTRICAL
    MANUFACTURING IN NI
    INSTITUTION OF PRODUCTION ENGINEERS
    BELFAST
    1953 2 10

2301 ROBERTS, G A
    IRISH LINEN
    GEOGR MAG 22 10!
    LONDON
    1950 2 01

2302 ROBERTS, G A
    THE IRISH LINEN INDUSTRY
    BANKER 87
    LONDON
    1948 2 01

2303 ROBINSON, J A
    THE LIQUID MILK AND FRESH CREAM INDUSTRY
    IN NI
    J SOC DAIRY TECHNOLOGY 21
    1964 2 01

2304 RODRIGUES, D; BRUINVELS, P
    BELFAST (ENTERPRISE ZONE)
    IN RODRIGUES, D; BRUINVELS, P
    LONDON
    1982 2 07

2305 SAMS, K I; SIMPSON, J V
    CASE STUDY OF A SHIPBUILDING REDUNDANCY
    IN NI
    SCOTT J POLIT ECON 15(3)
    1968 2 01

2306 SAYERS, J E
    ACTIVITY IN THE SHIPYARDS
    BANKER 83
    1947 2 01

2307 SAYERS, J E
    SHADOW OVER THE SHIPYARDS
    BANKER 91
    1949 2 01

2308 SAYERS, J E
    SHIPBUILDING IN NI
    BANKER 75
    1945 2 01

2309 SCALLY,J K
THE ECONOMIC GEOGRAPHY OF THE IRON ORES
AND BAUXITES OF COUNTY ANTRIM 1954
QUB MA
BELFAST
1954 2 04

2310 SCOPE
COOPERATIVES AND COMMUNITY DEVELOPMENT
SCOPE 10
BELFAST
1977 2 01

2311 SCOPE
NEWRY: A SCOPE PROFILE
SCOPE 41
BELFAST
1981 2 01

2312 SCOTT,W M
A HUNDRED YEARS OF MILLING
CARTER
BELFAST
1951 2 10

2313 SHIELDS,B F
AN ANALYSIS OF THE FINANCIAL ...
STATISTICS OF THE GREAT SOUTHERN ... AND
GREAT NORTHERN RAILWAY COMPANY 1938-1944
JSSISI 99
DUBLIN
1946 2 01

2314 SHORT BROS AND HARLAND
SHORTS STORY SOUVENIR ISSUE
SHORT BROS AND HARLAND
BELFAST
1949 2 10

2315 SIMPSON,A W
SOME ASPECTS OF FORESTRY IN NI SINCE
1922 COMPARED WITH THOSE IN GREAT
BRITAIN AND EIRE
QUART J FORESTRY 58
1964 2 01

2316 SIMPSON,J V
SHIP BUILDING ECONOMICS
MANAGEMENT
1980 2 01

2317 SIMPSON,N
THE BELFAST BANK 1827-1970
BLACKSTAFF
BELFAST
1975 2 02

2318 SINCLAIR,K
THE PORT OF BELFAST
JSSISI 19
DUBLIN
1957 2 01

2319 SINN FEIN (OFFICIAL)
THE GREAT IRISH OIL AND GAS ROBBERY
DEPT OF ECONOMIC AFFAIRS
DUBLIN
1975 1 09

2320 SINN FEIN (PROVISIONAL)
MINING AND ENERGY
DUBLIN
1974 2 09

2321 SMILEY,J
THE SOCIAL AND ECONOMIC BACKGROUND OF
THE IRISH LINEN TRADE
PACE 7(2/3)
1976 2 01

2322 SPENCE,W R
SOCIOLOGICAL ASPECTS OF THE ADOPTION OF
INNOVATIONS IN NI FARMING COMMUNITIES
QUB PHD
BELFAST
1971 2 04

2323 STEED,G
CHANGING LINKAGES AND INTERNAL
MULTIPLIER OF AN INDUSTRIAL COMPLEX
CANADIAN GEOG 14(3)
1970 2 01

2324 STEED,G
THE CHANGING MILIEU OF THE FIRM: A CASE
STUDY OF A SHIPBUILDING CONCERN
A AMER ASSOC GEOGR 58
1968 2 01

2325 STEED,G
INTERNAL ORGANIZATION, FIRM INTEGRATION
AND LOCATIONAL CHANGE: THE NI LINEN
COMPLEX
ECON GEOG 47
1971 2 01

2326 STEED,G
THE NI LINEN COMPLEX
A AMER ASSOC GEOGR 64(3)
LAWRENCE, KANSAS
1974 2 01

2327 STEVENSON,J
SOCIAL SECURITY IN NI, WITH SPECIAL
REFERENCE TO A SELECTED GROUP OF
INDUSTRIES
QUB PHD
BELFAST
1964 2 04

2328 STEWART,D
AFFORESTATION IN NI
IR FORESTRY 2
1945 2 01

2329 SWAN,T
DE LOREAN: THE AMERICAN DREAM IS ALIVE
AND FIGHTING FOR SURVIVAL IN NI
MOTOR TREND MAY
1981 2 01

2330 SWANN,J
FORTY YEARS OF AIR TRANSPORT IN NI
ULSTER FOLK MUSEUM
BELFAST
1979 2 02

2331 SYMONS,L
FARM SIZE AS A BASIS FOR INDICATING
PROFITABILITY OF HILL FARMS...
IR GEOG 6
1968 2 01

2332 SYMONS,L
HILL LAND UTILISATION
IN SYMONS,L (ED)
LONDON
1963 2 07

2333 SYMONS,L
HILL LAND UTILISATION IN ULSTER
DEPT GEOG QUB
BELFAST
1955 2 08

2334 SYMONS,L
THE IMPROVED LANDS
IN SYMONS,L (ED)
LONDON
1963 2 07

2335 SYMONS,L
ROUGH GRAZING, PEAT BOG, WOODLAND
IN SYMONS,L (ED)
LONDON
1963 2 07

2336 SYMONS,L; MCHUGH,B J
COUNTY LONDONDERRY
IN SYMONS,L (ED)
LONDON
1963 2 07

2337 THOMAS,D E L
ECONOMIC ASPECTS OF FORESTRY IN NI
JSSISI 115
DUBLIN
1961 2 01

2338 THOMAS,D E L
      FARM TYPES AND FARM INCOMES
      IN SYMONS,L (ED)
      1963 2 07

2339 THOMPSON,I M
      DUST AND SENSITIVITY IN THE LINEN
      INDUSTRY
      QUB MD
      BELFAST
      1956 2 04

2340 TOMLINSON,M
      THE ELECTRICITY INDUSTRY IN NI
      SCOPE MAY
      1980 2 01

2341 TYRRELL,W E
      HISTORY OF THE BELFAST SAVINGS BANK
      BELFAST SAVINGS BANK
      BELFAST
      1947 2 02

2342 ULSTER BANK LTD
      DECADES OF THE ULSTER BANK, 1836-1964
      ULSTER BANK
      BELFAST
      1965 2 02

2343 WALLACE,H
      ADMINISTRATION OF ESTATES (NI) ORDER
      1979
      NI LEG QUART 31
      BELFAST
      1981 2 01

2344 WALLWORK,K L
      MINING, QUARRYING AND DERELICT LAND: AN
      ASPECT OF LAND USE IN NI
      IR GEOG 6(5)
      DUBLIN
      1973 2 01

2345 WHATMOUGH,R
      LAND PRICES IN NI: THE BACKGROUND TO
      RECENT INCREASES
      J NI INST AGRIC SCI
      BELFAST
      1974 2 01

2346 WILCOX,D
      WATER RESOURCE MANAGEMENT IN NI
      IR GEOG 10
      1977 2 01

2347 WOODS,J C H
      THE ADVISORY SERVICE IN NI AND THE PILOT
      FARM SCHEME
      AGRICULTURAL PROGRESS 35
      1960 2 01

2348 ABRAHAMSON, M W
TRADE DISPUTES ACT: STRICT
INTERPRETATION IN IRELAND
MOD LAW R 24
LONDON
1961 2 01

2349 ALEXANDER, D J
FARM LABOUR FORCE IN NI
NI INST AGRIC SCI R 4
1956 2 01

2350 ALEXANDER, D J
FARMHAND MOBILITY AND ADJUSTMENTS IN
FARMING IN NI
JSSISI 21
1965 2 01

2351 ANDERSONSTOWN AND SUFFOLK INDUSTRIAL
PROMOTIONS ASSOCIATION
UNEMPLOYMENT IN ANDERSONSTOWN: A REPORT
ON A SURVEY...
NICRC
BELFAST
1972 2 10

2352 ANNING, N; NICHOLL, J
UNEMPLOYMENT'S TOP TOWN
NEW STATESMAN JAN 29
LONDON
1982 2 01

2353 BARLOW, P
INDUSTRIAL TRAINING: LONG NIGHT'S
JOURNEY INTO DAY
EDUC AND TRAINING 14(3)
1972 2 01

2354 BATES, J; BUCHANAN, R E; MCGRATH, D G;
REA, D
MANPOWER IN THE DISTRIBUTIVE INDUSTRY IN
NI TO 1980
DEPT BUSINESS STUD QUB
BELFAST
1975 2 02

2355 BATESON, P
THE INDUSTRIAL RELATIONS (NI) ORDERS
1976 NUMBERS 1 AND 2
NI LEG QUART 28
BELFAST
1977 2 01

2356 BATESON, P ET AL
INDUSTRIAL TRIBUNALS IN NI: MAIN WORK
AND SUPPLEMENT
SLS/FACULTY OF LAW QUB
BELFAST
1982 2 10

2357 BEARE, J M
LEGAL ASPECTS OF OCCUPATIONAL DERMATITIS
IN NI
CONTACT DERMATITIS 1
1980 2 01

2358 BELFAST AND DISTRICT TRADES COUNCIL
SHORT HISTORY
BELFAST AND DISTRICT TRADES COUNCIL
BELFAST
1951 2 99

2359 BELFAST JUNIOR CHAMBER OF COMMERCE
LEISURE AND THE SHORTER WORKING WEEK IN
NI
CHAMBER OF COMMERCE
BELFAST
1966 2 10

2360 BELFAST JUNIOR CHAMBER OF COMMERCE,
ECONOMIC AFFAIRS COMMISSION
REPORT ON UNEMPLOYMENT, OVEREMPLOYMENT,
AND LABOUR TRAINING
CHAMBER OF COMMERCE
BELFAST
1966 2 10

2361 BELL, T
STRUGGLE OF THE UNEMPLOYED IN BELFAST,
OCTOBER 1932
WORKER'S CLUB HISTORICAL REPRINT
CORK
1976 2 09

2362 BICO
LABOUR IN ULSTER
ATHOL BOOKS
BELFAST
1979 2 09

2363 BIRLEY, D
OPPORTUNITIES AT 16: REPORT OF A STUDY
GROUP
HMSO
BELFAST
1978 2 03

2364 BIRRELL, W D ET AL
SOME ASPECTS OF LABOUR MOBILITY IN NI
NUU
COLERAINE
1975 2 10

2365 BLACK, R D C
EMPLOYMENT PROSPECTS IN NI
CHRISTUS REX 18(4)
1964 2 01

2366 BLACK, W; JEFFERSON, C W
REGIONAL EMPLOYMENT PATTERNS IN NI
ESRI
DUBLIN
1974 2 10

2367 BLACK, W; SLATTERY, D G
REGIONAL AND NATIONAL VARIATIONS IN
EMPLOYMENT AND UNEMPLOYMENT - NI: A CASE
STUDY
SCOTT J POLIT ECON 22(2)
1975 2 01

2368 BLEAKLEY, D
NI TRADE UNION MOVEMENT
JSSISI 20
1960 2 01

2369 BLEAKLEY, D
SOCIAL AND INDUSTRIAL EFFECTS OF HIGH
UNEMPLOYMENT IN NI
TRANS ASSOC OF INDUSTRIAL MEDICAL
OFFICERS 11(3)
1961 2 01

2370 BLEAKLEY, D
TEACHING UNEMPLOYED BOYS IN BELFAST
EDUCATION 113
1959 2 01

2371 BLEAKLEY, D
TRADE UNION BEGINNINGS IN BELFAST AND
DISTRICT
QUB MA
BELFAST
1955 2 04

2372 BOOTH, D
THE PARADOX OF PEACE ON THE FACTORY
FLOOR
FINANCIAL TIMES 22 JAN
LONDON
1973 2 10

2373 BOWERS,J
ANATOMY OF REGIONAL ACTIVITY RATES
NATIONAL INSTITUTE OF ECONOMIC AND
SOCIAL RESEARCH
1970 2 01

2374 BOYD,A
RISE OF IRISH TRADE UNIONS
ANVIL
TRALEE
1972 2 02

2375 BREAKWELL,G
UNEMPLOYMENT AND YOUNG PEOPLE
BRIT PSYCHOL SOCIETY, NI REGIONAL OFFICE
CONF
BELFAST
1982 2 11

2376 BROWN,D N
LABOUR USE IN NI DAIRY HERDS
DEPT OF AGRICULTURE (NI)
BELFAST
1980 2 03

2377 BROWN,W
WORKER PARTICIPATION: THE HARLAND &
WOLFF EXPERIENCE
IN POLLOCK,H M (ED)
DUBLIN
1981 2 07

2378 BURNS,G ET AL
UNEMPLOYMENT: RECOMMENDATIONS FOR ACTION
WITHIN A STRATEGY FOR ECONOMIC
DEVELOPMENT: MAIN REPORT
ULSTER POLY
BELFAST
1982 2 10

2379 CAVE,E D
A FOLLOW UP STUDY OF THE SUBSEQUENT
CAREERS OF TWO MATCHED GROUPS OF
BORDERLINE PUPILS
QUB MA
BELFAST
1965 2 04

2380 CHALK,P
CLASS UNITY, NATIONALISM AND IRISH TRADE
UNIONS
IRL SOCIALIST R 2
LONDON
1978 2 01

2381 CHURCHES' INDUSTRIAL COUNCIL
CHURCHES' INDUSTRIAL COUNCIL NI
CHRISTUS REX 19(3)
1965 2 01

2382 CLARKSON,J D
LABOUR AND NATIONALISM IN IRELAND
AMS PRESS
NEW YORK
1970 2 02

2383 COMMISSION OF THE EUROPEAN COMMUNITIES
WOMEN AND EMPLOYMENT IN THE UNITED
KINGDOM, IRELAND AND DENMARK
BRUSSELS
COMMISSION OF THE EUROPEAN COMMUNITIES
1975 2 03

2384 COMPTON,P A
DEMOGRAPHIC AND GEOGRAPHICAL ASPECTS OF
THE UNEMPLOYMENT DIFFERENTIAL BETWEEN
PROTESTANTS AND ROMAN CATHOLICS
IN COMPTON,P A (ED)
BELFAST
1981 2 07

2385 CORMACK,R; OSBORNE,R D
YOUNG SCHOOL LEAVERS AND THE LABOUR
MARKET: THE BELFAST STUDY - 'INTO WORK
IN BELFAST?'
IN CORMACK,R; OSBORNE,R D (EDS)
BELFAST
1983 2 07

2386 CORMACK,R; OSBORNE,R D; THOMPSON,W
INTO WORK? YOUNG SCHOOL-LEAVERS AND THE
STRUCTURE OF OPPORTUNITIES IN BELFAST
FEA 5
BELFAST
1980 2 03

2387 COUGHLAN,A
TRADE UNIONISM IN IRELAND TODAY
CONNOLLY PUBLICATIONS
LONDON
1965 2 09

2388 CURRAGH,E G; MCGLEENON,C F
CAREERS EDUCATION IN POST-PRIMARY
SCHOOLS
NORTH TEACH 12(5)
BELFAST
1977 2 01

2389 CUTHBERT,N
EMPLOYMENT PROBLEM IN NI
BANKER
1952 2 01

2390 DEPT OF MANPOWER SERVICES (NI)
COHORT SURVEY OF THE UNEMPLOYED
HMSO
BELFAST
1979 2 03

2391 DEPT OF MANPOWER SERVICES (NI)
DMS GAZETTE NUMBERS 1-3 1978-79
DEPT OF MANPOWER SERVICES (NI)
BELFAST
1979 2 03

2392 DEPT OF MANPOWER SERVICES (NI)
GUIDE TO MANPOWER POLICY AND PRACTICES
HMSO
BELFAST
1978 2 03

2393 DITCH,J; OSBORNE,R D
WOMEN AND WORK IN NI: A SURVEY OF DATA
OCCASIONAL PAPER IN SOCIAL POLICY,
SCHOOL OF SOCIOLOGY AND SOCIAL POLICY
ULSTER POLY
BELFAST
1980 2 10

2394 DOHERTY,P
THE GEOGRAPHY OF UNEMPLOYMENT
IN BOAL,F W; DOUGLAS,J N H (EDS)
LONDON
1982 2 07

2395 DOHERTY,P
A GEOGRAPHY OF UNEMPLOYMENT IN THE
BELFAST URBAN AREA
QUB PHD
BELFAST
1977 2 04

2396 DOHERTY,P
PATTERNS OF UNEMPLOYMENT IN BELFAST
IR GEOG 13
DUBLIN
1980 2 01

2397 DOHERTY,P
THE UNEMPLOYED POPULATION OF BELFAST
IN COMPTON,P A (ED)
BELFAST
1980 2 07

2398 DRAUGHTSMAN'S AND ALLIED TECHNICIANS
ASSOCIATION, NUMBER 3 DIVISIONAL COUNCIL
TRADE UNIONISTS AND THE 'IRISH QUESTION'
THE DRAUGHTSMAN AUG
RICHMOND, SURREY
1964 2 01

2399 EAGLESON,E
EMPLOYMENT AND TRAINING OF GIRLS LEAVING
BELFAST SCHOOLS
QUB PHD
BELFAST
1958 2 04

Labour/Employment/

2400 EDWARDS,C J W
STRUCTURAL UNDEREMPLOYMENT ON FULL-TIME
FARMS IN NI
IR J AGRIC ECON RUR SOCIOL 8(2)
DUBLIN
1981 2 01

2401 FARLEY,M
THE YOUTH TRAINING PROGRAMME IN NI
NATIONAL ASSOC OF TEACHERS IN FURTHER
AND HIGHER EDUC J 8(2)
LONDON
1983 2 01

2402 FEA
A FINAL REPORT OF THE FAIR EMPLOYMENT
AGENCY FOR NI INTO THE EMPLOYMENT
PRACTICES OF THE NI ELECTRICITY SERVICE
FEA
BELFAST
1982 2 10

2403 FROGGATT,P
ONE DAY ABSENCE IN INDUSTRY
JSSISI
1965 2 01

2404 GARDNER,J J
PRACTICAL PERSONNEL AND INDUSTRIAL
RELATIONS MANAGEMENT
IN POLLOCK,H M (ED)
DUBLIN
1982 2 07

2405 GARMANY,J
EMPLOYMENT STRATEGY IN IRELAND
IR BANKING R JUNE
1978 2 01

2406 GARMANY,J
LABOUR RESERVES IN NI: WITH SPECIFIC
REFERENCE TO WEST ULSTER
IN RHODES,E; GARMANY,J (EDS)
DERRY
1966 2 07

2407 GARMANY,J
A SURVEY OF MANPOWER: LONDONDERRY,
COLERAINE, LIMAVADY AND STRABANE
JSSISI 21(2)
DUBLIN
1963 2 01

2408 GIBSON,N J
NOTE ON GOVERNMENT ECONOMIC POLICY IN NI
WITH SPECIAL REFERENCE TO EMPLOYMENT
AUTHOR
1973 2 08

2409 GIBSON,N J; SPENCER,J E
UNEMPLOYMENT AND WAGES IN NI
IN CRICK,B (ED)
LONDON
1981 2 07

2410 GIBSON,N J; SPENCER,J E
UNEMPLOYMENT AND WAGES IN NI
POLIT QUART 52(1)
1981 2 01

2411 GLASS,J C
FACTOR SUBSTITUTION AND DEMAND FOR
LABOUR IN THE NI ENGINEERING INDUSTRY
JSSISI
1972 2 01

2412 GORMALLY,B; LYNER,O; MULLIGAN,G;
WARDEN,M
UNEMPLOYMENT AND YOUNG OFFENDERS IN NI
NI ASSOCIATION FOR THE CARE AND
RESETTLEMENT OF OFFENDERS
BELFAST
1981 2 10

2413 GREER,J E; BROWN,W
THE INSPECTION OF RELIGIOUS EDUCATION IN
NI SCHOOLS
NORTH TEACH 13(4)
BELFAST
1981 2 01

2414 GRIEG,F W; SCOTT,W M
NI TRAINING AND ITS PLACE IN THE ECONOMY
PERSONNEL MANAGEMENT JUL
1971 2 01

2415 GUDGIN,G; MOORE,B; RHODES,J
EMPLOYMENT PROBLEMS IN THE CITIES AND
REGIONS OF THE UK: PROSPECTS FOR THE
1980S
CAMBRIDGE ECON R 8(2)
CAMBRIDGE
1982 2 01

2416 HARKIN,A M
AN ANALYSIS OF THE NEW LABOUR
LEGISLATION IN NI
QUB LLM
BELFAST
1977 2 04

2417 HARRISON,H
TRENDS IN AGRICULTURAL LAND, LABOUR,
FARMING UNITS IN NI FROM THE PRESENT
UNTIL 2000 A.D.
IR J AGRIC ECON AND RURAL SOCIOL 6
1976 2 01

2418 HARVEY,S; REA,D
AN EVALUATION OF THE EMPLOYER-BASED WORK
EXPERIENCE PROGRAMME
ULSTER POLY
BELFAST
1979 2 10

2419 HAUGHTON REPORT
REPORT ON THE EMPLOYMENT AND TRAINING OF
WOMEN IN NI
MINISTRY OF HEALTH AND SOCIAL SERVICES
(NI)
BELFAST
1969 2 03

2420 HENDERSON,I G
GENERAL TRAINING, GOVERNMENT
RESPONSIBILITY AND THE RURAL UNEMPLOYED
JSSISI
1973 2 01

2421 HENDERSON,I G
INDUSTRIAL TRAINING IN NI: THE EFFECTS
OF THE 1964 INDUSTRIAL TRAINING ACT
QUB MSC
BELFAST
1976 2 04

2422 HEPBURN,A C
EMPLOYMENT AND RELIGION IN BELFAST
1901-1971
FEA
BELFAST
1982 2 03

2423 HEPBURN,A C
EMPLOYMENT AND RELIGION IN BELFAST,
1901-1951
IN CORMACK,R; OSBORNE,R (EDS)
BELFAST
1983 2 07

2424 HILLERY,B
THE IRISH CONGRESS OF TRADE UNIONS
ADMIN (DUB) 24(1)
DUBLIN
1973 2 01

2425 HUTCHINSON,R
THE GOVERNMENT OF NI AND THE GENERAL
STRIKE, 1926
NUU MA
COLERAINE
1977 2 04

2426 ICTU
INDUSTRIAL RELATIONS IN NI
ICTU
BELFAST
1971 2 10

2427 ICTU
JOBS: AN ACTION PROGRAMME
ICTU
BELFAST
1979 2 99

2428 ICTU
REPEAL THE TRADES DISPUTES ACT
ICTU
BELFAST
1957 2 09

2429 ICTU
UNEMPLOYMENT: A CONSTRUCTIVE APPROACH TO
THE PROBLEM IN NI
ICTU
BELFAST
1952 2 09

2430 IRISH COUNCIL OF CHURCHES
A RIGHT TO WORK?
IRISH COUNCIL OF CHURCHES
BELFAST
1981 2 10

2431 ISLES,K S
PUBLIC FINANCE AND EMPLOYMENT
IPA
LONDON
1949 2 11

2432 JACKSON,J A; MILLER,R L
SIZE AND DETERMINANTS OF THE MARGINAL
LABOUR FORCE IN NI AND IRISH REPUBLIC
COMMISSION OF THE EUROPEAN COMMUNITIES,
DIRECTORATE-GENERAL FOR SOCIAL AFFAIRS
BRUXELLES
1978 2 03

2433 JENKS,R E
YOUTH EMPLOYMENT SERVICE: WHY, WHAT AND
HOW?
JSSISI
1963 2 01

2434 KIDD,C W
MORBIDITY TRENDS IN A COMMUNITY OF HIGH
UNEMPLOYMENT
TRANS ASSOC INDUSTRIAL MED OFFICERS
11(3)
1961 2 01

2435 LABOUR AND TRADE UNION CO-ORDINATING
GROUP
WORKERS BREAK THE STOPPAGE
LABOUR AND TRADE UNION CO-ORDINATING
GROUP
BELFAST
1977 1 09

2436 LABOUR RELATIONS AGENCY
EXTENSION OF TERMS AND CONDITIONS OF
EMPLOYMENT
LRA
BELFAST
1980 2 10

2437 LABOUR RELATIONS AGENCY
NI ADJUDICATION MACHINERY
LRA
BELFAST
1980 2 10

2438 LABOUR RELATIONS AGENCY
PRINCIPAL INDUSTRIAL RELATIONS AND
EMPLOYMENT LEGISLATION IN CONSOLIDATED
FORM
LRA
BELFAST
1981 2 03

2439 LARKIN,J
A COMMON LOYALTY - THE BRIDGE TO UNITY
ICTU
DUBLIN
1949 2 10

2440 LAW,D
WORK AND WAGE PATTERNS IN NI
CHRISTUS REX 18(2)
1964 2 01

2441 LOFTUS,B
MARCHING WORKERS
ARTS COUNCIL OF NI
BELFAST
1978 2 10

2442 LOWRY,H A
UNEMPLOYMENT IN NI: THE SOCIAL AND
ECONOMIC BACKGROUND
TRANS ASSOC INDUSTRIAL MEDICAL OFFICERS
11(3)
1961 2 01

2443 MACY,C
JOB DISCRIMINATION IN NI
HUMANIST 87(1)
1972 1 01

2444 MAGUIRE,M
TECHNOLOGICAL CHANGE AND CONTROL OF THE
WORKPLACE: AN EXAMINATION OF CHANGES IN
THE TELECOMMUNICATIONS INDUSTRY
SAI ANNUAL CONF
WEXFORD
1983 2 11

2445 MCALEER,W E; LYTTLE,J R
CASE STUDIES IN ARBITRATION
LRA
BELFAST
1981 2 03

2446 MCCARTHY,C
CIVIL STRIFE AND THE GROWTH OF TRADE
UNION UNITY: THE CASE OF IRELAND
GVT AND OPPOSITION 8(4)
1973 1 01

2447 MCCARTHY,C
DECADE OF UPHEAVAL: IRISH TRADE UNIONS
IN THE 1960'S
IPA
DUBLIN
1973 2 02

2448 MCCARTHY,C
THE EVOLUTION OF TRADE UNION
ORGANISATION IN IRELAND 1894-1960
TCD PHD
DUBLIN
1976 2 04

2449 MCCARTHY,C
FROM DIVISION TO DISSENSION: IRISH TRADE
UNIONS IN THE 1930S
ECON AND SOC R 5(3)
DUBLIN
1974 2 01

2450 MCCARTHY,C
TRADE UNIONS IN IRELAND 1894-1960
IPA
DUBLIN
1977 2 02

2451 MCCULLAGH,M
YOUTH UNEMPLOYMENT AND THE IDEOLOGY OF
CONTROL
IN CURTIN,C; KELLY,M; O'DOWD,L (EDS)
DUBLIN
1983 2 07

Labour/Employment/

2452 MCERLEAN, J
THE CRIMINAL LAW AND EMERGENCY AND
SPECIAL LEGISLATION IN RELATION TO TRADE
DISPUTES IN THE UK
QUB LLM
BELFAST
1970 1 04

2453 MCGANN, G
AN ANALYSIS OF THE GROWTH AND
DEVELOPMENT IN VOCATIONAL EDUCATION IN
IRELAND, 1950-1975
NUU MA
COLERAINE
1978 2 04

2454 MCGLADDERY, D R
IRISH CONGRESS OF TRADE UNIONS: A
UNIONIST VIEWPOINT
BELFAST
1963 2 09

2455 MCGUFFIN, S J
AN INVESTIGATION INTO THE FACTORS
INFLUENCING THE CHOICE OF CAREER BY BOYS
QUB MSC
BELFAST
1956 2 04

2456 MCINERNEY, M
TRADE UNIONS BID FOR PEACE IN NORTH
IRISH TIMES
DUBLIN
1970 1 10

2457 MCMULLAN, G
THE DEVELOPMENT OF CLERICAL TRADE
UNIONISM IN THE NORTH OF IRELAND DURING
THE TWENTIETH CENTURY
QUB PHD
BELFAST
1971 2 04

2458 MCNARRY, M
INTRODUCTION TO HEALTH EDUCATION IN
GOVERNMENT TRAINING CENTRES IN CO ANTRIM
HEALTH EDUC J 31(1)
1972 2 01

2459 MILLER, R L; OSBORNE, R D
RELIGION AND UNEMPLOYMENT: EVIDENCE FROM
A COHORT SURVEY
IN CORMACK, R; OSBORNE, R D (EDS)
BELFAST
1983 2 07

2460 MINISTRY OF EDUCATION (NI)
REPORT OF THE JOINT COMMITTEE ON THE
TRAINING OF APPRENTICES
HMSO CMD 231
BELFAST
1945 2 03

2461 MORGAN, A
POLITICS, THE LABOUR MOVEMENT AND THE
WORKING CLASS IN BELFAST 1905-1923
QUB PHD
BELFAST
1978 2 04

2462 MORONEY, M
TEACHERS UNIONS AND COLLECTIVE
BARGAINING
NORTH TEACH 13(3)
BELFAST
1980 2 01

2463 MORRISSEY, M; MORRISSEY, S
NI: WHY THE TRADE UNIONS ARE CENTRAL
MARXISM TODAY NOV
LONDON
1979 1 01

2464 MUNCK, R
CLASSE OUVRIERE ET QUESTION NATIONALE EN
IRLANDE
PLURIEL 29
1982 1 01

2465 MUNCK, R
A DIVIDED WORKING CLASS: PROTESTANT AND
CATHOLIC WORKERS IN NI
LABOUR, CAPITAL AND SOCIETY 13(1)
MONTREAL
1980 1 01

2466 MURIE, A S
SPATIAL ASPECTS OF UNEMPLOYMENT AND
ECONOMIC STRESS IN NI
IR GEOG 7
1974 2 01

2467 MURRAY, D; DARBY, J
THE VOCATIONAL ASPIRATIONS AND
EXPECTATIONS OF SCHOOL LEAVERS IN
LONDONDERRY AND STRABANE
FEA
BELFAST
1980 2 03

2468 MURRAY, D; DARBY, J
YOUNG SCHOOL LEAVERS AND THE LABOUR
MARKET: THE LONDONDERRY AND STRABANE
STUDY - OUT AND DOWN IN DERRY AND
STRABANE
IN CORMACK, R; OSBORNE, R D (EDS)
BELFAST
1983 2 07

2469 NATIONAL BOARD FOR PRICES AND INCOMES
PAY AND CONDITIONS OF BUSMEN EMPLOYED IN
BELFAST, GLASGOW AND LIVERPOOL
HMSO CMND 3646
LONDON
1968 2 03

2470 NEESON, W
THE AFTER-SCHOOL LIFE OF THE ADOLESCENT
LINEN WORKER
QUB MED
BELFAST
1951 2 04

2471 NI GOVERNMENT
REPORT OF THE COMMITTEE OF INQUIRY ON
VOCATIONAL GUIDANCE AND EMPLOYMENT
SERVICES FOR YOUNG PERSONS
HMSO CMD 394
BELFAST
1959 2 03

2472 NI REVIEW BODY ON INDUSTRIAL RELATIONS
INDUSTRIAL RELATIONS IN NI
HMSO
BELFAST
1979 2 03

2473 NI TRAINING EXECUTIVE
EMPLOYMENT LAW IN NI: A GENERAL GUIDE
FOR THOSE INVOLVED IN INDUSTRIAL
RELATIONS
NI TRAINING EXECUTIVE
BELFAST
1980 2 03

2474 NI YOUTH EMPLOYMENT SERVICE BOARD
INFORMATION OFFICE
OPPORTUNITY SURVEY OF CAREER
OPPORTUNITIES IN NI
NICHOLSON AND BASS
BELFAST
1973 2 02

2475 NICSS
INCREASING EMPLOYMENT IN RURAL AREAS IN
NI: A REPORT ON THE PAST, PRESENT AND
FUTURE USE OF PEAT LANDS
NICSS
BELFAST
1964 2 10

2476 NIEC
EMPLOYMENT PATTERNS IN NI 1950-1980
NIEC
BELFAST
1981 2 03

2477 NIEC
MANPOWER: AN APPRAISAL OF THE POSITION,
1964-1970
HMSO
BELFAST
1967   2   03

2478 NIEC
UNEMPLOYMENT IN NI 1974-79
NIEC
BELFAST
1980   2   03

2479 NIEC
YOUTH UNEMPLOYMENT AND TRAINING
NIEC
BELFAST
1982   2   03

2480 NILP
ULSTER LABOUR AND THE SIXTIES
NILP
BELFAST
1962   2   09

2481 NJUBA, S
LEGAL CONTROLS OVER...TRADE UNIONS IN
THE UNITED KINGDOM OF GREAT BRITAIN AND
NI, THE REPUBLIC OF IRELAND AND UGANDA
QUB LLM
BELFAST
1970   2   04

2482 NOLAN, P
THE IRISH TRADE UNION MOVEMENT NOW
CHRISTUS REX 23(1)
MAYNOOTH
1969   2   01

2483 O'BRIEN, F
NO JOBS, THAT'S THE PROBLEM
IN O'BRIEN, F (ED)
ROCKFORD, ILLINOIS
1971   1   07

2484 O'CONNELL, T J
HISTORY OF THE INTO, 1868-1968
INTO
DUBLIN
1969   2   02

2485 O'HERLIHY, C
ECONOMIC STUDIES IN NI LABOUR STATISTICS
JSSISI 21(2)
DUBLIN
1964   2   01

2486 O'KANE, P C
TWO CONTRASTING MANPOWER SCHEDULING
PROJECTS
PROC 7TH ANNUAL MEETING EUROPEAN WORKING
GROUP ON OPERATIONAL RESEARCH APPLIED TO
HEALTH SERVICES
TRONDHEIM
1981   2   11

2487 O'KANE, P C; HAMILTON, P
A COMMENTARY ON EXISTING NURSE ROTA
SYSTEMS IN TWO HOSPITALS IN THE NORTH
AND WEST BELFAST DISTRICT
HEALTH AND SOCIAL SERVICES MANAGEMENT
RESEARCH UNIT QUB
BELFAST
1981   2   10

2488 OSBORNE, R D
DENOMINATION AND UNEMPLOYMENT IN NI
AREA 10(4)
1978   2   01

2489 OSBORNE, R D
EQUALITY OF OPPORTUNITY AND
DISCRIMINATION: THE CASE OF RELIGION IN
NI
ADMIN (DUB) 29(4)
DUBLIN
1982   1   01

2490 OSBORNE, R D
RELIGIOUS DISCRIMINATION AND
DISADVANTAGE IN THE NI LABOUR MARKET
INT J SOC ECON 7(4)
BRADFORD
1980   2   01

2491 PALMER, D; JARDINE, M; FINNEGAN, G
FROM SCHOOLS TO WORK: WHAT NEXT?
STANDING CONFERENCE OF YOUTH
ORGANISATIONS
BELFAST
1980   2   10

2492 PARK, A T
OCCUPATIONAL MORTALITY IN NI (1960-62)
JSSISI 23
1966   2   01

2493 PATTERSON, H
CLASS, CONFLICT AND SECTARIANISM
BLACKSTAFF
BELFAST
1981   2   02

2494 PROVISIONAL UNITED TRADE UNION
ORGANISATION
DRAFT CONSTITUTION FOR A TRADE UNION
CENTRE FOR IRELAND
PROVISIONAL UNITED TRADE UNION
ORGANISATION
DUBLIN
1957   2   10

2495 PROVISIONAL UNITED TRADE UNION
ORGANISATION
REPORT OF THE DRAFTING SUB-COMMITTEE OF
THE JOINT COMMITTEE ON TRADE UNION UNITY
PROVISIONAL UNITED TRADE UNION
ORGANISATION
DUBLIN
1955   2   10

2496 PROVISIONAL UNITED TRADE UNION
ORGANISATION
SECOND REPORT
PROVISIONAL UNITED TRADE UNION
ORGANISATION
DUBLIN
1957   2   10

2497 PURDIE, B
BELFAST LABOURISM, 1905-1925
IRL SOCIALIST R 7
LONDON
1980   2   01

2498 REES, T L
STUDY OF SCHEMES OF DIRECT JOB CREATION
IN NI
COMMISSION OF EUROPEAN COMMUNITIES
BRUSSELS
1980   2   03

2499 REYNOLDS, F
A GUIDE TO INDUSTRIAL RELATIONS
LEGISLATION IN NI
THE INDUSTRIAL SOCIETY
LONDON
1977   2   10

2500 ROBERTS, R
TRADE UNION ORGANISATION IN IRELAND
JSSISI 20(2)
DUBLIN
1959   2   01

2501 ROBERTSON, N; SAMS, K I
INDUSTRIAL RELATIONS REFORMS IN NI
JSSISI
1975   2   01

2502 ROBERTSON, N; SAMS, K I
RESEARCH NOTE ON THE WORK PATTERN OF
UNION OFFICERS
INDUSTR RELAT J 9(1)
1978   2   01

2503 ROBERTSON,N; SAMS,K I
ROLE OF FULL TIME TRADE UNION OFFICIALS
IN NI
SSRC FINAL REPORT
LONDON
1976 2 08

2504 ROBERTSON,N; SAMS,K I
ROLE OF THE FULL TIME UNION OFFICER
ECON AND SOC R 8(1)
DUBLIN
1976 2 01

2505 ROBSON,P
ULSTER'S UNEMPLOYMENT PROBLEM
BANKER 108
LONDON
1958 2 01

2506 ROCHE,D J D ET AL
SOME DETERMINANTS OF LABOUR MOBILITY IN
NI
ECON AND SOC R 5(1)
DUBLIN
1973 2 01

2507 ROLSTON,B
CLASS, RELIGION AND SEX
NEW STATESMAN JULY 16
LONDON
1982 2 01

2508 ROLSTON,B
THE LIMITS OF TRADE UNIONISM
IN O'DOWD,L; ROLSTON,B; TOMLINSON,M
LONDON
1980 1 07

2509 ROLSTON,B
REFORMISM AND CLASS POLITICS IN NI: THE
CASE OF THE TRADE UNIONS
INSURGENT SOCIOLOGIST 10(2)
BINGHAMTON, NEW YORK
1980 1 01

2510 RUDD,J
ENTERPRISE ULSTER: LAYING THE
FOUNDATIONS FOR FULL EMPLOYMENT
COMM CARE 55
LONDON
1975 2 01

2511 SALT,J; JOHNSON,J
RECENT TRENDS IN THE LEVEL AND
DISTRIBUTION OF UNEMPLOYMENT IN NI
TIDJSCHR ECON SOC GEOGR 66(4)
1975 2 01

2512 SAMS,K I
THE APPEALS BOARD OF THE ICTU
BRIT J INDUSTR RELAT 6
LONDON
1968 2 01

2513 SAMS,K I
GOVERNMENT AND TRADE UNIONS: THE
SITUATION IN NI
BRIT J INDUSTR RELAT 2(2)
LONDON
1964 2 01

2514 SAMS,K I; SIMPSON,J V
CASE STUDY OF A SHIPBUILDING REDUNDANCY
IN NI
SCOTT J POLIT ECON 15(3)
1968 2 01

2515 SCOPE
JOB CREATION AND THE YOUNG UNEMPLOYED
SCOPE 9
BELFAST
1977 2 01

2516 SCOPE
NEWRY: A SCOPE PROFILE
SCOPE 41
BELFAST
1981 2 01

2517 SHEEHAN,J; HUTCHINSON,R W
DEMOGRAPHIC AND LABOUR FORCE STRUCTURE
IN THE REPUBLIC OF IRELAND AND NI
COOPERATION NORTH
BELFAST AND DUBLIN
1980 2 02

2518 SIMPSON,J V
ANATOMY OF UNEMPLOYMENT IN NI
MANAGEMENT 22(6/7)
LONDON
1976 1 01

2519 SIMPSON,J V
TEMPORARILY OUT OF STEP: RECENT CHANGES
IN INDUSTRIAL RELATIONS LAW
MANAGEMENT
1980 2 01

2520 SINCLAIR,B
TRADE UNIONS IN IRELAND
MARXISM TODAY 17(6)
1973 2 01

2521 SINCLAIR,B
UNEMPLOYMENT
COMMUNIST PARTY OF IRELAND
DUBLIN
1973 2 09

2522 SKILLEN,S M
A SURVEY OF SECRETARIAL TRAINING IN
NI...
QUB MSC
BELFAST
1978 2 04

2523 SMASH THE PREVENTION OF TERRORISM ACT
CAMPAIGN
TUC HANDS OFF IRELAND
REVOLUTIONARY COMMUNIST TENDENCY
LONDON
1981 1 09

2524 SMITH,J V
EMPLOYMENT EXPECTATIONS OF RURAL
SCHOOL-LEAVERS
JSSISI 123
DUBLIN
1970 2 01

2525 ST. LEGER,F J
OCCUPATIONAL ASPIRATIONS AND EDUCATION
IN THE COLERAINE TRIANGLE
SOC STUD 3(4)
MAYNOOTH
1974 2 01

2526 STANDING CONFERENCE OF YOUTH
ORGANISATIONS IN NI
YOUNG PEOPLE WITHOUT WORK
STANDING CONFERENCE OF YOUTH
ORGANISATIONS IN NI
BELFAST
1981 2 10

2527 STEELE,R
EMPLOYMENT LAW: TEN STEPS BACK
SCOPE 45
BELFAST
1981 2 01

2528 STEELE,R
EMPLOYMENT NOW IN NI
NI TRAINING EXECUTIVE
BELFAST
1980 2 03

2529 STEELE,R
LABOUR LAW IN ACTION
IN POLLOCK,H M (ED)
DUBLIN
1982 2 07

2530 STEELE,R
SCHEDULE 3 CLAIMS: THE EXTENSION OF
TERMS AND CONDITIONS OF EMPLOYMENT IN NI
NI LEG QUART 29
BELFAST
1978 2 01

2531 STEPHEN,F
WORKER'S PARTICIPATION: A BASIS FOR
DISCUSSION
ICTU
BELFAST
1975 2 10

2532 STEVENSON,J
THE ECONOMIC EFFECTS OF INDUSTRIAL
ACCIDENTS WITH SPECIAL REFERENCE TO NI
QUB MSC
BELFAST
1959 2 04

2533 TAYLOR,R
SHOPFLOOR ULSTER
NEW SOCIETY 23 MAY
LONDON
1974 2 01

2534 THOMPSON,W
UNEMPLOYMENT AMONG YOUNG MALES IN
BELFAST
BRIT PSYCHOL SOCIETY, NI REGIONAL OFFICE
CONF
BELFAST
1982 2 11

2535 THOMPSON,W; CORMACK,R; OSBORNE,R D
SOME ASPECTS OF OCCUPATIONAL CHOICE AND
PLACEMENT OF 16 YEAR-OLD BOYS IN BELFAST
IN HARBISON,J; HARBISON,J (EDS)
SHEPTON MALLET, SOMERSET
1980 2 07

2536 THORNLEY,D
THE DEVELOPMENT OF THE IRISH LABOUR
MOVEMENT
CHRISTUS REX 18(1)
MAYNOOTH
1964 2 01

2537 TOPLIS,G
ROLE ORIENTATIONS OF INDUSTRIAL TRAINING
BOARD MANAGEMENT TRAINING ADVISERS
NUU MA
COLERAINE
1975 2 04

2538 TOPPING,J W
THE HISTORY, LAW AND PRACTICE OF
PICKETING IN THE UK ...
QUB LLM
BELFAST
1979 2 04

2539 TRADE UNION SUBCOMMITTEE OF THE NATIONAL
H-BLOCKS COMMITTEE
TRADE UNIONS AND H-BLOCK
TRADE UNION SUBCOMMITTEE OF THE NATIONAL
H-BLOCKS COMMITTEE
BELFAST
1980 1 10

2540 TREWSDALE,J
REPORT ON UNEMPLOYMENT IN NI, 1974-79
NIEC 14
BELFAST
1980 2 03

2541 TREWSDALE,J
THE ROLE OF WOMEN IN THE NI ECONOMY
IN CORMACK,R; OSBORNE,R D (EDS)
BELFAST
1983 2 07

2542 TREWSDALE,J; TRAINOR,M
WOMANPOWER NO. 2: RECENT CHANGES IN THE
FEMALE LABOUR MARKET IN NI
EOC
BELFAST
1981 2 03

2543 TREWSDALE,J; TRAINOR,M
WOMANPOWER: A STATISTICAL SURVEY OF
WOMEN AND WORK IN NI
EOC
BELFAST
1979 2 03

2544 TURF LODGE DEVELOPMENT ASSOCIATION
REPORT ON EMPLOYMENT
TURF LODGE DEVELOPMENT ASSOCIATION
BELFAST
1972 2 10

2545 WALKER,B
INDUSTRIAL RELATIONS IN NI
CHRISTUS REX 21(3)
1967 2 01

2546 WALSH,B
THE LABOUR FORCE AND THE PROBLEM OF
UNEMPLOYMENT
IN GIBSON,N J; SPENCER,J E (EDS)
DUBLIN
1977 2 07

2547 WAYNE,N
LABOUR LAW IN IRELAND: A GUIDE TO
WORKERS RIGHTS
KINCORA PRESS/ITGWU
1980 2 10

2548 WILSON,J G
PEACE IN INDUSTRY: NI
CHRISTUS REX 19(2)
1965 2 01

2549 WORKERS' ASSOCIATION
WHAT TO DO ABOUT ULSTER TRADE UNIONISM
ATHOL BOOKS
BELFAST
1975 2 09

2550 WORKERS' ASSOCIATION
WHAT'S WRONG WITH ULSTER TRADE UNIONISM?
ATHOL BOOKS
BELFAST
1975 2 09

2551 WORKERS' RESEARCH UNIT
TRADE UNIONS IN NI
WRU BULLETIN 7
BELFAST
1979 2 10

2552 YOUNG,J R; MORONEY,M
THE EMPLOYER'S GUIDE TO EQUAL
OPPORTUNITIES FOR MEN AND WOMEN
EOC
BELFAST
1979 2 03

2553 AALEN, F H A
DEMOGRAPHY
IN GILLMOR, D A (ED)
DUBLIN
1968 2 07

2554 ADAMS, J
HOUSING AND POPULATION MOVEMENTS:
BALLYMENA
QUB MSC
BELFAST
1979 2 04

2555 AUNGER, E A
RELIGION AND CLASS: AN ANALYSIS OF 1971
CENSUS DATA
IN CORMACK, R; OSBORNE, R D (EDS)
BELFAST
1983 2 07

2556 AUNGER, E A
RELIGION AND OCCUPATIONAL CLASS IN NI
ECON AND SOC R 7(1)
1976 1 01

2557 BAMBER, J H; IRWIN, W G
CHARACTERISTICS OF SENIOR MEDICAL
STUDENTS AT BELFAST
MED EDUC 12
1978 2 01

2558 BIRRELL, W D ET AL
SOME ASPECTS OF LABOUR MOBILITY IN NI
NUU
COLERAINE
1975 2 10

2559 BLACK, W; JEFFERSON, C W
REGIONAL EMPLOYMENT PATTERNS IN NI
ESRI
DUBLIN
1974 2 10

2560 BLAND, R
STRUCTURAL AND EXCHANGE MOBILITY IN NI:
A RESEARCH NOTE
SCOTT J SOCIOL 4(3)
STIRLING
1980 2 01

2561 BOAL, F W
TERRITORIALITY AND CLASS: A STUDY OF TWO
RESIDENTIAL AREAS IN BELFAST
IR GEOG 4(3)
1971 2 01

2562 BOAL, F W; ROBINSON, A
CLOSE TOGETHER AND FAR APART: RELIGIOUS
AND CLASS DIVISIONS IN NI
COMM FORUM 2(3)
BELFAST
1972 1 02

2563 BOVENSKERK, F
ON THE CAUSES OF IRISH EMIGRATION
SOCIOLOGICA RURALIS 13(3/4)
1973 2 01

2564 BOYLE, J F
EDUCATIONAL ATTAINMENT, OCCUPATIONAL
ACHIEVEMENT AND RELIGION IN NI
ECON AND SOC R 8(2)
1977 2 01

2565 BOYLE, K
IRISH IMMIGRANT IN BRITAIN
NI LEG QUART 19(4)
1968 2 01

2566 BUCHANAN, G
DRIFT TO BELFAST: THE PROBLEM OF RURAL
DEPOPULATION
TOWN COUNTRY PLANN MARCH
1950 2 02

2567 BUSTEED, M A
GEOGRAPHY AND VOTING BEHAVIOUR
OUP
LONDON
1975 2 02

2568 COAKLEY, J
SPATIAL UNITS AND THE REPORTING OF IRISH
STATISTICAL DATA: REGIONAL DIVISIONS
ADMIN (DUB) 27(1)
1979 2 01

2569 COMPTON, P A
THE DEMOGRAPHIC BACKGROUND
IN WATT, D (ED)
LONDON
1981 2 07

2570 COMPTON, P A
THE DEMOGRAPHIC DIMENSION OF INTEGRATION
AND DIVISION IN NI
IN BOAL, F W; DOUGLAS, J N H (EDS)
LONDON
1982 1 07

2571 COMPTON, P A
THE DEMOGRAPHIC DIMENSION TO THE
ETHNIC-RELIGIOUS CONFLICT IN NI
SYMPOSIUM OF THE COMMISSION ON
POPULATION GEOGRAPHY OF THE
INTERNATIONAL GEOGRAPHICAL UNION
MINSK
1976 1 11

2572 COMPTON, P A
FERTILITY DIFFERENTIALS AND THEIR IMPACT
ON POPULATION DISTRIBUTION AND
COMPOSITION IN NI
ENVIRON AND PLANN 10(12)
1978 2 01

2573 COMPTON, P A
NI: A CENSUS ATLAS
GILL AND MACMILLAN
DUBLIN
1978 2 02

2574 COMPTON, P A
RELIGIOUS AFFILIATION AND DEMOGRAPHIC
VARIABILITY IN NI
TRANS INST BRIT GEOGR 1
1976 2 01

2575 COMPTON, P A
REVIEW OF POPULATION TRENDS IN NI,
1971-78
IN COMPTON, P A (ED)
BELFAST
1981 2 07

2576 CONNELL, K H
POPULATION OF IRELAND
GREENWOOD PRESS
CONNECTICUT
1975 2 02

2577 COOKE, J
DEVELOPMENT AND DISTRIBUTION OF
METHODISM IN IRELAND: A DEMOGRAPHIC
STUDY
QUB MA
BELFAST
1964 2 04

2578 COOPER, R; O'SHEA, T
NI: A NEW SOCIETY SURVEY OF THE SOCIAL
TRENDS
NEW SOCIETY
1973 2 10

2579 COUSENS,S
EMIGRATION AND DEMOGRAPHIC CHANGE IN
IRELAND 1951-1961
ECON HISTORY R 14
1962 2 01

2580 COVELLO,V T; ASHBY,J A
INEQUALITY IN A DIVIDED SOCIETY: AN
ANALYSIS OF DATA FROM NI
SOCIOL FOCUS 13(2)
AKRON
1980 2 01

2581 COVELLO,V T; BOLLEN,K A
STATUS CONSISTENCY IN COMPARATIVE
PERSPECTIVE: AN EXAMINATION OF
EDUCATIONAL, OCCUPATIONAL AND INCOME
DATA IN NINE SOCIETIES
SOC FORCES 58(2)
CHAPEL HILL
1979 2 01

2582 COWARD,J
THE FERTILITY OF ROMAN CATHOLICS IN
NORTHERN AND SOUTHERN IRELAND: TRENDS
AND COMPARISONS
IN COMPTON,P A (ED)
BELFAST
1981 2 07

2583 COWARD,J
IDEAL FAMILY SIZE IN NI
J BIOSOCIAL SCI 13(4)
1981 2 01

2584 COWARD,J
RECENT CHARACTERISTICS OF ROMAN CATHOLIC
FERTILITY IN NORTHERN AND SOUTHERN
IRELAND
POPUL STUD 34(1)
LONDON
1980 2 01

2585 DEPT OF EDUCATION (NI)
SCHOOLS AND DEMOGRAPHIC TRENDS: A
BACKCLOTH TO PLANNING
HMSO
BELFAST
1981 2 03

2586 DEPT OF MANPOWER SERVICES (NI)
DMS GAZETTE NUMBERS 1-3 1978-79
DEPT OF MANPOWER SERVICES (NI)
BELFAST
1979 2 03

2587 DOHERTY,P
SOCIAL GEOGRAPHY OF THE BELFAST URBAN
AREA
IR GEOG 11
1978 2 01

2588 ELWOOD,J H
DEMOGRAPHIC STUDY OF TORY ISLAND AND
RATHLIN ISLAND 1841-1964
ULSTER FOLKLIFE 17
1971 2 01

2589 ELWOOD,J H
POPULATION OF RATHLIN ISLAND
ULSTER MED J 37
1968 2 01

2590 FEA
INDUSTRIAL AND OCCUPATIONAL PROFILE OF
THE TWO SECTIONS OF THE POPULATION IN NI
FEA 1
BELFAST
1978 2 03

2591 FREEMAN,T W
AGRICULTURAL REGIONS AND RURAL
POPULATION OF IRELAND
B GEOGR SOC IRL 1(2)
1945 2 01

2592 FROGGATT,P
SHORT-TERM ABSENCE FROM INDUSTRY: A
STATISTICAL AND HISTORICAL SURVEY
QUB PHD
BELFAST
1967 2 04

2593 GEARY,R C; HUGHES,J G
MIGRATION BETWEEN NI AND THE REPUBLIC OF
IRELAND
IN WALSH,B M
DUBLIN
1970 2 07

2594 GLYNN,S
IRISH IMMIGRATION TO BRITAIN, 1911-1951:
PATTERNS AND POLICY
IR ECON AND SOC HIST R 8
DUNDALK
1981 2 01

2595 HARLAND,R W
SOCIOLOGICAL, ANATOMICAL AND
PHYSIOLOGICAL CHANGES IN FIRST-YEAR
STUDENTS ENTERING QUB OVER THIRTY YEARS,
1948-77
ULSTER MED J 49(1)
BELFAST
1980 2 01

2596 HARRISON,P
CULTURE AND MIGRATION: THE IRISH
ENGLISH
NEW SOCIETY 31(642)
LONDON
1973 2 01

2597 HARRISON,R L
POPULATION CHANGE AND HOUSING PROVISION
IN BELFAST
IN COMPTON,P A (ED)
BELFAST
1981 2 07

2598 JACKSON,J A
DETERMINANTS OF OCCUPATIONAL STATUS AND
MOBILITY IN NI AND IRELAND
SSRC FINAL REPORT
LONDON
1979 2 10

2599 JACKSON,J A
THE IRISH IN LONDON: A STUDY OF
MIGRATION AND SETTLEMENT IN THE LAST
HUNDRED YEARS
LONDON UNIV MA
LONDON
1958 2 04

2600 JACKSON,J A
IRISH OCCUPATIONAL INDEX: A NEW SCALE
FOR CODING IRISH OCCUPATIONAL DATA
ESRI
DUBLIN
1977 2 10

2601 JACKSON,J A
SURVEY OF SOCIAL AND OCCUPATIONAL
MOBILITY IN IRELAND: REPORT ON PROGRESS
IN SPENCER,A; O'DWYER,P A (EDS) PROC SAI
BELFAST
1976 2 11

2602 JACKSON,J A; MILLER,R L
SIZE AND DETERMINANTS OF THE MARGINAL
LABOUR FORCE IN NI AND IRISH REPUBLIC
COMMISSION OF THE EUROPEAN COMMUNITIES,
DIRECTORATE-GENERAL FOR SOCIAL AFFAIRS
BRUXELLES
1978 2 03

2603 JOHNSON,J H
POPULATION CHANGE IN IRELAND, 1961-1966
IR GEOG 5(5)
1968 2 01

2604 JOHNSON, J H
POPULATION CHANGES IN IRELAND, 1951-1961
GEOGR J 129
1963 2 01

2605 JONES, E
DISTRIBUTION AND SEGREGATION OF ROMAN
CATHOLICS IN BELFAST
SOCIOL R 4(2)
1956 2 01

2606 JONES, E
PROBLEMS OF PARTITION AND SEGREGATION IN
NI
J CONFLICT RESOL 4(1)
ANN ARBOR, MICHIGAN
1956 2 01

2607 KEANE, T
DEMOGRAPHIC TRENDS
IN HURLEY, M (ED)
DUBLIN
1970 2 07

2608 KENNEDY, R E
IRISH: EMIGRATION, MARRIAGE AND
FERTILITY
CALIFORNIA U P
1973 2 02

2609 KENNEDY, R E
MINORITY GROUP STATUS AND FERTILITY: THE
IRISH
AMER SOCIOL R 38(1)
NEW YORK
1973 2 01

2610 KENNEDY, S J
MIGRANTS IN BELFAST: A SOCIOLOLOGICAL
PERSPECTIVE
QUB MSSC
BELFAST
1973 2 04

2611 LESLIE, J
A STUDY OF RECENT MIGRATION TO COLERAINE
AND PORTSTEWART
NUU MSC
COLERAINE
1978 2 04

2612 MARTIN, D
MIGRATION WITHIN THE SIX COUNTIES OF NI
FROM 1911 TO 1937 WITH SPECIAL REFERENCE
TO... BELFAST
QUB MA
BELFAST
1977 2 04

2613 MCCULLAGH, M
THE POLITICAL AND SECTARIAN SIGNIFICANCE
OF CHANGES IN THE OCCUPATIONAL STRUCTURE
IN NI
SOC SCI TEACHER 12(2)
1983 2 01

2614 MCDERMOTT, R P; WEBB, D A
IRISH PROTESTANTISM TODAY AND TOMORROW:
A DEMOGRAPHIC STUDY
APCK
BELFAST
1945 2 02

2615 MCDONALD, J
MEDICAL RECORD LINKAGE: A STUDY OF
COMPUTER METHODS FOR LINKING NI BIRTH
AND DEATH REGISTRATION
QUB PHD
BELFAST
1979 2 04

2616 MILLER, R L
ATTITUDES TO WORK IN NI
FEA 2
BELFAST
1978 2 10

2617 MILLER, R L
A MODEL OF SOCIAL MOBILITY IN NI
IN COMPTON, P A (ED)
BELFAST
1981 2 07

2618 MILLER, R L
OCCUPATIONAL MOBILITY OF PROTESTANTS AND
ROMAN CATHOLICS IN NI: RESULTS AND
PROJECTIONS
FEA 4
BELFAST
1979 2 10

2619 MILLER, R L
SOCIAL MOBILITY IN NI
IN CORMACK, R; OSBORNE, R D (EDS)
BELFAST
1983 2 07

2620 NIHE
BELFAST HOUSEHOLD SURVEY 1978:
PRELIMINARY REPORT
NIHE
BELFAST
1979 2 03

2621 NIHE
NI HOUSEHOLD SURVEY 1975
NIHE
BELFAST
1976 2 10

2622 O'MUIRCHEARTHAIGH, C; WIGGINS, R D
SAMPLE DESIGN AND EVALUATION FOR AN
OCCUPATIONAL MOBILITY STUDY
ECON AND SOC R 8(2)
1977 2 01

2623 OFFICE OF POPULATION CENSUSES AND
SURVEYS
POPULATION PROJECTIONS 1977-2017:
ENGLAND AND WALES, WALES, SCOTLAND,
GREAT BRITAIN, NI, UNITED KINGDOM
HMSO
LONDON
1979 2 03

2624 PARK, A T
ANALYSIS OF HUMAN FERTILITY IN NI
JSSISI 21(1)
1963 2 01

2625 PATTON, J
DIRECTIONAL BIAS IN INTRA-URBAN
MIGRATION IN THE PUBLIC HOUSING SECTOR
OF THE BELFAST URBAN AREA
ULSTER POLY PHD
BELFAST
1981 2 04

2626 PINTER, F
POLARIZATION AND POPULATION MOVEMENT IN
BELFAST
LONDON UNIV
LONDON
1971 1 08

2627 PROUDFOOT, V B
CHANGES IN POPULATION AND FARM HOLDINGS
IN NI
IR GEOG 5(4)
1967 2 01

2628 ROBINSON, A
THE GEOGRAPHY OF HUMAN FERTILITY IN NI
(1961)
IR GEOG 5(4)
1965 2 01

2629 SAMS, K I
THE CREATION OF THE IRISH CONGRESS OF
TRADE UNIONS
J INDUSTR RELATIONS 8(1)
1966 2 01

2630 SCOPE
SCOPE PROFILE: FERMANAGH
SCOPE 43
BELFAST
1981 2 01

2631 SHEEHAN,J; HUTCHINSON,R W
DEMOGRAPHIC AND LABOUR FORCE STRUCTURE
IN THE REPUBLIC OF IRELAND AND NI
COOPERATION NORTH
BELFAST AND DUBLIN
1980 2 02

2632 SIMPSON,J V
POPULATION, EMPLOYMENT AND URBANISATION
TRENDS IN NI
JSSISI 23(3)
1976 2 01

2633 SINGLETON,D
PLANNING IMPLICATIONS OF POPULATION
TRENDS IN NI
IN COMPTON,P A (ED)
BELFAST
1981 2 07

2634 SLATTERY,D G; JONES,R M
SOME ASPECTS OF (NET) EMIGRATION FROM NI
JSSISI 24(1)
DUBLIN
1979 2 01

2635 SPENCER,A
THE RELATIVE FERTILITY OF THE TWO
RELIGIOUS-ETHNIC COMMUNITIES IN NI:
1947-1977
IN SPENCER,A (ED) PROC SAI
BELFAST
1979 2 07

2636 THOMPSON,H
THE SOCIAL ORGANISATION OF POPULATIONS
IN ULSTER: DRAPERSTOWN, CO DERRY
NUU MPHIL
COLERAINE
1971 2 04

2637 VAUGHAN,T D
A STUDY OF POPULATION IN NI WITH SPECIAL
REFERENCE TO CO. DOWN
QUB MA
BELFAST
1960 2 04

2638 VAUGHAN,W; FITZPATRICK,A
IRISH HISTORICAL STATISTICS: POPULATION
1821-1971
ROYAL IRISH ACADEMY
DUBLIN
1978 2 10

2639 WALSH,B
COMMENT ON CHAPTER BY COMPTON
IN WATT,D (ED)
LONDON
1981 2 07

2640 WALSH,B
IRELAND'S POPULATION PROSPECTS
SOC STUD 3(3)
1974 2 01

2641 WALSH,B
SOME IRISH POPULATION QUESTIONS
RECONSIDERED
ESRI
DUBLIN
1968 2 10

2642 WATERMAN,S
SOME COMMENTS ON STANDARD DISTANCE: A
NEW APPLICATION TO IRISH POPULATION
STATISTICS
IR GEOG 6(1)
1969 2 07

2643 WRIGHT,P; DAVIES,S
FERTILITY BEHAVIOUR OF A MINORITY
POPULATION - CATHOLICS IN NI
EKISTICS 37(221)
ATHENS
1974 2 01

2644 AALEN, F H A
RURAL AND URBAN SETTLEMENTS
IN GILLMOR, D A (ED)
DUBLIN
1968 2 07

2645 AITKEN, J M
NEW AND EXPANDING TOWNS IN NI
TOWN COUNTRY PLANN 34(1)
LONDON
1966 2 01

2646 AITKEN, J M
REGIONAL PLANNING IN NI
TOWN AND COUNTRY PLANNING SUMMER SCHOOL
BELFAST
1967 2 11

2647 ALCORN, D
WHO PLANS BELFAST?
SCOPE 52
BELFAST
1982 1 01

2648 ALLEN, L
NEW TOWNS AND THE TROUBLES: SOME
POLITICAL OBSERVATIONS ON NI
TOWN COUNTRY PLANN 50(11/12)
LONDON
1983 1 01

2649 ANTRIM AND BALLYMENA DEVELOPMENT
COMMISSION
ANTRIM: PROPOSALS FOR NEW TOWN CENTRE
ANTRIM AND BALLYMENA DEVELOPMENT
COMMISSION
BALLYMENA
1970 2 03

2650 ANTRIM STEERING COMMITTEE
ANTRIM NEW TOWN
HMSO
BELFAST
1965 2 03

2651 ARMSTRONG, W J
AN INTRODUCTION: THE ECONOMIC
PERSPECTIVE
IN CRUICKSHANK, J G; WILCOCK, D N (EDS)
BELFAST/COLERAINE
1982 2 07

2652 BALLYMENA STEERING COMMITTEE
BALLYMENA AREA PLAN
HMSO
1966 2 03

2653 BANNERMAN, A
NI'S NEW CITY
TOWN COUNTRY PLANN 35(1)
1967 2 01

2654 BARDON, J
BELFAST: AN ILLUSTRATED HISTORY
BLACKSTAFF
BELFAST
1982 2 02

2655 BARRINGTON, T J
ENVIRONMENT AND THE QUALITY OF LIFE
ADMIN (DUB) 21(4)
DUBLIN
1973 2 01

2656 BDP
BELFAST CENTRAL AREA: A REPORT TO
BELFAST CORPORATION ON PLANNING POLICY
IN THE CITY CENTRE
BDP
BELFAST
1969 2 10

2657 BDP
BELFAST DEVELOPMENT PLAN: REPORT TO THE
CITY CORPORATION OF BELFAST ON A
BUILDING PRESERVATION POLICY
BDP
BELFAST
1966 2 10

2658 BDP
BELFAST URBAN AREA PLAN
BDP
LONDON
1969 2 02

2659 BDP
HIGH BUILDINGS POLICY
BDP
BELFAST
1968 2 10

2660 BDP
PLANNING ASPECTS OF THE BELFAST URBAN
MOTORWAY
BDP
BELFAST
1968 2 10

2661 BDP
REDEVELOPMENT AND THE SMALL BUSINESS:
CITY OF BELFAST
BDP
BELFAST
1968 2 10

2662 BDP
REDEVELOPMENT AREAS PROGRAMME
BDP
BELFAST
1968 2 02

2663 BDP
REDEVELOPMENT OF THE SHANKILL
BDP
BELFAST
1967 2 10

2664 BECKETT, J C; DARWIN, K
BELFAST 1613-1963
ULSTER MUSEUM
BELFAST
1963 2 02

2665 BELFAST URBAN STUDIES GROUP
BELFAST URBAN STUDIES GROUP REPORT ON
THE BELFAST URBAN MOTORWAY
HOLY SMOKE PRESS
BELFAST
1973 2 10

2666 BETTS, N L
WATER SUPPLY IN NI
IR GEOG 2
DUBLIN
1978 2 01

2667 BETTS, N L; PRIOR, D B
FLOODING IN BELFAST
IR GEOG 7
DUBLIN
1974 2 01

2668 BLACK, W; SIMPSON, J V
GROWTH CENTRES IN IRELAND
IR BANKING R
1968 2 01

2669 BLAIR, T L
BELFAST: DIVIDED CITY
IN BLAIR, T L
1973 1 07

2670 BLAKE, P
NI
TOWN COUNTRY PLANN 45(2)
1977 2 01

2671 BLOMQUIST, P
THE LEISURE CENTRE BOOM
SCOPE 22
BELFAST
1979 2 01

2672 BOAL, F W
CONTEMPORARY BELFAST AND ITS FUTURE
DEVELOPMENT
IN BECKETT, J C; GLASSCOCK, R E (EDS)
LONDON
1967 2 07

2673 BOAL, F W
LONDONDERRY AREA REPORT 6, SHOPPING
REPORT
LONDONDERRY AREA STEERING COMM
1967 2 10

2674 BOAL, F W
NI
TOWN COUNTRY PLANN 41(1)
LONDON
1973 2 01

2675 BOAL, F W
NI: BELFAST
TOWN COUNTRY PLANN 39(9)
LONDON
1971 2 01

2676 BOAL, F W
PLANNING IN A TIGHT SITUATION: BELFAST
TOWN COUNTRY PLANN 39(9)
1971 1 01

2677 BOAL, F W
SOCIAL SPACE IN THE BELFAST URBAN AREA
IN JONES, E (ED)
1975 2 07

2678 BOAL, F W
SOCIAL SPACE IN THE BELFAST URBAN AREA
IN PEACH, C (ED)
1975 2 07

2679 BOAL, F W
SOCIAL SPACE IN THE BELFAST URBAN AREA
IN STEPHENS, N; GLASSCOCK, R E (EDS)
BELFAST
1970 2 07

2680 BOAL, F W
UK NEW TOWNS: NI
TOWN COUNTRY PLANN 41(1)
1973 2 01

2681 BOAL, F W
URBAN GROWTH AND LAND VALUE PATTERNS
PROFESSIONAL GEOGRAPHER 22(2)
1970 2 01

2682 BOAL, F W; MURRAY, R; POOLE, M A
PSYCHOLOGY AND THE THREATENING
ENVIRONMENT
ARCHITECTURAL PSYCHOL NEWSLETTER 5(4)
1975 1 01

2683 BOOTH, A G
BELFAST REDEVELOPMENT AREAS PROGRAMME:
STAGE 2
BELFAST CORPORATION CITY PLANNING
DEPARTMENT
BELFAST
1971 2 10

2684 BOOTHMAN, G
THE IMPACT OF URBAN RENEWAL ON
NEIGHBOURHOODS: THE YOUTH IN SHANKILL,
BELFAST
EKISTICS 44
ATHENS
1977 2 01

2685 BOYLE, J W
BELFAST AND THE ORIGINS OF NI
IN BECKETT, J C; GLASSCOCK, R E (EDS)
LONDON
1967 2 07

2686 BRANIFF, P
BELFAST: THE NEED FOR DISTRICT PLANS
SCOPE 32
BELFAST
1980 2 01

2687 BRETT, C E B
CONSERVATION AMID DESTRUCTION
COUNTRY LIFE OCT 10
1974 1 01

2688 BRETT, C E B
ULSTER'S ARCHITECTURAL HERITAGE
THE ARCHITECT 4(6)
1974 2 01

2689 BUCHANAN, R H
CHANGES IN RURAL SETTLEMENT IN NI
DEPT GEOG QUB
BELFAST
1969 2 08

2690 BUCHANAN, R H
FIVE YEAR PLAN FOR ULSTER
GEOGR MAG 42
1970 2 01

2691 BUCHANAN, R H
LANDSCAPE
IN CRUICKSHANK, J G; WILCOCK, D N (EDS)
BELFAST/COLERAINE
1982 2 07

2692 BUCHANAN, R H
RURAL SETTLEMENT IN IRELAND
IN STEPHENS, N; GLASSCOCK, R E (EDS)
1970 2 01

2693 CAMBLIN, G
ADMINISTRATIVE STRUCTURES FOR
DEVELOPMENT IN NI
IRISH REGIONAL STUD ASSOC CONFERENCE
GALWAY
1969 2 11

2694 CAMBLIN, G
NEW TOWNS AND NATIONAL PARKS IN NI
CHARTERED SURVEYOR 98
1965 2 01

2695 CAMBLIN, G
REGIONAL PLANNING IN NI
CHARTERED SURVEYOR 96(8)
1964 2 01

2696 CAMBLIN, G
STRUCTURES FOR DEVELOPMENT IN NI
ADMIN(DUB) 24(3)
1976 2 01

2697 CAMBLIN, G
THE TOWN IN ULSTER
MULLAN
BELFAST
1951 2 02

2698 CARLETON, S T
GROWTH OF SOUTH BELFAST
QUB MA
BELFAST
1967 2 04

2699 CASHELL, R
A STUDY OF ROAD NOISE IN URBAN
CONDITIONS
QUB MSC
BELFAST
1979 2 04

2700 CLARKE, P
RELATIONSHIP BETWEEN PHYSICAL AND
REGIONAL ECONOMIC PLANNING IN THEORY AND
PRACTICE WITH SPECIAL REFERENCE TO NI
LONDON UNIV COLLEGE MPHIL
LONDON
1971 2 04

2701 CLEARY, P G
SPATIAL EXPANSION AND URBAN ECOLOGY IN
BELFAST WITH SPECIAL REFERENCE TO THE
ROLE OF TRANSPORTATION
QUB PHD
BELFAST
1980 2 04

2702 CLERK, D
URBAN FIELDS OF NI: A STUDY IN
TOWN-COUNTRY RELATIONS
QUB PHD
BELFAST
1965 2 04

2703 CLERK, D
URBAN SETTLEMENTS OF COUNTY ANTRIM
QUB MA
BELFAST
1949 2 04

2704 COMMUNITY GROUP'S ACTION COMMITTEE ON
TRANSPORT IN BELFAST
ROADS TO DESTRUCTION
BELFAST
1979 2 10

2705 COMPTON, P A
CONFLICT AND ITS IMPACT ON THE URBAN
ENVIRONMENT OF NI
IN ENYEDI, G; MESZAROS, J (EDS)
BUDAPEST
1980 1 07

2706 COPCUTT, G
NEW CITY SURVEY
MINISTRY OF HEALTH AND LOCAL GOVERNMENT
(NI)
LURGAN
1963 2 03

2707 COWAN, R
BELFAST'S HIDDEN PLANNERS
TOWN COUNTRY PLANN 51(6)
LONDON
1982 1 01

2708 CRAIGAVON DEVELOPMENT COMMISSION
CRAIGAVON NEW CITY: REPORT ON SECTOR ONE
CRAIGAVON DEVELOPMENT COMMISSION
CRAIGAVON
1970 2 10

2709 CRAIGAVON DEVELOPMENT COMMISSION
CRAIGAVON NEW CITY: REPORT ON SECTOR TWO
CRAIGAVON DEVELOPMENT COMMISSION
CRAIGAVON
1970 2 10

2710 CRAIGAVON DEVELOPMENT COMMISSION
CRAIGAVON NEW CITY: STRATEGIC PLAN FOR
CENTRAL AREA
CRAIGAVON DEVELOPMENT COMMISSION
CRAIGAVON
1971 2 10

2711 CRILLY, E
NEWTOWNABBEY, RATHCOOLE AND BELFAST: A
STUDY IN URBAN RELATIONSHIPS
DEPT GEOGRAPHY QUB
BELFAST
1959 2 04

2712 CRONE, R
BELFAST: RISE OF A CITY
SCHOOLS CURRICULUM PROJECT
BELFAST
1976 2 10

2713 CURL, J T
CONSERVATION IN ACTION: PRESERVATION IN
A TROUBLED LAND
COUNTRY LIFE DEC 18
1975 2 01

2714 CUTHBERT, N; BLACK, W
TRANSPORT POLICY IN NI
IR BANKING R SEP
1964 2 01

2715 DEPT OF HOUSING, LOCAL GOVERNMENT AND
PLANNING (NI)
LONDONDERRY AREA PLAN: FURTHER STATEMENT
DEPT OF HOUSING, LOCAL GOVERNMENT AND
PLANNING (NI)
BELFAST
1975 2 03

2716 DEPT OF THE ENVIRONMENT (NI)
BELFAST URBAN AREA: PLANNING STATEMENT
AND PROGRESS REPORT
HMSO
BELFAST
1981 2 03

2717 DEPT OF THE ENVIRONMENT (NI)
EAST TYRONE AREA PLAN
HMSO
BELFAST
1978 2 03

2718 DEPT OF THE ENVIRONMENT (NI)
FERMANAGH AREA PLAN: A PHYSICAL
DEVELOPMENTAL PLAN FOR THE DISTRICT
HMSO
BELFAST
1978 2 03

2719 DEPT OF THE ENVIRONMENT (NI)
NI REGIONAL PHYSICAL DEVELOPMENT
STRATEGY, 1975-95
HMSO
BELFAST
1977 2 03

2720 DEPT OF THE ENVIRONMENT (NI)
POLEGLASS DEVELOPMENT SCHEME
HMSO
BELFAST
1976 2 03

2721 DEPT OF THE ENVIRONMENT (NI)
REVIEW OF RURAL PLANNING POLICY
HMSO
BELFAST
1978 2 03

2722 DEPT OF THE ENVIRONMENT (NI)
RIVER LAGAN: REPORT OF A WORKING PARTY
HMSO
BELFAST
1978 2 03

2723 DORAN, I G ET AL
CRAIGAVON NEW CITY: FIRST REPORT
CRAIGAVON DEVELOPMENT COMMISSION
CRAIGAVON
1967 2 10

2724 EVANS, E
BELFAST: THE SITE AND THE CITY
ULSTER J ARCHAEOLOGY 7
1945 2 01

2725 EVANS, E
THE GEOGRAPHICAL SETTING
IN BECKETT, J C; GLASSCOCK, R E (EDS)
BELFAST
1967 2 07

2726 EVANS, E; JONES, E
GROWTH OF BELFAST
TOWN PLANN R 26(2)
1955 2 01

2727 FORBES, J
TOWNS AND PLANNING IN IRELAND
IN STEPHENS, N; GLASSCOCK, R E (EDS)
BELFAST
1970 2 07

2728 FREEMAN, T W
URBAN HINTERLANDS IN IRELAND
GEOGR J 116
1950 2 01

2729 GLOVER, B
URBAN CHANGE AND COMMUNITY ACTION: A
CASE STUDY IN THE CLIFTON/OLDPARK AREA
ULSTER POLY MPHIL
BELFAST
1982 2 04

2730 GOSS, A
THE BELFAST STUDY: ATTITUDES TO
TRANSPORT
TRAFFIC ENGINEERING AND CONTROL 10(9)
1969 2 01

2731 GOSS, A
LONDONDERRY AREA PLAN
OFFICIAL ARCHITECTURE AND PLANNING 32
1969 2 01

2732 GOSS, A; MACMURRAY, T E
BELFAST'S TRANSPORTATION PLANS
TRAFFIC ENGINEERING AND CONTROL DEC
1969 2 01

2733 GREEN, F H W
SOME FEATURES OF THE RELATIONSHIP
BETWEEN TOWN AND COUNTRY IN NI
GEOG 34
1949 2 01

2734 GREER, P
THE TRANSPORT PROBLEM IN NI, 1921-48
NUU MA
COLERAINE
1977 2 04

2735 GUNN, P
IRISH PLANNING AND AN INTERSTATE BORDER
AREA
AN FORAS FORBARTHA
DUBLIN
1973 2 10

2736 HADDEN, T
IMPORTED BRITISH PLANNING
BUILT ENVIRONMENT 3(2)
1974 2 01

2737 HARLOE, M; HORROCKS, M
RESPONSIBILITY WITHOUT POWER: THE CASE
OF SOCIAL DEVELOPMENT
SOCIOLOGICAL SYMPOSIUM 13
BOWLING GREEN
1975 2 01

2738 HENDRY, J
CONSERVATION IN NI
TOWN PLANN R 48
1977 2 01

2739 HENDRY, J
THE ROLE OF CONSERVATION IN A HOUSING
PROGRAMME FOR NI
ULSTER ARCHITECTURAL HERITAGE SOCIETY
BELFAST
1971 2 10

2740 HENDRY, J
VILLAGE STRUCTURE IN THE CONSERVATION
PROCESS
HOUSING PLANN R 29(1)
1973 2 01

2741 HETHERINGTON, P
TUMBLEDOWN DERRY
COMM FORUM 4(2)
BELFAST
1972 1 01

2742 HODSON, R
LONDONDERRY COMMISSION AS A BLUE-PRINT
FOR THE FUTURE
FINANCIAL TIMES SURVEY ON NI 22 JAN
LONDON
1973 2 10

2743 HORNER, A A
PLANNING THE IRISH TRANSPORT NETWORK:
PARALLELS IN 19TH AND 20TH CENTURY
PROPOSALS
IR GEOG 10
1977 2 01

2744 HUTCHINSON, W R
TYRONE PRECINCT: A HISTORY OF THE
PLANTATION SETTLEMENT OF DUNGANNON AND
MOUNTJOY TO MODERN TIMES
ERSKINE MAYNE
BELFAST
1951 2 02

2745 IRISH COUNCIL OF CHURCHES AND ROMAN
CATHOLIC JOINT GROUP ON SOCIAL PROBLEMS
ENVIRONMENTAL PROBLEMS IN IRELAND
IRISH COUNCIL OF CHURCHES
BELFAST
1980 2 10

2746 JESS, P M H
A FUNCTIONAL APPROACH TO THE
GEOGRAPHICAL STUDY OF RURAL SETTLEMENT
WITH SPECIFIC REFERENCE TO SOUTHERN ARDS
PENINSULA, CO. DOWN
QUB PHD
BELFAST
1972 2 04

2747 JOHNSON, J H
THE GEOGRAPHY OF A BELFAST SUBURB
IR GEOG 3(3)
1956 2 01

2748 JOHSE, R B
EEN NEW TOWN IN NOORD IERLAND
TS KON NED ARDGENT 82(4)
1965 2 01

2749 JOINT WORKING PARTY ON THE RIVER LAGAN
THE RIVER LAGAN: STRANMILLIS WEIR TO THE
SEA: A REPORT
JOINT WORKING PARTY ON THE RIVER LAGAN
BELFAST
1979 2 03

2750 JONES, E
DELIMITATION OF SOME URBAN LANDSCAPE
FEATURES IN BELFAST
SCOTT GEOGR MAG 74(3)
1958 2 01

2751 JONES, E
THE SOCIAL GEOGRAPHY OF BELFAST
JSSISI 20
DUBLIN
1954 2 01

2752 JONES, E
SOCIAL GEOGRAPHY OF BELFAST
OUP
LONDON
1960 2 02

2753 JONES, E; SYMONS, L
URBAN AND INDUSTRIAL LAND USE
IN SYMONS, L (ED)
1967 2 07

2754 LAVERY REPORT
BELFAST URBAN AREA PLAN: REVIEW OF
TRANSPORTATION STRATEGY: REPORT ON
PUBLIC INQUIRY
DEPT OF THE ENVIRONMENT (NI)
BELFAST
1978 2 03

2755 LONDONDERRY DEVELOPMENT COMMISSION
AREA PLAN LONDONDERRY: 1972 REVIEW
LONDONDERRY DEVELOPMENT COMMISSION
LONDONDERRY
1972 2 10

2756 MACKENZIE,R H
THE NEW PLANNING LAW IN NI: PLANNING
(NI) ORDER 1972
J PLANN ENVIRONMENTAL LAW MAY
1974 2 01

2757 MARSHALL,A T; TAYLOR,W E
LONDONDERRY'S PLANNING AND POST-WAR
HOUSING
TOWN COUNTRY PLANN 16
LONDON
1948 2 01

2758 MATTHEW REPORT
BELFAST: REGIONAL SURVEY AND PLAN
HMSO
BELFAST
1964 2 03

2759 MATTHEW,R ET AL
COLERAINE AREA PLAN
HMSO CMD 458
BELFAST
1968 2 03

2760 MCCONNELL,R S
PLANNING FOR URBAN EXPANSION
CHARTERED SURVEYOR 100
1967 2 01

2761 MCCOURT,D
THE DYNAMIC QUALITY OF IRISH RURAL
SETTLEMENT
IN BUCHANAN,R H; JONES,E; MCCOURT,D
(EDS)
1971 2 07

2762 MCKINSTRY,R
REGIONAL ROUND-UP: NI
TOWN PLANN R 48
1977 2 01

2763 MCKINSTRY,R
RURAL PLANNING IN MID-DOWN
ARCHITECTS' J 158
1973 2 01

2764 MCNALLY,K
THE NARROW STREETS
BLACKSTAFF
BELFAST
1972 2 02

2765 MEADOWS,R
ANTRIM NEW TOWN
ARCHITECT AND BUILDING NEWS 229
1966 2 01

2766 MERCER,F
SANDY ROW - A STUDY BEFORE REDEVELOPMENT
DEPT SOC STUD QUB
BELFAST
1971 2 04

2767 MINISTRY OF DEVELOPMENT (NI)
ANTRIM NEW TOWN: AN OUTLINE PLAN
HMSO
BELFAST
1965 2 03

2768 MINISTRY OF DEVELOPMENT (NI)
ARMAGH AREA PLAN
HMSO
BELFAST
1973 2 03

2769 MINISTRY OF DEVELOPMENT (NI)
BALLYMENA AREA PLAN
HMSO
BELFAST
1966 2 03

2770 MINISTRY OF DEVELOPMENT (NI)
BELFAST URBAN AREA PLAN: STATEMENT BY
THE MINISTRY
HMSO
BELFAST
1973 2 03

2771 MINISTRY OF DEVELOPMENT (NI)
COLERAINE, PORTRUSH, PORTSTEWART: AREA
PLAN
HMSO
BELFAST
1968 2 03

2772 MINISTRY OF DEVELOPMENT (NI)
LIMAVADY AREA PLAN
HMSO
BELFAST
1973 2 03

2773 MINISTRY OF DEVELOPMENT (NI)
MOURNE
HMSO
BELFAST
      2 03

2774 MINISTRY OF DEVELOPMENT (NI)
NEWRY AREA PLAN
HMSO
BELFAST
1973 2 03

2775 MINISTRY OF DEVELOPMENT (NI)
NORTH DERRY AMENITY AND CONSERVATION
PLAN
HMSO
BELFAST
1969 2 03

2776 MINISTRY OF DEVELOPMENT (NI)
NORTH DOWN AREA PLAN
HMSO
BELFAST
1969 2 03

2777 MINISTRY OF DEVELOPMENT (NI)
TOWN AND COUNTRY PLANNING: PROPOSALS FOR
LEGISLATION
HMSO
BELFAST
1972 2 03

2778 MINISTRY OF DEVELOPMENT (NI)
WEST TYRONE AREA PLAN
HMSO
BELFAST
1972 2 03

2779 MINISTRY OF DEVELOPMENT (NI)
WEST TYRONE PRELIMINARY STUDY
HMSO
BELFAST
1969 2 03

2780 MINISTRY OF HEALTH AND LOCAL GOVERNMENT
(NI)
THE ADMINISTRATION OF TOWN AND COUNTRY
PLANNING IN NI
HMSO CMD 465
BELFAST
1964 2 03

2781 MINISTRY OF HEALTH AND LOCAL GOVERNMENT
(NI)
FIRST REPORT ON THE PROPOSED NEW CITY,
CO ARMAGH
HMSO
BELFAST
1964 2 03

2782 MINISTRY OF HEALTH AND LOCAL GOVERNMENT
(NI)
ROAD COMMUNICATIONS IN NI
HMSO CMD 241
BELFAST
1946 2 03

2783 MINISTRY OF HOME AFFAIRS (NI)
REPORT OF THE COMMITTEE ON THE NATURE OF
CONSERVATION IN NI
HMSO CMD 448
BELFAST
1962 2 03

2784 MINISTRY OF HOUSING AND LOCAL GOVERNMENT
     (NI)
     FIRST REPORT ON THE PROPOSED NEW CITY,
     COUNTY ARMAGH
     HMSO
     BELFAST
     1964 2 03

2785 MITCHELL, W F
     REPORT OF THE LONDONDERRY AREA PLAN
     PUBLIC INQUIRY
     HMSO
     BELFAST
     1975 2 03

2786 MITCHELL, W F
     REPORT OF THE NEWRY AREA PLAN PUBLIC
     INQUIRY
     HMSO
     BELFAST
     1978 2 03

2787 MORTON, R
     SOCIAL EFFECTS OF INDUSTRIAL CHANGE: NI
     ADMIN (DUB) 12(2)
     DUBLIN
     1964 2 01

2788 MOUGHTIN, C
     MARKETS AREA REDEVELOPMENT
     BUILT ENVIRONMENT 3(2)
     LONDON
     1974 2 01

2789 MUNCE, J
     LONDONDERRY AREA PLAN
     MUNCE PARTNERSHIP
     DERRY
     1974 2 10

2790 MURIE, A S
     PLANNING IN NI: A SURVEY
     TOWN PLANN R 44(4)
     1973 2 01

2791 NEILL, D G
     HOUSING AND THE SOCIAL ASPECTS OF TOWN
     AND COUNTRY PLANNING IN NI
     ADMIN (DUB) 2(3)
     DUBLIN
     1954 2 01

2792 NESBITT, N
     THE CHANGING FACE OF BELFAST
     ULSTER MUSEUM
     BELFAST
     1968 2 10

2793 NEWBOULD, P J
     OUTDOOR RECREATION, TOURISM AND
     CONSERVATION
     IN FORSYTH, J; BOYD, D (EDS)
     BELFAST
     1970 2 07

2794 NEWMAN, C F S
     SHORT HISTORY OF PLANNING IN NI
     J TOWN PLANN INST 52(2)
     1965 2 01

2795 NI AMENITY COUNCIL
     REPORT ON A CONFERENCE ON AMENITY AND
     CONSERVATION
     NI AMENITY COUNCIL
     BELFAST
     1972 2 10

2796 NI AMENITY COUNCIL
     REPORT ON THE THIRD CONFERENCE ON
     AMENITY AND CONSERVATION
     NI AMENITY COUNCIL
     BELFAST
     1974 2 10

2797 NI ASSEMBLY
     REPORT ON A CONSULTATION PAPER ISSUED BY
     THE DEPARTMENT OF THE ENVIRONMENT FOR
     NI, 'AREAS OF SPECIAL CONTROL AND
     OUTSTANDING NATURAL BEAUTY
     HMSO NIA 64
     BELFAST
     1983 2 03

2798 NI ASSEMBLY
     REPORT ON PROPOSAL FOR A DRAFT ACCESS TO
     THE COUNTRYSIDE (NI) ORDER
     HMSO NIA 40
     BELFAST
     1983 2 03

2799 NI GOVERNMENT
     PUBLIC TRANSPORT IN NI
     HMSO CMD 232
     BELFAST
     1946 2 03

2800 NI GOVERNMENT
     REPORT OF THE TRANSPORT TRIBUNAL
     HMSO CMD 310
     BELFAST
     1952 2 03

2801 NI PLANNING ADVISORY BOARD
     ULSTER COUNTRYSIDE
     NI PLANNING ADVISORY BOARD
     BELFAST
     1945 2 03

2802 NICSS
     THE OVERGROWTH OF BELFAST AND THE
     NEGLECT OF THE COUNTY TOWNS
     NICSS
     BELFAST
     1949 2 10

2803 NIEC
     PUBLIC EXPENDITURE PRIORITIES: ROADS
     NIEC
     BELFAST
     1981 2 03

2804 NORTH DOWN AREA PLAN STEERING COMMITTEE
     NORTH DOWN AREA PLAN
     HMSO
     BELFAST
     1972 2 03

2805 O'DOWD, L
     TOWARDS A STRUCTURAL ANALYSIS OF IRISH
     URBANIZATION
     IN SPENCER, A; TOVEY, H (EDS) PROC SAI
     BELFAST
     1978 2 01

2806 O'DOWD, L; TOMLINSON, M
     URBAN POLITICS IN BELFAST: TWO CASE
     STUDIES
     INT J URB REG RES 4(1)
     1980 2 01

2807 PARSON, D
     REGIONAL PLANNING, HOUSING POLICY, AND
     COMMUNITY ACTION IN NI
     UCLA MA
     LOS ANGELES
     1979 2 04

2808 PARSON, D
     URBAN RENEWAL AND HOUSING ACTION AREAS
     IN BELFAST: LEGITIMATION AND THE
     INCORPORATION OF PROTEST
     INT J URB REG RES 5
     LONDON
     1981 2 01

2809 PARSON, H J
     BANBRIDGE AREA PLAN: A DEVELOPMENTAL
     STRATEGY
     DOWN COUNTY COUNCIL
     DOWNPATRICK
     1970 2 10

2810 PD
A TRANSPORT POLICY RELATED TO THE NEEDS
OF THE PEOPLE
PD
BELFAST
1970 2 09

2811 PEARCE,D
NI
BUILT ENVIRONMENT 3(2)
1974 1 01

2812 PRESCOTT,T A N
ROAD SERVICES FOR A COUNTY
ADMIN (DUB) 10(2)
DUBLIN
1962 2 01

2813 PRIOR,D B; BETTS,N L
BELFAST FIGHTS FOR WATER
GEOGR MAG 45(12)
1973 2 01

2814 REES,M
INITIATIVES IN HOUSING AND PLANNING
BUILT ENVIRONMENT FEB
1974 2 01

2815 REID,J
COMMUNITY CONFLICT IN NI: ANALYSIS OF A
NEW TOWN PLAN
EKISTICS 213
ATHENS
1973 2 01

2816 RILEY,D W
THE BELFAST REGION: PROSPECTS FOR
PLANNED DEVELOPMENT IN NI
TOWN COUNTRY PLANN 33(1)
1965 2 01

2817 ROBINSON,A
LONDONDERRY, NI: A BORDER STUDY
SCOTT GEOGR MAG 86
1970 2 01

2818 ROBINSON,A
A SOCIAL GEOGRAPHY OF THE CITY OF
LONDONDERRY
QUB MA
BELFAST
1967 2 04

2819 RODEN STREET RESIDENTS ASSOCIATION
RODEN STREET: DEATH OF A COMMUNITY
GREATER WEST BELFAST COMMUNITY
ASSOCIATION
BELFAST
1973 2 02

2820 ROGERS,R S
PARKS POLICY IN NI
GEOGR MAG 46(8)
1974 2 01

2821 ROGERSON,F; O'HUIGINN,P
PLANNING IN IRELAND
AN FORAS FORBARTHA
DUBLIN
1967 2 02

2822 ROONEY,W
TWO COUNTY DOWN TOWNS, NEWCASTLE AND
CASTLEWELLAN: A COMPARATIVE STUDY IN
SOCIAL GEOGRAPHY
QUB MA
BELFAST
1965 2 04

2823 ROWAN,A
ULSTER'S ARCHITECTURAL IDENTITY
COUNTRY LIFE MAY 27
1971 2 01

2824 ROYAL SOCIETY OF ULSTER ARCHITECTS
PLANNING AND RECONSTRUCTION IN NI
ROYAL SOCIETY OF ULSTER ARCHITECTS
BELFAST
1945 2 10

2825 ROYAL SOCIETY OF ULSTER ARCHITECTS
TRANSPORTATION: THE NEED FOR
COORDINATION
ROYAL SOCIETY OF ULSTER ARCHITECTS
BELFAST
1970 2 08

2826 RUTHERFORD,B M
BELFAST URBAN AREA PLAN: REPORT OF A
PUBLIC INQUIRY TO THE MINISTRY OF
DEVELOPMENT
HMSO
BELFAST
1973 2 03

2827 SANDY ROW DEVELOPMENT ASSOCIATION
SANDY ROW AT THE PUBLIC ENQUIRY
BELFAST
1972 2 10

2828 SCOPE
ANATOMY OF AN INQUIRY
SCOPE 11
BELFAST
1977 2 01

2829 SCOPE
SCOPE PROFILE: FERMANAGH
SCOPE 43
BELFAST
1981 2 01

2830 SCOPE
WESTLINK: DOE NOISE FIGURES CHALLENGED
SCOPE 37
BELFAST
1980 2 01

2831 SINGLETON,D
PLANNING AND SECTARIANISM IN NI
PLANNER 63(1)
1977 1 01

2832 SINGLETON,D
PLANNING IMPLICATIONS OF POPULATION
TRENDS IN NI
IN COMPTON,P A (ED)
BELFAST
1981 2 07

2833 SINGLETON,D
POLEGLASS: A MICROCOSM OF PLANNING IN A
DIVIDED COMMUNITY
PLANNER 65(3)
1979 1 01

2834 SMITH-LORD,A ET AL
BALLYMENA: CONSULTANTS' PROPOSALS FOR
THE NEW TOWN CENTRE
ANTRIM AND BALLYMENA DEVELOPMENT
COMMISSION
BALLYMENA
1970 2 03

2835 SMYTH,A
DECISION-MAKING AND MODAL CHOICE BY
COMMUTERS IN THE BELFAST REGION
QUB PHD
BELFAST
1982 2 04

2836 SPAIN,R H
BELFAST REGIONAL SURVEY AND PLAN
TOWN PLANN INST J 51
1965 2 01

2837 SPENCER,A
URBANISATION AND THE PROBLEM OF IRELAND
AQUARIUS
BENBURB
1974 2 01

2838 ST. LEGER, F J
REPORT ON A SURVEY OF CRAIGAVON: NEW
TOWN
DEPT SOC ADMIN NUU
COLERAINE
1973 2 08

2839 STEMMAN, R
BELFAST: PRIORITY FOR A STRICKEN CITY
EUROPE 81 10
1981 2 01

2840 STEMMAN, R
WHAT NEXT FOR NI?
EUROPE 81 11
LONDON
1981 2 01

2841 STUART, J
AN ANALYSIS OF JOURNEYS TO WORK IN NI
NUU MSC
COLERAINE
1978 2 04

2842 TAYLOR, A
NEW ROADS FOR ULSTER
SURVEYOR 132
1968 2 01

2843 TOWN AND COUNTRY PLANNING
LONDONDERRY'S PLANNING AND POST WAR
HOUSING
TOWN COUNTRY PLANN 16(64)
LONDON
1948 2 01

2844 TOWN AND COUNTRY PLANNING
PLANNING WORLD: THE EMERALD ISLE
TOWN COUNTRY PLANN 42(2)
1974 2 01

2845 TOWN AND COUNTRY PLANNING
PORTAFERRY'S COTTAGE CONTROVERSY
TOWN COUNTRY PLANN 36
LONDON
1968 2 01

2846 TOWN AND COUNTRY PLANNING SERVICE (NI)
LONDONDERRY AREA PLAN
TOWN AND COUNTRY PLANNING SERVICE (NI)
BELFAST
1975 2 03

2847 TRAVERS MORGAN AND PARTNERS
BELFAST TRANSPORTATION PLAN
HMSO
BELFAST
1969 2 03

2848 TRAVERS MORGAN AND PARTNERS
REPORT ON BELFAST URBAN MOTORWAY
BELFAST
1967 2 10

2849 TRIMBLE, W D
PLANNING BLIGHT
NI LEG QUART 33
BELFAST
1982 2 01

2850 TRIMBLE, W D
THE PROCEDURE GOVERNING COMPULSORY
ACQUISITION OF LAND IN NI
NI LEG QUART 24(4)
BELFAST
1973 2 01

2851 VAUGHAN, T D
DROMORE: AN URBAN STUDY IN COUNTY DOWN
IR GEOG 4(2)
1960 2 01

2852 WALKER, R
A REGIONAL PLAN FOR IRELAND
ROYAL INST BRIT ARCHITECTS J 73(11)
1966 2 01

2853 WALLACE, H
LAND REGISTRY PRACTICE IN NI
SLS/FACULTY OF LAW QUB
BELFAST
1981 2 10

2854 WALLACE, M W
LAND UTILISATION OF CO ARMAGH
QUB MA
BELFAST
1951 2 04

2855 WIENER, R
THE BUS (BELFAST URBAN STUDIES) GUIDE TO
DISTRICT CENTRES
HOLY SMOKE PRESS
BELFAST
1974 2 10

2856 WIENER, R
POLITICS AND BOMBS DELAY BELFAST
PLANNING PROGRESS
MUNICIPAL ENGINEERING 151(31)
1974 1 01

2857 WIENER, R
THE RAPE AND PLUNDER OF THE SHANKILL
FARSET
BELFAST
1980 1 02

2858 WIENER, R
THE SHANKILL: POWER IN PARTICIPATION
PLANNER 62(4)
1976 1 01

2859 WILCOCK, D N
POST-WAR LAND DRAINAGE, FERTILISER USE
AND ENVIRONMENTAL IMPACT IN NI
J ENVIRONMENTAL MANAGEMENT 8(2)
1979 2 01

2860 ABBOTT, M
DISTRICT HEATING: THE TEMPERATURE IS
RISING
SCOPE 47
BELFAST
1981 2 01

2861 ADAMS, J
HOUSING AND POPULATION MOVEMENTS:
BALLYMENA
QUB MSC
BELFAST
1979 2 04

2862 ALCORN, D
WESTLINK PENSIONERS' DWELLINGS IN SHADOW
OF MAJOR NEW ROAD
SCOPE 38
BELFAST
1980 2 01

2863 ALCORN, D
WHOSE VANDALISM?
SCOPE 28
BELFAST
1979 2 01

2864 ANNING, N; NICHOLL, J
A PLAGUE ON ALL YOUR HOUSES
NEW STATESMAN OCT 23
LONDON
1981 2 01

2865 ARDOYNE EX-RESIDENTS ASSOCIATION
ARDOYNE - THE TRUE STORY
ARDOYNE EX-RESIDENTS ASSOCIATION
BELFAST
1973 1 10

2866 ASSOCIATION OF LOCAL ADVICE CENTRES
REPORT OF PUBLIC INQUIRY INTO HOUSING
CONDITIONS IN BELFAST
ASSOCIATION OF LOCAL ADVICE CENTRES
BELFAST
1981 2 10

2867 BAILLIE, B
SPECIAL NEEDS IN NI
HOUSING 15(10)
1979 2 01

2868 BDP
PEOPLE AND THEIR HOUSES
BDP
BELFAST
1967 2 10

2869 BELFAST CITY SURVEYOR'S DEPARTMENT -
TOWN PLANNING SECTION
REPORT ON CLEARING, HOUSING AND
REDEVELOPMENT
BELFAST CITY SURVEYOR'S DEPARTMENT
BELFAST
1959 2 03

2870 BELFAST COMMUNITY HOUSING ASSOCIATION
HOUSING ACTION AREA REPORT FOR LAGAN
VILLAGE AREA
BELFAST COMMUNITY HOUSING ASSOCIATION
BELFAST
1978 2 10

2871 BELFAST URBAN STUDY GROUP
A TO Z OF BELFAST HOUSING
HOLY SMOKE PRESS
BELFAST
1974 2 10

2872 BIRD, E L
WORK OF THE NI HOUSING TRUST
J RIBA
1949 2 01

2873 BIRRELL, W D ET AL
HOUSING REQUIREMENTS FOR NI
ECON AND SOC R 3(3)
1972 2 01

2874 BIRRELL, W D; MURIE, A S; CALVERT, J
HOUSING POLICY IN NI
COMM FORUM 2(2)
1972 2 01

2875 BIRRELL, W D; MURIE, A S; HILLYARD, P;
ROCHE, D J D
HOUSING IN NI
CENTRE FOR ENVIRONMENTAL STUDIES
LONDON
1971 2 10

2876 BIRRELL, W D; MURIE, A S; HILLYARD, P;
ROCHE, D J D
NI HOUSING EXECUTIVE
ADMIN(DUB) 19(3)
DUBLIN
1971 2 01

2877 BLACK, R
FLIGHT IN BELFAST
COMM FORUM 2(1)
1972 1 01

2878 BLACK, R; PINTER, F; OVERY, B
FLIGHT: A REPORT ON POPULATION MOVEMENT
IN BELFAST DURING AUGUST 1971
NICRC
BELFAST
1971 1 10

2879 BUILT ENVIRONMENT
THE HOUSING EXECUTIVE - INTERVIEW WITH
RAE EVANS
BUILT ENVIRONMENT FEBRUARY
LONDON
1974 2 01

2880 BYRNE, D
HOUSING IN BELFAST: REPRODUCTIVE
POLITICS AND CLASS POLITICS IN A
DIFFERENT PLACE
DEPT SOCIOL AND SOC POLICY ULSTER
COLLEGE
BELFAST
1979 2 08

2881 CALVERT, J
HOUSING POLICY IN NI: A CRITIQUE
COMM FORUM 2(2)
LONDON
1972 2 01

2882 CAPPER, N M
NI EXECUTIVE FACES ENORMOUS HOUSING
PROBLEMS
BUILDING SOCIETIES GAZETTE 108
1976 2 01

2883 CHAPMAN, P
HOUSING REFORM IN NI
J BUILT ENVIRON 35(3)
1972 2 01

2884 CLONARD HOUSING ASSOCIATION
DRAFT HOUSING ACTION AREA REPORT
NI FEDERATION OF HOUSING ASSOCIATIONS
BELFAST
1979 2 10

2885 CLONARD HOUSING ASSOCIATION
PLANNING OPTIONS FOR THE FORMULATION OF
A HOUSING ACTION AREA PLAN
NI FEDERATION OF HOUSING ASSOCIATIONS
BELFAST
1979 2 10

2886 CONNSWATER HOUSING ASSOCIATION
HOUSING ACTION AREA REPORT
CONNSWATER HOUSING ASSOCIATION
BELFAST
1977 2 10

2887 CRAIGAVON PLANNING SERVICE
BROWNLOW SURVEY 1974
DEPT OF HOUSING, LOCAL GOVERNMENT AND
PLANNING
CRAIGAVON
1975 2 03

2888 DARBY, J; MORRIS, G
INTIMIDATION IN HOUSING
NICRC
BELFAST
1974 1 03

2889 DEPT OF THE ENVIRONMENT (NI)
POLEGLASS DEVELOPMENT SCHEME
HMSO
BELFAST
1976 2 03

2890 DITCH, N
SHELTER (NI)
PACE 13(3)
BELFAST
1982 2 01

2891 DONNELLY, D
NI HOUSING TRUST
OFFICIAL ARCHITECT DEC
1948 2 01

2892 FETHERSTON, A H
THE RENT RESTRICTIONS ACT
NI LEG QUART 7(2)
BELFAST
1947 2 01

2893 FIELD, D
A REPORT ON UNSATISFACTORY TENANTS OF
BELFAST CORPORATION...
BELFAST COUNCIL OF SOCIAL WELFARE
BELFAST
1960 2 99

2894 FIELD, D; NEILL, D G
SURVEY OF NEW HOUSING ESTATES - HOUSING
TRUST 1945-54
DEPT SOC STUD QUB
BELFAST
1957 2 10

2895 FIELDING, N
PAYING THE PRICE: THE HOUSING CRISIS IN
NI
ROOF 8(3)
LONDON
1983 2 01

2896 FITZGERALD, M
NI: A HOUSING RECORD TO BE PROUD OF
LOCAL GOVT CHRON 5821
1978 2 01

2897 FLEMING, M C
CONVENTIONAL HOUSEBUILDING AND THE SCALE
OF OPERATIONS: A STUDY OF PRICES
OXFORD B ECON STATIST 29
1967 2 01

2898 FLEMING, M C
COSTS AND PRICES IN THE NI CONSTRUCTION
INDUSTRY, 1954-64
J INDUSTR ECON 14
1965 2 01

2899 FLEMING, M C
HOUSEBUILDING PRODUCTIVITY IN NI
URB STUD 4
1967 2 01

2900 FLEMING, M C
HOUSING IN NI
HEINEMANN
LONDON
1974 2 02

2901 FLEMING, M C
REVIEWS OF UK STATISTICAL SOURCES: VOL
3, HOUSING IN NI
HEINEMANN
LONDON
1974 2 10

2902 FLEMING, M C; NELLIS, J G
INFLATION OF HOUSE PRICES IN NI IN THE
1970S
ECON AND SOC R 13(1)
DUBLIN
1981 2 01

2903 FORSYTH, J
BELFAST'S STEPS AHEAD
ROOF 2(6)
LONDON
1977 2 01

2904 FRAZER, H; WYLIE, J C
THE RENT RESTRICTION LAW OF NI
NI LEG QUART 22(4)
1971 2 01

2905 GROVE HOUSING ASSOCIATION
HOUSING ACTION AREA REPORT
GROVE HOUSING ASSOCIATION
BELFAST
1978 2 10

2906 HADDEN, T
HOMELESSNESS IN NI
NI LEG QUART 32(1)
BELFAST
1981 2 01

2907 HADDEN, T
PUBLIC HEALTH AND HOUSING LEGISLATION:
TOWARDS AN INTEGRATED CODE OF PROCEDURE
NI LEG QUART 27
BELFAST
1976 2 01

2908 HARRISON, R L
POPULATION CHANGE AND HOUSING PROVISION
IN BELFAST
IN COMPTON, P A (ED)
BELFAST
1981 2 07

2909 HENDRY, J
HOUSE PLANS IN FOUR VILLAGES IN COUNTY
DOWN
ULSTER FOLKLIFE 20
1974 2 01

2910 HENDRY, J
HOUSING PROBLEMS IN NI
PACE 13(2)
BELFAST
1981 2 01

2911 HENDRY, J
HOUSING PROBLEMS IN NI
PACE 13(2)
BELFAST
1981 2 01

2912 HENDRY, J
THE ROLE OF CONSERVATION IN A HOUSING
PROGRAMME FOR NI
ULSTER ARCHITECTURAL HERITAGE SOCIETY
BELFAST
1971 2 10

2913 HENDRY, J; BRANIFF, P; HILLIS, A L
HOUSING ACTION AREA PROGRESS
DEPT TOWN AND COUNTRY PLANNING QUB
BELFAST
1981 2 01

2914 HILLYARD, P
RENTS, REPAIRS AND DESPAIR: A STUDY OF
THE PRIVATE RENTED SECTOR IN NI
AUTHOR
BELFAST
1982 2 02

2915 HILLYARD, P; ROCHE, D J D; MURIE, A S;
BIRRELL, W D
VARIATIONS IN THE STANDARD OF HOUSING
PROVISION IN NI
REG STUD 6(4)
1972   2   01

2916 HORTON, F J
NI: HOUSING AND THE HOUSING EXECUTIVE
HOUSING 9
1973   2   01

2917 HUGHES, D J
PUBLIC HEALTH LEGISLATION AND THE
IMPROVEMENT OF HOUSING CONDITIONS IN
ENGLAND AND WALES AND IN NI
NI LEG QUART 27(1)
BELFAST
1976   2   01

2918 IRIS
A COMMON EXPERIENCE ... BALLYMURPHY IN
WEST BELFAST AND BALLYMUN IN NORTH
DUBLIN
IRIS 3
DUBLIN
1982   2   01

2919 JOURNAL OF THE ROYAL INSTITUTE OF
BRITISH ARCHITECTS
THE WORK OF THE NI HOUSING TRUST
J RIBA MAY
LONDON
1954   2   01

2920 KEENAN, M
MOYARD: THE CASE FOR DEMOLITION
MOYARD HOUSING ACTION GROUP
BELFAST
1982   2   10

2921 KENNEDY, S J; BIRRELL, W D
HOUSING
IN DARBY, J; WILLIAMSON, A (EDS)
LONDON
1978   2   07

2922 KERR, G
ESTATE AGENT'S COMMISSION IN NI
NI LEG QUART 24(1)
BELFAST
1973   2   01

2923 KILMURRAY, A
THE MOST ARROGANT MAN IN NI? - INTERVIEW
WITH BILLY FLECK
SCOPE 43
BELFAST
1981   2   01

2924 LAZENBATT, J; EVANS, R
YOUR NEW HOME IN TWINBROOK
NIHE
BELFAST
1973   2   03

2925 LOWRY REPORT
BELFAST CORPORATION INQUIRY
HMSO CMD 440
BELFAST
1962   2   03

2926 MACGOUGAN, J
THE LONDONDERRY AIR: POVERTY, BAD
HOUSING AND OVERCROWDING
TOWN COUNTRY PLANN 16(63)
1948   2   01

2927 MACNEICE, D
FACTORY WORKERS' HOUSING IN COUNTIES
DOWN AND ARMAGH
QUB PHD
BELFAST
1982   2   04

2928 MAGEE, J K ET AL
SHELTERED TENANT SURVEY: A STUDY OF NI
HOUSING EXECUTIVE SCHEMES IN BELFAST
DHSS (NI)
BELFAST
1982   2   03

2929 MAGUIRE, J; GAY, P
HOUSING MANAGEMENT TRAINING AND
DEVELOPMENT IN NI
HOUSING 16(2)
LONDON
1980   2   01

2930 MARSHALL, A T; TAYLOR, W E
LONDONDERRY'S PLANNING AND POST-WAR
HOUSING
TOWN COUNTRY PLANN 16
LONDON
1948   2   01

2931 MINISTRY OF HEALTH AND LOCAL GOVERNMENT
(NI)
HOUSING COSTS INQUIRY
HMSO CMD 240
BELFAST
1946   2   03

2932 MINISTRY OF HEALTH AND LOCAL GOVERNMENT
(NI)
INSPECTOR'S REPORT ON BELFAST
CORPORATION HOUSING ALLOCATIONS INQUIRY
MINISTRY OF HEALTH AND LOCAL GOVERNMENT
(NI)
BELFAST
1954   2   03

2933 MORRISSEY, M
PUBLIC HOUSING POVERTY
QUEST 7
BELFAST
1977   2   01

2934 MURIE, A S
NEW BUILDING AND HOUSING NEEDS: A STUDY
OF CHAINS OF MOVES IN HOUSING IN NI
PERGAMON
OXFORD
1976   2   02

2935 MURIE, A S; BIRRELL, W D; HILLYARD, P
DEVELOPMENTS IN HOUSING POLICY AND
ADMINISTRATION IN NI SINCE 1945
SOC AND ECON ADM 6(1)
1972   2   01

2936 MURIE, A S; BIRRELL, W D; HILLYARD, P
HOUSING POLICY BETWEEN THE WARS; NI,
ENGLAND AND WALES
SOC AND ECON ADM 5(4)
1971   2   01

2937 MURIE, A S; HILLYARD, P; BIRRELL, W D;
ROCHE, D J D
NEW BUILDING AND HOUSING NEED - A STUDY
OF CHAINS OF MOVES IN HOUSING IN NI
PROGRESS IN PLANNING 6
1976   2   01

2938 MURIE, A S; HILLYARD, P; ROCHE, D J D
AN INDEX OF HOUSING CONDITIONS FOR
IRELAND
SOC STUD 1
1972   2   01

2939 MURRAY, R; BOAL, F W
FORCED RESIDENTIAL MOBILITY IN BELFAST
1969-72
IN HARBISON, J; HARBISON, J (EDS)
SHEPTON MALLET, SOMERSET
1980   1   07

2940 MURRAY, R; OSBORNE, R D
SEGREGATION ON HORN DRIVE - A CAUTIONARY
TALE
NEW SOCIETY 40(759)
LONDON
1977   1   01

2941 NATIONAL DEMOCRATIC GROUP
HOUSING: THE FACTS
NATIONAL DEMOCRATIC GROUP
BELFAST
1969 2 09

2942 NATIONAL DEMOCRATIC GROUP
A REAL HOUSING POLICY
NATIONAL DEMOCRATIC GROUP
BELFAST
1968 2 09

2943 NEILL, D C
HOUSING AND THE SOCIAL ASPECTS OF TOWN
AND COUNTRY PLANNING IN NI
ADMIN (DUB) 2(3)
DUBLIN
1954 2 01

2944 NI ASSEMBLY
REPORT OF CONSIDERATION ON PROPOSAL FOR
DRAFT PROPERTY (DISCHARGE OF MORTGAGE BY
RECEIPT) (NI) ORDER
HMSO NIA 31
BELFAST
1983 2 03

2945 NI ASSEMBLY
REPORT ON PROPOSAL FOR A DRAFT HOUSING
(NI) ORDER 1983
HMSO NIA 43
BELFAST
1983 2 03

2946 NI ASSEMBLY
REPORT ON PROPOSAL FOR A DRAFT HOUSING
BENEFITS (NI) ORDER
HMSO NIA 51
BELFAST
1983 2 03

2947 NI GOVERNMENT
HOUSING SURVEY: PROPOSALS FOR DEALING
WITH UNFIT HOUSING
HMSO CMD 398
BELFAST
1959 2 03

2948 NICRC
GUIDE FOR INTIMIDATED FAMILIES
NICRC
BELFAST
1974 1 03

2949 NICRC
HOUSING IN NI: PROCEEDINGS OF A
CONFERENCE
NICRC
BELFAST
1972 2 03

2950 NIEC
PUBLIC EXPENDITURE PRIORITIES: HOUSING
NIEC
BELFAST
1981 2 03

2951 NIHE
BELFAST HOUSEHOLD SURVEY 1978:
PRELIMINARY REPORT
NIHE
BELFAST
1979 2 03

2952 NIHE
BELFAST REDEVELOPMENT PROGRAMME
NIHE
BELFAST
1975 2 03

2953 NIHE
NI HOUSE CONDITION SURVEY 1979:
PRELIMINARY REPORT
NIHE
BELFAST
1980 2 10

2954 NIHE
NI HOUSEHOLD SURVEY 1975
NIHE
BELFAST
1976 2 10

2955 NIHE
NI HOUSING CONDITION SURVEY
NIHE
BELFAST
1974 2 03

2956 NIHE
THE WORK OF THE HOUSING EXECUTIVE
NIHE
BELFAST
1972 2 03

2957 NIHT
CITY OF BELFAST: GROSVENOR ROAD
REDEVELOPMENT
NIHT
BELFAST
1968 2 10

2958 NIHT
THE HOUSING TRUST: A SURVEY, 1945-1960
NIHT
BELFAST
1961 2 03

2959 O'BRIEN, L
THE NI HOUSING TRUST
JSSISI 19
1953 2 01

2960 PARSON, D
HOUSING POLICY IN BELFAST
INT J URB REG RES 5(2)
LONDON
1981 2 01

2961 PARSON, D
REGIONAL PLANNING, HOUSING POLICY, AND
COMMUNITY ACTION IN NI
UCLA MA
LOS ANGELES
1979 2 04

2962 PARSON, D
URBAN RENEWAL AND HOUSING ACTION AREAS
IN BELFAST: LEGITIMATION AND THE
INCORPORATION OF PROTEST
INT J URB REG RES 5
LONDON
1981 2 01

2963 PATTON, J
DIRECTIONAL BIAS IN INTRA-URBAN
MIGRATION IN THE PUBLIC HOUSING SECTOR
OF THE BELFAST URBAN AREA
ULSTER POLY PHD
BELFAST
1981 2 04

2964 PD
BELFAST HOUSING CRISIS
PD
BELFAST
1969 2 09

2965 PLANNING APPEALS COMMISSION
POLEGLASS AREA PUBLIC INQUIRY
HMSO
BELFAST
1977 1 03

2966 PORTER REPORT
COMMITTEE ON RENT RESTRICTION LAW OF NI
HMSO
BELFAST
1975 2 03

2967 REDPATH, J
£90,000 IS TOO MUCH FOR ONE HOUSE
SCOPE 4
BELFAST
1976 2 01

2968 REES,M
INITIATIVES IN HOUSING AND PLANNING
BUILT ENVIRONMENT FEB
1974   2   01

2969 ROCHE,D J D; MURIE,A S; BIRRELL,W D;
HILLYARD,P
HOUSING REQUIREMENTS FOR NI
ECON AND SOC R 3(3)
DUBLIN
1972   2   01

2970 ROLSTON,B
DIVIS FLATS
IRL SOCIALIST R 8
LONDON
1980   2   01

2971 ROSE,R; SIMPSON,H
WHERE CAN PEOPLE LIVE?
COMM FORUM 3(1)
LONDON
1973   2   01

2972 RUSSELL,J
HOUSING AMIDST CIVIL UNREST
CENTRE FOR ENVIRONMENTAL STUDIES
LONDON
1980   1   02

2973 SCOPE
PROFILE: HIGHFIELD ESTATE
SCOPE 31
BELFAST
1980   2   01

2974 SHELTER (NI)
THIS YEAR, NEXT YEAR, SOMETIME, NEVER
SHELTER (NI)
BELFAST
1981   2   10

2975 SIMPSON,H
THE NI HOUSING EXECUTIVE
HOUSING R 22/3
1973   2   01

2976 SINGLETON,D
'COUNCIL HOUSE' SALES IN NI
HOUSING R 31(2)
1981   2   01

2977 SINGLETON,D
HOUSING A DIVIDED COMMUNITY: THE PARADOX
OF REFORM IN NI
HOUSING R 31(3)
1982   2   01

2978 ST MATTHEW'S HOUSING ASSOCIATION
HOUSING ACTION AREA REPORT
ST MATTHEW'S HOUSING ASSOCIATION
BELFAST
1977   2   10

2979 TOMLINSON,M
HOUSING, THE STATE AND THE POLITICS OF
SEGREGATION
IN O'DOWD,L; ROLSTON,B; TOMLINSON,M
LONDON
1980   1   07

2980 TOWN AND COUNTRY PLANNING
LONDONDERRY'S PLANNING AND POST WAR
HOUSING
TOWN COUNTRY PLANN 16(64)
LONDON
1948   2   01

2981 UNIONIST RESEARCH DEPARTMENT
PUTTING PEOPLE FIRST IN HOUSING
UNIONIST RESEARCH DEPT
BELFAST
1973   2   09

2982 WALSH,D
HOUSING ACTION AREAS IN BELFAST
FACULTY OF LAW QUB
BELFAST
1980   2   10

2983 WIENER,R
THE A-Z OF BELFAST HOUSING
HOLY SMOKE PRESS
BELFAST
1974   1   10

2984 WOODVALE AND SHANKILL HOUSING
ASSOCIATION
HOUSING ACTION AREA REPORT
NI FEDERATION OF HOUSING ASSOCIATIONS
BELFAST
1977   2   10

2985 WYLIE,J C
LEASEHOLD (ENLARGEMENTS AND EXTENSION)
ACT (NI) 1971: A CRITIQUE
NI LEG QUART 22(4)
BELFAST
1971   2   01

2986 WEIR,S
THE KEYNESIANS ACROSS THE WATER
NEW SOCIETY 9 JUNE
LONDON
1983   2   01

2987 ACTION ON DEBT
STICKING THE KNIFE IN: DEBT AND DEBT
COLLECTION IN NI
ACTION ON DEBT
BELFAST
1980 2 09

2988 AGE CONCERN
THE NEEDS OF THE ELDERLY IN THE NEW
LODGE AREA - REPORT OF THE RESEARCH
PROJECT
AGE CONCERN
BELFAST
1977 2 10

2989 ALCORN, D
POVERTY: ULSTER AND THE UK
SCOPE 29
BELFAST
1979 2 01

2990 BERTHOUD, R
UNITED KINGDOM?
NEW SOCIETY JAN 14
LONDON
1982 2 01

2991 BIRRELL, W D
RELATIVE DEPRIVATION AS A FACTOR IN
CONFLICT IN NI
SOCIOL R 20(3)
1972 1 01

2992 BLACK, B
LOW PAY
IN BLACK, B; DITCH, J; MORRISSEY, M;
STEELE, R
LONDON
1980 2 07

2993 BLACK, B; STEELE, R
LOW PAY IN THE THREE NATIONS
LOW PAY UNIT B 25
LONDON
1979 2 01

2994 BOAL, F W; DOHERTY, P; PRINGLE, D G
SOCIAL PROBLEMS IN THE BELFAST URBAN
AREA: AN EXPLORATORY ANALYSIS
OCCASIONAL PAPER QUEEN MARY COLLEGE 12
LONDON
1978 2 10

2995 BOAL, F W; DOHERTY, P; PRINGLE, D G
SPATIAL DISTRIBUTION OF SOME SOCIAL
PROBLEMS IN THE BELFAST URBAN AREA
NICRC
BELFAST
1974 2 10

2996 BRETT, C E B
LEGAL AID AND ADVICE BILL (NI)
NI LEG QUART 15(3)
1964 2 01

2997 BUSH, L; MARSHALL, P
THE SOCIAL AND ECONOMIC CIRCUMSTANCES OF
DISADVANTAGED CHILDREN IN THE COMMUNITY
IN HARBISON, J (ED)
BELFAST
1983 1 07

2998 CALVERT, H
PARITY IN SOCIAL SECURITY IN NI
IR JURIST 5
DUBLIN
1970 2 01

2999 CASEY, J P
SOCIAL ASSISTANCE IN NI
NI LEG QUART 19(3)
1968 2 01

3000 CASEY, J P
SUPPLEMENTARY BENEFITS ACT: LAWYER'S LAW
ASPECTS
NI LEG QUART 19(1)
BELFAST
1968 2 01

3001 CAVES, W J
CONCEPT OF THE EDUCATIONAL PRIORITY AREA
AND ITS POSSIBLE APPLICATION TO THE CITY
OF BELFAST
QUB MED
BELFAST
1973 2 04

3002 COMMUNITY DEVELOPMENT FORUM
SOCIAL NEED AND SOCIAL NEED LEGISLATION
IN NI
COMM DEV FORUM
BELFAST
1972 2 99

3003 COMMUNITY ORGANISATIONS OF NI
POVERTY: THE BAN ANSWER?
COMMUNITY ORGANISATIONS OF NI
BELFAST
1979 2 10

3004 CORLEY, T A B
PERSONAL WEALTH OF NI 1920-1960
JSSISI
1963 2 01

3005 COUNCIL FOR CONTINUING EDUCATION
CONTINUING EDUCATION IN SOCIALLY
DISADVANTAGED AREAS OF NI
HMSO
BELFAST
1978 2 03

3006 COVELLO, V T; ASHBY, J A
INEQUALITY IN A DIVIDED SOCIETY: AN
ANALYSIS OF DATA FROM NI
SOCIOL FOCUS 13(2)
AKRON
1980 2 01

3007 COVELLO, V T; BOLLEN, K A
STATUS CONSISTENCY IN COMPARATIVE
PERSPECTIVE: AN EXAMINATION OF
EDUCATIONAL, OCCUPATIONAL AND INCOME
DATA IN NINE SOCIETIES
SOC FORCES 58(2)
CHAPEL HILL
1979 2 01

3008 CPAG
DOWNPATRICK SURVEY
CPAG
BELFAST
1972 2 10

3009 DEPT OF EDUCATION (NI)
REPORT OF A WORKING PARTY ON SOCIAL
PRIORITY SCHOOLS IN NI
HMSO
BELFAST
1979 2 03

3010 DEVLIN, P
THE LOW PAY SWAMP IN NI
IN POLLOCK, H M (ED)
DUBLIN
1981 2 07

3011 DEVLIN, P
THE STUDY OF THE USE OF OUTDOOR RELIEF
IN BELFAST 1920-1939
CRANFIELD INSTITUTE OF TECHNOLOGY MSC
CRANFIELD
1980 2 04

3012 DEVLIN, P
YES WE HAVE NO BANANAS: OUTDOOR RELIEF
IN BELFAST 1920-39
BLACKSTAFF
BELFAST
1981 2 02

3013 DITCH, J; MCWILLIAMS, M
THE SUPPLEMENTARY BENEFITS SYSTEM IN NI
1980-81
NI CONSUMER COUNCIL
BELFAST
1981 2 10

3014 DITCH, J; MORRISSEY, M
LIVING STANDARDS
IN BLACK, B; DITCH, J; MORRISSEY, M;
STEELE, R
LONDON
1980 2 07

3015 EVASON, E
BELFAST WELFARE RIGHTS PROJECT: MAIN
REPORT
ULSTER POLY
BELFAST
1980 2 10

3016 EVASON, E
ELDERLY IN ARMAGH
SOC WORK TODAY 5(16)
LONDON
1974 2 01

3017 EVASON, E
ENDS THAT WON'T MEET
CPAG
LONDON
1980 2 10

3018 EVASON, E
FAMILY POVERTY IN NI
CPAG
LONDON
1978 2 10

3019 EVASON, E
FINANCIAL AND OTHER CIRCUMSTANCES OF
ARMAGH'S ELDERLY
NUU
COLERAINE
1974 2 10

3020 EVASON, E
JUST ME AND THE KIDS: A STUDY OF
SINGLE-PARENT FAMILIES IN NI
EOC
BELFAST
1981 2 10

3021 EVASON, E
LOW INCOME HOUSEHOLDS IN A BELFAST
COMMUNITY: A STUDY OF NEEDS, DEFINITIONS
AND POLICIES
QUB MSSC
BELFAST
1972 2 04

3022 EVASON, E
MEASURING FAMILY POVERTY
SOC WORK TODAY 4(7)
LONDON
1974 2 01

3023 EVASON, E
NI: DEPRIVING THE DEPRIVED
POVERTY 45
LONDON
1980 2 01

3024 EVASON, E
POVERTY AND SOCIAL SECURITY IN NI
QUEST 2
BELFAST
1975 2 01

3025 EVASON, E
POVERTY: THE FACTS IN NI
CPAG
LONDON
1976 2 10

3026 EVASON, E
SUPPLEMENTARY SOCIAL BENEFITS IN NI
SOC STUD 2(1)
1973 2 01

3027 EVASON, E; DARBY, J; PEARSON, M
SOCIAL NEED AND SOCIAL PROVISION IN NI
NUU
COLERAINE
1976 2 10

3028 FARRELL, M
THE POOR LAW AND THE WORKHOUSE IN
BELFAST 1838-1948
PRONI
BELFAST
1978 2 03

3029 FLYNN, J; MORRISSEY, M
FUEL PRICES AND FUEL POVERTY IN NI
AUTHORS
CRAIGAVON
1978 2 10

3030 GREER, D S
LEGAL AID FOR SUMMARY TRIALS IN NI
NI LEG QUART 22(4)
1971 2 01

3031 GREER, D S
THE LEGAL AID, ADVICE AND ASSISTANCE
(NI) ORDER 1981 (NI STATUTES ANNOTATE D
NO. 1)
SLS/FACULTY OF LAW QUB
BELFAST
1982 2 10

3032 HARRISON, E M; MCKEOWN, M; O'SHEA, T
OLD AGE IN NI - A STUDY OF THE ELDERLY
IN A SEASIDE TOWN
ECON AND SOC R 3(1)
1971 2 01

3033 KNIGHT, I B
TWO-PARENT FAMILIES IN RECEIPT OF FIS
DHSS (NI)
BELFAST
1972 2 03

3034 LABOUR RELATIONS AGENCY
LOW PAY IN NI: THE ROLE OF THE LABOUR
RELATIONS AGENCY
LRA
BELFAST
1980 2 03

3035 LABOUR RELATIONS AGENCY
WAGES COUNCILS IN NI
LRA
BELFAST
1980 2 10

3036 LABOUR RELATIONS AGENCY
WAGES COUNCILS OPERATION IN NI
LRA
BELFAST
1978 2 03

3037 LAW SOCIETY OF NI
REPORT OF THE LAW SOCIETY OF NI ON THE
LEGAL AID SCHEME
HMSO
BELFAST
1979 2 03

3038 LYONS, P M
DISTRIBUTION OF PERSONAL WEALTH IN NI
ECON AND SOC R 3(2)
DUBLIN
1972 2 01

3039 MACGOUGAN, J
THE LONDONDERRY AIR: POVERTY, BAD
HOUSING AND OVERCROWDING
TOWN COUNTRY PLANN 16(63)
1948 2 01

3040 MCCAUGHEY, M
LOW PAY IN NEWRY
SCOPE 59
BELFAST
1983 2 01

3041 MCILREAVEY, F
THE NEED FOR LEGAL AID IN NI
NI LEG QUART 15(3)
1964 2 01

3042 MCKAY, J
SOCIAL SECURITY ABUSE AND TAX EVASION:
AN EXPLORATION OF CONTEMPORARY STATE
REACTION
QUB MSSC
BELFAST
1981 2 04

3043 MURIE, A S
FAMILY INCOME SUPPLEMENT AND LOW INCOMES
IN NI
SOC AND ECON ADM 8(1)
1974 2 01

3044 NARAIN, J
SOCIAL SECURITY APPEAL TRIBUNALS IN NI:
A SURVEY
NI LEG QUART 30(2)
BELFAST
1979 2 01

3045 NICSS
NEW LAW FOR OLD PEOPLE
NICSS
BELFAST
1948 2 10

3046 NICSS
POVERTY: THE IMPACT ON NI
NICSS
BELFAST
1981 2 10

3047 O'HAGAN, J W
SOCIAL SECURITY: AN APPENDIX TO CHAPTER
3
IN GIBSON, N J; SPENCER, J E (EDS)
1977 2 07

3048 PROJECT TEAM
BELFAST AREAS OF SPECIAL SOCIAL NEED
REPORT
HMSO
BELFAST
1976 2 03

3049 RAGG, N
BENEFITS IN NI
SOC WORK TODAY 2(13)
LONDON
1972 2 01

3050 RAINSFORD, T
SUPPLEMENTARY BENEFITS IN NI
SOC WORK TODAY 3(23)
LONDON
1973 2 01

3051 SCOPE
AREAS OF SPECIAL NEED: THE STORY SO FAR
SCOPE 12
BELFAST
1977 2 01

3052 SCOPE
BAN CASH
SCOPE 20
BELFAST
1979 2 01

3053 SCOPE
THE ELDERLY: THE FORGOTTEN POOR
SCOPE 16
BELFAST
1978 2 01

3054 SCOPE
FUEL POVERTY
SCOPE 33
BELFAST
1980 2 01

3055 SCOPE
LOW PAY: AN INTERVIEW WITH CHRIS POND
AND RICHARD STEELE
SCOPE 35
BELFAST
1980 2 01

3056 SCOPE
POVERTY AND THE ONE-PARENT FAMILY
SCOPE 14
BELFAST
1978 2 01

3057 SCOPE
PROFILE: HIGHFIELD ESTATE
SCOPE 31
BELFAST
1980 2 01

3058 SCOPE
RIP - SBC: INTERVIEW WITH RUAIDHRI
HIGGINS, CHAIRMAN OF THE SUPPLEMENTARY
BENEFITS COMMISSION
SCOPE 37
BELFAST
1980 2 01

3059 SPENCER, A
BALLYMURPHY: A TALE OF TWO SURVEYS
DEPT SOC STUD QUB
BELFAST
1973 1 10

3060 SPENCER, A
EDUCATIONAL PRIORITY: THE REPORT OF THE
WORKING PARTY OF THE EDUCATION COMMITTEE
ON NURSERY EDUCATION/EDUCATIONAL
PRIORITY AREAS 1973-1977
BELFAST EDUCATION AND LIBRARY BOARD
BELFAST
1977 2 10

3061 STEELE, R
MINIMUM WAGES
IN BLACK, B; DITCH, J; MORRISSEY, M;
STEELE, R
LONDON
1980 2 07

3062 STEVENSON, J
SOCIAL SECURITY IN NI, WITH SPECIAL
REFERENCE TO A SELECTED GROUP OF
INDUSTRIES
QUB PHD
BELFAST
1964 2 04

3063 TIPPING, B
SCROUNGING IN NI: THE BEGINNING OF AN
INVESTIGATION
ECON AND SOC R 13(3)
DUBLIN
1982 2 01

3064 TOWNSEND, P
HUMAN NEED IN ULSTER
NEW SOCIETY 25 NOVEMBER
LONDON
1971 2 01

3065 TOWNSEND, P
POVERTY IN THE UK
PELICAN
HARMONDSWORTH
1979 2 02

3066 TOWNSEND, P
      POVERTY IN ULSTER AND THE UK
      NICSS
      BELFAST
      1981 2 10

3067 WALL, D
      PROPOSED CHANGES IN DEBT LEGISLATION FOR
      NI
      BELFAST COMMUNITY LAW CENTRE
      BELFAST
      1980 2 08

3068 WILSON, J A; TREW, K
      THE EDUCATIONAL PRIORITY SCHOOL
      BRIT J EDUC PSYCHOL 45
      1975 2 01

3069 WOMEN'S INFORMATION DAY GROUP
      THE REAL COST OF LIVING IN NI
      WOMEN'S INFORMATION DAY GROUP
      BELFAST
      1982 2 09

3070 ABERNETHY,W R
REPORT ON THE HEALTH OF THE COUNTY
BOROUGH OF LONDONDERRY FOR THE YEAR 1946
STANDARD
LONDONDERRY
1946 2 10

3071 ACHENBACH,P
MENTAL SUBNORMALITY, 1324-1961
QUB PHD
BELFAST
1967 2 04

3072 ADAMS,G F
GERIATRICS IN NI
LANCET
1949 2 01

3073 ADAMS,G F; CHEESEMAN,E A
OLD PEOPLE IN NI
NI HOSPITALS AUTHORITY
BELFAST
1951 2 10

3074 AGE CONCERN
THE NEEDS OF THE ELDERLY IN THE NEW
LODGE AREA - REPORT OF THE RESEARCH
PROJECT
AGE CONCERN
BELFAST
1977 2 10

3075 ALCORN,D
'MODERNISE THE PUBLIC HEALTH ACT' -
DISTRICT COUNCILS
SCOPE 51
BELFAST
1982 2 01

3076 ALLISON,R S
THE VERY FACULTIES: A SHORT HISTORY
OF...OPTHALMOLOGICAL AND
OTORHINOLARYNGOLOGICAL SERVICES IN
BELFAST...
BAIRD
BELFAST
1969 2 02

3077 ANTRIM COUNTY HEALTH COMMITTEE
COMPREHENSIVE PROPOSALS FOR SERVICES TO
BE PROVIDED...DURING THE NEXT FIVE YEARS
ANTRIM COUNTY HEALTH COMMITTEE
BELFAST
1953 2 03

3078 ANTRIM COUNTY HEALTH COMMITTEE
HEALTH SERVICES IN THE COUNTY OF ANTRIM
BURROW AND CO
LONDON
1960 2 03

3079 ASHITEY,G
MULTIPLE SCLEROSIS IN NI: A STUDY OF THE
DATE AND PLACE OF BIRTH OF PATIENTS
ULSTER MED J 39(1)
1970 2 01

3080 ASHITEY,G
SOME EPIDEMIOLOGICAL CHARACTERISTICS OF
MULTIPLE SCLEROSIS IN NI
QUB MD
BELFAST
1969 2 04

3081 BALL,D
WARFARE WELFARE
NEW SOCIETY 18(481)
1971 1 01

3082 BAMBER,J H; IRWIN,W G
CHARACTERISTICS OF SENIOR MEDICAL
STUDENTS AT BELFAST
MED EDUC 12
1978 2 01

3083 BAMFORD,D
THE IMPACT OF CIVIL DISORDER ON SOCIAL
WORK IN NI
SOC WORK EDUC 8 AUG
1981 1 01

3084 BAMFORD,D
THE INTEGRATION OF SOCIAL SKILLS AND
SOCIAL WORK CONCEPTS IN AN UNDERGRADUATE
CQSW PROGRAMME
SOC WORK EDUC NOV
1981 2 01

3085 BARR,A
AN ACCOUNT OF TUBERCULOSIS IN IRELAND
QUB MSC
BELFAST
1953 2 04

3086 BARRITT,D P
SEVENTY YEARS OF SERVICE
SCOPE 4
BELFAST
1976 2 01

3087 BEARE,J M
LEGAL ASPECTS OF OCCUPATIONAL DERMATITIS
IN NI
CONTACT DERMATITIS 1
1980 2 01

3088 BELL,J S E; MCCREADY,P E
THE REORGANISATION OF HEALTH AND
PERSONAL SOCIAL SERVICES IN NI: SECOND
REPORT
DEPT BUSINESS STUD QUB/NUFFIELD
PROVINCIAL HOSPITALS TRUST
BELFAST
1976 2 10

3089 BIRRELL,W D
SOCIAL SERVICES IN NI
ADMIN (DUB) 20(4)
1972 2 01

3090 BIRRELL,W D; MURIE,A S
IDEOLOGY, CONFLICT AND SOCIAL POLICY
J SOC POL 4(3)
LONDON
1975 1 01

3091 BIRRELL,W D; MURIE,A S
SOCIAL POLICY IN NI
IN JONES,K (ED)
1972 2 01

3092 BLANEY,R
ALCOHOLISM IN IRELAND: MEDICAL AND
SOCIAL ASPECTS
JSSISI 23(1)
1974 2 01

3093 BLANEY,R; MACKENZIE,G
NI COMMUNITY HEALTH SURVEY
DHSS (NI)
BELFAST
1978 2 03

3094 BLANEY,R; MACKENZIE,G
THE PREVALENCE OF PROBLEM DRINKING IN
NI: A POPULATION STUDY
INT J EPIDEMIOLOGY 9(2)
1980 2 01

3095 BLANEY,R; RADFORD,I S
PREVALENCE OF ALCOHOLISM IN AN IRISH
TOWN
QUART J STUD ALCOHOLISM 34
1973 2 01

3096 BLANEY,R; RADFORD,I S; MACKENZIE,G
A BELFAST STUDY OF THE PREDICTION OF
OUTCOME IN THE TREATMENT OF ALCOHOLISM
BRIT J ADDICTION 70
1975 2 01

3097 BLEASE,M
MALADJUSTED SCHOOL CHILDREN IN A BELFAST
CENTRE
IN HARBISON,J (ED)
BELFAST
1983 1 07

3098 BOAL,F W; DOHERTY,P; PRINGLE,D C
SOCIAL PROBLEMS IN THE BELFAST URBAN
AREA: AN EXPLORATORY ANALYSIS
OCCASIONAL PAPER QUEEN MARY COLLEGE 12
LONDON
1978 2 10

3099 BOAL,F W; DOHERTY,P; PRINGLE,D G
SPATIAL DISTRIBUTION OF SOME SOCIAL
PROBLEMS IN THE BELFAST URBAN AREA
NICRC
BELFAST
1974 2 10

3100 BOYLE,L
COMMUNITY DEVELOPMENT AND COMMUNITY
RELATIONS: THE DEVELOPMENT OF THE NICRC
NUU
COLERAINE
1978 2 04

3101 BRADSHAW,J
FAMILIES CARING FOR HANDICAPPED CHILDREN
IN NI
DHSS (NI)
BELFAST
1976 2 03

3102 BRITISH MEDICAL JOURNAL
THE DOCTOR IN CONFLICT
BRIT MED J 1
1972 2 01

3103 BROOKER,D S; ROY,A D
BREAST DISEASE IN WOMEN UNDER THIRTY:
TEN YEAR REVIEW AND ASSESSMENT OF
CLINICAL SCREENING
ULSTER MED J 51(2)
BELFAST
1982 2 01

3104 BROWN,M J
DUBIOUS ADVANTAGES OF INTEGRATION
SOC WORK TODAY 10(27)
1979 2 01

3105 BROWN,M J
FOR THEY COULD BE JOLLY GOOD FELLOWS
COMM CARE 301
LONDON
1980 2 01

3106 BROWN,M J
NI'S MARRIAGE TROUBLED BY SEVEN YEAR
ITCH
HEALTH AND SOC SERVICES J 90
1980 2 01

3107 BROWNLOW COMMUNITY COUNCIL
THE BROWNLOW REPORT
BROWNLOW COMMUNITY COUNCIL
CRAIGAVON
1979 2 10

3108 BRYARS,J H
AN INVESTIGATION OF THE VISUALLY
HANDICAPPED CHILDREN IN NI
QUB MD
BELFAST
1977 2 04

3109 BYRNE,D; MCSHANE,E
A STUDY OF POLICY AND SERVICES FOR
PRE-SCHOOL CHILDREN IN NI
EOC
BELFAST
1978 2 03

3110 BYRNES,D P ET AL
PENETRATING CRANIOCEREBRAL MISSILE
INJURIES IN THE CIVIL DISTURBANCES IN NI
BRIT J SURGER 61
LONDON
1974 1 01

3111 CALWELL,H G
THE FOUNDATION AND EARLY DEVELOPMENT OF
THE ROYAL BELFAST HOSPITAL FOR SICK
CHILDREN
ULSTER MED J 38
BELFAST
1969 2 01

3112 CALWELL,H G
HISTORY OF THE ROYAL BELFAST HOSPITAL
FOR SICK CHILDREN, 1873-1948
QUB MA
BELFAST
1972 2 04

3113 CALWELL,H G
LIFE AND TIMES OF A VOLUNTARY HOSPITAL:
HISTORY OF ROYAL BELFAST HOSPITAL
BROUGH, COX AND DUNN
BELFAST
1973 2 02

3114 CAMPBELL,C M
REPORT OF THE COMMITTEE OF INQUIRY INTO
THE DEATH OF PAUL MCALOONE
DHSS (NI)
1980 2 03

3115 CAREY,G C R
AIR POLLUTION AND BRONCHITIS IN BELFAST
1961-1965
JSSISI
1967 2 01

3116 CAREY,G C R ET AL
BYSSINOSIS IN FLAX WORKERS IN NI
HMSO
BELFAST
1965 2 03

3117 CARSON,N A J
A BIOCHEMICAL STUDY OF MENTALLY RETARDED
INDIVIDUALS IN NI ...
QUB MD
BELFAST
1963 2 04

3118 CASEMENT,R S
HISTORY OF THE MATER INFIRMORUM
HOSPITAL, BELFAST
ULSTER MED J 38
BELFAST
1969 2 01

3119 CAUL,B
AN AREA BOARD REVISITED
SCOPE 35
BELFAST
1980 2 01

3120 CAUL,B
RESIDENTIAL WORK IN AREA BOARDS - THE
DEPRIVED CARING FOR THE DEPRIVED
QUEST 5
BELFAST
1976 2 01

3121 CHEESEMAN,E A
PULMONARY TUBERCULOSIS IN NI:
STATISTICAL DATA FOR 1948-1954
BRIT J SOC MED 10(3)
1956 2 01

3122 CHEESEMAN,E A ET AL
PHYSIQUE OF BELFAST SCHOOL CHILDREN
ULSTER MED J 23
1954 2 01

3123 COMMUNITY GROUPS CONFERENCE
COMMUNITY ACTION: THE WAY FORWARD
DERRY
1974 2 99

3124 COMPTON, P A; MURRAY, R
THE ELDERLY IN NI, WITH SPECIAL
REFERENCE TO THE CITY OF BELFAST
IN WARNES, A M (ED)
CHICHESTER
1982 2 07

3125 COMPTON, S A
PERFORATED PEPTIC ULCER AND THE CIVIL
DISTURBANCES IN NI
ULSTER MED J 45(2)
1976 1 01

3126 CONLON, J
COMMUNITY WORK IN A RURAL HEALTH AND
SOCIAL SERVICES DISTRICT
DHSS (NI)
BELFAST
1977 2 10

3127 CONLON, M; CONLON, J
RIGHT TO PARENT: A LONG-TERM FOSTERING
EXPERIENCE
DHSS (NI)
BELFAST
1978 2 10

3128 COURTNEY, R
THE NI FUND-RAISING HANDBOOK
SIMON COMMUNITY
BELFAST
1983 2 02

3129 CPAG
DOWNPATRICK SURVEY
CPAG
BELFAST
1972 2 10

3130 CRAIG, J; HARBISON, J
PATIENT ATTITUDES TO HEALTH CENTRES IN
NI
DHSS (NI)
BELFAST
1978 2 03

3131 CRAWFORD, J C
A STUDY OF TWO YEARS' WORK IN NI GENERAL
PRACTICE
BRIT J SOC MED 8(3)
1954 2 01

3132 CURRIE, J
AGE ACTION YEAR
SCOPE 2
BELFAST
1976 2 01

3133 DARBY, J; MORRIS, G
COMMUNITY GROUPS AND RESEARCH IN NI
COMM DEV J 10(2)
1975 2 01

3134 DARRAGH, P M
THE AETIOLOGY AND PREVALENCE OF SEVERE
MENTAL HANDICAP IN NI
QUB MD
BELFAST
1978 2 04

3135 DARRAGH, P M
THE PREVALENCE AND PREVENTION OF SEVERE
MENTAL HANDICAP IN NI
IR MED J JAN
1982 2 01

3136 DAVIDSON, S I
A REVIEW OF ESN SCHOOL LEAVERS IN NI
WITH SPECIAL REFERENCE TO VOCATIONAL
ADJUSTMENT
QUB MED
BELFAST
1972 2 04

3137 DEAN, G
LUNG CANCER AND BRONCHITIS IN NI 1960-2
BRIT MED J JUNE
LONDON
1966 2 01

3138 DEANE, E
COMMUNITY WORK IN THE 70'S
IN FRAZER, H ET AL
BELFAST
1981 1 07

3139 DEANE, E
NI: COMMUNITY WORK IN THE 70'S
CRANE BAG 4(2)
DUBLIN
1980 1 01

3140 DEENY, M
A SURVEY OF TB IN NI
QUB MD
BELFAST
1945 2 04

3141 DENTON, H C B
HANDICAPPED PERSONS IN NI: REPORT ON THE
SIZE AND NATURE OF SOME OF THE SPECIAL
PROBLEMS OF HANDICAPPED PERSONS IN NI
NICSS
BELFAST
1962 2 99

3142 DHSS (NI)
CONSULTATIVE PAPER ON THE STRUCTURE AND
MANAGEMENT OF HEALTH AND PERSONAL SOCIAL
SERVICES IN NI
HMSO
LONDON
1979 2 03

3143 DHSS (NI)
PRIVATE PRACTICE AND THE HEALTH SERVICE
IN NI
DHSS (NI)
BELFAST
1977 2 03

3144 DHSS (NI)
SERVICES FOR THE MENTALLY HANDICAPPED IN
NI: POLICY AND OBJECTIVES
HMSO
BELFAST
1978 2 03

3145 DHSS (NI)
A SURVEY OF GENERAL PRACTICE IN NI
DHSS (NI)
BELFAST
1978 2 03

3146 DICKINSON, C
CHILD ABUSE WITH REFERENCE TO EAST
BELFAST
NUU MSC
COLERAINE
1977 2 04

3147 DICKSON, D
MICROCOUNSELLING: AN EVALUATIVE STUDY OF
A PROGRAMME
ULSTER POLY PHD
BELFAST
1981 2 04

3148 DITCH, J; MORRISSEY, M
RECENT DEVELOPMENTS IN NI SOCIAL POLICY
IN BROWN, M; BALDWIN, S (EDS)
LONDON
1979 2 07

3149 DONAGHY, G; MAGUIRE, G
COMMUNITY WORK: STRUCTURES ARE NOT
ENOUGH
SCOPE 60
BELFAST
1983 2 01

3150 DONALDSON, N
POLIOMYELITIS IN NI
QUB MD
BELFAST
1966 2 04

3151 DRAPER, J
CENTRE RULES OK
COMM CARE OCT 18
1978 2 10

3152 DUDGEON, M Y; DAVIDSON, T W
SOME REACTIONS OF PATIENTS TO THEIR STAY
IN HOSPITAL
ULSTER MED J 37(1)
1968 2 01

3153 DUFF, N
COMMUNITY SELF-SURVEYS
COMM FORUM 3(1)
BELFAST
1973 2 01

3154 DUFF, R
A STUDY OF THE PROVISIONS OF THE WELFARE
SERVICES ACT NI 1949, AND THE CHILDREN
AND YOUNG PERSONS' ACT NI 1950
QUB MSC
BELFAST
1959 2 04

3155 DUFFY, F; PERCEVAL, R ET AL
COMMUNITY ACTION AND COMMUNITY
PERCEPTIONS OF SOCIAL SERVICES IN NI
NUU
COLERAINE
1975 2 10

3156 DUNHAM, A
COMMUNITY DEVELOPMENT AND COMMUNITY
RELATIONS IN NI
SOC SERVICE R 46(2)
1972 1 01

3157 DUNHAM, A
COMMUNITY ORGANISATIONS IN TIMES OF
CHANGE
COMM FORUM 2(1)
BELFAST
1972 2 01

3158 ELDER, A F
HEALTH SERVICES OF NI
BRIT J PREV SOC MED 7(3)
1953 2 01

3159 ELDER, A F
THE MIDWIFE IN NI
MED OFFICER 2067(99)
      2 01

3160 ELLIS, R; WHITTINGTON, D
A GUIDE TO SOCIAL SKILL TRAINING
CROOM HELM
LONDON
1981 2 02

3161 ELWOOD, J H
MAJOR CENTRAL NERVOUS-SYSTEM
MALFORMATIONS NOTIFIED IN NI 1969-1973
DEVELOPMENTAL MEDICINE AND CHILD
NEUROLOGY 18(4)
1976 2 01

3162 ELWOOD, J H
MEDICINE AND THE COMMUNITY: AN INAUGURAL
LECTURE
QUB
BELFAST
1980 2 10

3163 ELWOOD, J H
SECULAR TRENDS IN THE INCIDENCE OF
ANENCEPHALUS AND SPINA-BIFIDA IN BELFAST
IR J MED SCI 144(10)
1975 2 01

3164 ELWOOD, J H
SOME EPIDEMIOLOGICAL OBSERVATIONS ON
EARLY MORTALITY AND BIRTHWEIGHT IN
BELFAST
QUB PHD
BELFAST
1976 2 04

3165 ELWOOD, J H; CLINT, J; MALLAGHAN, M
TUBERCULOSIS IN BELFAST
IR J MED SCI 151
1982 2 01

3166 ELWOOD, J H; DARRAGH, P M
PREVALENCE OF MONGOLISM IN NI
J MENTAL DEFICIENCY RES 25(3)
1981 2 01

3167 ELWOOD, J H; DARRAGH, P M
SEVERE MENTAL HANDICAP IN NI
J MENTAL DEFICIENCY RES 25(3)
1981 2 01

3168 ELWOOD, J H; MACKENZIE, G; CRAN, G W
BIRTH-WEIGHT AND GESTATION OF SINGLE
BIRTHS IN BELFAST
IR J MED SCI 145(9)
1976 2 01

3169 ELWOOD, J H; MACKENZIE, G; CRAN, G W
OBSERVATIONS ON SINGLE BIRTHS TO WOMEN
RESIDENT IN BELFAST 1962-1966
J CHRONIC DISEASES 27
1974 2 01

3170 ELWOOD, J H; NEVIN, N C
FACTORS ASSOCIATED WITH ANENCEPHALUS AND
SPINA BIFIDA IN BELFAST
BRIT J PREV SOC MED 27(2)
1973 2 01

3171 EVANS, A E
ACCURACY OF HOSPITAL ACTIVITY ANALYSIS
DATA IN THE ROYAL VICTORIA HOSPITAL,
BELFAST 1973
IR MED J 71(12)
1978 2 01

3172 EVANS, A E
HOSPITAL ACTIVITY ANALYSIS IN NI
HOSPITAL HEALTH SERVICES R 70
1974 2 01

3173 EVASON, E
ELDERLY IN ARMAGH
SOC WORK TODAY 5(16)
LONDON
1974 2 01

3174 EVASON, E
FINANCIAL AND OTHER CIRCUMSTANCES OF
ARMAGH'S ELDERLY
NUU
COLERAINE
1974 2 10

3175 EVASON, E; DARBY, J; PEARSON, M
SOCIAL NEED AND SOCIAL PROVISION IN NI
NUU
COLERAINE
1976 2 10

3176 FARNDALE, W
HEALTH SERVICES TRAVELOGUE: NI, HOLLAND,
DENMARK AND USA
RAVENSWOOD PUBLICATIONS
BECKENHAM, KENT
1972 2 02

3177 FERGUSON, A C
A FRIEND IN NEED: A BEFRIENDING SCHEME
FOR HOLYWELL PSYCHIATRIC HOSPITAL, CO.
ANTRIM, NI
ROYAL SOCIETY HEALTH J 101(4)
1981 2 01

3178 FRASER, I J
THE BELFAST MEDICAL SCHOOL AND ITS
SURGEONS
ULSTER MED J 50
BELFAST
1981 2 01

3179 FRASER, M
COST OF COMMOTION
BRIT J PSYCHIATRY 118
1971 1 01

3180 FRASER,M
COST OF COMMOTION
COMM FORUM 1(1)
BELFAST
1971 1   01

3181 FRASER,M
MEDICINE IN A WORLD OF CHAOS
WLD MEDICINE JUN
1972 1   01

3182 FRASER,M
PSYCHIATRIC SEQUELAE OF THE 1969 BELFAST
RIOTS
BRIT J PSYCHIATRY 118
1971 1   01

3183 FRAZER,H
COMMUNITY WORK IN NI
COMM DEV J 14(3)
1979 2   01

3184 FRAZER,H
COMMUNITY WORK INTO THE 80'S
IN FRAZER,H ET AL
BELFAST
1981 2   07

3185 FRAZER,H
THE ROLE OF DISTRICT COUNCILS IN
COMMUNITY WORK
NICSS
BELFAST
1976 2   10

3186 FROGGATT,P
SHORT-TERM ABSENCE FROM INDUSTRY: A
STATISTICAL AND HISTORICAL SURVEY
QUB PHD
BELFAST
1967 2   04

3187 FROGGATT,P; LYNAS,M A; MACKENZIE,G
EPIDEMIOLOGY OF SUDDEN UNEXPECTED DEATH
IN INFANTS ('COT DEATH') IN NI
BRIT J PREV SOC MED 24
1971 2   01

3188 FRY,A
SOCIAL WORK IN THE FIRING LINE
COMM CARE 28
1974 1   01

3189 FRY,A
STRUGGLE FOR POWER IN NEWRY
COMM CARE 27
1974 3   01

3190 GAFFIKIN,F
SELF-HELP IN A CATHOLIC WORKING CLASS
COMMUNITY
QUB MSSC
BELFAST
1976 1   04

3191 GIBSON,E D; RITCHIE,J W K; ARMSTRONG,M J
THE CHANGING ROLE OF THE OBSTETRIC
FLYING SQUAD
ULSTER MED J 49
BELFAST
1981 2   01

3192 GIBSON,F
SOCIAL SERVICE RE-ORGANISATION IN NI
SOC WORK TODAY 2(18)
LONDON
1971 2   01

3193 GIBSON,M
THE ROLE OF SOCIAL WORK IN THE
REHABILITATION OF TRAUMATIC ONSET
DISABILITY
DHSS (NI)
BELFAST
1982 2   03

3194 GISH,O
EMIGRATION AND THE SUPPLY AND DEMAND FOR
MEDICAL MANPOWER: THE IRISH CASE
MINERVA 17(4)
1969 2   01

3195 CLANCY,B P
MONGOLISM IN NI
QUB MD
BELFAST
1958 2   04

3196 GLOVER,B
URBAN CHANGE AND COMMUNITY ACTION: A
CASE STUDY IN THE CLIFTON/OLDPARK AREA
ULSTER POLY MPHIL
BELFAST
1982 2   04

3197 GOODCHILD,N
BOGSIDE COMMUNITY DEVELOPMENT
ASSOCIATION
COMM FORUM 4(2)
BELFAST
1974 2   01

3198 GRAHAM,J
CHILDREN IN CARE IN NI
BRIT PSYCHOL SOC CONF
1979 2   11

3199 GRAHAM,J
CHILDREN IN CARE IN NI
SOCIAL WORK ADVISORY GROUP DHSS (NI)
BELFAST
1980 2   10

3200 GRANT,A P; BYRD,M W J
ASSESSMENT OF THE INCIDENCE OF CHRONIC
ALCOHOLISM IN NI
BRIT J ADDICTION 58
1967 2   01

3201 GRANT,D P
ALCOHOLISM AS A PUBLIC HEALTH PROBLEM IN
NI
ULSTER MED J 32
1963 2   01

3202 GREER,A E
FAMILY PLANNING IN NI
FAMILY PLANNING 11(2)
1962 2   01

3203 GREER,H L H; BELL,M; KIDD,C W
A REPORT OF AN INQUIRY INTO MATERNAL
DEATHS IN NI 1960-1963
HMSO
BELFAST
1965 2   03

3204 GREIG,M; PEMBERTON,J; HAY,I; MACKENZIE,G
A PROSPECTIVE STUDY OF THE DEVELOPMENT
OF CORONARY HEART DISEASE IN A GROUP OF
1202 MIDDLE-AGED MEN
J EPIDEMIOLOGY AND COMMUNITY HEALTH 34
1980 2   01

3205 GRIFFITHS,H
CARRYING ON IN THE MIDDLE OF VIOLENT
CONFLICT: SOME OBSERVATIONS OF
EXPERIENCE
IN JONES,D; MAYO,M (EDS)
1974 1   07

3206 GRIFFITHS,H
COMMUNITY DEVELOPMENT AND COMMUNITY
RELATIONS
COMM FORUM 1(2)
BELFAST
1971 1   01

3207 GRIFFITHS,H
COMMUNITY DEVELOPMENT: SOME MORE LESSONS
FROM THE RECENT PAST IN NI
COMM DEV J 10(1)
1975 2   01

3208 GRIFFITHS,H
NICRC
NEW COMM 1(2)
1972 2   01

3209 GRIFFITHS,H
THE NICRC: A CASE STUDY IN AGENCY
CONFLICT
NUU
COLERAINE
1974 2 10

3210 GRIFFITHS,H
PARAMILITARY GROUPS AND OTHER COMMUNITY
ACTION GROUPS IN NI TODAY
CENTRO SOCIALE 22
1975 1 01

3211 GRIFFITHS,H
PARAMILITARY GROUPS AND OTHER COMMUNITY
ACTION GROUPS IN NI TODAY
INT R COMM DEV
1975 1 01

3212 GUEST,I
ULSTER: COMMUNITY POWER OR FIRE POWER?
NEW INTERNATIONALIST 27
1975 1 01

3213 GUIRGUIS,E F
A REVIEW OF THE HOSTEL SITUATION IN
COUNTY DOWN, NI
INT J OF SOC PSYCHIAT 23(2)
1977 2 01

3214 GUTHRIE,D
FOOD FOR THOUGHT
SOC WORK TODAY 11(17)
1979 2 01

3215 GUTHRIE,D
REHABILITATION IN CO. FERMANAGH
FERMANAGH VOLUNTARY ASSOC FOR
HANDICAPPED
1979 2 10

3216 HADDEN,D R; MCDEVITT,D G
ENVIRONMENTAL STRESS AND THYROTONICOSIS:
ABSENCE OF ASSOCIATION
LANCET
1974 2 01

3217 HAIRE,T R
THE CONCEPT OF MENTAL DEFECT WITH
SPECIAL REFERENCE TO INTELLECTUAL
SUBNORMALITY
QUB MD
BELFAST
1954 2 04

3218 HALL,R A
VIOLENCE AND ITS EFFECTS ON THE
COMMUNITY
MEDICO-LEGAL J 43(3)
1975 1 01

3219 HARGIE,O
AN EVALUATION OF MICROTEACHING PROGRAMME
ULSTER POLY PHD
BELFAST
1980 2 04

3220 HARLAND,R W
SOCIOLOGICAL, ANATOMICAL AND
PHYSIOLOGICAL CHANGES IN FIRST-YEAR
STUDENTS ENTERING QUB OVER THIRTY YEARS,
1948-77
ULSTER MED J 49(1)
BELFAST
1980 2 01

3221 HARRISON,E M
SECOND INTERIM REPORT: ADMINISTRATION
AND ORGANISATION OF THE HOME HELP
SERVICE
CENTRAL PERSONAL SOCIAL SERVICES
BELFAST
1978 2 10

3222 HARRISON,E M; MCKEOWN,M; O'SHEA,T
OLD AGE IN NI - A STUDY OF THE ELDERLY
IN A SEASIDE TOWN
ECON AND SOC R 3(1)
1971 2 01

3223 HAYES,M
COMMUNITY RELATIONS AND THE ROLE OF THE
COMMUNITY RELATIONS COMMISSION IN NI
RUNNYMEDE TRUST
LONDON
1972 1 10

3224 HAYES,M
ROLE OF THE COMMUNITY RELATIONS
COMMISSION IN NI
ADMIN (DUB) 20(4)
DUBLIN
1972 2 01

3225 HEALTH AND SOCIAL SERVICES JOURNAL
TIDINGS FROM ULSTER
HEALTH SOC SERVICES J 86
1976 2 01

3226 HERRON,S
HOW MANY SOCIAL WORKERS FOR BELFAST?
QUEST 2
BELFAST
1975 2 01

3227 HERRON,S; CAUL,B
A SERVICE FOR PEOPLE: ORIGINS AND
DEVELOPMENT OF THE PERSONAL SOCIAL
SERVICES
AUTHORS
BELFAST
1980 2 10

3228 HOLLAND,E L ET AL
ASSOCIATIONS BETWEEN PELVIC ANATOMY,
HEIGHT AND YEAR OF BIRTH OF MEN AND
WOMEN IN BELFAST
A HUMAN BIOLOGY 9(2)
1982 2 01

3229 HUGHES,D J
PUBLIC HEALTH LEGISLATION AND THE
IMPROVEMENT OF HOUSING CONDITIONS IN
ENGLAND AND WALES AND IN NI
NI LEG QUART 27(1)
BELFAST
1976 2 01

3230 HYNAM,C A S
COMMUNITY DEVELOPMENT UNDER CRISIS
CONDITIONS: FLEETING IMPRESSIONS
J COMM DEV SOC 4(1)
COLUMBIA, MISSOURI
1973 1 01

3231 INTER-DEPARTMENTAL COMMITTEE ON FAMILY
PROBLEMS
FAMILY PROBLEMS: A COMMENTARY ON THE
IMPLEMENTATION IN NI OF THE
RECOMMENDATIONS OF THE FINER REPORT ON
ONE-PARENT FAMILIES AND VIOLENCE IN
MARRIAGE
COMMITTEE ON FAMILY PROBLEMS
BELFAST
1977 2 10

3232 INTER-DEPARTMENTAL COMMITTEE ON FAMILY
PROBLEMS
FAMILY PROBLEMS: A GUIDE TO PROGRESS ON
THE RECOMMENDATIONS OF THE COMMITTEE
COMMITTEE ON FAMILY PROBLEMS
BELFAST
1977 2 10

3233 IRISH COUNCIL OF CHURCHES AND ROMAN
CATHOLIC JOINT GROUP ON SOCIAL PROBLEMS
REPORT OF THE WORKING PARTY ON TEENAGE
DRINKING
IRISH COUNCIL OF CHURCHES JOINT GROUP ON
SOCIAL PROBLEMS
BELFAST
1974 2 10

3234 IRISH COUNCIL OF CHURCHES AND ROMAN
CATHOLIC JOINT GROUP ON SOCIAL PROBLEMS
REPORT OF THE WORKING PARTY ON THE USE
OF DRUGS
IRISH COUNCIL OF CHURCHES
1972 2 10

3235 IRWIN,W G
A NEW ACADEMIC CAREER STRUCTURE IN
GENERAL PRACTICE IN NI
J ROYAL COLLEGE OF GENERAL PRACTITIONERS
30
LONDON
1980 2 01

3236 IRWIN,W G; BAMBER,J H
CHARACTERISTICS OF SENIOR MEDICAL
STUDENTS AT BELFAST
MED EDUC 12(2)
1978 2 01

3237 IRWIN,W G; BAMBER,J H
AN EVALUATION OF A COURSE FOR
UNDER-GRADUATE TEACHING OF GENERAL
PRACTICE
MED EDUC 12
1978 2 01

3238 JAMES,W V; LAWSON,G T N
REHABILITATION PROGRESS IN NI
MUSGRAVE PARK HOSPITAL
BELFAST
1979 2 08

3239 JOHNSTON,S
SERIOUS EYE INJURIES CAUSED BY THE CIVIL
DISTURBANCES IN BELFAST
ULSTER MED J 40(1)
1971 1 01

3240 KELLY,G
A BLACK PICTURE OF THE FUTURE
SOC WORK TODAY 12(1)
LONDON
1980 2 01

3241 KELLY,G
JOINT FUNDING
SOC WORK TODAY 9(46)
LONDON
1978 2 01

3242 KELLY,G
SOCIAL WORK AND THE COURTS IN NI
IN PARKER,H (ED)
LONDON
1979 2 07

3243 KELLY,G
SOCIAL WORK IN NI
SOC WORK TODAY 10(27)
LONDON
1979 2 01

3244 KELLY,K
COMMUNITY ACTIVITY AND DUNGANNON
COMM FORUM 4(2)
BELFAST
1974 2 01

3245 KELLY,M P
THE NI HOSPITALS AUTHORITY AND CATHOLICS
QUINN
BELFAST
1962 2 11

3246 KIDD,C B
COMPARATIVE STUDY OF OLD PEOPLE IN
GERIATRIC AND MENTAL HOSPITALS, WITH
PARTICULAR REFERENCE TO SOCIOLOGICAL,
PHYSICAL AND PSYCHOLOGICAL ASSESSMENT
QUB MD
BELFAST
1961 2 04

3247 KIDD,C W
THE MEASUREMENT OF MORBIDITY WITH
PARTICULAR REFERENCE TO NATIONAL
INSURANCE RECORDS IN NI
QUB PHD
BELFAST
1959 2 04

3248 KIDD,C W
MORBIDITY TRENDS IN A COMMUNITY OF HIGH
UNEMPLOYMENT
TRANS ASSOC INDUSTRIAL MED OFFICERS
11(3)
1961 2 01

3249 KIDD,C W; PARK,A T
BRONCHITIS IN THE INSURED POPULATION OF
NI
BRIT J PREV SOC MED 13(4)
1960 2 01

3250 KILMURRAY,A
'WHEN THE BOUGH BREAKS': NSPCC AT WORK
SCOPE 55
BELFAST
1982 2 01

3251 KILMURRAY,A
THE MENTALLY HANDICAPPED: A LOW
PRIORITY?
SCOPE 45
BELFAST
1981 2 01

3252 KING,R
SOME ASPECTS OF THE EDUCATION OF
PHYSICALLY HANDICAPPED CHILDREN IN NI
QUB MED
BELFAST
1972 2 04

3253 KNOX,E W
CHRONIC BRONCHITIS IN THE WATERSIDE
DISTRICT OF LONDONDERRY CO. BOROUGH
QUB MD
BELFAST
1961 2 04

3254 KNOX,S J
A GUIDE TO THE MENTAL HEALTH ACT (NI)
1961
NI ASSOCIATION FOR MENTAL HEALTH
BELFAST
1974 2 10

3255 LANCET
NEW HOSPITALS IN ULSTER
LANCET 19
1960 2 01

3256 LAWRENCE,R J
HEALTH SERVICES IN NI
PUBL ADM 34(3)
LONDON
1956 2 01

3257 LENNON,M
CORONARY CARE IN BELFAST
NURSING TIMES 67
1971 2 01

3258 LIVINGSTON,R H
THEY COMFORT ME: THE HISTORY OF NURSING
IN BELFAST
ULSTER MED J APR
BELFAST
1981 2 01

3259 LOVETT,T
THE CHALLENGE OF COMMUNITY EDUCATION IN
SOCIAL AND POLITICAL CHANGE
CONVERGENCE 11(1)
TORONTO
1978 1 01

3260 LOVETT,T
COMMUNITY EDUCATION AND COMMUNITY ACTION
SCOPE 9
BELFAST
1977   2   01

3261 LOVETT,T
THE FUTURE OF COMMUNITY ACTION IN NI
SCOPE 59
BELFAST
1983   2   01

3262 LOVETT,T; MACKAY,L
ADULT EDUCATION AND THE WORKING CLASS: A
CASE STUDY
URB R 9(3)
1976   2   01

3263 LOVETT,T; PERCEVAL,R
POLITICS, CONFLICT AND COMMUNITY ACTION
IN NI
IN CURNO,P (ED)
LONDON
1978   2   07

3264 LUKIANOWICZ,N
BATTERED CHILDREN
PSYCHIATRICA CLINICA 4(5)
1971   2   01

3265 LUKIANOWICZ,N
INFANTICIDE
PSYCHIATRICA CLINICA 4(3)
1971   2   01

3266 LUKIANOWICZ,N
REJECTED CHILDREN
PSYCHIATRICA CLINICA 5(3)
1972   2   01

3267 LUKIANOWICZ,N
REVIEW OF ONE HUNDRED UNSELECTED CHILD
GUIDANCE CLINIC REFERRALS
PSYCHIATRICA CLINICA 5(6)
1972   2   01

3268 LUKIANOWICZ,N
SUICIDAL BEHAVIOUR: AN ATTEMPT TO MODIFY
THE ENVIRONMENT
PSYCHIATRICA CLINICA 6(3)
1973   2   01

3269 LUKIANOWICZ,N
A SURVEY OF THE REASONS FOR REFERRAL OF
URBAN AND RURAL PRIMARY SCHOOL CHILDREN
TO CHILD GUIDANCE CLINICS IN COUNTY
ANTRIM
PAPERS IN PSYCHOL 1(1)
1967   2   01

3270 LYONS,H A
ATTEMPTED SUICIDE BY SELF-POISONING
J IR MED ASSOC 65(17)
1972   2   01

3271 LYONS,H A
DEPRESSIVE ILLNESS AND AGGRESSION IN
BELFAST
BRIT MED J 1(5796)
1972   2   01

3272 LYONS,H A
EFFECTS OF CIVIL DISTURBANCES ON MENTAL
HEALTH
MEDICAL ASSOC FOR PREVENTION WAR 2(3)
1971   1   01

3273 LYONS,H A
HEALTH SERVICES
IN DARBY,J; WILLIAMSON,A (EDS)
LONDON
1978   2   07

3274 LYONS,H A
LEGACY OF VIOLENCE IN NI
INT J OFFENDER THERAPY AND COMP CRIM
19(3)
1975   1   01

3275 LYONS,H A
PSYCHIATRIC EFFECTS OF CIVIL DISTURBANCE
WLD MED 21 APR
1971   1   01

3276 LYONS,H A
PSYCHIATRIC SEQUELAE OF THE BELFAST
RIOTS
BRIT PSYCHIATRY 118(544)
1971   1   01

3277 LYONS,H A
PSYCHOLOGICAL EFFECTS OF THE CIVIL
DISTURBANCES
AQUARIUS
BENBURB
1974   1   01

3278 LYONS,H A
PSYCHOLOGICAL EFFECTS OF THE CIVIL
DISTURBANCES ON CHILDREN
NORTH TEACH 11(1)
BELFAST
1973   1   01

3279 LYONS,H A
TERRORISTS' BOMBING AND THE
PSYCHOLOGICAL SEQUELAE
J IR MED ASSOC 67(1)
1974   1   01

3280 LYONS,H A
VIOLENCE IN BELFAST - A REVIEW OF THE
PSYCHOLOGICAL EFFECTS
PUBL HEALTH 87(6)
1973   1   01

3281 LYONS,H A
VIOLENCE IN BELFAST: A REVIEW OF THE
PSYCHOLOGICAL EFFECTS
COMM HEALTH 5(3)
1973   1   01

3282 LYONS,H A; BINDAL,K K
ATTEMPTED SUICIDE IN BELFAST:
CONTINUATION OF A STUDY IN A DISTRICT
GENERAL HOSPITAL
IR MED J 70(11)
1977   2   01

3283 MACBEATH,A
FIFTY YEARS OF SOCIAL WORK, 1906-1956: A
BRIEF HISTORY OF THE WORK OF BELFAST
COUNCIL OF SOCIAL WELFARE
COUNCIL OF SOCIAL WELFARE
BELFAST
1957   2   10

3284 MACKAY,D N
CHANGING PATTERNS IN THE PREVALENCE OF
MENTAL SUBNORMALITY IN NI
ULSTER MED J 43
BELFAST
1974   2   01

3285 MACKAY,D N
MENTAL SUBNORMALITY IN NI
J MENTAL DEFICIENCY RES 15(1)
1971   2   01

3286 MACKAY,D N; ELLIOTT,R
SUBNORMALS UNDER COMMUNITY AND HOSPITAL
CARE
J MENTAL DEFICIENCY RES 19(1)
1975   2   01

3287 MACKAY,D N; MCDONALD,G
DON'T UNDERESTIMATE THE SUBNORMAL
COMM CARE 140
LONDON
1976   2   01

3288 MAGEE UNIVERSITY COLLEGE CONFERENCE
A PERSON OF NO CONSEQUENCE? A STUDY OF
RETIREMENT...
EXTRA-MURAL STUD MAGEE UNIV COLLEGE
DERRY
1968   2   11

3289 MAGUIRE,G
COMMUNITY WORK IN MOURNEVIEW
IN HENDERSON,P; WRIGHT,A; WYNCOLL,K
(EDS)
LONDON
1982 2 07

3290 MANNING,M
CARING IN A WASTELAND
COMM CARE 196
1978 1 01

3291 MARSHALL,R
50 YEARS ON THE GROSVENOR ROAD: AN
ACCOUNT OF THE RVH 1903-53
ROYAL VICTORIA HOSPITAL
BELFAST
1953 2 10

3292 MARSHALL,R; KELLY,K N M
THE STORY OF THE ULSTER HOSPITAL,
1873-1973
ULSTER HOSPITAL
BELFAST
1973 2 02

3293 MARTIN,W J
LIBRARY SERVICES TO THE DISADVANTAGED:
NOT QUITE WHAT THEY SEEM
AN LEABHARLANN 9
DUBLIN
1980 2 01

3294 MAYNARD,J ; MCREADY,P
THE REORGANISATION OF HEALTH AND
PERSONAL SOCIAL SERVICES IN NI
DEPT BUS STUD QUB
BELFAST
1974 2 10

3295 MCAULEY,R
BEHAVIOUR THERAPY VERSUS ELECTRIC
THERAPY: A COMPARISON OF TWO TREATMENTS
CONDUCTED IN A ROUTINE PSYCHIATRIC
SETTING
QUB MD
BELFAST
1980 2 04

3296 MCCAFFERTY,W H
BELFAST DOMESTIC MISSION 1853-1953: A
CENTURY OF SOCIAL SERVICE
MAGOWAN
BELFAST
1953 2 10

3297 MCCARNEY,W G
GLUE-SNIFFING: CAUSE FOR CONCERN?
SCOPE 43
BELFAST
1981 2 01

3298 MCCLELLAND,J
THE DEVELOPMENT OF EDUCATIONAL
FACILITIES FOR HANDICAPPED CHILDREN
QUB MA
BELFAST
1965 2 04

3299 MCCLURE,G; KEILTY,S; REID,M; RITCHIE,J W K;
SCOTT,M J
NEONATAL DEATH IN NI
BRIT MED J 2
1978 2 01

3300 MCCLURE,G; RITCHIE,J W K; REID,M;
SCOTT,M J; KEILTY,S
REGIONAL NEONATAL CARE BY BELFAST STUDY
GROUP
J IR MED ASSOC 70(14)
DUBLIN
1977 2 01

3301 MCCOY,K
CHILD CARE TRENDS: A REVIEW OF
STATISTICAL RETURNS 1970-1979
SOCIAL WORK ADVISORY GROUP DHSS (NI)
BELFAST
1982 2 03

3302 MCCOY,K
HEALTH AND SOCIAL SERVICES FOR THE VERY
OLD AT HOME
DHSS (NI)
BELFAST
1982 2 03

3303 MCCOY,K
OTHER PEOPLES CHILDREN
DHSS (NI)
BELFAST
1980 2 03

3304 MCCREARY,A
THE ROYAL BELFAST HOSPITAL FOR SICK
CHILDREN: ONE HUNDRED YEARS OF CARING
1873-1973
ROYAL BELFAST HOSPITAL FOR SICK CHILDREN
BELFAST
1973 2 10

3305 MCCREARY,A
SURVIVORS
AUTHOR
BELFAST
1976 1 02

3306 MCDONALD,G; MACKAY,D W
ADMISSION AND DISCHARGE HISTORIES OF
HIGH GRADE SUB-NORMALS IN A HOSPITAL IN
NI
BRIT J MENTAL SUBNORMALITY 21(40)
1975 2 01

3307 MCDONALD,G; MACKAY,D W
MENTAL SUBNORMALITY IN NI
J MENTAL DEFICIENCY RES 22
1978 2 01

3308 MCDONALD,G; MCCABE,P; MACKLE,B
SYMPOSIUM ON STRUCTURED TEACHING AND
TRAINING: SELF-HELP SKILLS IN THE
PROFOUNDLY SUBNORMAL
BRIT J MENTAL SUBNORMALITY 22
1976 2 01

3309 MCDONALD,J
MEDICAL RECORD LINKAGE: A STUDY OF
COMPUTER METHODS FOR LINKING NI BIRTH
AND DEATH REGISTRATION
QUB PHD
BELFAST
1979 2 04

3310 MCDOWELL,I
LOOKING AHEAD IN NI
TRAINING SCHOOL B 53
1956 2 01

3311 MCGUFFIN,S J
HEALTH EDUCATION IN NI SCHOOLS: A SURVEY
OF TEACHERS' ATTITUDES
STRANMILLIS COLLEGE
BELFAST
1976 2 08

3312 MCGUFFIN,S J
HEALTH EDUCATION IN NI SCHOOLS: A SURVEY
OF THE ATTITUDES OF PARENTS AND PUPILS
STRANMILLIS COLLEGE
BELFAST
1976 2 08

3313 MCGUFFIN,S J
HEALTH EDUCATION IN NI: A SURVEY OF
CURRENT PRACTICE IN POST-PRIMARY SCHOOLS
J INST HEALTH EDUC 14(1)
1976 2 01

3314 MCGUFFIN,S J
HEALTH EDUCATION IN POST-PRIMARY
SCHOOLS: A SURVEY OF CURRENT PRACTICE
STRANMILLIS COLLEGE
BELFAST
1975 2 08

3315 MCGUFFIN,S J
HEALTH EDUCATION IN PRIMARY SCHOOLS IN
NI
NORTH TEACH 12(3)
BELFAST
1977 2 01

3316 MCGUFFIN,S J
HEALTH EDUCATION IN PRIMARY SCHOOLS IN
NI: A SURVEY OF CURRENT PRACTICE
STRANMILLIS COLLEGE
BELFAST
1976 2 08

3317 MCGUFFIN,S J
KNOWLEDGE OF REPRODUCTION AND CHILDCARE
POSSESSED BY 16 YEAR OLDS IN NI
PUBL HEALTH 94(4)
1980 2 01

3318 MCGUFFIN,S J
RECENT DEVELOPMENT IN HEALTH EDUCATION
IN SCHOOLS IN NI
ULSTER MED J 47(1)
BELFAST
1978 2 01

3319 MCGUFFIN,S J
VENEREAL DISEASE: ITS PLACE IN HEALTH
EDUCATION IN SCHOOLS
BRIT J VENEREAL DISEASES 53(4)
1977 2 01

3320 MCGUFFIN,S J
WHAT NI TEACHERS THINK ABOUT HEALTH
EDUCATION
J INST HEALTH EDUC 14(1)
1978 2 01

3321 MCKENNA,M
A STUDY OF EDUCATIONALLY SUB-NORMAL
CHILDREN WHO WERE EVENTUALLY DECLARED TO
BE IN NEED OF SPECIAL CARE
QUB MA
BELFAST
1973 2 04

3322 MCNARRY,M
INTRODUCTION TO HEALTH EDUCATION IN
GOVERNMENT TRAINING CENTRES IN CO ANTRIM
HEALTH EDUC J 31(1)
1972 2 01

3323 MCNEILL,M
CHILDREN'S GUARDIANS IN NI
HOWARD J 7(1)
1945 2 01

3324 MCNEILLY,R H
A STUDY OF THE EPIDEMIOLOGY OF 998 FATAL
CASES OF CORONARY ARTERY DISEASE IN
BELFAST
QUB MD
BELFAST
1967 2 04

3325 MCSHANE,E
SOCIAL POLICY AND PROVISION FOR
PRE-SCHOOL CHILDREN
QUEST 2
BELFAST
1975 2 01

3326 MERRETT,J D
SOCIAL CLASS DISTRIBUTION OF RESPIRATORY
TUBERCOLOSIS NOTIFICATIONS IN NI 1949-53
BRIT J PREV SOC MED 13(4)
1960 2 01

3327 MERRETT,J D; HADDEN,W A; RUTHERFORD,W H
THE INJURIES OF TERRORIST BOMBING: A
STUDY OF 1532 CONSECUTIVE PATIENTS
BRIT J SURGERY 65
1978 1 01

3328 MERRETT,J D; MCHENRY,J C; NEVIN,N C
COMPARISON OF CENTRAL NERVOUS SYSTEM
MALFORMATIONS IN SPONTANEOUS ABORTIONS IN
NI AND SOUTH-EAST ENGLAND
BRIT MED J 1
LONDON
1979 2 01

3329 MILLAR,B
PAST AND PRESENT TRENDS IN INFANT
MORTALITY
QUB MD
BELFAST
1947 2 04

3330 MILLER,R; RUTHERFORD,W H; JOHNSTON,S;
MALHOTRA,V J
INJURIES CAUSED BY RUBBER BULLETS: A
REPORT ON NINETY PATIENTS
BRIT J SURGERY 62
1975 1 01

3331 MINISTRY OF HEALTH AND LOCAL GOVERNMENT
(NI)
REPORT OF THE COMMITTEE ON THE HEALTH
SERVICES IN NI
HMSO CMD 334
BELFAST
1955 2 03

3332 MINISTRY OF HEALTH AND LOCAL GOVERNMENT
(NI)
SUMMARY OF THE HOSPITAL BUILDING
PROGRAMME OF THE NI HOSPITALS AUTHORITY
MINISTRY OF HEALTH AND LOCAL GOVERNMENT
(NI)
BELFAST
1963 2 03

3333 MINISTRY OF HEALTH AND SOCIAL SERVICES
(NI)
ADMINISTRATIVE STRUCTURE OF HOSPITAL
MANAGEMENT COMMITTEES
HMSO
BELFAST
1966 2 03

3334 MINISTRY OF HEALTH AND SOCIAL SERVICES
(NI)
HOSPITAL PLAN FOR NI 1966-75
HMSO CMD 417
BELFAST
1966 2 03

3335 MINISTRY OF HEALTH AND SOCIAL SERVICES
(NI)
PRESCRIBING AND SICKNESS BENEFIT COSTS
IN NI
HMSO CMD 528
BELFAST
1969 2 03

3336 MINISTRY OF HEALTH AND SOCIAL SERVICES
(NI)
REVIEW OF THE HOSPITAL PLAN FOR NI
1968-78
HMSO CMD 524
BELFAST
1968 2 03

3337 MINISTRY OF HEALTH AND SOCIAL SERVICES
(NI)
SECOND REVIEW OF THE HOSPITAL PLAN FOR
NI
HMSO CMD 556
BELFAST
1971 2 03

3338 MINISTRY OF HEALTH AND SOCIAL SERVICES
(NI)
A SURVEY OF GENERAL PRACTICE IN NI
MINISTRY OF HEALTH AND SOCIAL SERVICES
(NI)
BELFAST
1970 2 03

3339 MINISTRY OF HOME AFFAIRS (NI)
REPORT ON LEGAL AID AND ADVICE IN NI
HMSO CMD 417
BELFAST
1960 2 03

3340 MITCHEL, N C
BOCIO EN IRLANDA DEL NORTE
REUNION ESPECIAL DE LA COMMISSION DE
GEOGRAFICA MEDICA 6
1967 2 01

3341 MITCHEL, N C
ESCLEROSIS MULTIPLE EN IRELANDA DEL
NORTE
REUNION ESPECIAL DE LA COMMISSION DE
GEOGRAFICA MEDICA 6
1967 2 01

3342 MOFFETT, J
SOCIAL WORK IN A HEALTH CENTRE
DHSS (NI)
BELFAST
1978 2 03

3343 MOLE, S; WHITEBREAD, S B
STAGE ONE REPORT OF SURVEY - ACTION
HANDICAP SURVEY IN NI
OUTSET
LONDON
1979 2 10

3344 MOORE, R
PSYCHIATRIC SEQUELAE OF THE BELFAST
RIOTS: A REPLY TO LYONS
BRIT J PSYCHIATRY 120(557)
LONDON
1972 1 01

3345 MOOREHEAD, R A
EXCITING DEVELOPMENTS IN ULSTER
NURSING MIRROR AND MIDWIVES J 132
1971 2 01

3346 MORRISSEY, M
COMMUNITY ACTION IN THE MONTIAGHS
NEW SOCIETY MAR
LONDON
1974 1 01

3347 MORRISSEY, M
THE LIMITS OF COMMUNITY ACTION
ULSTER POLY MPHIL
BELFAST
1981 2 04

3348 MORRISSEY, M; DITCH, J
SOCIAL POLICY IMPLICATIONS OF EMERGENCY
LEGISLATION
ANNUAL SOC ADMIN CONF
CAMBRIDGE
1979 1 08

3349 MORRISSEY, M; DITCH, J
SOME RECENT DEVELOPMENTS IN NI SOCIAL
POLICY
IN BROWN, M; BALDWIN, S (EDS)
LONDON
1980 2 07

3350 MORTON, P
CONGENITAL HEART DISEASE IN NI
QUB MD
BELFAST
1963 2 04

3351 MULDREW, T
A STUDY OF GENERAL PRACTICE PHARMACY IN
NI
QUB PHD
BELFAST
1981 2 04

3352 MURIE, A S; BIRRELL, W D
SOCIAL SERVICES IN NI
ADMIN (DUB) 20(4)
1972 2 01

3353 MYCO, F
THE IMPLEMENTATION OF NURSING RESEARCH
RELATED TO THE NURSING PROFESSION IN NI
J ADVANCED NURSING 6(1)
OXFORD
1981 2 01

3354 NEILL, D G
SOME PROBLEMS OF INTEGRATION IN THE
HOSPITAL SERVICE IN NI
JSSISI 19
DUBLIN
1956 2 01

3355 NEILL, D G
THE UNFINISHED BUSINESS OF THE WELFARE
STATE
BOYD
BELFAST
1958 2 10

3356 NEILL, G A W
TYPHUS FEVER IN COUNTY TYRONE
PUBL HEALTH, JUNE
1949 2 01

3357 NELSON, M G; MERRETT, J D
EPIDEMIOLOGY OF LEUKAEMIA IN NI
IR J MED SCI 489
1966 2 01

3358 NEVIN, G B; NEVIN, N C; REDMOND, A D
CYSTIC-FIBROSIS IN NI
J MED GENETICS 16(2)
1979 2 01

3359 NEVIN, N C; MCDONALD, J R; WALBY, A L
COMPARISON OF NEURAL TUBE DEFECTS...IN
NI
INT J EPIDEMIOLOGY 7(4)
1978 2 01

3360 NEWE, G B
STORY OF NI COUNCIL FOR SOCIAL SERVICES,
1938-63
NICSS
BELFAST
1963 2 10

3361 NI ASSOCIATION FOR MENTAL HEALTH
THE FUTURE OF CHILD GUIDANCE IN NI
NI ASSOCIATION FOR MENTAL HEALTH
BELFAST
1965 2 10

3362 NI CHILD WELFARE COUNCIL
CHILDREN IN CARE: A REPORT
HMSO
BELFAST
1956 2 03

3363 NI COMMITTEE FOR THE INTERNATIONAL YEAR
OF THE CHILD
PROCEEDINGS OF STUDY DAY ON UNDER-AGE
DRINKING
ULSTER POLY
BELFAST
1979 2 08

3364 NI COUNCIL FOR NURSES AND MIDWIVES
A SUMMARY OF THE WORK OF THE COUNCIL
1971-1975
NI COUNCIL FOR NURSES AND MIDWIVES
BELFAST
1976 2 10

3365 NI HOSPITALS AUTHORITY
THE DEVELOPMENT OF HOSPITAL AND
SPECIALIST SERVICES
NI HOSPITALS AUTHORITY
BELFAST
1963 2 03

3366 NI HOSPITALS AUTHORITY
GROSVENOR ROAD SITE DEVELOPMENT: THE
FUTURE DEVELOPMENT OF THE ROYAL VICTORIA
HOSPITAL
NI HOSPITALS AUTHORITY
BELFAST
1968 2 03

3367 NI HOSPITALS AUTHORITY
REPORT OF THE SPECIAL COMMITTEE ON THE
HOSPITAL AND SPECIALIST SERVICES
HMSO
BELFAST
1944 2 03

3368 NI MEDICAL MANPOWER ADVISORY COMMITTEE
REPORT OF THE GENERAL MEDICAL
PRACTITIONER AND GP TRAINING GRADES
SUB-COMMITTEE ON MEDICAL STAFFING IN
GENERAL PRACTICE
NI MEDICAL MANPOWER ADVISORY COMMITTEE
BELFAST
1975 2 10

3369 NI REGIONAL HOSPITALS COUNCIL
THE RED BOOK: A PLAN FOR THE HOSPITAL
SERVICES OF NI
NI REGIONAL HOSPITALS COUNCIL
BELFAST
1946 2 03

3370 NI REVIEW COMMITTEE ON MENTAL HEALTH
LEGISLATION
REPORT OF REVIEW COMMITTEE ON MENTAL
HEALTH LEGISLATION
HMSO
BELFAST
1981 2 03

3371 NICRC
PEOPLE AT CENTRE: BUILDING A COMMUNITY
CENTRE
NICRC
BELFAST
1971 2 10

3372 NICSS
ACCESS GUIDE - A SURVEY OF ACCESS
FACILITIES FOR THE DISABLED IN NI
NICSS
BELFAST
1978 2 29

3373 NICSS
THE CHILD IN THE COMMUNITY: THE
CHALLENGE
NICSS
BELFAST
1962 2 08

3374 NICSS
HANDICAPPED PERSONS IN NI
NICSS
BELFAST
1962 2 10

3375 NICSS
REGISTER OF VOLUNTARY ASSOCIATIONS IN NI
NICSS
BELFAST
1977 2 10

3376 NICSS
WELFARE STATE AND WELFARE SOCIETY
NICSS
BELFAST
1966 2 10

3377 NICSS
THE YOUNG CHRONIC SICK IN NI: A SURVEY
NICSS
BELFAST
1972 2 10

3378 NIEC
PUBLIC EXPENDITURE PRIORITIES: HEALTH
AND PERSONAL SOCIAL SERVICES
NIEC
BELFAST
1982 2 03

3379 NORTHERN HEALTH AND SOCIAL SERVICES
BOARD
DEVELOPMENT OF HOSPITAL SERVICES IN THE
AREA OF THE NORTHERN HEALTH AND SOCAL
SERVICES BOARD
NORTHERN HEALTH AND SOCIAL SERVICES
BOARD
BALLYMENA
1977 2 03

3380 NOWLAN, D
LAST COMMUNITY LINK IN ULSTER: THE
FAMILY DOCTOR
WLD MED 7(1)
1971 2 01

3381 O'BLEINE, R
ALCOLACHT: FADHB AR LEITH IN EIRINN?
ULTACH 53(12)
1976 2 01

3382 O'BLEINE, R
EIPIDEIMEOLAIOCHT NA SCLEAROISE SIOLTA
ULTACH 53(10)
1976 2 01

3383 O'BRIEN, D
FROM RESIDENTIAL UNIT TO DAY ASSESSMENT
CENTRE
SOC WORK TODAY 10(27)
LONDON
1979 2 01

3384 O'KANE, P C ET AL
THE NHS IN NI
RES PAPERS ROYAL COMMISSION ON THE NHS 2
LONDON
1978 2 03

3385 O'KANE, P C; HAMILTON, P
A COMMENTARY ON EXISTING NURSE ROTA
SYSTEMS IN TWO HOSPITALS IN THE NORTH
AND WEST BELFAST DISTRICT
HEALTH AND SOCIAL SERVICES MANAGEMENT
RESEARCH UNIT QUB
BELFAST
1981 2 10

3386 O'KANE, P C; MCCLEAN, P; SHEPPARD, C R
AN INVESTIGATION INTO METHODS OF
DECREASING PATIENT WAITING TIME IN THE
ACCIDENT AND EMERGENCY DEPARTMENT OF THE
ROYAL VICTORIA HOSPITAL
HEALTH AND SOCIAL SERVICES MANAGEMENT
RESEARCH UNIT QUB
BELFAST
1980 2 10

3387 O'KANE, P C; SHEPPARD, C R
AN INVESTIGATION OF STOCKHOLDING
POLICIES IN HOSPITAL PHARMACIES
HEALTH AND SOCIAL SERVICES MANAGEMENT
RESEARCH UNIT QUB
BELFAST
1980 2 10

3388 O'KANE, P C; WALKER, R ET AL
THE NHS IN NI: MANAGEMENT OF HEALTH
RESOURCES
RES PAP ROYAL COMMISSION ON NHS 2
1978 2 10

3389 O'MALLEY, P P
ATTEMPTED SUICIDE BEFORE AND AFTER
COMMUNAL VIOLENCE IN BELFAST AUG 1969
J IR MED ASSOC 56(5)
1971 1 01

3390 O'MALLEY, P P
ATTEMPTED SUICIDE; SUICIDE AND COMMUNAL
VIOLENCE
IR MED J 68(5)
1975 1 01

3391 ODLUM, D
INTEGRATION OF PSYCHIATRY IN GENERAL
MEDICINE IN GB AND NI
INT J SOC PSYCHIATRY 1(2)
1955 2 01

3392 OLIVER, J
PRE-SUPPOSITIONS AND IMPLICATIONS OF THE
WELFARE STATE
QUB PHD
BELFAST
1951 2 04

3393 OMAGH COMMUNITY DEVELOPMENT PROJECT
THREE YEARS ON
OMAGH COMMUNITY DEVELOPMENT PROJECT
OMAGH
1981 2 10

3394 OUTSET
'ACTION HANDICAP' SURVEY IN NI: STAGE
ONE REPORT
OUTSET
LONDON
1979 2 10

3395 OUTSET
'ACTION ON HANDICAP' SURVEY IN NI: A
REPORT ON A SURVEY OF THE HANDICAPPED IN
LARNE AND CARRICKFERGUS HEALTH AND
SOCIAL SERVICES
OUTSET
LONDON
1981 2 10

3396 OUTSET
ACTION ON HANDICAP: A REPORT OF THE
ONE-DAY CONFERENCE TO DISCUSS OUTSET'S
SURVEY OF THE HANDICAPPED IN NI
OUTSET
LONDON
1978 2 10

3397 PALLEY, C
ADOPTION ACT (NI) 1967
NI LEG QUART 21(3)
1970 2 01

3398 PANTRIDGE, J F; GEDDES, J S
A MOBILE INTENSIVE-CARE UNIT IN THE
MANAGEMENT OF MYOCARDIAL INFRACTION
LANCET 5 AUG
1967 2 01

3399 PARK, A T
OCCUPATIONAL MORTALITY IN NI (1960-62)
JSSISI 23
1966 2 01

3400 PARKER, J G; DAMOGLOU, A P; STEWART, D A
FAECAL BACTERIA IN THE RIVER LAGAN
ESTUARY
RECORD OF AGRICULTURAL RES
BELFAST
1979 2 01

3401 PATTEN, P
LOCAL GOVERNMENT REFORM: HEALTH AND
SOCIAL SERVICES
COMM FORUM 3(1)
BELFAST
1973 2 01

3402 PEMBERTON, J
SMOKING SURVEYS AT ROYAL BELFAST
ACADEMICAL INSTITUTION
HEALTH EDUC J 35(2)
1976 2 01

3403 PHILLIPS, J G
PLASTIC BULLET INJURY: A CASE REPORT
BRIT J ORAL SURGERY 3
1977 1 01

3404 REDGRAVE, P
PLASTIC BULLETS: THE MEDICAL FACTS
WLD MEDICINE 5 FEB
1983 1 01

3405 REILLY, L
HUMAN TUBERCULOSIS OF BOVINE ORIGIN IN
NI
J HYGIENE 48(4)
1951 2 01

3406 REVIEW COMMITTEE ON HEALTH AND PERSONAL
SOCIAL SERVICES FOR ELDERLY PEOPLE IN NI
PAST 65: WHO CARES?
HMSO
BELFAST
1982 2 03

3407 ROBB, J
HEALTH AND DISEASE
SCOPE 44
BELFAST
1981 2 01

3408 ROBB, J; MATTHEWS, J G
THE INJURIES AND MANAGEMENT OF RIOT
CASUALTIES
BRIT J SURGERY 58(6)
1971 1 01

3409 ROBINSON, J; NIC GIOLLA CHOILLE, T
REGISTER OF VOLUNTARY ORGANISATIONS IN
NI
NICSS
BELFAST
1977 2 10

3410 ROCH, E
FOLK MEDICINE AND FAITH HEALING IN NI
QUB PHD
BELFAST
1981 2 04

3411 RODDIE, I
AN EXCELLENT MEDICAL SCHOOL, AN
INAUGURAL LECTURE
QUB
BELFAST
1975 2 10

3412 ROGERS, S; TITTERINGTON, J
A SURVEY OF NON-ACCIDENTAL INJURY
REGISTERS IN NI
ULSTER POLY
BELFAST
1978 2 10

3413 ROLSTON, B
COMMUNITY DEVELOPMENT AND THE CAPITALIST
STATE: THE CASE OF THE NI COMMUNITY
RELATIONS COMMISSION
QUB PHD
BELFAST
1978 1 04

3414 ROLSTON, B
COMMUNITY POLITICS
IN O'DOWD, L; ROLSTON, B; TOMLINSON, M
LONDON
1980 1 07

3415 ROLSTON, B
COMMUNITY WORK: CONTROL OR LIBERATION?
IN SPENCER, A; CORMACK, R; O'DOWD, L;
TOVEY, H (EDS) PROC SAI
BELFAST
1977 1 01

3416 ROLSTON, B
THE FUTURE OF COMMUNITY WORK: VISION OR
NIGHTMARE
SCOPE 59
BELFAST
1983 2 01

3417 ROLSTON, B
IRON FISTS, KID GLOVES
CASE CON 20
LONDON
1975 1 01

3418 ROLSTON, B
REFORMING THE ORANGE STATE: PROBLEMS OF
THE NI COMMUNITY RELATIONS COMMISSION
IN DOWNING, J D; ROLSTON, B; SMYTH, J
LONDON
1977 1 10

3419 ROLSTON, B
SECTARIANISM AND COMMUNITY POLITICS
IN FRAZER, H ET AL
BELFAST
1981 1 07

3420 ROLSTON, B
SOME THOUGHTS ON THE PASSING OF THE
COMMUNITY RELATIONS COMMISSION
NEW COMM 5(3)
LONDON
1976 1 01

3421 ROLSTON, B; SMYTH, M
THE SPACES BETWEEN CASES: RADICAL SOCIAL
WORK IN NI
IN BAILEY, R; LEE, P (EDS)
OXFORD
1982 2 07

3422 RUSSELL, J
LIVING ALONE IN NI
SOC POL AND ADM 17(1)
OXFORD
1983 2 01

3423 RUSSELL, M F
A CONTROLLED STUDY OF THE RELATIONSHIP
BETWEEN GYNAECOLOGICAL ILLNESS AND
MARITAL PROBLEMS IN A BELFAST GENERAL
PRACTICE
QUB MD
BELFAST
1968 2 04

3424 RUTHERFORD, W H
ALCOHOLIC PROBLEMS AS SEEN FROM A LARGE
BELFAST HOSPITAL
BRIT J ALCHOLISM 12(4)
1977 2 01

3425 RUTHERFORD, W H
THE INJURIES OF CIVIL DISORDER
COMM HEALTH 6(14)
1974 1 01

3426 SARGAISON, E
GROWING OLD IN COMMON LODGINGS...IN
BELFAST
NUFFIELD PROVINCIAL HOSPITALS TRUST
LONDON
1957 2 10

3427 SCALLY, B G
MARRIAGE AND MENTAL HANDICAP: SOME
OBSERVATIONS IN NI
IN DE LA CRUZ, F; LAVECK, G D (EDS)
NEW YORK
1973 2 07

3428 SCALLY, B G; MACKAY, D N
THE SPECIAL CARE SERVICE IN NI: ORIGINS
AND STRUCTURE
IR J MED SCI 462
1964 2 01

3429 SCOPE
ALCOHOL: WHAT MORE COULD WE DO?
SCOPE 19
BELFAST
1978 2 01

3430 SCOPE
DISTRICT COMMITTEES: HOW WELL DO THEY
DO?
SCOPE 8
BELFAST
1977 2 01

3431 SCOPE
DISTRICT COUNCILS AND COMMUNITY WORK
SCOPE 3
BELFAST
1976 2 01

3432 SCOPE
DISTRICT COUNCILS AND COMMUNITY WORK:
TWENTY MONTHS ON
SCOPE 13
BELFAST
1977 2 01

3433 SCOPE
THE HANDICAPPED: A DISADVANTAGED
MINORITY
SCOPE 15
BELFAST
1978 2 01

3434 SCOPE
INTERVIEW WITH DOUGLAS SMYTH
SCOPE 22
BELFAST
1979 2 01

3435 SCOPE
INTERVIEW WITH HYWEL GRIFFITHS
SCOPE 1
BELFAST
1975 2 01

3436 SCOPE
INTERVIEW WITH LORD MELCHETT
SCOPE 11
BELFAST
1977 2 01

3437 SCOPE
INTERVIEW WITH PETER MCLACHLAN
SCOPE 3
BELFAST
1976 2 01

3438 SCOPE
SOCIAL POLICIES AND THE POLITICAL
PARTIES
SCOPE 18
BELFAST
1978 2 01

3439 SCOPE
THE UNDER-FIVES CRISIS
SCOPE 25
BELFAST
1979 2 01

3440 SCOPE
VOLUNTARY ORGANISATIONS: THE NEW WELFARE
STATE?
SCOPE 17
BELFAST
1978 2 01

3441 SCOPE
THE WISE MAN AND THE MINISTER
SCOPE 23
BELFAST
1979 2 01

3442 SCOPE
YOUTH SERVICE IN SEARCH OF A POLICY
SCOPE 1
BELFAST
1975 1 01

3443 SCOTT, M J; MCCLURE, G; REID, M; RITCHIE, J
W K; KEILTY, S
NEONATAL DEATH IN NI
BRIT MED J 2
1978 2 01

3444 SCOTT, M J; RITCHIE, J W K
A STUDY OF THE WORLD HEALTH ORGANISATION
PERINATAL DEATH CERTIFICATE IN NI
PROC 8TH STUDY GROUP ROYAL COLLEGE
OBSTETRICS AND GYNAECOLOGY
LONDON
1980 2 11

3445 SHANAHAN, P
NEGOTIATING THE DEFINITION OF COMMUNITY
WORK IN RURAL IRELAND
COMM DEV J 15(2)
1980 2 01

3446 SHAW, J
PULMONARY CONTASION IN CHILDREN DUE TO
RUBBER BULLET INJURIES
BRIT MED J 2
LONDON
1972 1 01

3447 SLEATH, S
VOLUNTEER RECRUITMENT AND MOBILISATION
OF VOLUNTEERS VIA TELEVISION IN NI
SOC ACTION AND THE MEDIA 4
1979 2 01

3448 SMEATON, B
COMMUNITY WORK, SOCIAL CHANGE AND THE
UNIVERSITIES
SCOPE 2
BELFAST
1976 2 01

3449 SMILEY, J
BACKGROUND TO BYSSINOSIS IN ULSTER
BRIT J INDUSTRIAL MED 18
1961 2 01

3450 SMITH, J P
INFANT MORTALITY AND HANDICAP IN NI
J ADVANCED NURSING 6(2)
1981 2 01

3451 SMYTH, S
COMMUNITY CONVENTION
NORTH BELFAST RESOURCE CENTRE
BELFAST
1975 1 08

3452 SMYTH, S
THE GREATER WEST BELFAST COMMUNITY
ASSOCIATION
COMM FORUM 3(3)
1973 1 09

3453 SOCIAL WORK TODAY
SPECIAL FEATURE ON SOCIAL WORK IN NI
SOC WORK TODAY 10(27)
LONDON
1979 2 01

3454 SONA, G
THE BLOOMFIELD STUDY
NETWORK 1(1)
BELFAST
1980 2 01

3455 SPARE RIB
A PLAYGROUP CALLED FREEDOM
SPARE RIB 41
LONDON
1975 1 10

3456 STEPHEN, E
HANDICAP IN NI: A SPECIAL CASE
IN SWAN, W (ED)
LONDON
1981 2 07

3457 STRAHAN, J
AGRICULTURAL INJURIES IN NI
QUB MCH
BELFAST
1971 1 04

3458 STRAIN, R W M
THE HISTORY OF THE ULSTER MEDICAL
SOCIETY
ULSTER MED J 36
BELFAST
1967 2 01

3459 SUBCOMMITTEE ON PERSONAL SOCIAL SERVICES
FOR BLIND, PARTIALLY SIGHTED PEOPLE
REPORT ON SERVICES FOR HEARING IMPAIRED
PEOPLE
CENTRAL SOCIAL SERVICES ADVISORY
COMMITTEE
BELFAST
1977 2 10

3460 TAGGART, J
COMMUNITY HEALTH SERVICES UNDER STRESS
PUBL HEALTH(87)
LONDON
1973 2 01

3461 TAGGART, J
FAMILY PLANNING FOR ULSTER
WRIGHT
BRISTOL
1969 2 11

3462 TANNER REPORT
REPORT OF THE COMMITTEE ON HEALTH
SERVICES IN NI
HMSO CMD 334
BELFAST
1955 2 03

3463 TAYLOR, A
SEX EDUCATION AND ITS PROVISION IN NI
SECONDARY AND GRAMMAR SCHOOLS
QUB MED
BELFAST
1967 2 04

3464 THEN, B L
A COMPARATIVE STUDY OF THE MEANING OF
'CHARITY' IN MALAYA, ENGLAND, NI AND THE
IRISH REPUBLIC...
QUB LLM
BELFAST
1968 2 04

3465 THOMPSON, I M
DUST AND SENSITIVITY IN THE LINEN
INDUSTRY
QUB MD
BELFAST
1956 2 04

3466 TITTMAR, H; HARGIE, O; DICKSON, D
SOCIAL SKILLS TRAINING AT ULSTER COLLEGE
PROGRAM LEARN ED TECH 4
1977 2 01

3467 TOWNSEND, M
THE NEED FOR CARE: A CENSUS OF RESIDENTS
IN HOMES FOR THE ELDERLY
SOCIAL WORK ADVISORY GROUP DHSS (NI)
BELFAST
1977 2 03

3468 TRAUB, A I; BOYLE, D D; THOMPSON, W
THE ESTABLISHMENT OF AN AID CLINIC IN NI
ULSTER MED J 48
BELFAST
1979 2 01

3469 TRAUB, A I; GIBSON, E D; THOMPSON, W
HYSTERECTOMY IN YOUNG WOMEN: A THIRTY
YEAR REVIEW
BRIT J CLINICAL PRACTICE 34
1980 2 01

3470 TWEED, B
COMMUNITY WORK COMMENT IN NI
SOC WORK TODAY 2(15)
1971 1 01

3471 VUOPALA, U H
RESUMPTION OF WORK AFTER MYOCARDIAL
INFRACTION IN NI
OULU UNIV MD
1972 2 04

3472 WADDINGTON, P
COMMUNITY WORK IN 1980: SOME ISSUES AND
DILEMMAS
IN FRAZER, H ET AL
BELFAST
1980 2 07

3473 WALKER,R; GOLDBERG,E; FRUIN,D
SOCIAL WORKERS AND THEIR WORKLOADS IN NI
WELFARE DEPARTMENTS
NAT INST FOR SOC WORK TRAINING
LONDON
1972 2 10

3474 WALLACE,W F M ET AL
A STUDY OF APPENDICECTOMIES IN BELFAST
IN 1958
ULSTER MED J 32
BELFAST
1963 2 01

3475 WALSH,N
NI'S SICK CHILDREN
STUDIES 62
DUBLIN
1973 2 01

3476 WEIR,T W
LEGISLATION AND MENTAL HEALTH IN NI
J MENTAL SCI 95
1949 2 01

3477 WHITE,J G
CLINICAL PSYCHOLOGY IN NI: THE FIRST
SEVEN YEARS
BRIT PSYCHOL SOC BULL 20
LONDON
1967 2 01

3478 WHITLOCK,R I; GORMAN,J M
SOME MISSILE INJURIES DUE TO CIVIL
UNREST IN NI
INT J ORAL SURGERY 4
1978 1 01

3479 WICKEN,A
ENVIRONMENTAL AND PERSONAL FACTORS IN
LUNG CANCER AND BRONCHITIS MORTALITY
TOBACCO RESEARCH COUNCIL
LONDON
1966 2 10

3480 WIENER,R
COMMUNITY SELF SURVEY: A DO IT YOURSELF
GUIDE
NICRC
BELFAST
1972 2 10

3481 WIENER,R
CONSEQUENCES OF A SELF-SURVEY BY A
BELFAST COMMUNITY
J SOC PSYCHOL 93(2)
PROVINCETOWN
1974 2 01

3482 WIENER,R
THE RAPE AND PLUNDER OF THE SHANKILL
FARSET
BELFAST
1980 1 02

3483 WILLIAMSON,A
THE BEGINNINGS OF STATE CARE FOR THE
MENTALLY ILL IN IRELAND
ECON AND SOC R 1(2)
DUBLIN
1970 2 01

3484 WILLIAMSON,A
NEW FRONTIERS IN SOCIAL ADMINISTRATION
NUU
COLERAINE
1973 2 10

3485 WILLIAMSON,A; DARBY,J
SOCIAL WELFARE SERVICES
IN DARBY,J; WILLIAMSON,A (EDS)
LONDON
1978 1 07

3486 WILLIAMSON,F
DAY HOSPITAL IN A TROUBLED
COMMUNITY...BELFAST
NURSING TIMES DEC 28
1972 1 01

3487 WILLIAMSON,F
A DAY HOSPITAL WITHIN THE DIVISIONS OF A
TROUBLED COMMUNITY
INT J SOC PSYCHIATRY 24(2)
1978 1 01

3488 WILTON,G
HIGH RISE HOSPITAL
HEALTH SOC SERVICES J NOVEMBER 5
LONDON
1981 2 01

3489 WILTON,G
A LITTLE IRISH REJIG
HEALTH SOC SERVICES J, SEPTEMBER 11
LONDON
1981 2 01

3490 WORKERS' RESEARCH UNIT
HEALTH AND WEALTH IN THE SIX COUNTIES
WRU BULLETIN 3
BELFAST
1978 1 09

3491 BELFAST WOMEN'S COLLECTIVE AND WOMEN IN
MEDIA
SCARLET WOMEN
SCARLET WOMEN COLLECTIVE
NORTH SHIELDS, TYNE AND WEAR
1980 1 10

3492 BICO
WOMEN'S LIBERATION IN BRITAIN AND
IRELAND
ATHOL BOOKS
BELFAST
1974 2 09

3493 BOYD, R; FELIX, P; ARDILL, S; KELLY, B
WOMEN IN IRELAND: OUR STRUGGLE
SPARE RIB 130
LONDON
1983 I 01

3494 BOYLE, C
VIOLENCE AGAINST WIVES: THE CRIMINAL LAW
IN RETREAT?
NI LEG QUART 31(1)
1980 2 01

3495 BROMLEY, P M; PASSINGHAM, B
DIVORCE LAW REFORM IN NI
DEPT LAW QUB
BELFAST
1978 2 10

3496 BROOKER, D S; ROY, A D
BREAST DISEASE IN WOMEN UNDER THIRTY:
TEN YEAR REVIEW AND ASSESSMENT OF
CLINICAL SCREENING
ULSTER MED J 51(2)
BELFAST
1982 2 01

3497 BRYANS, H
WOMAN POWER
SCOPE 26
BELFAST
1979 2 01

3498 BUCKLEY, S; LONGERAN, P
WOMEN OF THE TROUBLES, 1969-1980
IN ALEXANDER, Y; O'DAY, A (EDS)
LONDON
1983 1 07

3499 BURNS, G
THE LAW AND GAYS IN NI
NORTHERN GAY RIGHTS ASSOCIATION
BELFAST
1981 2 09

3500 CLARKE, M T
MEN, WOMEN AND POST-PRIMARY
PRINCIPALSHIP IN NI
CORE 3(1)
1979 2 01

3501 CLARKE, M T
MEN, WOMEN AND POST-PRIMARY
PRINCIPALSHIP IN NI
EOC
BELFAST
1978 2 03

3502 COMMISSION OF THE EUROPEAN COMMUNITIES
WOMEN AND EMPLOYMENT IN THE UNITED
KINGDOM, IRELAND AND DENMARK
BRUSSELS
COMMISSION OF THE EUROPEAN COMMUNITIES
1975 2 03

3503 COMPTON, P A ET AL
RELIGION AND LEGAL ABORTION IN NI
J BIOSOCIAL SCI 6
1974 2 01

3504 CONLON, L
CUMANN NA MBAN AND THE WOMEN OF IRELAND
KILKENNY PEOPLE LTD
KILKENNY
1969 2 02

3505 COREA, G
NI: THE VIOLENCE ISN'T ALL IN THE STREET
MS 8
1979 2 01

3506 COURTNAY, A
THE FEMINIST CASE AGAINST ABORTION
SCOPE 45
BELFAST
1981 2 01

3507 CREIGHTON, W B
THE SEX DISCRIMINATION (NI) ORDER 1976
NI LEG QUART 29(3/4)
BELFAST
1978 2 01

3508 CROMIE, S
WOMEN AS MANAGERS IN NI
J OCCUPATIONAL PSYCHOL 54(2)
1981 2 01

3509 D'ARCY, M
TELL THEM EVERYTHING
PLUTO
LONDON
1981 1 02

3510 DITCH, J; OSBORNE, R D
WOMEN AND WORK IN NI: A SURVEY OF DATA
OCCASIONAL PAPER IN SOCIAL POLICY,
SCHOOL OF SOCIOLOGY AND SOCIAL POLICY
ULSTER POLY
BELFAST
1980 2 10

3511 DOGGETT, A; HICKMAN, M
WOMEN AND NATIONALISM
IRL SOCIALIST R 8
LONDON
1981 1 01

3512 EAGLESON, E
EMPLOYMENT AND TRAINING OF GIRLS LEAVING
BELFAST SCHOOLS
QUB PHD
BELFAST
1958 2 04

3513 EDGERTON, L
WOMEN IN NI
QUB STUDENT UNION
BELFAST
1974 2 10

3514 EOC
CASES IN EQUAL PAY AND SEX
DISCRIMINATION LAW IN NI 1979-1982
EOC
BELFAST
1983 2 10

3515 EOC
GIRLS AND EDUCATION: A NI STATISTICAL
ANALYSIS
EOC
BELFAST
1981 2 03

3516 EOC
A GUIDE TO WOMEN'S VOLUNTARY
ORGANISATIONS IN NI
EOC
BELFAST
1980 2 03

3517 EOC
REPORT OF A FORMAL INVESTIGATION INTO
FURTHER EDUCATION IN NI
EOC
BELFAST
1981 2 03

3518 EVASON, E
HIDDEN VIOLENCE: A STUDY OF BATTERED
WOMEN IN NI
FARSET
BELFAST
1982 2 02

3519 EVASON, E
JUST ME AND THE KIDS: A STUDY OF
SINGLE-PARENT FAMILIES IN NI
EOC
BELFAST
1981 2 10

3520 EVASON, E
WOMEN IN NI: EMPLOYMENT, LAW AND SOCIAL
PROVISION
NEW COMM 5(1-2)
1976 2 01

3521 EVE, J
DOMESTIC PROCEEDINGS IN MAGISTRATES'
COURTS: A DISCUSSION OF THE DOMESTIC
PROCEEDINGS (NI) ORDER 1980
SLS/FACULTY OF LAW QUB
BELFAST
1981 2 08

3522 EZEKIEL, J
WOMEN IN NI
RADICAL AMERICA 14(6)
1980 1 01

3523 GOLDSTROM, J M
ABORTION AND THE LAW IN NI
SCOPE 45
BELFAST
1981 2 01

3524 GREER, H L H; BELL, M; KIDD, C W
A REPORT OF AN INQUIRY INTO MATERNAL
DEATHS IN NI 1960-1963
HMSO
BELFAST
1965 2 03

3525 HAUGHTON REPORT
REPORT ON THE EMPLOYMENT AND TRAINING OF
WOMEN IN NI
MINISTRY OF HEALTH AND SOCIAL SERVICES
(NI)
BELFAST
1969 2 03

3526 HINDS, B
LEGISLATIVE INEQUALITY: THE NEED FOR
SOCIAL REFORMS
SCOPE 5
BELFAST
1976 2 01

3527 IPA
WOMEN IN IRELAND
IPA
DUBLIN
1975 2 02

3528 IRIS
A PEOPLE'S ARMY
IRIS 4
DUBLIN
1982 1 01

3529 KELLY, R M; BOUTILIER, M
THE MAKING OF POLITICAL WOMEN: A STUDY
OF SOCIALISATION AND ROLE CONFLICT
NELSON-HALL
CHICAGO
1978 1 02

3530 KILMURRAY, A
RAPE: ADDING INSULT TO INJURY
SCOPE 50
BELFAST
1982 2 01

3531 KINGHAN, N
UNITED WE STOOD: THE STORY OF THE ULSTER
WOMEN'S UNIONIST COUNCIL 1911-1974
APPLETREE PRESS
BELFAST
1975 2 02

3532 MACNALLY, M F
MARITAL EXPECTATIONS AND ATTITUDES OF A
GROUP OF WOMEN REARED IN A WORKING-CLASS
SUBURB
QUB MA
BELFAST
1975 2 04

3533 MCCAFFERTY, N
THE ARMAGH WOMEN
CO-OP BOOKS
DUBLIN
1981 1 09

3534 MCCAULEY, L
THE WOMEN OF ULSTER
WEEKEND 17 MAR
1979 2 01

3535 MESSENGER, B
'YOU WILL EASY KNOW A DOFFER': THE
FOLKLORE OF THE LINEN INDUSTRY IN NI
EIRE-IRELAND 14(1)
ST PAUL
1979 2 01

3536 MESSENGER, B
FOLKLORE OF THE NORTHERN IRISH LINEN
INDUSTRY 1900-1935
INDIANA UNIV PHD
1975 2 04

3537 MESSENGER, B
PICKING UP THE LINEN THREADS
BLACKSTAFF
BELFAST
1980 2 02

3538 MIDDLETON, A
THE WOMANS LIBERATION MOVEMENT AND
WOMENS AID: VIOLENCE AND THE STATE
BELFAST WOMENS AID
BELFAST
1978 2 08

3539 MOONEY, M
WOMEN IN IRELAND
LABOUR MONTHLY 61(2)
1979 2 01

3540 NELLIS, M; HUTCHINSON, N
DERRY RELATIVES' ACTION
IN CURNO, A ET AL (EDS)
LONDON
1982 1 07

3541 NICHOLSON, M
IRELAND: WAR AND PEACE
SPARE RIB 52
1976 1 01

3542 O'CONNOR, F
DIVERSITY AND DIVISION
LEFT PERSPECTIVES 2(1)
DUBLIN
1981 1 01

3543 O'GORMAN, E C
DIFFICULTIES ASSOCIATED WITH MARRIAGES
BETWEEN HETEROSEXUALS AND HOMOSEXUALS
BRIT J SEXUAL MED 8(72)
1981 2 01

3544 O'GORMAN,E C
A PRELIMINARY REPORT ON TRANSSEXUALISM
IN NI
ULSTER MED J 50(1)
BELFAST
1981 2 01

3545 PALLEY,C
WIVES, CREDITORS AND THE MATRIMONIAL
HOME
NI LEG QUART 20(2)
BELFAST
1969 2 01

3546 POWER OF WOMEN COLLECTIVE
NI: THE POWER OF THE GHETTO
IN EDMOND,W; FLEMING,S (EDS)
BRISTOL
1975 1 07

3547 REID,N; GOLDIE,R
NI WOMEN IN HIGHER EDUCATION
EOC
BELFAST
1981 2 10

3548 REVOLUTIONARY STRUGGLE
REBEL SISTER
REVOLUTIONARY STRUGGLE
DUBLIN
1976 1 09

3549 ROSE,C
THE FEMALE EXPERIENCE: HISTORY OF THE
WOMEN'S MOVEMENT IN IRELAND
ARLEN
GALWAY
1975 2 02

3550 RUSSELL,M F
A CONTROLLED STUDY OF THE RELATIONSHIP
BETWEEN GYNAECOLOGICAL ILLNESS AND
MARITAL PROBLEMS IN A BELFAST GENERAL
PRACTICE
QUB MD
BELFAST
1968 2 04

3551 SINN FEIN (PROVISIONAL)
WOMEN IN THE NEW IRELAND
SINN FEIN (PROVISIONAL)
DUBLIN
1982 2 09

3552 SINN FEIN DEPARTMENT OF WOMEN'S AFFAIRS
THE OPPRESSION OF WOMEN
IRIS 1(2)
DUBLIN
1981 2 01

3553 SINN FEIN NATIONAL WOMENS COMMITTEE
WOMENS RIGHTS IN IRELAND
DUBLIN
1975 2 09

3554 SPARE RIB
A PLAYGROUP CALLED FREEDOM
SPARE RIB 41
LONDON
1975 1 10

3555 SPARE RIB
REPUBLICANISM: WHAT OUR IRISH SISTERS
THINK
SPARE RIB 99
LONDON
1980 1 01

3556 TRAUB,A I; GIBSON,E D; THOMPSON,W
HYSTERECTOMY IN YOUNG WOMEN: A THIRTY
YEAR REVIEW
BRIT J CLINICAL PRACTICE 34
1980 2 01

3557 TREWSDALE,J
THE ROLE OF WOMEN IN THE NI ECONOMY
IN CORMACK,R; OSBORNE,R D (EDS)
BELFAST
1983 2 07

3558 TREWSDALE,J; TRAINOR,M
WOMANPOWER NO. 2: RECENT CHANGES IN THE
FEMALE LABOUR MARKET IN NI
EOC
BELFAST
1981 2 03

3559 TREWSDALE,J; TRAINOR,M
WOMANPOWER: A STATISTICAL SURVEY OF
WOMEN AND WORK IN NI
EOC
BELFAST
1979 2 03

3560 WARD,M
MARGINALITY AND MILITANCY: CUMANN NA
MBAN 1914-1936
IN MORGAN A; PURDIE B (EDS)
LONDON
1980 2 07

3561 WARD,M
UNMANAGEABLE REVOLUTIONARIES
PLUTO/BRANDON
LONDON/DINGLE
1983 1 02

3562 WOMEN AGAINST IMPERIALISM
WOMEN PROTEST FOR POLITICAL STATUS IN
ARMAGH GAOL
WAI
BELFAST
1980 1 09

3563 WOMEN AND IRELAND GROUP
IRISH WOMEN AT WAR
WOMEN AND IRELAND GROUP
LONDON
1977 1 11

3564 WOMEN IN MEDIA
A WOMAN'S CHOICE: THE CASE FOR FREE,
SAFE, LEGAL ABORTION IN NI
WOMEN IN MEDIA
BELFAST
1980 2 10

3565 WORKERS' RESEARCH UNIT
WOMEN IN NI
WRU BULLETIN 5
BELFAST
1978 1 09

3566 YOUNG,J R; MORONEY,M
THE EMPLOYER'S GUIDE TO EQUAL
OPPORTUNITIES FOR MEN AND WOMEN
EOC
BELFAST
1979 2 03

3567 ARTHUR, A
ATTITUDE CHANGE AND NEUROTICISM AMONG
NORTHERN IRISH CHILDREN PARTICIPATING IN
JOINT-FAITH HOLIDAYS
QUB MSC
BELFAST
1974 2 04

3568 BAMBER, J H
THE FACTORIAL STRUCTURE OF ADOLESCENT
RESPONSES TO A FEAR SURVEY SCHEDULE
J GENETIC PSYCHOL 130
1977 2 01

3569 BAMBER, J H
THE FEARS OF ADOLESCENTS
J GENETIC PSYCHOL 125
1974 2 01

3570 BAMBER, J H
THE FEARS OF ADOLESCENTS: AN EMPIRICAL
INVESTIGATION
QUB PHD
BELFAST
1975 2 04

3571 BAMBER, J H
THE JUNIOR P.E.N. INVENTORY IN NI
IR J PSYCHOL 2(1)
1973 2 01

3572 BAXTER, T
LOCKING UP THE CHILDREN IN NI
SCOPE 35
BELFAST
1980 2 01

3573 BINAYISA, C N
COMPARATIVE STUDY OF SOME JUVENILE
JUSTICE INSTITUTIONS...
QUB LLM
BELFAST
1969 2 04

3574 BIRLEY, D
OPPORTUNITIES AT 16: REPORT OF A STUDY
GROUP
HMSO
BELFAST
1978 2 03

3575 BLACK REPORT
LEGISLATION AND SERVICES FOR CHILDREN
AND YOUNG PERSONS IN NI
DHSS (NI)
BELFAST
1979 2 03

3576 BLAKSTAD, M
CHILDREN IN CROSSFIRE
LISTENER 91(2346)
LONDON
1974 1 01

3577 BLANCHE, P G
MORAL REASONING AND SOCIAL-POLITICAL
ATTITUDES IN NI ADOLESCENT MALES
PENNSYLVANIA UNIV PHD
1978 1 04

3578 BLEAKLEY, D
YOUNG ULSTER AND RELIGION IN THE
SIXTIES: AN INQUIRY INTO ATTITUDES
AUTHOR
BELFAST
1964 2 10

3579 BLEASE, M
MALADJUSTED SCHOOL CHILDREN IN A BELFAST
CENTRE
IN HARBISON, J (ED)
BELFAST
1983 1 07

3580 BOOTHMAN, G
THE IMPACT OF URBAN RENEWAL ON
NEIGHBOURHOODS: THE YOUTH IN SHANKILL,
BELFAST
EKISTICS 44
ATHENS
1977 2 01

3581 BREAKWELL, G
UNEMPLOYMENT AND YOUNG PEOPLE
BRIT PSYCHOL SOCIETY, NI REGIONAL OFFICE
CONF
BELFAST
1982 2 11

3582 BUSH, L; MARSHALL, P
THE SOCIAL AND ECONOMIC CIRCUMSTANCES OF
DISADVANTAGED CHILDREN IN THE COMMUNITY
IN HARBISON, J (ED)
BELFAST
1983 1 07

3583 BYRNE, D; MCSHANE, E
A STUDY OF POLICY AND SERVICES FOR
PRE-SCHOOL CHILDREN IN NI
EOC
BELFAST
1978 2 03

3584 CAIRNS, E
DEVELOPMENT OF ETHNIC DISCRIMINATION IN
CHILDREN IN NI
IN HARBISON, J; HARBISON, J (EDS)
SHEPTON MALLET, SOMERSET
1980 1 07

3585 CAIRNS, E
INVESTIGATION OF SALIENCE FOR YOUNG
CHILDREN IN NI OF ADULT GENERATED
STEREOTYPIC PROTESTANT AND CATHOLIC
FIRST NAMES
BRIT PSYCHOL SOC CONF
1977 3 11

3586 CAIRNS, E
THE POLITICAL SOCIALISATION OF
TOMORROW'S PARENTS: VIOLENCE, POLITICS
AND THE MEDIA
IN HARBISON, J (ED)
BELFAST
1983 1 07

3587 CAIRNS, E ET AL
YOUNG CHILDREN'S AWARENESS OF VIOLENCE
IN NI: THE INFLUENCE OF NI TELEVISION IN
SCOTLAND AND NI
BRIT J SOC CLINIC PSYCHOL 19
LONDON
1980 1 01

3588 CAIRNS, E; DURIEZ, B
INFLUENCE OF ACCENT ON THE RECALL OF
CATHOLIC AND PROTESTANT CHILDREN IN NI
BRIT J SOC CLIN PSYCH 15
1976 2 01

3589 CAIRNS, E; HOSIN, A
THE IMPACT OF POLITICAL CONFLICT UPON
CHILDREN'S RATIONAL PERCEPTIONS
INT ASSOC CROSS-CULTURAL PSYCHOL CONF
ABERDEEN
1982 1 11

3590 CAIRNS, E; MERCER, G W
ADOLESCENT SOCIAL IDENTITY IN NI: THE
IMPORTANCE OF DENOMINATIONAL IDENTITY
NUU
COLERAINE
1978 1 08

3591 CARTER, F
JUVENILE DELINQUENCY AREAS IN BELFAST
QUB MED
BELFAST
1953 2 04

3592 COLES, R
BELFAST'S CHILDREN
NEW REPUBLIC 185(15)
1981 1 01

3593 COLES, R
CHILDREN OF CRISIS
LITTLE, BROWN AND CO
NEW YORK
1982 1 02

3594 COLES, R
ULSTER'S CHILDREN
ATLANTIC DEC
BOSTON
1980 2 01

3595 COMMUNITY HOMES SCHOOL GAZETTE
EFFECTS OF RELATIONS WITH STAFF ON
ATTITUDES AND BEHAVIOUR OF DELINQUENT
BOYS
COMMUNITY HOMES SCHOOL GAZ 72(8)
1978 2 01

3596 CONROY, J
ULSTER'S LOST GENERATION
NEW YORK TIMES MAG AUG 2
NEW YORK
1981 1 01

3597 CORMACK, R; OSBORNE, R D
YOUNG SCHOOL LEAVERS AND THE LABOUR
MARKET: THE BELFAST STUDY - 'INTO WORK
IN BELFAST?'
IN CORMACK, R; OSBORNE, R D (EDS)
BELFAST
1983 2 07

3598 CORMACK, R; OSBORNE, R D; THOMPSON, W
INTO WORK? YOUNG SCHOOL-LEAVERS AND THE
STRUCTURE OF OPPORTUNITIES IN BELFAST
FEA 5
BELFAST
1980 2 03

3599 CROOKS, S H
THE LEVEL AND PATTERNS OF RESPONSE OF A
SAMPLE OF NORTHERN IRISH CHILDREN
QUB MSC
BELFAST
1973 2 04

3600 CRUTCHLY, J
JOYRIDING PROBLEM: WEST BELFAST
CONSTABULARY GAZETTE MAY
1982 1 01

3601 CURRAN, J D; JARDINE, E; HARBISON, J
FACTORS ASSOCIATED WITH THE DEVELOPMENT
OF DEVIANT ATTITUDES IN NI SCHOOLBOYS
IN HARBISON, J; HARBISON, J (EDS)
1980 1 07

3602 CURRAN, J D; JARDINE, E; HARBISON, J
PERSONALITY AND ATTITUDES IN NI SCHOOL
CHILDREN
IR PSYCHOL OCT
1977 1 07

3603 DAVIDSON, S I
A REVIEW OF ESN SCHOOL LEAVERS IN NI
WITH SPECIAL REFERENCE TO VOCATIONAL
ADJUSTMENT
QUB MED
BELFAST
1972 2 04

3604 DICKINSON, C
CHILD ABUSE WITH REFERENCE TO EAST
BELFAST
NUU MSC
COLERAINE
1977 2 04

3605 DUFF, R
A STUDY OF THE PROVISIONS OF THE WELFARE
SERVICES ACT NI 1949, AND THE CHILDREN
AND YOUNG PERSONS' ACT NI 1950
QUB MSC
BELFAST
1959 2 04

3606 ELLIOTT, R; LOCKHART, W H
CHARACTERISTICS OF SCHEDULED OFFENDERS
AND JUVENILE DELINQUENTS
IN HARBISON, J; HARBISON, J (EDS)
1980 1 07

3607 FARLEY, M
THE YOUTH TRAINING PROGRAMME IN NI
NATIONAL ASSOC OF TEACHERS IN FURTHER
AND HIGHER EDUC J 8(2)
LONDON
1983 2 01

3608 FARTHING, B D
ADOLESCENTS' PERCEPTION OF THE
GENERATION GAP
NUU MA
COLERAINE
1977 2 04

3609 FEE, F
RESPONSES TO A BEHAVIOURAL QUESTIONNAIRE
OF A GROUP OF BELFAST CHILDREN
IN HARBISON, J; HARBISON, J (EDS)
1980 1 07

3610 FIELDS, R
CHILD TERROR VICTIMS AND ADULT
TERRORISTS
J PSYCHOHIST 7(1)
1979 1 01

3611 FIELDS, R
PSYCHOLOGICAL GENOCIDE: THE CHILDREN OF
NI
J PSYCHOHIST 3
1975 1 01

3612 FOLEY, T; GRAHAM, P
RIGHTS AND RESPONSIBILITIES: A YOUNG
PERSON'S GUIDE TO THE LAW AND EMERGENCY
LEGISLATION IN NI
PEACE PEOPLE
BELFAST
1980 1 09

3613 FRASER, M
AT SCHOOL DURING GUERRILLA WAR
SPECIAL EDUCATION 61
1972 1 01

3614 FRASER, M
CHILDREN IN CONFLICT
SECKER AND WARBURG
LONDON
1973 1 02

3615 FRASER, M
ULSTER'S CHILDREN OF CONFLICT
NEW SOCIETY 17(446)
LONDON
1971 1 01

3616 FRASER, M; OVERY, R; RUSSELL, J; DUNLAP, R;
BOURNE, R
CHILDREN AND CONFLICT
COMM FORUM 2(2)
BELFAST
1972 1 01

3617 FROGGATT, P; LYNAS, M A; MACKENZIE, G
EPIDEMIOLOGY OF SUDDEN UNEXPECTED DEATH
IN INFANTS ('COT DEATH') IN NI
BRIT J PREV SOC MED 24
1971 2 01

3618 GORMALLY, B
PICK THEM UP OR PUT THEM DOWN: AN
ASSESSMENT OF THE BLACK REPORT
HOWARD J 16
1978 2 01

3619 GRAHAM, J
CHILDREN IN CARE IN NI
BRIT PSYCHOL SOC CONF
1979 2 11

3620 GRAHAM,J
CHILDREN IN CARE IN NI
SOCIAL WORK ADVISORY GROUP DHSS (NI)
BELFAST
1980   2   10

3621 GREER,J E
THE CHILD'S UNDERSTANDING OF CREATION
EDUC RES 24(2)
1972   2   01

3622 GREER,J E
THE PERSISTENCE OF RELIGION: A STUDY OF
ADOLESCENTS IN NI
CHARACTER POTENTIAL 9(3)
1980   2   01

3623 GREER,J E
A QUESTIONING GENERATION
CHURCH OF IRELAND BOARD OF EDUC
1972   2   10

3624 GREER,J E
RELIGIOUS ATTITUDES AND THINKING IN
BELFAST PUPILS
EDUC RES 23(3)
1981   2   01

3625 GREER,J E
RELIGIOUS BELIEF AND CHURCH ATTENDANCE
OF SIXTH FORM PUPILS AND THEIR PARENTS
IR J EDUC 5(2)
1971   2   01

3626 HARBISON,J
CHILDREN IN A SOCIETY IN TURMOIL
IN HARBISON,J (ED)
BELFAST
1983   1   07

3627 HARBISON,J
CHILDREN OF NI
NEW SOCIETY 52(915)
LONDON
1980   1   01

3628 HARVEY,S; REA,D
AN EVALUATION OF THE EMPLOYER-BASED WORK
EXPERIENCE PROGRAMME
ULSTER POLY
BELFAST
1979   2   10

3629 HERRON,C
THE INVOLVEMENT OF SIXTEEN YEAR OLD
SCHOOL LEAVERS IN PHYSICAL ACTIVITY
ULSTER POLY MPHIL
BELFAST
1981   2   04

3630 HESKIN,K
CHILDREN AND YOUNG PEOPLE IN NI: A
RESEARCH REVIEW
IN HARBISON,J; HARBISON,J (EDS)
SHEPTON MALLET, SOMERSET
1980   1   07

3631 HOLMES,E; THORNTON,A M
CHILDREN IN DISTRESS: EFFECTS OF THE
DISTURBANCES ON PUPILS IN ARDOYNE
SECONDARY SCHOOLS
NORTH TEACH 10(4)
1972   1   01

3632 HOSIN,A; CAIRNS,E
POLITICAL CONSCIOUSNESS IN CHILDREN IN
NI
IN MCWHIRTER,L (ED)
ABERDEEN
1980   1   11

3633 INTERDEPARTMENTAL COMMITTEE ON MATTERS
RELATING TO THE ALIENATION OF YOUNG
PEOPLE
REPORT
INTERDEPARTMENTAL COMMITTEE ON MATTERS
RELATING TO THE ALIENATION OF YOUNG
PEOPLE
BELFAST
1974   2   03

3634 IRISH ASSOCIATION FOR CULTURAL, ECONOMIC
AND SOCIAL RELATIONS
ATTITUDES OF SCHOOL LEAVERS: A SURVEY
COMM FORUM 3(3)
BELFAST
1973   2   01

3635 IRISH COUNCIL OF CHURCHES AND ROMAN
CATHOLIC JOINT GROUP ON SOCIAL PROBLEMS
REPORT OF THE WORKING PARTY ON TEENAGE
DRINKING
IRISH COUNCIL OF CHURCHES JOINT GROUP ON
SOCIAL PROBLEMS
BELFAST
1974   2   10

3636 IRISH COUNCIL OF CHURCHES AND ROMAN
CATHOLIC JOINT GROUP ON SOCIAL PROBLEMS
REPORT OF THE WORKING PARTY ON THE USE
OF DRUGS
IRISH COUNCIL OF CHURCHES
1972   2   10

3637 JAHODA,G; HARRISON,S
BELFAST CHILDREN: SOME EFFECTS OF A
CONFLICT ENVIRONMENT
IR J PSYCHOL 3(1)
1975   1   01

3638 JARDINE,E
INTRODUCTION TO THE SYMPOSIUM ON
JUVENILE DELINQUENCY - A NI PERSPECTIVE
B BRIT PSYCHOL SOC MAY
1980   2   01

3639 JARDINE,E
MODELS OF DIVERSION IN INTERVENTION WITH
ALIENATED ADOLESCENTS
IN HARBISON,J (ED)
BELFAST
1983   2   07

3640 JARDINE,E
SOME SOCIAL, EDUCATIONAL AND
PSYCHOLOGICAL VARIABLES ASSOCIATED WITH
THE ADJUSTMENT OF BOYS IN TWO NI
TRAINING SCHOOLS
QUB MSC
BELFAST
1978   2   04

3641 JARDINE,E; CURRAN,J D; HARBISON,J
YOUNG OFFENDERS AND THEIR OFFENCES: SOME
COMPARISONS BETWEEN NI, ENGLAND AND
SCOTLAND
BRIT PSYCHOL SOCIETY, NI REGIONAL OFFICE
CONF
BELFAST
1978   2   11

3642 JENKINS,R
HIGHTOWN RULES: GROWING UP IN A BELFAST
HOUSING ESTATE
NATIONAL YOUTH BUREAU
LEICESTER
1982   1   01

3643 JENKINS,R
LADS, CITIZENS AND ORDINARY KIDS
RKP
LONDON
1983   1   01

3644 JENKS,R E
YOUTH EMPLOYMENT SERVICE: WHY, WHAT AND
HOW?
JSSISI
1963   2   01

3645 JENVEY,S
SONS AND HATERS: ULSTER YOUTH IN
CONFLICT
NEW SOCIETY 21(512)
1972 1 01

3646 KENNEDY,H P
REPORT OF A PUBLIC INQUIRY INTO
THE...USE OF LISNEVIN SCHOOL...AS A
TRAINING REMAND HOME...
HMSO
BELFAST
1979 2 03

3647 KERR,G
CUSTODY OF CHILDREN ON BREAKDOWN OF
MARRIAGE IN NI
SLS/FACULTY OF LAW QUB
BELFAST
       2 10

3648 KILMURRAY,A
HYDEBANK: BARRING THE WAY TO BLACK?
SCOPE 46
BELFAST
1981 2 01

3649 KIRK,J M
THE RUC AND YOUNG PEOPLE
PACE 14(3)
BELFAST
1983 1 01

3650 LOCKHART,W H
THE OUTCOMES OF INDIVIDUAL
CLIENT-CENTRED COUNSELLING WITH YOUNG
OFFENDERS IN SECURE RESIDENTIAL CARE
IN HARBISON,J (ED)
BELFAST
1983 1 07

3651 LOCKHART,W H; ELLIOTT,R
CHANGES IN ATTITUDES OF YOUNG OFFENDERS
IN AN INTEGRATED ASSESSMENT CENTRE
IN HARBISON,J; HARBISON,J (EDS)
SHEPTON MALLET, SOMERSET
1980 1 07

3652 LUKIANOWICZ,N
BATTERED CHILDREN
PSYCHIATRICA CLINICA 4(5)
1971 2 01

3653 LUKIANOWICZ,N
INFANTICIDE
PSYCHIATRICA CLINICA 4(3)
1971 2 01

3654 LUKIANOWICZ,N
JUVENILE OFFENDERS: SECOND GROUP OF 50
GIRLS FROM A REMAND HOME IN NI
ACTA PSYCHIAT SCAN 48(4)
       2 01

3655 LUKIANOWICZ,N
REJECTED CHILDREN
PSYCHIATRICA CLINICA 5(3)
1972 2 01

3656 LUKIANOWICZ,N
REVIEW OF ONE HUNDRED UNSELECTED CHILD
GUIDANCE CLINIC REFERRALS
PSYCHIATRICA CLINICA 5(6)
1972 2 01

3657 MANNING,M
NO PLACE TO BE YOUNG
COMM CARE 181
LONDON
1977 1 01

3658 MCAULEY,R; TROY,M
THE IMPACT OF URBAN CONFLICT AND
VIOLENCE ON CHILDREN REFERRED TO A CHILD
PSYCHIATRY CLINIC
IN HARBISON,J (ED)
BELFAST
1983 1 07

3659 MCCAFFERTY,N
IF WE WERE GIVEN A CHANCE...
NICRC
BELFAST
1974 1 10

3660 MCCARNEY,W G
GLUE-SNIFFING: CAUSE FOR CONCERN?
SCOPE 43
BELFAST
1981 2 01

3661 MCCARNEY,W G
JOYRIDING: A QUEST FOR IDENTITY
YOUTH IN SOCIETY 53
LONDON
1981 1 01

3662 MCCLURE,G; KEILTY,S; REID,M; RITCHIE,J W K;
SCOTT,M J
NEONATAL DEATH IN NI
BRIT MED J 2
1978 2 01

3663 MCCONAGHY,E M
SOME CHARACTERISTICS OF ... DELINQUENTS
ADMITTED TO TRAINING SCHOOLS IN NI
QUB MED
BELFAST
1971 2 04

3664 MCCORMACK,P; RHODES,E
YOUTH IN DERRY
MAGEE UNIV COLLEGE
DERRY
1972 1 10

3665 MCCOY,K
CHILD CARE TRENDS: A REVIEW OF
STATISTICAL RETURNS 1970-1979
SOCIAL WORK ADVISORY GROUP DHSS (NI)
BELFAST
1982 2 03

3666 MCCOY,K
OTHER PEOPLES CHILDREN
DHSS (NI)
BELFAST
1980 2 03

3667 MCCREARY,A
THE ROYAL BELFAST HOSPITAL FOR SICK
CHILDREN: ONE HUNDRED YEARS OF CARING
1873-1973
ROYAL BELFAST HOSPITAL FOR SICK CHILDREN
BELFAST
1973 2 10

3668 MCCULLAGH,M
YOUTH UNEMPLOYMENT AND THE IDEOLOGY OF
CONTROL
IN CURTIN,C; KELLY,M; O'DOWD,L (EDS)
DUBLIN
1983 2 07

3669 MCDOWELL,I
LOOKING AHEAD IN NI
TRAINING SCHOOL B 53
1956 2 01

3670 MCGUFFIN,S J
KNOWLEDGE OF REPRODUCTION AND CHILDCARE
POSSESSED BY 16 YEAR OLDS IN NI
PUBL HEALTH 94(4)
1980 2 01

3671 MCKERNAN,J; RUSSELL,J
DIFFERENCES OF RELIGION AND SEX IN THE
VALUE SYSTEMS OF NI ADOLESCENTS
BRIT J SOC CLINIC PSYCHOL 10(2)
1980 2 01

3672 MCSHANE,E
SOCIAL POLICY AND PROVISION FOR
PRE-SCHOOL CHILDREN
QUEST 2
BELFAST
1975 2 01

3673 MCWHIRTER, L
THE CHILDREN OF ULSTER
PSYCHOL NEWS 31
1982 1 01

3674 MCWHIRTER, L
THE INFLUENCE OF CONTACT ON THE
DEVELOPMENT OF INTERPERSONAL AWARENESS
IN NI CHILDREN
B BRIT PSYCHOL SOC APR
1982 2 01

3675 MCWHIRTER, L
LOOKING BACK AND LOOKING FORWARD: AN
INSIDE PERSPECTIVE
IN HARBISON, J (ED)
BELFAST
1983 1 07

3676 MCWHIRTER, L
THE MEANING OF VIOLENCE FOR NI CHILDREN
CYCLE OF VIOLENCE CONF
BELFAST
1982 1 11

3677 MCWHIRTER, L
NI: GROWING UP WITH THE 'TROUBLES'
IN GOLDSTEIN, A P; SEGALL, M (EDS)
NEW YORK
1983 1 07

3678 MCWHIRTER, L
NORTHERN IRISH CHILDREN'S CONCEPTIONS OF
VIOLENT CRIME
HOWARD J 21
1982 1 01

3679 MCWHIRTER, L
VIOLENCE IN NI: CHILDREN'S CONCEPTIONS
INT SOCIETY FOR THE STUDY OF BEHAVIOURAL
DEVELOPMENT CONF
TORONTO
1981 1 11

3680 MCWHIRTER, L
YOKED BY VIOLENCE TOGETHER: STRESS AND
COPING IN CHILDREN IN NI
COMM CARE 4 NOV
LONDON
1982 1 01

3681 MCWHIRTER, L; TREW, K
CHILDREN IN NI: A LOST GENERATION?
IN ANTHONY, E J; CHILAND, C (EDS)
NEW YORK
1982 1 07

3682 MCWHIRTER, L; TREW, K
SOCIAL AWARENESS IN NI
B BRIT PSYCHOL SOC 34
1981 1 01

3683 MCWHIRTER, L; YOUNG, V; MAJURY, J
AWARENESS OF DEATH IN BELFAST CHILDREN
IN MCWHIRTER, L (ED)
1980 2 07

3684 MCWHIRTER, L; YOUNG, V; MAJURY, J
BELFAST CHILDREN'S AWARENESS OF VIOLENT
DEATH
BRIT J SOC PSYCHOL 44
1982 1 01

3685 MERCER, G W; BUNTING, B
SOME MOTIVATIONS OF ADOLESCENT
DEMONSTRATORS IN NI CIVIL DISTURBANCES
IN HARBISON, J; HARBISON, J (EDS)
SHEPTON MALLET, SOMERSET
1980 1 07

3686 MILLAR, B
PAST AND PRESENT TRENDS IN INFANT
MORTALITY
QUB MD
BELFAST
1947 2 04

3687 MINISTRY OF EDUCATION (NI)
DEVELOPMENT OF THE YOUTH SERVICE
HMSO CMD 424
BELFAST
1961 2 03

3688 MURRAY, D; DARBY, J
THE VOCATIONAL ASPIRATIONS AND
EXPECTATIONS OF SCHOOL LEAVERS IN
LONDONDERRY AND STRABANE
FEA
BELFAST
1980 2 03

3689 MURRAY, D; DARBY, J
YOUNG SCHOOL LEAVERS AND THE LABOUR
MARKET: THE LONDONDERRY AND STRABANE
STUDY - OUT AND DOWN IN DERRY AND
STRABANE
IN CORMACK, R; OSBORNE, R D (EDS)
BELFAST
1983 2 07

3690 NATIONAL OPINION POLLS MARKET RESEARCH
LTD
YOUNG PEOPLE IN NI
NATIONAL OPINION POLLS MARKET RESEARCH
LTD
LONDON
1968 2 10

3691 NEESON, W
THE AFTER-SCHOOL LIFE OF THE ADOLESCENT
LINEN WORKER
QUB MED
BELFAST
1951 2 04

3692 NELSON, M A
INTERMEDIATE TREATMENT
DHSS (NI)
BELFAST
1979 2 03

3693 NEWSWEEK
ULSTER: THE CHILDREN OF VIOLENCE
NEWSWEEK APR 19
NEW YORK
1971 1 01

3694 NI ASSOCIATION FOR MENTAL HEALTH
THE FUTURE OF CHILD GUIDANCE IN NI
NI ASSOCIATION FOR MENTAL HEALTH
BELFAST
1965 2 10

3695 NI CHILD WELFARE COUNCIL
CHILDREN IN CARE: A REPORT
HMSO
BELFAST
1956 2 03

3696 NI COMMITTEE FOR THE INTERNATIONAL YEAR
OF THE CHILD
PROCEEDINGS OF STUDY DAY ON UNDER-AGE
DRINKING
ULSTER POLY
BELFAST
1979 2 08

3697 NI GOVERNMENT
REPORT OF THE COMMITTEE OF INQUIRY ON
VOCATIONAL GUIDANCE AND EMPLOYMENT
SERVICES FOR YOUNG PERSONS
HMSO CMD 394
BELFAST
1959 2 03

3698 NI GOVERNMENT
REPORT ON THE PROTECTION AND WELFARE OF
THE YOUNG AND THE TREATMENT OF YOUNG
OFFENDERS
HMSO CMD 264
BELFAST
1948 2 03

3699 NICSS
THE CHILD IN THE COMMUNITY: THE
CHALLENGE
NICSS
BELFAST
1962 2 08

3700 NICSS
     THE YOUNG CHRONIC SICK IN NI: A SURVEY
     NICSS
     BELFAST
     1972 2 10

3701 NIEC
     YOUTH UNEMPLOYMENT AND TRAINING
     NIEC
     BELFAST
     1982 2 03

3702 OSBOROUGH, N
     BORSTAL IN IRELAND
     IPA
     DUBLIN
     1975 2 02

3703 OSBOROUGH, N
     PARTITION AND THE NORTHERN BORSTAL BOY
     1921-7
     DUBLIN UNIV LAW R 1(1)
     DUBLIN
     1969 2 01

3704 RHODES, E; MCCORMACK, P
     YOUTH IN DERRY: A SURVEY REPORT
     MAGEE UNIV COLLEGE
     DERRY
     1972 2 10

3705 ROGERS, S; TITTERINGTON, J
     A SURVEY OF NON-ACCIDENTAL INJURY
     REGISTERS IN NI
     ULSTER POLY
     BELFAST
     1978 2 10

3706 ROSENBLATT, R
     CHILDREN OF WAR
     READER'S DIGEST APRIL
     1982 1 01

3707 RUSSELL, J
     MOTIVATIONS FOR VANDALISM IN NI:
     RESEARCH PAPER
     IN MULCAHY, D G (ED)
     CORK
     1977 1 07

3708 RUSSELL, J
     SOME ASPECTS OF CIVIC EDUCATION OF
     SECONDARY SCHOOLBOYS IN NI
     NICRC
     BELFAST
     1972 1 01

3709 RUSSELL, J; SCHELLENBERG, J A
     POLITICAL ATTITUDE STRUCTURE OF
     SCHOOLBOYS IN NI
     INT J PSYCH 3(2)
     1976 1 01

3710 SALTERS, J
     ATTITUDES TOWARDS SOCIETY IN PROTESTANT
     AND ROMAN CATHOLIC SCHOOLCHILDREN IN
     BELFAST
     QUB MED
     BELFAST
     1975 1 04

3711 SCHELLENBERG, J A; RUSSELL, J
     INTERGROUP ATTITUDES OF SCHOOLBOYS IN NI
     INT J GROUP TENSIONS 6(1-2)
     1976 1 01

3712 SCOPE
     CHILDREN'S COMMUNITY HOLIDAY SCHEMES
     SCOPE 7
     BELFAST
     1976 1 01

3713 SCOPE
     FAIR PLAY FOR 5-10 YEAR OLDS
     SCOPE 12
     BELFAST
     1977 2 01

3714 SCOPE
     JOB CREATION AND THE YOUNG UNEMPLOYED
     SCOPE 9
     BELFAST
     1977 2 01

3715 SCOPE
     MOBILE YOUNG PEOPLE AT RISK
     SCOPE 6
     BELFAST
     1976 2 01

3716 SCOPE
     THE UNDER-FIVES CRISIS
     SCOPE 25
     BELFAST
     1979 2 01

3717 SCOPE
     THE YEAR OF THE CHILD
     SCOPE 20
     BELFAST
     1979 2 01

3718 SCOPE
     YOUNG PEOPLE: CARE OR CONTROL?
     SCOPE 10
     BELFAST
     1977 2 01

3719 SCOPE
     YOUTH SERVICE IN SEARCH OF A POLICY
     SCOPE 1
     BELFAST
     1975 1 01

3720 SKINNER, R E G
     THE BELFAST CHILD'S EXPERIENCE AND
     CONCEPTUALISATION OF DEATH
     QUB MA
     BELFAST
     1976 1 04

3721 SMITH, J P
     INFANT MORTALITY AND HANDICAP IN NI
     J ADVANCED NURSING 6(2)
     1981 2 01

3722 STANDING CONFERENCE OF YOUTH
     ORGANISATIONS IN NI
     YOUNG PEOPLE WITHOUT WORK
     STANDING CONFERENCE OF YOUTH
     ORGANISATIONS IN NI
     BELFAST
     1981 2 10

3723 THOMPSON, W
     UNEMPLOYMENT AMONG YOUNG MALES IN
     BELFAST
     BRIT PSYCHOL SOCIETY, NI REGIONAL OFFICE
     CONF
     BELFAST
     1982 2 11

3724 THOMPSON, W; CORMACK, R; OSBORNE, R D
     SOME ASPECTS OF OCCUPATIONAL CHOICE AND
     PLACEMENT OF 16 YEAR-OLD BOYS IN BELFAST
     IN HARBISON, J; HARBISON, J (EDS)
     SHEPTON MALLET, SOMERSET
     1980 2 07

3725 TOMLINSON, M
     PROFESSIONAL GROUPS AND AGENCIES AND
     YOUNG PEOPLE
     IN TAYLOR, L; NELSON, S (EDS)
     BELFAST
     1977 2 07

3726 TURNER, E B
     RELIGIOUS UNDERSTANDING AND RELIGIOUS
     ATTITUDES IN MALE URBAN ADOLESCENTS
     QUB PHD
     BELFAST
     1970 1 04

3727 TURNER, I F
     PROBABILITY AND THE BEHAVIOUR OF
     CHILDREN IN SEQUENTIAL TWO-CHOICE
     SITUATIONS
     QUB PHD
     BELFAST
     1967 2   04

3728 UNGOED-THOMAS, J
     PATTERNS OF ADOLESCENT BEHAVIOUR AND
     RELATIONSHIPS IN NI
     J MORAL EDUC OCT
     1972 2   01

3729 VINCENT, S
     THE BELFAST JOY-RIDERS
     NEW SOCIETY 17 JUNE
     LONDON
     1982 1   01

3730 WALSH, N
     NI'S SICK CHILDREN
     STUDIES 62
     DUBLIN
     1973 2   01

3731 WAUGH, J L
     A SURVEY OF ATTITUDES TOWARD YOUTH CLUB
     MEMBERSHIP IN NI
     QUB MSC
     BELFAST
     1969 2   04

3732 WEINREICH, P
     IDENTITY DEVELOPMENT IN PROTESTANT AND
     ROMAN CATHOLIC ADOLESCENT BOYS AND GIRLS
     IN BELFAST
     INT ASSOC FOR CHILD AND ADOLESCENT
     PSYCHIATRY CONF
     DUBLIN
     1982 2   11

3733 WHYTE, D
     A SOCIAL PSYCHOLOGICAL EVALUATION OF A
     COMMUNITY SERVICE PROGRAMME FOR YOUNG
     OFFENDERS IN A NI TRAINING SCHOOL
     QUB MSSC
     BELFAST
     1981 2   04

3734 WHYTE, J
     EVERYDAY LIFE FOR 11 AND 12 YEAR OLDS IN
     A TROUBLED AREA OF BELFAST: DO 'THE
     TROUBLES' INTRUDE?
     IN HARBISON, J (ED)
     BELFAST
     1983 1   07

3735 WOODS, E
     PATTERNS OF LEISURE TELEVISION VIEWING
     AMONG A SAMPLE OF FOURTEEN YEAR OLDS
     QUB MED
     BELFAST
     1973 2   04

3736 WORKERS' PARTY REPUBLICAN CLUBS
     BEING YOUNG IN WEST BELFAST
     WORKERS' PARTY REPUBLICAN CLUBS
     BELFAST
     1981 1   09

3737 ABUKUTSA,J L
THE UNIVERSITY LIBRARY AND THE NEEDS OF
THE ACADEMIC COMMUNITY
QUB MA
BELFAST
1972 2 04

3738 ADVISORY COUNCIL FOR EDUCATION IN NI
RURAL EDUCATION
HMSO CMD 300
BELFAST
1952 2 03

3739 ADVISORY COUNCIL FOR EDUCATION IN NI
SCHOOL ATTENDANCE IN NI
HMSO CMD 362
BELFAST
1956 2 03

3740 ADVISORY COUNCIL FOR EDUCATION IN NI
SECONDARY SCHOOL ORGANISATION,
CONDITIONS OF RECOGNITION, SUPPLY OF
TEACHERS AND SELECTION PROCEDURE
HMSO CMD 471
BELFAST
1964 2 03

3741 ADVISORY COUNCIL FOR EDUCATION IN NI
SELECTION OF PUPILS FOR SECONDARY
SCHOOLS
HMSO CMD 301
BELFAST
1952 2 03

3742 ADVISORY COUNCIL FOR EDUCATION IN NI
SELECTION OF PUPILS FOR SECONDARY
SCHOOLS
HMSO CMD 419
BELFAST
1960 2 03

3743 ADVISORY COUNCIL FOR EDUCATION IN NI
SPECIAL EDUCATIONAL TREATMENT
HMSO CMD 331
BELFAST
1955 2 03

3744 AKENSON,D H
EDUCATION AND ENMITY: THE CONTROL OF
SCHOOLING IN NI 1920-1950
DAVID AND CHARLES
NEWTON ABBOT
1973 2 02

3745 ALCORN,D
WEST BELFAST SCHOOLS STILL GIVING
PROBLEMS
SCOPE 60
BELFAST
1983 2 01

3746 ALLEN,R
PRESBYTERIAN COLLEGE, BELFAST 1853-1953
MULLAN
BELFAST
1954 2 10

3747 ANTHONY,P G J
A REVIEW OF TRENDS IN RELIGIOUS
EDUCATION IN NI
QUB MA
BELFAST
1977 2 04

3748 ASSOCIATION OF NI EDUCATION AND LIBRARY
BOARDS
VANDALISM AND DISCIPLINE IN SCHOOLS
ASSOC NI EDUC AND LIBRARY BOARDS
BELFAST
1976 2 02

3749 AUSTIN,S
TO BE CALLED STUPID... THE EDUCATION OF
NON-EXAMINATION PUPILS IN FOUR BELFAST
SECONDARY SCHOOLS
SCHOOLS CURRICULUM PROJECT
BELFAST
1975 2 10

3750 BAMFORD,D
THE INTEGRATION OF SOCIAL SKILLS AND
SOCIAL WORK CONCEPTS IN AN UNDERGRADUATE
CQSW PROGRAMME
SOC WORK EDUC NOV
1981 2 01

3751 BARLOW,P
INSTITUTE OF CONTINUING EDUCATION
COMM FORUM 14(2)
1974 2 01

3752 BEATTIE,D R
A STUDY OF A GUIDANCE SCHEME IN A
BELFAST SECONDARY SCHOOL
QUB MA
BELFAST
1970 2 04

3753 BELFAST EDUCATION AND LIBRARY BOARD
ADULT AND COMMUNITY EDUCATION IN
BELFAST: REPORT OF A WORKING PARTY
BELFAST EDUCATION AND LIBRARY BOARD
BELFAST
1981 2 03

3754 BELFAST EDUCATION AND LIBRARY BOARD
FINAL REPORT OF A WORKING PARTY...TO
CONSIDER THE WORK AND STRUCTURE OF
SCHOOL MANAGEMENT COMMITTEES
BELFAST EDUCATION AND LIBRARY BOARD
BELFAST
1977 2 03

3755 BELFAST EDUCATION AND LIBRARY BOARD
THE REPORT OF THE WORKING PARTY ON
NURSERY EDUCATION 1973-1977
BELFAST EDUCATION AND LIBRARY BOARD
BELFAST
1977 2 03

3756 BELL,W
EXPERIMENT IN EDUCATION
BRITAIN TODAY
1951 2 01

3757 BENTON,E
INTEGRATED EDUCATION
SCOPE 29
BELFAST
1979 1 01

3758 BILL,J M
EARLY LEAVING IN NI
NICER
BELFAST
1974 2 10

3759 BILL,J M
ENVIRONMENTAL STRESS AND EDUCATIONAL
OUTCOMES
NORTH TEACH 11(1)
1973 3 01

3760 BILL,J M
NI SECONDARY SCHOOL SURVEY
NICER
BELFAST
1972 2 10

3761 BILL,J M; TREW,K; WILSON,J A
EARLY LEAVING IN NI
NICER
BELFAST
1974 2 10

3762 BLEAKLEY, D
TEACHING UNEMPLOYED BOYS IN BELFAST
EDUCATION 113
1959 2 01

3763 BOAL, F W
BELFAST 1979: AN INTERVIEW WITH
EDUCATIONAL ADMINISTRATORS
TEACH 3
1979 2 01

3764 BOAL, F W
THE INTERIM-ALTERNATIVE-REVISED TRANSFER
SYSTEM
TEACH 1
1978 2 01

3765 BOYD, G H S
SOCIO-ECONOMIC AND EDUCATIONAL FACTORS
INFLUENCING THE DECLINE OF THE ONE-,
TWO-, AND THREE-TEACHER ELEMENTARY
SCHOOLS
QUB PHD
BELFAST
1972 2 04

3766 BOYLE, J F
MODELS OF EDUCATION IN NI
INT SOCIOL ASSOC
DUBLIN
1977 2 11

3767 BRADLEY, A M
EDUCATIONAL ATTITUDES AND THE
PROBATIONARY TEACHER
NUU MA
COLERAINE
1978 2 04

3768 BRADY, B
CATHOLIC EDUCATION IN NI: THE CHILVER
CHALLENGE
AUTHOR
BELFAST
1982 2 10

3769 BREMNER, A
A STUDY OF COUNSELLING SCHEMES IN A
SAMPLE OF SECONDARY SCHOOLS IN THE
GREATER BELFAST AREA
QUB MED
BELFAST
1974 2 04

3770 BROWN, G A
THE EFFECTS OF TRAINING UPON THE
PERFORMANCE OF STUDENTS IN TEACHING
SITUATIONS
NUU DPHIL
COLERAINE
1973 2 04

3771 BROWN, G A
A NOTE ON CONCURRENT AND CONSECUTIVE
COURSES IN BRITAIN
RESEARCH IN EDUC 14
1975 2 01

3772 BROWN, G A
THE PERFORMANCE OF NON-GRADUATE STUDENT
TEACHERS IN UNIVERSITY COURSES
BRIT J EDUC PSYCHOL 41(3)
1971 2 01

3773 BURNS, F
THE EFFECTS OF TEACHER COMMUNICATION
STYLE ON PERFORMANCE IN REMEDIAL PUPILS
QUB MED
BELFAST
1981 2 04

3774 CALDWELL, J C; SETH, G
PERSONALITY AND ATTAINMENT
NICER
BELFAST
1972 2 10

3775 CALDWELL, L
THE DIFFERENCE IN LANGUAGE STRUCTURE AND
PATTERNS BETWEEN MIDDLE-CLASS AND
WORKING-CLASS...BELFAST PRIMARY SCHOOL
CHILDREN
QUB MSC
BELFAST
1970 2 04

3776 CAMPBELL, J A
GEOGRAPHY AT QUEENS: AN HISTORICAL
SURVEY
DEPT GEOG QUB
BELFAST
1978 2 10

3777 CAMPBELL, J J
CATHOLIC SCHOOLS: A SURVEY OF A NI
PROBLEM
FALLONS
BELFAST
1963 2 02

3778 CAMPBELL, J J
VOLUNTARY SCHOOLS IN NI
IR ECCLESIASTICAL RECORD FEB
1952 2 01

3779 CAMPBELL, K
SOCIAL CLASS DIFFERENCES AND LANGUAGE: A
COMPARATIVE STUDY...OF TWO GROUPS IN A
BELFAST PRIMARY SCHOOL
QUB MSC
BELFAST
1968 2 04

3780 CARRY ON LEARNING PROJECT
'CARRY ON LEARNING': REPORT OF AN
EXPERIMENTAL PROJECT IN COMMUNITY
EDUCATION
COMMUNITY EDUCATION PROJECT QUB
BELFAST
1977 2 10

3781 CARTER, A
USE AND ABUSE OF HISTORY IN NORTHERN
SCHOOLS
THE WORLD AND THE SCHOOL
1970 3 01

3782 CARVILLE, J B
A STUDY OF THE LESS-ABLE SECONDARY
MODERN SCHOOL PUPILS IN BELFAST ...
QUB MA
BELFAST
1966 2 04

3783 CATHCART, R
TO BUILD ANEW
NORTH TEACH 11(1)
1973 2 01

3784 CAVE, E D
THE EFFECTS OF 11+ RESULTS ON THE
SUBSEQUENT CAREERS OF PUPILS
BRIT J EDUC PSYCHOL 37(1)
1967 2 01

3785 CAVE, E D
A FOLLOW UP STUDY OF THE SUBSEQUENT
CAREERS OF TWO MATCHED GROUPS OF
BORDERLINE PUPILS
QUB MA
BELFAST
1965 2 04

3786 CAVEN, N; HARBISON, J
PERSISTENT SCHOOL NON-ATTENDANCE
HARBISON, J; HARBISON, J (EDS)
SHEPTON MALLET, SOMERSET
1980 2 07

3787 CAVES, W J
CONCEPT OF THE EDUCATIONAL PRIORITY AREA
AND ITS POSSIBLE APPLICATION TO THE CITY
OF BELFAST
QUB MED
BELFAST
1973 2 04

3788 CENTRAL ECONOMIC SERVICE
PERSISTENT SCHOOL ABSENTEEISM IN NI
DEPT OF FINANCE (NI)
BELFAST
1978 2 03

3789 CHASTY,H T
STUDIES OF THE LANGUAGE DEVELOPMENT AND
ABSTRACT THINKING IN NI PUPILS...
QUB PHD
BELFAST
1973 2 04

3790 CHILVER REPORT
THE FUTURE OF HIGHER EDUCATION IN NI
HMSO
BELFAST
1982 2 03

3791 CLARKE,D
. . . A CRITICAL ANALYSIS OF THE
POLICIES FOR ADULT EDUCATION PUT FORWARD
IN THE DOCUMENT 'FOCUS FOR ACTION'
NUU MA
COLERAINE
1977 2 04

3792 CLARKE,M T
MEN, WOMEN AND POST-PRIMARY
PRINCIPALSHIP IN NI
CORE 3(1)
1979 2 01

3793 CLARKE,M T
MEN, WOMEN AND POST-PRIMARY
PRINCIPALSHIP IN NI
EOC
BELFAST
1978 2 03

3794 COCHRANE,A C
THE SCHOOLS LIBRARY SERVICE IN NI
AN LEABHARLANN 9
DUBLIN
1980 2 01

3795 COFFEY,A
PLACE AND TEACHING OF ENGLISH IN THE
SECONDARY INTERMEDIATE SCHOOL IN NI
QUB MA
BELFAST
1959 2 04

3796 COLGAN,J
HOME AND SCHOOL: A SOCIOLOGICAL APPROACH
TO PARENT-TEACHER RELATIONSHIPS IN NI
PRIMARY SCHOOLS
QUB MA
BELFAST
1976 2 04

3797 COLGAN,J
HOME-SCHOOL CONTACTS
NORTH TEACH 12(4)
1977 2 01

3798 CONWAY,W
CATHOLIC SCHOOLS
VERITAS
DUBLIN
1971 2 10

3799 CORKEY,W
EPISODE IN THE HISTORY OF PROTESTANT
ULSTER 1923-47
DORMAN
BELFAST
1960 2 02

3800 CORRIGAN,J; CRONE,R
A SIXTH-FORM EXPERIMENT
PRACTICE '73
BELFAST
1973 2 99

3801 COUNCIL FOR CONTINUING EDUCATION
CONTINUING EDUCATION IN SOCIALLY
DISADVANTAGED AREAS OF NI
HMSO
BELFAST
1978 2 03

3802 CRONE,R; CORRIGAN,J
LOCAL STUDIES IN THE JUNIOR SCHOOLS
APPLETREE PRESS
BELFAST
1976 2 02

3803 CRONE,R; MALONE,J
CONTINUITIES IN EDUCATION: THE NI
SCHOOLS CURRICULUM PROJECT
BELFAST
1979 2 10

3804 CRONE,R; MALONE,J
THE HUMAN CURRICULUM: THE EXPERIENCE OF
THE NI SCHOOLS SUPPORT SERVICE 1978-82
FARSET
BELFAST
1983 2 02

3805 CROSSLAND,B
SCHOOL AND INDUSTRY
NORTH TEACH 12(3)
BELFAST
1977 2 01

3806 CROWE,W H
BEYOND THE HILLS: AN ULSTER HEADMASTER
REMEMBERS
DUNDALGAN PRESS
DUNDALK
1971 2 02

3807 CROWE,W H
IN BANBRIDGE TOWN
W MULLAN
BELFAST
1964 2 02

3808 CURRAGH,E F
CAREERS EDUCATION IN POST-PRIMARY
SCHOOLS
NORTH TEACH 12(5)
BELFAST
1978 2 01

3809 CURRAGH,E G; MCGLEENON,C F
CAREERS EDUCATION IN POST-PRIMARY
SCHOOLS
NORTH TEACH 12(5)
BELFAST
1977 2 01

3810 CUSDIN,L
A FUNCTIONAL ANALYSIS OF THE RELATION
BETWEEN PARTICIPATION IN SPORT AND
ATTAINMENT IN FINAL DEGREE EXAMINATIONS
BY UNDERGRADUATES
QUB MSSC
BELFAST
1981 2 04

3811 DALLAT,M
INTEGRATED EDUCATION
COMM FORUM 2(1)
BELFAST
1972 2 01

3812 DALY,E
INTEGRATED EDUCATION
THE FURROW 32(6)
1981 2 01

3813 DARBY,J
DENOMINATIONAL SCHOOLING IN NI
IN SPENCER,A; TOVEY,H (EDS) PROC SAI
BELFAST
1978 2 11

3814 DARBY,J
DIVISIVENESS IN EDUCATION: ITS EXTENT
AND EFFECTS IN NI
NORTH TEACH 11(1)
BELFAST
1973 2 01

3815 DARBY,J
EDUCATION AND CONFLICT IN NI
NETWORK 1(1)
1980 1 01

3816 DARBY,J
EDUCATION PROVISION IN NI
NORTH TEACH 12(4)
BELFAST
1977 2 01

3817 DARBY,J
HISTORY IN THE SCHOOL: A REVIEW ARTICLE
COMM FORUM 4(2)
BELFAST
1974 2 01

3818 DARBY,J
NI: BONDS AND BREAKS IN EDUCATION
BRIT J EDUC STUD 26(3)
        2 01

3819 DARBY,J
RACE AND RELIGION: SOME OBSERVATIONS ON
DESEGREGATION IN AMERICA AND NI
INTEGRATED EDUC 18(5-6)
1980 1 01

3820 DARBY,J
SEGREGATED SCHOOLING - DOES IT
CONTRIBUTE TO SECTARIANISM?
IN SOCIAL STUDY CONFERENCE
DUBLIN
1974 1 07

3821 DARBY,J ET AL
EDUCATION AND COMMUNITY IN NI: SCHOOLS
APART?
CORE 2(3)
1978 1 01

3822 DARBY,J; MURRAY,D; BATTS,D; DUNN,S;
FARREN,S; MORRIS,J
EDUCATION AND COMMUNITY IN NI: SCHOOLS
APART?
NUU
COLERAINE
1977 2 10

3823 DENT,G I
THE LAW OF EDUCATION IN NI AND THE
INFLUENCE OF ENGLISH LAW
LONDON UNIV
LONDON
1965 2 04

3824 DEPT OF EDUCATION (NI)
ADULT EDUCATION IN NI
HMSO CMD 473
BELFAST
1964 2 03

3825 DEPT OF EDUCATION (NI)
EDUCATION IN NI IN 1978
HMSO
LONDON
1979 2 03

3826 DEPT OF EDUCATION (NI)
HIGHER EDUCATION IN NI: THE FUTURE
STRUCTURE
HMSO
BELFAST
1982 2 03

3827 DEPT OF EDUCATION (NI)
HOME-SCHOOL LINKS: REPORT OF THE WORKING
PARTY ON EDUCATIONAL WELFARE
HMSO
BELFAST
1976 2 03

3828 DEPT OF EDUCATION (NI)
REORGANISATION OF SECONDARY EDUCATION IN
NI: A CONSULTATIVE DOCUMENT
HMSO
BELFAST
1976 2 03

3829 DEPT OF EDUCATION (NI)
REPORT OF A WORKING PARTY ON SOCIAL
PRIORITY SCHOOLS IN NI
HMSO
BELFAST
1979 2 03

3830 DEPT OF EDUCATION (NI)
REPORT OF THE WORKING PARTY ON THE
MANAGEMENT OF SCHOOLS IN NI
HMSO
BELFAST
1979 2 03

3831 DEPT OF EDUCATION (NI)
SCHOOLS AND DEMOGRAPHIC TRENDS: A
BACKCLOTH TO PLANNING
HMSO
BELFAST
1981 2 03

3832 DICKSON,D
ASPECTS OF THE TEACHING PERFORMANCES OF
CONSECUTIVE AND CONCURRENT STUDENTS
NUU MA
COLERAINE
1974 2 04

3833 DICKSON,D
MICROCOUNSELLING: AN EVALUATIVE STUDY OF
A PROGRAMME
ULSTER POLY PHD
BELFAST
1981 2 04

3834 DOLAN,C
SOME IMPLICATIONS OF COMPREHENSIVE
EDUCATION
NORTH TEACH 10(6)
BELFAST
1973 2 01

3835 DONAGHY,P
A STUDY OF THE SECONDARY SCHOOL SYSTEM
OF NI 1947-69
QUB MA
BELFAST
1970 2 04

3836 DOUGLAS,F
'O' LEVELS AND 'A' LEVELS AS PREDICTORS
OF SUCCESS IN THE BELFAST TEACHER
TRAINING COLLEGES
IN MCKERNAN,J (ED)
COLERAINE
1978 2 07

3837 DOUGLAS,F
A PARTIAL COST-EFFECTIVENESS ANALYSIS OF
THE CAREERS COURSE AT ST. AUGUSTINE'S
BOYS' SECONDARY SCHOOL, BELFAST
NUU MA
COLERAINE
1976 2 04

3838 DOWLING,P
HISTORY OF IRISH EDUCATION
MERCIER
CORK
1971 2 02

3839 DOWNEY,A; O'DWYER,L
THE INITIATION AND EARLY IMPLEMENTATION
OF A MASS ADULT LITERACY SCHEME: THE NI
EXPERIENCE
AONTAS 2(1)
DUBLIN
1980 2 01

3840 DOWNEY,N G
A COMPARATIVE STUDY OF THE ROLE AND
PROVISION OF SELECTED TEACHERS' CENTRES
IN ENGLAND AND NI...
NUU MA
COLERAINE
1977 2 04

3841 DOWNEY,R
COMMUNITY SCHOOLS IN ACTION
NUU MA
COLERAINE
1980 2 04

3842 DOWNING,J D
NOTHING TO HIDE: THE BOEHRINGER CASE AND
ACADEMIC FREEDOM IN NI
COUNCIL FOR ACADEMIC FREEDOM AND
DEMOCRACY
LONDON
1974 2 10

3843 DUNCAN,T
HISTORY OF IRISH EDUCATION FROM 1800
WITH SPECIAL REFERENCE TO MANUAL
INSTRUCTION
DRAGON BOOKS
BALA
1972 2 02

3844 DUNN,S; MORGAN,V
A COMPARATIVE DEMOGRAPHIC STUDY OF
STUDENT TEACHERS FROM THE NORTH AND
SOUTH OF IRELAND
COMP EDUC FEB
1979 2 01

3845 DUNN,S; MORGAN,V
A CROSS-BORDER COMPARISON OF STUDENT
TEACHER ATTITUDES TO PRIMARY EDUCATION
PROC EDUC STUD ASSOC IRELAND
DUBLIN
1980 2 08

3846 DUNN,S; MORGAN,V
RECRUITS TO TEACHING IN IRELAND
CORE 3(1)
1979 2 01

3847 DYNAN,J
HIDDEN CURRICULUM OF A CATHOLIC BOYS
SCHOOL
NUU MA
COLERAINE
1980 2 04

3848 EATON,M
PERSISTENT ABSENTEEISM: A SCHOOL BASED
PREVENTATIVE APPROACH
TEACH 3
BELFAST
1979 2 01

3849 ELLIS,R; WHITTINGTON,D
A GUIDE TO SOCIAL SKILL TRAINING
CROOM HELM
LONDON
1981 2 02

3850 ELLIS,T H
NOISY MANSIONS: REFLECTIONS ON A CAREER
IN ULSTER SCHOOLS
WHITEHORN PRESS
LISNASKEA
1983 2 02

3851 ENWRIGHT,N C
THE USE OF A VOLUNTARY ASSOCIATION AS A
LINKING MECHANISM BETWEEN ADULTS IN THE
COMMUNITY AND COURSES OF EDUCATIONAL
PROVISION
NUU MA
COLERAINE
1975 2 04

3852 EOC
GIRLS AND EDUCATION: A NI STATISTICAL
ANALYSIS
EOC
BELFAST
1981 2 03

3853 EOC
REPORT OF A FORMAL INVESTIGATION INTO
FURTHER EDUCATION IN NI
EOC
BELFAST
1981 2 03

3854 FAHEY,J
PEACE EDUCATION: ITS RELEVANCE TO NI
NORTH TEACH 12(5)
BELFAST
1978 1 01

3855 FEE,F
EDUCATIONAL CHANGE IN BELFAST SCHOOL
CHILDREN, 1975-1981
IN HARBISON,J (ED)
BELFAST
1983 2 07

3856 FEE,F
READING AND DISTURBANCE IN BELFAST
SCHOOLS
EDUCATION AND LIBRARY BOARD
BELFAST
1977 1 10

3857 FEE,F
WORKING PARTY REPORT OF BELFAST
EDUCATION AND LIBRARY BOARD
EDUCATION AND LIBRARY BOARD
BELFAST
1977 2 10

3858 FISHER,G S
TEACHERS' PERCEPTIONS OF STUDENTS IN
FURTHER EDUCATION
QUB MED
BELFAST
1977 2 04

3859 FITZPATRICK,S
SIGNIFICANCE OF GEOGRAPHY IN IRISH
EDUCATION
GEOGR VIEWPOINT 3
1974 2 01

3860 FOOTE,T P
INITIAL REPORT ON TEACHER
SHORTAGE/SURPLUS AREAS
NICER
BELFAST
1978 2 10

3861 FORBES,J
DISTRIBUTION OF INTELLIGENCE AMONG
ELEMENTARY SCHOOL CHILDREN IN NI
BRIT J EDUC PSYCHOL NOV
1945 2 01

3862 FORSTER,D
A STUDY OF THE PREDICTION OF ACADEMIC
SUCCESS IN QUB
QUB MA
BELFAST
1959 2 04

3863 FORSTER,M
AUDIT OF ACADEMIC PERFORMANCE, QUB
BOYD
BELFAST
1959 2 99

3864 FRENCH,P G
A STUDY OF THE EXAMINATION MARKS
OBTAINED BY THIRD YEAR PUPILS IN
SELECTED SECONDARY SCHOOLS IN NI
NUU MPHIL
COLERAINE
1973 2 04

3865 FULTON,J
THE BEGINNINGS OF VOCATIONAL GUIDANCE IN
NI
NORTH TEACH 13(3)
BELFAST
1980 2 01

3866 FULTON,J
A NOTE ON THE WORK OF SCHOOL COUNSELLORS
NORTH TEACH 12(1)
BELFAST
1975 2 01

3867 FULTON, J
RECENT DEVELOPMENTS IN VOCATIONAL
GUIDANCE IN NI
NORTH TEACH 13(4)
BELFAST
1981 2 01

3868 FULTON, J
SOME REFLECTIONS ON CATHOLIC SCHOOLS IN
NI
STUDIES 58
1969 2 01

3869 FULTON, J F
EDUCATIONAL RESEARCH IN NI
IN COHEN, L; THOMAS, J; MANION, L (EDS)
WINDSOR
1982 2 07

3870 GAMBLE, H M
THE DEVELOPMENT OF THE PROVINCIAL
TECHNICAL COLLEGES IN NI
QUB MA
BELFAST
1973 2 04

3871 GAMBLE, R
AN INVESTIGATION INTO THE SOCIAL
INTERACTION, IDENTITY AND RELIGIOUS
ATTITUDES OF INTEGRATED SCHOOL PUPILS
QUB MSC
BELFAST
1982 2 04

3872 GEDDES, A; CRONE, R
FIRST YEAR READING PROGRAMME IN A
SECONDARY SCHOOL
NORTH TEACH 13(2)
BELFAST
1978 2 01

3873 GIBBS, I
THE EFFECTIVENESS OF THREE METHODS OF
TEACHER TRAINING
NUU PHD
COLERAINE
1978 2 04

3874 GIBBS, I
SOME RESPONSES OF STUDENTS AT THE NEW
UNIVERSITY OF ULSTER TO MICROTEACHING
NUU MPHIL
COLERAINE
1973 2 04

3875 GLASSCOCK, R E
GEOGRAPHY IN THE IRISH UNIVERSITIES
IR GEOG 5(5)
1968 2 01

3876 GLENNY, J B
PROBLEMS OF PUPILS IN A LARGE
CO-EDUCATIONAL SCHOOL
NUU MA
COLERAINE
1978 2 04

3877 GLOCKLING, B
COGNITIVE VARIABLES ASSOCIATED WITH
A-LEVEL ARTS AND SCIENCE PUPILS
QUB MED
BELFAST
1976 2 04

3878 GRAHAM, A
ATTITUDES TOWARDS SCIENCE AMONG FOURTH
FORMERS IN BELFAST GRAMMAR SCHOOLS
QUB MED
BELFAST
1968 2 04

3879 GRAHAM, E S D
RELIGION AND EDUCATION: THE
CONSTITUTIONAL PROBLEM
NI LEG QUART 33
BELFAST
1982 2 01

3880 GRAHAM, J M
A SAMPLE SURVEY OF THE SCHOOL CAREER...
OF PUPILS ADMITTED... TO NI GRAMMAR
SCHOOLS IN 1978
QUB MA
BELFAST
1968 2 04

3881 GREENWOOD, J
THE PERSONAL CHARACTERISTICS AND
PERFORMANCE OF A GROUP OF COLLEGE OF
EDUCATION STUDENTS
QUB MED
BELFAST
1972 2 04

3882 GREER, J E
THE ATTITUDES OF PARENTS AND PUPILS TO
RELIGION IN SCHOOLS
IR J EDUC 4
1970 2 01

3883 GREER, J E
RELIGION IN IRELAND: A SCHOOL BASED
CURRICULUM DEVELOPMENT PROJECT
LEARNING FOR LIVING 17(2)
1977 2 01

3884 GREER, J E
RELIGIOUS EDUCATION IN STATE PRIMARY
SCHOOLS IN NI
NORTH TEACH 13(2)
BELFAST
1978 2 01

3885 GREER, J E
RELIGIOUS EXPERIENCE AND RELIGIOUS
EDUCATION
SEARCH 4(1)
1981 2 01

3886 GREER, J E
SIXTH FORM RELIGION IN NI
NUU MPHIL
COLERAINE
1972 2 04

3887 GREER, J E
SIXTH FORM RELIGION IN NI
SOC STUD 1(3)
1972 2 01

3888 GREER, J E
TEACHERS AND RELIGIOUS EDUCATION
RELIGIOUS EDUCATION COUNCIL
BELFAST
1973 2 10

3889 GREER, J E; BROWN, G A
THE EFFECTS OF NEW APPROACHES TO
RELIGIOUS EDUCATION IN THE PRIMARY
SCHOOL
J CURRICULUM STUD 5(11)
1973 2 01

3890 GREER, J E; BROWN, W
THE INSPECTION OF RELIGIOUS EDUCATION IN
NI SCHOOLS
NORTH TEACH 13(4)
BELFAST
1981 2 01

3891 GREER, J E; MCCULLAGH, J J; MCELHINNEY, E P
TEACHING RELIGION IN IRELAND
NUU
COLERAINE
1980 2 10

3892 GUILD OF CATHOLIC TEACHERS
DIOCESE OF DOWN AND CONNOR: ASPECTS OF
CATHOLIC EDUCATION
ST JOSEPH'S COLL OF EDUC
BELFAST
1971 2 10

3893 HAINSWORTH, P
SOME COMMENTS ON ADULT LITERACY
PROVISION IN NI
J FURTHER HIGHER EDUC 5(2)
LONDON
1981 2 01

3894 HAMBLY, G E
COMPARISON OF THE PERFORMANCE OF
CHILDREN FROM PREPARATORY...(AND)
PRIMARY SCHOOLS IN THE QUALIFYING
EXAMINATION. . .1948
QUB MED
BELFAST
1949 2 04

3895 HARBISON, J; CAVEN, N
PERSISTENT SCHOOL ABSENTEEISM IN NI
DEPT OF FINANCE (NI)
BELFAST
1977 2 03

3896 HARBISON, J; FEE, F; CAVEN, N
CHARACTERISTICS OF A GROUP OF PERSISTENT
NON-ATTENDERS AT SCHOOL
IN HARBISON, J; HARBISON, J (EDS)
SHEPTON MALLET, SOMERSET
1980 1 07

3897 HARGIE, O
AN EVALUATION OF MICROTEACHING PROGRAMME
ULSTER POLY PHD
BELFAST
1980 2 04

3898 HAYES, D P
THE CONSTRUCTION OF AN ATTITUDE SCALE
TOWARDS MATHEMATICS....
QUB MED
BELFAST
1971 2 04

3899 HIGHER EDUCATION REVIEW GROUP
THE FUTURE STRUCTURE OF TEACHER
EDUCATION IN NI
HMSO
BELFAST
1980 2 03

3900 HOLDEN, J C
LOCAL GEOGRAPHY AND LOCAL STUDIES IN NI
SCHOOLS
QUB MA
BELFAST
1958 2 04

3901 HOLMES, E
PUBLIC OPINION AND EDUCATIONAL REFORM IN
THE NORTH OF IRELAND 1900-54
QUB
BELFAST
1968 2 04

3902 HOLMES, R F C
MAGEE 1865-1965
BELFAST NEWSLETTER, LTD
BELFAST
1965 2 02

3903 HUALLACHAIN, C
LANGUAGES OF INSTRUCTION IN IRELAND
1904-1977
INT R EDUC 24(4)
1978 2 01

3904 HUTCHINSON, B; MCALEER, J
INNOVATIONS IN THE SCHOOL: HOW CAN
RESEARCHERS HELP?
IN MCKERNAN, J (ED)
COLERAINE
1978 2 07

3905 HUTCHINSON, B; MCALEER, J
THE TEACHER'S CURRICULUM PROJECT
NORTH TEACH 13(2)
1970 2 01

3906 HUTCHINSON, W B D
AN INVESTIGATION OF VARIABLES ASSOCIATED
WITH VARIOUS FORMS OF CLASS ORGANIZATION
QUB MED
BELFAST
1972 2 04

3907 IRWIN, W G
A NEW ACADEMIC CAREER STRUCTURE IN
GENERAL PRACTICE IN NI
J ROYAL COLLEGE OF GENERAL PRACTITIONERS
30
LONDON
1980 2 01

3908 IRWIN, W G; BAMBER, J H
AN EVALUATION OF A COURSE FOR
UNDER-GRADUATE TEACHING OF GENERAL
PRACTICE
MED EDUC 12
1978 2 01

3909 JACQUES, W
THE CHIEF FACTORS DETERMINING THE
DEVELOPMENTS IN PRIMARY EDUCATION,
IRELAND, 1831-1947
QUB PHD
BELFAST
1952 2 04

3910 JAMIESON, J
HISTORY OF THE ROYAL BELFAST ACADEMICAL
INSTITUTION 1810-1960
MULLAN
BELFAST
1959 2 02

3911 JOHNSTON REPORT
EXAMINATIONS FOR SECONDARY INTERMEDIATE
(INCLUDING TECHNICAL INTERMEDIATE)
SCHOOLS
HMSO CMD 413
BELFAST
1960 2 03

3912 JOHNSTON, D H
THE DICKSON PLAN FOR CO. ARMAGH: A STUDY
IN LOCAL EDUCATIONAL PLANNING AND
DEVELOPMENT, 1965-1971
QUB MED
BELFAST
1971 2 04

3913 KARAGEORGOS, D L
MATHEMATICAL MODELS IN EDUCATIONAL
PLANNING
NUU PHD
COLERAINE
1977 2 04

3914 KEANE, T B
ATTITUDES TO RELIGIOUS INTEGRATION IN
SCHOOLS IN A SAMPLE OF SECONDARY SCHOOL
CHILDREN IN NEWRY AND SOUTH DOWN AREA
IN MCKERNAN, J (ED)
COLERAINE
1978 2 07

3915 KEANE, T B
ATTITUDES TO THE RELIGIOUS INTEGRATION
OF SCHOOLS IN NI
QUB MA
BELFAST
1977 2 04

3916 KELLY, T F
EDUCATION
IN HURLEY, M (ED)
DUBLIN
1970 2 07

3917 KELLY, V
EXTENT AND CAUSES OF EARLY AND PREMATURE
LEAVING IN SIX SELECTED NI GRAMMAR
SCHOOLS
QUB MA
BELFAST
1969 2 04

3918 KENNEDY, D
CATHOLIC EDUCATION IN NI, 1921-1970
ST JOSEPH'S COLL OF EDUC
BELFAST
1971 2 02

Education/

3919 KENNEDY,D
TOWARDS A UNIVERSITY
CATHOLIC DEAN OF RESIDENCE
BELFAST
1946 2 10

3920 KERR,J F
THE DEVELOPMENT OF THE TEACHING OF
SCIENCE IN IRELAND SINCE 1800
QUB PHD
BELFAST
1957 2 04

3921 KING,R
SOME ASPECTS OF THE EDUCATION OF
PHYSICALLY HANDICAPPED CHILDREN IN NI
QUB MED
BELFAST
1972 2 04

3922 KINNEN,J W D
CREATIVITY: ITS IDENTIFICATION AND
ENHANCEMENT IN PRIMARY SCHOOL EDUCATION
QUB MED
BELFAST
1978 2 04

3923 KNOX,H M
RELIGIOUS SEGREGATION IN THE SCHOOLS OF
NI
BRIT J EDUC STUD 21(3)
1973 2 01

3924 L'AIMIE,A
THE SCHOOLS CULTURAL STUDIES PROJECT
TEACH 13(1)
1981 2 01

3925 LAMBON,A J
A FOLLOW-UP STUDY OF SPECIAL EMPHASIS ON
READING PROGRESS OF 75 BOYS IN A BELFAST
PRIMARY SCHOOL
QUB MED
BELFAST
1973 2 04

3926 LAMMEY,M
COMMUNITY SERVICE: AN APPROACH THROUGH
MODE III CSE
TEACH 3
1979 2 01

3927 LARMOUR,J; FARRELL,G
PROBLEMS OF EDUCATION DURING THE CIVIL
UNREST
NORTH TEACH 11(1)
BELFAST
1973 1 01

3928 LATCHEM,C R
EDUCATIONAL DEVELOPMENT SYSTEM FOR NI
COUNCIL FOR EDUCATIONAL TECHNOLOGY
LONDON
1979 2 02

3929 LATCHEM,C R
FEASIBILITY STUDY ON THE ORGANIZATION OF
EDUCATIONAL TECHNOLOGY IN NI
COUNCIL FOR EDUCATIONAL TECHNOLOGY
LONDON
1977 2 10

3930 LAU,S B C
THE ECONOMICS OF EDUCATION IN NI FROM
1959/60 - 1968/69
QUB MSC
BELFAST
1973 2 04

3931 LEONARD,J J D
ACADEMIC MOTIVATION AND REWARD
PREFERENCES IN RELATION TO
DIFFERENTIATION AND POLARISATION IN A
GIRLS' GRAMMAR SCHOOL
QUB MED
BELFAST
1973 2 04

3932 LOCKWOOD REPORT
HIGHER EDUCATION IN NI
HMSO CMD 475
BELFAST
1965 2 03

3933 LONDONDERRY CITY AND BOROUGH COUNCIL
SUBMISSION TO THE GOVERNMENT OF NI,
PRESENTING THE CASE FOR THE PROMOTION OF
A UNIVERSITY AT LONDONDERRY
D. IRVINE
LONDONDERRY
1963 2 10

3934 LOUGHRAN,G
MORAL EDUCATION PROJECT IN NI
COMM FORUM 1(2)
BELFAST
1971 2 01

3935 LOVETT,T
THE CHALLENGE OF COMMUNITY EDUCATION IN
SOCIAL AND POLITICAL CHANGE
CONVERGENCE 11(1)
TORONTO
1978 1 01

3936 LOVETT,T
COMMUNITY EDUCATION AND COMMUNITY ACTION
SCOPE 9
BELFAST
1977 2 01

3937 LOVETT,T; MACKAY,L
ADULT EDUCATION AND THE WORKING CLASS: A
CASE STUDY
URB R 9(3)
1976 2 01

3938 LUKIANOWICZ,N
A SURVEY OF THE REASONS FOR REFERRAL OF
URBAN AND RURAL PRIMARY SCHOOL CHILDREN
TO CHILD GUIDANCE CLINICS IN COUNTY
ANTRIM
PAPERS IN PSYCHOL 1(1)
1967 2 01

3939 MACINTYRE,D G
THE NI COUNCIL FOR CONTINUING EDUCATION
AONTAS 1(2)
DUBLIN
1979 2 01

3940 MACKEY,M M
COUNSELLING IN FIVE BELFAST SECONDARY
SCHOOLS
QUB MSC
BELFAST
1974 2 04

3941 MACLOCK,M C
ATTITUDES OF SECONDARY SCHOOL PUPILS
TOWARDS PARTICIPATION IN PHYSICAL
ACTIVITY
QUB MSC
BELFAST
1970 2 04

3942 MAGEE,J
THE TEACHING OF IRISH HISTORY IN IRISH
SCHOOLS
NORTH TEACH 10(1)
BELFAST
1970 2 01

3943 MAGEE,J
TEACHING OF IRISH HISTORY IN SCHOOLS
NICRC
BELFAST
1971 2 10

3944 MALONE,J
SCHOOLS AND COMMUNITY RELATIONS
NORTH TEACH 11(1)
1973 1 01

3945 MALONE,J
SCHOOLS PROJECT IN COMMUNITY RELATIONS
NICRC
BELFAST
1972 1 10

3946 MALONE,J; CRONE,R
APPROACHES TO INNOVATIONS IN SCHOOLS
NORTH TEACH 12(1)
1975 2 01

3947 MALONE,J; CRONE,R
NEW APPROACH TO INNOVATION IN SCHOOLS
EDUC RES 20
1978 2 01

3948 MANNING,P
SPECIAL EDUCATION: A STUDY OF UNIT
PROVISION IN NI
NUU MA
COLERAINE
1978 2 04

3949 MARGRAIN,S; MCWHIRTER,L
THE WORK OF THE PSYCHOLOGY TEACHER IN
POLYTECHNICS: A SURVEY
PSYCHOL TEACHING 6(2)
1978 2 01

3950 MARSHALL,R
METHODIST COLLEGE BELFAST: THE FIRST
HUNDRED YEARS
METHODIST COLLEGE
BELFAST
1968 2 02

3951 MATIER,M
THE ORGANISATIONAL STRUCTURE OF THE
EDUCATION SYSTEM IN NI: A SOCIOLOGICAL
AND COMPARATIVE ANALYSIS
QUB MED
BELFAST
1981 2 04

3952 MCALEER,J; HUTCHINSON,B
CASE STUDY: TEACHERS' EXPECTATIONS AND
THE STUDY OF EDUCATION: A DIALOGICAL
APPROACH TO AN IN-SERVICE B ED
BRIT J IN-SERVICE EDUC 5(3)
NAFFERTON, NORTH HUMBERSIDE
1979 2 01

3953 MCALEER,J; WOODHOUSE,P C
IN-SERVICE B ED PROGRAMME AT THE
ENNISKILLEN OUT CENTRE
BRIT J IN-SERVICE EDUC 7(1)
NAFFERTON, NORTH HUMBERSIDE
1980 2 01

3954 MCALEER,J; WOODHOUSE,P C
THE USE OF THE LOUDSPEAKING TELEPHONE TO
CONDUCT SEMINARS AT AN OUT CENTRE
EDUC CHANGE DEVELOP 4(1)
SHEFFIELD
1981 2 01

3955 MCALLISTER,M A
CULTURAL AND INTELLECTUAL DEVELOPMENT IN
CONTEMPORARY SOCIETY ... STUDY OF
BELFAST SCHOOLGIRLS AND FEMALE
UNIVERSITY STUDENTS
QUB MA
BELFAST
1972 2 04

3956 MCCANN,J
NORTHERN SCHOOLS AND INTEGRATION
CHRISTUS REX 23(3)
1969 2 01

3957 MCCARNEY,W G
A SOCIOLOGICAL STUDY OF THE PROBLEMS OF
TRUANCY
QUB MA
BELFAST
1980 2 04

3958 MCCARNEY,W G
TRUANCY
NORTH TEACH 12(4)
1977 2 01

3959 MCCLELLAND,J
THE DEVELOPMENT OF EDUCATIONAL
FACILITIES FOR HANDICAPPED CHILDREN
QUB MA
BELFAST
1965 2 04

3960 MCCONNELL,G A
THE TEACHING OF ECONOMICS AS PART OF A
LEVEL NI GCE COURSE IN ECONOMICS...
QUB MED
BELFAST
1976 2 04

3961 MCCULLOUGH,S
AN INQUIRY INTO GEOGRAPHY WITH REGARD TO
THE CERTIFICATE OF SECONDARY EDUCATION
QUB MED
BELFAST
1974 2 04

3962 MCDONALD,G; MCCABE,P; MACKLE,B
SYMPOSIUM ON STRUCTURED TEACHING AND
TRAINING: SELF-HELP SKILLS IN THE
PROFOUNDLY SUBNORMAL
BRIT J MENTAL SUBNORMALITY 22
1976 2 01

3963 MCDOWELL,J
THE DEVELOPMENT OF FURTHER EDUCATION IN
NI 1947-75
NUU MA
COLERAINE
1978 2 04

3964 MCELLIGOTT,T
EDUCATION IN IRELAND
DUBLIN
1966 2 02

3965 MCEWEN,A
SCHOOL ORGANISATION AND MANAGEMENT:
FUNCTIONS AND DYSFUNCTIONS
NORTH TEACH 13
BELFAST
1978 2 01

3966 MCEWEN,A
URBAN EDUCATION
NORTH TEACH 11
BELFAST
1975 2 01

3967 MCGANN,G
AN ANALYSIS OF THE GROWTH AND
DEVELOPMENT IN VOCATIONAL EDUCATION IN
IRELAND, 1950-1975
NUU MA
COLERAINE
1978 2 04

3968 MCGEOWN,V
DIMENSIONS OF TEACHER INNOVATIVENESS
CORE 3(2)
1979 2 01

3969 MCGEOWN,V
SELECTED LEADERSHIP FUNCTIONS OF THE
SCHOOL PRINCIPAL
EDUCATIONAL ADMINISTRATION 8(1)
1979 2 01

3970 MCGEOWN,V
TEACHER PARTICIPATION IN SCHOOL DECISION
MAKING
NORTH TEACH 4
BELFAST
1980 2 01

3971 MCGILL,P
EDUCATION: REPRESENTATION FOR PARENTS?
SCOPE 34
BELFAST
1980 2 01

3972 MCGILTON,J
NI COUNCIL FOR EDUCATIONAL RESEARCH,
1963-1973
NORTH TEACH 10(6)
1973 2 01

3973 MCGILTON, J
SOME COMPARATIVE STUDIES OF EDUCATION IN
THE US AND THE UK
NORTH TEACH 12(2)
1976   2   01

3974 MCGILTON, J
THE VERBAL ATTITUDES OF REPRESENTATIVE
GROUPS OF PRIMARY SCHOOL CHILDREN
QUB PHD
BELFAST
1958   2   04

3975 MCGLERNON, C F
PERSPECTIVES OF A CAREERS EDUCATION
CURRICULUM,....
QUB MA
BELFAST
1977   2   04

3976 MCGRATTAN, G
A SURVEY OF HOME SCHOOL LIAISON IN WEST
BELFAST
NUU MA
COLERAINE
1979   2   04

3977 MCGRENERA, S
THE ROLE OF THE EDUCATION WELFARE
OFFICER IN NI
NUU MSC
COLERAINE
1978   2   04

3978 MCGUFFIN, S J
HEALTH EDUCATION IN NI SCHOOLS: A SURVEY
OF TEACHERS' ATTITUDES
STRANMILLIS COLLEGE
BELFAST
1976   2   08

3979 MCGUFFIN, S J
HEALTH EDUCATION IN NI SCHOOLS: A SURVEY
OF THE ATTITUDES OF PARENTS AND PUPILS
STRANMILLIS COLLEGE
BELFAST
1976   2   08

3980 MCGUFFIN, S J
HEALTH EDUCATION IN NI: A SURVEY OF
CURRENT PRACTICE IN POST-PRIMARY SCHOOLS
J INST HEALTH EDUC 14(1)
1976   2   01

3981 MCGUFFIN, S J
HEALTH EDUCATION IN POST-PRIMARY
SCHOOLS: A SURVEY OF CURRENT PRACTICE
STRANMILLIS COLLEGE
BELFAST
1975   2   08

3982 MCGUFFIN, S J
HEALTH EDUCATION IN PRIMARY SCHOOLS IN
NI
NORTH TEACH 12(3)
BELFAST
1977   2   01

3983 MCGUFFIN, S J
HEALTH EDUCATION IN PRIMARY SCHOOLS IN
NI: A SURVEY OF CURRENT PRACTICE
STRANMILLIS COLLEGE
BELFAST
1976   2   08

3984 MCGUFFIN, S J
AN INVESTIGATION INTO THE FACTORS
INFLUENCING THE CHOICE OF CAREER BY BOYS
QUB MSC
BELFAST
1956   2   04

3985 MCGUFFIN, S J
RECENT DEVELOPMENT IN HEALTH EDUCATION
IN SCHOOLS IN NI
ULSTER MED J 47(1)
BELFAST
1978   2   01

3986 MCGUFFIN, S J
RECENT DEVELOPMENTS IN POST-PRIMARY
SCIENCE TEACHING IN NI SCHOOLS
NORTH TEACH 11(2)
BELFAST
1974   2   01

3987 MCGUFFIN, S J
THE SCHOOLS COUNCIL INTEGRATED SCIENCE
PROJECT IN NI SCHOOLS, 1970-73
QUB MA
BELFAST
1974   2   04

3988 MCGUFFIN, S J
VENEREAL DISEASE: ITS PLACE IN HEALTH
EDUCATION IN SCHOOLS
BRIT J VENEREAL DISEASES 53(4)
1977   2   01

3989 MCGUFFIN, S J
WHAT NI TEACHERS THINK ABOUT HEALTH
EDUCATION
J INST HEALTH EDUC 14(1)
1978   2   01

3990 MCIVOR, J A
POPULAR EDUCATION IN THE IRISH
PRESBYTERIAN CHURCH
SCEPTER
DUBLIN
1969   2   02

3991 MCIVOR, M
ENVIRONMENTAL UNDERSTANDING IN NI
INT SOCIETY FOR THE STUDY OF BEHAVIOURAL
DEVELOPMENT CONF
TORONTO
1981   1   11

3992 MCKAY, J R; KEITH, A
HIGHER EDUCATION IN SCOTLAND AND NI
WHERE? 15
1966   2   01

3993 MCKAY, R
NI: AN INFRASTRUCTURE FOR EDUCATIONAL
CHANGE
TEACH 5
BELFAST
1981   2   01

3994 MCKENNA, M
A STUDY OF EDUCATIONALLY SUB-NORMAL
CHILDREN WHO WERE EVENTUALLY DECLARED TO
BE IN NEED OF SPECIAL CARE
QUB MA
BELFAST
1973   2   04

3995 MCKEOWN, G
THE TEACHING OF GEOGRAPHY IN THE
SECONDARY (INTERMEDIATE) SCHOOLS OF NI
QUB MA
BELFAST
1972   2   04

3996 MCKEOWN, M
CIVIL UNREST: SECONDARY SCHOOLS SURVEY
NORTH TEACH 11(1)
1973   1   01

3997 MCKEOWN, M
EDUCATION
IN DARBY, J; WILLIAMSON, A (EDS)
1978   1   07

3998 MCKERNAN, J
AN EXPERIMENT IN SCHOOL-BASED CURRICULUM
DEVELOPMENT IN A NI SECONDARY SCHOOL
SECONDARY TEACHER 6(4)
1977   2   01

3999 MCKERNAN, J
PUPIL VALUE SYSTEMS IN STATE AND
CATHOLIC SECONDARY SCHOOLS IN NI
IN MULCAHY, D G (ED)
CORK
1977   2   07

4000 MCKERNAN,J
PUPIL VALUES AS SOCIAL INDICATORS OF
INTER-GROUP DIFFERENCES IN NI
IN HARBISON,J; HARBISON,J (EDS)
SHEPTON MALLET, SOMERSET
1980 1 07

4001 MCKERNAN,J
A SURVEY OF TEACHER DOGMATISM IN NI:
OPEN-MINDED OR CLOSED-MINDED TEACHING
IR J PSYCHOL 5(1)
1981 2 01

4002 MCKERNAN,J
TEACHING CONTROVERSIAL ISSUES
NUU DPHIL
COLERAINE
1978 1 04

4003 MCKERNAN,J
TRANSFER AT 14: A STUDY OF THE CRAIGAVON
TWO-TIER SYSTEM AS AN ORGANISATIONAL
INNOVATION IN EDUCATION
NICER
BELFAST
1981 2 10

4004 MCKINNIE,O
ASPECTS OF RELIGIOUS SEGREGATION IN
SCHOOLS IN NI
COMPARE 7(2)
1977 2 01

4005 MCMAHON,H F
CURRICULUM DEVELOPMENT IN NI
IN HARRIS,A ET AL (EDS)
LONDON
1975 2 07

4006 MCMAHON,H F; MCCONNELLOGUE,P; ANDERSON,J
S A
COMPUTER MANAGED LEARNING IN NI
NORTH TEACH 22(5)
1978 2 01

4007 MCMAHON,N
THE REVISION OF THE OSERETSKY TESTS OF
MOTOR PROFICIENCY FOR USE...IN PRIMARY
SCHOOL IN NI
NUU MPHIL
COLERAINE
1978 2 04

4008 MCNEILLY,N
EXACTLY 50 YEARS - BELFAST EDUCATION
AUTHORITY AND ITS WORK 1923-73
BELFAST
1974 2 02

4009 MCNEILLY,N
INTEGRATION IN EDUCATION, PAST, PRESENT
AND FUTURE
BELFAST NATURAL HISTORY AND
PHILOSOPHICAL SOCIETY PROC 9
BELFAST
1976 2 01

4010 MCQUIGG,O
INVOLVING PARENTS
TEACH 5
1981 2 01

4011 MCSTAVICK,B
A STUDY OF SCHOOL ORGANISATION AND
CURRICULUM PROVISIONS FOR THE 14+ PUPIL
QUB MA
BELFAST
1974 2 04

4012 MCWHIRTER,L
CONTACT AND CONFLICT: THE QUESTION OF
INTEGRATED EDUCATION
IR J PSYCHOL 6(1)
DUBLIN
1983 1 01

4013 MCWHIRTER,L
SEGREGATED EDUCATION AND SOCIAL CONFLICT
IN NI
INT PERSPECTIVES ON CHILD DEVELOPMENT
AND SOC POLICY CONF
TORONTO
1981 1 11

4014 MCWHIRTER,L; MARGRAIN,S
FLEXIBILITY OF TRANSFER BETWEEN COURSES:
AN AID TO STUDENT ASSESSMENT
PSYCHOL TEACHING 5(2)
1977 2 01

4015 MEHAFFEY,D J
ATTITUDES TOWARDS SPECIAL EDUCATION
NUU MA
COLERAINE
1978 2 04

4016 MEHAFFEY,H
THE RESPONSE TO THE STUDY OF ENGLISH
LITERATURE IN EIGHT NI GRAMMAR AND
SENIOR HIGH SCHOOLS
QUB MED
BELFAST
1974 2 04

4017 MILLER,D W
EDUCATION AND SECTARIAN CONFLICT IN NI
AMER HISTORICAL ASSOC
1969 1 08

4018 MILLER,R L
OPINIONS ON SCHOOL DE-SEGREGATION IN NI
IN SPENCER,A; TOVEY,H (EDS) PROC SAI
BELFAST
1978 2 01

4019 MILNE,K
NEW APPROACHES TO THE TEACHING OF IRISH
HISTORY
HISTORICAL ASSOCIATION
LONDON
1979 2 10

4020 MINISTRY OF EDUCATION (NI)
EDUCATIONAL DEVELOPMENT IN NI 1964
HMSO CMD 470
BELFAST
1964 2 03

4021 MINISTRY OF EDUCATION (NI)
EDUCATIONAL RECONSTRUCTION IN NI: THE
FIRST TEN YEARS
HMSO
BELFAST
1959 2 03

4022 MINISTRY OF EDUCATION (NI)
THE EXISTING SELECTION PROCEDURE FOR
SECONDARY EDUCATION IN NI 1971
HMSO CMD 551
BELFAST
1971 2 03

4023 MINISTRY OF EDUCATION (NI)
LOCAL EDUCATION AUTHORITIES AND
VOLUNTARY SCHOOLS
HMSO CMD 513
BELFAST
1967 2 03

4024 MINISTRY OF EDUCATION (NI)
PUBLIC EDUCATION IN NI
HMSO
BELFAST
1964 2 03

4025 MINISTRY OF EDUCATION (NI)
THE REORGANISATION OF SECONDARY
EDUCATION IN NI
HMSO CMD 574
BELFAST
1973 2 03

4026 MINISTRY OF EDUCATION (NI)
REPORT OF THE PRIMARY SCHOOLS PROGRAMME
COMMITTEE
HMSO
BELFAST
1956 2 03

4027 MINISTRY OF EDUCATION (NI)
RURAL EDUCATION: A REPORT OF THE
ADVISORY COUNCIL FOR EDUCATION IN NI
HMSO CMD 300
BELFAST
1951 2 03

4028 MINNIS, N
THE PROFESSIONAL IDEOLOGY OF TEACHERS OF
SOCIOLOGY IN SECONDARY SCHOOLS AND
FURTHER EDUCATION COLLEGES IN NI
QUB MSSC
BELFAST
1981 2 04

4029 MITCHELL, W
EDUCATION FOR PEACE
BELFAST CHRISTIAN JOURNALS
BELFAST
1978 1 10

4030 MOLES, W
INTEGRATED EDUCATION
COMM FORUM 2(1)
1972 2 01

4031 MOORE, E M
PARENT-TEACHER COMMUNICATION IN RURAL
AREAS: A NI STUDY
IR J AGRIC ECON RUR SOCIOL 3(2)
1971 2 01

4032 MOORE, M E
SOME SYNTACTIC, LEXICAL AND PHONETIC
CHARACTERISTICS OF...PASSAGES WRITTEN
BY... ADOLESCENT PUPILS IN NI GRAMMAR
SCHOOLS
QUB PHD
BELFAST
1976 2 04

4033 MOORE, T
AGRICULTURE EDUCATION IN NI
AGRICULTURAL PROGRESS 44
1969 2 01

4034 MORONEY, M
TEACHERS UNIONS AND COLLECTIVE
BARGAINING
NORTH TEACH 13(3)
BELFAST
1980 2 01

4035 MURPHY, M
EDUCATION IN IRELAND: NOW AND THE FUTURE
MERCIER
CORK
1970 2 02

4036 MURRAY, D
EDUCATION AND COMMUNITY IN NI
NORTH TEACH 13(2)
BELFAST
1978 2 01

4037 MURRAY, D
EDUCATION AND COMMUNITY IN NI: SCHOOLS
APART?
IN MCKERNAN, J (ED)
COLERAINE
1978 1 01

4038 MURRAY, R; OSBORNE, R D
EDUCATIONAL QUALIFICATIONS AND RELIGIOUS
AFFILIATION
IN CORMACK, R; OSBORNE, R D (EDS)
BELFAST
1983 2 07

4039 MUSSON, J
THE TRAINING OF TEACHERS IN IRELAND FROM
1811 TO THE PRESENT DAY
QUB PHD THESIS
1955 2 04

4040 NEILL, D G
EDUCATIONAL ADMINISTRATION IN NI
ADMIN (DUB) 3(1)
1955 2 01

4041 NEILL, D G ET AL
THE ROLE OF EDUCATIONAL INSTITUTIONS IN
NI
COMM FORUM 2(1)
1972 2 01

4042 NI ASSEMBLY
REPORT ON THE RATIONALISATION OF SCHOOLS
HMSO NIA 34
BELFAST
1983 2 03

4043 NI ASSOCIATION FOR COMPREHENSIVE
EDUCATION
COMPREHENSIVE CHALLENGE
NI ASSOCIATION FOR COMPREHENSIVE
EDUCATION
BELFAST
1978 2 10

4044 NI COMMITTEE FOR EDUCATIONAL TECHNOLOGY
PLANNING FOR EDUCATIONAL TECHNOLOGY IN
NI: REPORT OF THE COMMITTEE
NI COMMITTEE FOR EDUCATIONAL TECHNOLOGY
BANGOR
1976 2 03

4045 NI COUNCIL FOR CONTINUING EDUCATION
CONTINUING EDUCATION IN NI: A STRATEGY
FOR DEVELOPMENT
NI COUNCIL FOR CONTINUING EDUCATION
BELFAST
1980 2 03

4046 NI GOVERNMENT
REPORT OF THE COMMITTEE ON LEGAL
EDUCATION IN NI
HMSO CMD 579
BELFAST
1973 2 03

4047 NI GOVERNMENT
REPORT OF THE COMMITTEE ON THE POSSIBLE
DEVELOPMENT OF MAGEE UNIVERSITY COLLEGE
HMSO CMD 275
BELFAST
1950 2 03

4048 NI GOVERNMENT
REPORT OF THE COMMITTEE ON THE
RECRUITMENT AND TRAINING OF TEACHERS
HMSO CMD 254
BELFAST
1947 2 03

4049 NI SCHOOLS CURRICULUM COMMITTEE
ULSTER CHILDREN SPEAKING AND WRITING
MINISTRY OF EDUCATION (NI)
BANGOR
         2 10

4050 NICER
EARLY LEAVING IN NI
NICER
BELFAST
1974 2 10

4051 NICER
PERSONALITY AND ATTAINMENT
NICER
BELFAST
1972 2 10

4052 NICER
TEACHERS AND RESEARCH: A REPORT OF A
CONFERENCE
NICER
BELFAST
1969 2 08

4053 NICHOLLS, S
THE PEDAGOGICAL TREATMENT OF INDIVIDUAL
PUPILS: AN INVESTIGATION OF PRIMARY AND
SECONDARY SCHOOLS IN TWO AREAS IN NI
QUB MED
BELFAST
1981 2   04

4054 NIEC
PUBLIC EXPENDITURE PRIORITIES: EDUCATION
NIEC
BELFAST
1982 2   03

4055 NIKJOO, N
READING DIFFICULTIES AND PERCEPTUAL TASK
COMPETENCIES OF ADULT ILLITERATES
QUB MA
BELFAST
1977 2   04

4056 NOLAN, M B
ANALYSIS OF PUPIL'S SELF-REPORTS OF
ADAPTATION TO THE TRANSITION TO
SECONDARY SCHOOL
QUB MA
BELFAST
1979 2   04

4057 NURSERY SCHOOLS ASSOCIATION OF GB AND NI
NURSERY CLASSES IN PRIMARY SCHOOLS
LONDON UNIV
LONDON
1957 2   10

4058 O'BRIEN, J
SCIENCE AND CATHOLIC EDUCATION
CATHOLIC TEACHERS J 9(5)
1966 2   01

4059 O'CONNELL, J I
APPROACHES TO THE TEACHING OF HISTORY IN
SECONDARY INTERMEDIATE SCHOOLS IN NI
QUB MED
BELFAST
1961 2   04

4060 O'CONNELL, T J
HISTORY OF THE INTO, 1868-1968
INTO
DUBLIN
1969 2   02

4061 O'CONNOR, S
CHOCOLATE CREAM SOLDIERS: EVALUATING AN
EXPERIMENT IN NON-SECTARIAN EDUCATION IN
NI
J CURRICULUM STUD 12(3)
1980 1   01

4062 ORR, J A E; BOAL, F W
RECENT TRENDS IN SCHOOL ENROLMENTS IN
BELFAST
IR GEOG 13
DUBLIN
1980 2   01

4063 OSBORNE, R D
THE LOCKWOOD REPORT AND THE LOCATION OF
A SECOND UNIVERSITY IN NI
IN BOAL, F W; DOUGLAS, J N H (EDS)
LONDON
1982 2   07

4064 OSBORNE, R D; CORMACK, R; REID, N;
WILLIAMSON, A
POLITICAL ARITHMETIC AND HIGHER
EDUCATION IN NI
IN CORMACK, R; OSBORNE, R D (EDS)
BELFAST
1983 2   07

4065 OSBORNE, R D; MURRAY, R
EDUCATIONAL QUALIFICATIONS AND RELIGIOUS
AFFILIATION IN NI
FEA 3
BELFAST
1978 2   10

4066 OTTERBURN, M K
MATHEMATICS FOR THE CERTIFICATE OF
SECONDARY EDUCATION WITH SPECIAL
REFERENCE TO NI
QUB MA
BELFAST
1975 2   04

4067 PALMER, D; JARDINE, M; FINNEGAN, G
FROM SCHOOLS TO WORK: WHAT NEXT?
STANDING CONFERENCE OF YOUTH
ORGANISATIONS
BELFAST
1980 2   10

4068 PAUL, J A
THE STUDY AND TEACHING OF SENIOR
CERTIFICATE HISTORY IN...NI GRAMMAR
SCHOOL
QUB MED
BELFAST
1962 2   04

4069 PRICE, A
EVERYTHING OUT OF NOTHING
EDUCATION 121(28)
1963 2   01

4070 PRITCHARD, R M O
RECONSTRUCTION - STRATEGY FOR A BRIGHTER
FUTURE?
NORTH TEACH 12(1)
BELFAST
1976 1   01

4071 PRITCHARD, R M O
SCHOOL LANGUAGE LABORATORIES IN NI
IR J EDUC 10(2)
DUBLIN
1976 2   01

4072 PRITCHARD, R M O
SCHOOL LANGUAGE LABORATORIES IN NI
NUU PHD
COLERAINE
1974 2   04

4073 RAWLES, M E
RELIGIOUS EDUCATION FOR SLOW-LEARNING
ADOLESCENTS
NUU MA
BELFAST
1970 2   04

4074 RAY, D
THE CASE AGAINST PRIMARY SCHOOL CLOSURES
SCOPE 49
BELFAST
1982 2   01

4075 REA, D
A DISCUSSION OF SOCIAL CLASS BACKGROUND
WITH SPECIAL REFERENCE TO STUDENTS
JSSISI 21(4)
DUBLIN
1968 2   01

4076 REA, D
THE UNIVERSITY AS AN ORGANISATION WITH
PARTICULAR REFERENCE TO THE PERSONNEL
FUNCTION
QUB PHD
BELFAST
1973 2   04

4077 REID, N; GOLDIE, R
NI WOMEN IN HIGHER EDUCATION
EOC
BELFAST
1981 2   10

4078 REYNOLDS, A W
PEER GROUP VALUES AND FRIENDSHIP
PATTERNS IN A GRAMMAR SCHOOL FIFTH
FORM...AND THEIR RELATIONSHIP TO
EDUCATIONAL ACHIEVEMENT
NUU MA
BELFAST
1972 2   04

4079 RHODES, E
COMPREHENSIVE SECONDARY EDUCATION
MAGEE UNIV COLLEGE
DERRY
1969 2 11

4080 ROBINSON, A
EDUCATION AND SECTARIAN CONFLICT IN NI
NEW ERA JAN
1971 1 10

4081 ROBINSON, A
THE SCHOOLS CULTURAL STUDIES PROJECT
TEACH 1
BELFAST
1979 2 01

4082 ROBINSON, A
SOCIAL STUDIES IN NI: THE SCHOOLS
CULTURAL STUDIES PROJECT
SOC SCI TEACHER 9(3)
1980 2 01

4083 ROCKS, J F
AN OPPORTUNITY LOST: THE NI EDUCATION
SYSTEM 1921-30
NUU MA
COLERAINE
1978 2 04

4084 RODDIE, I
AN EXCELLENT MEDICAL SCHOOL, AN
INAUGURAL LECTURE
QUB
BELFAST
1975 2 10

4085 ROGERS, P S; O'NEILL, B
ACTIVITY TEACHING IN MATHEMATICS IN THE
PRIMARY SCHOOL
NORTH TEACH 13(3)
BELFAST
1979 2 01

4086 ROWLANDS, D ET AL
THE COMMUNITY EDUCATION PROJECT: FINAL
REPORT
QUB
BELFAST
1979 2 02

4087 RUSSELL, J
INTEGRATED SCHOOLING
SECONDARY TEACHER 7(1)
1977 2 01

4088 SALTERS, J
INTEGRATED EDUCATION IN NI: SOME
ASSUMPTIONS TO BE EXAMINED
PROC IRISH EDUC SOC
1976 2 11

4089 SALTERS, J
INTEGRATION: A SOCIOLOGICAL PERSPECTIVE
IN GUILD OF CATHOLIC TEACHERS
1978 2 07

4090 SALTERS, M G
...RELIGIOUS INSTRUCTION IN GRANT-AIDED
SCHOOLS IN THE UNITED KINGDOM WITH
SPECIAL REFERENCE TO...NI
QUB MED
BELFAST
1967 2 04

4091 SCOPE
INTERVIEW WITH NICHOLAS SCOTT
SCOPE 62
BELFAST
1983 2 01

4092 SCOTT, R D
UNIVERSITY UNDER STRESS: THE PECULIAR
PROBLEMS OF TEACHING IN ULSTER
VESTES 16
1973 1 01

4093 SHAW, T
ENVIRONMENTAL EDUCATION IN NI: CONCERN
AND DEVELOPMENT
B ENVIRONMENTAL EDUC 131
1982 2 01

4094 SHORTT, J A
PRIMARY SCHOOL HISTORY TEACHING: A
SURVEY OF PRACTICE IN A SAMPLE OF
SCHOOLS IN THE GREATER BELFAST AREA
QUB MED
BELFAST
1972 2 04

4095 SHRUM, R
ACROSS THE SEA IN IRELAND
NEW TIMES 9
1977 2 01

4096 SKILBECK, M
THE SCHOOL AND CULTURAL DEVELOPMENT
NORTH TEACH 11(1)
BELFAST
1973 2 01

4097 SMEATON, B
COMMUNITY WORK, SOCIAL CHANGE AND THE
UNIVERSITIES
SCOPE 2
BELFAST
1976 2 01

4098 SMYTH, W
IRISH HISTORY IN SECONDARY
(INTERMEDIATE) SCHOOLS IN NI...
QUB MA
BELFAST
1974 2 04

4099 SPELMAN, B J
DEVELOPMENT OF POST PRIMARY EDUCATION IN
NI: A RESEARCH PERSPECTIVE
NORTH TEACH 11(4)
BELFAST
1975 2 01

4100 SPELMAN, B J
PUPIL ADAPTATION TO SECONDARY SCHOOL IN
NI
NICER
BELFAST
1979 2 10

4101 SPENCE, W R
THE GROWTH AND DEVELOPMENT OF THE
SECONDARY INTERMEDIATE SCHOOL IN NI...
QUB MA
BELFAST
1959 2 04

4102 SPENCER, A
EDUCATIONAL PRIORITY: THE REPORT OF THE
WORKING PARTY OF THE EDUCATION COMMITTEE
ON NURSERY EDUCATION/EDUCATIONAL
PRIORITY AREAS 1973-1977
BELFAST EDUCATION AND LIBRARY BOARD
BELFAST
1977 2 10

4103 SPENCER, A
FINAL REPORT OF A WORKING PARTY OF THE
EDUCATION COMMITTEE TO CONSIDER THE WORK
AND STRUCTURE OF SCHOOL MANAGEMENT
COMMITTEES
BELFAST EDUCATION AND LIBRARY BOARD
BELFAST
1977 2 10

4104 SPENCER, A
SCHOOL AS A SOURCE OF PASTORAL CARE
PROBLEMS
IN MCCAFFERTY, N (ED)
1977 2 07

4105 ST JOSEPH'S COLL OF EDUCATION
ASPECTS OF CATHOLIC EDUCATION
ST JOSEPH'S COLL OF EDUCATION
BELFAST
1971 2 10

4106 ST. JOHN BROOKS,C
THE HISTORY AND DEVELOPMENT OF
EDUCATIONAL BROADCASTING IN IRELAND
NUU MA
COLERAINE
1971 2 04

4107 ST. LEGER,F J
OCCUPATIONAL ASPIRATIONS AND EDUCATION
IN THE COLERAINE TRIANGLE
SOC STUD 3(4)
MAYNOOTH
1974 2 01

4108 STARR,J W
DISCIPLINE AND CORPORAL PUNISHMENT IN
SCHOOLS: A LONGTITUDINAL STUDY
EDUC RES 19
1978 2 01

4109 STEPHEN,E
HANDICAP IN NI: A SPECIAL CASE
IN SWAN,W (ED)
LONDON
1981 2 07

4110 SUTHERLAND,A E
CURRICULUM PROJECTS IN PRIMARY SCHOOLS:
AN INVESTIGATION OF PROJECT ADOPTION
AND IMPLEMENTATION IN 185 NI SCHOOLS
NICER
BELFAST
1981 2 10

4111 SUTHERLAND,M
EDUCATION IN NI
IN BELL R (ED)
LONDON
1973 2 07

4112 SUTHERLAND,M
PROGRESS AND PROBLEMS OF EDUCATION IN NI
1952-1982
BRIT J EDUC STUD 30(1)
1982 2 01

4113 TAYLOR,A
SEX EDUCATION AND ITS PROVISION IN NI
SECONDARY AND GRAMMAR SCHOOLS
QUB MED
BELFAST
1967 2 04

4114 THOMPSON,W
IN PLACE OF SELECTION
NORTH TEACH 12(4)
BELFAST
1977 2 01

4115 TITTMAR,H; HARGIE,O; DICKSON,D
SOCIAL SKILLS TRAINING AT ULSTER COLLEGE
PROGRAM LEARN ED TECH 4
1977 2 01

4116 TODD,H L
SOME ASPECTS OF THE GENERAL ASSEMBLY AND
RELIGIOUS EDUCATION IN PRIMARY SCHOOLS
1921-1971
QUB MED
BELFAST
1972 2 04

4117 TOULSON,S
TRAINING ULSTER'S TEACHERS...AND
ULSTER'S NEW UNIVERSITY
TEACHER 13(4)
1969 2 01

4118 TRACEY,J P
SOME DIVERGENT TRENDS IN IRISH EDUCATION
SINCE 1922
QUB MED
BELFAST
1963 2 04

4119 TRAINOR,B
IN NI
ADMIN (DUB) 1(2)
DUBLIN
1953 2 01

4120 TRANT,A
ROADS TO RECONCILIATION: THE ROLE OF
EDUCATION
IN SOCIAL STUDY CONFERENCE
DUBLIN
1974 1 07

4121 TREW,K
ASPECTS OF CLASSROOM PRACTICES IN THE
UPPER PRIMARY SCHOOL
PROC IRISH EDUC SOCIETY CONF
GALWAY
1976 2 11

4122 TREW,K
A DISCUSSION AND EXPERIMENTAL
INVESTIGATION OF ENVIRONMENTAL
INFLUENCES ON THE DEVELOPMENT OF THE
PERCEPTION OF SPEECH
QUB PHD
BELFAST
1971 2 04

4123 TREW,K
EDUCATIONAL RESEARCH IN NI
PAPERS IN PSYCHOL 5(1)
1971 2 01

4124 TREW,K
THE PHYSICAL ENVIRONMENT OF A
REPRESENTATIVE SAMPLE OF NI PRIMARY
SCHOOLS
NORTH TEACH 10(3)
BELFAST
1971 2 01

4125 TREW,K
TEACHER PRACTICES AND CLASSROOM
RESOURCES
NICER
BELFAST
1977 2 10

4126 TREW,K
TEACHING READING IN THE URBAN SCHOOL: A
STUDY AND ITS METHODOLOGY
IN GREANY,V (ED)
1977 2 07

4127 TRUSTEES OF THE CATHOLIC EDUCATION
COLLEGES
CATHOLIC EDUCATION AND THE CHILVER
PROPOSALS
TRUSTEES OF THE CATHOLIC EDUCATION
COLLEGES
BELFAST
1981 2 10

4128 TURNER,E B; TURNER,I F; REID,A
RELIGIOUS ATTITUDES IN TWO TYPES OF
URBAN SECONDARY SCHOOL: A DECADE OF
CHANGE
IR J EDUC 14
1980 2 01

4129 TURNER,E B; AGNEW,J B
THE INTELLIGENCE AND EDUCATIONAL
ATTAINMENT OF BORSTAL TRAINEES IN NI
IR J EDUC 11(1)
DUBLIN
1977 2 01

4130 TURNER,I F
COGNITIVE EFFECTS OF PLAYGROUP
ATTENDANCE
IR J EDUC 8(1-2)
1974 2 01

4131 TURNER,I F
PRE-SCHOOL EXPERIENCE AND PSYCHOLOGICAL
DEVELOPMENT
PRE-SCHOOL PLAYGROUP ASSOC
BELFAST
1977 2 10

155

4132 TURNER,I F
PRE-SCHOOL PLAYGROUPS RESEARCH AND
EVALUATION PROJECT
DHSS (NI)
BELFAST
1977 2 10

4133 TURNER,I F
SUPERVISOR BEHAVIOUR AND THE ARTISTIC
DEVELOPMENT OF CHILDREN IN PRESCHOOL
CENTRES
INT J EARLY CHILDHOOD 10(2)
1978 2 01

4134 TURNER,I F; WHYTE,J
THE LANGUAGE DIMENSION: AN ACTION
PROGRAMME IN THE RECEPTION CLASS
NICER
BELFAST
1979 2 10

4135 TYRONE EDUCATION COMMITTEE
YOUTH IN THE COUNTRY
TYRONE EDUC COMMITTEE
OMAGH
1972 2 10

4136 VAUGHAN,T D
SOME ASPECTS OF THE DISTRIBUTION OF
EXAMINATION SUCCESS IN CO. DOWN
QUB MED
BELFAST
1965 2 04

4137 WARD,W
A STUDY OF SOME EFFECTS OF
OPEN-CLOSED-PLAN CLASSROOM ARCHITECTURES
ON PRIMARY SCHOOL PUPILS' PERFORMANCE
QUB MED
BELFAST
1981 2 04

4138 WATSON,E
CATHOLIC SCHOOLS: SOME SOCIOLOGICAL
ASPECTS
GUILD OF CATHOLIC TEACHERS
BELFAST
2 10

4139 WELTON,J
HOME-SCHOOL LINKS PROJECT: ISSUES IN THE
DEVELOPMENT OF POLICY-RELATED RESEARCH
IN MCKERNAN,J (ED)
COLERAINE
1978 2 07

4140 WHYTE,J
ADULT LITERACY IN NI
READING NEWS 3(1)
1978 2 01

4141 WHYTE,J
CAN WE RELIEVE THE STRESS? A CASE STUDY
IN INTERVENTION IN AN INFANT SCHOOL
IN HARBISON,J; HARBISON,J (EDS)
SHEPTON MALLET, SOMERSET
1980 1 07

4142 WHYTE,J
EDUCATIONAL ENRICHMENT WITH DEPRIVED
CHILDREN: THE LONG-TERM CONSEQUENCES
IN HARBISON,J (ED)
BELFAST
1983 2 07

4143 WHYTE,J
INTERVENING IN EDUCATIONAL DISADVANTAGE:
THE NI CONTEXT
ASSOC EDUC PSYCHOL J 5(4)
1980 2 01

4144 WHYTE,J
LANGUAGE AND READING: A STUDY OF ADULT
LITERACY STUDENTS IN NI
J OF READING 24(7)
1981 2 01

4145 WHYTE,J
LANGUAGE IN THE RECEPTION CLASS: A PILOT
PROJECT IN NI
SCHOOL PSYCHOL INT 1(5)
1981 2 01

4146 WILKINSON,C W
A CONSIDERATION OF THE CONCEPT OF THE
COMMUNITY SCHOOL... AND ITS INFLUENCE ON
SOME SECONDARY SCHOOLS IN NI
QUB MED
BELFAST
1972 2 04

4147 WILKINSON,G M
INNOVATIONS IN THE TEACHING AND
ASSESSMENT OF SCIENCE IN A BELFAST
SECONDARY SCHOOL
QUB MA
BELFAST
1970 2 04

4148 WILSON,D
ADULT EDUCATION IN A WORKING CLASS
COMMUNITY
NUU MA
COLERAINE
1978 2 04

4149 WILSON,D
AN APPROACH TO SOME EARLY SCHOOL LEAVERS
COMM FORUM 1
LONDON
1971 2 01

4150 WILSON,J A
ADJUSTMENT IN THE CLASSROOM: PATTERNS OF
ADAPTATION
RES IN EDUC 11
1974 2 01

4151 WILSON,J A
ADJUSTMENT IN THE CLASSROOM: TEACHERS'
RATINGS OF DEVIANT BEHAVIOUR
RES IN EDUC 10
1973 2 01

4152 WILSON,J A
BRIGHTNESS, SOCIAL ADVANTAGE AND SCHOOL
EFFECTIVENESS
IR J PSYCHOL 4(1)
1978 2 01

4153 WILSON,J A
COEDUCATION AND RELIGIOUS INTEGRATION AS
ISSUES IN RE-ORGANSATION OF SECONDARY
EDUCATION
NORTH TEACH 12(4)
BELFAST
1977 2 01

4154 WILSON,J A
DEVELOPMENTAL AND SOCIAL INTERACTION IN
CATEGORIES OF WORD-DEFINITION
BRIT J EDUC PSYCHOL 45
1975 2 01

4155 WILSON,J A
THE ENVIRONMENT AND PRIMARY EDUCATION
NICER
BELFAST
1971 2 10

4156 WILSON,J A
INCIDENCE AND READING STANDARDS OF
HEARING-IMPAIRED PUPILS OF SECONDARY
SCHOOL AGE
NICER
BELFAST
1975 2 10

4157 WILSON,J A
THE NI COUNCIL FOR EDUCATIONAL RESEARCH
B BRIT EDUC RES ASSOC 1
1975 2 01

4158 WILSON, J A
     THE ORGANISATION OF SECONDARY EDUCATION:
     REPORT OF AN INQUIRY AMONG TEACHERS IN
     PRIMARY, SECONDARY AND FURTHER
     EDUCATION...
     NICER
     BELFAST
     1977 2 10

4159 WILSON, J A
     OVER AND UNDER-ACHIEVEMENT IN READING
     AND MATHEMATICS
     IR J EDUC 9(2)
     DUBLIN
     1975 2 01

4160 WILSON, J A
     PERSONALITY AND ATTAINMENT IN THE
     PRIMARY SCHOOL
     RES IN EDUC 6
     1972 2 01

4161 WILSON, J A
     PUPIL ACHIEVEMENT IN NI PRIMARY SCHOOLS:
     25 YEARS OF FINDINGS AND ISSUES
     IR J EDUC 7
     1973 2 01

4162 WILSON, J A
     QUESTION CHOICE IN A-LEVEL PHYSICS
     J CURRICULUM STUD 8(1)
     1976 2 01

4163 WILSON, J A
     READING STANDARDS IN NI
     IR J PSYCHOL 2(2)
     1973 2 01

4164 WILSON, J A
     READING STANDARDS IN NI
     NICER
     BELFAST
     1973 2 10

4165 WILSON, J A
     READING STANDARDS IN NI
     NICER
     BELFAST
     1975 2 10

4166 WILSON, J A
     READING STANDARDS IN 1976
     NICER
     BELFAST
     1977 2 10

4167 WILSON, J A
     REGIONAL ASPECTS OF EDUCATIONAL
     DISADVANTAGE
     IN HARBISON, J; HARBISON, J (EDS)
     SHEPTON MALLET, SOMERSET
     1980 2 07

4168 WILSON, J A
     A SURVEY OF VANDALISM AND INDISCIPLINE
     IN SCHOOLS
     IN NI EDUCATION AND LIBRARY BOARDS
     BELFAST
     1976 2 07

4169 WILSON, J A
     1972 READING SURVEYS IN NI
     B BRIT PSYCHOL SOC 27
     1974 2 01

4170 WILSON, J A; BILL, J M
     THE STRUCTURE OF OLIVER'S 'SURVEY OF
     OPINIONS ABOUT EDUCATION'
     BRIT J EDUC PSYCHOL 46
     1976 2 01

4171 WILSON, J A; FOOTE, T P
     PRIMARY SCHOOL SIZE AND THE
     PUPIL/TEACHER RATIO
     NORTH TEACH 13(4)
     BELFAST
     1981 2 01

4172 WILSON, J A; FOOTE, T P
     THE STAFFING NEEDS OF SCHOOLS
     NICER
     BELFAST
     1978 2 10

4173 WILSON, J A; IRVINE, S A
     EDUCATION AND BEHAVIOUR PROBLEMS IN NI
     BEHAVIORAL DISORDERS 3(4)
     1978 2 01

4174 WILSON, J A; SPELMAN, B J
     THE ORGANIZATION OF SECONDARY EDUCATION
     NICER
     BELFAST
     1977 2 10

4175 WILSON, J A; SPELMAN, B J; TREW, K
     EXPERIMENTAL VALIDATION OF TWO CLASSROOM
     OBSERVATION SYSTEMS
     J EDUC PSYCHOL 68(6)
     1976 2 01

4176 WILSON, J A; TREW, K
     THE EDUCATIONAL PRIORITY SCHOOL
     BRIT J EDUC PSYCHOL 45
     1975 2 01

4177 WILSON, R
     AN EMPIRICAL STUDY OF VARIABLES RELATING
     TO READING DISABILITY IN A SECONDARY
     SCHOOL
     QUB MED
     BELFAST
     1972 2 04

4178 ALLEN, R
PRESBYTERIAN COLLEGE, BELFAST 1853-1953
MULLAN
BELFAST
1954 2 10

4179 ANDERSON, A C
STORY OF THE PRESBYTERIAN CHURCH IN
IRELAND
BELL, LOGAN AND CARSWELL
BELFAST
1965 2 02

4180 ANTHONY, P G J
A REVIEW OF TRENDS IN RELIGIOUS
EDUCATION IN NI
QUB MA
BELFAST
1977 2 04

4181 BARKLEY, J M
ANGLICAN-PRESBYTERIAN RELATIONS
IN HURLEY, M (ED)
DUBLIN
1970 2 07

4182 BARKLEY, J M
CATHOLICS THROUGH PROTESTANT EYES
NEWMAN R 1(1)
1969 2 01

4183 BARKLEY, J M
ECUMENISM AND SECTARIANISM IN IRELAND
IN SOCIAL STUDY CONFERENCE
DUBLIN
1975 2 07

4184 BARKLEY, J M
PRESBYTERIAN-ROMAN CATHOLIC RELATIONS IN
IRELAND 1780-1975
DOCTRINE AND LIFE 31(6)
1981 2 01

4185 BARKLEY, J M
PRESBYTERIANISM
BELFAST
1951 2 02

4186 BARKLEY, J M
ROMEWARD TREND IN IRISH PRESBYTERIANISM
PRESBYTERIAN COLLEGE
BELFAST
1968 2 99

4187 BARKLEY, J M
SHORT HISTORY OF THE PRESBYTERIAN CHURCH
IN IRELAND
PRESBYTERIAN CHURCH
BELFAST
1960 2 99

4188 BARKLEY, J M ET AL
CHALLENGE AND CONFLICT: ESSAYS IN IRISH
PRESBYTERIAN HISTORY AND DOCTRINE
W AND G BAIRD
BELFAST
1981 2 02

4189 BIRRELL, W D; GREER, J E; ROCHE, D J D
POLITICAL ROLE AND INFLUENCE OF THE
CLERGY IN NI
SOCIOL R 27(3)
1979 2 01

4190 BIRRELL, W D; ROCHE, D J D
POLITICAL ROLE AND INFLUENCE OF
CLERGYMEN IN NI
IN SPENCER, A; TOVEY, H (EDS) PROC SAI
BELFAST
1978 2 11

4191 BIRRELL, W D; ROCHE, D J D
THEOLOGY, POLITICAL ATTITUDES AND PARTY
PREFERENCE AMONG CLERGYMEN IN NI
IN SPENCER, A; TOVEY, H (EDS) PROC SAI
BELFAST
1978 2 01

4192 BLANCHARD, J
CHURCH IN CONTEMPORARY IRELAND
CLONMORE AND REYNOLDS
DUBLIN
1963 2 02

4193 BLANSHARD, P
NI AND PARTITION
IN BLANSHARD, P
BOSTON
1953 2 07 .

4194 BLEAKLEY, D
YOUNG ULSTER AND RELIGION IN THE
SIXTIES: AN INQUIRY INTO ATTITUDES
AUTHOR
BELFAST
1964 2 10

4195 BRADY, B
CATHOLIC EDUCATION IN NI: THE CHILVER
CHALLENGE
AUTHOR
BELFAST
1982 2 10

4196 BRADY, J C
THE LAW RELATING TO RELIGIOUS CHARITIES
IN NI
QUB PHD
BELFAST
1970 2 04

4197 BROWN, T
THE MAJORITY'S MINORITIES - PROTESTANT
DENOMINATIONS IN THE NORTH
CRANE BAG 5(1)
DUBLIN
1981 2 01

4198 CAMPBELL, J
FUTURE OF PROTESTANTISM IN IRELAND
STUDIES 24(12)
1945 2 01

4199 CAMPBELL, J J
CATHOLIC SCHOOLS: A SURVEY OF A NI
PROBLEM
FALLONS
BELFAST
1963 2 02

4200 CATHERWOOD, F
A BETTER WAY: THE CASE FOR A CHRISTIAN
SOCIAL ORDER
INTER-VARSITY PRESS
LONDON
1975 3 02

4201 CATHERWOOD, F
CHRISTIAN DUTY IN ULSTER TODAY
EVANGELICAL PRESS
LONDON
1970 1 10

4202 CHILLINGWORTH, H R
RELIGION AND THE IRISH PROBLEM
MODERN CHURCHMAN
1952 2 01

4203 CHURCHES' INDUSTRIAL COUNCIL
CHURCHES' INDUSTRIAL COUNCIL NI
CHRISTUS REX 19(3)
1965 2 01

4204 COHAN, A S
RELIGIOUS VALUES AND AN END TO PARTITION
LANCASTER
1971 1 08

4205 COLE, R L
ONE METHODIST CHURCH, 1860-1960
IRISH METHODIST PUBLISHING COMPANY
BELFAST
1960 2 02

4206 CONNOLLY, P
THE CHURCH IN IRELAND SINCE THE SECOND
VATICAN COUNCIL
ET IRL 3
LILLE
1978 2 01

4207 CONWAY, W
CATHOLIC SCHOOLS
VERITAS
DUBLIN
1971 2 10

4208 COOKE, J
DEVELOPMENT AND DISTRIBUTION OF
METHODISM IN IRELAND: A DEMOGRAPHIC
STUDY
QUB MA
BELFAST
1964 2 04

4209 COOKE, R
CRISIS IN NI: A BIBLE PROTESTANT
VIEWPOINT
WORD OF TRUTH PUBLICATIONS
LOS ANGELES
1972 1 02

4210 COOKE, R
THUNDER OF PAPAL PROPAGANDA
AUTHOR
PASADENA
1969 3 02

4211 CORISH, P J
IRISH ECCLESIASTICAL HISTORY SINCE 1500
IN LEE, J (ED)
CORK
1981 2 07

4212 CORKEY, W
EPISODE IN THE HISTORY OF PROTESTANT
ULSTER 1923-47
DORMAN
BELFAST
1960 2 02

4213 DALY, C B
A VISION OF ECUMENISM IN IRELAND
EIRE-IRELAND 17(1)
ST PAUL
1982 1 01

4214 DAVISON, G
RELIGIOUS PARTICIPATION AND PRACTICE
QUB MSSC
BELFAST
1975 2 04

4215 DAVISON, W
A CRITICAL ANALYSIS OF THE DECISIONS OF
THE PRESBYTERIAN CHURCH 1921-70
QUB PHD
BELFAST
1978 2 04

4216 DOWDEN, R
NI AND THE CATHOLIC CHURCH IN BRITAIN
COMMISSION FOR INT JUSTICE AND PEACE OF
ENGLAND AND WALES
ABBOTS LANGLEY
1975 2 10

4217 DUFF, F
TRUE DEVOTION TO THE NATION
DUNDALGAN PRESS
DUNDALK
1967 2 99

4218 DYNAN, J
HIDDEN CURRICULUM OF A CATHOLIC BOYS
SCHOOL
NUU MA
COLERAINE
1980 2 04

4219 EASTHOPE, G
RELIGIOUS WAR IN NI
SOCIOLOGY 10(3)
LONDON
1976 1 01

4220 ECCLESTONE, G; ELLIOTT, E
THE IRISH PROBLEM AND OURSELVES
GENERAL SYNOD BOARD
LONDON
1977 1 10

4221 FAHY, P
ROMAN CATHOLIC PRIESTS AND LOCAL
POLITICS IN NI: AN EXPLORATORY STUDY
STRATHCLYDE UNIV MSC
GLASGOW
1971 2 04

4222 FAHY, P
SOME POLITICAL BEHAVIOUR PATTERNS AND
ATTITUDES OF ROMAN CATHOLIC PRIESTS IN A
RURAL PART OF NI
ECON AND SOC R
DUBLIN
1971 2 01

4223 FENNELL, D
CHANGING FACE OF CATHOLIC IRELAND
CHAPMAN
LONDON
1968 2 02

4224 FENNELL, D
THE NORTHERN CATHOLIC
IRISH TIMES
DUBLIN
1959 2 10

4225 FLYNN, T
CHARISMATIC RENEWAL AND THE IRISH
EXPERIENCE
HODDER AND STOUGHTON
LONDON
1974 2 02

4226 FORDE, B; SPENCER, C
HOPE IN BOMB CITY
MARSHALL, MORGAN AND SCOTT
LONDON
1980 1 02

4227 FORDE, B; SPENCER, C
LOVE IN BOMB CITY
MARSHALLS
LONDON
1982 1 02

4228 FULTON, J
IS THE IRISH CONFLICT RELIGIOUS?
SOC STUD 5(3-4)
    1 01

4229 FULTON, J
SOME REFLECTIONS ON CATHOLIC SCHOOLS IN
NI
STUDIES 58
1969 2 01

4230 GALLAGHER, E
BETTER WAY OF LIFE FOR IRISH PROTESTANTS
AND ROMAN CATHOLICS
METHODIST MISSION BOARD
BELFAST
1973 1 10

4231 GALLAGHER, E
ROADS TO RECONCILIATION: THE PROTESTANT
CONTRIBUTION
IN SOCIAL STUDY CONFERENCE
DUBLIN
1974 1 07

4232 GALLAGHER,E; WORRALL,S
CHRISTIANS IN ULSTER 1968-1980
OUP
OXFORD
1982 1 01

4233 GALLAGHER,T
RELIGION, REACTION AND REVOLT IN NI: THE
IMPACT OF PAISLEYISM IN ULSTER
J CHURCH AND STATE 23
1981 1 01

4234 GRAHAM,E S D
RELIGION AND EDUCATION: THE
CONSTITUTIONAL PROBLEM
NI LEG QUART 33
BELFAST
1982 2 01

4235 GREER,J E
THE ATTITUDES OF PARENTS AND PUPILS TO
RELIGION IN SCHOOLS
IR J EDUC 4
1970 2 01

4236 GREER,J E
THE CHILD'S UNDERSTANDING OF CREATION
EDUC RES 24(2)
1972 2 01

4237 GREER,J E
THE PERSISTENCE OF RELIGION: A STUDY OF
ADOLESCENTS IN NI
CHARACTER POTENTIAL 9(3)
1980 2 01

4238 GREER,J E
A QUESTIONING GENERATION
CHURCH OF IRELAND BOARD OF EDUC
1972 2 10

4239 GREER,J E
RELIGION IN IRELAND: A SCHOOL BASED
CURRICULUM DEVELOPMENT PROJECT
LEARNING FOR LIVING 17(2)
1977 2 01

4240 GREER,J E
RELIGIOUS ATTITUDES AND THINKING IN
BELFAST PUPILS
EDUC RES 23(3)
1981 2 01

4241 GREER,J E
RELIGIOUS BELIEF AND CHURCH ATTENDANCE
OF SIXTH FORM PUPILS AND THEIR PARENTS
IR J EDUC 5(2)
1971 2 01

4242 GREER,J E
RELIGIOUS EDUCATION IN STATE PRIMARY
SCHOOLS IN NI
NORTH TEACH 13(2)
BELFAST
1978 2 01

4243 GREER,J E
RELIGIOUS EXPERIENCE AND RELIGIOUS
EDUCATION
SEARCH 4(1)
1981 2 01

4244 GREER,J E
SIXTH FORM RELIGION IN NI
NUU MPHIL
COLERAINE
1972 2 04

4245 GREER,J E
SIXTH FORM RELIGION IN NI
SOC STUD 1(3)
1972 2 01

4246 GREER,J E
TEACHERS AND RELIGIOUS EDUCATION
RELIGIOUS EDUCATION COUNCIL
BELFAST
1973 2 10

4247 GREER,J E; BROWN,G A
THE EFFECTS OF NEW APPROACHES TO
RELIGIOUS EDUCATION IN THE PRIMARY
SCHOOL
J CURRICULUM STUD 5(11)
1973 2 01

4248 GREER,J E; MCCULLAGH,J J; MCELHINNEY,E P
TEACHING RELIGION IN IRELAND
NUU
COLERAINE
1980 2 10

4249 GUILD OF CATHOLIC TEACHERS
DIOCESE OF DOWN AND CONNOR: ASPECTS OF
CATHOLIC EDUCATION
ST JOSEPH'S COLL OF EDUC
BELFAST
1971 2 10

4250 HANLY,J
IRELAND CALLING: A PLAN FOR
THE...RECOVERY OF IRELAND BASED ON
CHRISTIAN SOCIAL PRINCIPLES. . . .
PARKSIDE PRESS
DUBLIN
1958 2 02

4251 HANSON,R
POLITICS AND THE PULPIT
COMM FORUM 13(3)
BELFAST
1973 3 01

4252 HICKEY,J
RELIGION AS A VARIABLE IN THE
SOCIOLOGICAL ANALYSIS OF NI
SOC STUD 5(3-4)
1977 2 01

4253 HOLMES,R F G
IRISH PRESBYTERIANISM AND MODERN IRISH
NATIONALISM
IN BAKER,D; MEWS,S (EDS)
OXFORD
1981 2 07

4254 HUGHES,C G
THE CATHOLIC CHURCH AND THE CRISIS IN
ULSTER
PENNSYLVANIA STATE UNIV PHD
1976 1 04

4255 HURLEY,M
THE FUTURE
IN HURLEY,M (ED)
DUBLIN
1970 2 07

4256 INDEPENDENT TELEVISION AUTHORITY
RELIGION IN GREAT BRITAIN AND NI
INDEPENDENT TELEVISION AUTHORITY
LONDON
1970 2 02

4257 IRISH CHRISTIAN YOUTH ASSEMBLY
BRIDGE THAT GAP
IRISH ASSEMBLY
BELFAST
1971 2 10

4258 IRISH EPISCOPAL CONFERENCE
DIRECTORY ON ECUMENISM FOR IRELAND
IRISH EPISCOPAL CONFERENCE
DUBLIN
1976 2 10

4259 JEFFREY,F
ANGLICAN-METHODIST RELATIONS
IN HURLEY,M (ED)
DUBLIN
1970 2 07

4260 JEFFREY,F
IRISH METHODISM: AN HISTORICAL ACCOUNT
OF THE TRADITIONS, THEOLOGY AND
INFLUENCE
IRISH METHODIST PUBLISHING COMPANY
BELFAST
1964 2 02

4261 JOHNSTON, T J ET AL
HISTORY OF THE CHURCH OF IRELAND
APCK
DUBLIN
1953 2 02

4262 KEANE, T
DEMOGRAPHIC TRENDS
IN HURLEY, M (ED)
DUBLIN
1970 2 07

4263 KEANE, T B
ATTITUDES TO RELIGIOUS INTEGRATION IN
SCHOOLS IN A SAMPLE OF SECONDARY SCHOOL
CHILDREN IN NEWRY AND SOUTH DOWN AREA
IN MCKERNAN, J (ED)
COLERAINE
1978 2 07

4264 KEANE, T B
ATTITUDES TO THE RELIGIOUS INTEGRATION
OF SCHOOLS IN NI
QUB MA
BELFAST
1977 2 04

4265 KELLY, M P
THE NI HOSPITALS AUTHORITY AND CATHOLICS
QUINN
BELFAST
1962 2 11

4266 KELLY, T F
EDUCATION
IN HURLEY, M (ED)
DUBLIN
1970 2 07

4267 KENNEDY, D
ASPECTS OF THE NI SITUATION
IN HURLEY, M (ED)
DUBLIN
1970 2 07

4268 KENNEDY, D
CATHOLIC EDUCATION IN NI, 1921-1970
ST JOSEPH'S COLL OF EDUC
BELFAST
1971 2 02

4269 LENNON, S
ROADS TO RECONCILIATION - A CATHOLIC
CONTRIBUTION
IN SOCIAL STUDY CONFERENCE
DUBLIN
1974 1 07

4270 LOCKINGTON, J
AN ANALYSIS OF THE PRACTICE AND
PROCEDURE IN IRISH PRESBYTERIANISM
QUB PHD
BELFAST
1980 2 04

4271 MACOURT, M
NATURE OF RELIGION IN IRELAND
IN HILL, M (ED)
LONDON
1973 2 07

4272 MACY, C
RELIGIOUS FACTOR IN ULSTER
HUMANIST 87(1)
1972 1 01

4273 MADELEY, J
POLITICS AND THE PULPIT: THE CASE OF
PROTESTANT EUROPE
WESTERN EUROPEAN POLITICS 5(2)
LONDON
1982 2 01

4274 MAWHINNEY, B; WELLS, R
CONFLICT AND CHRISTIANITY IN NI
LION
BECKHAMPSTEAD
1975 1 02

4275 MCALLISTER, I
THE DEVIL, MIRACLES AND THE AFTERLIFE:
THE POLITICAL SOCIOLOGY OF RELIGION
BRIT J SOCIOL 33(3)
LONDON
1982 1 01

4276 MCCAFFERTY, W H
BELFAST DOMESTIC MISSION 1853-1953: A
CENTURY OF SOCIAL SERVICE
MAGOWAN
BELFAST
1953 2 10

4277 MCDERMOTT, R P; WEBB, D A
IRISH PROTESTANTISM TODAY AND TOMORROW:
A DEMOGRAPHIC STUDY
APCK
BELFAST
1945 2 02

4278 MCIVOR, J A
POPULAR EDUCATION IN THE IRISH
PRESBYTERIAN CHURCH
SCEPTER
DUBLIN
1969 2 02

4279 MENENDEZ, A J
THE BITTER HARVEST: CHURCH AND STATE IN
NI
ROBERT B LUCE
NEW YORK
1973 1 02

4280 MILLER, D W
CHURCH, STATE AND NATION IN IRELAND
GILL AND MACMILLAN
DUBLIN
1973 2 02

4281 MILLER, D W
PRESBYTERIANISM AND MODERNIZATION IN
ULSTER
PAST AND PRESENT 80
1978 2 01

4282 MILNE, K
THE CHURCH OF IRELAND: A HISTORY
APCK
DUBLIN
1966 2 02

4283 MORROW, J
PEACE AND PEACEMAKING - CHURCH AND
COMMUNITY IN NI
QUB PHD
BELFAST
1976 1 04

4284 MOXON-BROWNE, E
ATTITUDES TOWARDS RELIGION IN NI: SOME
COMPARISONS BETWEEN CATHOLICS AND
PROTESTANTS
PACE 12
BELFAST
1980 2 01

4285 MURPHY, J A
RELIGIOUS MAJORITIES AND MINORITIES THEN
AND NOW
CRANE BAG 5(1)
DUBLIN
1981 2 01

4286 MURRAY, S W
THE CITY MISSION STORY
BELFAST CITY MISSION
BELFAST
1976 1 10

4287 NUM
TRIBALISM AND CHRISTIANITY IN IRELAND
NUM
BELFAST
1973 1 10

Religion/

4288 NUSIGHT
THE CHURCHES DURING THE CRISIS
NUSIGHT OCT
1969 1 01

4289 O'BRIEN, J
SCIENCE AND CATHOLIC EDUCATION
CATHOLIC TEACHERS J 9(5)
1966 2 01

4290 OPINION RESEARCH CENTRE
RELIGION IN NI
OPINION RESEARCH CENTRE
LONDON
1970 2 10

4291 PAISLEY, I R K
CASE AGAINST ECUMENISM
COMM FORUM 1(1)
BELFAST
1971 2 01

4292 PATTERSON, M
HUNGRY SHEEP OF ULSTER
PLATFORM PUBLICATIONS
BELFAST
1974 1 02

4293 PATTERSON, T A
THE CHURCH IN A SITUATION OF CONFLICT
PACE 13(2)
BELFAST
1981 1 01

4294 PRO MUNDI VITA
IRISH CONFLICT AND CHRISTIAN CONSCIENCE:
A SPECIAL REPORT
THE FURROW 24(9)
LONDON
1973 1 01

4295 RAWLES, M E
RELIGIOUS EDUCATION FOR SLOW-LEARNING
ADOLESCENTS
NUU MA
BELFAST
1970 2 04

4296 REDMOND, J
CHURCH, STATE, INDUSTRY IN EAST BELFAST
1827-1929
AUTHOR
BELFAST
1961 2 02

4297 RICHARDSON, J T; REIDY, M: VINCENT, T
NEO-PENTECOSTALISM IN IRELAND: A
COMPARISON WITH THE AMERICAN EXPERIENCE
SOC STUD 5(3-4)
MAYNOOTH
1977 2 01

4298 ROBERTS, D
ORANGE ORDER IN IRELAND: A RELIGIOUS
INSTITUTION
BRIT J SOCIOL 22(3)
1971 2 01

4299 ROCHE, D J D; BIRRELL, W D; GREER, J E
A SOCIO-POLITICAL OPINION PROFILE OF
CLERGYMEN IN NI
SOC STUD 4(2)
DUBLIN
1975 1 01

4300 RYAN, V
RECENT LITURGICAL REFORM
IN HURLEY, M (ED)
DUBLIN
1970 2 07

4301 SALTERS, M G
...RELIGIOUS INSTRUCTION IN GRANT-AIDED
SCHOOLS IN THE UNITED KINGDOM WITH
SPECIAL REFERENCE TO...NI
QUB MED
BELFAST
1967 2 04

4302 SCHMID, V
RENEWED DEDICATION TO PEACE IN IRELAND
CHRISTIAN CENTURY 95
1978 1 01

4303 SCOTT, F E
THE POLITICAL PREACHING TRADITION IN
ULSTER: PRELUDE TO PAISLEY
WESTERN SPEECH COMMUNICATION 40(4)
1976 1 01

4304 SHEEHY, M
IS IRELAND DYING? CULTURE AND CHURCH IN
MODERN IRELAND
TAPLINGER
NEW YORK
1968 2 02

4305 SLOAN, H
ECUMENISM
COMM FORUM 1(1)
1971 2 01

4306 SPENCER, A
THE RELIGIOUS AND THE SACRED IN THE NI
CONFLICT
IN SPENCER, A; CORMACK, R; O'DOWD, L;
TOVEY, H (EDS) PROC SAI
BELFAST
1977 1 01

4307 ST JOHN'S AND CORPUS CHRISTI PARISH
COUNCIL STEERING COMMITTEE
OPEN THE WINDOW, LET IN THE LIGHT
ST JOHN'S AND CORPUS CHRISTI PARISH
COUNCIL STEERING COMMITTEE
BELFAST
1975 2 10

4308 ST JOSEPH'S COLL OF EDUCATION
ASPECTS OF CATHOLIC EDUCATION
ST JOSEPH'S COLL OF EDUCATION
BELFAST
1971 2 10

4309 STACK, C M
UNITY, THE REPUBLIC AND THE CHURCH OF
IRELAND
THE BELL 16(4)
1951 2 01

4310 STANFORD, W
FAITH AND FACTION IN IRELAND NOW
APCK
DUBLIN
1946 2 02

4311 STUDENT CHRISTIAN MOVEMENT
UNKNOWN IRELAND
SCM
DUBLIN
1976 2 10

4312 TAYLOR, D
IAN PAISLEY AND THE IDEOLOGY OF ULSTER
PROTESTANTISM
IN CURTIN, C; KELLY, M; O'DOWD, L (EDS)
DUBLIN
1983 2 07

4313 THOMPSON, J
ASPECTS OF EVANGELIZATION IN IRISH
PRESBYTERIANISM, 1880-1965
QUB MTH
BELFAST
1971 2 04

4314 TODD, H L
SOME ASPECTS OF THE GENERAL ASSEMBLY AND
RELIGIOUS EDUCATION IN PRIMARY SCHOOLS
1921-1971
QUB MED
BELFAST
1972 2 04

4315 TRUSTEES OF THE CATHOLIC EDUCATION
     COLLEGES
     CATHOLIC EDUCATION AND THE CHILVER
     PROPOSALS
     TRUSTEES OF THE CATHOLIC EDUCATION
     COLLEGES
     BELFAST
     1981 2 10

4316 TURNER,E B
     RELIGIOUS UNDERSTANDING AND RELIGIOUS
     ATTITUDES IN MALE URBAN ADOLESCENTS
     QUB PHD
     BELFAST
     1970 1 04

4317 TURNER,E B; TURNER,I F; REID,A
     RELIGIOUS ATTITUDES IN TWO TYPES OF
     URBAN SECONDARY SCHOOL: A DECADE OF
     CHANGE
     IR J EDUC 14
     1980 2 01

4318 WARD,C
     SOCIO-RELIGIOUS RESEARCH IN IRELAND
     SOC COMPASS 11(3-4)
     1964 2 01

4319 WATSON,E
     CATHOLIC SCHOOLS: SOME SOCIOLOGICAL
     ASPECTS
     GUILD OF CATHOLIC TEACHERS
     BELFAST
              2 10

4320 WHYTE,J H
     CHURCH AND STATE IN MODERN IRELAND
     1923-1979
     GILL AND MACMILLAN
     DUBLIN
     1980 2 02

4321 WORKERS' RESEARCH UNIT
     CHURCHES IN NI
     WRU BULLETIN 8
     BELFAST
     1980 2 10

4322 AGNEW, P
FEAR AND LOATHING IN FERMANAGH
MAGILL 4(6)
DUBLIN
1981 1 01

4323 AKENSON, D H
EDUCATION AND ENMITY: THE CONTROL OF
SCHOOLING IN NI 1920-1950
DAVID AND CHARLES
NEWTON ABBOT
1973 2 02

4324 ALCOCK, A E
PERIPHERAL REGIONS AND DIVIDED
COMMUNITIES IN EUROPE: THE CASE OF NI
INT INST MINORITY RIGHTS AND REGIONALISM
BOLZONO
1978 1 08

4325 ALL-PARTY ANTI-PARTITION CONFERENCE
DISCRIMINATION: A STUDY IN INJUSTICE TO
A MINORITY
ALL-PARTY ANTI-PARTITION CONFERENCE
DUBLIN
1950 2 09

4326 ALL-PARTY ANTI-PARTITION CONFERENCE
ONE VOTE EQUALS TWO: A STUDY IN THE
PRACTICE AND PURPOSE OF BOUNDARY
MANIPULATION
ALL-PARTY ANTI-PARTITION CONFERENCE
DUBLIN
1950 2 09

4327 ARDOYNE EX-RESIDENTS ASSOCIATION
ARDOYNE - THE TRUE STORY
ARDOYNE EX-RESIDENTS ASSOCIATION
BELFAST
1973 1 10

4328 ARTHUR, A
ATTITUDE CHANGE AND NEUROTICISM AMONG
NORTHERN IRISH CHILDREN PARTICIPATING IN
JOINT-FAITH HOLIDAYS
QUB MSC
BELFAST
1974 2 04

4329 AUNGER, E A
IN SEARCH OF POLITICAL STABILITY: A
COMPARATIVE STUDY OF NEW BRUNSWICK AND
NI
MCGILL - QUEEN'S U P
TORONTO
1981 1 02

4330 AUNGER, E A
RELIGION AND CLASS: AN ANALYSIS OF 1971
CENSUS DATA
IN CORMACK, R; OSBORNE, R D (EDS)
BELFAST
1983 2 07

4331 AUNGER, E A
RELIGION AND OCCUPATIONAL CLASS IN NI
ECON AND SOC R 7(1)
1976 1 01

4332 AUNGER, E A
SOCIAL FRAGMENTATION AND POLITICAL
STABILITY: COMPARATIVE STUDY OF NEW
BRUNSWICK AND NI
CALIFORNIA UNIV PHD
DAVIS, CALIFORNIA
1978 2 04

4333 BARKLEY, J M
CATHOLICS THROUGH PROTESTANT EYES
NEWMAN R 1(1)
1969 2 01

4334 BARKLEY, J M
ECUMENISM AND SECTARIANISM IN IRELAND
IN SOCIAL STUDY CONFERENCE
DUBLIN
1975 2 07

4335 BARRITT, D P
NI: THE PROBLEM OF A DIVIDED COMMUNITY
MANCHESTER STATISTICAL SOCIETY
MANCHESTER
1972 1 11

4336 BARRITT, D P; BOOTH, A
ORANGE AND GREEN: A QUAKER STUDY OF
COMMUNITY RELATIONS IN NI
NORTHERN FRIENDS PEACE BOARD
SEDBURGH, YORKSHIRE
1969 1 10

4337 BEACH, S W
RELIGION AND POLITICAL CHANGE IN NI
SOCIOL ANALYSIS 38(1)
1977 1 01

4338 BENTON, E
INTEGRATED EDUCATION
SCOPE 29
BELFAST
1979 1 01

4339 BLACK, R
FLIGHT IN BELFAST
COMM FORUM 2(1)
1972 1 01

4340 BLACK, R; PINTER, F; OVERY, B
FLIGHT: A REPORT ON POPULATION MOVEMENT
IN BELFAST DURING AUGUST 1971
NICRC
BELFAST
1971 1 10

4341 BLACKBURN, A
NI ELECTORAL LAW 1921-1972: THE QUESTION
OF DISCRIMINATION
QUB LLM
BELFAST
1981 1 04

4342 BOAL, F W
AFTERWORD
IN CORMACK, R; OSBORNE, R D (EDS)
BELFAST
1983 2 07

4343 BOAL, F W
CLOSE TOGETHER AND FAR APART: RELIGIOUS
AND CLASS DIVISIONS IN BELFAST
IN BOURNE, L S (ED)
NEW YORK
1982 1 07

4344 BOAL, F W
ETHNIC RESIDENTIAL SEGREGATION
IN HERBERT, D; JOHNSON, R J (EDS)
LONDON
1976 1 07

4345 BOAL, F W
RESIDENTIAL SEGREGATION AND MIXING IN A
SITUATION OF ETHNIC AND NATIONAL
CONFLICT: BELFAST
IN COMPTON, P A (ED)
BELFAST
1981 1 07

4346 BOAL, F W
SEGREGATING AND MIXING: SPACE AND
RESIDENCE IN BELFAST
IN BOAL, F W; DOUGLAS, J N H (EDS)
LONDON
1982 2 07

4347 BOAL,F W
SEGREGATION IN WEST BELFAST
AREA 1
1970 1 01

4348 BOAL,F W
TERRITORIALITY AND CLASS: A STUDY OF TWO
RESIDENTIAL AREAS IN BELFAST
IR GEOG 4(3)
1971 2 01

4349 BOAL,F W
TERRITORIALITY ON THE SHANKILL/FALLS
DIVIDE IN BELFAST
IR GEOG 6(18)
1969 1 01

4350 BOAL,F W
TERRITORIALITY ON THE SHANKILL/FALLS
DIVIDE: THE PERSPECTIVE FROM 1976
IN LANEGRAN,D A; PALM,R (EDS)
NEW YORK
1978 1 07

4351 BOAL,F W
URBAN RESIDENTIAL SUB-COMMUNITY - A
CONFLICT INTERPRETATION
AREA 4(3)
1972 3 01

4352 BOAL,F W; COMPTON,P A
ASPECTS OF THE INTERCOMMUNITY BALANCE IN
NI
ECON AND SOC R 1(4)
1970 1 01

4353 BOAL,F W; MURRAY,R
CITY IN CONFLICT (BELFAST)
GEOGR MAG 49
1977 1 01

4354 BOAL,F W; MURRAY,R; POOLE,M A
BELFAST: THE URBAN ENCAPSULATION OF A
NATIONAL CONFLICT
IN CLARKE,S C; OBLER,J L (EDS)
CHAPEL HILL, NORTH CAROLINA
1976 1 01

4355 BOAL,F W; ORR,J A E
ETHNIC AND TEMPORAL DIMENSIONS OF
REGIONAL RESIDENTIAL PREFERENCES: A NI
EXAMPLE
IR GEOG 11
1978 2 01

4356 BOAL,F W; POOLE,M A; MURRAY,R
RELIGIOUS SEGREGATION AND RESIDENTIAL
DECISION-MAKING IN A BELFAST URBAN AREA
CURR ANTHROPOL 19
1978 2 01

4357 BOAL,F W; POOLE,M A; MURRAY,R; KENNEDY,S
J
RELIGIOUS RESIDENTIAL SEGREGATION AND
RESIDENTIAL DECISION-MAKING IN BELFAST
SSRC FINAL REPORT
LONDON
1976 1 07

4358 BOAL,F W; ROBINSON,A
CLOSE TOGETHER AND FAR APART: RELIGIOUS
AND CLASS DIVISIONS IN NI
COMM FORUM 2(3)
BELFAST
1972 1 02

4359 BOYD,A
BELFAST RIOTS 1935
AQUARIUS
BENBURB
1972 2 01

4360 BOYD,A
HOLY WAR IN BELFAST
ANVIL
TRALEE
1969 2 02

4361 BOYLE,J F
EDUCATIONAL ATTAINMENT, OCCUPATIONAL
ACHIEVEMENT AND RELIGION IN NI
ECON AND SOC R 8(2)
1977 2 01

4362 BURTON,F
IDEOLOGICAL SOCIAL RELATIONS IN NI
BRIT J SOCIOL 30(1)
1979 1 01

4363 BURTON,F
POLITICS OF LEGITIMACY: STRUGGLES IN A
BELFAST COMMUNITY
RKP
LONDON
1978 1 02

4364 BURTON,F
SOCIAL MEANINGS OF CATHOLICISM IN
IRELAND
LONDON UNIV PHD
LONDON
1976 1 04

4365 CAIRNS,E
DEVELOPMENT OF ETHNIC DISCRIMINATION IN
CHILDREN IN NI
IN HARBISON,J; HARBISON,J (EDS)
SHEPTON MALLET, SOMERSET
1980 1 07

4366 CAIRNS,E
INTERGROUP CONFLICT IN NI
IN TAJFEL,H (ED)
CAMBRIDGE
1981 1 07

4367 CAIRNS,E
INVESTIGATION OF SALIENCE FOR YOUNG
CHILDREN IN NI OF ADULT GENERATED
STEREOTYPIC PROTESTANT AND CATHOLIC
FIRST NAMES
BRIT PSYCHOL SOC CONF
1977 3 11

4368 CAIRNS,E; DURIEZ,B
INFLUENCE OF ACCENT ON THE RECALL OF
CATHOLIC AND PROTESTANT CHILDREN IN NI
BRIT J SOC CLIN PSYCH 15
1976 2 01

4369 CAIRNS,E; MERCER,G W
ADOLESCENT SOCIAL IDENTITY IN NI: THE
IMPORTANCE OF DENOMINATIONAL IDENTITY
NUU
COLERAINE
1978 1 08

4370 CAIRNS,E; MERCER,G W
AUTHORITARIANISM AND ITS RELATIONSHIP TO
GENERAL AND SPECIFIC ETHNOCENTRISM
NUU
COLERAINE
1978 2 08

4371 CAMPAIGN FOR SOCIAL JUSTICE IN NI
PLAIN TRUTH
CAMPAIGN FOR SOCIAL JUSTICE IN NI
DUNGANNON
1969 1 09

4372 CAVANAGH,C
HOW WE ALL BECOME SECTARIAN
IN FRAZER,H ET AL
BELFAST
1981 1 07

4373 COMMINS,B; LOCKWOOD,J
EFFECTS ON INTERGROUP RELATIONS OF
MIXING ROMAN CATHOLICS AND PROTESTANTS
EUROP J SOC PSYCHOL 8
1978 2 01

4374 COMPTON,P A
DEMOGRAPHIC AND GEOGRAPHICAL ASPECTS OF
THE UNEMPLOYMENT DIFFERENTIAL BETWEEN
PROTESTANTS AND ROMAN CATHOLICS
IN COMPTON,P A (ED)
BELFAST
1981 2 07

4375 COMPTON,P A
THE DEMOGRAPHIC BACKGROUND
IN WATT,D (ED)
LONDON
1981 2 07

4376 COMPTON,P A
THE DEMOGRAPHIC DIMENSION OF INTEGRATION
AND DIVISION IN NI
IN BOAL,F W; DOUGLAS,J N H (EDS)
LONDON
1982 1 07

4377 COMPTON,P A
THE DEMOGRAPHIC DIMENSION TO THE
ETHNIC-RELIGIOUS CONFLICT IN NI
SYMPOSIUM OF THE COMMISSION ON
POPULATION GEOGRAPHY OF THE
INTERNATIONAL GEOGRAPHICAL UNION
MINSK
1976 1 11

4378 COMPTON,P A
FERTILITY DIFFERENTIALS AND THEIR IMPACT
ON POPULATION DISTRIBUTION AND
COMPOSITION IN NI
ENVIRON AND PLANN 10(12)
1978 2 01

4379 COMPTON,P A
RELIGIOUS AFFILIATION AND DEMOGRAPHIC
VARIABILITY IN NI
TRANS INST BRIT GEOGR 1
1976 2 01

4380 COMPTON,P A ET AL
RELIGION AND LEGAL ABORTION IN NI
J BIOSOCIAL SCI 6
1974 2 01

4381 DALLAT,M
INTEGRATED EDUCATION
COMM FORUM 2(1)
BELFAST
1972 2 01

4382 DALY,E
INTEGRATED EDUCATION
THE FURROW 32(6)
1981 2 01

4383 DARBY,J
CONFLICT IN NI: THE DEVELOPMENT OF A
POLARIZED COMMUNITY
GILL AND MACMILLAN
DUBLIN
1976 1 02

4384 DARBY,J
DENOMINATIONAL SCHOOLING IN NI
IN SPENCER,A; TOVEY,H (EDS) PROC SAI
BELFAST
1978 2 11

4385 DARBY,J
DIVISIVENESS IN EDUCATION: ITS EXTENT
AND EFFECTS IN NI
NORTH TEACH 11(1)
BELFAST
1973 2 01

4386 DARBY,J
EDUCATION AND CONFLICT IN NI
NETWORK 1(1)
1980 1 01

4387 DARBY,J
NI: BONDS AND BREAKS IN EDUCATION
BRIT J EDUC STUD 26(3)
        2 01

4388 DARBY,J
RACE AND RELIGION: SOME OBSERVATIONS ON
DESEGREGATION IN AMERICA AND NI
INTEGRATED EDUC 18(5-6)
1980 1 01

4389 DARBY,J
SEGREGATED SCHOOLING - DOES IT
CONTRIBUTE TO SECTARIANISM?
IN SOCIAL STUDY CONFERENCE
DUBLIN
1974 1 07

4390 DARBY,J ET AL
EDUCATION AND COMMUNITY IN NI: SCHOOLS
APART?
CORE 2(3)
1978 1 01

4391 DARBY,J; MORRIS,G
INTIMIDATION IN HOUSING
NICRC
BELFAST
1974 1 03

4392 DARBY,J; MURRAY,D; BATTS,D; DUNN,S;
FARREN,S; MORRIS,J
EDUCATION AND COMMUNITY IN NI: SCHOOLS
APART?
NUU
COLERAINE
1977 2 10

4393 DAVEY,R
CORRYMEELA IS NOT AN ISLAND
COMM FORUM 1(2)
BELFAST
1971 1 01

4394 DEMPSEY,P
THE FAIR EMPLOYMENT AGENCY: AN EMPTY
EXERCISE IN 'REFORM'
IRIS 4
DUBLIN
1982 1 01

4395 DERRYNANE
STORMONT, THE PUPPET GOVERNMENT: A STUDY
IN LEGAL CODOLOGY
CONNOLLY PUBLICATIONS
LONDON
1965 1 09

4396 DILLON,M; LEHANE,D
POLITICAL MURDER IN NI
PENGUIN
LONDON
1973 1 02

4397 DOUGLAS,J N H
NI: SPATIAL FRAMEWORKS AND COMMUNITY
RELATIONS
IN BOAL,F W; DOUGLAS,J N H (EDS)
LONDON
1982 1 07

4398 DREW,P
ACCUSATIONS: THE OCCASIONAL USE OF
MEMBERS' KNOWLEDGE OF RELIGIOUS
GEOGRAPHY
SOCIOLOGY 12
LONDON
1978 1 01

4399 DUTTER,L E
NI AND THEORIES OF ETHNIC POLITICS
J CONFLICT RESOL 24(4)
LONDON
1980 1 01

4400 EASTHOPE,G
RELIGIOUS WAR IN NI
SOCIOLOGY 10(3)
LONDON
1976 1 01

4401 ERCMAN,S
THE PROBLEM OF DISCRIMINATION AND
MEASURES WHICH SHOULD BE TAKEN FOR ITS
ELIMINATION
ANNALES DE LA FACULTE DE DROIT
D'ISTANBUL
ISTANBUL
1970 1 01

Protestant/Catholic Division/

4402 FAIRLEIGH, J
PERSONALITY AND SOCIAL FACTORS IN
RELIGIOUS PREJUDICE
IN SOCIAL STUDY CONFERENCE
DUBLIN
1974 1 07

4403 FEA
A FINAL REPORT OF THE FAIR EMPLOYMENT
AGENCY FOR NI INTO THE EMPLOYMENT
PRACTICES OF THE NI ELECTRICITY SERVICE
FEA
BELFAST
1982 2 10

4404 FEA
INDUSTRIAL AND OCCUPATIONAL PROFILE OF
THE TWO SECTIONS OF THE POPULATION IN NI
FEA 1
BELFAST
1978 2 03

4405 FERMANAGH CIVIL RIGHTS ASSOCIATION
FERMANAGH FACTS
FERMANAGH CIVIL RIGHTS ASSOCIATION
ENNISKILLEN
1969 1 09

4406 GALLAGHER, A
INTERGROUP RELATIONS AND POLITICAL
ATTITUDES IN NI
QUB MSC
BELFAST
1982 1 04

4407 GALLAGHER, E
BETTER WAY OF LIFE FOR IRISH PROTESTANTS
AND ROMAN CATHOLICS
METHODIST MISSION BOARD
BELFAST
1973 1 10

4408 GALLAGHER, E
ROADS TO RECONCILIATION: THE PROTESTANT
CONTRIBUTION
IN SOCIAL STUDY CONFERENCE
DUBLIN
1974 1 07

4409 GALLAGHER, F
INDIVISIBLE ISLAND
GOLLANCZ
LONDON
1957 2 02

4410 GALWAY, R N
THE PERCEPTION AND MANIPULATION OF THE
RELIGIOUS IDENTITIES IN A NORTHERN IRISH
COMMUNITY
QUB MA
BELFAST
1978 1 04

4411 GAMBLE, R
AN INVESTIGATION INTO THE SOCIAL
INTERACTION, IDENTITY AND RELIGIOUS
ATTITUDES OF INTEGRATED SCHOOL PUPILS
QUB MSC
BELFAST
1982 2 04

4412 GIBSON, N J
SECTARIANISM - ROADS TO RECONCILIATION
IN SOCIAL STUDY CONFERENCE
DUBLIN
1974 1 07

4413 GRAHAM, D
NI: A STATE BEYOND REFORM
SAI ANNUAL CONF
WEXFORD
1983 1 11

4414 GRAY, T
PSALMS AND SLAUGHTER: A STUDY IN BIGOTRY
HEINEMANN
LONDON
1972 1 02

4415 GRAY, T
THE RELIGIOUS DIMENSION
NEW HUMANIST MARCH
1973 1 01

4416 HARKIN, B
PROTESTANTS THROUGH CATHOLIC EYES
NEWMAN R I(1)
1969 1 01

4417 HARRIES, D; PEACOCK, A
RECONCILIATION IN BOGSIDE
YOUNG QUAKER 14(10)
1969 1 01

4418 HARRIS, R
COMMUNITY RELATIONSHIPS IN NORTHERN AND
SOUTHERN IRELAND
SOCIOL R 27(1)
KEELE
1979 2 01

4419 HARRIS, R
PREJUDICE AND TOLERANCE IN ULSTER: A
STUDY OF NEIGHBOURS AND STRANGERS IN A
BORDER COMMUNITY
MANCHESTER U P
MANCHESTER
1972 2 02

4420 HARRIS, R
SOCIAL RELATIONS AND ATTITUDES IN A
NORTHERN IRISH RURAL AREA
LONDON UNIV MA
LONDON
1954 2 04

4421 HAYES, M
COMMUNITY RELATIONS AND THE ROLE OF THE
COMMUNITY RELATIONS COMMISSION IN NI
RUNNYMEDE TRUST
LONDON
1972 1 10

4422 HAYES, M
ROLE OF THE COMMUNITY RELATIONS
COMMISSION IN NI
ADMIN (DUB) 20(4)
DUBLIN
1972 2 01

4423 HEATLEY, F
CIVIL RIGHTS IN THE SIX COUNTIES
IN CELTIC LEAGUE ANNUAL
DUBLIN
1969 1 07

4424 HEISLER, M O
ETHNIC CONFLICT IN THE WORLD TODAY
A AMER ACAD POLIT SOC SCI 433
PHILADELPHIA
1977 1 01

4425 HEPBURN, A C
EMPLOYMENT AND RELIGION IN BELFAST
1901-1971
FEA
BELFAST
1982 2 03

4426 HEPBURN, A C
EMPLOYMENT AND RELIGION IN BELFAST,
1901-1951
IN CORMACK, R; OSBORNE, R D (EDS)
BELFAST
1983 2 07

4427 HEWITT, C
CATHOLIC GRIEVANCES, CATHOLIC
NATIONALISM AND VIOLENCE IN NI DURING
THE CIVIL RIGHTS PERIOD - A
CONSIDERATION
BRIT J SOCIOL 32(3)
LONDON
1981 1 01

4428 HICKEY, J
RELIGION AS A VARIABLE IN THE
SOCIOLOGICAL ANALYSIS OF NI
SOC STUD 5(3-4)
1977 2 01

4429 HOWARD, P
IRISH SECTARIAN PERIODICALS
SMOOTHIE PUBLICATIONS
BRIGHTON, ENGLAND
1973 2 02

4430 HOWARD, P ET AL
WHAT THE OTHER PAPERS SAY
COMM FORUM 2(2)
BELFAST
1972 1 01

4431 IRISH CHRISTIAN YOUTH ASSEMBLY
BRIDGE THAT GAP
IRISH ASSEMBLY
BELFAST
1971 2 10

4432 JENKINS, R
CONFLICT AND POLARISATION
BRITISH SOCIOLOGICAL ASSOCIATION
1968 1 11

4433 JENKINS, R
CONFLICT AND POLARISATION
PEACE RESEARCH CENTRE
LANCASTER UNIV
1968 1 10

4434 JENKINS, R
ETHNICITY AND THE RISE OF CAPITALISM IN
ULSTER
SSRC RESEARCH UNIT ON ETHNIC RELATIONS
ASTON
1982 1 08

4435 JENKINS, R
RELIGIOUS CONFLICT IN NI
IN MARTIN, D (ED)
1969 1 07

4436 JENKINS, R; MACRAE, J
RELIGION, CONFLICT AND POLARIZATION IN
NI
IN ROLING, B (ED)
ASSEN
1968 1 07

4437 JENKINS, R; SMOKER, P
NI: A CASE STUDY IN POLARISATION
PEACE RESEARCH CENTRE
LANCASTER UNIV
1971 1 10

4438 JENVEY, S
SONS AND HATERS: ULSTER YOUTH IN
CONFLICT
NEW SOCIETY 21(512)
1972 1 01

4439 JONES, E
DISTRIBUTION AND SEGREGATION OF ROMAN
CATHOLICS IN BELFAST
SOCIOL R 4(2)
1956 2 01

4440 JONES, E
PROBLEMS OF PARTITION AND SEGREGATION IN
NI
J CONFLICT RESOL 4(1)
ANN ARBOR, MICHIGAN
1956 2 01

4441 KARCH, C
ANGLO-SAXON ETHNOCENTRISM: ITS ROOTS AND
CONSEQUENCES IN NI AND THE SOUTHERN
UNITED STATES
IN LEGETT, J (ED)
NEW YORK
1973 1 07

4442 KENNEDY, D
CATHOLICS IN NI: 1926-1939
IN MACMANUS, F (ED)
DUBLIN
1967 2 07

4443 KIRK, T
RELIGIOUS DISTRIBUTION OF LURGAN WITH
SPECIAL REFERENCE TO SEGREGATIONAL
ECOLOGY
QUB MA
BELFAST
1967 2 04

4444 KNOX, H M
RELIGIOUS SEGREGATION IN THE SCHOOLS OF
NI
BRIT J EDUC STUD 21(3)
1973 2 01

4445 LARKIN, G V
STABILITY IN A SECTARIAN SOCIETY: A LOOK
AT THE NETHERLANDS
NEW SOCIOL 1(2)
KINGSTON-ON-THAMES
1972 1 01

4446 LEAHY, F S
FEARS AND CONVICTIONS OF ULSTER
PROTESTANTS
THE BELL 16(3)
DUBLIN
1950 2 01

4447 LEAHY, F S; GILMORE, G
FEARS OF ULSTER PROTESTANTS
THE BELL 17(1)
DUBLIN
1951 2 01

4448 LEBOW, R N
ORIGINS OF SECTARIAN ASSASSINATION: THE
CASE OF BELFAST
J INT AFFAIRS 32(1)
1978 1 01

4449 LENNON, S
ROADS TO RECONCILIATION - A CATHOLIC
CONTRIBUTION
IN SOCIAL STUDY CONFERENCE
DUBLIN
1974 1 07

4450 LOCKWOOD, J
WORKING FOR THEM, WORKING FOR US: A
THEORETICAL CASE STUDY IN INTERGROUP
RELATIONS
IN STRINGER, M (ED)
1980 2 07

4451 LOWRY, D R
LEGISLATION IN A SOCIAL VACUUM: THE
FAILURE OF THE FAIR EMPLOYMENT (NI) ACT
NEW YORK UNIV J INT LAW AND POLITICS
9(3)
NEW YORK
1977 1 01

4452 MACGREIL, M
PREJUDICE AND TOLERANCE IN IRELAND
COLLEGE OF INDUSTRIAL RELATIONS
DUBLIN
1977 2 02

4453 MACRAE, J
POLARISATION IN NI: A PRELIMINARY REPORT
PEACE RESEARCH CENTRE
LANCASTER
1966 2 99

4454 MACY, C
JOB DISCRIMINATION IN NI
HUMANIST 87(1)
1972 1 01

4455 MCANALLEN, M
MINORITY INTERACTION IN A SMALL NI
VILLAGE
QUB MA
BELFAST
1977 2 04

4456 MCCANN, J
NORTHERN SCHOOLS AND INTEGRATION
CHRISTUS REX 23(3)
1969 2 01

4457 MCCLUNG LEE, A
INTER-ETHNIC CONFLICT IN THE BRITISH
ISLES
SSSP
NEW YORK
1978 1 99

4458 MCCLUNG LEE, A
INTER-ETHNIC CONFLICT PATTERNS IN NI
DEPT SOCIOL AND ANTHROPOL CUNY
NEW YORK
        1 01

4459 MCCLUNG LEE, A
IS ULSTER'S CONFLICT RELIGIOUS?
CHURCH AND STATE 29
1976 1 01

4460 MCCLUNG LEE, A
NORTHERN IRISH SOCIALISATION IN CONFLICT
PATTERNS
INT R MODERN SOCIOL 5
1976 1 01

4461 MCCREARY, A
CORRYMEELA: HILL OF HARMONY IN NI
HAWTHORN BOOKS
NEW YORK
1976 1 02

4462 MCCREARY, A
CORRYMEELA: THE SEARCH FOR PEACE
CHRISTIAN JOURNALS
BELFAST
1975 1 10

4463 MCCRUDDEN, J C
DISCRIMINATION AGAINST MINORITY GROUPS
IN EMPLOYMENT: A COMPARISON OF LEGAL
REMEDIES IN THE UNITED KINGDOM AND THE
UNITED STATES
OXFORD UNIV DPHIL
OXFORD
1981 2 04

4464 MCCRUDDEN, J C
THE EXPERIENCE OF THE LEGAL ENFORCEMENT
OF THE FAIR EMPLOYMENT (NI) ACT 1976
IN CORMACK, R; OSBORNE, R D (EDS)
BELFAST
1983 2 07

4465 MCCULLAGH, M
THE POLITICAL AND SECTARIAN SIGNIFICANCE
OF CHANGES IN THE OCCUPATIONAL STRUCTURE
IN NI
SOC SCI TEACHER 12(2)
1983 2 01

4466 MCFARLANE, W G
MIXED MARRIAGES IN BALLYCUAN, NI
J COMPARATIVE FAMILY STUD 10(2)
CALGARY
1979 2 01

4467 MCKERNAN, J
PUPIL VALUES AS SOCIAL INDICATORS OF
INTER-GROUP DIFFERENCES IN NI
IN HARBISON, J; HARBISON, J (EDS)
SHEPTON MALLET, SOMERSET
1980 1 07

4468 MCKERNAN, J
THE STRUCTURE OF VALUE SYSTEMS AND RACE
RELATIONS IN AMERICA AND NI
IN MCWHIRTER, L (ED)
1980 1 07

4469 MCKERNAN, J
VALUE SYSTEMS AND RACE RELATIONS IN NI
AND AMERICA
ETHNIC AND RACIAL STUDIES 5(2)
1982 1 01

4470 MCKINNIE, O
ASPECTS OF RELIGIOUS SEGREGATION IN
SCHOOLS IN NI
COMPARE 7(2)
1977 2 01

4471 MCLAUGHLIN, J
DISCRIMINATION IN NI: HISTORICAL ROOTS
AND CONTEMPORARY PATTERNS
ST. PATRICK'S COLL MA
MAYNOOTH
1979 1 04

4472 MCNABB, P
A PEOPLE UNDER PRESSURE
LANCASTER CONFERENCE ON NI
LANCASTER
1971 1 11

4473 MCNEILLY, N
INTEGRATION IN EDUCATION, PAST, PRESENT
AND FUTURE
BELFAST NATURAL HISTORY AND
PHILOSOPHICAL SOCIETY PROC 9
BELFAST
1976 2 01

4474 MCTIERNAN, T J; KNOX, R E
IRISH STUDENTS' STEREOTYPES ABOUT SOME
NATIONAL AND SUBNATIONAL GROUPS WITHIN
IRELAND AND GREAT BRITAIN
SOC BEHAVIOR AND PERSONALITY 7(1)
1979 2 01

4475 MCWHIRTER, L
CONTACT AND CONFLICT: THE QUESTION OF
INTEGRATED EDUCATION
IR J PSYCHOL 6(1)
DUBLIN
1983 1 01

4476 MCWHIRTER, L
THE IMPACT OF POLITICAL AND SECTARIAN
VIOLENCE IN NI
IN DEREGOWSKI, J B; DZIURAWIEC, S; ANNIS, R
C (EDS)
LISSE
1983 1 07

4477 MCWHIRTER, L
LOOKING BACK AND LOOKING FORWARD: AN
INSIDE PERSPECTIVE
IN HARBISON, J (ED)
BELFAST
1983 1 07

4478 MCWHIRTER, L
SEGREGATED EDUCATION AND SOCIAL CONFLICT
IN NI
INT PERSPECTIVES ON CHILD DEVELOPMENT
AND SOC POLICY CONF
TORONTO
1981 1 11

4479 MCWHIRTER, L; GAMBLE, R
DEVELOPMENT OF ETHNIC AWARENESS IN THE
ABSENCE OF PHYSICAL CUES
IR J PSYCHOL 5(2)
1982 1 01

4480 MERCER, G W; CAIRNS, E
CONSERVATISM AND ITS RELATIONSHIP TO
GENERAL AND SPECIFIC ETHNOCENTRISM IN NI
BRIT J SOC PSYCHOL 20(1)
1981 2 01

4481 MERCER, G W; CAIRNS, E; BUNTING, B
NI STEREOTYPES
B BRIT PSYCHOL SOC 31
1978 1 01

4482 MILLER, D W
EDUCATION AND SECTARIAN CONFLICT IN NI
AMER HISTORICAL ASSOC
1969 1 08

4483 MILLER, R L
ATTITUDES TO WORK IN NI
FEA 2
BELFAST
1978 2 10

Protestant/Catholic Division/

4484 MILLER,R L
OCCUPATIONAL MOBILITY OF PROTESTANTS AND
ROMAN CATHOLICS IN NI: RESULTS AND
PROJECTIONS
FEA 4
BELFAST
1979 2 10

4485 MILLER,R L
OPINIONS ON SCHOOL DE-SEGREGATION IN NI
IN SPENCER,A; TOVEY,H (EDS) PROC SAI
BELFAST
1978 2 01

4486 MILLER,R L; OSBORNE,R D
RELIGION AND UNEMPLOYMENT: EVIDENCE FROM
A COHORT SURVEY
IN CORMACK,R; OSBORNE,R D (EDS)
BELFAST
1983 2 07

4487 MINISTRY OF HEALTH AND SOCIAL SERVICES
(NI)
REPORT AND RECOMMENDATIONS OF THE
WORKING PARTY OF DISCRIMINATION IN THE
PRIVATE SECTOR OF EMPLOYMENT
HMSO
BELFAST
1973 1 03

4488 MOLES,W
INTEGRATED EDUCATION
COMM FORUM 2(1)
1972 2 01

4489 MOORE,R
RACE RELATIONS IN THE SIX COUNTIES,
COLONIALISM, INDUSTRIALIZATION AND
STRATIFICATION IN IRELAND
RACE 14(1)
1972 1 01

4490 MURPHY,D
A PLACE APART
PENGUIN
HARMONDSWORTH
1979 1 02

4491 MURRAY,D
EDUCATION AND COMMUNITY IN NI
NORTH TEACH 13(2)
BELFAST
1978 2 01

4492 MURRAY,D
EDUCATION AND COMMUNITY IN NI: SCHOOLS
APART?
IN MCKERNAN,J (ED)
COLERAINE
1978 1 01

4493 MURRAY,R; BOAL,F W
FORCED RESIDENTIAL MOBILITY IN BELFAST
1969-72
IN HARBISON,J; HARBISON,J (EDS)
SHEPTON MALLET, SOMERSET
1980 1 07

4494 MURRAY,R; BOAL,F W
THE SOCIAL ECOLOGY OF URBAN VIOLENCE
IN HERBERT,D; SMITH,D (EDS)
LONDON
1979 1 07

4495 MURRAY,R; OSBORNE,R
EDUCATIONAL QUALIFICATIONS AND RELIGIOUS
AFFILIATION
IN CORMACK,R; OSBORNE,R D (EDS)
BELFAST
1983 2 07

4496 MURRAY,R; OSBORNE,R D
SEGREGATION ON HORN DRIVE - A CAUTIONARY
TALE
NEW SOCIETY 40(759)
LONDON
1977 1 01

4497 NATIONAL DEMOCRATIC GROUP
HOUSING: THE FACTS
NATIONAL DEMOCRATIC GROUP
BELFAST
1969 2 09

4498 NEILSEN,S L
INTER-GROUP CONFLICT AND VIOLENCE,
BELFAST 1968
PSYCHOSOCIAL STUD 4
BERGEN UNIV NORWAY
1972 1 01

4499 NEWE,G B
LIVING TOGETHER
COMM FORUM 2(3)
1972 1 01

4500 NEWE,G B
A WAY TO IMPROVE COMMUNITY RELATIONS:
CORRYMEELA FAMILY WEEK
NEWMAN R 1
1969 1 01

4501 NICRC
GUIDE FOR INTIMIDATED FAMILIES
NICRC
BELFAST
1974 1 03

4502 NOLAN,J T
THE STATUS OF THE CATHOLIC MINORITY IN
NI 1920-1939: A STUDY IN INTERETHNIC
RELATIONS
FORDHAM UNIV PHD
NEW YORK
1953 2 04

4503 NUM
TRIBALISM AND CHRISTIANITY IN IRELAND
NUM
BELFAST
1973 1 10

4504 O'CONNOR,S
CHOCOLATE CREAM SOLDIERS: EVALUATING AN
EXPERIMENT IN NON-SECTARIAN EDUCATION IN
NI
J CURRICULUM STUD 12(3)
1980 1 01

4505 O'DONNELL,E
THE CONFLICT IN NI: A STUDY IN
STEREOTYPES
SOUTHERN CALIFORNIA UNIV PHD
1976 1 04

4506 O'DONNELL,E
NORTHERN IRISH STEREOTYPES
COLLEGE INDUSTRIAL RELATIONS
DUBLIN
1977 1 02

4507 OSBORNE,R D
DENOMINATION AND UNEMPLOYMENT IN NI
AREA 10(4)
1978 2 01

4508 OSBORNE,R D
EQUALITY OF OPPORTUNITY AND
DISCRIMINATION: THE CASE OF RELIGION IN
NI
ADMIN (DUB) 29(4)
DUBLIN
1982 1 01

4509 OSBORNE,R D
FAIR EMPLOYMENT IN COOKSTOWN? A NOTE ON
ANTI-DISCRIMINATION POLICY IN NI
J SOC POL 11(4)
1982 2 01

4510 OSBORNE,R D
FAIR EMPLOYMENT IN NI
NEW COMM 8(1-2)
LONDON
1980 1 01

4511 OSBORNE, R D
INEQUALITY IN NI
SOCIOL FOCUS 14(2)
AKRON
1981 2 01

4512 OSBORNE, R D
RELIGIOUS DISCRIMINATION AND
DISADVANTAGE IN THE NI LABOUR MARKET
INT J SOC ECON 7(4)
BRADFORD
1980 2 01

4513 OSBORNE, R D; CORMACK, R; REID, N;
WILLIAMSON, A
POLITICAL ARITHMETIC AND HIGHER
EDUCATION IN NI
IN CORMACK, R; OSBORNE, R D (EDS)
BELFAST
1983 2 07

4514 OSBORNE, R D; MURRAY, R
EDUCATIONAL QUALIFICATIONS AND RELIGIOUS
AFFILIATION IN NI
FEA 3
BELFAST
1978 2 10

4515 PINTER, F
POLARIZATION AND POPULATION MOVEMENT IN
BELFAST
LONDON UNIV
LONDON
1971 1 08

4516 POLITICAL AND ECONOMIC PLANNING
TOWARDS BETTER COMMUNITY RELATIONS: A
STUDY OF COMMUNITY RELATIONS IN NI
PEP
LONDON
1970 1 10

4517 POOLE, M A
RELIGIOUS RESIDENTIAL SEGREGATION IN
URBAN NI
IN BOAL, F W; DOUGLAS, J N H (EDS)
LONDON
1982 1 07

4518 POOLE, M A; BOAL, F W
RELIGIOUS RESIDENTIAL SEGREGATION IN
BELFAST IN MID-1969
IN CLARK, B; CLEAVE, M (EDS)
LONDON
1973 1 07

4519 ROBINSON, A
EDUCATION AND SECTARIAN CONFLICT IN NI
NEW ERA JAN
1971 1 10

4520 ROBINSON, A
LONDONDERRY: CITY OF COMMUNITIES
COMM FORUM 4(2)
LONDON
1974 2 01

4521 ROLSTON, B
CLASS, RELIGION AND SEX
NEW STATESMAN JULY 16
LONDON
1982 2 01

4522 ROLSTON, B
SECTARIANISM AND COMMUNITY POLITICS
IN FRAZER, H ET AL
BELFAST
1981 1 07

4523 RUSSELL, J
INTEGRATED SCHOOLING
SECONDARY TEACHER 7(1)
1977 2 01

4524 RUSSELL, J
REPLICATION OF INSTABILITY: POLITICAL
SOCIALIZATION IN NI
BRIT J POLIT SCI 7
1977 1 01

4525 RUSSELL, J
SOCIALISATION INTO CONFLICT
PROC IR EDUC SOC
1976 1 11

4526 RUSSELL, J
SOCIALIZATION INTO CONFLICT
STRATHCLYDE UNIV PHD
GLASGOW
1974 1 04

4527 RUSSELL, J
SOME ASPECTS OF CIVIC EDUCATION OF
SECONDARY SCHOOLBOYS IN NI
NICRC
BELFAST
1972 1 01

4528 RUSSELL, J; SCHELLENBERG, J A
POLITICAL ATTITUDE STRUCTURE OF
SCHOOLBOYS IN NI
INT J PSYCH 3(2)
1976 1 01

4529 SALTERS, J
INTEGRATED EDUCATION IN NI: SOME
ASSUMPTIONS TO BE EXAMINED
PROC IRISH EDUC SOC
1976 2 11

4530 SALTERS, J
INTEGRATION: A SOCIOLOGICAL PERSPECTIVE
IN GUILD OF CATHOLIC TEACHERS
1978 2 07

4531 SCHELLENBERG, J A; RUSSELL, J
INTERGROUP ATTITUDES OF SCHOOLBOYS IN NI
INT J GROUP TENSIONS 6(1-2)
1976 1 01

4532 SCHMITT, D
THE CONSEQUENCES OF ADMINISTRATIVE
EMPLOYEES IN EQUAL OPPORTUNITY
STRATEGIES: COMPARATIVE ANALYSIS OF THE
UNITED STATES AND NI
AMER POLIT SCI ASSOC ANNUAL CONF
1981 2 11

4533 SCHMITT, D
EQUAL OPPORTUNITY AS A TECHNIQUE TOWARD
THE CONTROL OF POLITICAL VIOLENCE: THE
CASE OF THE FEA
CURRENT RESEARCH PEACE AND VIOLENCE
1980 1 01

4534 SCHMITT, D
ETHNIC CONFLICT IN NI
IN ESMAN, M (ED)
ITHACA
1977 1 07

4535 SCHMITT, D
VIOLENCE IN NI: ETHNIC CONFLICT AND
RADICALISATION IN AN INTERNATIONAL
SETTING
GENERAL LEARNING PRESS
NEW JERSEY
1974 1 02

4536 SCOTT, O
THE CULTURAL DIVIDE
LANCASTER CONFERENCE ON NI
LANCASTER
1971 1 08

4537 SIMPSON, G; YINGER, J
RACIAL AND CULTURAL MINORITIES
HARPER AND ROW
NEW YORK
1965 1 07

4538 SINGLETON, D
PLANNING AND SECTARIANISM IN NI
PLANNER 63(1)
1977 1 01

4539 SINGLETON, D
POLEGLASS: A MICROCOSM OF PLANNING IN A
DIVIDED COMMUNITY
PLANNER 65(3)
1979 1 01

4540 SINNOTT,R; DAVIS,E E
POLITICAL MOBILIZATION, POLITICAL
INSTITUTIONALIZATION AND THE MAINTENANCE
OF ETHNIC CONFLICT
ETHNIC AND RACIAL STUDIES 4(4)
LONDON
1981 1 01

4541 SMITH,M
GEOGRAPHY OF SECTARIANISM
IRL SOCIALIST R 8
LONDON
1981 2 01

4542 SPENCER,A
THE RELATIVE FERTILITY OF THE TWO
RELIGIOUS-ETHNIC COMMUNITIES IN NI:
1947-1977
IN SPENCER,A (ED) PROC SAI
BELFAST
1979 2 07

4543 STRINGER,M
THE RELATIVE STRENGTH OF THREE
DENOMINATIONAL CUES IN NI
B BRIT PSYCHOL SOC 34
1980 1 01

4544 STRINGER,M; CAIRNS,E
AN INVESTIGATION INTO DENOMINATIONAL
ATTITUDES IN NI
IN MCWHIRTER,L (ED)
ABERDEEN
1980 2 07

4545 TAYLOR,B M
BRASS MONEY AND WOODEN SHOES: PROTESTANT
SECTARIANISM AND ETHNIC COMPETITION IN
NI
MICHIGAN UNIV PHD
1979 1 04

4546 TAYLOR,R
BRIDGING THE SECTARIAN DIVIDE
RACE TODAY 3(7)
LONDON
1971 1 01

4547 TRANT,A
ROADS TO RECONCILIATION: THE ROLE OF
EDUCATION
IN SOCIAL STUDY CONFERENCE
DUBLIN
1974 1 07

4548 TREW,K
GROUP IDENTIFICATION IN A DIVIDED
SOCIETY
IN HARBISON,J (ED)
BELFAST
1983 1 07

4549 TREW,K
INTERGROUP RELATIONS AND THE DEVELOPMENT
OF SOCIAL IDENTITY IN NI
INT SOCIETY FOR THE STUDY OF BEHAVIOURAL
DEVELOPMENT CONF
TORONTO
1981 1 11

4550 WEINREICH,P
IDENTITY DEVELOPMENT IN PROTESTANT AND
ROMAN CATHOLIC ADOLESCENT BOYS AND GIRLS
IN BELFAST
INT ASSOC FOR CHILD AND ADOLESCENT
PSYCHIATRY CONF
DUBLIN
1982 2 11

4551 WHITE,C
COMMUNITIES IN TENSION AND CONFLICT
SOC STUD 2(1)
MAYNOOTH
1973 1 01

4552 WHYTE,J H
COMPARING NI WITH SECTARIAN TENSIONS
ABROAD
MONTH AUGUST
1978 1 01

4553 WHYTE,J H
HOW MUCH DISCRIMINATION WAS THERE UNDER
THE UNIONIST REGIME, 1921-1968?
IN GALLAGHER,T; O'CONNELL,J (EDS)
MANCHESTER
1983 2 07

4554 WILSON,J A
COEDUCATION AND RELIGIOUS INTEGRATION AS
ISSUES IN RE-ORGANSATION OF SECONDARY
EDUCATION
NORTH TEACH 12(4)
BELFAST
1977 2 01

4555 WILSON,J A
THE RESIDENTIAL SEGREGATION OF CATHOLICS
AND PROTESTANTS IN ARMAGH URBAN AREA
NUU MSC
COLERAINE
1978 3 04

4556 ACKROYD,C; MARGOLIS,K; ROSENHEAD,J;
SHALLICE,T
THE TECHNOLOGY OF POLITICAL CONTROL
PLUTO
LONDON
1980 1 02

4557 BAIN,R E D
SABOTAGE AT BELFAST WATER WORKS
SURVEYOR DEC 19
1969 1 01

4558 BANKS,M
THE ARMY IN NI
BRASSEYS ANNUAL
LONDON
1972 1 01

4559 BARKER,D
BANDIT COUNTRY
IN BARKER,D
LONDON
1981 1 07

4560 BARTHORP,M
CRATER TO THE CREGGAN: A HISTORY OF THE
ROYAL ANGLIAN REGIMENT 1964-1974
LONDON
1976 2 02

4561 BARZILAY,D
BRITISH ARMY IN ULSTER (VOLUME 1)
CENTURY SERVICES
BELFAST
1973 1 02

4562 BARZILAY,D
BRITISH ARMY IN ULSTER (VOLUME 2)
CENTURY SERVICES
BELFAST
1975 1 02

4563 BARZILAY,D
BRITISH ARMY IN ULSTER (VOLUME 3)
CENTURY SERVICES
BELFAST
1978 1 02

4564 BARZILAY,D; MURRAY,M
FOUR MONTHS IN WINTER
ROYAL REGIMENT OF FUSILIERS
BELFAST
1972 1 02

4565 BAYLEY,J; LOIZOS,P
BOGSIDE OFF ITS KNEES
NEW SOCIETY
1969 1 01

4566 BEER,C
IMPRESSIONS FROM ULSTER
ARMY QUART AND DEFENCE J 102(3)
1972 1 01

4567 BELL,C
IRELAND: THE DYNAMICS OF INSURGENCY
NEW SOCIETY 18(478)
LONDON
1971 1 01

4568 BELL,J B
ESCALATION OF INSURGENCY: THE
PROVISIONAL IRA'S EXPERIENCE
R POLITICS 35(3)
1973 1 01

4569 BELL,J B
THE IRISH REPUBLICAN ARMY
IN CARLTON,D; SCHAERF,C (EDS)
LONDON
1982 1 07

4570 BELL,J B
THE IRISH REPUBLICAN MOVEMENT: TRADITION
AND TECHNIQUES
IN BELL,J B (ED)
WASHINGTON, D.C.
1975 1 07

4571 BELL,J B
MEN WITHOUT GUNS: THE LEGITIMACY OF
VIOLENT DISSENT
IN DEITCH,B (ED)
1979 1 07

4572 BELL,J B
SECRET ARMY
ACADEMY PRESS
DUBLIN
1979 1 02

4573 BELL,J B
SOCIETAL PATTERNS AND LESSONS: THE IRISH
CASE
IN HIGHAM,R (ED)
LEXINGTON
1972 2 07

4574 BELL,J B
STRATEGY, TACTICS AND TERROR: AN IRISH
PERSPECTIVE
IN ALEXANDER,Y (ED)
NEW YORK
1976 1 07

4575 BENNETT,J
FOURTEEN DAYS OF FASCIST TERROR
IRISH DEMOCRAT BOOKS
LONDON
1974 1 09

4576 BERKE,A
DERRY - HOW THE PEOPLE FOUGHT
SOLIDARITY 5(11)
          1 01

4577 BEW,P
THE PROBLEM OF ULSTER TERRORISM: THE
HISTORICAL ROOTS
IN ALEXANDER,Y; O'DAY,A (EDS)
LONDON
1983 1 07

4578 BIDWELL,R G S
THE ROLE OF THE ARMED FORCES IN
PEACE-KEEPING IN THE 1970'S
RUSI
LONDON
1973 1 02

4579 BISHOP,J W
LAW IN THE CONTROL OF TERRORISM AND
INSURRECTION: THE BRITISH LABORATORY
EXPERIENCE
LAW AND CONTEMPORARY SOC PROBLEMS 42(2)
DURHAM N. CAROLINA
1978 1 01

4580 BLAXLAND,G
THE LONE SENTRY (1966-1970)
IN BLAXLAND,G
LONDON
1971 1 07

4581 BLOCH,J; FITZGERALD,P
BRITISH INTELLIGENCE AND COVERT ACTION
BRANDON/JUNCTION BOOKS
DINGLE/LONDON
1983 1 02

4582 BOGSIDE REPUBLICAN APPEAL FUND
BATTLE OF BOGSIDE
BOGSIDE REPUBLICAN APPEAL FUND
BELFAST
1969 1 10

4583 BOSSY,J
PATTERNS OF VIOLENCE
ENCOUNTER 52
LONDON
1979 1 01

4584 BOULTON,D
THE UVF: 1966-1973
TORC
DUBLIN
1973 1 02

4585 BOWDEN,T
IRA AND THE CHANGING TACTICS OF
TERRORISM
POLIT QUART 47(4)
1976 1 01

4586 BOYCE,D G
WATER FOR THE FISH: TERRORISM AND PUBLIC
OPINION
IN ALEXANDER,Y; O'DAY,A (EDS)
LONDON
1983 1 07

4587 BOYLE,K; CHESNEY,R; HADDEN,T
WHO ARE THE TERRORISTS?
NEW SOCIETY 36(709)
1976 1 01

4588 BOYLE,L
ULSTER WORKERS' COUNCIL STRIKE, MAY 1974
IN DARBY,J; WILLIAMSON,A (EDS)
LONDON
1978 1 07

4589 BRADY,B; FAUL,D; MURRAY,R
BRITISH ARMY MURDER: LEO NORNEY (17
YEARS) DECEMBER 1975
AUTHOR
DUNGANNON
1975 1 10

4590 BRADY,B; FAUL,D; MURRAY,R
BRITISH ARMY TERROR TACTICS, WEST
BELFAST, SEPTEMBER-OCTOBER 1976
AUTHOR
DUNGANNON
1977 1 10

4591 BRENNAN,P
LA TRADITION REVOLUTIONAIRE IRLANDAISE
TEMPS MODERNES 311
1972 1 01

4592 BREWER,J; SMYTH,J
THE PARAMETERS OF A PUZZLE: CONFLICT
MANAGEMENT IN NI AND SOUTH AFRICA
ECPR
ESSEX
1983 1 11

4593 BRITISH SOCIETY FOR SOCIAL
RESPONSIBILITY IN SCIENCE
NEW TECHNOLOGY OF REPRESSION: LESSONS
FROM IRELAND
BRITISH SOCIETY FOR SOCIAL
RESPONSIBILITY IN SCIENCE
LONDON
1970 1 09

4594 BROWNE,V
"THERE WILL BE NO MORE CEASEFIRES UNTIL
THE END" - INTERVIEW WITH PROVISIONAL
IRA
MAGILL 1(11) AUGUST
DUBLIN
1978 1 01

4595 BROWNE,V
THE NEW IRA STRATEGY
MAGILL 5(2)
DUBLIN
1981 1 01

4596 BROWNE,V
WHY WE KILLED AIREY NEAVE - THE INLA
MAGILL 2(7)
DUBLIN
1979 1 01

4597 BUCKLEY,A D; OLSON,D D
INTERNATIONAL TERRORISM: CURRENT
RESEARCH AND FUTURE DEVELOPMENTS
AVERY PUBLICATIONS
WAYNE, NEW JERSEY
1980 1 02

4598 BURKE,V; MURPHY,S
SPRINGFIELD RIOT REPORT
NEWMAN R 3(1)
1971 1 01

4599 BURTON,A
URBAN TERRORISM: THEORY, PRACTICE AND
RESPONSE
COOPER
LONDON
1975 1 07

4600 BYRNES,D P ET AL
PENETRATING CRANIOCEREBRAL MISSILE
INJURIES IN THE CIVIL DISTURBANCES IN NI
BRIT J SURGER 61
LONDON
1974 1 01

4601 CAMERON COMMISSION
DISTURBANCES IN NI: REPORT OF THE
COMMISSION APPOINTED BY THE GOVERNOR OF
NI
HMSO CMD, 532
BELFAST
1969 1 03

4602 CAMPAIGN FOR SOCIAL JUSTICE IN NI
NI - THE MAILED FIST
CAMPAIGN FOR SOCIAL JUSTICE IN NI
DUNGANNON
1971 1 09

4603 CARROLL,T
DISOBEDIENCE AND VIOLENCE IN NI
COMP POLIT STUD 14
BEVERLY HILLS
1981 1 01

4604 CARROLL,T
ENDS AND MEANS IN NI
DEPT POLIT SCI ST CATHERINE'S
ONTARIO
1976 1 08

4605 CARROLL,T
POLITICAL ACTIVISTS IN DISAFFECTED
COUNTRIES: DISSIDENCE, DISOBEDIENCE,
REBELLION...
CARLETON UNIV
OTTAWA
1974 1 04

4606 CARROLL,T
REGULATING CONFLICTS: THE CASE OF ULSTER
POLIT QUART 51(4)
LONDON
1980 1 01

4607 CARSON,H M
RIOTS AND RELIGION
HENRY WALTERS
WORTHING
1970 1 10

4608 CHALFONT,A
THE ARMY AND THE IRA
NEW STATESMAN APRIL 2
LONDON
1971 1 01

4609 CHALFONT,A
BALANCE OF MILITARY FORCES
IN CROZIER,B; MOSS,R (EDS)
LONDON
1972 1 07

4610 CHALK,P
SURVEILLANCE, THE LAW AND MILITARY RULE
IN NI
IRL SOCIALIST R 4
LONDON
1979 1 01

4611 CHARTERS, D
CHANGING FORMS OF CONFLICT IN NI
CONFLICT QUART 1(2)
LONDON
1980 1 01

4612 CHARTERS, D
INTELLIGENCE AND PSYCHOLOGICAL WARFARE
OPERATIONS IN NI
RUSI J 122(3)
LONDON
1977 1 01

4613 CLAIR-LOUIS, J
PROBLEMS OF NI
R MILITAIRE GENERALE 7
1970 1 01

4614 CLANN NA HEIREANN
BATTLE OF BELFAST
CLANN NA HEIREANN
LONDON
1971 1 09

4615 CLANN NA HEIREANN
LITTLEJOHN MEMORANDUM
CLANN NA HEIREANN
LONDON
1974 1 09

4616 CLARK, D
TERRORISM IN IRELAND: RENEWAL OF A
TRADITION
IN LIVINGSTON, M H (ED)
1978 1 07

4617 CLARK, D
WHICH WAY THE IRA?
COMMONWEAL 13
1973 1 01

4618 CLARK, H
WHY AN ULSTER DEFENCE REGIMENT
SOLON 1(2)
1970 1 01

4619 CLARKE, A F N
CONTACT
SECKER AND WARBURG
LONDON
1983 1 02

4620 CLUTTERBUCK, R
COMMENT ON CHAPTER BY COLE
IN WATT, D (ED)
LONDON
1981 1 07

4621 CLUTTERBUCK, R
GUERRILLAS AND TERRORISTS
FABER
LONDON
1977 1 02

4622 CLUTTERBUCK, R
PROTEST AND THE URBAN GUERRILLA
CASSELL
LONDON
1973 1 02

4623 CLUTTERBUCK, R
TERRORISM AND THE SECURITY FORCES IN
EUROPE
ARMY QUART AND DEFENCE J 111(1)
1981 1 01

4624 CLUTTERBUCK, R
TERRORISM: A SOLDIER'S VIEW
IN RUSI
LONDON
1979 1 07

4625 CLUTTERBUCK, R
TERRORIST INTERNATIONAL
ARMY QUART AND DEFENCE J 104(2)
1974 1 01

4626 COLE, J
SECURITY CONSTRAINTS
IN WATT, D (ED)
LONDON
1981 1 07

4627 CONLON, L
CUMANN NA MBAN AND THE WOMEN OF IRELAND
KILKENNY PEOPLE LTD
KILKENNY
1969 2 02

4628 CONNOLLY O'BRIEN, N
WE SHALL RISE AGAIN
MOSQUITO PRESS
LONDON
1981 1 02

4629 COOGAN, T P
THE IRA
FONTANA
LONDON
1979 1 02

4630 COOPER, G L C
SOME ASPECTS OF CONFLICT IN ULSTER
MILITARY R 53(9)
FORT LEAVENWORTH
1973 1 01

4631 CORFE, T
POLITICAL ASSASSINATION IN THE IRISH
TRADITION
IN ALEXANDER, Y; O'DAY, A (EDS)
LONDON
1983 1 07

4632 CORRADO, R
ETHNIC AND STUDENT TERRORISM IN WESTERN
EUROPE
IN STOHL, M (ED)
NEW YORK
1979 1 07

4633 COSTELLO, D
INTERNATIONAL TERRORISM AND THE
DEVELOPMENT OF THE PRINCIPLE AUT DEDERE
AUT JUDICARE
IR JURIST 9(2)
1974 1 01

4634 CRENSHAW, M
THE PERSISTENCE OF IRA TERRORISM
COLLOQUIUM
1979 1 08

4635 CRENSHAW, M
THE PERSISTENCE OF IRA TERRORISM
IN ALEXANDER, Y; O'DAY, A (EDS)
LONDON
1983 1 07

4636 CRITCHLEY, J
ULSTER AND THE URBAN GUERRILLA
WLD SURVEY 40
1972 1 01

4637 CRONIN, S
THE IDEOLOGY OF THE IRA AND THE ROOTS OF
CONFLICT IN NI
NEW SCHOOL FOR SOCIAL RESEARCH PHD
NEW YORK
1979 1 04

4638 CRONIN, S
THE MCGARRITY PAPERS: REVELATIONS OF THE
IRISH REVOLUTIONARY MOVEMENT IN IRELAND
AND AMERICA, 1900-1940
ANVIL
TRALEE
1972 2 02

4639 CUNNINGHAM, M
MONAGHAN: COUNTY OF INTRIGUE
AUTHOR
CAVAN
1979 1 02

4640 CURTIS,L
THEY SHOOT CHILDREN: THE USE OF RUBBER
AND PLASTIC BULLETS IN THE NORTH OF
IRELAND
INFORMATION ON IRELAND
LONDON
1982 1 10

4641 DALY,E
DERRY MASSACRE
IN O'CONNOR,U (ED)
1974 1 07

4642 DANE,M
FERMANAGH 'B' SPECIALS
IMPARTIAL REPORTER
ENNISKILLEN
1970 2 10

4643 DANKER,G
ANTITERROR STRATEGIE
HUBER
FRAUENFELD (SWITZERLAND)
1978 1 02

4644 DAWSON,J; STRINGER,W
IRISH POLITICAL PRISONERS
IRL SOCIALIST R
LONDON
1978 1 01

4645 DEANE-DRUMMOND,A
RIOT CONTROL
RUSI
LONDON
1975 1 02

4646 DESPORTE,I P
PSYCHOLOGICAL WEAPON IN NI
RECH SOC (PARIS) 35
PARIS
1973 1 01

4647 DEUTSCH,R
LA GREVE LOYALIST DE MAI 1974: NOTES
BIBLIOGRAPHIQUE
ET IRL 4
1975 1 01

4648 DEUTSCH,R
LA GREVE LOYALISTE DE MAI 1977
ET IRL 2
1977 1 01

4649 DEVLIN,P
TUZO, WHITELAW AND THE TERROR IN NI
AUTHOR
BELFAST
1973 1 09

4650 DILLON,M; LEHANE,D
POLITICAL MURDER IN NI
PENGUIN
LONDON
1973 1 02

4651 DOBSON,C; PAYNE,R
THE WEAPONS OF TERROR: INTERNATIONAL
TERRORISM AT WORK
MACMILLAN
LONDON
1979 1 02

4652 DODD,N L
THE CORPORAL'S WAR: INTERNAL SECURITY
OPERATIONS
MILITARY R 56(7)
1976 1 01

4653 DOWLING,K
CIVIL RIGHTS, HUMAN RIGHTS AND TERRORISM
IN NI
J INTERGROUP RELATIONS 7(4)
1979 1 01

4654 DOWNEY,J
CONFLICT AND CRIME IN NI
OHIO UNIV PHD
1978 1 04

4655 DOWNEY,J
A NOTE ON VIOLENT CRIME IN NI
WISCONSIN SOCIOLOGIST 15(4)
1978 1 01

4656 ECONOMIST
BOMBS ALONG THE BORDER
ECONOMIST 202 17 FEB
1962 2 10

4657 EDMONDS,S
THE GUN, THE LAW AND THE IRISH PEOPLE
ANVIL
TRALEE
1971 1 02

4658 ENLOE,C
POLICE AND MILITARY IN ULSTER:
PEACEKEEPING OR PEACE-SUBVERTING FORCES
J PEACE RES 15(3)
1978 1 01

4659 EVELEGH,R
PEACE-KEEPING IN A DEMOCRATIC SOCIETY:
THE LESSONS OF NI
HURST
LONDON
1978 1 02

4660 FALIGOT,R
BRITAIN'S MILITARY STRATEGY IN IRELAND:
THE KITSON EXPERIMENT
BRANDON
DINGLE
1983 1 02

4661 FALIGOT,R
GUERRE SPECIALE EN IRLANDE
TEXTS FLAMMARIAN
PARIS
1980 1 02

4662 FALIGOT,R
LA RESISTANCE IRLANDAISE, 1916-1976
MASPERO
PARIS
1977 1 02

4663 FALIGOT,R
NOUS AVONS TUE MOUNTBATTEN: L'IRA PARLE
EDITIONS JEAN PICOLLEC
PARIS
1981 1 02

4664 FALIGOT,R
SPECIAL WAR IN IRELAND
CRANE BAG 4(2)
DUBLIN
1980 1 01

4665 FARRELL,M
ARMS OUTSIDE THE LAW: PROBLEMS OF THE
ULSTER SPECIAL CONSTABULARY 1920-22
STRATHCLYDE UNIV MSC
GLASGOW
1978 2 04

4666 FARRELL,M
ESTABLISHMENT OF THE ULSTER SPECIAL
CONSTABULARY
IN MORGAN,A; PURDIE,B (EDS)
1980 2 07

4667 FAUL,D
MAJELLA O'HARE
AUTHOR
DUNGANNON
1976 1 10

4668 FAUL,D; MURRAY,R
BRITISH ARMY AND SPECIAL BRANCH RUC
BRUTALITIES DEC 1971-1972
AUTHORS
CAVAN
1972 1 10

4669 FAUL, D; MURRAY, R
THE BRITISH DIMENSION: BRUTALITY, MURDER
AND LEGAL DUPLICITY IN NI
AUTHORS
DUNGANNON
1980 1 10

4670 FAUL, D; MURRAY, R
DANNY BARRETT: A BRITISH ARMY MURDER
AUTHORS
DUNGANNON
1982 1 10

4671 FAUL, D; MURRAY, R
HOODED MEN: BRITISH TORTURE IN IRELAND
AUTHORS
DUNGANNON
1974 1 10

4672 FAUL, D; MURRAY, R
PLASTIC BULLETS - PLASTIC GOVERNMENT
AUTHORS
DUNGANNON
1982 1 10

4673 FAUL, D; MURRAY, R
RUBBER AND PLASTIC BULLETS KILL AND MAIM
AUTHORS
DUNGANNON
1981 1 10

4674 FIELDS, R
CHILD TERROR VICTIMS AND ADULT
TERRORISTS
J PSYCHOHIST 7(1)
1979 1 01

4675 FIELDS, R
ULSTER: A PSYCHOLOGICAL EXPERIMENT?
NEW HUMANIST 88(11)
1973 1 01

4676 FISK, R
THE EFFECT OF SOCIAL AND POLITICAL CRIME
ON THE POLICE AND BRITISH ARMY IN NI
IN LIVINGSTON, M H (ED)
WESTPORT, CONNECTICUT
1978 1 07

4677 FISK, R
THE POINT OF NO RETURN: THE STRIKE WHICH
BROKE THE BRITISH IN ULSTER
DEUTSCH
LONDON
1975 1 02

4678 FOLEY, G
IRELAND IN REBELLION
PATHFINDER PRESS
NEW YORK
1971 1 09

4679 FOLEY, G
PROBLEMS OF THE IRISH REVOLUTION: CAN
THE IRA MEET THE CHALLENGE?
PATHFINDER PRESS
NEW YORK
1972 1 09

4680 GALE, R
OLD PROBLEM, NEW SETTING
RUSI J 117
1972 1 01

4681 GARRETT, B
TEN YEARS OF BRITISH TROOPS IN NI
INT SECURITY 4
1980 1 01

4682 GELLNER, J
EXTREMES IN VIOLENCE: THE IRA AND THE
WEATHERMEN
IN GELLNER, J
NEW YORK
1974 1 07

4683 GERAGHTY, T
TEN YEARS OF TERRORISM
IN RUSI
LONDON
1979 1 07

4684 GERAGHTY, T
WHO DARES WINS: THE STORY OF THE SPECIAL
AIR SERVICE 1950-1980
ARMS AND ARMOUR PRESS
LONDON
1980 1 02

4685 GIBSON, B
THE BIRMINGHAM BOMBS
BARRY ROSE
LONDON
1976 1 02

4686 GIFFORD, T
CIRCUMSTANCES SURROUNDING DEATHS OF
SEAMUS CUSACK AND GEORGE DESMOND BEATTIE
NI SOCIALIST RESEARCH CENTRE
BELFAST
1972 1 10

4687 GIFFORD, T
DEATH ON THE STREETS OF DERRY
NCCL
LONDON
1982 1 09

4688 GOULDING, C
ENTWICKLUNG UND ZIELE DER IRISH
REPUBLICAN ARMY (IRA)
BLATTER DEUTSCHE U INT POL 18
COLOGNE
1973 1 01

4689 GRAHAM, P W
LOW-LEVEL CIVIL-MILITARY CO-ORDINATION,
BELFAST 1970-1973
RUSI J
LONDON
1974 1 01

4690 GREER, D S
LEGAL CONTROL OF MILITARY OPERATIONS: A
MISSED OPPORTUNITY
NI LEG QUART 31
BELFAST
1980 1 01

4691 GREER, S
MILITARY INTERVENTION IN CIVIL
DISTURBANCES: THE LEGAL BASIS
RECONSIDERED
PUBL LAW
LONDON
1983 1 01

4692 GREIG, I
SUBVERSION, PROPAGANDA, AGITATION AND
THE SPREAD OF THE PEOPLE'S WAR
TOM STACEY
LONDON
1973 1 02

4693 GREY, LORD
POLITICAL PROBLEMS OF TERRORISM AND
SOCIETY
IN RUSI
LONDON
1979 1 07

4694 GRIFFITHS, H
PARAMILITARY GROUPS AND OTHER COMMUNITY
ACTION GROUPS IN NI TODAY
CENTRO SOCIALE 22
1975 1 01

4695 GRIFFITHS, H
PARAMILITARY GROUPS AND OTHER COMMUNITY
ACTION GROUPS IN NI TODAY
INT R COMM DEV
1975 1 01

4696 GRIMALDI, F; NORTH, S
BLOOD IN THE STREET
PD/LOTTA CONTINUA
1972 1 09

4697 GUELKE,A
THE 'BALLOT BOMB': THE NI ASSEMBLY
ELECTION AND THE PROVISIONAL IRA
ECPR
ESSEX
1983 1 11

4698 GUELKE,A
THE CHANGING POLITICS OF ULSTER'S
VIOLENT MEN
NEW SOCIETY 29 JULY
LONDON
1982 1 01

4699 HACHEY,T E
POLITICAL TERRORISM: A PERSPECTIVE OF
THE BRITISH EXPERIENCE SINCE 1815
IN ALEXANDER,Y (ED)
NEW YORK
1976 2 07

4700 HAGGERTY,J J
THE WAR THAT NEVER STOPPED BLEEDING
MILITARY R 59
FORT LEAVONWORTH, KANSAS
1979 1 01

4701 HARDY,Y
L'IRA: ANALYSE ET INTERVIEWS
TEMPS MODERNES 311
1972 1 01

4702 HARRIS,J
THE MORALITY OF TERRORISM
RADICAL PHILOSOPHY SPRING
LEEDS
1983 1 01

4703 HASWELL,J
THE BRITISH ARMY, A CONCISE HISTORY
THAMES
LONDON
1975 2 02

4704 HAYES,P
SHOOT TO KILL: THE UNCHANGING FACE OF
REPRESSION
IRIS 5
DUBLIN
1983 1 01

4705 HEDERMAN,M
INTERVIEW WITH SEAMUS TWOMEY
CRANE BAG 1(1)
DUBLIN
1977 1 01

4706 HESKIN,K
THE PSYCHOLOGY OF TERRORISM IN NI
IN ALEXANDER,Y; O'DAY,A (EDS)
LONDON
1983 1 07

4707 HEWITT,C
MAJORITIES AND MINORITIES: A
COMPARATIVE SURVEY OF ETHNIC VIOLENCE
ANNALS OF THE AMERICAN ACADEMY
1977 1 01

4708 HEWITT,C
VIOLENCE IN ULSTER 1968-71: AN ANALYSIS
AND A TEST OF SOME HYPOTHESES
MARYLAND UNIV
        1 08

4709 HEZLETT,A
B SPECIALS: A HISTORY OF THE ULSTER
SPECIAL CONSTABULARY
PAN BOOKS
1973 1 02

4710 HIGGINS,J
IRISH POLITICAL PRISONERS IN ENGLAND:
SPECIAL CATEGORY 'A'
SINN FEIN POW DEPARTMENT
DUBLIN
1980 1 09

4711 HILLYARD,P
ARMY IN NI: FROM ACCEPTANCE TO
REJECTION
QUB
BELFAST
        1 08

4712 HOGAN,G
ALWAYS ON CALL
SOLDIER NOV
1970 1 01

4713 HOGGART,S
ARMY PR MEN OF NI
NEW SOCIETY 26(575)
LONDON
1973 1 01

4714 HOLLAND,C
THE BLACK, THE RED AND THE ORANGE:
SYSTEM TERRORISM VERSUS REGIME TERROR
SSSP
NEW YORK
1981 1 08

4715 HOLLAND,J
INSIDE THE IRA
NATION 229 OCT 27
1979 1 01

4716 HOLLAND,M
DEATH OF AN OFFICER AND A GENTLEMAN
NEW STATESMAN 21 OCT
LONDON
1977 1 01

4717 HOLLAND,M
A PROVISIONAL RETURN
NEW STATESMAN 4 FEB
LONDON
1977 1 01

4718 HOLLOWAY,D
BRITISH ARMY IN NI
NEW EDINBURGH R 17
1972 1 01

4719 HOWTON,H
IN THE STREETS OF BROKEN GLASS
SOLDIER 27(6)
LONDON
1971 1 01

4720 HUDSON,P
INTERNAL SECURITY OPERATIONS IN NI
THE INFANTRYMAN 9
1970 1 01

4721 HUTTON,J
SUBVERTERS OF LIBERTY
ALLEN AND UNWIN
LONDON
1973 1 02

4722 HYAMS,E
TERRORISTS AND TERRORISM
DENT
LONDON
1975 1 02

4723 INFORMATION ON IRELAND
BRITISH SOLDIERS SPEAK OUT ON IRELAND
INFORMATION ON IRELAND
LONDON
1979 1 09

4724 INSTITUTE FOR THE STUDY OF CONFLICT
ULSTER POLITICS AND TERRORISM
CONFLICT STUD 36
1973 1 01

4725 INSTITUTE FOR THE STUDY OF CONFLICT
ULSTER: POLITICS AND TERRORISM
CONFLICT STUD 36
LONDON
1973 1 01

4726 INTELLECT
STOPPING VIOLENCE IN NI
INTELLECT 105(2384)
1977 1 01

4727 IRA
IRISH RESISTANCE TO BRITISH AGGRESSION
IRA
DUBLIN/NEW YORK
1955 2 02

4728 IRA (OFFICIAL)
IN THE 70'S THE IRA SPEAKS
REPSOL
DUBLIN
1970 1 09

4729 IRA (PROVISIONAL)
FREEDOM STRUGGLE
IRA(PROVISIONAL)
DUNDALK
1973 1 02

4730 IRIS
FOUR YEARS ON THE BLANKET
IRIS 1(2)
DUBLIN
1981 1 01

4731 IRIS
IRA INTERVIEW: IRIS TALKS TO A MEMBER OF
THE IRA'S HEADQUARTERS STAFF
IRIS 1(1)
DUBLIN
1981 1 01

4732 IRIS
THE IRON FIST IN THE VELVET GLOVE
IRIS 1(1)
DUBLIN
1981 1 01

4733 IRIS
A PEOPLE'S ARMY
IRIS 4
DUBLIN
1982 1 01

4734 IRIS
PLASTIC BULLETS
IRIS 1(2)
DUBLIN
1981 1 01

4735 IRIS
THE POLITICS OF REPRESSION
IRIS 3
DUBLIN
1982 1 01

4736 IRIS
RESISTANCE ON ALL FRONTS: INTERVIEW WITH
IRA SPOKESPERSON
IRIS 3
DUBLIN
1982 1 01

4737 JANKE, P
ULSTER: A DECADE OF VIOLENCE
CONFLICT STUD 108
1979 1 01

4738 KEARNEY, R
THE IRA'S STATEGY OF FAILURE
CRANE BAG 4(2)
1980 1 01

4739 KEARNEY, R
MYTH AND TERROR
CRANE BAG 1(2)
1977 1 01

4740 KEARNEY, R
TERRORISME ET SACRIFICE, LE CAS DE
L'IRLANDE DU NORD
ESPRIT 4
PARIS
1979 1 01

4741 KELLEY, K
THE LONGEST WAR: NI AND THE IRA
BRANDON
DINGLE
1982 1 02

4742 KELLY, K J
THE SURVIVAL OF THE IRA
AMERICA MAY 24
1980 1 01

4743 KENNALLY, D; PRESTON, E
BELFAST, AUGUST 1971: A CASE TO BE
ANSWERED
INDEPENDENT LABOUR PARTY
LONDON
1971 1 09

4744 KENNEDY, E M
ON THE DERRY KILLINGS
IN O'CONNOR, U (ED)
1974 1 07

4745 KITSON, F
LOW INTENSITY OPERATIONS: SUBVERSION,
INSURGENCY AND PEACEKEEPING
FABER
LONDON
1971 1 02

4746 KRUMPACH, R
TERRORISM IN NI
KRIMINALISTIK 32(1)
1978 1 01

4747 KRUMPACH, R
TERRORISM IN NI - SYNOPSIS
KRIMINALISTIK 32(2)
1978 1 01

4748 KUPER, L; KUPER, H
TERRORISM AND THE MIDDLE GROUND:
REFLECTIONS ON NI
IN KAPFERER, B (ED)
1978 1 07

4749 LABOUR AND TRADE UNION CO-ORDINATING
GROUP
WORKERS BREAK THE STOPPAGE
LABOUR AND TRADE UNION CO-ORDINATING
GROUP
BELFAST
1977 1 09

4750 LAQUEUR, W
GUERILLA: A CRITICAL AND HISTORICAL
STUDY
WEIDENFELD AND NICOLSON
LONDON
1977 2 02

4751 LAQUEUR, W
INTERPRETATIONS OF TERRORISM: FACT,
FICTION AND POLITICAL SCIENCE
J CONTEMP HIST 12
1977 1 01

4752 LAQUEUR, W
TERRORISM
WEIDENFELD AND NICOLSON
LONDON
1977 1 02

4753 LE BAILLY, J
HEROIQUE ET TENEBREUSE IRA
PRESSES DE LA CITE
PARIS
1972 1 02

4754 LEBOW, R N
ORIGINS OF SECTARIAN ASSASSINATION: THE
CASE OF BELFAST
J INT AFFAIRS 32(1)
1978 1 01

4755 LINDSAY, K
AMBUSH AT TULLYWEST: THE BRITISH
INTELLIGENCE SERVICES IN ACTION
DUNDROD PRESS
DUNDALK
1979 1 09

4756 LINDSAY, K
THE BRITISH INTELLIGENCE SERVICES IN
ACTION
DUNDROD PRESS
DUNDALK
1980 1 09

4757 LOWRY, D R
DETENTION
COLUMBIA HUMAN RIGHTS LAW R 8
NEW YORK
1977 1 01

4758 LOWRY, D R
INTERNMENT
HUM RIGHTS R 1
LONDON
1977 1 01

4759 LOWRY, D R
INTERNMENT IN NI
TOLEDO UNIV LAW R 8(1)
USA
1976 1 01

4760 LOWRY, D R
TERRORISM AND HUMAN RIGHTS
NOTRE DAME LAWYER 53
1977 1 01

4761 LUNT, J D
SOLDIERS ARE NOT POLICEMEN
ARMY QUART AND DEFENCE J 104(4)
1974 1 01

4762 LYONS, H A
RIOTS AND RIOTERS IN BELFAST
COMM FORUM 3(2)
BELFAST
1973 1 01

4763 LYONS, H A
RIOTS AND RIOTERS IN BELFAST -
DEMOGRAPHIC ANALYSIS OF 1,674 ARRESTEES
ECON AND SOC R 3(4)
DUBLIN
1972 1 01

4764 MAC AN AILI, C
THE PROVISIONAL IRA: THEIR ORIGINS AND
OBJECTIVES
IN O'CONNELL, U (ED)
DUBLIN
1974 1 07

4765 MACEOIN, G
IRISH REPUBLICAN ARMY
EIRE-IRELAND 9(2)
1974 1 01

4766 MACSTIOFAIN, S
MEMOIRS OF A REVOLUTIONARY
GORDON CREMONESI
LONDON
1975 1 02

4767 MACY, C
SINN FEIN AND THE IRAS: PARTS 1 AND 2
HUMANIST 87(1)
1972 1 01

4768 MAGILL
BRITISH INTELLIGENCE OPERATIONS IN
IRELAND
MAGILL 2(9)
1979 1 01

4769 MAGUIRE, M
TO TAKE ARMS: A YEAR IN THE PROVISIONAL
IRA
MACMILLAN/QUARTET
LONDON
1973 1 02

4770 MAGUIRE, P
POLITICAL GENERAL STRIKES
NI LEG QUART 28(3)
1977 1 01

4771 MALLIN, J
TERRORISM AS A MILITARY WEAPON
AIR UNIV R 28(2)
1977 1 01

4772 MANHATTAN, A
CATHOLIC TERROR TODAY
PARAVISION
LONDON
1969 1 02

4773 MANHATTAN, A
RELIGIOUS TERROR IN IRELAND
PARAVISION
LONDON
1970 1 02

4774 MANSFIELD, D
THE IRISH REPUBLICAN ARMY AND NI
IN O'NEILL, B E; HEATON, W R; ALBERTS, D J
(EDS)
BOULDER, COLORADO
1980 1 07

4775 MCCANN, E
THE LOYALIST STRIKE: FASCISTS OR
REVOLUTIONARIES
TIME OUT 223 JUNE
LONDON
1974 1 01

4776 MCCARTNEY, D
THE IRISH REVOLUTIONARY TRADITION
IN O'BRIEN, F (ED)
ROCKFORD, ILLINOIS
1971 2 07

4777 MCCLUNG LEE, A
THE DYNAMICS OF TERRORISM IN NI
1968-1980
SOC RES 48(1)
NEW YORK
1981 1 01

4778 MCCLUNG LEE, A
EFFORTS TO CONTROL INSURGENCY IN NI
INT J GROUP TENSIONS 4(3)
LONDON
1974 1 01

4779 MCCLUNG LEE, A
INSURGENCY AND 'PEACEKEEPING' VIOLENCE
IN NI
SSSP
NEW YORK
1972 1 11

4780 MCCLUNG LEE, A
INSURGENT AND 'PEACE-KEEPING' VIOLENCE
IN NI
SOC PROBL 20(4)
NEW YORK-ROCHESTER, MICHIGAN
1973 1 01

4781 MCGARRITY, J
RESISTANCE: THE STORY OF THE STRUGGLE IN
BRITISH OCCUPIED IRELAND
IRISH FREEDOM PRESS
DUBLIN
1957 2 09

4782 MCGOVERN, E
INTERNMENT AND DETENTION IN THE LIGHT OF
THE EUROPEAN CONVENTION ON HUMAN RIGHTS
IN BRIDGE, J W (ED)
LONDON
1973 1 07

4783 MCGUFFIN, J
THE GUINEAPIGS
PENGUIN
HARMONDSWORTH
1974 1 02

4784 MCGUFFIN, J
INTERNMENT
ANVIL
TRALEE
1973 1 02

4785 MCKINLEY, M
THE INTERNATIONAL DIMENSIONS OF
TERRORISM IN IRELAND
IN ALEXANDER, Y; O'DAY, A (EDS)
LONDON
1983 1 07

4786 MERRETT, J D; HADDEN, W A; RUTHERFORD, W H
THE INJURIES OF TERRORIST BOMBING: A
STUDY OF 1532 CONSECUTIVE PATIENTS
BRIT J SURGERY 65
1978 1 01

4787 MILLER, R; RUTHERFORD, W H; JOHNSTON, S;
MALHOTRA, V J
INJURIES CAUSED BY RUBBER BULLETS: A
REPORT ON NINETY PATIENTS
BRIT J SURGERY 62
1975 1 01

4788 MILLS, S; BAILIE, R
THE MANIPULATORS: THE REVOLUTIONARY
STRATEGY FOR AN EXPLOSION IN ULSTER
UUP
BELFAST
1969 1 09

4789 MOLONEY, E
THE IRA
MAGILL 3(12)
1980 1 01

4790 MOLONEY, E
THE SAS IN NI
MAGILL 1(12)
DUBLIN
1978 1 01

4791 MOODIE, M
THE PATRIOT GAME: THE POLITICS OF
VIOLENCE IN NI
IN LIVINGSTON, M H (ED)
WESTPORT, CONNECTICUT
1978 1 07

4792 MOSS, R
THE SPREADING IRISH CONFLICT 2: THE
SECURITY OF ULSTER
CONFLICT STUD 17
1971 1 10

4793 MOSS, R
URBAN GUERRILLAS
MAURICE TEMPLE SMITH
LONDON
1972 1 02

4794 MOSS, R
THE WAR FOR THE CITIES
NEW YORK
1972 1 02

4795 MOXON-BROWNE, E
TERRORISM IN NI: THE CASE OF THE
PROVISIONAL IRA
IN LODGE, J (ED)
OXFORD
1981 1 02

4796 MOXON-BROWNE, E
THE WATER AND THE FISH: PUBLIC OPINION
AND THE PROVISIONAL IRA IN NI
IN WILKINSON, P (ED)
LONDON
1981 1 07

4797 MULVENNA, J
INTERNMENT, WHAT NOW?
AQUARIUS
BENBURB
1974 1 01

4798 MURPHY, J A
COMMENT ON CHAPTER BY VAIZEY
IN WATT, D (ED)
LONDON
1981 1 07

4799 MURPHY, J A
THE NEW IRA, 1925-62
IN WILLIAMS, T D (ED)
1973 2 07

4800 MURPHY, S; BURKE, V
RIOTING ON THE UPPER SPRINGFIELD ROAD,
EASTER 1970
NEWMAN R 3(1)
1971 1 01

4801 MURRAY, R
'DOORSTEP' MURDERS IN BELFAST
INST BRIT GEOGR ANN CONF
1980 1 11

4802 MURRAY, R
POLITICAL VIOLENCE IN NI, 1969-1977
IN BOAL, F W; DOUGLAS, J N H (EDS)
LONDON
1982 1 07

4803 MYERS, K
THE RIFLES OF THE IRA
MAGILL 1(6)
DUBLIN
1978   01

4804 NEILSEN, S L
INTER-GROUP CONFLICT AND VIOLENCE,
BELFAST 1968
PSYCHOSOCIAL STUD 4
BERGEN UNIV NORWAY
1972 1 01

4805 NELSON, S
THE EFFECTS OF TERRORISM ON NI SOCIETY
OXFORD CONFERENCE - ARMS AND MEN
OXFORD
1978 1 11

4806 NELSON, S
ULSTER: GUNMEN IN POLITICS
NEW SOCIETY 1 MAY
1975 1 01

4807 NELSON, S
ULSTER'S UNCERTAIN DEFENDERS: LOYALISTS
IN POLITICAL, PARAMILITARY AND COMMUNITY
ORGANISATIONS
STRATHCLYDE UNIV PHD
GLASGOW
1979 1 04

4808 NI GOVERNMENT
A COMMENTARY...TO ACCOMPANY THE CAMERON
REPORT, INCORPORATING AN ACCOUNT OF
PROGRESS AND A PROGRAMME OF ACTION
HMSO
BELFAST
1969 1 03

4809 NICRA
MASSACRE AT DERRY
NICRA
BELFAST
1972 1 10

4810 O'BALLANCE, E
IRA LEADERSHIP AND PROBLEMS
IN WILKINSON, P (ED)
LONDON
1981 1 07

4811 O'BALLANCE, E
TERROR IN IRELAND
PRESIDIO PRESS
NOVATO, CALIFORNIA
1981 1 02

4812 O'BOYLE, M P
TORTURE AND EMERGENCY POWERS UNDER THE
EUROPEAN CONVENTION ON HUMAN RIGHTS
AMER J INT LAW 71(4)
1977 1 01

4813 O'BRIEN, C C
HEROD: REFLECTIONS ON POLITICAL VIOLENCE
HUTCHINSON
LONDON
1978 1 02

4814 O'BRIEN,C C
LIBERTY AND TERROR, ILLUSION OF
VIOLENCE, DELUSIONS OF LIBERATION
ENCOUNTER 49(4)
1977 1 01

4815 O'BRIEN,C C
VIOLENCE IN IRELAND: ANOTHER ALGERIA?
NEW YORK R BOOKS 17
1971 1 01

4816 O'FEARGHALL,S
LAW(?) AND ORDERS: THE BELFAST CURFEW OF
3-5 JULY 1970
CENTRAL CITIZENS' DEFENCE COMMITTEE
BELFAST
1970 1 10

4817 O'NEILL,T P
IN SEARCH OF A POLITICAL PATH: IRISH
REPUBLICANISM 1922 TO 1927
HISTORICAL STUD 10
1976 2 01

4818 O'RIAIN,S
PROVOS: PATRIOTS OR TERRORISTS?
IRISH BOOK BUREAU
DUBLIN
1974 1 09

4819 O'SUILLEABHAIN,D
TOWARDS IRELAND BRITLESS
IRISH FREEDOM PRESS
DUBLIN
1978 1 09

4820 O'SULLIVAN,P M
PATRIOT GRAVES: RESISTANCE IN IRELAND
FOLLETT
CHICAGO
1972 1 02

4821 PAINE,L
TERRORISTS
ROBERT HALE
LONDON
1975 1 02

4822 PALETZ,D L; FOZZARD,P A; AYANIAN,J Z
THE IRA, THE RED BRIGADES AND THE FALN
IN THE NEW YORK TIMES
J COMMUNICATION 32(2)
1982 1 01

4823 PATRICK,D
FETCH FELIX: THE FIGHT AGAINST THE
ULSTER BOMBERS 1976-1977
HAMISH HAMILTON
LONDON
1981 1 02

4824 PEROFF,K; HEWITT,C
RIOTING IN NI
J CONFLICT RESOL 24(4)
LONDON
1980 1 01

4825 PHILLIPS,J G
PLASTIC BULLET INJURY: A CASE REPORT
BRIT J ORAL SURGERY 3
1977 1 01

4826 PINCHER,C
INSIDE STORY
SIDGWICK AND JACKSON
LONDON
1979 1 02

4827 PISTOI,P
OPERATION MOTORMAN IN BALLYMURPHY
ESSEX UNIVERSITY
COLCHESTER, ENGLAND
1972 1 04

4828 PRICE,D L
SECURITY ATTRITION TACTICS
CONFLICT STUD 50
LONDON
1974 1 01

4829 PRICE,H E
STRATEGY AND TACTICS OF REVOLUTIONARY
TERRORISM
COMP STUD SOC HIST 19
THE HAGUE - ANN ARBOR, MICHIGAN
1977 1 01

4830 PURCELL,H
REVOLUTIONARY WAR: GUERILLA WARFARE AND
TERRORISM IN OUR TIME
HAMISH HAMILTON
LONDON
1980 1 02

4831 RAYMOND,R J
THE UNITED STATES AND TERRORISM IN
IRELAND, 1969-1981
IN ALEXANDER,Y; O'DAY,A (EDS)
LONDON
1983 1 07

4832 RED PATRIOT
AN ANALYSIS OF THE SIGNIFICANCE OF THE
ULSTER WORKERS' STRIKE 1974
DUBLIN
1974 1 09

4833 REDGRAVE,P
PLASTIC BULLETS: THE MEDICAL FACTS
WLD MEDICINE 5 FEB
1983 1 01

4834 REED,J
ATTENTION BY TERROR
WAR MONTHLY 9(12)
1981 1 01

4835 REES,M
TERRORISM IN IRELAND AND BRITAIN'S
RESPONSE
IN WILKINSON,P (ED)
LONDON
1981 1 07

4836 RESETTLEMENT ASSOCIATION OF NI
FIRST REPORT
RESETTLEMENT ASSOC NI
BELFAST
1975 2 10

4837 RISTOW,W; SHALLICE,T
TAKING THE HOOD OFF BRITISH TORTURE
NEW SCIENTIST 5 AUG
1976 1 01

4838 ROBB,J; MATTHEWS,J G
THE INJURIES AND MANAGEMENT OF RIOT
CASUALTIES
BRIT J SURGERY 58(6)
1971 1 01

4839 ROBERTS,A
THE BRITISH ARMED FORCES AND SOCIETY
ARMED FORCES AND SOC 3(4)
1977 1 01

4840 ROBERTS,A
ULSTER: ONLY THE PROVISIONAL ENDURES
NEW SOCIETY 9 JAN
LONDON
1977 1 10

4841 ROBINSON,P
CAPITAL PUNISHMENT FOR CAPITAL CRIME
DEMOCRATIC UNIONIST PARTY
BELFAST
      1 09

4842 ROBINSON,P
SAVAGERY AND SUFFERING: A GLIMPSE AT THE
BUTCHERY AND BRUTALITY OF THE IRA
DEMOCRATIC UNIONIST PARTY
BELFAST
1981 1 09

4843 ROLSTON,B
IRON FISTS, KID GLOVES
CASE CON 20
LONDON
1975 1 01

4844 ROSENHEAD, J
A NEW LOOK AT 'LESS LETHAL' WEAPONS
NEW SCIENTIST 16 DEC
LONDON
1976 1   01

4845 ROSENHEAD, J
SOLDIER BLUE
NEW SOCIALIST MAY/JUN
LONDON
1982 1   01

4846 ROSENHEAD, J
THE TECHNOLOGY OF RIOT CONTROL
NEW SCIENTIST 23 JULY
LONDON
1981 1   01

4847 ROWTHORN, B
IRELAND'S INTRACTABLE CRISIS: EXCLUSIVE
INTERVIEWS WITH UDA AND PROVISIONALS
MARXISM TODAY 25(12)
LONDON
1981 1   01

4848 RUTHERFORD, W H
THE INJURIES OF CIVIL DISORDER
COMM HEALTH 6(14)
1974 1   01

4849 SALMON, T C
THE CHANGING NATURE OF IRISH DEFENCE
POLICY
WLD TODAY 35(11)
LONDON
1979 1   01

4850 SAYERS, J E
AN ERUPTION IN LONDONDERRY
ROUND TABLE 59(233)
BELFAST
1969 1   01

4851 SCARMAN, LORD
VIOLENCE AND CIVIL DISTURBANCE IN NI
1969
HMSO CMD 566
BELFAST
1972 1   03

4852 SCHELLENBERG, J A
AREA VARIATIONS OF VIOLENCE IN NI
SOCIOL FOCUS 10(1)
1977 1   01

4853 SCHELLENBERG, J A
VIOLENCE IN NI 1965-75
INT J GROUP TENSIONS 6
1976 1   07

4854 SCHLESINGER, P
'TERRORISM', THE MEDIA AND THE
LIBERAL-DEMOCRATIC STATE: A CRITIQUE OF
THE ORTHODOXY
SOC RES 48(1)
NEW YORK
1981 1   01

4855 SCOTT, S; CAMPBELL, D
THE SECRET WAR FOR IRELAND
NEW STATESMAN
LONDON
1979 1   01

4856 SHALLICE, T
THE HARMLESS BULLET THAT KILLS
NEW STATESMAN AUG 14
LONDON
1981 1   01

4857 SHALLICE, T
THE ULSTER DEPTH INTERROGATION
TECHNIQUES
COGNITION 1(4)
1973 1   01

4858 SHAW, J
PULMONARY CONTASION IN CHILDREN DUE TO
RUBBER BULLET INJURIES
BRIT MED J 2
LONDON
1972 1   01

4859 SHAW, J ET AL
TEN YEARS OF TERRORISM
RUSI
LONDON
1979 1   02

4860 SILENT TOO LONG
SILENT TOO LONG: THE ASSOCIATION OF THE
FAMILIES OF INNOCENT VICTIMS OF
LOYALIST, UDR, RUC AND BRITISH ARMY
VIOLENCE
SILENT TOO LONG
BELFAST
1982 1   09

4861 SINN FEIN (OFFICIAL)
THE IRA SPEAKS
SINN FEIN (OFFICIAL)
DUBLIN
1970 1   09

4862 SINN FEIN (OFFICIAL)
SPIES IN IRELAND: THE LITTLEJOHN
MEMORANDUM
LONDON
       1   09

4863 SINN FEIN (PROVISIONAL)
THE H-BLOCK CONVEYOR BELT
SINN FEIN POW DEPARTMENT
DUBLIN
1979 1   09

4864 SINN FEIN (PROVISIONAL)
THE INFORMERS
SINN FEIN (PROVISIONAL)
DUBLIN
1983 1   09

4865 SMYTH, C
THE AXIS AGAINST ULSTER: THE IRA, EIRE
AND THE CHURCH OF ROME
PURITAN PRINTING
BELFAST
1972 1   09

4866 SMYTH, J
CIVIL LIBERTIES AND RIOT CONTROL IN NI
ECPR
ESSEX
1983 1   11

4867 SMYTH, J
NI: COUNTER INSURGENCY AS STATE POLICY
ECPR
ESSEX
1983 1   11

4868 SOBEL, L
NI
IN SOBEL, L
OXFORD
1975 1   01

4869 SOBEL, L
NI
IN SOBEL, L
OXFORD
1978 1   01

4870 SPJUT, R
TORTURE UNDER THE EUROPEAN CONVENTION ON
HUMAN RIGHTS
AMER J INT LAW 73(2)
WASHINGTON
1979 1   01

4871 STAFFORD, L
HOW TWO BOYS DIED
NEW STATESMAN JAN 29
LONDON
1982 1   01

4872 STERLING, C
THE TERROR NETWORK: THE SECRET WAR OF
INTERNATIONAL TERRORISM
WEIDENFELD AND NICOLSON
LONDON
1981 1 02

4873 STERLING, C
TERRORISM: TRACING THE INTERNATIONAL
NETWORK
NY TIMES MAG MAR 1
NEW YORK
1981 1 01

4874 STETLER, R
THE BATTLE OF THE BOGSIDE
SHEED AND WARD
LONDON
1970 1 02

4875 STETLER, R
NI FROM CIVIL RIGHTS TO ARMED STRUGGLE
MONTHLY R NOV
NEW YORK
1970 1 01

4876 STRAWSON, J
THE ARMY TODAY
BLACKWOOD'S MAG 314
1973 1 01

4877 STYLES, G
BOMBS HAVE NO PITY
LUSCOMBE
LONDON
1975 1 02

4878 TAYLOR, P
BEATING THE TERRORISTS?
PENGUIN
HARMONDSWORTH
1980 1 02

4879 TERRAINE, J ET AL
TERRORISM AND THE MEDIA
IN RUSI
LONDON
1979 1 07

4880 TITTMAR, H
CROWD CONTROL: A COMPARATIVE VIEWPOINT
RUSI J 124
1979 1 01

4881 TOMLINSON, M
POLICING THE PERIPHERY: IDEOLOGIES OF
REPRESSION IN NI
B SOC POL 5
1980 1 01

4882 TOMLINSON, M
REFORMING REPRESSION
IN O'DOWD, L; ROLSTON, B; TOMLINSON, M
LONDON
1980 1 07

4883 TUGWELL, M
POLITICS AND PROPAGANDA OF THE
PROVISIONAL IRA
IN WILKINSON, P (ED)
LONDON
1981 1 07

4884 ULSTER DEFENCE ASSOCIATION
THE SHANKILL DISTURBANCES
UDA
BELFAST
1972 1 09

4885 ULSTER UNIONIST PARTY
ULSTER - THE FACTS: BORN IN THE SHADOWS
- THE PLOT TO SEIZE ULSTER
UUP
BELFAST
1971 1 09

4886 ULSTER UNIONIST PARTY
ULSTER THE FACTS - 96 HOURS - THE
ANATOMY OF AN UPRISING
UUP
BELFAST
1969 1 09

4887 ULSTER UNIONIST PARTY
ULSTER: STEPPING STONE FOR COMMUNISM
UUP
BELFAST
1972 1 09

4888 ULSTER WORKERS COUNCIL
ULSTER GENERAL STRIKE
BELFAST
1974 1 09

4889 ULSTER YOUNG UNIONIST COUNCIL
GUNMEN AND THE LAW ...INVESTIGATION INTO
WAYS OF STRENGTHENING THE LAW TO DEFEAT
TERRORISM
ULSTER YOUNG UNIONIST COUNCIL
BELFAST
1981 1 09

4890 UNIONIST RESEARCH DEPARTMENT
THE CASE FOR INTERNMENT
UUP
BELFAST
1971 1 09

4891 UNITED ULSTER UNIONIST COUNCIL
SECURITY IN NI
BELFAST
1975 1 09

4892 VAIZEY, J
THE MIND OF REPUBLICANISM
IN WATT, D (ED)
LONDON
1981 1 07

4893 VAN STRAUBENZEE, W R
INTERNATIONAL LAW AND TERRORISM
IN RUSI
LONDON
1979 1 07

4894 VERRIER, A
THROUGH THE LOOKING GLASS
CAPE
LONDON
1983 1 02

4895 VILLIERS, P
WHERE ANGELS FEAR TO TREAD: AN EXCURSION
INTO IRISH POLITICS
INSTITUTE FOR DEFENCE STUD J 124(3)
1979 1 01

4896 WALKER, C
THE NEW IRISH TERRORISM
SPECTATOR 19 MAY
1979 1 01

4897 WALSH, S P
ENGLISH COLONIALISM VS. IRA 'TERRORISM':
THE LEGACY OF HATRED
USA TODAY JAN
1981 1 01

4898 WARD, M
MARGINALITY AND MILITANCY: CUMANN NA
MBAN 1914-1936
IN MORGAN A; PURDIE B (EDS)
LONDON
1980 2 07

4899 WARD, M
UNMANAGEABLE REVOLUTIONARIES
PLUTO/BRANDON
LONDON/DINGLE
1983 1 02

4900 WHITLOCK, R I; GORMAN, J M
SOME MISSILE INJURIES DUE TO CIVIL
UNREST IN NI
INT J ORAL SURGERY 4
1978 1 01

4901 WIDGERY, LORD
REPORT OF THE WIDGERY TRIBUNAL
HMSO
LONDON
1972 1 03

4902 WIENER, R; BAYLEY, J
BRITISH TROOPS AND ULSTER'S POLITICAL
LEADERS
NEW SOCIETY AUG 20
LONDON
1970 1 10

4903 WILKINSON, P
CAN A STATE BE 'TERRORIST'?
INT AFFAIRS (LONDON) 57(3)
LONDON
1981 1 01

4904 WILKINSON, P
POLITICAL TERRORISM
MACMILLAN
LONDON
1974 1 02

4905 WILKINSON, P
THE PROVISIONAL IRA: AN ASSESSMENT IN
THE WAKE OF THE 1981 HUNGER STRIKE
GVT AND OPPOSITION SPRING
1982 1 01

4906 WILKINSON, P
TERRORISM AND THE LIBERAL STATE
MACMILLAN
LONDON
1977 1 02

4907 WINBLAD, L
IRA INIFRAN - EN EUROPEISK GERILLA
TRYCKT
1972 1 02

4908 WORKERS' RESEARCH UNIT
REPRESSION: THE VELVET GLOVE AND THE
IRON FIST
WRU BULLETIN 2
BELFAST
1977 1 09

4909 WORLD TODAY
NI: COULD THE UN KEEP THE PEACE?
WLD TODAY JULY
1981 1 01

4910 WRIGHT, S
THE CAMPAIGN OF THE BRITISH ARMY IN NI:
A CASE OF SELF-LEGITIMATION
LANCASTER UNIV
LANCASTER
1978 1 11

4911 YOUNG, R; ADAMS, J
THE CASE FOR DETENTION
BOW PUBLICATIONS
LONDON
1974 1 09

4912 ZUMULINA, L A
THE IRISH REPUBLICAN ARMY
VOPROSY ISTORII 8
MOSCOW
1973 1 01

4913 AMNESTY INTERNATIONAL
REPORT OF AN AMNESTY INTERNATIONAL
MISSION TO NI
AMNESTY INTERNATIONAL
LONDON
1978 1   10

4914 AMNESTY INTERNATIONAL
REPORT OF AN INQUIRY INTO ALLEGATIONS OF
ILL TREATMENT IN NI
AMNESTY INTERNATIONAL
LONDON
1975 1   10

4915 AMNESTY INTERNATIONAL
REPORT ON TORTURE
DUCKWORTH
LONDON
1975 1   11

4916 ASSOCIATION FOR LEGAL JUSTICE
TORTURE - THE RECORD OF BRITISH
BRUTALITY IN IRELAND
ASSOCIATION FOR LEGAL JUSTICE AND
NORTHERN AID
BELFAST
1971 1   09

4917 BARTON, B
THE GOVERNMENT OF NI, 1920-23
ATHOL BOOKS
BELFAST
1980 2   09

4918 BARTON, B
NI GOVERNMENT POLICY IN RELATION TO LAW
AND ORDER AND LOCAL GOVERNMENT 1920-1923
NUU MA
COLERAINE
1977 2   04

4919 BAXTER, T
LOCKING UP THE CHILDREN IN NI
SCOPE 35
BELFAST
1980 2   01

4920 BENNETT REPORT
REPORT OF THE COMMITTEE OF INQUIRY INTO
POLICE INTERROGATION PROCEDURES IN NI
HMSO CMND 7497
LONDON
1979 1   03

4921 BINAYISA, C N
COMPARATIVE STUDY OF SOME JUVENILE
JUSTICE INSTITUTIONS...
QUB LLM
BELFAST
1969 2   04

4922 BISHOP, J W
LAW IN THE CONTROL OF TERRORISM AND
INSURRECTION: THE BRITISH LABORATORY
EXPERIENCE
LAW AND CONTEMPORARY SOC PROBLEMS 42(2)
DURHAM N. CAROLINA
1978 1   01

4923 BLACK REPORT
LEGISLATION AND SERVICES FOR CHILDREN
AND YOUNG PERSONS IN NI
DHSS (NI)
BELFAST
1979 2   03

4924 BLAKE, N
CIVIL LIBERTIES AND SOCIALISM IN NI
NIASL
BELFAST
1983 1   10

4925 BOEHRINGER, G H
BEYOND HUNT: A POLICING POLICY FOR NI
SOC STUD 2(4)
1973 1   01

4926 BOEHRINGER, G H
FUTURE OF POLICING IN NI
COMM FORUM 3(2)
1973 1   01

4927 BOEHRINGER, G H
MEMORANDUM ON DETENTION UNDER EMERGENCY
REGULATIONS IN NI - AND IN THE UNITED
KINGDOM
AUTHOR
BELFAST
1972 1   08

4928 BOEHRINGER, G H
MEMORANDUM TO THE PARKER COMMITTEE ON
INTERROGATION PROCEDURES
AUTHOR
BELFAST
1971 1   08

4929 BOEHRINGER, G H
TOWARDS A THEORETICAL ORIENTATION IN THE
SOCIOLOGY OF POLICING: THE NI CASE
BSA SOCIOL OF LAW STUDY GROUP
1973 1   08

4930 BONNER, D
IRELAND V. UNITED KINGDOM
INT COMP LAW QUART 27
1975 1   01

4931 BOWDEN, T
BREAKDOWN OF PUBLIC SECURITY
SAGE
LONDON
1977 2   07

4932 BOWDEN, T
MAN IN THE MIDDLE: THE UK POLICE
CONFLICT STUD 68
1978 2   01

4933 BOYCE, D G
NORMAL POLICING: PUBLIC ORDER IN NI
SINCE PARTITION
EIRE-IRELAND 14(4)
ST PAUL
1979 1   01

4934 BOYD, R; FELIX, P; ARDILL, S; KELLY, B
WOMEN IN IRELAND: OUR STRUGGLE
SPARE RIB 130
LONDON
1983 I   01

4935 BOYLE, C
VIOLENCE AGAINST WIVES: THE CRIMINAL LAW
IN RETREAT?
NI LEG QUART 31(1)
1980 2   01

4936 BOYLE, K
THE DISEASE CONCEPT OF CRIME: THE
MINIMUM SENTENCES ACT
NI LEG QUART 11(4)
1970 2   01

4937 BOYLE, K
EMERGENCY CONDITIONS
IN CAMPBELL, C M (ED)
LONDON
1980 1   07

4938 BOYLE, K
POLICE AND POLICE REFORMS IN NI
QUB
BELFAST
1970 1   08

4939 BOYLE,K; HADDEN,T; HILLYARD,P
LAW AND STATE: THE CASE OF NI
MARTIN ROBERTSON
LONDON
1975 1   02

4940 BOYLE,K; HADDEN,T; HILLYARD,P
TEN YEARS ON IN NI
COBDEN TRUST
LONDON
1981 1   02

4941 BOYLE,K; HANNUM,H
IRELAND IN STRASBOURG
IR JURIST 7
1972 1   01

4942 BOYLE,K; HANNUM,H
IRELAND IN STRASBOURG: FINAL DECISIONS
IR JURIST 11
1976 1   01

4943 BRADY,B; FAUL,D; MURRAY,R
CORRUPTION OF LAW: MEMORANDUM TO
GARDINER COMMITTEE
AUTHOR
DUNGANNON
1974 1   09

4944 BREATHNACH,S
IRISH POLICE
ANVIL
DUBLIN
1974 2   02

4945 BRETT,C E B
LEGAL AID AND ADVICE BILL (NI)
NI LEG QUART 15(3)
1964 2   01

4946 BROCKWAY,F
NI BILL OF RIGHTS
CONNOLLY PUBLICATIONS
LONDON
1973 1   09

4947 BURNS,G
THE LAW AND GAYS IN NI
NORTHERN GAY RIGHTS ASSOCIATION
BELFAST
1981 2   09

4948 CALVERT,H
HUMAN RIGHTS IN NI
R INT COMMISSION OF JURISTS
1969 2   01

4949 CALVERT,H
SPECIAL POWERS EXTRAORDINARY
NI LEG QUART 20(1)
1968 1   01

4950 CAMPBELL,C M
THE HOSTILE ENVIRONMENT
IN CAMPBELL,C M (ED)
LONDON
1980 1   07

4951 CAMPBELL,C M
LAW CENTRES AND LEGAL SERVICES
NI OFFICE
BELFAST
1980 2   03

4952 CARLIN,T
A CHARTER FOR NI
IN CAMPBELL,C M (ED)
LONDON
1980 1   07

4953 CARROLL,W D
SEARCH FOR JUSTICE IN NI
NEW YORK UNIV J INT LAW AND POLITICS
6(1)
1973 1   01

4954 CARTER,F
JUVENILE DELINQUENCY AREAS IN BELFAST
QUB MED
BELFAST
1953 2   04

4955 CENTRAL CITIZENS' DEFENCE COMMITTEE
BLACK PAPER: THE STORY OF THE POLICE
CENTRAL CITIZENS' DEFENCE COMMITTEE
BELFAST
1973 1   09

4956 CENTRAL CITIZENS' DEFENCE COMMITTEE
THE TRUE STORY - TERROR IN NI
CENTRAL CITIZENS' DEFENCE COMMITTEE
DERRY
1969 1   10

4957 CLUTTERBUCK,R
INTIMIDATION OF WITNESSES AND JURIES
ARMY QUART AND DEFENCE J 104(3)
1974 1   01

4958 COHEN,S
STATE, THE LAW AND IRELAND
NCCL
MANCHESTER
1974 1   10

4959 COMMUNITY HOMES SCHOOL GAZETTE
EFFECTS OF RELATIONS WITH STAFF ON
ATTITUDES AND BEHAVIOUR OF DELINQUENT
BOYS
COMMUNITY HOMES SCHOOL GAZ 72(8)
1978 2   01

4960 COMPTON,E
REPORT OF ENQUIRY INTO ALLEGATIONS...OF
PHYSICAL BRUTALITY IN NI...
HMSO CMND 4823
LONDON
1971 1   03

4961 COOGAN,T P
ON THE BLANKET
WARD RIVER PRESS
DUBLIN
1980 1   02

4962 COSTELLO,D
INTERNATIONAL TERRORISM AND THE
DEVELOPMENT OF THE PRINCIPLE AUT DEDERE
AUT JUDICARE
IR JURIST 9(2)
1974 1   01

4963 CRAWFORD,C
LONG KESH: AN ALTERNATIVE PERSPECTIVE
CRANFIELD INSTITUTE OF TECHNOLOGY MSC
CRANFIELD
1979 1   04

4964 CRUTCHLY,J
JOYRIDING PROBLEM: WEST BELFAST
CONSTABULARY GAZETTE MAY
1982 1   01

4965 D'ARCY,M
TELL THEM EVERYTHING
PLUTO
LONDON
1981 1   02

4966 DALY,C B
SPECIAL POWERS ACT
NEWMAN R 3(1)
1971 1   01

4967 DASH,S
JUSTICE DENIED
INT LEAGUE FOR RIGHTS OF MAN
1972 1   10

4968 DASH,S
JUSTICE DENIED: A CHALLENGE TO LORD
WIDGERY'S REPORT ON BLOODY SUNDAY
NCCL
LONDON
1972 1   10

4969 DAWSON,J; STRINGER,W
IRISH POLITICAL PRISONERS
IRL SOCIALIST R
LONDON
1978 1 01

4970 DEUTSCH,R
LA PRISON DE MAZE
ET IRL 6
LILLE
1981 1 01

4971 DICKEY,A
ANTI-INCITEMENT LEGISLATION IN NI
NEW COMM 1(2)
1972 1 01

4972 DIPLOCK REPORT
REPORT OF COMMISSION TO CONSIDER LEGAL
PROCEDURES TO DEAL WITH TERRORIST
ACTIVITIES IN NI
HMSO CMND 5185
LONDON
1972 1 03

4973 DONALDSON,A
FUNDAMENTAL RIGHTS IN THE CONSTITUTION
OF NI
CANADIAN BAR R 37
1959 2 01

4974 DOWLING,K
CIVIL RIGHTS, HUMAN RIGHTS AND TERRORISM
IN NI
J INTERGROUP RELATIONS 7(4)
1979 1 01

4975 DOWNEY,J
CONFLICT AND CRIME IN NI
OHIO UNIV PHD
1978 1 04

4976 DOWNEY,J
A NOTE ON VIOLENT CRIME IN NI
WISCONSIN SOCIOLOGIST 15(4)
1978 1 01

4977 EDWARDS,J
SPECIAL POWERS IN NI
CRIMINAL LAW R
1956 1 01

4978 EL SIMAT,E
NON-FATAL CRIMES OF VIOLENCE: A
COMPARATIVE STUDY OF LEGAL DEFINITIONS
AND CLASSIFICATION AND MODES OF
TREATMENT OF OFFENCES...
QUB LLM
BELFAST
1971 2 04

4979 ELLIOTT,R; LOCKHART.W H
CHARACTERISTICS OF SCHEDULED OFFENDERS
AND JUVENILE DELINQUENTS
IN HARBISON,J; HARBISON,J (EDS)
1980 1 07

4980 EUROPEAN COMMISSION OF HUMAN RIGHTS
IRELAND AGAINST THE UNITED KINGDOM OF
GREAT BRITAIN AND NI
COUNCIL OF EUROPE
STRASBOURG
1976 1 03

4981 EUROPEAN COURT OF HUMAN RIGHTS
CASE OF IRELAND AGAINST THE UNITED
KINGDOM, 1976-1978
EUROPEAN COURT OF HUMAN RIGHTS
COLOGNE
1980 1 02

4982 EVE,J
DOMESTIC PROCEEDINGS IN MAGISTRATES'
COURTS: A DISCUSSION OF THE DOMESTIC
PROCEEDINGS (NI) ORDER 1980
SLS/FACULTY OF LAW QUB
BELFAST
1981 2 08

4983 FABIAN SOCIETY
EMERGENCY POWERS: A FRESH START
FABIAN SOCIETY
LONDON
1972 1 09

4984 FAIRWEATHER,E
A VISIT TO PATRICK 'ON THE BLANKET'
NEW SOCIETY 7 MAY
LONDON
1981 1 01

4985 FARRELL,M; MCCULLOUGH,P
BEHIND THE WIRE
PD
BELFAST
1974 1 09

4986 FAUL,D; MURRAY,R
THE BIRMINGHAM FRAMEWORK
AUTHORS
DUNGANNON
1976 1 10

4987 FAUL,D; MURRAY,R
BRITISH ARMY AND SPECIAL BRANCH RUC
BRUTALITIES DEC 1971-1972
AUTHORS
CAVAN
1972 1 10

4988 FAUL,D; MURRAY,R
THE BRITISH DIMENSION: BRUTALITY, MURDER
AND LEGAL DUPLICITY IN NI
AUTHORS
DUNGANNON
1980 1 10

4989 FAUL,D; MURRAY,R
CASTLEREAGH FILE
AUTHORS
DUNGANNON
1978 1 10

4990 FAUL,D; MURRAY,R
FLAMES OF LONG KESH
AUTHORS
DUNGANNON
1974 1 10

4991 FAUL,D; MURRAY,R
H BLOCKS: BRITISH JAIL FOR IRISH
POLITICAL PRISONERS
AUTHORS
DUNGANNON
1979 1 10

4992 FAUL,D; MURRAY,R
INIQUITY OF INTERNMENT, 9 AUG 1971 - 9
AUG 1974
AUTHORS
DUNGANNON
1974 1 10

4993 FAUL,D; MURRAY,R
THE RUC: THE BLACK AND BLUE BOOK
AUTHORS
DUNGANNON
1973 1 10

4994 FAUL,D; MURRAY,R
WHITELAW'S TRIBUNALS: LONG KESH
INTERNMENT CAMP NOV 1972-JAN 1973
AUTHORS
DUNGANNON
1973 1 10

4995 FEENEY,H
IN THE CARE OF HER MAJESTY'S PRISONS
REPUBLICAN PRESS CENTRE
BELFAST
1976 1 09

4996 FOLEY,T; GRAHAM,P
RIGHTS AND RESPONSIBILITIES: A YOUNG
PERSON'S GUIDE TO THE LAW AND EMERGENCY
LEGISLATION IN NI
PEACE PEOPLE
BELFAST
1980 1 09

4997 FORDE,B; SPENCER,C
HOPE IN BOMB CITY
MARSHALL, MORGAN AND SCOTT
LONDON
1980 1 02

4998 FORDE,B; SPENCER,C
LOVE IN BOMB CITY
MARSHALLS
LONDON
1982 1 02

4999 GARDINER REPORT
MEASURES TO DEAL WITH TERRORISM IN NI
HMSO CMND 5847
LONDON
1975 1 03

5000 GARDINER,LORD
INTERROGATION PROCEDURES
R INT COMMISSION OF JURISTS 8
1972 1 01

5001 GARRETT,B
PROBLEMS AND PROSPECTS
IN CAMPBELL,C M (ED)
LONDON
1980 1 07

5002 GIBSON,B
THE BIRMINGHAM BOMBS
BARRY ROSE
LONDON
1976 1 02

5003 GORMALLY,B
PICK THEM UP OR PUT THEM DOWN: AN
ASSESSMENT OF THE BLACK REPORT
HOWARD J 16
1978 2 01

5004 GORMALLY,B; LYNER,O; MULLIGAN,G;
WARDEN,M
UNEMPLOYMENT AND YOUNG OFFENDERS IN NI
NI ASSOCIATION FOR THE CARE AND
RESETTLEMENT OF OFFENDERS
BELFAST
1981 2 10

5005 GRAHAM,E S D
JUDICIAL REVIEW: FROM THE FROG TO MICKEY
MOUSE
NI LEG QUART 32
BELFAST
1981 2 01

5006 GRAHAM,E S D
JUDICIAL REVIEW: THE NEW PROCEDURES IN
NI
NI LEG QUART 31
BELFAST
1980 2 01

5007 GRALTON
DIPLOCKING THEM UP
GRALTON 2
DUBLIN
1982 1 01

5008 GREER,D S
THE ADMISSIBILITY OF CONFESSIONS UNDER
THE NI (EMERGENCY PROVISIONS) ACT
NI LEG QUART 31(3)
BELFAST
1980 1 01

5009 GREER,D S
LEGAL AID FOR SUMMARY TRIALS IN NI
NI LEG QUART 22(4)
1971 2 01

5010 GREER,D S
THE LEGAL AID, ADVICE AND ASSISTANCE
(NI) ORDER 1981 (NI STATUTES ANNOTATE D
NO. 1)
SLS/FACULTY OF LAW QUB
BELFAST
1982 2 10

5011 GREER,D S
LEGAL CONTROL OF MILITARY OPERATIONS: A
MISSED OPPORTUNITY
NI LEG QUART 31
BELFAST
1980 1 01

5012 GREER,D S
SMALL CLAIMS: THE NEW PROCEDURE IN NI
SLS/FACULTY OF LAW QUB
BELFAST
1981 2 10

5013 GREER,D S
SOME RECENT DEVELOPMENTS IN THE LAW OF
NEGLIGENCE AND ASSESSMENT OF DAMAGES
BELFAST SOLICITORS' ASSOCIATION
BELFAST
1978 2 10

5014 GREER,D S; LEONARD,L M
SMALL CLAIMS IN NI
NI CONSUMER COUNCIL
BELFAST
1980 2 03

5015 GREER,D S; MITCHELL,V A
COMPENSATION FOR CRIMINAL INJURIES TO
PERSONS IN NI
NI LEG QUART (SUPPL)
1978 2 01

5016 GREER,S
MILITARY INTERVENTION IN CIVIL
DISTURBANCES: THE LEGAL BASIS
RECONSIDERED
PUBL LAW
LONDON
1983 1 01

5017 GRIFFITHS,B
A UNIQUE SERVICE ON PROBATION
COMM CARE 154
1977 2 01

5018 HADDEN,T
DEBACLE OF ULSTER INTERNMENT
NEW SOCIETY 31(644)
LONDON
1975 1 01

5019 HADDEN,T; BOYLE,K
HUNT REPORT - CONVINCING JUSTICE
NEW LAW J
LONDON
1969 1 01

5020 HADDEN,T; HILLYARD,P
JUSTICE IN A CRISIS
NEW SOCIETY 18 OCT
LONDON
1973 1 01

5021 HADDEN,T; HILLYARD,P
JUSTICE IN NI: A STUDY IN SOCIAL
CONFIDENCE
COBDEN TRUST
LONDON
1973 1 02

5022 HADDEN,T; HILLYARD,P; BOYLE,K
'TROOPS OUT' IS NO ANSWER
NEW SOCIETY 20 NOV
LONDON
1980 1 01

5023 HADDEN,T; HILLYARD,P; BOYLE,K
HOW FAIR ARE THE ULSTER TRIALS?
NEW SOCIETY 13 NOV
LONDON
1980 1 01

5024 HADDEN,T; HILLYARD,P; BOYLE,K
NI: THE COMMUNAL ROOTS OF VIOLENCE
NEW SOCIETY 6 NOV
LONDON
1980 1 01

5025 HADDEN,T; WRIGHT,S
A TERRORIST TRIAL IN CRUMLIN ROAD
NEW SOCIETY 28 JUN
LONDON
1979 1   01

5026 HADFIELD,B
THE ONUS OF PROOF IN DISCRIMINATION
CASES
NI LEG QUART 32(1)
BELFAST
1981 1   01

5027 HADFIELD,B
A SOCIO-HISTORICAL ANALYSIS OF THE
PROVISION OF LEGAL SERVICES
QUB LLM
BELFAST
1977 2   04

5028 HANNA,T
MONEY BEHIND BARS: THE COST OF RUNNING
THE MAZE
TRADE AND INDUSTRY IN NI 5(6)
BELFAST
1982 1   01

5029 HARVEY,R
DIPLOCK AND THE ASSAULT ON CIVIL
LIBERTIES: TIME TO REPEAL NI'S EMERGENCY
LEGISLATION
HALDANE SOCIETY OF SOCIALIST LAWYERS
LONDON
1981 1   10

5030 HEATLEY,P; TOMLINSON,M
THE POLITICS OF IMPRISONMENT IN IRELAND:
AN HISTORICAL OVERVIEW
DEPT SOC STUD QUB
BELFAST
1981 1   08

5031 HEATLEY,P; TOMLINSON,M
THE POLITICS OF IMPRISONMENT IN IRELAND:
SOME HISTORICAL NOTES
IN HILLYARD,P; SQUIRES,P (EDS)
BRISTOL
1982 1   07

5032 HERMON,J
ROYAL ULSTER CONSTABULARY
POLICE J OCT/DEC
LONDON
1981 1   01

5033 HEWITT,P
THE ABUSE OF POWER: CIVIL LIBERTIES IN
THE UNITED KINGDOM
MARTIN ROBERTSON
OXFORD
1981 1   02

5034 HEWITT,P
DEFENDING CIVIL LIBERTIES
IN CAMPBELL,C M (ED)
LONDON
1980 1   07

5035 HIGGINS,J
IRISH POLITICAL PRISONERS IN ENGLAND:
SPECIAL CATEGORY 'A'
SINN FEIN POW DEPARTMENT
DUBLIN
1980 1   09

5036 HILLYARD,P
THE NATURE AND EXTENT OF CRIME IN
IRELAND
KEELE UNIV MA
1969 2   04

5037 HILLYARD,P
POLICE AND PENAL SERVICES
IN DARBY,J; WILLIAMSON,A (EDS)
LONDON
1978 1   07

5038 HILLYARD,P
PUBLIC ATTITUDES TOWARDS THE POLICE IN A
MEDIUM-SIZED TOWN IN NI
IR JURIST 7(1)
DUBLIN
1972 1   01

5039 HILLYARD,P; BOYLE,K
THE DIPLOCK COURT STRATEGY: SOME
REFLECTIONS ON LAW AND THE POLITICS OF
LAW
IN KELLY,M; O'DOWD,L; WICKHAM,J (EDS)
DUBLIN
1982 1   07

5040 HITCHENS,C
HUMAN RIGHTS IN ULSTER - WITHOUT
IDENTIFIABLE CULPRITS
NATION 229(6)
1979 1   01

5041 HOLLAND,J
THE SECRET TORTURERS
NATION 229 SEPT 8
1979 1   01

5042 HOLLAND,M
ROY MASON'S GUILT
MAGILL 2(7)
1979 1   01

5043 HUNT,LORD
REPORT OF THE ADVISORY COMMITTEE ON
POLICE IN NI
HMSO CMD 535
BELFAST
1969 1   03

5044 INTERNATIONAL COMMISSION OF JURISTS'
REVIEW
HUMAN RIGHTS IN NI
INT COMMISSION OF JURISTS' R 2
1969 1   01

5045 IRIS
FOUR YEARS ON THE BLANKET
IRIS 1(2)
DUBLIN
1981 1   01

5046 IRIS
SIXTY YEARS OF REPRESSION: AN OUTLINE
HISTORY OF THE RUC
IRIS 3
DUBLIN
1982 1   01

5047 IRISH COUNCIL OF CHURCHES ADVISORY FORUM
THE H-BLOCK ISSUE: AN INTERIM STUDY
IRISH COUNCIL OF CHURCHES
BELFAST
1980 1   10

5048 JACKSON,J D
THE 'MENS REA' OF MURDER IN NI
NI LEG QUART 32(2)
BELFAST
1981 1   01

5049 JARDINE,E
INTRODUCTION TO THE SYMPOSIUM ON
JUVENILE DELINQUENCY - A NI PERSPECTIVE
B BRIT PSYCHOL SOC MAY
1980 2   01

5050 JARDINE,E
SOME SOCIAL, EDUCATIONAL AND
PSYCHOLOGICAL VARIABLES ASSOCIATED WITH
THE ADJUSTMENT OF BOYS IN TWO NI
TRAINING SCHOOLS
QUB MSC
BELFAST
1978 2   04

5051 JARDINE,E; CURRAN,J D; HARBISON,J
YOUNG OFFENDERS AND THEIR OFFENCES: SOME
COMPARISONS BETWEEN NI, ENGLAND AND
SCOTLAND
BRIT PSYCHOL SOCIETY, NI REGIONAL OFFICE
CONF
BELFAST
1978 2 11

5052 JORGENSEN,B
DEFENDING THE TERRORISTS: QUEEN'S
COUNSEL BEFORE THE DIPLOCK COURTS
IN HILLYARD,P; SQUIRES,P (EDS)
BRISTOL
1982 1 07

5053 JORGENSEN,B
DEFENDING THE TERRORISTS: QUEEN'S
COUNSEL BEFORE THE DIPLOCK COURTS OF NI
J LAW AND SOC 9(1)
OXFORD
1982 1 01

5054 KAYE,J
THE IRISH PRISONERS
NEW SOCIETY 6 SEPT
1973 1 01

5055 KELLY,C
A BLACK PICTURE OF THE FUTURE
SOC WORK TODAY 12(1)
LONDON
1980 2 01

5056 KELLY,C
SOCIAL WORK AND THE COURTS IN NI
IN PARKER,H (ED)
LONDON
1979 2 07

5057 KENNALLY,D; PRESTON,E
BELFAST, AUGUST 1971: A CASE TO BE
ANSWERED
INDEPENDENT LABOUR PARTY
LONDON
1971 1 09

5058 KENNEDY,A
ROYAL ULSTER CONSTABULARY
POLICE J 40(2)
1967 2 01

5059 KENNEDY,H P
REPORT OF A PUBLIC INQUIRY INTO
THE...USE OF LISNEVIN SCHOOL...AS A
TRAINING REMAND HOME...
HMSO
BELFAST
1979 2 03

5060 KENNY,J
THE ADVANTAGES OF A WRITTEN CONSTITUTION
INCORPORATING A BILL OF RIGHTS
NI LEG QUART 30(3)
BELFAST
1979 2 01

5061 KERR,C
CUSTODY OF CHILDREN ON BREAKDOWN OF
MARRIAGE IN NI
SLS/FACULTY OF LAW QUB
BELFAST
          2 10

5062 KILMURRAY,A
HYDEBANK: BARRING THE WAY TO BLACK?
SCOPE 46
BELFAST
1981 2 01

5063 KILMURRAY,A
RAPE: ADDING INSULT TO INJURY
SCOPE 50
BELFAST
1982 2 01

5064 KILMURRAY,A
THE WHITEFIELD EXPERIMENT: SWIMMING
AGAINST THE CURRENT?
SCOPE 52
BELFAST
1982 2 01

5065 KIRK,J M
THE RUC AND YOUNG PEOPLE
PACE 14(3)
BELFAST
1983 1 01

5066 LANHAM,D
GARDINER REPORT ON NI
CRIMINAL LAW R
1975 1 01

5067 LAW ENFORCEMENT COMMISSION
REPORT TO THE MINISTER FOR JUSTICE OF
IRELAND AND THE SECRETARY OF STATE FOR
NI
GOVERNMENT STATIONERY OFFICE PRL 3822
DUBLIN
1975 1 03

5068 LAW SOCIETY OF NI
REPORT OF THE LAW SOCIETY OF NI ON THE
LEGAL AID SCHEME
HMSO
BELFAST
1979 2 03

5069 LEE,C
CONSTITUTION AND STATE OF EMERGENCY
IR LAW STUDIES 103
1969 1 01

5070 LINDSAY,J R
THE SUPREME COURT OF NI
NI LEG QUART 7(1)
BELFAST
1946 2 01

5071 LIPMAN,M
THE ABROGATION OF DOMESTIC HUMAN RIGHTS:
NI AND THE RULE OF BRITISH LAW
IN ALEXANDER,Y; MYERS,K (EDS)
LONDON
1982 1 07

5072 LOCKHART,W H
THE OUTCOMES OF INDIVIDUAL
CLIENT-CENTRED COUNSELLING WITH YOUNG
OFFENDERS IN SECURE RESIDENTIAL CARE
IN HARBISON,J (ED)
BELFAST
1983 1 07

5073 LOCKHART,W H; ELLIOTT,R
CHANGES IN ATTITUDES OF YOUNG OFFENDERS
IN AN INTEGRATED ASSESSMENT CENTRE
IN HARBISON,J; HARBISON,J (EDS)
SHEPTON MALLET, SOMERSET
1980 1 07

5074 LORD HIGH CHANCELLOR
COURTS IN NI: THE FUTURE PATTERN
HMSO
LONDON
1977 2 03

5075 LOWRY,D R
DETENTION
COLUMBIA HUMAN RIGHTS LAW R 8
NEW YORK
1977 1 01

5076 LOWRY,D R
ILL-TREATMENT, BRUTALITY AND TORTURE:
SOME THOUGHTS ON TREATMENT OF IRISH
POLITICAL PRISONERS
DEPAUL LAW R 22
CHICAGO
1973 1 01

5077 LOWRY, D R
INTERNMENT
HUM RIGHTS R 1
LONDON
1977 1 01

5078 LOWRY, D R
INTERNMENT IN NI
TOLEDO UNIV LAW R 8(1)
USA
1976 1 01

5079 LOWRY, D R
TERRORISM AND HUMAN RIGHTS
NOTRE DAME LAWYER 53
1977 1 01

5080 LOWRY, D R
1978 EMERGENCY POWERS
NOTRE DAME LAW R
USA
1978 1 01

5081 LOWRY, D R; SPJUT, R
BILL OF RIGHTS FOR NI
WARWICK LAW PAPER 4
COVENTRY
1977 1 10

5082 LOWRY, D R; SPJUT, R J
EUROPEAN CONVENTION AND HUMAN RIGHTS IN
NI
CASE WESTERN RESERVE J INT LAW 10(2)
CLEVELAND, OHIO
1978 1 01

5083 LOWRY, D R; SPJUT, R J
EUROPEAN CONVENTION IN NI
VANDERBILT INT LAW R
MEMPHIS, TENN
1978 1 01

5084 LUKIANOWICZ, N
JUVENILE OFFENDERS: SECOND GROUP OF 50
GIRLS FROM A REMAND HOME IN NI
ACTA PSYCHIAT SCAN 48(4)
       2 01

5085 MACBRIDE, S
THE SPECIAL POWERS ACT OF NI
QUIS CUSTODIET (TCD) 24
1969 1 01

5086 MACDERMOTT, J C
THE DECLINE OF THE RULE OF LAW
NI LEG QUART 23(4)
1972 1 01

5087 MACDERMOTT, J C
LAW AND PRACTICE IN NI
NI LEG QUART 10(2)
1953 2 01

5088 MAGUIRE, P
THE REPORTS OF THE EXAMINER OF STATUTORY
RULES FOR NI 1974-78
NI LEG QUART 30(4)
BELFAST
1979 2 01

5089 MAGUIRE, P
THE STANDING ADVISORY COMMITTEE ON HUMAN
RIGHTS
NI LEG QUART 32
BELFAST
1981 2 01

5090 MANNING, M
SUNNINGDALE AND THE LAW
GARDA R 2(2)
1974 1 01

5091 MARTIN, P
A PROPOS DE L'ARTICLE 3 DE LA CONVENTION
EUROPEENE DE DROITS DE L'HOMME...
L'AFFAIRE IRLANDE C. ROYAUME-UNI
R GENERALE DE DR INT PUB 83(1)
PARIS
1979 1 01

5092 MASIME, J O
A COMPARATIVE STUDY OF...PENAL TREATMENT
WITH REFERENCE TO THE CALIFORNIAN, NI
AND KENYA PENAL SYSTEMS
QUB LLM
BELFAST
1969 2 04

5093 MCCAFFERTY, N
THE ARMAGH WOMEN
CO-OP BOOKS
DUBLIN
1981 1 09

5094 MCCARNEY, W G
JOYRIDING: A QUEST FOR IDENTITY
YOUTH IN SOCIETY 53
LONDON
1981 1 01

5095 MCCARNEY, W G
POSITIVE POLICING: THE ROAD TO DIVIS
YOUTH IN SOCIETY 62
LONDON
1982 1 01

5096 MCCLUNG LEE, A
HUMAN RIGHTS IN THE NI CONFLICT 1968-80
INT J POL 10(7)
NEW YORK
1980 1 01

5097 MCCONAGHY, E M
SOME CHARACTERISTICS OF ... DELINQUENTS
ADMITTED TO TRAINING SCHOOLS IN NI
QUB MED
BELFAST
1971 2 04

5098 MCCULLOUGH, H M
THE ROYAL ULSTER CONSTABULARY
POLICE STUD 4
1982 1 01

5099 MCERLEAN, J
THE CRIMINAL LAW AND EMERGENCY AND
SPECIAL LEGISLATION IN RELATION TO TRADE
DISPUTES IN THE UK
QUB LLM
BELFAST
1970 1 04

5100 MCGOVERN, E
INTERNMENT AND DETENTION IN THE LIGHT OF
THE EUROPEAN CONVENTION ON HUMAN RIGHTS
IN BRIDGE, J W (ED)
LONDON
1973 1 07

5101 MCGUFFIN, J
THE GUINEAPIGS
PENGUIN
HARMONDSWORTH
1974 1 02

5102 MCGUFFIN, J
INTERNMENT
ANVIL
TRALEE
1973 1 02

5103 MCILREAVEY, F
THE NEED FOR LEGAL AID IN NI
NI LEG QUART 15(3)
1964 2 01

5104 MCLEAN, J; NEWARK, F H; WYLIE, J C
SOME DEVELOPMENTS IN NI SINCE 1921
NI LEG QUART 23(1)
1972 2 01

5105 MCMAHON, B
THE IMPAIRED ASSET: A LEGAL COMMENTARY
ON THE REPORT OF THE WIDGERY TRIBUNAL
AUTHOR
CORK
1972 1 99

Criminal Justice System/

5106 MELCHETT,P
     LEGAL RIGHTS AND POLITICAL CONTROL
     IN CAMPBELL,C M (ED)
     LONDON
     1980 1 07

5107 MERTENS,C
     REPORT ON CIVIL AND SOCIAL RIGHTS IN NI
     HUM RIGHTS J 2(3)
     1969 1 01

5108 MERTENS,P
     L'AFFAIRE IRLANDE CONTRE ROYAUME-UNIS
     DEVANT LA COMMISSION EUROPEENE DES
     DROITS DE L'HOMME
     R BELGE DE DR INT 13(1-2)
     1977 1 01

5109 MINISTRY OF HOME AFFAIRS (NI)
     REPORT OF FINDINGS OF A POLICE INQUIRY
     HMSO CMD 498
     BELFAST
     1966 2 03

5110 MINISTRY OF HOME AFFAIRS (NI)
     REPORT ON LEGAL AID AND ADVICE IN NI
     HMSO CMD 417
     BELFAST
     1960 2 03

5111 MINISTRY OF HOME AFFAIRS (NI)
     RUC RESERVE
     HMSO CMD 536
     BELFAST
     1969 1 03

5112 MITCHELL,V A
     SOME RECENT DEVELOPMENTS IN THE CRIMINAL
     LAW IN NI
     BELFAST SOLICITORS' ASSOCIATION
     BELFAST
     1979 2 10

5113 MORRISSEY,M; DITCH,J
     SOCIAL POLICY IMPLICATIONS OF EMERGENCY
     LEGISLATION
     ANNUAL SOC ADMIN CONF
     CAMBRIDGE
     1979 1 08

5114 MULVENNA,J
     INTERNMENT, WHAT NOW?
     AQUARIUS
     BENBURB
     1974 1 01

5115 MYERS,K
     H-BLOCK HELL HOLE
     MAGILL 1(9)
     DUBLIN
     1978 1 01

5116 NARAIN,J
     PUBLIC LAW IN NI
     APPLETREE PRESS
     BELFAST
     1973 1 02

5117 NCCL
     CRISIS IN NI: REPRESENTATIONS OF NCCL TO
     HM GOVERNMENT
     NCCL
     LONDON
     1971 1 10

5118 NCCL
     MEMORANDUM ON THE PREVENTION OF
     TERRORISM ACT
     NCCL
     LONDON
     1979 1 10

5119 NCCL
     NI (EMERGENCY PROVISIONS) ACT:
     MEMORANDUM FOR MEMBERS OF PARLIAMENT ON
     THE FIRST YEAR'S OPERATION OF THE ACT
     NCCL
     LONDON
     1974 1 10

5120 NCCL
     REPORT OF THE FIRST FOUR MONTHS OF THE
     PREVENTION OF TERRORISM ACT 1974
     NCCL
     LONDON
     1975 1 10

5121 NCCL
     THE RUC: A REPORT ON COMPLAINTS
     PROCEDURE
     NCCL
     LONDON
     1975 1 10

5122 NCCL
     THE SPECIAL POWERS ACT OF NI (ORIGINALLY
     PUBLISHED 1936)
     NCCL
     LONDON
     1972 1 10

5123 NELLIS,M; HUTCHINSON,N
     DERRY RELATIVES' ACTION
     IN CURNO,A ET AL (EDS)
     LONDON
     1982 1 07

5124 NELSON,M A
     INTERMEDIATE TREATMENT
     DHSS (NI)
     BELFAST
     1979 2 03

5125 NEWARK,F H
     NOTES ON IRISH LEGAL HISTORY
     MAYNE/BOYD
     BELFAST
     1960 2 10

5126 NEWARK,F H; MCLEAN,J; WYLIE,J C
     BRINGING OF ENGLISH LAW TO IRELAND -
     SOME DEVELOPMENTS SINCE 1921
     NI LEG QUART 23(1)
     1972 2 01

5127 NEWMAN,K
     PREVENTION IN EXTREMIS: THE PREVENTIVE
     ROLE OF THE POLICE IN NI
     IN BROWN,J (ED)
     LONDON
     1979 1 07

5128 NI ASSOCIATION OF SOCIALIST LAWYERS
     MANIFESTO AND CONSTITUTION
     NIASL
     BELFAST
     1980 2 10

5129 NI GOVERNMENT
     LAW REFORM IN NI
     HMSO CMD 507
     BELFAST
     1967 2 03

5130 NI GOVERNMENT
     REPORT OF THE COMMITTEE ON LEGAL
     EDUCATION IN NI
     HMSO CMD 579
     BELFAST
     1973 2 03

5131 NI GOVERNMENT
     REPORT OF THE WORKING PARTY ON PUBLIC
     PROSECUTIONS
     HMSO CMD 554
     BELFAST
     1971 1 03

5132 NI GOVERNMENT
     REPORT ON THE PROTECTION AND WELFARE OF
     THE YOUNG AND THE TREATMENT OF YOUNG
     OFFENDERS
     HMSO CMD 264
     BELFAST
     1948 2 03

5133 NI LEGAL QUARTERLY (SPECIAL ISSUE)
     SPECIAL POWERS EXTRAORDINARY
     NI LEG QUART 20(1)
     1969 1 01

Criminal Justice System/

5134 NICRA
BILL OF RIGHTS (NI) ACT 1975: PRESENTED
TO THE PEOPLE OF NI BY NICRA
NICRA
BELFAST
1975   1   09

5135 NICRA
BRITISH GOVERNMENT VIOLATIONS OF HUMAN
RIGHTS IN NI
NICRA
BELFAST
        1   10

5136 NICRA
NI (EMERGENCY PROVISIONS) ACT 1973:
SUBMISSION PREPARED FOR GARDINER
COMMITTEE BY NICRA
NICRA
BELFAST
1973   1   09

5137 NUM
TOWARDS THE RETURN OF THE RULE OF LAW
NUM
BELFAST
1972   1   10

5138 O'BOYLE,M P
EMERGENCY SITUATIONS AND THE PROTECTION
OF HUMAN RIGHTS
NI LEG QUART 28(2)
1977   1   01

5139 O'BOYLE,M P
TORTURE AND EMERGENCY POWERS UNDER THE
EUROPEAN CONVENTION ON HUMAN RIGHTS
AMER J INT LAW 71(4)
1977   1   01

5140 O'DUILL,P
H-BLOCKS: CAN WE REMAIN SILENT?
NATIONAL H-BLOCK COMMITTEE
DUBLIN
1980   1   09

5141 O'HIGGINS,P
ANGLO-IRISH EXTRADITION
NEW LAW J 116(1)
1965   2   01

5142 O'HIGGINS,P
ENGLISH LAW AND THE IRISH QUESTION
IR JURIST 1(1)
1966   2   01

5143 O'HIGGINS,P
THE IRISH EXTRADITION ACT 1965
INT COMP LAW QUART APRIL
1966   2   01

5144 OSBOROUGH,N
BORSTAL IN IRELAND
IPA
DUBLIN
1975   2   02

5145 OSBOROUGH,N
HOMICIDE AND CRIMINAL RESPONSIBILITY
BILL (NI) 1963
NI LEG QUART 16(1)
BELFAST
1965   2   01

5146 OSBOROUGH,N
PARTITION AND THE NORTHERN BORSTAL BOY
1921-7
DUBLIN UNIV LAW R 1(1)
DUBLIN
1969   2   01

5147 OSBOROUGH,N
PROBATION IN NI
IR JURIST 9(2)
1974   2   01

5148 OSBOROUGH,N
THE SUSPENDED SENTENCE IN NI
IR JURIST 2
1967   2   01

5149 PALLEY,C
CONSTITUTIONAL LAW AND MINORITIES
MINORITY RIGHTS GROUP
LONDON
1978   2   10

5150 PARKER REPORT
REPORT OF PRIVY COUNCILLORS APPOINTED TO
CONSIDER AUTHORISED PROCEDURE FOR
INTERROGATION
HMSO CMND 4901
LONDON
1972   1   03

5151 PD
PRISONERS OF PARTITION: H-BLOCK/ARMAGH
PD
BELFAST
1980   1   09

5152 PEACE PEOPLE
THE (TEMPORARY) EMERGENCY PROVISIONS
ACT: TIME FOR A CHANGE
PEACE PEOPLE
BELFAST
1980   1   10

5153 PEACOCK,A
ROYAL ULSTER CONSTABULARY
SOLON 1(2)
1970   1   01

5154 PEOPLE AGAINST THE PREVENTION OF
TERRORISM ACT
APARTHEID IN BRITAIN: AN ANALYSIS OF THE
PREVENTION OF TERRORISM ACT
PAPTA
LONDON
1977   1   09

5155 POLICE AUTHORITY OF NI
FIRST THREE YEARS
POLICE AUTHORITY OF NI
BELFAST
1973   1   10

5156 POOLE,C
THE COMMUNITY RELATIONS ROLE OF THE
POLICE
NUU MSC
COLERAINE
1976   1   04

5157 RAUCH,E
THE COMPATIBILITY OF THE DETENTION OF
TERRORISTS ORDER...
NEW YORK UNIV J INT LAW AND POLITICS
6(1)
NEW YORK
1973   1   01

5158 RITCHIE,J
THE INN OF COURT IN NI: ITS FOUNDATION,
DEVELOPMENT AND FUNCTIONING
NI LEG QUART 15(4)
BELFAST
1964   2   01

5159 ROBERTSON,A H
HUMAN RIGHTS IN EUROPE
INT R 4
1975   1   01

5160 ROBINSON,P
SELF-INFLICTED: AN EXPOSURE OF THE
H-BLOCK ISSUE
DEMOCRATIC UNIONIST PARTY
BELFAST
1980   1   09

5161 ROLSTON,B; TOMLINSON,M
SPECTATORS AT THE 'CARNIVAL OF
REACTION'? ANALYSING POLITICAL CRIME IN
IRELAND
IN KELLY,M; O'DOWD,L; WICKHAM,J (EDS)
DUBLIN
1982   1   07

5162 ROWE,A
ON THE BLANKET
CANADIAN DIMENSION 15(5)
1981 1 01

5163 ROYAL ULSTER CONSTABULARY
MEMORANDUM TO THE HUNT ADVISORY BOARD
BELFAST
1969 1 10

5164 RUDD,J
LOOKING AFTER THE MEN IN LONG KESH
COMM CARE 45
LONDON
1975 1 01

5165 SANDS,B
THE DIARY OF BOBBY SANDS
SINN FEIN PUBLICITY DEPT
DUBLIN
1981 1 09

5166 SCOPE
YOUNG PEOPLE: CARE OR CONTROL?
SCOPE 10
BELFAST
1977 2 01

5167 SCORER,C
THE PREVENTION OF TERRORISM ACTS: A
REPORT ON THE OPERATION OF THE LAW
NCCL
LONDON
1976 1 09

5168 SCORER,C; HEWITT,P
THE PREVENTION OF TERRORISM ACT: THE
CASE FOR REPEAL
NCCL
LONDON
1981 1 09

5169 SHALLICE,T
THE ULSTER DEPTH INTERROGATION
TECHNIQUES
COGNITION 1(4)
1973 1 01

5170 SHERIDAN,L A
THE LEGAL SYSTEM
IN KEETON,G W; LLOYD,D (EDS)
LONDON
1955 2 07

5171 SHIRLEY,J
AND ONE LAW FOR THE IRISH
MAGILL 1(2)
DUBLIN
1977 1 01

5172 SINCLAIR,R J K; SCULLY,F J M
ARRESTING MEMORIES: CAPTURED MOMENTS IN
CONSTABULARY LIFE
RUC DIAMOND JUBILEE COMMITTEE
BELFAST
1982 1 02

5173 SINN FEIN (PROVISIONAL)
THE H-BLOCK CONVEYOR BELT
SINN FEIN POW DEPARTMENT
DUBLIN
1979 1 09

5174 SINN FEIN (PROVISIONAL)
PRISON STRUGGLE
REPUBLICAN PRESS CENTRE
BELFAST
1977 1 09

5175 SMITH,P
EMERGENCY LEGISLATION: THE PREVENTION OF
TERRORISM ACTS
IN HILLYARD,P; SQUIRES,P (EDS)
BRISTOL
1982 1 07

5176 SMYTH,J
CIVIL LIBERTIES AND RIOT CONTROL IN NI
ECPR
ESSEX
1983 1 11

5177 SPJUT,R
EXECUTIVE DETENTION IN NI: GARDINER
REPORT AND NI (EPA AMENDMENT) 1975
IR JURIST 10(2)
1975 1 01

5178 SPJUT,R
THE PREVENTION OF TERRORISM ACT 1974:
MEMORANDUM ON LEGAL ASPECTS
NCCL
LONDON
1974 1 09

5179 SPJUT,R
TORTURE UNDER THE EUROPEAN CONVENTION ON
HUMAN RIGHTS
AMER J INT LAW 73(2)
WASHINGTON
1979 1 01

5180 SPJUT,R; LOWRY,D R
A PROPOSED BILL OF RIGHTS PREPARED FOR
SUBMISSION TO THE PEOPLE OF THE UNITED
KINGDOM
ULSTER CITIZENS' CIVIL LIBERTIES CENTRE
BELFAST
1975 1 09

5181 STREET,M
THE PREVENTION OF TERRORISM ACT OF 1974
CRIMINAL LAW R APRIL
LONDON
1975 1 01

5182 TAYLOR,P
BEATING THE TERRORISTS?
PENGUIN
HARMONDSWORTH
1980 1 02

5183 THORNBERRY,C
INTERNATIONAL LAW AND EMERGENCY
SITUATIONS
COMM FORUM 3(2)
LONDON
1973 1 01

5184 TOBIAS,J
THE POLICING OF IRELAND
CRIMINOLOGIST 5
1970 2 01

5185 TOMLINSON,M
POLICING THE PERIPHERY: IDEOLOGIES OF
REPRESSION IN NI
B SOC POL 5
1980 1 01

5186 TOMLINSON,M
REFORMING REPRESSION
IN O'DOWD,L; ROLSTON,B; TOMLINSON,M
LONDON
1980 1 07

5187 TRADE UNION SUBCOMMITTEE OF THE NATIONAL
H-BLOCKS COMMITTEE
TRADE UNIONS AND H-BLOCK
TRADE UNION SUBCOMMITTEE OF THE NATIONAL
H-BLOCKS COMMITTEE
BELFAST
1980 1 10

5188 TURNER,E B; AGNEW,J B
THE INTELLIGENCE AND EDUCATIONAL
ATTAINMENT OF BORSTAL TRAINEES IN NI
IR J EDUC 11(1)
DUBLIN
1977 2 01

5189 TWINING,W L
EMERGENCY POWERS AND CRIMINAL PROCESS:
THE DIPLOCK REPORT
CRIMINAL LAW R
1973 1 01

5190 ULSTER CITIZENS CIVIL LIBERTIES CENTRE
A PROPOSED BILL OF RIGHTS
ULSTER CITIZENS CIVIL LIBERTIES CENTRE
BELFAST
1975 1 09

Criminal Justice System/

5191 ULSTER YOUNG UNIONIST COUNCIL
     GUNMEN AND THE LAW ...INVESTIGATION INTO
     WAYS OF STRENGTHENING THE LAW TO DEFEAT
     TERRORISM
     ULSTER YOUNG UNIONIST COUNCIL
     BELFAST
     1981 1   09

5192 UNIONIST RESEARCH DEPARTMENT
     THE CASE FOR INTERNMENT
     UUP
     BELFAST
     1971 1   09

5193 UNITED ULSTER UNIONIST COUNCIL
     SECURITY IN NI
     BELFAST
     1975 1   09

5194 VAN STRAUBENZEE,W R
     INTERNATIONAL LAW AND TERRORISM
     IN RUSI
     LONDON
     1979 1   07

5195 WAGHORN,J H
     CIVILIANISATION OF THE RUC
     LOC GOVT CHRONICLE MARCH
     1971 1   01

5196 WALSH,D
     ARREST AND INTERROGATION: NI 1981
     J LAW AND SOC 9(1)
     OXFORD
     1982 1   01

5197 WHYTE,D
     A SOCIAL PSYCHOLOGICAL EVALUATION OF A
     COMMUNITY SERVICE PROGRAMME FOR YOUNG
     OFFENDERS IN A NI TRAINING SCHOOL
     QUB MSSC
     BELFAST
     1981 2   04

5198 WILSON,W J
     THE ROYAL ULSTER CONSTABULARY AND POLICE
     COMMUNITY RELATIONS IN NI
     CRANFIELD INSTITUTE OF TECHNOLOGY MSC
     CRANFIELD
     1978 1   04

5199 WOMEN AGAINST IMPERIALISM
     WOMEN PROTEST FOR POLITICAL STATUS IN
     ARMAGH GAOL
     WAI
     BELFAST
     1980 1   09

5200 WORKERS' RESEARCH UNIT
     ROUGH JUSTICE: THE LAW IN NI
     WRU BULLETIN 10
     BELFAST
     1982 1   09

5201 YOUNG,R; ADAMS,J
     THE CASE FOR DETENTION
     BOW PUBLICATIONS
     LONDON
     1974 1   09

5202 YOUNG,T
     INCITEMENT TO DISAFFECTION
     COBDEN TRUST
     LONDON
     1975 1   02

5203 ACHESON,A
MEDIA AND THE CRISIS
CHURCH OF IRELAND GAZETTE 28 JUNE
1972 1 01

5204 AUDLEY,R
THE PROBLEM OF IMPARTIALITY: A CASE
STUDY OF BBC POLICY...IN RELATION TO THE
TROUBLES OF NI DURING 1971 AND 1972
QUB MSSC
BELFAST
1982 1 04

5205 BBC
PRINCIPLES AND PRACTICE: NEWS AND
CURRENT AFFAIRS
BBC
LONDON
1977 2 99

5206 BELL,M
REPORTING ULSTER
LISTENER 5 OCT
LONDON
1972 1 01

5207 BELL,M
VIEWS
LISTENER 6 JAN
LONDON
1972 1 01

5208 BLUMLER,J
ULSTER ON THE SMALL SCREEN
NEW SOCIETY
1971 1 01

5209 BRESLIN,S
IRISH JOURNALISM: AN EVALUATION
EVERYMAN 2
1969 2 01

5210 BROWN,S
PRESS IN IRELAND: A SURVEY AND A GUIDE
LEMMA PUBL CORP
NEW YORK
1971 2 02

5211 BURROWES,J
THE 1000 YEAR WAR
IN BURROWES,J
EDINBURGH
1982 1 07

5212 CAIRNS,E
THE POLITICAL SOCIALISATION OF
TOMORROW'S PARENTS: VIOLENCE, POLITICS
AND THE MEDIA
IN HARBISON,J (ED)
BELFAST
1983 1 07

5213 CAIRNS,E ET AL
YOUNG CHILDREN'S AWARENESS OF VIOLENCE
IN NI: THE INFLUENCE OF NI TELEVISION IN
SCOTLAND AND NI
BRIT J SOC CLINIC PSYCHOL 19
LONDON
1980 1 01

5214 CAMERAWORK
REPORTING BACK ON NI
CAMERAWORK
LONDON
1981 1 09

5215 CAMERAWORK
REPORTING ON NI
CAMERAWORK
1979 1 10

5216 CAMPAIGN FOR FREE SPEECH ON IRELAND
THE BRITISH MEDIA IN IRELAND
CAMPAIGN FOR FREE SPEECH ON IRELAND
LONDON
1979 1 09

5217 CANAVAN,A J
IRISH POLITICAL AND PRESS REACTIONS TO
EUROPEAN EVENTS 1935-1939
ULSTER POLY PHD
BELFAST
1981 2 04

5218 CHIBNALL,S
LAW-AND-ORDER NEWS
TAVISTOCK
LONDON
1977 1 02

5219 CLUTTERBUCK,R
THE MEDIA AND POLITICAL VIOLENCE
MACMILLAN
LONDON
1981 1 02

5220 CORBETT,J R
PRESS BIAS IN NI
OHIO STATE UNIV PHD
1981 1 04

5221 CURTIS,L
HOW THE BRITISH MEDIA REPORTED BLOODY
SUNDAY
IRIS 5
DUBLIN
1983 1 01

5222 DAVIES,M
ROLE OF THE PRESS IN THE RECENT NI
CRISIS
LSE
LONDON
1970 1 04

5223 DAVIS,R
ULSTER PROTESTANTS AND SINN FEIN PRESS,
1914-22
EIRE-IRELAND 15(4)
ST PAUL
1980 2 01

5224 DEUTSCH,R
AS OTHERS SEE US: FRANCE
COMM FORUM 4(1)
BELFAST
1974 1 01

5225 DEUTSCH,R
INTRODUCTION TO NI POLITICAL NEWSPAPERS
ET IRL 4
1975 1 01

5226 ELLIOTT,P
IMAGES OF CONFLICT: A STUDY OF NORTHERN
IRISH NEWS IN PRESS AND TELEVISION
UNIV LEICESTER
1976 1 10

5227 ELLIOTT,P
MISREPORTING ULSTER: NEWS AS A
FIELD-DRESSING
NEW SOCIETY 38(738)
LONDON
        1 01

5228 ELLIOTT,P
PRESS PERFORMANCE AS POLITICAL RITUAL
IN CHRISTIAN,H (ED)
KEELE
1980 1 07

5229 ELLIOTT,P
REPORTING NI
IN O'HALLORAN,J ET AL
1977 1 07

5230 ELLIOTT,P; MURDOCK,G; SCHLESINGER,P
THE STATE AND 'TERRORISM' ON BRITISH
TELEVISION
22ND INT R OF SOCIAL DOCUMENTARY FILM
FLORENCE
1981 1 11

5231 FOOT,P
ULSTER COVERAGE OR COVER UP?
INK 7 JAN
1972 1 10

5232 FRANCIS,R
BROADCASTING TO A COMMUNITY IN CONFLICT:
THE EXPERIENCE OF NI
BBC
LONDON
1977 1 10

5233 GAGEBY,D
THE MEDIA 1945-70
IN LEE,J (ED)
DUBLIN
1979 2 07

5234 GARDNER,C
TV COVERAGE OF THE WAR IN IRELAND TEN
YEARS ON
IRL SOCIALIST R 4
LONDON
1979 1 01

5235 GIULIANI,P
IMAGES DE L'IRLANDE DANS LE CINEMA
ET IRL 5
ROUEN
1980 3 01

5236 GLANDON,V E
THE IRISH PRESS AND REVOLUTIONARY IRISH
NATIONALISM 1900-1922
EIRE-IRELAND 16(1) ·
ST PAUL, MINNESOTA
1981 2 01

5237 HALL,S
DEVIANCE, POLITICS AND THE MEDIA
IN ROCK,P; MCINTOSH,M (EDS)
LONDON
1974 2 07

5238 HAWTHORNE,J
REPORTING VIOLENCE: LESSONS FROM NI?
BBC
LONDON
1981 1 10

5239 HICKEY,N
THE BATTLE FOR NI: HOW TV TIPS THE
BALANCE
TV GUIDE SEPT 26
1981 1 02

5240 HICKMAN,M
THE MEDIA AND NI
SOCIAL SCIENCE TEACHER 10(1)
1980 1 01

5241 HOGGART,R
ULSTER: A 'SWITCH-OFF' TV SUBJECT?
LISTENER 103(2651)
LONDON
1980 2 01

5242 HOGGART,S
ARMY PR MEN OF NI
NEW SOCIETY 26(575)
LONDON
1973 1 01

5243 HOWARD,P
IRISH SECTARIAN PERIODICALS
SMOOTHIE PUBLICATIONS
BRIGHTON, ENGLAND
1973 2 02

5244 HOWARD,P ET AL
WHAT THE OTHER PAPERS SAY
COMM FORUM 2(2)
BELFAST
1972 1 01

5245 HOWKINS,J
CENSORSHIP 1977-78: A BACKGROUND PAPER
EDINBURGH TV FESTIVAL BROCHURE
1978 2 10

5246 HUCZYNSKI,A
CONTENT ANALYSIS OF ENGLISH, EIRE AND
ULSTER NEWSPAPERS BETWEEN AUGUST 11-16
1969
LSE
LONDON
1970 1

5247 KIRKALDY,J
ENGLISH CARTOONISTS: ULSTER REALITIES
EIRE-IRELAND 16(3)
ST PAUL MINNESOTA
1981 1 01

5248 KIRKALDY,J
NI AND FLEET STREET: MISREPORTING A
CONTINUING TRAGEDY
IN ALEXANDER,Y; O'DAY,A (EDS)
LONDON
1983 1 07

5249 KIRKALDY,J
STEREOTYPING AND REPORTING OF THE
ENGLISH PRESS IN RELATION TO NI
CONFLICT, 1968-73
NEW SOUTH WALES UNIV PHD
KENSINGTON, AUSTRALIA
1979 1 04

5250 KIRKCALDY,J
BLOODY AWFUL COUNTRY: ENGLISH PRESS
IMAGES OF THE IRISH, 1968-76
DEPT HISTORY UNIV OF NEW SOUTH WALES
1978 1 08

5251 KUSNIR,J
COVERING BELFAST: MEDIA PEOPLE AND THE
BLOOD OF IRISHMEN
ALTERNATIVE MEDIA SPRING
NEW YORK
1982 1 01

5252 MACCONGHAILL,M
TELEVISION AND POLITICS
GILL AND MACMILLAN
DUBLIN
1972 2 02

5253 MCCANN,E
THE BRITISH PRESS AND NI
IN COHEN,S; YOUNG,J (EDS)
LONDON
1978 1 07

5254 MCCANN,E
THE BRITISH PRESS AND NI
NI SOCIALIST RESEARCH CENTRE
BELFAST
1971 1 10

5255 MCCLUNG LEE,A
MASS MEDIA MYTHMAKING IN THE UK'S
INTERETHNIC STRUGGLES
ETHNICITY 8(1)
1981 1 01

5256 MCFEE,T
ULSTER THROUGH A LENS
NEW STATESMAN 17 MAR
LONDON
1978 1 01

5257 PALETZ,D L; FOZZARD,P A; AYANIAN,J Z
THE IRA, THE RED BRIGADES AND THE FALN
IN THE NEW YORK TIMES
J COMMUNICATION 32(2)
1982 1 01

Mass Media/

5258 SAYERS,J E
THE RELATIONSHIPS OF THE PRESS AND
PUBLIC ADMINISTRATION
IN RHODES,E (ED)
DERRY
1967 2 07

5259 SCHLESINGER,P
'TERRORISM', THE MEDIA AND THE
LIBERAL-DEMOCRATIC STATE: A CRITIQUE OF
THE ORTHODOXY
SOC RES 48(1)
NEW YORK
1981 1 01

5260 SCHLESINGER,P
REPORTING NI
IN SCHLESINGER,P
LONDON
1977 1 07

5261 SCOPE
THE ALTERNATIVE NEWSPAPERS
SCOPE 29
BELFAST
1979 1 01

5262 SCOPE
THE MEDIA AND THE COMMUNITY
SCOPE 26
BELFAST
1979 2 01

5263 SLEATH,S
VOLUNTEER RECRUITMENT AND MOBILISATION
OF VOLUNTEERS VIA TELEVISION IN NI
SOC ACTION AND THE MEDIA 4
1979 2 01

5264 SMITH,A
BIAS IN BROADCASTING
THIS WEEK SEPT
DUBLIN
1972 1 01

5265 SMITH,A
TELEVISION COVERAGE OF NI
INDEX ON CENSORSHIP SUMMER
1972 1 01

5266 ST. JOHN BROOKS,C
THE HISTORY AND DEVELOPMENT OF
EDUCATIONAL BROADCASTING IN IRELAND
NUU MA
COLERAINE
1971 2 04

5267 STEPHEN,A
A REPORTERS LIFE IN BELFAST
OBSERVER 29 FEB
LONDON
1976 1 10

5268 TAYLOR,P
REPORTING NI
INDEX ON CENSORSHIP (6)
1978 1 01

5269 TAYLOR,R
IMAGES OF THE IRISH
NEW SOCIETY 28 NOVEMBER
LONDON
1974 3 01

5270 TERRAINE,J ET AL
TERRORISM AND THE MEDIA
IN RUSI
LONDON
1979 1 07

5271 WARD,K
ULSTER TERRORISM: THE U.S. NETWORK NEWS
COVERAGE OF NI
IN ALEXANDER,Y; O'DAY,A (EDS)
LONDON
1983 1 07

5272 WINCHESTER,S
AS OTHERS SEE US: THE USA
COMM FORUM 4(1)
LONDON
1974 1 01

5273 WINCHESTER,S
IN HOLY TERROR
FABER
LONDON
1974 1 02

5274 WINCHESTER,S
NI IN CRISIS: REPORTING THE NI TROUBLES
NEW YORK
1975 1 02

5275 WOODS,E
PATTERNS OF LEISURE TELEVISION VIEWING
AMONG A SAMPLE OF FOURTEEN YEAR OLDS
QUB MED
BELFAST
1973 2 04

5276 WORKERS' ASSOCIATION
WARMONGERING: THE 'IRISH PRESS' AND THE
TROUBLES IN NI
WORKERS' ASSOCIATION
BELFAST
1973 1 09

5277 WORKERS' RESEARCH UNIT
MEDIA MISREPORT NI
WRU BULLETIN 6
BELFAST
1979 1 10

5278 AALEN, F H A
MAN AND THE LANDSCAPE IN IRELAND
ACADEMIC PRESS
LONDON
1978 2 02

5279 ADAMS, G
FALLS MEMORIES
BRANDON
DINGLE
1982 2 02

5280 ADAMS, G
PAWN SHOPS AND POLITICS
THE RACE TODAY R 14(5)
LONDON
1983 2 01

5281 ADAMS, G B
ASPECTS OF MONOGLOTTISM IN ULSTER
ULSTER FOLKLIFE 22
1976 2 01

5282 ADAMS, G B
AN INTRODUCTION TO THE STUDY OF ULSTER
DIALECTS
ROYAL IR ACADEMY PROC 52
DUBLIN
1948 2 01

5283 ADAMS, G B
LANGUAGE AND MAN IN IRELAND
ULSTER FOLKLIFE 16
1970 2 01

5284 ADAMS, G B
ULSTER DIALECTS: AN INTRODUCTORY
SYMPOSIUM
ULSTER FOLK MUSEUM
BELFAST
1964 2 10

5285 ANDREWS, E
ULSTER FOLKLORE
E P PUBLISHERS
WAKEFIELD
1977 2 02

5286 ARMSTRONG-INGRAM, R
AN ANALYSIS OF A COLLECTION OF LOYALIST
VERSE TEXTS
QUB MA
BELFAST
1981 3 04

5287 BALLARD, L M
ULSTER ORAL NARRATIVE: THE STRESS ON
AUTHENTICITY
ULSTER FOLKLIFE 26
BELFAST
1980 2 01

5288 BEBBINGTON, J
BELFAST IN LITERATURE
PROC BELFAST NATURAL HISTORY AND
PHILOSOPHICAL SOCIETY 4
BELFAST
1955 2 01

5289 BELL, D
COMMUNITY STUDIES: THE SOCIAL
ANTHROPOLOGICAL HERITAGE AND ITS
POPULARITY IN IRELAND
INT J SOCIOL SOC POL 1(2)
STIRLING
1981 2 01

5290 BELL, S H
THE THEATRE IN ULSTER
GILL AND MACMILLAN
DUBLIN
1972 2 02

5291 BENNETT, T J G
NORTH ANTRIM FAMILIES
VOLTURNA PRESS
ABERDEENSHIRE
1974 2 02

5292 BICO
'HIDDEN ULSTER' EXPLORED
ATHOL BOOKS
BELFAST
1973 2 09

5293 BLACKING, J
INTRODUCTION TO ASPECTS OF FAMILY LIFE
IN IRELAND
J COMPARATIVE FAMILY STUD 10
1979 2 01

5294 BROWNE, J
THE LITERATURE OF VIOLENCE: THE WRITER
AND NI
IN SULLIVAN, E ET AL (EDS)
GAINESVILLE, FLORIDA
1976 1 07

5295 BUCHANAN, R H
THE BARONY OF LECALE, CO DOWN: A STUDY
OF REGIONAL PERSONALITY
QUB PHD
BELFAST
1958 2 04

5296 BUCHANAN, R H
THE FOLKLORE OF AN IRISH TOWNLAND
ULSTER FOLKLIFE 2
1956 2 01

5297 BUCHANAN, R H
THE PLANTER AND THE GAEL: CULTURAL
DIMENSIONS OF THE NI PROBLEM
IN BOAL, F W; DOUGLAS, J N H (EDS)
LONDON
1982 2 07

5298 BUCHANAN, R H
RURAL CHANGE IN AN IRISH TOWNLAND,
1890-1955
ADVANCEMENT OF EDUC 56
1958 2 01

5299 BUCHANAN, R H
TRADITION AND CHANGE IN RURAL ULSTER
FOLKLIFE 3
1970 2 01

5300 BUCKLEY, A
A GENTLE PEOPLE: A STUDY OF A PEACEFUL
COMMUNITY IN ULSTER
ULSTER FOLK AND TRANSPORT MUSEUM
BELFAST
1982 2 02

5301 BUCKLEY, A
UNOFFICIAL HEALING IN ULSTER
ULSTER FOLKLIFE 26
BELFAST
1980 2 01

5302 BUFWACK, M S
VILLAGE WITHOUT VIOLENCE: AN EXAMINATION
OF A NORTHERN IRISH COMMUNITY
SCHENKMAN
CAMBRIDGE, MASS
1980 1 02

5303 CAMPBELL, C L
SOCIAL RELATIONS IN GLENARM: A NI
VILLAGE
QUB MA
BELFAST
1978 2 04

5304 CATTO,M
ART IN ULSTER VOLUME 2
BLACKSTAFF
BELFAST
1977 2 02

5305 CROWE,W H
THE RING OF MOURNE
DUNDALGAN PRESS
DUNDALK
1968 2 02

5306 CURLEY,P B
NORTHERN IRISH POETS AND THE LAND SINCE
1800
QUB MA
BELFAST
1977 2 04

5307 DE BREFFNY,B
HERITAGE OF IRELAND
WEIDENFELD AND NICOLSON
LONDON
1979 2 02

5308 DE BREFFNY,B
THE LAND OF IRELAND
THAMES AND HUDSON
LONDON
1979 2 02

5309 DE FREINE,S
DIVIDED MIND: IRELAND'S CULTURAL DILEMNA
SOC STUD 5(3-4)
1976 2 02

5310 DE FREINE,S
GREAT SILENCE
FOILSEACHAIN NAISIUNTA TEO
DUBLIN
1965   02

5311 DE PAOR,L
CULTURAL TRADITIONS
ADMIN (DUB) 20(4)
DUBLIN
1972 2 01

5312 DEANE,S
THE ARTIST AND THE TROUBLES
IN COOGAN,T P (ED)
LONDON
1983 1 07

5313 DEANE,S
POETRY IN NI
TWENTIETH CENTURY STUD 4
1970 2 01

5314 DEPT OF THE ENVIRONMENT (NI)
SOCIAL ENTERTAINMENT IN THE BELFAST CITY
CENTRE: REPORT OF A WORKING PARTY...
HMSO
BELFAST
1979 2 03

5315 DEUTSCH,R
SELECTION DISCOGRAPHIQUE DES BALLADES
INSPIREES PAR LES EVENEMENTS D'IRELANDE
DU NORD
ET IRL 3
1974 1 01

5316 DEUTSCH,R
WITHIN TWO SHADOWS: THE TROUBLES IN NI
IN RAFROIDI,P; HARMAN,M (EDS)
1976 1 07

5317 DORAN,J S
MY MOURNE
MOURNE OBSERVER PRESS
NEWCASTLE
1976 2 02

5318 DOUGLAS,E
A SOCIOLINGUISTIC STUDY OF ARTICLAVE, CO
DERRY
NUU DPHIL
COLERAINE
1976 2 04

5319 EVANS,E
IRISH FOLKWAYS
RKP
LONDON
1957 2 02

5320 EVANS,E
IRISH HERITAGE
DUNDALGAN PRESS
DUNDALK
1949 2 02

5321 EVANS,E
THE IRISHNESS OF THE IRISH
IRISH ASSOCIATION
1967 2 99

5322 EVANS,E
MOURNE COUNTRY
DUNDALGAN PRESS
DUNDALK
1967 2 02

5323 EVANS,E
NI: A PORTRAIT
COLLINS
LONDON
1951 2 02

5324 EVANS,E
NORTHERN HERITAGE
AQUARIUS
1971 2 99

5325 EVANS,E
PERSONALITY OF IRELAND
CUP
CAMBRIDGE
1973 2 02

5326 EVANS,E
PERSONALITY OF ULSTER
TRANSACTION 51
1970 2 01

5327 EVANS,E
PORTRAIT OF NI
COLLINS
LONDON
1951 2 02

5328 FIRESTONE,M
CHRISTMAS MUMMING AND SYMBOLIC
INTERACTIONISM
ETHOS 6(2)
1978 2 01

5329 FOSTER,J
FORCES AND THEMES IN ULSTER FICTION
GILL AND MACMILLAN
DUBLIN
1974 2 02

5330 GAELIC ATHLETIC ASSOCIATION
SIXTY GLORIOUS YEARS OF THE GAA
GAELIC ATHLETIC ASSOCIATION
DUBLIN
1947 2 10

5331 GAILEY,A
SCOTS ELEMENT IN NORTH IRISH POPULAR
CULTURE
ETHNOLOGIA EUROPAEA 8(1)
1975 2 01

5332 GAILEY,A
ULSTER FOLK WAYS: AN INTRODUCTION
EASON
BELFAST
1978 2 10

5333 GAILEY,A; O'DANACHAIR,C
ETHNOLOGICAL MAPPING IN IRELAND
ETHNOLOGIA EUROPAEA 9(1)
1976 2 01

5334 GALLAGHER,C
ALL AROUND THE LONEY-O
AUTHOR
BELFAST
1978 2 10

Culture and the Arts/

5335 GLASSIE,H H
PASSING THE TIME IN BALLYMENONE: CULTURE
AND HISTORY OF AN ULSTER COMMUNITY
PHILADELPHIA U P
PHILADELPHIA
1982 2 02

5336 GRAECEN,R
DRAMA UP NORTH
THE BELL 13(5)
DUBLIN
1947 2 01

5337 HAMILTON,C
THE SESSION: A SOCIO-MUSICAL PHENOMENON
IN IRISH TRADITIONAL MUSIC
QUB MA
BELFAST
1978 2 04

5338 HAYWARD,R
BELFAST THROUGH THE AGES
DUNDALGAN PRESS
DUNDALK
1952 2 10

5339 HAYWARD,R
PROVINCE OF ULSTER
IN GORMAN,M (ED)
LONDON
1963 2 07

5340 HAYWARD,R
ULSTER AND THE CITY OF BELFAST
BARKER
LONDON
1950 2 99

5341 HEANEY,S
THE WRITER AND THE TROUBLES
THRESHOLD 25
1974 1 01

5342 HERRON,C
THE INVOLVEMENT OF SIXTEEN YEAR OLD
SCHOOL LEAVERS IN PHYSICAL ACTIVITY
ULSTER POLY MPHIL
BELFAST
1981 2 04

5343 HEWITT,J
ART IN ULSTER, VOL 1
BLACKSTAFF
BELFAST
1977 2 02

5344 HEWITT,J
THE BITTER GROUND: SOME PROBLEMS OF THE
ULSTER WRITER
LAGAN 3
1945 2 01

5345 HEWITT,J
THE COURSE OF WRITING IN ULSTER
RANN 20
1953 2 01

5346 HEWITT,J
POETRY AND ULSTER: A SURVEY
POETRY IRELAND 8
1950 2 01

5347 HEWITT,J
SOME NOTES ON WRITING IN ULSTER
THE BELL 18(4)
DUBLIN
1952 2 01

5348 JAMISON,K
THE ARTS IN A SMALL COMMUNITY
ARTS COUNCIL OF NI
BELFAST
1969 2 10

5349 JOHNSTON,E
FOLK ART IN ULSTER
ARCHITECTURAL R
1970 2 01

5350 JONES,W R
ENGLAND AGAINST THE CELTIC FRINGE: A
STUDY IN CULTURAL STEREOTYPES
J WLD HIST 13
LONDON
1971 2 01

5351 KEARNEY,T
THE POETRY OF THE NORTH: A
POST-MODERNIST PERSPECTIVE
CRANE BAG 3(2)
DUBLIN
1979 2 01

5352 KENNEDY,D
THE THEATRE IN ULSTER 1944-1953
RANN 20
1953 2 01

5353 KENNEDY,D
THE ULSTER REGION AND THE THEATRE
LAGAN 4
1946 2 01

5354 KERSNOWSKI,F
THE POET IN NI: A WAY IN OR OUT?
IN SULLIVAN,E ET AL (EDS)
GAINESVILLE, FLORIDA
1976 1 07

5355 KING,N
THE FLUTE BAND IN NI
QUB MA
BELFAST
1977 2 04

5356 LARSEN,S S
THE GLORIOUS TWELFTH: THE POLITICS OF
LEGITIMATION IN KILBRONEY
IN COHEN,A P (ED)
MANCHESTER
1982 2 07

5357 LARSEN,S S
THE TWO SIDES OF THE HOUSE: IDENTITY AND
SOCIAL ORGANISATION IN KILBRONEY, NI
IN COHEN,A P (ED)
MANCHESTER
1982 2 07

5358 LAVER,M J
CULTURAL ASPECTS OF LOYALTY: ON
HIRSCHMAN AND LOYALISM IN ULSTER
POLIT STUD (OXFORD) 24(4)
OXFORD
1976 1 01

5359 LAVER,M J
CULTURAL ASPECTS OF LOYALTY: SOCIAL
LOYALTY AND THE ULSTER LOYALIST
DEPT POLITICS LIVERPOOL UNIV
LIVERPOOL
1974 1 08

5360 LEYTON,E H
CONSCIOUS MODELS AND DISPUTE REGULATION
IN AN ULSTER VILLAGE
MAN 1(4)
LONDON
1966 2 01

5361 LEYTON,E H
DUAL ORGANISATION IN KILDARRAGH
MEMORIAL UNIV PHD
NEWFOUNDLAND
1971 2 04

5362 LEYTON,E H
KINSHIP AND CLASS IN AN ULSTER VILLAGE
TORONTO UNIV PHD
TORONTO
1972 2 04

5363 LEYTON,E H
ONE BLOOD: KINSHIP AND CLASS IN AN IRISH
VILLAGE
MEMORIAL U P
NEWFOUNDLAND
1975 2 02

Culture and the Arts/

5364 LEYTON, E H
OPPOSITION AND INTEGRATION IN ULSTER
MAN 9(2)
LONDON
1974 2 01

5365 LEYTON, E H
SPHERES OF INHERITANCE IN AUGHNABOY
AMER ANTHROPOLOGIST
WASHINGTON, D C
1970 2 01

5366 LOFTUS, R J
NATIONALISM IN MODERN ANGLO-IRISH POETRY
WISCONSIN UNIV PHD
MADISON
1962 2 04

5367 LOUDAN, J
ULSTER AND A SUBSIDISED THEATRE
LAGAN 4
1946 2 01

5368 LOUGHBOROUGH RECREATION PLANNING
CONSULTANTS
CRAIGAVON RECREATION REPORT
CRAIGAVON DEVELOPMENT COMMISSION
CRAIGAVON
1973 2 02

5369 MACKILLOP, J
ULSTER VIOLENCE IN FICTION
IN SULLIVAN, E ET AL (EDS)
GAINESVILLE, FLORIDA
1976 1 07

5370 MACKLOCK, R B
AN ANALYSIS OF OUTDOOR RECREATION
CONSUMPTION BEHAVIOUR AT TWO FOREST
PARKS
QUB PHD
BELFAST
1971 2 04

5371 MAXWELL, D E S
IMAGINING THE NORTH: VIOLENCE AND ITS
WRITERS
EIRE-IRELAND 8(2)
1973 1 01

5372 MCFARLANE, W G
GOSSIP AND SOCIAL RELATIONS IN A
NORTHERN IRISH COMMUNITY
IN STUCHLIK, M (ED)
BELFAST
1977 2 07

5373 MCFARLANE, W G
GOSSIP AND SOCIAL RELATIONSHIPS IN A NI
VILLAGE
QUB PHD
BELFAST
1978 2 04

5374 MCFARLANE, W G
SOCIAL LIFE IN NI
SSRC NEWSLETTER 42
LONDON
1980 2 01

5375 MCKENDRY, E
COMPUTER-AIDED CONTRIBUTIONS TO THE
STUDY OF IRISH DIALECTS
QUB PHD
BELFAST
1982 2 04

5376 MCMINN, J
CONTEMPORARY NOVELS ON THE 'TROUBLES'
ET IRL 5
1980 1 01

5377 MILROY, J
REGIONAL ACCENTS OF ENGLISH: BELFAST
BLACKSTAFF
BELFAST
1981 2 02

5378 MILROY, L
INVESTIGATING LINGUISTIC VARIATION IN
THREE BELFAST WORKING CLASS COMMUNITIES
IN SPENCER, A; CORMACK, R; O'DOWD, L;
TOVEY, H (EDS) PROC SAI
BELFAST
1977 2 01

5379 MILROY, L
LANGUAGE AND SOCIAL NETWORK IN BELFAST
QUB PHD
BELFAST
1979 2 04

5380 MILROY, L
LANGUAGE AND SOCIAL NETWORKS
BLACKWELL
OXFORD
1980 2 02

5381 MILROY, L; MILROY, J
BELFAST: CHANGE AND VARIATION IN AN
URBAN VERNACULAR
IN TRUDGILL, P (ED)
LONDON
1978 2 07

5382 MINISTRY OF EDUCATION (NI)
PROVISION OF RECREATIONAL, SOCIAL AND
PHYSICAL TRAINING FACILITIES IN NI
HMSO CMD 246
BELFAST
1947 2 03

5383 MOGEY, J M
CHARACTERISTICS OF THE RURAL COMMUNITY
IN NI
RUR SOCIOL 18(3)
1953 2 01

5384 MOGEY, J M
THE COMMUNITY IN NI
MAN 48
1948 2 01

5385 MOGEY, J M
RURAL LIFE IN NI
OUP
OXFORD
1947 2 02

5386 MOGEY, J M
RURAL LIFE IN NI
QUB DSC
BELFAST
1948 2 04

5387 MOGEY, J M
ULSTER'S SIX COUNTIES
IN WILSON, T (ED)
OXFORD
1955 2 07

5388 MORRELL, R
REFLECTIONS ON THE LANGUAGE OF THE NI
TROUBLES
CONTEMP R 239
LONDON
1981 1 01

5389 MURPHY, M J
MOUNTAIN YEAR: LIFE ON THE SLOPES OF
SLIEVE GALLION
DUFOUR
CHESTER SPRINGS, PA
1964 2 02

5390 MURPHY, M J
TYRONE FOLK QUEST
BLACKSTAFF
BELFAST
1975 2 02

5391 O'BRIEN, J
VIOLENCE IN THE NORTH OF IRELAND: THE
POETS' RESPONSE
IN SULLIVAN, E ET AL (EDS)
GAINESVILLE, FLORIDA
1976 1 07

5392 O'DONNELL, D
BEAUTY AND BELFAST: A NOTE ON 'ODD MAN
OUT'
THE BELL 14(2)
DUBLIN
1947 2 01

5393 O'SNODAIGH, P
HIDDEN ULSTER
CLODHANNA TEO
DUBLIN
1973 2 10

5394 QUINN, H
BELFAST STREET SONGS
RANN 16
1952 2 01

5395 RAFROIDI, P
POLITIQUE ET LITTERATURE: LUTTES
FRATRICIDES EN IRLANDE DU NORDE
LE MONDE DIPLOMATIQUE 22
1974 1 01

5396 REDMOND, T
A SENSE OF COMMUNITY: BROUGHSHANE (CO.
ANTRIM)
COMM FORUM 3(3)
BELFAST
1973 2 01

5397 ROBINSON, A
CULTURE AND IDENTITY IN NI
NETWORK 1(2)
DERRY
1980 1 01

5398 ROBINSON, A; JOHNSTON, R
THE BALLYARNET/SHANTALLOW RECREATION
CENTRE
COMM FORUM 4(2)
BELFAST
1974 2 01

5399 ROCH, E
FOLK MEDICINE AND FAITH HEALING IN NI
QUB PHD
BELFAST
1981 2 04

5400 ROLSTON, B
ESCAPING FROM BELFAST: CLASS, IDEOLOGY
AND LITERATURE IN NI
RACE AND CLASS 20(1)
LONDON
1978 1 01

5401 ROSENFIELD, R
THEATRE IN BELFAST: ACHIEVEMENT OF A
DECADE
THRESHOLD 2(1)
BELFAST
1958 2 01

5402 SCOPE
WHAT IS COMMUNITY ART?
SCOPE 21
BELFAST
1979 2 01

5403 SCULLION, F
THE LAMBEG DRUM IN ULSTER
QUB MA
BELFAST
1982 2 04

5404 SERGEANT, H
ULSTER REGIONALISM
RANN 20
1953 2 01

5405 SEYMOUR, ST JOHN D
IRISH WITCHCRAFT AND DEMONOLOGY
CAUSEWAY
NEW YORK
1973 2 02

5406 SILKE, E
DRAMA IN BELFAST
THE BELL 15(4)
DUBLIN
1948 2 01

5407 STEPHENS, M
LINGUISTIC MINORITIES OF WESTERN EUROPE
WALES
1976 2 02

5408 TITLEY, A
ROUGH RUG-HEADED KERNS: THE IRISH GUNMAN
IN THE POPULAR NOVEL
EIRE-IRELAND 15(4)
ST PAUL
1980 1 01

5409 TORODE, B
IRELAND THE TERRIBLE
IN CURTIN, C; KELLY, M; O'DOWD, L (EDS)
DUBLIN
1983 2 07

5410 WAGNER, H; O'BAOILL, C
LINGUISTIC ATLAS AND SURVEY OF IRISH
DIALECTS: VOL. 4: THE DIALECTS OF ULSTER
AND THE ISLE OF MAN
INST ADVANCED STUD
DUBLIN
1969 2 02

5411 WALKER, I
BARRACKROOM BALLADS OF NI
NEW SOCIETY 24 APR
LONDON
1980 1 01

5412 ADAMSON, I
THE CRUITHIN: A HISTORY OF THE ULSTER
LAND AND PEOPLE
DONARD
BELFAST
1978 1 02

5413 AMERICAN GEOGRAPHICAL SOCIETY
NI
AMERICAN GEOGRAPHICAL SOCIETY
1973 2 10

5414 BLAND, F E
THE UNITED KINGDOM OF GREAT BRITAIN AND
NI
COUNTRY PROFILES FEB
1975 2 01

5415 BOEHRINGER, G H
SOCIOLOGY, SOCIAL PROBLEMS AND SOCIAL
CONTROL
SOC STUD 3(4)
1974 1 01

5416 BRITISH INFORMATION SERVICES
NI
CENTRAL OFFICE OF INFORMATION
LONDON
1978 1 03

5417 BROWN, R H
I AM OF IRELAND
HARPER AND ROW
NEW YORK
1974 3 02

5418 BRYANS, R
ULSTER: A JOURNEY THROUGH THE SIX
COUNTIES
FABER
LONDON
1975 2 02

5419 BUCKLAND, P
ULSTER UNIONISM AND THE ORIGINS OF NI
1885-1923
GILL AND MACMILLAN
DUBLIN
1973 2 02

5420 BUCKLAND, P
UNITY OF ULSTER UNIONISM 1886-1939
HISTORY 60(199)
1975 2 01

5421 BUSTEED, M A
COUNTRY IN SEARCH OF IDENTITY
GEOGR MAG 49
1977 2 01

5422 BUSTEED, M A
NI
OUP
LONDON
1974 2 02

5423 BUSTEED, M A
NI: GEOGRAPHICAL ASPECTS OF A CRISIS
SCHOOL OF GEOGR RES PAPER 3
OXFORD
1972 1 10

5424 BUTLIN, R
HISTORICAL GEOGRAPHY AND LOCAL STUDIES
IN IRELAND
GEOGR VIEWPOINT 1(3)
1966 2 01

5425 BUTLIN, R
IRELAND IN AN INTERNATIONAL WORLD - THE
DIVIDED ISLAND
GEOGR MAG 49
1977 2 01

5426 CATHCART, R
LETS LOOK AT ULSTER
UTV
BELFAST
1977 2 02

5427 COLUMBIA BROADCASTING SYSTEM
NI: GLOSSARY OF TERMS, ASSOCIATIONS AND
PERSONALITIES
COLUMBIA BROADCASTING SYSTEM
NEW YORK
1969 1 99

5428 COMMON, R
SOME CONCERNS OF REGIONAL GEOGRAPHY WITH
ILLUSTRATIONS FROM NI
SCOTT GEOGR MAG 87
1971 2 01

5429 CONWAY, J; CONWAY, L
MOST NATURAL THING IN THE WORLD
NEW YORK
1974 1 02

5430 COOGAN, T P
THE IRISH - A PERSONAL VIEW
PHAIDON
LONDON
1975 2 02

5431 COWIE, D
IRELAND: THE LAND AND THE PEOPLE
BARNES
NEW JERSEY
1976 2 02

5432 DARBY, J
CLEARER PERSPECTIVES ON ULSTER: A REVIEW
ARTICLE
NEW COMM 4(4)
1976 1 01

5433 DARBY, J
TRYING TO SEE IRELAND
NEW COMM 1(2)
1972 2 01

5434 DEUTSCH, R; MAGOWAN, V
NI: CHRONOLOGY OF EVENTS VOLUME ONE:
1968-71
BLACKSTAFF
BELFAST
1973 1 06

5435 DEUTSCH, R; MAGOWAN, V
NI: CHRONOLOGY OF EVENTS VOLUME THREE:
1974
BLACKSTAFF
BELFAST
1975 1 06

5436 DEUTSCH, R; MAGOWAN, V
NI: CHRONOLOGY OF EVENTS VOLUME TWO:
1972-73
BLACKSTAFF
BELFAST
1974 1 06

5437 DOHRS, F
NI
J AMER GEOGR SOCIETY
1967 2 01

5438 DOYLE, C
PEOPLE AT WAR
FDR TEORANTA
DUBLIN
1975 1 02

5439 DUFF, C
IRELAND AND THE IRISH
BOARDMAN AND CO
LONDON
1952 2 99

5440 DURES,A
MODERN IRELAND
WAYLAND
HOVE
1973 2 02

5441 ECONOMIST
JOHN BULL'S MODEL IRELAND: ULSTER
ECONOMIST 6 OCT
1956 2 10

5442 ECONOMIST
NI: THE OTHER ULSTER (SUPPLEMENT)
ECONOMIST 275 JUNE 28
LONDON
1980 1 01

5443 EMERSON,P J
THAT SONS MAY BURY THEIR FATHERS
POLAND STREET PUBLICATIONS
LONDON
1979 1 02

5444 EXIT PHOTOGRAPHY GROUP
SURVIVAL PROGRAMMES IN BRITAIN'S INNER
CITIES
OPEN UNIVERSITY
MILTON KEYNES
1982 1 02

5445 FLACKES,W
NI: A POLITICAL DIRECTORY
GILL AND MACMILLAN
DUBLIN
1980 1 02

5446 FREEMAN,T W
FORTY YEARS OF GEOGRAPHY
IR GEOG 5(5)
DUBLIN
1968 2 01

5447 FREEMAN,T W
IRELAND: A GENERAL AND REGIONAL
GEOGRAPHY
METHUEN
LONDON
1972 2 02

5448 FREEMAN,T W
IRELAND: ITS PHYSICAL, HISTORICAL AND
SOCIAL GEOGRAPHY
METHUEN
LONDON
1950 2 99

5449 FREEMAN,T W
TWO LANDSCAPES: SOUTHWEST SCOTLAND AND
NORTHEAST IRELAND
IN MILLER,R; WATSON,J W (EDS)
LONDON
1959 2 07

5450 GIBSON,N J
ECONOMIC AND SOCIAL RESEARCH AND NI
SSRC NEWSLETTER 20
LONDON
1973 2 01

5451 GILLMOR,D A
A SYSTEMATIC GEOGRAPHY OF IRELAND
GILL AND MACMILLAN
DUBLIN
1971 2 02

5452 GOODYEAR,P M
SOCIAL COMPARISONS, REFERENCE GROUPS AND
DISSENT IN NI
ANTIPODE 11(2)
WORCESTER, MASS
1980 1 01

5453 GRIFFITHS,H; NIC GIOLLA CHOILLE,T;
ROBINSON,J
YESTERDAY'S HERITAGE AND TOMORROW'S
RESOURCES: A STUDY OF VOLUNTARY
ORGANISATIONS...IN NI
NUU
COLERAINE
1978 2 10

5454 CUIFFAN,J; VERRIERE,J; RAFROIDI,P
L'IRLANDE: MILIEU ET HISTOIRE
PARIS
1971 2 02

5455 HAHN,E
FRACTURED EMERALD: IRELAND
DOUBLEDAY
NEW YORK
1971 1 02

5456 HANNA,D O
FACE OF ULSTER
BATSFORD
LONDON
1952 2 02

5457 HARBISON,J; HARBISON,J
UNLESS YOU'RE FROM THE PLACE YOU CAN'T
START TO UNDERSTAND IT
IN HARBISON,J; HARBISON,J (EDS)
SHEPTON MALLET, SOMERSET
1980 1 07

5458 HARRIS,R
RANDOM NOTES ON ULSTER
IN O'CONNOR,U (ED)
1974 1 07

5459 HAUGHTON,J P; GILLMOR,D A
THE GEOGRAPHY OF IRELAND
DEPT OF FOREIGN AFFAIRS
DUBLIN
1979 2 03

5460 HEATLEY,E ET AL
REGISTER OF ARCHIVES FOR NI
IR COMMITTEE HISTORICAL SC1 B 3(68)
1954 2 01

5461 HESLINGA,M W
GEOGRAPHY AND NATIONALITY
DEPT GEOG QUB
BELFAST
1978 1 08

5462 HESLINGA,M W
THE IRISH BORDER AS A CULTURAL DIVIDE
GORCUM AND COMPANY
ASSEN, NETHERLANDS
1962 2 02

5463 HILL,D A
NI
CUP
CAMBRIDGE
1974 2 10

5464 HODGSON,B
WAR AND PEACE IN NI
NATIONAL GEOGRAPHIC APR
1981 2 01

5465 INSTITUTE OF COMMONWEALTH STUDIES
COLLECTED CONFERENCE PAPERS ON IRELAND,
BRITAIN AND EUROPE
INST COMMONWEALTH STUD
LONDON
1971 2 11

5466 IRISH GOVERNMENT
IRELAND: THE STORY IN PICTURES OF THE
NORTH'S DISTRESS
GOVERNMENT INFORMATION BUREAU
DUBLIN
1969 1 03

5467 LANE,P
IRELAND
BATSFORD
LONDON
1974 2 10

5468 MACAODHA,B S; CURRIE,E A
IRELAND: A SYSTEMATIC AND REGIONAL
GEOGRAPHY
1968 2 02

5469 MCCREARY, A
PROFILES OF HOPE
CHRISTIAN JOURNALS
BELFAST
1981 1 10

5470 MCGOVERN, P D
NI: PEOPLE WITH A PURPOSE
GEOGR MAG 37
1965 2 02

5471 MOROWITZ, H J
SOCIAL IMPLICATIONS OF A BIOLOGICAL
PRINCIPLE
IN MOROWITZ, H J
NEW YORK
1979 1 07

5472 NATIONAL LABOUR MOVEMENT DELEGATION TO
IRELAND
REPORT
NATIONAL LABOUR MOVEMENT DELEGATION
LONDON
1976 1 10

5473 NEW SOCIETY
NI: A SOCIAL STUDIES READER
NEW SOCIETY PUBLICATIONS
LONDON
1973 1 99

5474 NEWCASTLE ON TYNE TRADES COUNCIL
FIVE DAYS IN IRELAND
NEWCASTLE ON TYNE TRADES COUNCIL
NEWCASTLE
1979 2 10

5475 NEWE, G B
GETTING INVOLVED IN MANKIND
EVERYMAN
BENBURB
1970 3 01

5476 NEWE, G B
NATIONAL DEVELOPMENT: SOCIAL AND
CULTURAL
IN RHODES, E (ED)
DERRY
1967 2 07

5477 NICHOLS, H
ADMINISTRATION OF LOCAL STUDIES
COLLECTIONS IN GB AND NI
J LIBRARIANSHIP 8(4)
1976 2 10

5478 NICSS
PROGRESS IN ULSTER SINCE 1921
NICSS
BELFAST
1960 2 10

5479 O'FAOLAIN, S
THE IRISH
PENGUIN
HARMONDSWORTH
1969 2 02

5480 O'GRADA, S
ARE YOU IRISH OR NORMAL?
KAYE AND WARD
LONDON
1970 3 02

5481 O'HANLON, J
THE IRISH: SINNERS, SAINTS ... AND OTHER
PROUD NATIVES OF THE FABLED ISLE
HARPER AND ROW
NEW YORK
1975 1 02

5482 PICKLES, T
GREAT BRITAIN AND IRELAND
DENT
LONDON
1961 2 02

5483 PROUDFOOT, V B
NI, PEOPLES AND PLACES
AUCKLAND STUD GEOG 2(1)
AUCKLAND, NEW ZEALAND
1967 2 01

5484 QUB
THE PURSUIT OF KNOWLEDGE: A COLLECTION
OF ESSAYS ON CURRENT RESEARCH IN QUB
QUB
BELFAST
1959 2 10

5485 RIDDELL, P
THE IRISH - ARE THEY REAL?
HAMISH HAMILTON
LONDON
1972 2 02

5486 SMITH, R H
NI: A REGIONAL GEOGRAPHY
NI GOVT INFORMATION SERVICE
BELFAST
1971 2 03

5487 SMYTH, P
THIRTY YEARS ON
IR ARCHIVAL B 5
1975 2 01

5488 STAMP, L D; BEAVER, S H
THE BRITISH ISLES: A GEOGRAPHIC AND
ECONOMIC SURVEY
LONGMANS
LONDON
1954 2 02

5489 SYMONS, L; HANNA, L
NI: A GEOGRAPHICAL INTRODUCTION
LONDON U P
LONDON
1967 2 02

5490 TIERNEY, M
MODERN IRELAND 1850-1950
GILL AND MACMILLAN
DUBLIN
1972 2 02

5491 TIERNEY, M
MODERN IRELAND: TWO INTERPETATIONS
STUDIES DEC
DUBLIN
1952 2 01

5492 UNKNOWN
MICROFICHE OF NI POLITICAL LITERATURE,
1968-1975
CLEARWATER PUBLISHING CO.
NEW YORK
         1 10

5493 URIS, J; URIS, L
IRELAND: A TERRIBLE BEAUTY
CORGI
LONDON
1979 1 02

5494 WALLACE, M
THE IRISH: HOW THEY LIVE AND WORK
DAVID AND CHARLES
NEWTON ABBOT
1972 1 02

Any Other General Topic

5495 ALEVY,D; BUNKER,B; DOOB,L; FOLTZ,W;
FRENCH,N; KLEIN,E; MILLER,J
RATIONALE, RESEARCH AND ROLE
RELATIONSHIPS IN THE STIRLING WORKSHOP
J CONFLICT RESOL 18(2)
1974 1 01

5496 ARMSTRONG.R
THROUGH THE AGES TO NEWTOWNABBEY
SHANWAY PUBLICATIONS
MUCKAMORE, CO ANTRIM
1980 2 02

5497 ASSISSI FELLOWSHIP COMMITTEE
ITINERANTS IN NI
ASSISSI FELLOWSHIP COMMITTEE
BELFAST
1966 2 02

5498 BILL,J M
METHODOLOGICAL STUDY OF THE INTERVIEW
AND QUESTIONNAIRE APPROACH TO
INFORMATION GATHERING
RES IN EDUC 9
1973 2 01

5499 BLAIR,S A
ULSTER'S COUNTRY YOUTH: THE FIRST FIFTY
YEARS OF THE YOUNG FARMERS' CLUBS OF
ULSTER
YOUNG FARMERS' CLUB OF ULSTER
BELFAST
1978 2 02

5500 BOAL,F W; JOHNSON,D B
RANK-SIZE CURVE: A DIAGNOSTIC TOOL?
PROFESSIONAL GEOGRAPHER 17
1965 2 01

5501 BOEHRINGER,G H; ZEROULIS,V; BAYLEY,J;
BOEHRINGER,K
STIRLING: THE DESTRUCTIVE APPLICATION OF
GROUP TECHNIQUES TO A CONFLICT
J CONFLICT RESOL 18(2)
1974 1 01

5502 BOWEN,D
BALLYMURPHY ESTATE
CONTEMP R 218(1264)
1971 1 01

5503 BOYD,H A
RATHLIN ISLAND, NORTH OF ANTRIM
SCARLETT
BALLYCASTLE
1947 2 02

5504 BRETT.C E B
LONG SHADOWS CAST BEFORE: NINE LIVES IN
ULSTER, 1625-1977
J BARTHOLOMEW
EDINBURGH
1978 2 02

5505 BROWN,R H
BOOKS AND BOMBS
PUBLISHERS WEEKLY JAN 23
1981 1 01

5506 BROWN,R H
LIBRARIES IN NI: SERVICE GOES ON
LIBRARY J 106(11)
1981 1 01

5507 BRUNT,R M
A NI LIBRARY NETWORK?
AN LEABHARLANN 5
DUBLIN
1976 2 01

5508 BURNETT,R
LONDONDERRY SCENE
SOLON 1(2)
1970 3 01

5509 BURTON,F; CARLEN,P
OFFICIAL DISCOURSE
ECON AND SOCIETY 6(4)
LONDON
1977 1 01

5510 BURTON,F; CARLEN,P
OFFICIAL DISCOURSE: ON DISCOURSE
ANALYSIS, GOVERNMENT PUBLICATIONS,
IDEOLOGY AND THE STATE
RKP
LONDON
1979 1 02

5511 CALDWELL,T ET AL
TAXONOMIC ANALYSIS OF EVENTS IN NI AND
OUTLINE OF EVENTS-BASED SIMULATION
PROGAMME PEACE RESEARCH
LANCASTER UNIV SOCIOLOGY DEPT
1971 1 08

5512 CARSON,W
DERRY THROUGH THE LENS
BALLYSHANNON
1976 1 02

5513 CARTER,C E; RIPPEY,B
WATER QUALITY IN FOUR BAYS IN LOUGH
NEAGH, NI
IR J ENVIRONMENTAL SCI 11(1)
DUBLIN
1982 2 01

5514 CHINOY,M
HOW NOT TO RESOLVE A CONFLICT
NEW SOCIETY 4 SEPT
LONDON
1975 1 01

5515 CLARK,W
RATHLIN: DISPUTED ISLAND
VOLTURNA PRESS
PORTLAW, WATERFORD
1971 2 02

5516 CLARKSON,L A
INTRODUCTION: K.H. CONNELL AND ECONOMIC
AND SOCIAL HISTORY AT QUB
IN GOLDSTROM,J M; CLARKSON,L A (EDS)
OXFORD
1981 2 07

5517 COCHRANE,A C
GOOD NEWS FROM A TROUBLED PROVINCE
LIBRARY ASSOC RECORD 81
1979 2 01

5518 COCHRANE,A C
INFORMATION DEVELOPMENTS IN NI
AN LEABHARLANN 10
DUBLIN
1981 2 01

5519 COX,C
MILITAR GEOGRAPHISCHE ANGABEN UBER
IRLAND
AN COSANTOIR 35(3)
1976 2 01

5520 DARWIN,K
THE PUBLIC RECORD OFFICE OF NI
ARCHIVES 6
1964 2 01

5521 DARWIN,K
THE PUBLIC RECORD OFFICE OF NI
IR ANCESTOR 1
1969 2 01

5522 DAVIDSON, J
ATTITUDES TO AGGRESSION AND ETHICAL
BEHAVIOUR IN ...RUGBY UNION FOOTBALL
PLAYERS IN ENGLAND, IRELAND, SCOTLAND
AND WALES
QUB MED
BELFAST
1980 2 04

5523 DAVIES, G L
THOMAS WALTER FREEMAN AND THE GEOGRAPHY
OF IRELAND: A TRIBUTE
IR GEOG 6(5)
DUBLIN
1973 2 01

5524 DAVIES, G L
TWENTY-SEVEN YEARS OF IRISH GEOGRAPHY
IR GEOG 6(2)
1970 2 01

5525 DAVISON, R S
THE GERMAN AIR RAIDS ON BELFAST OF...
MAY 1941, AND THEIR CONSEQUENCES
QUB PHD
BELFAST
1979 2 04

5526 DELAIGLES, J; GONZALEZ, E
IRELAND AND THE NORTH ATLANTIC TREATY
R POLIT INT (MADRID) 162
MADRID
1979 2 01

5527 DOOB, L; FOLTZ, W
BELFAST WORKSHOP: AN APPLICATION OF
GROUP TECHNIQUES TO A DESTRUCTIVE
CONFLICT
J CONFLICT RESOL 17(3)
1973 1 01

5528 DOOB, L; FOLTZ, W
IMPACT OF A WORKSHOP UPON GRASS ROOTS
LEADERS IN BELFAST
J CONFLICT RESOL 18(2)
1974 1 01

5529 DOUGHTY, P
THE PUBLIC OF THE ULSTER MUSEUM: A
STATISTICAL SURVEY
MUSEUMS J 68
1968 2 01

5530 DUNCAN, M
THE EFFECTS OF SOCIAL CONFLICT ON
RECREATION PATTERNS IN BELFAST
US INT UNIV CALIF PHD
         1 04

5531 EDWARDS, R D
IRISH FAMILIES: THE ARCHIVAL ASPECT
NATIONAL UNIV OF IRELAND
DUBLIN
1974 2 10

5532 EIDE, A
PEACE RESEARCH AS COMMUNICATION: HOW,
WITH WHOM, FOR WHAT PURPOSE
CURRENT RES ON PEACE AND VIOLENCE 1(2)
OSLO
1971 1 01

5533 EVANS, E
ARCHAEOLOGY IN ULSTER SINCE 1920
ULSTER J ARCHAEOLOGY 31
1968 2 01

5534 EVE, J
INHERITANCE (PROVISION FOR FAMILY AND
DEPENDANTS) (NI) ORDER 1979
NI LEG QUART 30
BELFAST
1979 2 01

5535 FALLS, C
NI AND THE DEFENCE OF THE BRITISH ISLES
IN WILSON, T (ED)
OXFORD
1955 2 07

5536 FALLS, C
NI AS AN OUTPOST OF DEFENCE
WLD R (OCT)
1951 2 01

5537 FREEMAN, T W
MAN-MADE WALLS OF ULSTER
GEOGR MAG 46(11)
1974 2 01

5538 GAILEY, I B; GILLESPIE, W F; HASSETT, J
ACCOUNT OF THE TERRITORIALS IN NI,
1947-78
TERRITORIAL ARMY
BELFAST
1979 2 02

5539 GINGERBREAD
AS WE SEE IT: PROBLEMS OF ONE-PARENT
FAMILIES, TOLD IN THEIR OWN WORDS
GINGERBREAD
BELFAST
       2 10

5540 GMELCH, G
TO SHORTEN THE ROAD
O'BRIEN PRESS
DUBLIN
1978 2 02

5541 GMELCH, G; GMELCH, S B
THE EMERGENCE OF AN ETHNIC GROUP: THE
IRISH TINKERS
ANTHROPOLOGICAL QUART 44(4)
WASHINGTON, D C
1976 2 01

5542 GMELCH, S B
TINKERS AND TRAVELLERS
O'BRIEN PRESS
DUBLIN
1975 2 02

5543 GRAHAM, T R
WATER POLLUTION CONTROL, WITH PARTICULAR
REFERENCE TO NI
WATER POLLUTION CONTROL 66(6)
1967 2 01

5544 HALSTOCK, M
RATS: THE STORY OF A DOG SOLDIER
GOLLANCZ
LONDON
1981 1 02

5545 HAMILTON, P
UP THE SHANKILL
BLACKSTAFF
BELFAST
1979 2 02

5546 HARBISON, J; JARDINE, E; CURRAN, J D
USE OF THE JESNESS INVENTORY WITH NI
POPULATIONS
BRIT J CRIMINOLOGY 18(4)
1978 2 01

5547 HARKNESS, E
SALE OF GOODS: SOME RECENT DEVELOPMENTS
SLS/FACULTY OF LAW QUB
BELFAST
1981 2 10

5548 HARRIS, R
SELECTION OF LEADERS IN BALLYBEG
SOCIOL R 9(2)
KEELE
1961 2 01

5549 HEDERMAN, M
THE CRANE BAG AND THE NORTH OF IRELAND
CRANE BAG 4(2)
1980 1 01

5550 HEWITT, J
NO ROOTLESS COLONIST
AQUARIUS
BENBURB
1972 1 01

Any Other Specific Topic/

5551 KENNEDY, L
RECENT DEVELOPMENTS IN ORAL HISTORY IN
NI
ORAL HISTORY 10(1)
1982 2 01

5552 KERR, G; EVE, J
THE FAMILY LAW REFORM (NI) ORDER 1977
NI LEG QUART 28
BELFAST
1977 2 01

5553 KIRK, B
THE KLONDYKE BAR: PHOTOGRAPHS FROM THE
LIFE OF A BELFAST PUBLIC HOUSE
BLACKSTAFF
BELFAST
1975 2 02

5554 KIRK, T
SENSE OF COMMUNITY: PARK, COUNTY
LONDONDERRY
COMM FORUM 3(3)
BELFAST
1973 2 01

5555 KLEINEBERGER, H R
IRELAND THROUGH GERMAN EYES 1844-1957
STUDIES 49
1960 2 01

5556 KNOX, E
EFFECTS ON MORAL JUDGEMENT OF SOCIAL
PRESSURE
QUB
BELFAST
        2 04

5557 LIBRARY ASSOCIATION NI BRANCH
DIRECTORY OF NI LIBRARIES
LIBRARY ASSOC (NI BRANCH)
1967 2 10

5558 LIVINGSTONE, P
FERMANAGH STORY: A DOCUMENTARY HISTORY
OF CO FERMANAGH FROM THE EARLIEST TIMES
TO THE PRESENT DAY
CUMANN SEANCHAIS CHLOCHAIR
ENNISKILLEN
1969 2 02

5559 LOCKWOOD, J
CONDUCTING RESEARCH IN NI: A PERSONAL
VIEW
IN STRINGER, P (ED)
1982 2 07

5560 LOGAN, B
THE SHANKILL
FARSET
BELFAST
1979 1 02

5561 LONETTO, R; FLEMING, S; MERCER, G W
THE STRUCTURE OF DEATH ANXIETY: A FACTOR
ANALYTIC STUDY
J PERSONALITY ASSESSMENT 43(4)
1979 1 01

5562 LONETTO, R; MERCER, G W; FLEMING, S;
BUNTING, B; CLARE, M
THE DEATH ANXIETY OF UNIVERSITY STUDENTS
IN NI AND CANADA
J PSYCHOL 104
1980 2 01

5563 LYNN, R
SOCIAL ECOLOGY OF INTELLIGENCE IN THE
BRITISH ISLES
BRIT J SOC CLINIC PSYCHOL 18
LONDON
1979 2 01

5564 MACDERMOTT, F
THE WAR AND IRISH UNITY
POLIT QUART 10(4)
LONDON
1959 2 01

Any Other Specific Topic/

5565 MACKEY, W J N
IRISH HISTORY: FACT OR FICTION
BELFAST CHURCHES CENTRAL COMMITTEE FOR
COMMUNITY WORK
1975 1 10

5566 MALCOLMSON, A P W
THE PUBLICATIONS PROGRAMME OF THE PUBLIC
RECORD OFFICE OF NI
IR BOOKLORE 1(2)
DUBLIN
1971 2 01

5567 MANNING, P I
THE ROLE OF THE GEOLOGICAL SURVEY OF NI
IN HIGHWAY CONSTRUCTION PROBLEMS
QUART J ENGINEERING GEOLOGY 5(1-2)
1972 2 01

5568 MCCARTNEY, J B; O'MAHONEY, D S
THE LEGAL RESPONSIBILITIES OF
PSYCHOLOGISTS
B BRIT PSYCHOL SOC 30
1977 2 01

5569 MCCORMACK, V
AUTHORITARIANISM
DEPT PSYCHOL QUB
BELFAST
1970 2 08

5570 MCCOURT, D
INNOVATION DIFFUSION IN IRELAND: AN
HISTORICAL CASE STUDY
PROC R IR ACAD 73(1)
1973 2 01

5571 MCFARLANE, W G
POLITICAL ECONOMY AND COMMUNITY RESEARCH
IN IN: AN ASSESSMENT
DEPT SOC ANTHROPOL QUB
BELFAST
1983 2 11

5572 MCKEOWN, M
CHRONICLES: A REGISTER OF NI'S
CASUALTIES 1969-80
CRANE BAG 4(2)
1980 1 01

5573 MCKEOWN, M
THE FIRST 500
IRISH NEWS
BELFAST
1972 2 10

5574 MCWHIRTER, L
RESEARCHING THE NI CONFLICT: SOME
PERSONAL ISSUES
BRIT PSYCHOL SOCIETY, DEVELOPMENTAL
PSYCHOL SECTION NEWSLETTER 3
1983 1 01

5575 MCWHIRTER, L; GAMBLE, R
DEVELOPMENT OF GROUP UNDERSTANDING: FROM
PERCEPTION TO PRAGMATICS AND PROCEDURES
ANNUAL CONF DEVELOPMENT SECTION BRIT
PSYCHOL SOC
EDINBURGH
1980 2 11

5576 MERCER, G W; BUNTING, B
CHRONIC ENVIRONMENTAL THREAT AND
REPRESSION OF DEATH-RELATED COGNITIONS
J DEATH AND DYING 3(2)
1979 1 01

5577 MERCER, G W; BUNTING, B; SNOOK, S
EFFECTS OF LOCATION EXPERIENCES WITH...
DISTURBANCES AND RELIGION ON DEATH
ANXIETY... IN A SAMPLE OF NI UNIVERSITY
STUDENTS
BRIT J SOC CLINIC PSYCHOL 18
1980 1 01

5578 MERCER, G W; BUNTING, B; SNOOK, S
NI UNIVERSITY STUDENTS: CONTACT WITH THE
CIVIL DISTURBANCES
SCHOOL OF BIOLOGY/ENVIRONMENTAL SCI NUU
COLERAINE
1978 1 08

5579 MERCER, G W; BUNTING, B; SNOOK, S
SOME PSYCHOLOGICAL AND SOCIAL ATTITUDE
CORRELATES OF NI UNIVERSITY STUDENTS'
CONTACT WITH THE CIVIL DISTURBANCES
J APPLIED SOC PSYCHOL 10(3)
LAFAYETTE
1980 1 01

5580 MILNE, A J M
PHILOSOPHY AND POLITICAL ACTION: THE
CASE FOR CIVIL RIGHTS
POLIT STUD (OXFORD) 21(4)
1973 1 01

5581 MOORE, P
ARMAGH OBSERVATORY: A HISTORY, 1790-1967
ARMAGH OBSERVATORY
ARMAGH
1967 2 02

5582 MOORE, T
THE SOCIAL CONTROL OF DRUG USE IN NI
DEPT SOC STUD QUB
BELFAST
1978 2 04

5583 MURRAY, R; BOAL, F W; POOLE, M A
PSYCHOLOGY AND THE THREATENING
ENVIRONMENT
ARCHIT PSYCHOL NEWSL 5(4)
1975 1 01

5584 NI OFFICE
REPORT OF THE INTERDEPARTMENTAL REVIEW
BODY ON INTOXICATING LIQUOR LICENSING IN
NI
HMSO
LONDON
1979 2 03

5585 O'BRIEN, F
LONDONDERRY AIRS
IN O'BRIEN, F (ED)
ROCKFORD, ILLINOIS
1971 3 07

5586 O'DOWD, L
INTELLECTUALS ON THE ROAD TO MODERNITY:
ASPECTS OF SOCIAL IDEOLOGY IN THE 1950S
SAI ANNUAL CONF
BALLYVAUGHAN, CO CLARE
1982 2 11

5587 O'REILLY, D V
THE DEVELOPMENT AND EVALUATION OF A
LEARNING GAME BASED ON THE NI
POLITICO-RELIGIOUS CONFLICT
DENVER UNIV
DENVER
1975 1 04

5588 PAISLEY, I R K
AMERICA'S DEBT TO ULSTER
MARTYRS' MEMORIAL PUBLICATIONS
BELFAST
1976 2 09

5589 PARKINSON, R E
HISTORY OF THE GRAND LODGE OF FREE AND
ACCEPTED MASONS OF IRELAND
LODGE OF RESEARCH
DUBLIN
1957 2 02

5590 PRIOR, D B; BETTS, N L
FLOODING IN BELFAST
IR GEOG 7
DUBLIN
1974 2 01

5591 PUXON, G; PUXON, V
VICTIMS: ITINERANTS IN IRELAND
AISTI EIREANNACHA
DUBLIN
1967 2. 99

5592 RANKIN, H
ON THE PSYCHOSTASIS OF ULSTER
PSYCHOTHERAPY AND PSYCHOSOMATICS 19
LONDON
1971 1 01

5593 RESEARCH SERVICES LIMITED
READERSHIP SURVEY OF NI
RSL
LONDON
1970 2 10

5594 ROBINSON, A
GEOGRAPHICAL FIELDWORK IN AN IRISH
BORDER AREA: LONDONDERRY/MOVILLE
BISHOP GROSSTESTE COLL EDUC
LINCOLN
1969 2 02

5595 ROBINSON, A
GEOGRAPHICAL FIELDWORK IN AN IRISH
BORDER AREA: LONDONDERRY/MOVILLE
MAGEE UNIV COLLEGE
DERRY
1969 2 10

5596 SAVORY, D
THE WAR EFFORT OF NI
UUC
BELFAST
1947 2 09

5597 SHERIDAN, L A
THE LAW OF PROPERTY
IN KEETON, G W; LLOYD, D (EDS)
LONDON
1955 2 07

5598 SHERRIN, C H
DISINHERITANCE OF A SPOUSE: A
COMPARATIVE STUDY OF THE LAW IN THE UK
AND THE REPUBLIC OF IRELAND
NI LEG QUART 31(1)
BELFAST
1980 2 01

5599 SHILLMAN, B
A SHORT HISTORY OF THE JEWS IN IRELAND
EASON
DUBLIN
1945 2 02

5600 SPENCER, A; BELL, Y
DATA ARCHIVE FOR IRELAND
IN SPENCER, A; TOVEY, H (EDS) PROC SAI
BELFAST
1978 2 01

5601 STEPHAN, E
SPIES IN IRELAND
MACDONALD
LONDON
1963 2 02

5602 STEWART, A T Q
THE ULSTER CRISIS
FABER
LONDON
1967 2 02

5603 SURRENCY, E
RESEARCH IN THE LAW OF NI
NI LEG QUART 15(1)
BELFAST
1964 2 01

5604 TAYLOR, W R
THE ORDNANCE SURVEY OF NI: AN OUTLINE OF
THE HISTORY AND PRESENT MAPPING TASKS
CARTOGRAPHIC J 6(2)
1969 2 01

5605 TEELING, W
THE WAR AND IRELAND
IN TEELING, W
LONDON
1970 2 07

5606 TREW, K
SOCIAL AND PSYCHOLOGICAL RESEARCH IN NI:
A CRITICAL APPRAISAL
IN MCWHIRTER, L (ED)
ABERDEEN
1980 1 07

5607 TURNER, B S
     DISTRIBUTIONAL ASPECTS OF FAMILY NAME
     STUDY ILLUSTRATED IN THE GLENS OF ANTRIM
     QUB PHD
     BELFAST
     1974 2 04

5608 USHERWOOD, B
     BOOKS, BOMBS AND BULLETS: LIBRARIES IN
     NI
     WILSON LIBRARY R 46
     1972 1 01

5609 VEITCH, E
     A LAW REFORM (BEREAVED SPOUSES) ACT
     (NI)?
     NI LEG QUART 22(3)
     BELFAST
     1971 2 01

5610 WALKER, T
     LIBRARIES AND LIBRARIANSHIP IN NI
     AN LEABHARLANN 13(1)
     1955 2 01

5611 WALLACE, H
     FINANCIAL PROVISIONS ON DEATH
     GAZETTE INCORPORATED LAW SOCIETY NI
     BELFAST
     1980 2 01

5612 WHYTE, J H
     IS RESEARCH ON THE NI PROBLEM
     WORTHWHILE? - INAUGURAL LECTURE
     QUB
     BELFAST
     1983 1 10

5613 WILLIAMS, D
     NULLITY JURISDICTION IN NI
     MOD LAW R NOV
     1956 1 01

5614 WILSON, R; MCKNIGHT, C: BANNON, T
     ATTRACTION PREFERENCES AND ASSORTATIVE
     MATING IN A NI SAMPLE
     B BRIT PSYCHOL SOC 34
     1981 2 01

5615 WYLIE, J C
     IRISH LAND LAW
     INCORPORATED LAW SOCIETY
     DUBLIN
     1970 2 02

5616 WYLIE, J C
     IRISH LAND LAW AND IRISH CONVEYANCING
     LAW
     QUB LLD
     BELFAST
     1980 2 02

5617 BOCCA,G
     BEAUTY AND THE BOMBS
     HORIZON MAR
     1982 1   01

5618 GRUBB INSTITUTE INTERGROUP PROJECT
     WORKING PAPER NO. 4
     GRUBB INSTITUTE
     LONDON
     1972 1   08

5619 NEUHAUS,R J
     BELFAST BLUES
     WORLDVIEW 16(11)
     1973 1   01

5620 TIMES
     NI - A SPECIAL REPORT
     TIMES 20 NOV
     1967 2   10

5621 ALEXANDER,Y (ED)
INTERNATIONAL TERRORISM: NATIONAL,
REGIONAL AND GLOBAL PERSPECTIVES
PRAEGER
NEW YORK
1976

5622 ALEXANDER,Y; GLEASON,J (EDS)
BEHAVIORAL AND QUANTITATIVE PERSPECTIVES
ON TERRORISM
PERGAMON
NEW YORK
1981

5623 ALEXANDER,Y; MYERS,K (EDS)
TERRORISM IN EUROPE
CROOM HELM
LONDON
1982

5624 ALEXANDER,Y; O'DAY,A (EDS)
TERRORISM IN IRELAND
CROOM HELM
LONDON
1983

5625 ALLEN,K ET AL (EDS)
REGIONAL PROBLEMS AND POLICIES IN THE
EUROPEAN COMMUNITIES: A BIBLIOGRAPHY
SAXON HOUSE
FARNBOROUGH
1979

5626 ANTHONY,E J; CHILAND,C (EDS)
THE CHILD IN HIS FAMILY: CHILDREN IN
TURMOIL - TOMORROW'S PARENTS
WILEY
NEW YORK
1982

5627 BAILEY,R; LEE,P (EDS)
THEORY AND PRACTICE IN SOCIAL WORK
BASIL BLACKWELL
OXFORD
1982

5628 BAKER,D; MEWS,S P (EDS)
RELIGION AND NATIONAL IDENTITY: STUDIES
IN CHURCH HISTORY
BLACKWELL
OXFORD
1981

5629 BARKER,D
SOLDIERING ON: AN UNOFFICIAL PORTRAIT OF
THE BRITISH ARMY
DEUTSCH
LONDON
1981

5630 BATES,J ET AL (EDS)
INDUSTRIAL RELATIONS IN NI
HMSO
BELFAST
1979

5631 BECKETT,J C; GLASSCOCK,R E (EDS)
BELFAST: THE ORIGIN AND GROWTH OF AN
INDUSTRIAL CITY
BBC
LONDON
1967

5632 BELL,J B (ED)
ON REVOLUTIONARY STRATEGIES OF NATIONAL
LIBERATION
HARVARD U P
CAMBRIDGE, MASS
1976

5633 BELL,J B (ED)
TRANSNATIONAL TERROR
AMERICAN ENTERPRISE INSTITUTE FOR PUBLIC
POLICY RESEARCH
WASHINGTON D.C.
1975

5634 BELL,R (ED)
EDUCATION IN GREAT BRITAIN AND IRELAND
RKP
LONDON
1973

5635 BELL,S H (ED)
ARTS IN ULSTER
HARRAP
LONDON
1951

5636 BELL,W; FREEMAN,W (EDS)
ETHNICITY AND NATION BUILDING:
COMPARATIVE INTERNATIONAL AND HISTORICAL
PERSPECTIVES
SAGE
BEVERLY HILLS
1974

5637 BENEWICK,R; SMITH,T (EDS)
DIRECT ACTION AND DEMOCRATIC POLITICS
ALLEN AND UNWIN
LONDON
1972

5638 BLACK,B; DITCH,J; MORRISSEY,M; STEELE,R
LOW PAY IN NI
LOW PAY UNIT
LONDON
1980

5639 BLACK,R D C (ED)
STATISTICAL AND SOCIAL INQUIRY SOCIETY
OF IRELAND: CENTENARY VOLUME,
1847-1947
JSSISI
DUBLIN
1949

5640 BLAIR,T L
POVERTY OF PLANNING
MACDONALD
LONDON
1973

5641 BLANSHARD,P
THE IRISH AND CATHOLIC POWER
BEACON
BOSTON, MASS
1953

5642 BLAXLAND,G
THE REGIMENTS DEPART: A HISTORY OF THE
BRITISH ARMY, 1945-1973
KIMBER
LONDON
1971

5643 BOAL,F W; DOUGLAS,J N H (EDS)
INTEGRATION AND DIVISION: GEOGRAPHICAL
PERSPECTIVES ON THE NI PROBLEM
ACADEMIC PRESS
LONDON
1982

5644 BOURNE,L S (ED)
INTERNAL STRUCTURE OF THE CITY
OUP
NEW YORK
1982

5645 BOWEN,E; CARTER,H; TAYLOR,J (EDS)
GEOGRAPHY AT ABERYSTWYTH
ABERYSTWYTH
1968

5646 BRANIFF,P; EUSTACE,J (EDS)
REPORT ON IRISH LEAGUE OF CREDIT UNIONS
IRISH LEAGUE OF CREDIT UNIONS
DUBLIN
1981

5647 BRIDGE,J W (ED)
FUNDAMENTAL RIGHTS
SWEET AND MAXWELL
LONDON
1973

5648 BRITISH ASSOCIATION FOR THE ADVANCEMENT
OF SCIENCE
BELFAST IN ITS REGIONAL SETTING: A
SCIENTIFIC SURVEY
BRITISH ASSOCIATION FOR THE ADVANCEMENT
OF SCIENCE
LONDON
1952

5649 BROWN,G (ED)
THE RED PAPER ON SCOTLAND
EUSPB
EDINBURGH
1975

5650 BROWN,J
THE CRANFIELD PAPERS: PROCEEDINGS OF THE
1978 CRANFIELD CONFERENCE ON THE
PREVENTION OF CRIME IN EUROPE
PEEL PRESS
LONDON
1979

5651 BROWN,M; BALDWIN,S (EDS)
THE YEAR BOOK OF SOCIAL POLICY IN
BRITAIN
RKP
LONDON
1979

5652 BUCHANAN,R H (ED)
RECENT RESEARCH ON IRISH RURAL
SETTLEMENT
DEPT GEOG QUB
BELFAST
1963

5653 BUCHANAN,R H; JONES,E; MCCOURT,D (EDS)
MAN AND HIS HABITAT: ESSAYS PRESENTED TO
EMYR ESTYN EVANS
RKP
LONDON
1971

5654 BUDGE,I; CREWER,J; FARLE,D (EDS)
PARTY IDENTIFICATION AND BEYOND
WILEY
NEW YORK
1976

5655 BURROWES,J
FRONTLINE REPORT: A JOURNALIST'S
NOTEBOOK
MAINSTREAM PUBLISHING
EDINBURGH
1982

5656 BUTLER,D E (ED)
BRITISH GENERAL ELECTION 1951
MACMILLAN
LONDON
1952

5657 BUTLER,D E; KING,A (EDS)
BRITISH GENERAL ELECTION 1966
MACMILLAN
LONDON
1966

5658 BUTTERWORTH,E; WEIR,D (EDS)
SOCIAL PROBLEMS OF MODERN BRITAIN
FONTANA
LONDON
1972

5659 CAMPBELL,C M (ED)
DO WE NEED A BILL OF RIGHTS?
TEMPLE SMITH
LONDON
1980

5660 CARLTON,C (ED)
BIGOTRY AND BLOOD: DOCUMENTS ON THE
ULSTER TROUBLES
NELSON
CHICAGO
1977

5661 CARLTON,D; SCHAERF,C (EDS)
CONTEMPORARY TERROR: STUDIES IN
SUB-STATE VIOLENCE
MACMILLAN
LONDON
1982

5662 CARPENTER,A (ED)
PLACE, PERSONALITY AND THE IRISH WRITER
G SMYTHE
BUCKS
1977

5663 CELTIC LEAGUE
SIGNIFICANCE OF FREEDOM - CELTIC LEAGUE
ANNUAL
CELTIC LEAGUE
DUBLIN
1969

5664 CENTRE FOR AGRICULTURAL STRATEGY
THE FUTURE OF UPLAND BRITAIN
READING UNIV
READING
1978

5665 CHRISTIAN,H (ED)
THE SOCIOLOGY OF JOURNALISM AND THE
PRESS
SOCIOLOGICAL R MONOGRAPH 29
KEELE
1980

5666 CLARK,B; CLEAVE,M (EDS)
SOCIAL PATTERNS IN CITIES
LONDON
1973

5667 CLARKE,S C; OBLER,J L (EDS)
URBAN ETHNIC CONFLICT: A COMPARATIVE
PERSPECTIVE
NORTH CAROLINA UNIV
CHAPEL HILL, NORTH CAROLINA
1976

5668 COHEN,A P (ED)
BELONGING: IDENTITY AND SOCIAL
ORGANISATION IN BRITISH RURAL CULTURES
MANCHESTER U P
MANCHESTER
1982

5669 COHEN,L; THOMAS,J; MANION,L (EDS)
EDUCATIONAL RESEARCH AND DEVELOPMENT IN
GREAT BRITAIN
NATIONAL FOUNDATION FOR EDUCATIONAL
RESEARCH
WINDSOR
1982

5670 COHEN,S; YOUNG,J (EDS)
THE MANUFACTURE OF NEWS
CONSTABLE
LONDON
1978

5671 COMPTON,P A (ED)
THE CONTEMPORARY POPULATION OF NI AND
POPULATION-RELATED ISSUES
INST IRISH STUD QUB
BELFAST
1981

5672 COOGAN,T P (ED)
IRELAND AND THE ARTS
NAMARA PRESS
LONDON
1983

5673 CORMACK,R; OSBORNE,R D (EDS)
RELIGION, EDUCATION AND EMPLOYMENT
APPLETREE
BELFAST
1983

5674 CREWE,I (ED)
BRITISH POLITICAL SOCIOLOGY YEARBOOK 11
CROOM HELM
LONDON
1975

5675 CRICK,B (ED)
UNEMPLOYMENT
METHUEN
LONDON
1981

5676 CRITCHLEY,J (ED)
ULSTER AT WAR
ATLANTIC INFORMATION CENTRE FOR TEACHERS
LONDON
1971

5677 CRONIN,S; ROCHE,R (EDS)
FREEDOM THE WOLFE TONE WAY
ANVIL
TRALEE
1977

5678 CRONNE,H A; MOODY,T W; QUINN,D B (EDS)
ESSAYS ON BRITISH AND IRISH HISTORY IN
HONOUR OF JAMES EADIE TODD
FREDERICK MULLER
LONDON
1949

5679 CROZIER,B (ED)
ULSTER: POLITICS AND TERRORISM
CONFLICT STUD 36
1973

5680 CROZIER,B; MOSS,R (EDS)
ULSTER DEBATE
BODLEY HEAD
LONDON
1972

5681 CRUICKSHANK,W J; WILCOCK,D N (EDS)
NI: ENVIRONMENT AND NATURAL RESOURCES
QUB/NUU
BELFAST/COLERAINE
1982

5682 CSPP
UK POLITICS 1977 VOLUME 1
STRATHCLYDE UNIV
GLASGOW
1977

5683 CULLEN,L M (ED)
FORMATION OF THE IRISH ECONOMY
MERCIER
CORK
1969

5684 CURNO,A ET AL (EDS)
WOMEN IN COLLECTIVE ACTION
ASSOCIATION OF COMMUNITY WORKERS
LONDON
1982

5685 CURNO,P (ED)
POLITICAL ISSUES AND COMMUNITY WORK
RKP
LONDON
1978

5686 CURTIN,C; KELLY,M; O'DOWD,L (EDS)
CULTURE AND IDEOLOGY IN IRELAND
TUROE PRESS
DUBLIN
1983

5687 DARBY,J; WILLIAMSON,A (EDS)
VIOLENCE AND THE SOCIAL SERVICES IN NI
HEINEMANN
LONDON
1978

5688 DAWSON,J; DOORNKAMP,J (EDS)
EVALUATING THE HUMAN ENVIRONMENT
ARNOLD
LONDON
1973

5689 DE LA CRUZ,F; LAVECK,G D (EDS)
HUMAN SEXUALITY AND THE MENTALLY
HANDICAPPED
BRUNNER/MAZEL
NEW YORK
1973

5690 DEITCH,B (ED)
LEGITIMATION OF REGIMES
SAGE
LONDON
1979

5691 DEREGOWSKI,J B; DZIURAWIEC,S; ANNIS,R C
(EDS)
EXPLORATIONS IN CROSS-CULTURAL
PSYCHOLOGY
SWETS AND ZEITLINGER
LISSE
1983

5692 DOFNY,J; AKIWOWO,A (EDS)
NATIONAL AND ETHNIC MOVEMENTS
SAGE
LONDON
1980

5693 DOWNING,J D; SMYTH,J; ROLSTON,B
NI
THAMES POLYTECHNIC
LONDON
1977

5694 EDMOND,W; FLEMING,S (EDS)
ALL WORK AND NO PAY: WOMEN, HOUSEWORK
AND THE WAGES DUE
POWER OF WOMEN COLLECTIVE AND FALLING
WALL PRESS
BRISTOL
1975

5695 EDWARDS,O D (ED)
CONOR CRUISE O'BRIEN INTRODUCES IRELAND
DEUTSCH
LONDON
1969

5696 EDWARDS,O D ET AL
CELTIC NATIONALISM
RKP
LONDON
1968

5697 ELDRIDGE,A F (ED)
LEGISLATURES IN PLURAL SOCIETIES
DUKE U P
DURHAM, N CAROLINA
1977

5698 ENYEDI,G; MESZAROS,J (EDS)
THE GEOGRAPHY OF SETTLEMENT SYSTEMS
AKADEMI KIADO
BUDAPEST
1980

5699 ESMAN,M (ED)
ETHNIC CONFLICT IN THE WESTERN WORLD
CORNELL U P
ITHACA, NEW YORK
1977

5700 EVENDEN,L; CUNNINGHAM,F (EDS)
CULTURAL DISCORD IN THE MODERN WORLD
BBC RESEARCH SERIES NO. 20
LONDON
1974

5701 FINER,S E (ED)
ADVERSARY POLITICS AND ELECTORAL REFORM
WIGRAM
LONDON
1975

(Edited) Books/

5702 FORSYTH, J; BOYD, D (EDS)
CONSERVATION IN THE DEVELOPMENT OF NI
DEPT EXTRA-MURAL STUD QUB
BELFAST
1970

5703 FRAZER, H ET AL
COMMUNITY WORK IN A DIVIDED SOCIETY
FARSET
BELFAST
1981

5704 FURBER, E C (ED)
CHANGING VIEWS ON BRITISH HISTORY
HARVARD U P
CAMBRIDGE, MASS
1966

5705 GALLAGHER, T; O'CONNELL, J (EDS)
CONTEMPORARY IRISH STUDIES
MANCHESTER U P
MANCHESTER
1983

5706 GELLNER, J
BAYONETS IN THE STREETS
COLLIER MACMILLAN
NEW YORK
1974

5707 GIBSON, N J (ED)
ECONOMIC AND SOCIAL IMPLICATIONS OF THE
POLITICAL ALTERNATIVES . . . .
NUU
COLERAINE
1974

5708 GIBSON, N J; SPENCER, J E (EDS)
ECONOMIC ACTIVITY IN IRELAND: A STUDY
OF TWO OPEN ECONOMIES
GILL AND MACMILLAN
DUBLIN
1977

5709 GILLMOR, D A (ED)
IRISH RESOURCES AND LAND USE
IPA
DUBLIN
1979

5710 GILLMOR, D A (ED)
RESOURCES AND ECONOMIC ACTIVITY
(ENCYCLOPEDIA OF IRELAND)
ALLEN FIGGIS
DUBLIN
1968

5711 GMELCH, S B (ED)
IRISH LIFE
O'BRIEN PRESS
DUBLIN
1979

57,12 GOLDSTEIN, A P; SEGALL, M (EDS)
AGGRESSION IN GLOBAL PERSPECTIVE
PERGAMON
NEW YORK
1983

5713 GOLDSTROM, J M; CLARKSON, L A (EDS)
IRISH POPULATION, ECONOMY AND SOCIETY:
ESSAYS IN HONOUR OF THE LATE K.H.
CONNELL
CLARENDON PRESS
OXFORD
1981

5714 GORMAN, M (ED)
IRELAND BY THE IRISH
GALLEY PRESS
LONDON
1963

5715 GREANY, V (ED)
STUDIES IN READING
EDUCATIONAL CO
DUBLIN
1977

5716 GREENBERG, S B (ED)
RACE AND STATE IN CAPITALIST DEVELOPMENT
YALE U P
NEW HAVEN, CONNECTICUT
1980

5717 GREER, D S (ED)
INDEX TO CASES DECIDED IN THE COURTS OF
NI 1921-70
INCORP CO LAW REPORTING
BELFAST
1975

5718 GUILD OF CATHOLIC TEACHERS
TEACHING RELIGION
GUILD OF CATHOLIC TEACHERS
1978

5719 HALL, R (ED)
ETHNIC AUTONOMY: COMPARATIVE DYNAMICS
PERGAMON
LONDON
1979

5720 HARBISON, J (ED)
CHILDREN OF THE TROUBLES
THE LEARNING RESOURCES UNIT, STRANMILLIS
COLLEGE
BELFAST
1983

5721 HARBISON, J; HARBISON, J (EDS)
A SOCIETY UNDER STRESS
OPEN BOOKS
SHEPTON MALLET, SOMERSET
1980

5722 HARRIS, A ET AL (EDS)
CURRICULUM INNOVATION
CROOM HELM
LONDON
1975

5723 HARVEY, S; REA, D (EDS)
THE NI ECONOMY
DECISION PARTNERSHIP
BELFAST
1983

5724 HAWTHORNE, J (ED)
TWO CENTURIES OF IRISH HISTORY
BBC
1974

5725 HENDERSON, G; LEBOW, R N; STOESSINGER, J
(EDS)
DIVIDED NATIONS IN A DIVIDED WORLD
MCKAY
NEW YORK
1972

5726 HENDERSON, P; WRIGHT, A; WYNCOLL, K (EDS)
SUCCESSES AND STRUGGLES ON COUNCIL
ESTATES: TENANT ACTION AND COMMUNITY
WORK
ASSOCIATION OF COMMUNITY WORKERS
LONDON
1982

5727 HEPBURN, A C (ED)
MINORITIES IN HISTORY
IR CONF OF HISTORIANS 13
COLERAINE
1977

5728 HERBERT, D; JOHNSTON, R J (EDS)
SOCIAL AREAS IN CITIES: VOL 1 - SPATIAL
FORM AND PROCESS
WILEY
LONDON
1978

5729 HERBERT, D; SMITH, D (EDS)
SOCIAL PROBLEMS AND THE CITY:
GEOGRAPHICAL PERSPECTIVES
OUP
LONDON
1979

5730 HERMAN,V; HAGGER,M (EDS)
THE LEGISLATION OF DIRECT ELECTIONS TO
THE EUROPEAN PARLIAMENT
GOWER
FARNBOROUGH
1980

5731 HERMANS,F A (ED)
VERFASSUNG UND VERFASSUNGSWIRKLICH-KEIT
WESTDEUTSCHVERLAG
KOLN
1969

5732 HEWITT,J (ED)
EYE-WITNESSES TO IRELAND IN REVOLT
OSPREY PUBLISHING
READING
1974

5733 HIGHAM,R (ED)
CIVIL WARS IN THE 20TH CENTURY
KENTUCKY U P
LEXINGTON
1972

5734 HILL,M (ED)
SOCIOLOGICAL YEARBOOK OF RELIGION IN
BRITAIN
SCM PRESS
LONDON
1973

5735 HILLYARD,P; SQUIRES,P (EDS)
SECURING THE STATE: POLITICS OF INTERNAL
SECURITY IN EUROPE
EUROPEAN GROUP FOR THE STUDY OF DEVIANCE
AND SOCIAL CONTROL
BRISTOL
1982

5736 HOPE,R (ED)
NI YOUTH SERVICE DIRECTORY
STANDING CONFERENCE OF YOUTH
ORGANISATIONS
BELFAST
1979

5737 HOUSE,J W (ED)
NORTHERN GEOGRAPHICAL ESSAYS
DEPT GEOG NEWCASTLE UNIV
NEWCASTLE ON TYNE
1966

5738 HURLEY,M (ED)
IRISH ANGLICANISM, 1869-1969
FIGGIS
DUBLIN
1970

5739 JACKSON,T A
IRELAND HER OWN: AN OUTLINE HISTORY OF
THE IRISH STRUGGLE FOR NATIONAL FREEDOM
AND INDEPENDENCE
LAWRENCE AND WISHART
LONDON
1971

5740 JARDINE,E; MCCAVERA,P; MCCOY,K (EDS)
CO-ORDINATING CARE AND THE SCHOOL:
PROCEEDINGS OF A CONFERENCE
DHSS (NI)
BELFAST
1983

5741 JONES,D; MAYO,M (EDS)
COMMUNITY WORK ONE
RKP
LONDON
1974

5742 JONES,E (ED)
BELFAST IN ITS REGIONAL SETTING: A
SCIENTIFIC SURVEY
BELFAST
1952

5743 JONES,E (ED)
READINGS IN SOCIAL GEOGRAPHY
OUP
LONDON
1975

5744 JONES,K (ED)
THE YEAR BOOK OF SOCIAL POLICY IN
BRITAIN
RKP
LONDON
1972

5745 KEETON,G W; LLOYD,D (EDS)
UNITED KINGDOM. BRITISH COMMONWEALTH.
TWO VOLUMES. THE DEVELOPMENT OF ITS LAWS
AND CONSTITUTION
STEVENS
LONDON
1955

5746 KELLY,M; O'DOWD,L; WICKHAM,J (EDS)
POWER, CONFLICT AND INEQUALITY
TUROE PRESS
DUBLIN
1982

5747 KERR,G (ED)
CUSTODY OF CHILDREN ON BREAKDOWN OF
MARRIAGE
SLS/FACULTY OF LAW QUB
BELFAST
1981

5748 KOLINSKY,M (ED)
DIVIDED LOYALTIES: BRITISH REGIONAL
ASSERTION AND EUROPEAN INTEGRATION
MANCHESTER U P
MANCHESTER
1978

5749 LANE,D A (ED)
IRELAND, LIBERATION AND THEOLOGY
ORBIS BOOKS
LONDON
1978

5750 LANEGRAN,D A; PALM,R (EDS)
INVITATION TO GEOGRAPHY
MCGRAW-HILL
NEW YORK
1978

5751 LEE,J (ED)
IRELAND, 1945-1970
GILL AND MACMILLAN
DUBLIN
1979

5752 LEE,J (ED)
IRISH HISTORIOGRAPHY, 1970-79
CORK U P
CORK
1981

5753 LEES,J D; KIMBER,R (EDS)
POLITICAL PARTIES IN MODERN BRITAIN
RKP
LONDON
1972

5754 LEGETT,J (ED)
TAKING STATE POWER
HARPER AND ROW
NEW YORK
1973

5755 LIVINGSTON,M H (ED)
INTERNATIONAL TERRORISM IN THE
CONTEMPORARY WORLD
GREENWOOD PRESS
WESTPORT, CONNECTICUT
1978

5756 LODGE,J (ED)
TERRORISM: A CHALLENGE TO THE STATE
MARTIN ROBERTSON
OXFORD
1981

(Edited) Books/

5757 MACDONACH,O; MANDLE,W F; TRAVERS,P (EDS)
IRISH CULTURE AND NATIONALISM, 1750-1950
GILL AND MACMILLAN
DUBLIN
1983

5758 MACMANUS,F (ED)
THE YEARS OF THE GREAT TEST
MERCIER
CORK
1967

5759 MADCWICK,P; ROSE,R (EDS)
UK POLITICS
MACMILLAN
LONDON
1981

5760 MANSBACH,R (ED)
NI: HALF A CENTURY OF PARTITION
FACTS ON FILE
NEW YORK
1973

5761 MARTIN,F X; BYRNE,F J (EDS)
THE SCHOLAR REVOLUTIONARY: EOIN MACNEILL
1867-1945, AND THE MAKING OF THE NEW
IRELAND
IRISH U P
SHANNON
1973

5762 MCCAFFERTY,N (ED)
CONTENT OF A SERIES OF CONFERENCES ON
PASTORAL CARE
MAGEE UNIV COLL
DERRY
1977

5763 MCCAFFREY,L (ED)
IRISH NATIONALISM AND THE AMERICAN
CONTRIBUTION
NEW YORK
1976

5764 MCCARTAN,W (ED)
COMMUNITY RESPONSIBILITY AND THE
ALCOHOLIC
BEACON HOUSE
BELFAST
1963

5765 MCKERNAN,J (ED)
PROCEEDINGS OF THE 3RD ANNUAL EDUCATION
CONFERENCE, EDUCATIONAL STUDIES
ASSOCIATION OF IRELAND
NUU
COLERAINE
1978

5766 MCWHIRTER,L (ED)
POLITICAL AND SOCIAL AWARENESS IN NI:
MYTH AND REALITY
ANNUAL CONF BRIT PSYCHOL
ABERDEEN
1980

5767 METCALFE,J E
BRITISH MINING FIELDS
INSTITUTE OF MINING AND METALLURCY
LONDON
1960

5768 MILLER,R; WATSON,J W (EDS)
GEOGRAPHICAL ESSAYS IN MEMORY OF ALAN C.
OGILVIE
NELSON
LONDON
1959

5769 MOODY,T W (ED)
IRISH HISTORIOGRAPHY, 1936-1970
IRISH COMMITTEE OF HIST SCI
DUBLIN
1971

5770 MOODY,T W; BECKETT,J C (EDS)
ULSTER SINCE 1800 VOL 1 AND 2
BBC
LONDON
1957

5771 MOODY,T W; MARTIN,F X (EDS)
THE COURSE OF IRISH HISTORY
MERCIER
CORK
1967

5772 MORGAN,A; PURDIE,B (EDS)
IRELAND: DIVIDED NATION. DIVIDED CLASS
INK LINKS
LONDON
1980

5773 MOROWITZ,H J
THE WINE OF LIFE AND OTHER ESSAYS ON
SOCIETIES, ENERGY AND LIVING THINGS
ST MARTIN'S PRESS
NEW YORK
1979

5774 MULCAHY,D G (ED)
PROCEEDINGS OF THE EDUCATION CONFERENCE
1977
UNIV COLLEGE CORK
CORK
1977

5775 NEWARK,F H ET AL (EDS)
DEVOLUTION OF GOVERNMENT: THE EXPERIMENT
IN NI
ALLEN AND UNWIN
LONDON
1953

5776 NI EDUCATION AND LIBRARY BOARDS
VANDALISM AND INDISCIPLINE IN SCHOOLS
NI EDUCATION AND LIBRARY BOARDS
BELFAST
1976

5777 NOSSITER,B (ED)
BRITAIN: A FUTURE THAT WORKS
DEUTSCH
LONDON
1978

5778 NOWLAN,K B (ED)
TRAVEL AND TRANSPORT IN IRELAND
GILL AND MACMILLAN
DUBLIN
1973

5779 NOWLAN,K B; WILLIAMS,T D (EDS)
IRELAND IN THE WAR YEARS AND AFTER
GILL AND MACMILLAN
DUBLIN
1969

5780 O'BRIEN,F (ED)
DIVIDED IRELAND
ROCKFORD COLL U P
ROCKFORD, ILLINOIS
1971

5781 O'BRIEN,K (ED)
DIGEST OF IRISH AFFAIRS 1969-78
ACADEMY PRESS
DUBLIN
1980

5782 O'CONNOR,U (ED)
IRISH LIBERATION
GROVE PRESS
NEW YORK
1974

5783 O'DOWD,L; ROLSTON,B; TOMLINSON,M
NI: BETWEEN CIVIL RIGHTS AND CIVIL WAR
CSE BOOKS
LONDON
1980

5784 O'HALLORAN,J ET AL
ETHNICITY AND THE MEDIA
UNESCO
PARIS
1977

(Edited) Books/

5785 O'NEILL,B E; HEATON,W R; ALBERTS,D J
     (EDS)
     INSURGENCY IN THE MODERN WORLD
     WESTVIEW PRESS
     BOULDER, COLORADO
     1980

5786 OAKLEY,R; ROSE,P
     THE POLITICAL YEAR 1971
     PITMAN
     LONDON
     1971

5787 OREL,H (ED)
     IRISH HISTORY AND CULTURE: ASPECTS OF A
     PEOPLE'S HERITAGE
     WOLFHOUND PRESS
     DUBLIN
     1979

5788 PAISLEY,I R K (ED)
     ULSTER: THE FACTS
     CROWN PUBLICATIONS
     BELFAST
     1982

5789 PARKER,H (ED)
     SOCIAL WORK AND THE COURTS
     ARNOLD
     LONDON
     1979

5790 PEACH,C (ED)
     URBAN SOCIAL SEGREGATION
     CROOM HELM
     LONDON
     1981

5791 PEELE,G; COOKE,C (EDS)
     THE POLITICS OF REAPPRAISAL 1918-1939
     MACMILLAN
     LONDON
     1975

5792 POLLOCK,H M (ED)
     INDUSTRIAL RELATIONS IN PRACTICE
     O'BRIEN PRESS
     DUBLIN
     1981

5793 POLLOCK,H M (ED)
     REFORM OF INDUSTRIAL RELATIONS
     O'BRIEN PRESS
     DUBLIN
     1982

5794 RAFROIDI,P; HARMAN,M (EDS)
     IRISH NOVEL IN OUR TIME
     LILLE UNIV
     LILLE
     1976

5795 RAFROIDI,P; JOANNON,P (EDS)
     IRELAND AT THE CROSSROADS: THE ACTS OF
     THE LILLE SYMPOSIUM, JUNE-JULY 1978
     LILLE UNIV
     LILLE
     1979

5796 REA,D (ED)
     POLITICAL CO-OPERATION IN DIVIDED
     SOCIETIES
     GILL AND MACMILLAN
     DUBLIN
     1982

5797 RHODES,E (ED)
     DEVELOPING COMMUNITIES CONFERENCE REPORT
     MAGEE UNIV COLLEGE
     DERRY
     1968

5798 RHODES,E (ED)
     HOUSING PROBLEM
     MAGEE UNIV COLLEGE
     DERRY
     1969

5799 RHODES,E (ED)
     A PERSON OF NO CONSEQUENCE? A STUDY OF
     RETIREMENT
     MAGEE UNIV COLLEGE
     DERRY
     1968

5800 RHODES,E (ED)
     PUBLIC ADMINISTRATION IN NI
     MAGEE UNIV COLLEGE
     DERRY
     1967

5801 RHODES,E; GARMANY,J (EDS)
     THE DEVELOPMENT OF AN AREA: WEST ULSTER
     MAGEE UNIV COLLEGE
     DERRY
     1966

5802 ROBSON,W (ED)
     THE POLITICAL QUARTERLY IN THE THIRTIES
     ALLEN LANE
     LONDON
     1971

5803 ROCK,P; MCINTOSH,M (EDS)
     DEVIANCE AND SOCIAL CONTROL
     TAVISTOCK
     LONDON
     1974

5804 RODRIGUES,D; BRUINVELS,P
     ZONING IN ON ENTERPRISE
     KOGAN PAGE
     LONDON
     1982

5805 ROEBUCK,P (ED)
     PLANTATION TO PARTITION: ESSAYS IN
     ULSTER HISTORY IN HONOUR OF J L
     MCCRACKEN
     BLACKSTAFF
     BELFAST
     1981

5806 ROMANOS,M C (ED)
     WESTERN EUROPEAN CITIES IN CRISIS
     LEXINGTON BOOKS
     LEXINGTON, MASSACHUSETTS
     1979

5807 ROSE,P
     BACKBENCHER'S DILEMMA
     FREDERICK MULLER
     LONDON
     1981

5808 ROSE,R (ED)
     ELECTORAL BEHAVIOUR: A COMPARATIVE
     HANDBOOK
     FREE PRESS
     NEW YORK
     1974

5809 RUSI
     TEN YEARS OF TERRORISM: COLLECTED VIEWS
     RUSI
     LONDON
     1979

5810 SCHLESINGER,P
     PUTTING REALITY TOGETHER: BBC NEWS
     CONSTABLE
     LONDON
     1977

5811 SCOTT,H (ED)
     HOW SHALL I VOTE?
     BODLEY HEAD
     LONDON
     1976

5812 SOBEL,L
     POLITICAL TERRORISM, VOLUME 1
     CLIO PRESS
     OXFORD
     1975

(Edited) Books/

5813 SOBEL, L
POLITICAL TERRORISM, VOLUME 2 1974-78
CLIO PRESS
OXFORD
1978

5814 SOCIAL STUDY CONFERENCE
SECTARIANISM: ROADS TO RECONCILIATION
THREE CANDLES PRESS
DUBLIN
1974

5815 SPENCER, A (ED)
PROCEEDINGS OF SOCIOLOGICAL ASSOCIATION
OF IRELAND: FIFTH ANNUAL CONFERENCE
QUB
BELFAST
1979

5816 SPENCER, A; CORMACK, R; O'DOWD, L; TOVEY, H
(EDS)
PROCEEDINGS OF SOCIOLOGICAL ASSOCIATION
OF IRELAND: THIRD ANNUAL CONFERENCE
QUB
BELFAST
1977

5817 SPENCER, A; O'DWYER, P A (EDS)
PROCEEDINGS OF SOCIOLOGICAL ASSOCIATION
OF IRELAND: SECOND ANNUAL CONFERENCE
QUB
BELFAST
1976

5818 SPENCER, A; TOVEY, H (EDS)
PROCEEDINGS OF SOCIOLOGICAL ASSOCIATION
OF IRELAND: FIRST AND FOURTH ANNUAL
QUB
BELFAST
1978

5819 STEPHENS, N; GLASSCOCK, R E (EDS)
IRISH GEOGRAPHICAL STUDIES IN HONOUR OF
ESTYN EVANS
QUB
BELFAST
1970

5820 STOHL, M (ED)
THE POLITICS OF TERRORISM
MARCEL DEKKER
NEW YORK
1979

5821 STRINGER, M (ED)
APPLYING SOCIAL PSYCHOLOGY, VOLUME 2
ACADEMIC PRESS
1980

5822 STRINGER, P (ED)
CONFRONTING SOCIAL ISSUES
ACADEMIC PRESS
LONDON
1982

5823 SULLIVAN, E ET AL (EDS)
CONFLICT IN IRELAND
FLORIDA UNIV
GAINESVILLE, FLORIDA
1976

5824 SWAN, W (ED)
SPECIAL NEEDS IN EDUCATION
BLACKWELL/OPEN UNIV
LONDON
1981

5825 SYMONS, L (ED)
LAND USE IN NI
LONDON U P
LONDON
1963

5826 TAJFEL, H (ED)
HUMAN GROUPS AND SOCIAL CATEGORIES
CUP
CAMBRIDGE
1981

5827 TAYLOR, L; NELSON, S (EDS)
YOUNG PEOPLE AND CIVIL CONFLICT IN NI
DHSS (NI)
BELFAST
1978

5828 TEELING, W
CORRIDORS OF FRUSTRATION
JOHNSON
LONDON
1970

5829 THOMPSON, F G (ED)
THE CELTIC EXPERIENCE: PAST AND PRESENT
CELTIC LEAGUE
DUBLIN
1972

5830 THORNHILL, W (ED)
THE MODERNISATION OF BRITISH GOVERNMENT
PITMAN
LONDON
1975

5831 TRUDGILL, P (ED)
SOCIOLINGUISTIC PATTERNS IN BRITISH
ENGLISH
ARNOLD
LONDON
1978

5832 UNKNOWN
LE DROIT A L'AUTODETERMINATION
PRESSES D'EUROPE
PARIS AND NICE
1980

5833 VAIZEY, J (ED)
ECONOMIC SOVEREIGNTY AND REGIONAL
POLICY: A SYMPOSIUM ON REGIONAL PROBLEMS
IN BRITAIN AND IRELAND
GILL AND MACMILLAN
DUBLIN
1975

5834 WALSH, B
RELIGION AND DEMOGRAPHIC BEHAVIOUR IN
IRELAND
ESRI
DUBLIN
1970

5835 WARNES, A M (ED)
GEOGRAPHICAL PERSPECTIVES ON THE ELDERLY
WILEY
CHICHESTER
1982

5836 WATT, D (ED)
THE CONSTITUTION OF NI: PROBLEMS AND
PROSPECTS
HEINEMANN
LONDON
1981

5837 WILKINSON, P (ED)
BRITISH PERSPECTIVES ON TERRORISM
ALLEN AND UNWIN
LONDON
1981

5838 WILLIAMS, T D (ED)
THE IRISH STRUGGLE (1916-1926)
RKP
LONDON
1966

5839 WILLIAMS, T D (ED)
SECRET SOCIETIES IN IRELAND
GILL AND MACMILLAN
DUBLIN
1973

5840 WILSON, T (ED)
PAPERS ON REGIONAL DEVELOPMENT
BASIL BLACKWELL
OXFORD
1965

(Edited) Books/

5841 WILSON,T (ED)
ULSTER UNDER HOME RULE: A STUDY OF THE
POLITICAL AND ECONOMIC PROBLEMS OF NI
OUP
OXFORD
1955

5842 WORRALL,S (ED)
WHO ARE WE?
CHRISTIAN JOURNALS
1977

5841 WILSON,T (ED)
ULSTER UNDER HOME RULE: A STUDY OF THE
POLITICAL AND ECONOMIC PROBLEMS OF NI
OUP
OXFORD
1955

(Edited) Books

```
##############################
JOURNAL ABBREVIATIONS/INDEX
##############################
```

BLATTER DEUTSCHE U INT POL
Blatter fur deutsche und internationale
Politik

BRIT J ADDICTION
British Journal of Addiction

BRIT J ALCHOLISM
British Journal of Alcoholism

BRIT J CLINICAL PRACTICE
British Journal of Clinical Practice

BRIT J CRIMINOLOGY
British Journal of Criminology

BRIT J EDUC PSYCHOL
British Journal of Educational Psychology

BRIT J EDUC STUD
British Journal of Educational Studies

BRIT J IN-SERVICE EDUC
British Journal of In-Service Education

BRIT J INDUSTR RELAT
British Journal of Industrial Relations

BRIT J INDUSTRIAL MED
British Journal of Industrial Medicine

BRIT J MENTAL SUBNORMALITY
British Journal of Mental Subnormality

BRIT J ORAL SURGERY
British Journal of Oral Surgery

BRIT J POLIT SCI
British Journal of Political Science

BRIT J PREV SOC MED
British Journal of Preventive Social Medicine

BRIT J PSYCHIATRY
British Journal of Psychiatry

BRIT J SEXUAL MED
British Journal of Sexual Medicine

BRIT J SOC CLIN PSYCH
British Journal of Social and Clinical
Psychology

BRIT J SOC MED
British Journal of Social Medicine

BRIT J SOC PSYCHOL
British Jounral of Social Psychology

BRIT J SOCIOL
British Journal of Sociology

BRIT J SURGER
British Journal of Surgery

BRIT J VENEREAL DISEASES
British Journal of Venereal Diseases

BRIT MED J
British Medical Journal

BRIT PSYCHIATRY
British Psychiatry

BRIT PSYCHOL SOC BULL
British Psychological Society Bulletin

BRITAIN TODAY

BRITISH SURVEY

BUILDING AND CONTRACT J

BUILDING SOCIETIES GAZETTE

BUILDING TRADES J

BUILT ENVIRONMENT

BULL DEPT FOREIGN AFFAIRS
Bulletin of the Department of Foreign Affairs

BUS WEEK
Business Week

CAH COMMUNISME
Cahiers Communisme

CAMBRIA

CAMBRIDGE ECON R
Cambridge Economic Review

CAMBRIDGE J ECON
Cambridge Journal of Economics

CAMBRIDGE R

CAMERAWORK

CANADIAN BAR R

CANADIAN DIMENSION

CANADIAN GEOG
Canadian Geography

CANADIAN GEOGR J
Canadian Geographical Journal

CANB SER ADMIN STUD
Canberra Series in Administrative Studies

CAPITAL AND CLASS

CAPUCHIN ANNUAL

CARTOGRAPHIC J

CASE CON

CASE WESTERN RESERVE J INT LAW
Case Western Reserve Journal of International
Law

CATHOLIC TEACHERS J

CENTER MAG
Center Magazine

CENTRO SOCIALE

CHARACTER POTENTIAL

CHARTERED SURVEYOR

CHRISTIAN CENTURY

CHRISTIAN HERALD

CHRISTIANITY TODAY

CHRISTUS REX

CHURCH AND STATE

CHURCH HISTORY

CHURCH OF IRELAND GAZETTE

THE CHURCHMAN

CITHERA

CIVILTA CATTOLICA

CIVITAS

COGNITION

COLLOQUIUM

COLUMBIA HUMAN RIGHTS LAW R

COLUMBIA J WLD BUS
Columbia Journal of World Business

COMM CARE
Community Care

COMM DEV J
Community Development Journal

COMM FORUM
Community Forum

COMM HEALTH
Community Health

COMMENTARY

COMMONWEAL

COMMUNIST COMMENT

COMMUNITY HOMES SCHOOL GAZ
Community Homes School Gazette

COMP EDUC
Comparative Education

COMP POLIT STUD
Comparative Political Studies

COMP STUD SOC HIST
Comparative Studies in Society and History

COMPARE

CONFLICT QUART
Conflict Quarterly

CONFLICT STUD
Conflict Studies

CONSTABULARY GAZETTE

CONTACT DERMATITIS

CONTEMP R
Contemporary Review

CONVERGENCE

CORE

AN COSANTOIR

COUNTRY LIFE

COUNTRY PROFILES

COURIER

CRAIGAVON HIST SOC R
Craigavon Historical Society Review

CRANE BAG

CRIME AND SOCIAL JUSTICE

CRIMINAL LAW R

CRIMINOLOGIST

CRIT SOCIOL (ROMA)
Critica Sociologica (Roma)

CROSSBOW

CURR ANTHROPOL
Current Anthropology

CURRENT BIOGRAPHY

CURRENT HISTORY

CURRENT LEG PROBLEMS
Current Legal Problems

CURRENT RES ON PEACE AND VIOLENCE
Current Research on Peace and Violence

DALHOUSIE R

DEPAUL LAW R

DEPT OF STATE BULL
Department of State Bulletin

DER SPIEGEL

DEVELOPMENTAL MEDICINE AND CHILD NEUROLOGY

DIE ZEIT

DISSENT

DOCTRINE AND LIFE

THE DRAUGHTSMAN

DUBLIN UNIV LAW R
Dublin University Law Review

ECON AND SOC R
Economic and Social Review

ECON AND SOCIETY
Economy and Society

ECON BULL
Economic Bulletin

ECON GEOG
Economic Geography

ECON HISTORY R
Economic History Review

ECON J
Economic Journal

ECONOMIST

EDUC AND TRAINING
Education and Training

EDUC CHANGE DEVELOP
Educational Change and Development

EDUC RES
Educational Research

EDUCATION

EDUCATIONAL ADMINISTRATION

EIRE-IRELAND

EKISTICS

ENCOUNTER

ENERGY WLD
Energy World

ENGINEER

ENGINEERING

ENVIRON AND PLANN
Environment and Planning

ESCRITS DE PARIS

ESPRIT

ET IRL
Etudes Irlandes

ETHNIC AND RACIAL STUDIES

ETHNICITY

ETHNOLOGIA EUROPAEA

ETHOS

EUROP J POLIT RES
European Journal of Political Research

EUROP J SOCIOL
European Journal of Sociology

EUROP R
European Review

EUROPA ARCHIV

EUROPE 81

EVERYMAN

FAMILY PLANNING

FARM AND FOOD RES
Farm and Food Research

FLETCHER FORUM

FOCUS

FOLKLIFE

FOREIGN AFFAIRS

FOREIGN POLICY

FOREIGN SERVICE J

FORTNIGHT

FORTUNE

FRANCE LIBRE

FREEDOM AT ISSUE

THE FURROW

GARDA R

GAZ INCORP LAW SOC IR
Gazette of the Incorporated Law Society of
Ireland

GEOFORUM

GEOFR RUNDSCHAU
Geographische Rundschau

GEOG
Geography

GEOGR J
Geographical Journal

GEOGR MAG
Geographical Magazine

GEOGR R
Geographical Review

GEOGR VIEWPOINT
Geographical Viewpoint

GEOLOGY IN NI

GRALTON

GVT AND OPPOSITION
Government and Opposition

HARPER'S MAG
Harper's Magazine

HASTINGS CENTER REPORT

HEALTH EDUC J
Health Education Journal

HEALTH SOC SERVICES J
Health and Social Services Journal

HERDER CORRESPONDENCE

HIBERNIAN J

HIST OF ECONOMIC THOUGHT NEWSLETTER
History of Economic Thought Newsletter

HISTORIAN

HISTORICAL STUD
Historical Studies

HISTORY TODAY

HISTORY

HOLY CROSS QUART
Holy Cross Quarterly

HORIZON

HOSPITAL HEALTH SERVICES R

HOUSING PLANN R
Housing and Planning Review

HOUSING R

HOUSING

HOWARD J

HUM RIGHTS J
Human Rights Journal

HUM RIGHTS R
Human Rights Review

HUMAN BIOLOGY

HUMANIST

INDEX ON CENSORSHIP

INDIAN ADMINISTRATIVE AND MANAGEMENT R

INDUSTR RELAT J
Industrial Relations Journal

INDUSTRY

INK

INQUABA YA BASEBENZI

INSIDE STORY

INST BANK IRL J
Institute of Bankers in Ireland Journal

INSTITUTE FOR DEFENCE STUD J
Institute for Defence Studies Journal

INSURGENT SOCIOLOGIST

INT AFF (LONDON)
International Affairs (London)

INT COMP LAW QUART
International Comparative Law Quarterly

INT J EARLY CHILDHOOD
International Journal of Early Childhood

INT J EPIDEMIOLOGY
International Journal of Epidemiology

INT J GROUP TENSIONS
International Journal of Group Tensions

INT J OF SOC PSYCHIAT
International Journal of Social Psychiatry

INT J OFFENDER THERAPY AND COMP CRIM
International Journal of Offender Therapy and
Comparative Criminology

INT J ORAL SURGERY
International Journal of Oral Surgery

INT J POL
International Journal of Politics

INT J PSYCH
International Journal of Psychology

INT J SOC ECON
International Journal of Social Economics

INT J SOC PSYCHIATRY
International Journal of Social Psychiatry

INT J SOCIOL SOC POL
International Journal of Sociology and Social
Policy

INT J URB REG RES
International Journal of Urban and Regional
Research

INT PEACE RES SOC PAP
International Peace Research Society Papers

INT POLIT (BERGEN)
International Politics (Bergen)

INT R COMM DEV
International Review of Community Development

INT R EDUC
International Review of Education

INT R MODERN SOCIOL
International Review of Modern Sociology

INT R
International Review

INT RELAT (LONDON)
International Relations (London)

INT SECURITY
International Security

INT SOCIALISM
International Socialism

INT SOCIALIST
International Socialist

INT TOURISM QUART
International Tourism Quarterly

INTEGRATED EDUC
Integrated Education

INTELLECT

INTERROGATIONS

IR ANCESTOR
Irish Ancestor

IR ARCHIVAL B
Irish Archival Bulletin

IR BANKING R
Irish Banking Review

IR BOOKLORE
Irish Booklore

IR COMMITTEE HISTORICAL SCI B
Irish Committee of Historical Science Bulletin

IR ECCLESIASTICAL RECORD
Irish Ecclesiastical Record

IR ECON AND SOC HIST R
Irish Economic and Social History Review

IR FORESTRY
Irish Forestry

IR GEOG
Irish Geography

IR HIST STUD
Irish Historical Studies

IR J AGRIC ECON AND RURAL SOCIOL
Irish Journal of Agricultural Economics and
Rural Sociology

IR J EDUC
Irish Journal of Education

IR J ENVIRONMENTAL SCI
Irish Journal of Environmental Science

IR J MED SCI
Irish Journal of Medical Science

IR J PSYCHOL
Irish Journal of Psychology

IR JURIST
Irish Jurist

IR LAW STUDIES
Irish Law Studies

IR MED J
Irish Medical Journal

IR MONTHLY
Irish Monthly

IR PSYCHOL
Irish Psychology

IR STUD INT AFF
Irish Studies in International Affairs

IRIS

IRL SOCIALIST R
Ireland Socialist Review

J ADVANCED NURSING

J AGRIC ECON
Journal of Agricultural Economics

J AMER GEOGR SOCIETY
Journal of the American Geographical Society

J APPLIED SOC PSYCHOL
Journal of Applied Social Psychology

J BIOSOCIAL SCI
Journal of Biosocial Science

J BRIT STUD
Journal of British Studies

J BUILT ENVIRON
Journal of the Built Environment

J CAPA

J CHRONIC DISEASES

J CHURCH AND STATE

J COMM DEV SOC
Journal of the Community Development Society
of America

J COMMERCE

J COMMON MARKET STUD
Journal of Common Market Studies

J COMMONWEALTH COMP POLIT
Journal of Commonwealth and Comparative
Politics

J COMMUNICATION

J CONFLICT RESOL
Journal of Conflict Resolution

J CONTEMP HIST
Journal of Contemporary History

J CURRICULUM STUD
Journal of Curriculum Studies

J DEATH AND DYING

J DEV STUD
Journal of Development Studies

J EDUC PSYCHOL
Journal of Educational Psychology

J ENVIRONMENTAL MANAGEMENT

J EPIDEMIOLOGY AND COMMUNITY HEALTH

J ETHNIC STUD
Journal of Ethnic Studies

J FURTHER HIGHER EDUC
Journal of Further and Higher Education

J GENETIC PSYCHOL
Journal of Genetic Psychology

J HYGIENE

J INDUSTR ECON
Journal of Industrial Economics

J INDUSTR RELATIONS
Journal of Industrial Relations

J INST HEALTH EDUC
Journal of the Institute of Health Education

J INT AFF
Journal of International Affairs

J INTERGROUP RELATIONS

J IR BUS ADM RES
Journal of Irish Business Administrative
Research

J IR MED ASSOC
Journal of the Irish Medical Association

J LAW AND SOC
Journal of law and Society

J LIBRARIANSHIP

J MED GENETICS
Journal of Medical Genetics

J MENTAL DEFICIENCY RES
Journal of Mental Deficiency Research

J MENTAL SCI
Journal of Mental Science

J MILK MARKETING BOARD NI

J MORAL EDUC
Journal of Moral Education

J NI INST AGRIC SCI
Journal of the Northern Ireland Institute of
Agricultural Science

J OCCUPATIONAL PSYCHOL
Journal of Occupational Psychology

J OF READING

J PEACE RES
Journal of Peace Research

J PEACE SCI
Journal of Peace Science

J PERSONALITY ASSESSMENT

J PLANN ENVIRONMENTAL LAW
Journal of Planning and Environmental Law

J POLIT
Journal of Politics

J PORT ECON E FINS

J PSYCHOHIST
Journal of Psychohistory

J PSYCHOL
Journal of Psychology

J RIBA

J ROYAL COLLEGE OF GENERAL PRACTITIONERS

J SOC AND POLIT STUD
Journal of Social and Political Studies

J SOC DAIRY TECHNOLOGY
Society of Dairy Technology Journal

J SOC HIST
Journal of Social History

J SOC POL
Journal of Social Policy

J SOC PSYCHOL
Journal of Social Psychology

J TOWN PLANN INST
Journal of the Town Planning Institute

J WLD HIST
Journal of World History

JERUSALEM J INT RELAT
Jerusalem Journal of International Relations

JSSISI
Statistical and Social Inquiry Society of
Ireland Journal

KOLNER Z SOZ SZ-PSY
Kolner Zeitschrift fur Sociologie und
Socialpsychologie

KRIMINALISTIK

LABOUR MONTHLY

LABOUR, CAPITAL AND SOCIETY

LAGAN

LAKEHEAD UNIV R
Lakehead University Review

LANCET

LAW AND CONTEMPORARY SOC PROBLEMS
Law and Contemporary Social Problems

LE MONDE DIPLOMATIQUE

AN LEABHARLANN

LEARNING FOR LIVING

LEFT PERSPECTIVES

LES TEMPS MODERNES

LIBERATION

LIBRARIANSHIP

LIBRARY ASSOC RECORD
Library Association Record

LIBRARY J

LIFE

LINK MAGAZINE

LISTENER

LOC GOVT CHRON
Local Government Chronicle

LOC GOVT R
Local Government Review

LOC GOVT STUD
Local Government Studies

LONDON R OF BOOKS

LOW PAY UNIT B
Low Pay Unit Bulletin

MACLEANS

MAGILL

MAN

MANAGEMENT

MARXISM TODAY

MED EDUC
Medical Education

MED OFFICER
Medical Officer

MEDICAL ASSOC FOR PREVENTION WAR
Medical Association for the Prevention of War

MEDICO-LEGAL J

MELBOURNE J POLIT
Melbourne Journal of Politics

MIDLAND BANK R

MIDWEST J POLIT SCI
Midwest Journal of Political Science

MILIEU

MILITARY R

MINERVA

MOD LAW R
Modern Law Review

MODERN CHURCHMAN

MONTH

MONTHLY R

MOTOR TREND

MS

MUNICIPAL AND PUBL SERVICES J
Municipal and Public Services Journal

MUNICIPAL ENGINEERING

MUNICIPAL R

MUSEUMS J

NAT INST ECON R
National Institute Economic Review

NAT R
National Review

NAT WESTMINSTER BANK QUART R
National Westminster Bank Quarterly Review

NATION

NATIONAL ASSOC OF TEACHERS IN FURTHER AND
HIGHER EDUC J
National Association of Teachers in Further
and Higher Education Journal

NATIONAL CATHOLIC REPORTER

NATIONAL GEOGRAPHIC

NETWORK

NEW BLACKFRIARS

NEW COMM
New Community

NEW COMMONWEALTH

NEW EDINBURGH R

NEW ERA

NEW HUMANIST

NEW INTERNATIONALIST

NEW LAW J

NEW LEADER

NEW LEFT R

NEW OUTLOOK

NEW R

NEW REPUBLIC

NEW SCIENTIST

NEW SOCIALIST

NEW SOCIETY

NEW SOCIOL
New Sociology

NEW STATESMAN

NEW TIMES

NEW YORK

NEW YORK R BOOKS
New York Review of Books

NEW YORK UNIV J INT LAW AND POLITICS
New York University Journal of International
Law and Politics

NEW YORKER

NEWMAN R

NEWSWEEK

NI INST AGRIC SCI R
Northern Ireland Institute of Agricultural
Science Review

NI LEG QUART
Northern Ireland Legal Quarterly

NOROIS

NORSK MILITAERT TIDSSKRIFT

NORTH TEACH
Northern Teacher

NOTRE DAME LAW R

NOTRE DAME LAWYER

NOUV CRITIQUE
Nouvelle Critique

NOUV R INT
Nouvelle Revue Internationale

NOVAIA I NOVEISHAIA ISTORIIA

NOWE DROGI

NURSING MIRROR AND MIDWIVES J

NURSING TIMES

NUSIGHT

NY TIMES MAG
New York Times Magazine

OFFICIAL ARCHITECT

OFFICIAL ARCHITECTURE AND PLANNING

ORAL HISTORY

ORBIS

OSTERREICH IN GESCHICHTE UND LITERATUR

OXFORD B ECON STATIST
Oxford Bulletin of Economics and Statistics

PACE
Protestant and Catholic Encounter

PAP PEACE SCI SOC INT
Papers of the International Peace Science
Society

PAPERS IN PSYCHOL
Papers in Psychology

PARL AFFAIRS
Parliamentary Affairs

PAST AND PRESENT

PENSEE

PEOPLE

PERSONNEL MANAGEMENT

THE PLAIN TRUTH

PLANNER

PLURIEL

POETRY IRELAND

POLICE J

POLICE STUD
Police Studies

POLICY

POLICY STUD
Policy Studies

POLIT QUART
Political Quarterly

POLIT STUD (OXFORD)
Political Studies (Oxford)

POLITICS AND SOC
Politics and Society

POLITICS TODAY

PONTE

POPUL STUD
Population Studies

POVERTY

PREUVES

PROC BELFAST NATURAL HISTORY AND PHILOSOPHICAL
SOCIETY
Proceedings of the Belfast Natural History and
Philosophy Society

PROC INST CIVIL ENGINEERS
Proceedings of the Institute of Civil
Engineers

PROC R IR ACAD
Proceedings of the Royal Irish Academy

PROFESSIONAL GEOGRAPHER

PROGRAM LEARN ED TECH
Programmed Learning and Educational Technology

PROGRESS IN PLANNING

PSYCHIATRICA CLINICA

PSYCHOL NEWS
Psychology News

PSYCHOL TEACHING
Psychology Teaching

PSYCHOSOCIAL STUD
Psychosocial Studies

PSYCHOTHERAPY AND PSYCHOSOMATICS

PUBL ADM
Public Administration

PUBL HEALTH
Public Health

PUBL LAW
Public Law

PUBLISHERS WEEKLY

QUART J ENGINEERING GEOLOGY
Quarterly Journal of Engineering Geology

QUART J FORESTRY
Quarterly Journal of Forestry

QUART J STUD ALCOHOLISM
Quarterly Journal of Studies in Alcoholism

QUARTERLY

QUEST

QUIS CUSTODIET (TCD)

R BELGE DE DR INT
Revue Belge de Droit International

R DEFENSE NATIONALE

R DR PUB SCI POLIT
Revue du Droit Public et de la Science
Politique en France

R EGYPT DR INT
Revue Egyptienne de Droit International

R ESTUD POLIT
Revista de Estudios Politicos

R FRAN SCI POLIT
Revue Francaise de Science Politique

R GENERALE DE DR INT PUB
Revue Generale de Droit International Public

R INT COMMISSION OF JURISTS
Review of the International Commission of
Jurists

R MILITAIRE GENERALE

R POLIT INT (MADRID)
Revista de Politica Internacional

R POLITICS
Review of Politics

R RADICAL POLIT ECON
Review of Radical Political Economy

RACE AND CLASS

THE RACE TODAY R

RACE TODAY

RACE

RADICAL AMERICA

RADICAL PHILOSOPHY

RADIO TIMES

RAMPARTS

RANN

READER'S DIGEST

READING NEWS

RECH SOC (PARIS)
Recherches Sociologiques (Paris)

RECORD OF AGRICULTURAL RES
Record of Agricultural Research

REG STUD
Regional Studies

REG URB ECON
Regional and Urban Economics

THE REMINDER

RES IN EDUC
Research in Education

RESEARCH

REVOLUTIONARY COMMUNIST

REVOLUTIONARY COMMUNIST PAPERS

RIPENING OF TIME

ROLLING STONE

ROOF

ROTE SKIZZE

ROUND TABLE

ROYAL INST BRIT ARCHITECTS J
Royal Institute of British Architects Journal

ROYAL IR ACADEMY PROC
Royal Irish Academy Proceedings

ROYAL SOCIETY ANTIQUARIES OF IRELAND J

ROYAL SOCIETY HEALTH J

RUR SOCIOL
Rural Sociology

RUSI J
Royal United Services Institute Journal

SAMTIDEN

SAOTHAR

SATURDAY R

SCHOOL PSYCHOL INT
School Psychology International

SCIENTIFIC AMERICAN

SCOPE

SCOTT GEOGR MAG
Scottish Geographical Magazine

SCOTT J POLIT ECON
Scottish Journal of Political Economy

SCOTT J SOCIOL
Scottish Journal of Sociology

SCOTTISH FORESTRY

SEARCH

SECONDARY TEACHER

SEED POTATO

SENIOR SCHOLASTIC

SERIES WORLD AFFAIRS

SOC ACTION AND THE MEDIA
Social Action and the Media

SOC AND ECON ADM
Social and Economic Administration

SOC BEHAVIOR AND PERSONALITY
Social Behaviour and Personality

SOC COMPASS
Social Compass

SOC DYNAMICS
Social Dynamics

SOC FORCES
Social Forces

SOC POL AND ADM
Social Policy and Administration

SOC PROBL
Social Problems

SOC RES
Social Research

SOC SCI TEACHER
Social Science Teacher

SOC SERVICE R
Social Service Review

SOC STUD
Social Studies

SOC WORK EDUC
Social Work Education

SOC WORK TODAY
Social Work Today

SOCIALIST R

SOCIALIST REGISTER

SOCIALIST STANDARD

SOCIOL ANALYSIS
Sociological Analysis

SOCIOL FOCUS
Sociological Focus

SOCIOL INQUIRY
Sociological Inquiry

SOCIOL QUART
Sociological Quarterly

SOCIOL R
Sociological Review

SOCIOL SOC WELFARE
Sociology and Social Welfare

SOCIOLOGICA RURALIS

SOCIOLOGICAL SYMPOSIUM

SOCIOLOGY

SOLDIER

SOLIDARITY

SOLON

SOUTHERN SPEECH COMMUNICATION J

SPARE RIB

SPECIAL EDUCATION

SPECTATOR

SPIEGEL HIST

SPRAWY MIEDZYNARODOWE

SSRC NEWSLETTER

STATIST

STUD IN HISTORY AND SOCIETY
Studies in History and Society

STUD PUBL POL
Studies in Public Policy

STUDIA HIBERNICA

STUDIES

SURVEY

SURVEYOR

SWISS R WLD AFFAIRS
Swiss Review of World Affairs

SYNTHESES

TEACH

TEACHER

TECHNOLOGY IRELAND

TEMPS MODERNES

THIS WEEK

THREE BANKS R

THRESHOLD

TIJDSCHR ECON SOC GEOGR
Tijdschrift voor Economische en Sociale
Geografie

TIME

TIME OUT

TIMES R INDUSTR TECH
Times Review of Industrial Technology

TOLEDO UNIV LAW R
Toledo University Law Review

TORONTO UNIV LAW J
Toronto University Law Journal

TOWN COUNTRY PLANN
Town and Country Planning

TOWN PLANN INST J
Town Planning Institute Journal

TOWN PLANN R
Town Planning Review

TRADE AND INDUSTRY IN NI

TRAFFIC ENGINEERING AND CONTROL

TRAINING SCHOOL B
Training School Bulletin

TRANS ASSOC INDUSTRIAL MED OFFICERS
Transactions of the Association of Industrial
Medical Officers

TRANS INST BRIT GEOGR
Transactions of the Institute of British
Geographers

TRANSACTION

TS KON NED ARDGENT

TV GUIDE

TWENTIETH CENTURY STUD
Twentieth Century Studies

ULSTER FOLKLIFE

ULSTER J ARCHAEOLOGY

ULSTER MED J
Ulster Medical Journal

ULTACH

URB R
Urban Review

URB STUD
Urban Studies

US CATHOLIC

US NEWS AND WORLD REPORT

USA TODAY

VANDERBILT INT LAW R
Vanderbilt International Law Review

VESTES

VITAL SPEECHES

VOPROSY ISTORII

WAR MONTHLY

WASHINGTON R STRATEGIC AND INT STUD
Washington Review of Strategic and
International Studies

WATER POLLUTION CONTROL

WEEKEND

WELTGESCHEHEN

WELTWOCHE

WESTERN EUROPEAN POLITICS

WESTERN SPEECH COMMUNICATION

WHERE?

WILSON LIBRARY R

WISCONSIN SOCIOLOGIST

WLD AFFAIRS
World Affairs

WLD MARXIST R
World Marxist Review

WLD MED
World Medicine

WLD POLITICS
World Politics

WLD PRESS R
World Press Review

WLD R
World Review

WLD SURVEY
World Survey

WLD TODAY
World Today

WOMAN

THE WORLD AND THE SCHOOL

WORLDVIEW

WRU BULLETIN
Workers Research Unit Bulletin

YALE R

YOUNG QUAKER

YOUTH IN SOCIETY

ACAD
Academy

ADMIN
Administration

AFF
Affairs

AGRIC
Agriculture

AMER
American

ANN
Annual

ANTHROPOL
Anthropology, Anthropological

APCK
Association for the Promotion of Christian
Knowledge

ASA
American Sociological Association

ASSOC
Association

ATL INFOR CENT TEACHERS
Atlantic Information Center for Teachers

B
Bulletin

B ED
Bachelor of Education

BAN
Belfast Areas of Need

BBC
British Broadcasting Corporation

BDP
Building Design Partnership

BICO
British and Irish Communist Organisation

BRIT
British

BSA
British Sociological Association

BUS
Business, Belfast Urban Studies

CALIF
California

CBI
Confederation of British Industry

CHIEF ELECT OFF FOR NI
Chief Electoral Officer for Northern Ireland

COLL
College

COMM
Community, Commission

COMM DEV FORUM
Community Development Forum

COMMUNIST PARTY GB
Communist Party of Great Britain

CONF
Conference

CPAG
Child Poverty Action Group

CQSW
Certificate of Qualification in Social Work

CSE
Conference of Socialist Economists,
Certificate of Secondary Education

CSPP
Centre for the Study of Social Problems

CUNY
City University of New York

CUP
Cambridge University Press

DEPT
Department

DHSS (NI)
Department of Health and Social Services (NI)

DMS
Department of Manpower Services

DOE
Department of the Environment

DPHIL
Doctor of Philosophy

DSC
Doctor of Science

DUP
Democratic Unionist Party

ECON
Economics

ECPR
European Consortium for Political Research

ED
Editor

EDS
Editors

EDUC
Education

EEC
European Economic Community

EOC
Equal Opportunities Commission

EPA
Emergency Provisions Act

ESN
Educationally Subnormal

ESRI
Economic and Social Research Unit

FEA
Fair Employment Agency

GAA
Gaelic Athletic Association

GB
Great Britain

GCE
General Certificate of Education

GEOG
Geography

```
GOVT                                    MSC
Government                              Master of Science

GP                                      MSC (ECON)
General Practitioner                    Master of Science (Economics)

HIST                                    MSSC
History                                 Master of Social Science

HMSO                                    MTH
Her/His Majesty's Stationery Office     Master of Theology

ICTU                                    NAT
Irish Congress of Trade Unions          National

IDB                                     NCCL
Industrial Development Board            National Council of Civil Liberties

INLA                                    NCSA
Irish National Liberation Army          North Central Sociological Association

INST                                    NHS
Institute                               National Health Service

INT                                     NI
International                            Northern Ireland

INTO                                    NIA
Irish National Teachers' Organisation   Northern Ireland Assembly

IPA                                     NIASL
Institute of Public Administration      Northern Ireland Association of Socialist
                                        Lawyers
IR
Irish                                   NICER
                                        Northern Ireland Council for Educational
IRA                                     Research
Irish Republican Army
                                        NICRA
IRL                                     Northern Ireland Civil Rights Association
Ireland
                                        NICRC
ITGWU                                   Northern Ireland Community Relations
Irish Transport and General Workers' Union  Commission

J                                       NICSS
Journal                                 Northern Ireland Council of Social Service

LEDU                                    NIEC
Local Enterprise Development Unit       Northern Ireland Economic Council

LLD                                     NIHE
Doctor of Law                           Northern Ireland Housing Executive

LLM                                     NIHT
Master of Law                           Northern Ireland Housing Trust

LIB                                     NILP
Library                                 Northern Ireland Labour Party

LRA                                     NSPCC
Labour Relations Agency                 National Society for the Prevention of
                                        Cruelty to Children
LSE
London School of Economics              NUM
                                        New Ulster Movement
M COMM SC
Master of Commercial Science            NUPRG
                                        New Ulster Political Research Group
MA
Master of Arts                          NUU
                                        New University of Ulster
MBA
Master of Business Administration       NY
                                        New York
MCH
Master of Chemistry                     ORGAN
                                        Organisation
MD
Doctor of Medicine                      OUP
                                        Oxford University Press
MED
Master of Education                     PAPTA
                                        People Against the Prevention of Terrorism
MPHIL                                   Act
Master of Philosophy
                                        PD
                                        Peoples Democracy
```

PEP
Political and Economic Planning

PHD
Doctor of Philosophy

POLIT
Politics

POLY
Polytechnic

POW
Prisoners of War

PR
Proportional Representation, Public Relations

PROC
Proceedings

PRONI
Public Record Office of Northern Ireland

PSYCHOL
Psychology

QUB
Queen's University, Belfast

R
Review, Royal

RES
Research

RKP
Routledge and Kegan Paul

RUC
Royal Ulster Constabulary

RUSI
Royal United Services Institute

RVH
Royal Victoria Hospital

SAI
Sociological Association of Ireland

SAS
Special Air Services

SBC
Supplementary Benefits Commission

SCI
Science

SCM
Student Christian Movement

SDLP
Social Democratic and Labour Party

SLS
Servicing the Legal System

SOC
Social

SOCIOL
Sociology

SSRC
Social Science Research Council

SSSP
Society for the Study of Social Problems

STUD
Studies

STV
Single Transferable Vote

TB
Tuberculosis

TCD
Trinity College, Dublin

TUC
Trade Union Congress

U P
University Press

UCD
University College, Dublin

UCLA
University of California, Los Angeles

UDA
Ulster Defence Association

UDR
Ulster Defence Regiment

UK
United Kingdom

ULCCC
Ulster Loyalist Central Coordinating Committee

UNIV
University

URB
Urban

US
United States

UTV
Ulster Television

UUC
Ulster Unionist Council

UUP
Ulster Unionist Party

UVF
Ulster Volunteer Force

WAI
Women Against Imperialism

WLD
World

Other Abbreviations

AALEN, F H A - 2553, 2644, 5278
ABBOTT, M - 2860
ABERG, A - 203
ABERNETHY, W R - 3070
ABRAHAMSON, M W - 2348
ABUKUTSA, J L - 3737
ACHENBACH, P - 3071
ACHESON, A - 5203
ACKROYD, C - 4556
ACTION ON DEBT - 2987
ADAMS, G - 204, 5279-5280
ADAMS, G B - 5281-5284
ADAMS, C F - 3072-3073
ADAMS, J - 2554, 2861
ADAMS, J - 4911, 5201
ADAMSON, I - 5412
ADVERTISERS' WEEKLY - 1724
ADVISORY COUNCIL FOR EDUCATION IN NI - 3738-3743
AGE CONCERN - 2988, 3074
AGNEW, J B - 4129, 5188
AGNEW, N - 1725
AGNEW, P - 205, 4322
AITKEN, J M - 2645-2646
AJEMIAN, R - 1044
AKENSON, D H - 90, 3744, 4323
AKIWOWO, A - 5692, (929)
ALBERT, T - 1045, (4774)
ALBERTS, D J - 5785
ALBREKTSEN, B - 206
ALCOCK, A E - 207, 1726, 4324
ALCORN, D - 2647, 2862-2863, 2989, 3075, 3745
ALEVY, D - 5495
ALEXANDER, A - 1279
ALEXANDER, D J - 1727-1728, 2349-2350
ALEXANDER, J M - 208-214
ALEXANDER, Y - 5621-5624
ALL-PARTY ANTI-PARTITION CONFERENCE - 1280-1281, 4325-4326
ALLEN, K - 1, 5625
ALLEN, L - 2648
ALLEN, R - 3746, 4178
ALLEN, W E D - 2092
ALLISON, D - 1729
ALLISON, R S - 3076
ALLISTER, J H - 215
ALLUM, P - 216-217
ALTER, P - 218
ALVAREZ, G - 219, 1282
AMERICAN GEOGRAPHICAL SOCIETY - 5413
AMNESTY INTERNATIONAL - 4913-4915
AN FORAS FORBARTHA - 25
ANDERSON, A C - 4179
ANDERSON, J - 220
ANDERSON, J S A - 4006
ANDERSON, T J - 1857
ANDERSONSTOWN AND SUFFOLK INDUSTRIAL PROMOTIONS ASSOCIATION - 2351
ANDREWS, E - 5285
ANDREWS, J H - 1283
ANNING, N - 2352, 2864
ANNIS, R C - 5691, (4476)
ANTHONY, E J - 5626, (3681)
ANTHONY, P G J - 3747, 4180
ANTRIM AND BALLYMENA DEVELOPMENT COMMISSION - 2649
ANTRIM COUNTY HEALTH COMMITTEE - 3077-3078
ANTRIM COUNTY LIBRARY - 2
ANTRIM STEERING COMMITTEE - 2650
ARBLASTER, A - 221
ARCHER, J R - 222, 1284
ARDEN, J - 1046
ARDILL, S - 3493, 4934
ARDOYNE EX-RESIDENTS ASSOCIATION - 2865, 4327
ARGAL, A - 223
ARLOW, B - 1730, 2093
ARMSTRONG, D L - 1731, 2094
ARMSTRONG, J - 1732
ARMSTRONG, M J - 3191
ARMSTRONG, R - 5496
ARMSTRONG, W J - 2651
ARMSTRONG-INGRAM, R - 5286
ARNOLD, B - 224-226, 1285

ARTHUR, A - 3567, 4328
ARTHUR, P - 227-229, 1286-1290, 1659-1660
ASHBY, J A - 2580, 3006
ASHITEY, G - 3079-3080
ASHLEY, L R - 230
ASSISSI FELLOWSHIP COMMITTEE - 5497
ASSOCIATION FOR LEGAL JUSTICE - 4916
ASSOCIATION OF LOCAL ADVICE CENTRES - 2866
ASSOCIATION OF NI EDUCATION AND LIBRARY - BOARDS - 3748
ATKINS, H - 231
ATKINSON, C - 1291
ATLANTIC INFORMATION CENTRE FOR TEACHERS - 232, 1292
ATTWOOD, E A - 1733
AUDLEY, R - 5204
AUGHEY, A - 1734
AUNGER, E A - 1293-1294, 2555-2556, 4329-4332
AUSTIN, J - 1954
AUSTIN, S - 3749
AYANIAN, J Z - 4822, 5257

BABY, N - 233
BAILEY, A - 234
BAILEY, R - 5627, (3421)
BAILIE, R - 4788
BAILLIE, B - 2867
BAIN, H - 235
BAIN, R E D - 4557
BAKER, D - 5628, (595, 4253)
BALDWIN, S - 5651, (3148, 3349)
BALL, D - 3081
BALLARD, L M - 5287
BALLYMENA STEERING COMMITTEE - 2652
BALTHROP, V W - 236
BAMBER, J H - 2557, 3082, 3236-3237, 3568-3571, 3908
BAMBERY, C - 619
BAMFORD, D - 3083-3084, 3750
BANKER - 1735
BANKERS' MAGAZINE - 1736
BANKS, M - 4558
BANNERMAN, A - 2653
BANNON, T - 5614
BANNOV, B G - 237
BARDON, J - 2654
BARKER, A J - 238
BARKER, D - 4559, 5629, (4559)
BARKLEY, J M - 4181-4188, 4333-4334
BARLEY, C - 239
BARLOW, P - 2353, 3751
BARON, V O - 240-241
BARR, A - 1737, 3085
BARRINGTON, D - 242-243, 1295-1296
BARRINGTON, T J - 2655
BARRITT, D P - 244-249, 3086, 4335-4336
BARROW, G L - 1738
BARRY, B - 250
BARTHORP, M - 4560
BARTON, B - 1297-1298, 4917-4918
BARZILAY, D - 4561-4564
BATES, J - 1739-1742, 2095, 2354, 5630
BATES, P J - 2097
BATESON, P - 2096, 2355-2356
BATTS, D - 3822, 4392
BAXTER, L - 1661
BAXTER, R - 251
BAXTER, T - 3572, 4919
BAXTER-MOORE, N - 1441-1442
BAYLEY, J - 252, 1743, 4565, 4902, 5501
BBC - 5205
BDP - 1744, 2656-2663, 2868
BEACH, S W - 253, 1662, 4337
BEARE, J M - 2357, 3087
BEATTIE, D R - 3752
BEATTIE, G W - 254
BEATTIE, R P - 2097
BEATTY, J - 255, 1047
BEAVER, S H - 5488
BEBBINGTON, J - 5288

BRESLIN, J - 1054
BRESLIN, S - 5209
BRETT, C E B - 1322, 2687-2688, 2996, 4695, 5504
BREWER, J - 348, 4592
BRIDGE, J W - 5647, (4782, 5100)
BRIDGES, G - (743)
BRISTOW, J - 1759-1761
BRITISH ASSOCIATION FOR THE ADVANCEMENT OF SCIENCE - 5648, (1958)
BRITISH INFORMATION SERVICES - 5416
BRITISH MEDICAL JOURNAL - 3102
BRITISH SOCIETY FOR SOCIAL RESPONSIBILITY IN SCIENCE - 4593
BROAD, R - 104
BROCKWAY, F - 4946
BROMLEY, P M - 3495
BROOKE, A C - 1762
BROOKEBOROUGH, B - 349
BROOKER, D S - 3103, 3496
BROWN, A J - 1763
BROWN, D - 350
BROWN, D N - 2376
BROWN, G - 5649, (457)
BROWN, G A - 3770-3772, 3889, 4247
BROWN, J - 437, 5650, (5127)
BROWN, L T - 2110
BROWN, M - 5651, (3148)
BROWN, M J - 3104-3106
BROWN, R H - 5417, 5505-5506
BROWN, S - 5210
BROWN, T - 4197
BROWN, W - 2111, 2377, 2413, 3890
BROWNE, J - 5294
BROWNE, V - 351, 1055-1061, 4594-4596
BROWNLOW COMMUNITY COUNCIL - 3107
BRUCE, A - 352
BRUINVELS, P - 2304, 5804, (2304)
BRUNT, R M - 8, 5507
BRYANS, H - 3497
BRYANS, R - 5418
BRYARS, J H - 3108
BUCHANAN, G - 2566
BUCHANAN, R E - 2095, 2354
BUCHANAN, R H - 312, 1317, 1764-1765, 2689-2692, 5295-5299, 5652-5653, (2671)
BUCKLAND, P - 105-109, 1062, 5419-5420
BUCKLEY, A - 5300-5301, 4597
BUCKLEY, S - 3498
BUCKMAN, P - 1063
BUDGE, I - 353, 1323-1325, 1564, 5654, (1149)
BUFWACK, M S - 5302
BUGLER, J - 1326
BUICK, A - 354
BUILT ENVIRONMENT - 2879
BUNDRED, S - 355, 1668
BUNKER, B - 5495
BUNTING, B - 3685, 4481, 5562, 5576-5579
BUNTING, R T - 1327
BURKE, V - 4598, 4800
BURKETT, T - 356
BURNETT, R - 5508
BURNISON, G - 1766-1767
BURNS, F - 3773
BURNS, G - 1768, 2378, 3499, 4947
BURRIDGE, K - 9
BURROWES, J - 5211, 5655, (5211)
BURTON, A - 4599
BURTON, F - 357, 4362-4364, 5509-5510
BUSH, L - 2997, 3582
BUSINESS WEEK - 1769, 2112
BUSTEED, M A - 1328-1330, 1770-1771, 2567, 5421-5423
BUTLER, D - 1064, (1527, 1557)
BUTLER, D E - 5656-5657
BUTLER, H - 358
BUTLIN, R - 5424-5425
BUTTERWECK, H - 359
BUTTERWORTH, E - 5658
BYRD, M W J - 3200
BYRNE, D - 360-361, 1772, 2880, 3109, 3583
BYRNE, F J - 5761, (1120)
BYRNES, D P - 3110, 4600

CAGIANELLI, G - 362
CAHILL, G A - 1331
CAHILL, K M - 363-364

CAIRNS, E - 3584-3590, 3632, 4365-4370, 4380-4481, 4544, 5212-5513
CALDWELL, J C - 3774
CALDWELL, J H - 2113
CALDWELL, L - 3775
CALDWELL, T - 5511
CALLAGHAN, J - 365
CALLENDER, L - 1669-1670
CALVERT, D - 1671
CALVERT, H - 366, 1332-1334, 2998, 4948-4949
CALVERT, J - 367, 2874, 2881
CALWELL, H G - 3111-3113
CAMBLIN, G - 1335, 1773, 2693-2697
CAMBRIDGE REVIEW - 368
CAMERAWORK - 5214-5215
CAMERON COMMISSION - 1336, 4601
CAMPAIGN FOR FREE SPEECH ON IRELAND - 5216
CAMPAIGN FOR LABOUR REPRESENTATION IN NI - 1672
CAMPAIGN FOR SOCIAL JUSTICE IN NI - 1337, 4371-4602
CAMPBELL, A D - 1774
CAMPBELL, B M S - 10
CAMPBELL, C L - 5303
CAMPBELL, C M - 3114, 4950-4951, 5659, (4937, 4950, 4952, 5001, 5034, 5106)
CAMPBELL, D - 4855
CAMPBELL, H M - 2114
CAMPBELL, J - 4198
CAMPBELL, J A - 3776
CAMPBELL, J J - 110, 3777-3778, 4199
CAMPBELL, K - 3779
CAMPBELL, N - 1673
CANAVAN, A J - 5217
CAPPER, N M - 2882
CARASSO, J P - 369
CAREY, G C R - 3115-3116
CARLEN, P - 5509-5510
CARLETON, S T - 2698
CARLETON, W - 370
CARLIN, T - 4952
CARLOW, P - 371
CARLTON, C - 5660
CARLTON, D - 5661, (1040, 4569)
CARNDUFF, T - 372, 1065
CARPENTER, A - 5662
CARROLL, F M - 111
CARROLL, J T - 112
CARROLL, T - 4603-4606
CARROLL, W D - 4953
CARRY ON LEARNING PROJECT - 3780
CARSANIGA, G - 373
CARSON, H M - 4607
CARSON, N A J - 3117
CARSON, W - 1775
CARSON, W - 5512
CARSON, W H - 2115
CARSON, W R H - 11
CARTER, A - 3781
CARTER, C E - 5513
CARTER, C F - 249, 1776-1781
CARTER, F - 3591, 4954
CARTER, H - 5645, (443)
CARTER, J - 1066
CARTER, W - 2116-2117
CARTY, R K - 1338
CARVILLE, J B - 3782
CASE, H J - 2118
CASEMENT, R S - 3118
CASEY, J P - 2999-3000
CASHELL, R - 2699
CASTERAN, C - 374
CATHCART, R - 3783, 5426
CATHERWOOD, F - 375, 4200-4201
CATHOLIC TRUTH SOCIETY - 1067
CATTELAIN, J P - 376
CATTO, M - 5304
CAUL, B - 1339, 3119-3120, 3227
CAVANAGH, C - 4372
CAVE, E D - 2379, 3784-3785
CAVEN, N - 3786, 3895-3896
CAVES, W J - 3001, 3787
CELTIC LEAGUE - 5663, (1414, 4423)
CENTRAL CITIZENS' DEFENCE COMMITTEE - 4955, 4956
CENTRAL ECONOMIC SERVICE - 3788
CENTRE FOR AGRICULTURAL STRATEGY - 5664, (2180)
CHALFONT, A - 4608-4609

CRONNE,H A - 5678
CROOKS,S H - 3599
CROSSBOW - 415
CROSSEY,J H - 2138
CROSSLAND,B - 1795, 3805
CROTTY,R - 1796
CROWE,W H - 3806-3807, 5305
CROZIER,B - 5679-5680, (95, 375, 746, 1478,
        4609)
CRUICKSHANK,J G - 2139-2140, (2651, 2691)
CRUICKSHANK,M M - 2139
CRUICKSHANK,W J - 5681
CRUTCHLY,J - 3600, 4964
CRYAN,M - 2141
CSPP - 5682, (69, 747, 910, 1306, 1311,
        1403, 1487, 1853)
CULLEN,B - 1797
CULLEN,L M - 1798, 5683
CULTURAL RELATIONS COMMITTEE OF IRELAND - 16
CUNNINGHAM,F - 5700, (1364)
CUNNINGHAM,M - 4639
CURL,J T - 2713
CURLEY,P B - 5306
CURNO,A - 5684, (3540, 5123)
CURNO,P - 5685, (3263)
CURRAGH,E G - 2388, 3809
CURRAN,J - 416-417, 1347-1348
CURRAN,J D - 3601-3602, 3641, 5051, 5546
CURRAN,R G - 1799
CURRENT BIOGRAPHY - 1078
CURRIE,E A - 5468
CURRIE,J - 3132
CURRIE,J R L - 2142
CURTIN,C - 5686, (1713, 2451, 3668, 4312,
        5409)
CURTIS,L - 4640, 5221
CURTIS,L P - 120
CUSDIN,L - 3810
CUTHBERT,N - 1800-1808, 1885-1887, 2050,
        2143, 2389, 2714

D'ARCY,M - 3509, 4965
DALLAT,M - 3811, 4381
DALY,C B - 418-420, 1349, 4213, 4966
DALY,E - 3812, 4382, 4641
DAMOGLOU,A P - 3400
DANE,M - 4642
DANIEL,T K - 421
DANKER,G - 4643
DARBY,J - 17-18, 422-425, 1350, 2467-2468,
        2888, 3027, 3133, 3175, 3485, 3688-
        3689, 3813-3822, 4383-4392, 5432-
        5433, 5687, (1645, 2921, 3273, 3485,
        3997, 4558, 5037)
DARRAGH,P M - 3134-3167
DARWIN,K - 2664, 5520-5521
DASH,S - 4967-4968
DAUFOUY,P - 195-196
DAVEY,R - 4393
DAVIDSON,J - 5522
DAVIDSON,S - 1079
DAVIDSON,S I - 3136, 3603
DAVIDSON,T W - 3152
DAVIES,C - 426-427, 1809
DAVIES,G L - 2144, 5523-5524
DAVIES,K - 19
DAVIES,M - 5222
DAVIES,R - 1810-1811
DAVIES,S - 2643
DAVIS,E E - 428, 1624, 4540
DAVIS,J - 2145-2150
DAVIS,K C - 2151
DAVIS,R - 5223
DAVISON,B - 1812
DAVISON,G - 4214
DAVISON,M - 429
DAVISON,R S - 5525
DAVISON,W - 4215
DAWSON,J - 2152-2156, 4644, 4969, 5688,
        (445)
DE BREFFNY,B - 5307-5308
DE FREINE,S - 5309-5310
DE LA CRUZ,F - 5689, (3427)
DE PAOR,L - 121, 430, 5311
DEAN,G - 3137
DEANE,E - 3138-3139

DEANE,S - 2157, 5312-5313
DEANE-DRUMMOND,A - 4645
DEEDES,W - 431
DEENY,M - 3140
DEES,D - 1080
DEITCH,B - 5690, (4571)
DELAIGLES,J - 5526
DELANEY,S - 1677
DELANOE,N - 432
DEMPSEY,P - 1351, 4394
DENNISON,S R - 1813
DENT,G I - 3823
DENTON,H C B - 3141
DEPT OF AGRICULTURE (NI) - 1814, 2158-2163
DEPT OF EDUCATION (NI) - 2585, 3009, 3824-
        3831
DEPT OF HOUSING, LOCAL GOVERNMENT AND
        PLANNING (NI) - 2715
DEPT OF MANPOWER SERVICES (NI) - 2390-2392,
        2586
DEPT OF THE ENVIRONMENT (NI) - 2716-2722,
        2889, 5314
DER SPIEGEL - 1081
DEREGOWSKI,J B - 5691, (4476)
DERRY LABOUR PARTY - 1082
DERRYNANE - 1352, 4395
DERWIN,D - 433
DESPORTE,I P - 4646
DEUTSCH,R - 20, 623-624, 1083-1087, 1353,
        4647-4648, 4970, 5224-5225, 5315-
        5316, 5434-5436
DEVLIN,B - 1088-1089
DEVLIN,P - 434, 1090, 3010-3012, 4649
DEWAR,M - 435-437
DHSS (NI) - 1354, 3142-3145
DICKEY,A - 4971
DICKIE-CLARK,H - 438
DICKINSON,C - 3146, 3604
DICKSON,D - 3147, 3466, 3832-3833, 4115
DILLON,M - 2164, 4396, 4650
DIPLOCK REPORT - 4972
DITCH,J - 1355-1357, 2165, 2393, 3013-3014,
        3148, 3348-3349, 3510, 5113, 5638,
        (2992, 3014, 3061)
DITCH,N - 2890
DOBSON,C - 4651
DODD,N L - 4652
DODGE,N - 18
DOFNY,J - 5692, (929)
DOGGETT,A - 439, 3511
DOHERTY,P - 440, 2394- 2397, 2587, 2994-
        2995, 3098-3099,
DOHRS,F - 2166, 5437
DOLAN,G - 3834
DONAGHY,B - 1091
DONAGHY,G - 3149
DONAGHY,P - 3835
DONALDSON,A - 1358-1362, 4973
DONALDSON,N - 3150
DONNELLY,D - 2167, 2891
DONNISON,D - 1363
DONOGHUE,D - 1092
DOOB,L - 5495, 5527-5528
DOOLEY CLARKE,D - 1093
DOORNKAMP,J - 5688, (445)
DORAN,I G - 2723
DORAN,J S - 5317
DORLAND,A C - 441
DORN,R - 442
DOUGHTY,P - 5529
DOUGLAS,E - 5318
DOUGLAS,F - 3836-3837
DOUGLAS,J N H - 313, 443-447, 731, 1364-1366,
        4397, 5643, (313, 446, 1579-1580,
        1873, 2394, 2570, 4063, 4346, 4376,
        4517, 4802, 5297)
DOUGLAS,W - 448
DOWDEN,R - 4216
DOWLING,B R - 1367, 1815
DOWLING,K - 4653, 4974
DOWLING,P - 3838
DOWNEY,A - 3839
DOWNEY,J - 4654-4655, 4975-4976
DOWNEY,N G - 3840
DOWNEY,R - 3841
DOWNING,J D - 449, 3842, 5693, (449, 953,
        3418)
DOYLE,C - 5438
DOYLE,D N - 122
DRAPER,J - 3151

GUIRGUIS, E F - 3213
GUNN, P - 2735
GUTHRIE, D - 3214-3215

HACHEY, T E - 541-542, 4699
HADDEN, D R - 3216
HADDEN, P - 543-544
HADDEN, T - 339-340, 545-547, 2736, 2906-2907,
        4587, 4939-4940, 5018-5025
HADDEN, W A - 3327, 4786
HADFIELD, B - 1408, 5026-5027
HAEGER, R A - 548-550
HAGGER, M - 5730, (749)
HAGGERTY, J J - 4700
HAHN, E - 5455
HAINSWORTH, P - 551, 1409, 3893
HAIRE, T R - 3217
HALL REPORT - 1855
HALL, F G - 2190
HALL, R - 5719, (416)
HALL, R A - 3218
HALL, S - 5237
HALSTOCK, M - 5544
HAMBLY, G E - 3894
HAMILL, J - 552
HAMILL, P - 553
HAMILTON, A J - 136
HAMILTON, C - 5337
HAMILTON, I - 554-556
HAMILTON, P - 2487, 3385, 5545
HANCOCK, G - 557
HAND, G J - 558, 1120, 1410
HANLY, J - 559, 4250
HANNA, D O - 5456
HANNA, F - 560
HANNA, L - 2191, 5489
HANNA, T - 5028
HANNUM, H - 4941-4942
HANSON, R - 561, 4251
HARBINSON, J F - 1686-1687
HARBINSON, R - 1121
HARBISON, J - 3130, 3601-3602, 3641, 3786,
        3895-3896, 5051, 5457, 5546, 5721,
        (269, 2535, 2939, 3601, 3606, 3609,
        3630, 3651, 3685, 3724, 3786, 3896,
        4000, 4141, 4167, 4365, 4467, 4493)
HARBISON, J - 3626-3727, 5457, 5720-5721,
        (269, 2535, 2939, 2997, 3097, 3579,
        3582, 3584, 3596, 3601, 3606, 3609,
        3626, 3630, 3639, 3650-3651, 3658,
        3675, 3685, 3724, 3734, 3855, 3896,
        4000, 4141-4142, 4167, 4365, 4467,
        4477, 4493, 4548, 4979, 5072-5073,
        5212, 5457)
HARDY, Y - 4701
HARGIE, O - 3219, 3466, 3897, 4115
HARKIN, A M - 2416
HARKIN, B - 562, 4416
HARKNESS, D A E - 1411, 1856
HARKNESS, D W - 137-139, 1370, 1412
HARKNESS, E - 5547
HARLAND AND WOLFF, LTD. - 31
HARLAND, R W - 2595, 3220
HARLOE, M - 2737
HARMAN, C - 563
HARMAN, M - 5794
HARRIES, D - 4417
HARRIS, A - 5722
HARRIS, H - 564
HARRIS, J - 4702
HARRIS, R - 4418-4420, 5458, 5548
HARRISON, E M - 3032, 3221-3222
HARRISON, H - 2192, 2417
HARRISON, M - 2061
HARRISON, P - 565, 2596
HARRISON, R L - 2597, 2908
HARRISON, R T - 1857
HARRISON, S - 3637
HARVEY, R - 5029
HARVEY, S - 1858-1859, 2418, 3628, 5723,
        (1777, 1838, 1859, 1888, 1912,
        2022)
HARWOOD, J - 566
HASLETT, E - 140
HASSETT, J - 5538
HASTINGS, M - 1122-1123
HASWELL, J - 4703
HAUGHEY, C - 567
HAUGHTON REPORT - 2419, 3525

HAUGHTON, J P - 5459
HAUPTFUHRER, F - 1124
HAUSER, R - 568
HAWTHORNE, J - 5238, 5724, (198)
HAY, I - 3204
HAYES, D P - 3898
HAYES, M - 1413, 3223-3224, 4421-4422
HAYES, P - 4704
HAYES, R J - 32
HAYWARD, R - 5338-5340
HEADEY, B - 1860
HEALTH AND SOCIAL SERVICES JOURNAL - 3225
HEALY, J - 569-570
HEANEY, S - 5341
HEATEN, W R - 5785, (4774)
HEATLEY, E - 5460
HEATLEY, F - 571, 1414, 4423
HEATLEY, P - 5030-5031
HEATON, W R - 5785
HECHTER, M - 572-578, 1861-1867
HEDERMAN, M - 4705
HEDERMAN, M P - 5549
HEISLER, M O - 579, 580, 4424
HEMEL HEMPSTEAD CONSTITUENCY LABOUR PARTY -
        581, 1688
HEMMING, M F W - 1868
HENDERSON, G - 5725, (655)
HENDERSON, I G - 2420-2421
HENDERSON, P - 5726
HENDRY, J - 2738-2740, 2909-2913
HENEGHAN, P - 2193
HEPBURN, A C - 18, 117, 141, 914, 2422-2423,
        4425-4426, 5727, (1345)
HEPPLE, B A - 33
HERBERT, D - 5728-5729, (4434, 4494)
HERDER CORRESPONDENCE - 1125
HERMAN, V - 5730, (749)
HERMANS, F A - 5731, 1560)
HERMLE, R - 582
HERMON, J - 5032
HERRON, C - 3629, 5342
HERRON, S - 3226-3227
HESKIN, K - 583-584, 3630, 4706
HESLINGA, M W - 5461-5462
HETHERINGTON, P - 2741
HEUSAFF, A - 585
HEWITT, C - 1415, 4427, 4707-4708, 4824
HEWITT, J - 142, 5343-5347, 5550, 5732
HEWITT, P - 5033-5034, 5168
HEWITT, V N - 2194
HEZLETT, A - 4709
HIBERNIAN JOURNAL - 1126
HICKEY, J - 4252, 4428
HICKEY, N - 5239
HICKIE, J - 461
HICKMAN, M - 439, 3511
HICKMAN, M - 5240
HIGGINS, J - 4710, 5035
HIGHAM, R - 5733, (4573)
HIGHER EDUCATION REVIEW GROUP - 3899
HILL, D - 1416-1417
HILL, D A - 1869-1870, 2195-2198, 5463
HILL, M - 5734, (4271)
HILLAN, J J - 1418
HILLERY, B - 2424
HILLERY, P J - 1127
HILLIS, A L - 2913
HILLYARD, P - 339-340, 546-547, 1956-1957,
        2875-2876, 2914-2915, 2935-2938,
        2969, 4711, 4939-4940, 5020-5024,
        5036-5039, 5735, (5031, 5052, 5175)
HINCKLE, W - 1128
HINDS, B - 3526
HINDSLEY, W R - 143
HITCHENS, C - 586, 1129, 5040
HOARE, A G - 1871-1875
HOBART, A E L - 34
HOBSON, B - 144
HODGSON, E - 5464
HODSON, R - 1419, 2742
HOFFMAN, J - 587
HOGAN, G - 4712
HOGBERG, G H - 588
HOGGART, R - 5241
HOGGART, S - 4713, 5242
HOGWOOD, B - 1420, 1876
HOLDEN, J C - 3900
HOLLAND, C - 4714

HOLLAND,E L   - 3228
HOLLAND,J - 589-592, 1130-1133, 4715, 5041
HOLLAND,M - 593, 1134-1143, 1689, 4716-4717,
          5042
HOLLOWAY,D - 4718
HOLLOWAY,G R - 2097
HOLMES,E - 594, 1421-1422, 3631, 3901
HOLMES,R F G - 595, 3902, 4253
HOME OFFICE - 1423
HOPE,R - 5736
HOPKINS,S - 596
HORNER,A A - 2743
HORROCKS,M - 2737
HORTON,F J - 2916
HOSENBALL,M - 1144
HOSIN,A - 3589, 3632
HOUSE,J W - 5737, (1786)
HOUSTON,J - 1877
HOWARD,N - 235
HOWARD,P - 4429-4430, 5243-5244
HOWKINS,J - 5245
HOWTON,H - 4719
HUALLACHAIN,C - 3903
HUCZYNSKI,A - 5246
HUDSON,P - 4720
HUGHES,C G - 597-598, 4254
HUGHES,D J - 2917, 3229
HUGHES,J G - 2593
HUGHES,N - 35
HUGHES,P H - 2199-2201
HULL,C - 599
HULL,R H - 600-601
HUMANIST - 602
HUME,J - 603, 1145
HUMPHREYS,A L - 36
HUNT,LORD - 5043
HUNTER,J - 604
HUNTER,W I - 2202
HURLEY,M - 4255, 5738, (2607, 3916, 4181,
          4255, 4259, 4262, 4266-4267, 4300)
HUTCHINSON,B - 3904-3905, 3952
HUTCHINSON,N - 3540, 5123
HUTCHINSON,R - 2425
HUTCHINSON,R W - 1878, 2517, 2631
HUTCHINSON,W B D - 3906
HUTCHINSON,W R - 2744
HUTTON,J - 4721
HYAMS,E - 4722
HYDE,H M - 1146, 2203
HYNAM,C A S - 3230

ICTU - 605-606, 1879-1880, 2426-2429
INDEPENDENT TELEVISION AUTHORITY - 4256
INFORMATION ON IRELAND - 4723
INGLIS,B - 145
INK - 607
INSIDE STORY - 608
INSTITUTE FOR THE STUDY OF CONFLICT - 609,
          4724-4725
INSTITUTE OF BANKERS IN IRELAND - 1881
INSTITUTE OF COMMONWEALTH STUDIES - 5465
INSTITUTE OF CONTINUING EDUCATION - 2204
INSTITUTE OF MECHANICAL ENGINEERS - 2205
INTERNATIONAL SOCIALISM - 610
INTELLECT - 4726
INTER-DEPARTMENTAL COMMITTEE ON FAMILY
          PROBLEMS - 3231-3232
INTERDEPARTMENTAL COMMITTEE ON MATTERS
          RELATING TO THE ALIENATION OF YOUNG
          PEOPLE - 3633
INTERNATIONAL COMMISSION OF JURISTS' REVIEW
          5044
INTERNATIONAL REVIEW OF ADMINISTRATIVE
          SCIENCES - 37
IPA - 3527
IRA - 4727
IRA (OFFICIAL) - 4728
IRA (PROVISIONAL) - 4729
IRELAND,D - 611, 1147-1148
IRELAND,J - 332
IRIS - 1149-1150, 1424, 1690, 2918, 3528,
          4730-4736, 5045-5046
IRISH ASSOCIATION FOR CULTURAL, ECONOMIC AND
          SOCIAL RELATIONS - 3634
IRISH CHRISTIAN YOUTH ASSEMBLY - 4257, 4431
IRISH COMMUNIST ORGANISATION - 612, 1425

IRISH COUNCIL OF CHURCHES - 613, 2430
IRISH COUNCIL OF CHURCHES ADVISORY FORUM -
          5047
IRISH COUNCIL OF CHURCHES AND ROMAN CATHOLIC
          JOINT GROUP ON SOCIAL PROBLEMS -
          2745, 3233-3236
IRISH EPISCOPAL CONFERENCE - 4258
IRISH FREEDOM MOVEMENT - 614
IRISH GOVERNMENT - 5466
IRISH NEWS - 1426
IRVINE,S A - 4173
IRWIN,W G - 2557, 3082, 3235-3237, 3907-3908
IRWIN,W L - 2206
ISLES,K S - 1882-1887, 2431

JACKSON,H - 615
JACKSON,J A - 333-337, 616, 902, 2432, 2598-
          2602
JACKSON,J D - 5048
JACKSON,T A - 5739, (527)
JACOBSEN,J K - 1151
JACOBSON,A - 1899
JACQUES,W - 3909
JAEGER,J - 1888
JAHODA,G - 3637
JAMES,M - 617
JAMES,T - 1152
JAMES,W V - 3238
JAMIESON,J - 3910
JAMISON,D - 1427
JAMISON,K - 5348
JANKE,P - 618, 4737
JARDINE,E - 3601-3602, 3638-3641, 5049-5051,
          5546, 5740
JARDINE,M - 2491, 4067
JEFFERSON,C W - 1889, 1890, 1891, 1892, 2051,
          2366, 2559
JEFFREY,F - 4259-4260
JENKINS,G - 619
JENKINS,P - 1428
JENKINS,R - 1893, 3642-3643, 4434
JENKINS,R - 4432-4433, 4435-4437
JENKS,R E - 2433, 3644
JENVEY,S - 3645, 4438
JESS,P M H - 2746
JOANNON,P - 38-39, 146, 620-624, 5795
JOHNSON,D B - 2207, 5500
JOHNSON,D S - 1153-1154, 1894-1895, 2208
JOHNSON,J - 2511
JOHNSON,J H - 625, 1429, 2209, 2603-2604,
          2747
JOHNSON,P - 147
JOHNSON,R W - 626
JOHNSON,S - 40
JOHNSTON REPORT - 3911
JOHNSTON,D H - 3912
JOHNSTON,E - 5349
JOHNSTON,I S - 1896
JOHNSTON,J - 1897, 2149, 2210
JOHNSTON,M - 41
JOHNSTON,R - 5398
JOHNSTON,R J - 5728, (4344)
JOHNSTON,S - 3239-3330, 4787
JOHNSTON,T J - 4261
JOHSE,R B - 2748
JOINT WORKING PARTY ON THE ECONOMY OF NI -
          1898
JOINT WORKING PARTY ON THE RIVER LAGAN - 2749
JONES,A - 1155-1156
JONES,D - 5741, (3205)
JONES,E - 2605-2606, 2726, 2750-2753, 4439-
          4440, 5653, 5742-5743, (2677, 2761)
JONES,G W - 1430
JONES,J B - 42
JONES,K - 5744, (3091)
JONES,M W - 1157
JONES,R M - 2634
JONES,W R - 5350
JORDAN,R J - 1910
JORGENSEN,B - 5052-5053
JOURNAL OF THE ROYAL INSTITUTE OF BRITISH
          ARCHITECTS - 2919

KANE,J J - 627
KANNER,B - 2211
KAPFERER,B - 5746, (4748)
KARAGEORGOS,D L - 3913
KARCH,C - 628, 4441

MILLER, R L - 333-337, 902, 2432, 2459, 2602,
         2616-2619, 4018, 4483-4486
MILLS, S - 4788
MILNE, A J M - 5580
MILNE, K - 4019, 4282
MILNOR, A - 729
MILOTTE, M - 1704, 1705
MILROY, J - 5377, 5381
MILROY, L - 5378-5381
MINISTRY OF AGRICULTURE (NI) - 1941-1943,
         2253
MINISTRY OF COMMERCE (NI) - 1944, 2254-2255
MINISTRY OF DEVELOPMENT (NI) - 1517, 2767-
         2779
MINISTRY OF EDUCATION (NI) - 1518, 2460, 3687,
         4020-4027, 5382
MINISTRY OF HEALTH AND LOCAL GOVERNMENT (NI)
         1519, 2256, 2780-2782, 2931-2932,
         3331-3332
MINISTRY OF HEALTH AND SOCIAL SERVICES (NI)
         1520-1521, 3333-3338, 4487
MINISTRY OF HOME AFFAIRS (NI) - 2783, 3339,
         5109-5111
MINNIS, N - 4028
MINNS, R - 1522, 1945
MITCHEL, N C - 730-731, 2252, 2257-2258, 3340-
         3341
MITCHELL, I - 732
MITCHELL, J K - 733
MITCHELL, R - 734
MITCHELL, V A - 5015, 5112
MITCHELL, W - 4029
MITCHELL, W F - 2785-2786
MOFFETT, J - 3342
MOFFETT, W - 1946
MOGEY, J M - 5383-5387
MOHN, A H - 735
MOHRING, H - 736
MOIR, P - 737
MOLE, S - 3343
MOLES, W - 4030, 4488
MOLONEY, E - 1199-1200, 4789-4790
MONDAY, M - 738
MOODIE, M - 739, 4791
MOODY, T W - 168-171, 5768-5771, (164, 169-
         170, 172, 1617, 1883)
MOONEY, M - 3539
MOORE, B - 1947, 2415
MOORE, E M - 4031
MOORE, J - 1523
MOORE, J - 2259
MOORE, J D - 2260
MOORE, M E - 4032
MOORE, P - 5581
MOORE, R - 740, 4489
MOORE, R - 1948-1951
MOORE, R - 3344
MOORE, T - 1952, 4033, 5582
MOOREHEAD, R A - 3345
MORGAN, A - 741-742, 2461, 5772, (276, 587,
         670, 742, 879, 952, 3560, 4666,
         4898)
MORGAN, R - 1930
MORGAN, V - 3844-3846
MORONEY, M - 2462, 2552, 3566, 4034
MOROWITZ, H J - 5471, 5773, (5471)
MORRELL, R - 5388
MORRIS, D E - 2261
MORRIS, C - 2888, 3133, 4391
MORRIS, J - 3822, 4392
MORRISON, A M - 2262
MORRISON, J - 1958
MORRISSEY, M - 743-744, 1953-1954, 2165, 2463,
         2933, 3014, 3029, 3148, 3346-3349,
         5113, 5638, (2992, 3014, 3061)
MORRISSEY, S - 2463
MORROW, J - 4283
MORTON, P - 3350
MORTON, R - 1955, 2787
MOSKIN, J R - 745
MOSS, J E - 2264-2265
MOSS, R - 556, 746, 4792-4794, 5681, (95, 375,
         1478, 4609)
MOUGHTIN, C - 2788
MOUNT, F - 1201
MOXON-BROWNE, E - 747-752, 4284, 4795-4796
MULCAHY, D C - 5774, (3707, 3999)

MULDREW, T - 3351
MULLEN, L - 1202
MULLEN, M - 753
MULLER VAN ISSEN, G - 2214
MULLIGAN, G - 2412, 5004
MULVENNA, J - 4797, 5114
MULVEY, H - 49-50, 172
MULVIHILL, R F - 754
MUMFORD, D - 1706
MUNCE, J - 2789
MUNCK, R - 755-758, 2465, 2564
MUNRO, H - 759-762
MURDOCK, G - 5230
MURIE, A S - 1313, 1956-1957, 2466, 2790,
         2874-2876, 2915, 2934-2938, 2969,
         3043, 3090-3091, 3352
MURNAGHAN, S - 1707
MURPHY, D - 4490
MURPHY, J A - 173, 763-764, 4285, 4798-4799
MURPHY, M - 765
MURPHY, M - 1524
MURPHY, M - 4035
MURPHY, M J - 5389-5390
MURPHY, P - 385, 690
MURPHY, S - 4598, 4800
MURRAY, D - 2467-2468, 3688-3689, 3822, 4036-
         4037, 4392, 4491-4492
MURRAY, H T - 1203
MURRAY, M - 4564
MURRAY, R - 2682, 2939-2940, 3124, 4038, 4065,
         4353-4354, 4356-4357, 4493-4496,
         4514, 4589-4590, 4668-4673, 4801-
         4802, 4943, 4986-4994
MURRAY, R B - 1930
MURRAY, S - 766
MURRAY, S W - 4286
MUSKETT, A E - 1958
MUSSON, J - 4039
MYANT, C - 1525
MYCO, F - 3353
MYERS, K - 1204, 4803, 5115
MYERS, K - 5623, (5071)

NAIRN, T - 767, 768
NARAIN, J - 3044, 5116
NASH, G C - 2266
NATIONAL ASSOCIATION OF BRITISH MANUFACTURERS
         - 1959
NATIONAL BOARD FOR PRICES AND INCOMES - 2469
NATIONAL BUILDING AGENCY - 51
NATIONAL DEMOCRATIC GROUP - 2941-2942, 4497
NATIONAL INSTITUTE FOR ECONOMIC AND SOCIAL
         RESEARCH - 1960
NATIONAL LABOUR MOVEMENT DELEGATION TO
         IRELAND - 5472
NATIONAL LIBRARY OF IRELAND - 52
NATIONAL OPINION POLLS MARKET RESEARCH LTD -
         769, 3690
NCCL - 5117-5122
NEALON, T - 1526
NEESON, J M - 33
NEESON, W - 2470, 3691
NEILL, D B - 2267
NEILL, D G - 1527-1529, 2791, 2894, 2943,
         3354-3355, 4040-4041
NEILL, G A W - 3356
NEILL, K - 174
NEILSEN, S L - 4498, 4804
NELLIS, J G - 2902
NELLIS, M - 3540, 5123
NELSON, M A - 3692, 5124
NELSON, M G - 3357
NELSON, S - 770-771, 1503, 1530, 4805-4807,
         5827, (3725)
NESBITT, N - 2792
NEUHAUS, R J - 5619
NEVIN, E - 1531, 1961
NEVIN, G B - 3358
NEVIN, N C - 3170, 3328, 3358-3359
NEW OUTLOOK - 772
NEW REVIEW - 773
NEW SOCIETY - 774, 5473
NEW ULSTER POLITICAL RESEARCH GROUP (UDA) -
         775, 1532
NEW YORKER - 1205
NEWARK, F H - 1533-1536, 5104, 5125-5126,
         5775, (1388, 1411, 1528, 1788, 1856)
NEWBOULD, P J - 2793
NEWCASTLE ON TYNE TRADES COUNCIL - 5474

REGIONAL PLANNING AND RESEARCH TEAM - 2027
REID,A - 4128, 4317
REID,J - 2815
REID,M - 3299-3300, 3443, 3662
REID,N - 3547, 4064, 4077, 4513
REID,P - 9
REIDY,M - 4297
REIK,M - 888
REILLY,L - 3405
RESEARCH SERVICES LIMITED - 5593
RESETTLEMENT ASSOCIATION OF NI - 4836
REVIEW COMMITTEE ON HEALTH AND PERSONAL
          SOCIAL SERVICES FOR ELDERLY PEOPLE
          IN NI -
          3406
REVOLUTIONARY COMMUNIST GROUP - 889-890, 1712
REVOLUTIONARY MARXIST GROUP - 891-892
REVOLUTIONARY STRUGGLE - 851, 893-894, 3548
REYNOLDS,A W - 4078
REYNOLDS,F - 2499
RHODES,E - 3664, 3704, 4079, 5797-5801,
          (1393, 1413, 1435, 1466, 1477, 1505,
          1602, 1606, 1762, 2015, 2176, 2291,
          2406, 5258, 5476)
RHODES,J - 1947, 2415
RICE,R - 1237
RICHARDSON,J T - 4297
RIDDELL,P - 895, 5485
RILEY,D W - 2816
RINGLAND,J - 2300
RIPPEY,B - 5513
RISTOW,W - 4837
RITCHIE,J - 5158
RITCHIE,J W K - 3191, 3300, 3443-3444
RITCHIE,K - 3299, 3662
ROBB,J - 896-898, 3407-3408, 4838
ROBERTS,A - 1238, 4839, 4840
ROBERTS,D - 899, 4298
ROBERTS,G A - 1239-1240, 2301-2302
ROBERTS,R - 2500
ROBERTSON,A H - 5159
ROBERTSON,J - 1241
ROBERTSON,N - 2501-2504
ROBINSON,A - 2562, 2628, 2817-2818, 4080-
          4082, 4358, 4519-4520, 5397-5398,
          5594-5595
ROBINSON,D P - 900
ROBINSON,E - 901
ROBINSON,J - 3409, 5453
ROBINSON,J A - 2303
ROBINSON,M - 1596
ROBINSON,P - 1242, 4841-4842, 5160
ROBSON,M - 1781
ROBSON,P - 2028-2033, 2505
ROBSON,W - 5802, (1033)
ROCH,E - 3410, 5399
ROCHE,D J D - 1956-1957, 2034, 2506, 2875-
          2876, 2915, 2937-2938, 2969, 4189-
          4191, 4299
ROCHE,R - 5677, (272)
ROCHE,S - 333-337, 616, 902
ROCK,P - 5803, (5237)
ROCKS,J F - 4083
RODDIE,I - 3411, 4084
RODEN STREET RESIDENTS ASSOCIATION - 2819
RODRIGUES,D - 2304, 5804, (2304)
ROEBUCK,P - 5805, (1895)
ROGERS,P S - 4085
ROGERS,R S - 2820
ROGERS,S - 3412, 3705
ROGERSON,F - 2821
ROLING,B - (4436)
ROLSTON,B - 815-816, 2292, 2507-2509, 2970,
          3413-3421, 4521-4522, 4843, 5161,
          5400, 5693, 5783, (449, 814, 953,
          1627, 2001, 2508, 2979, 3414, 3418,
          4882, 5186)
ROMANOS,M C - 5806
ROONEY,E - 1713
ROONEY,W - 2822
ROSE,C - 3549
ROSE,P - 903-906, 1219, 5786, 5807, (903,
          1219)
ROSE,R - 74, 907-910, 1504, 1597-1600, 2971,
          5759-5808, (694, 1023)
ROSENBLATT,R - 3706
ROSENFIELD,R - 2035, 5401
ROSENHEAD,J - 4556, 4844-4846
ROSENHEIM,A - 911
ROTH,A - 1243

ROUAT,J - 912
ROUND TABLE - 1244
ROWAN,A - 2823
ROWE,A - 5162
ROWLANDS,D - 4086
ROWTHORN,B - 2036, 4847
ROY,A D - 3103, 3496
ROYAL SOCIETY OF ULSTER ARCHITECTS - 2824-
          2825
ROYAL ULSTER CONSTABULARY - 5163
RUDD,J - 2510, 5164
RUDDOCK,A - 75
RULLI,G - 913
RUMPF,E - 914
RUSI - 5809, (4578, 4624, 4645, 4693, 4859,
          4879, 4893, 5194, 5270, 5809)
RUSSELL,G - 1245-1246
RUSSELL,H - 76-80
RUSSELL,J - 915, 2972, 3422, 3616, 3671,
          3707-3709, 3711, 4087, 4523-4528,
          4531
RUSSELL,M F - 3423, 3550
RUTAN,G - 916, 1601
RUTHERFORD,B M - 2826
RUTHERFORD,W - 917
RUTHERFORD,W H - 3327, 3330, 3424-3425, 4786-
          4848
RYAN,E - 918
RYAN,J L - 1602
RYAN,V - 4300

SAATY,T L - 214, 235
SALMON,T C - 4849
SALT,J - 2511
SALTERS,J - 3710, 4088-4089, 4529-4530
SALTERS,M G - 4090, 4301
SAMS,K I - 1811, 2305, 2501-2504, 2512-2514,
          2629
SANDFORD,E - 2037
SANDS,B - 1247, 5165
SANDY ROW DEVELOPMENT ASSOCIATION - 2827
SARGAISON,E - 3426
SAVAGE,K - 1714
SAVORY,D - 183, 684, 919, 1603-1604, 5596
SAYERS,J E - 1248-250, 1605-1606, 1715, 2038,
          2306-2308, 4850, 5258
SCALLY,B G - 3427-3428
SCALLY,J K - 2309
SCARMAN,LORD - 4851
SCHAERF,C - 5661, (1040, 4569)
SCHELLENBERG,J A - 920, 3709, 3711, 4528,
          4531-4853
SCHLESINGER,P - 4854, 5230, 5259-5260, 5810,
          (5260)
SCHMITT,D - 921, 1607-1608, 4532-4535
SCHUTZ,B - 922
SCHWARTZ,M - 1251
SCOPE - 1609-1612, 1716, 2310-2311, 2515-
          2515, 2630, 2828-2830, 2973, 3051-
          3058, 3429-3442, 3712-3719, 4091,
          5166, 5261-5262, 5402
SCORER,C - 5167-5168
SCOTT,D - 81, 301, 922
SCOTT,F E - 923, 4303
SCOTT,H - 5811
SCOTT,M D - 924
SCOTT,M J - 3299-3300, 3443-3444, 3662
SCOTT,O - 4536
SCOTT,R D - 184, 925-927, 1613-1614, 4092
SCOTT,S - 2241, 4855
SCOTT,W - 2039-2040
SCOTT,W M - 2312, 2414
SCULLION,F - 5403
SCULLY,F J M - 5172
SEAMUS COSTELLO MEMORIAL COMMITTEE - 1252
SEE,K O'S - 928-929
SEGALL,M - 5712, (3677)
SERGEANT,H - 5404
SETH,G - 3774
SEYMOUR,ST JOHN D - 5405
SHALLICE,T - 4556, 4837, 4856-4857, 5169
SHANAHAN,P - 3445
SHANN,R - 1253
SHANNON,M O - 82
SHARKIE,B R - 83
SHAW,J - 3446, 4858-4859
SHAW,T - 4093
SHEA,P - 1615

WALSH, F - 876
WALSH, N - 3475, 3730
WALSH, S P - 4897
WARD, C - 4318
WARD, K - 5271
WARD, M - 3560-3561, 4898-4899
WARD, W - 4137
WARDEN, M - 2412, 5004
WARNES, A M - 5835, (3124)
WARREN, J - 1525
WATERMAN, S - 2642
WATKINS, D - 2156
WATSON, A - 1274
WATSON, E - 4138, 4319
WATSON, J W - 5768, (5449)
WATT, D - 1014, 5836, (92, 157, 225, 786, 967,
          1014, 1428, 1443, 1584, 1644, 1917,
          1921, 2569, 2639, 4375, 4620, 4626,
          4798, 4892)
WAUGH, J L - 3731
WAYNE, N - 2547
WEBB, D A - 2614, 4277
WEINREICH, P - 3732, 4550
WEIR, D - 5658, (461)
WEIR, S - 2986
WEIR, T W - 3476
WELLS, R - 692, 4274
WELTGESHEHEN - 1015
WELTON, J - 4139
WEST ULSTER UNIONIST COUNCIL - 1016
WHALE, J - 1017, 1643
WHATMOUGH, R - 2345
WHEELER, M - 1275
WHELAN, M - 87
WHIPPLE, C - 1276
WHITE, B - 1644-1646
WHITE, C - 4551
WHITE, J - 1018
WHITE, J G - 3477
WHITE, T DE VERE - 200
WHITEBREAD, S B - 3343
WHITLOCK, R I - 3478, 4900
WHITTAKER, P - 687, 1697
WHITTINGTON, D - 3160, 3849
WHYTE, D - 3733, 5197
WHYTE, J - 3734, 4134, 4140-4145
WHYTE, J H - 1019-1026, 1648-1651, 1721, 4320,
          4552-4553, 5612
WICKEN, A - 3479
WICKHAM, J - 5746, (2002, 5039, 5161)
WIDGERY, LORD - 4901
WIENER, R - 2855-2858, 2983, 3480-3482, 4902
WIGGINS, R D - 2622
WILCOCK, D N - 2859, 5681, (2651, 2691)
WILCOX, D - 2346
WILES, P - 1652
WILKINSON, C W - 4146
WILKINSON, G M - 4147
WILKINSON, P - 4903-4906, 5837, (4796, 4810,
          4835, 4883)
WILLIAMS, D - 5613
WILLIAMS, T D - 5779, 5838-5839, (150, 838,
          4799)
WILLIAMSON, A - 3483-3485, 4064, 4513, 5687,
          (1645, 2921, 3273, 3485, 3997, 4588,
          5073)
WILLIAMSON, A P - 1027
WILLIAMSON, F - 3486-3487
WILSON REPORT - 2086
WILSON, B - 1703, 1722
WILSON, D - 1028-1029, 2087, 4148-4149
WILSON, E - 2088
WILSON, H - 1030-1031
WILSON, J A - 88, 3068, 3761, 4150-4176, 4554-
          4555
WILSON, J G - 2548
WILSON, R - 1032, 4177, 5614
WILSON, S - 1277
WILSON, T - 1033, 1653-1656, 2038, 2089-2090,
          5840-5841, (1535, 1605, 1653, 1715,
          1885, 1887, 2028, 2185, 5387, 5535)
WILSON, W J - 5198
WILTON, G - 3488-3489
WINBLAD, L - 4907
WINCHESTER, S - 5272-5274
WINDELSHAM, LORD - 1657-1658

WINTOUR, P - 1278
WOMEN AGAINST IMPERIALISM - 3562, 5199
WOMEN AND IRELAND GROUP - 3563
WOMEN IN MEDIA - 3564
WOMEN'S INFORMATION DAY GROUP - 3069
WOODHOUSE, P G - 3953-3954
WOODS, E - 3735, 5275
WOODS, J C H - 2347
WOODVALE AND SHANKILL HOUSING ASSOCIATION -
          2984
WOODWARD, J W O - 201
WOODWARD, V - 2091
WORKERS' ASSOCIATION - 1034-1035, 1723, 2549-
          2550, 5276
WORKERS' PARTY REPUBLICAN CLUBS - 3736
WORKERS' RESEARCH UNIT - 1036-1037, 2551,
          3490, 3565, 4321, 4908, 5200, 5277
WORLD SURVEY - 1038
WORLD TODAY - 4909
WORRALL, S - 4232, 5842
WRIGHT, A - 5726, (3289)
WRIGHT, F - 1039-1040
WRIGHT, J E - 89
WRIGHT, P - 2643
WRIGHT, S - 1041-1043, 4910, 5025
WYLIE, J C - 2904, 2985, 5104, 5126, 5615-5616
WYNCOLL, K - 5726, (3289)

YINGER, J - 4537
YOUNG, J - 5670, (5253)
YOUNG, J R - 2552, 3566
YOUNG, R - 4911, 5201
YOUNG, T - 5202
YOUNG, V - 3683-3684
YOUNGER, C - 202

ZEROULIS, V - 5501
ZUMULINA, L A - 4912

inter-ethnic conflict, 4458
inter-ethnic struggles, 5255
ETHNIC GROUP, 5541
ETHNIC MOVEMENTS, 819; national and, 5692
ETHNIC, -national movements, 929; politics,
        455; -religious conflict, 2571, 4377;
        terrorism, 4632; violence, 4707
ETHNICITY, 1893, 4434, 5784; and nation
        building, 5635
ETHNOCENTRISM, 4370, 4480; Anglo-saxon,
        4441
ETHNOLOGICAL MAPPING, 5333
EUROPEAN COMMUNITY (EEC), 1, 1356, 1734,
        1787, 1820, 2021; policies, 1888;
        see common market
EUROPEAN CONVENTION ON HUMAN RIGHTS, 4782,
        4812, 4870, 5082-5083, 5100, 5139,
        5179
EUROPEAN, integration, 5748; free trade,
        1745; monetary system, 1999;
        Parliament, 5730; unity, 629
EVANGELIZATION, 4313
EVANS, Rae, 2879
EVANS, Estyn, 5819
EWART W AND SON LTD, 2173
EWART-BIGGS MEMORIAL LECTURES, 802
EWE FLOCK PERFORMANCE, 2159, 2226;
        lamb finishing, 2230;
        sheep farms, 2264
EXAMINATION SUCCESS, 4136
EXPENDITURE AND PRICE ELASTICITIES, 1830
EXPORTING, 2135;
        export drive, 1997
EXTERNAL TRADE, 2007
EXTREMISM, 554
EYE INJURIES, 3239

FACTORY WORKERS' HOUSING, 2927
FAECAL BACTERIA, 3400
FAIR EMPLOYMENT, 1571-1572, 4509-4510
FAIR EMPLOYMENT AGENCY (FEA), 1345, 1351,
        1608, 2402, 4394, 4403, 4533
FAIR EMPLOYMENT (NI) ACT (1976), 1510, 4451,
        4464
FAITH HEALING, 3410, 5399
FALLS, Memories, 5279; Road, 1253; /Shankill
        divide, 4349-4350
FAMILY, child in, 5626; doctor, 3380; life,
        5293; name study, 5607; planning, 3202;
        problems, 3231-3232; size, 2583;
        Irish families, 5531;
        north Antrim families, 5291
FAMILY LAW REFORM (NI) ORDER (1977), 5552
FARM(S), enterprise systems, 2171; full-time,
        2400; hill, 2331; holdings, 2297;
        income(s), 1829, 2338; labour force,
        2349; land mobility on, 1819;
        management standards, 2161; pilot
        scheme, 2347; planning, 1908; size,
        2331; small, 2203; structure, 1727;
        types, 2338; see agriculture, farming
FARMING, 1728, 1823, 2202, 2243, 2290;
        communities, 2322; part-time, 2163,
        2264; units, 2192, 2417;
        farmers, 1950-1951;
        farm hand mobility, 1727, 2350;
        see agriculture, farm(s)
FASCISM, 849;
        Fascist Terror, 4575
FATSTOCK AND CARCASE MEAT INDUSTRY, 2251
FAULKNER, Brian, 1051, 1053
FEAR SURVEY SCHEDULE, 3568
FEDERAL IRELAND, 1367; economic implications,
        1815;
        federalism, 1625
FERTILISER USE, 2859
FERTILITY, 2608-2609; behaviour, 2643;
        differentials, 2572, 4378; human, 2624,
        2628; relative, 2635, 4542; of Roman
        Catholics, 2582, 2584
FIANNA FAIL, 1256
FICTION, Ulster, 5329; violence in, 5369
FINANCE ACT (1965), 2050
FINANCIAL SYSTEM OF NI, 1984
FISHERIES, in Lough Neagh Basin, 2258; Lower
        Bann, 2252; salmon and inland, 2271;
        fishing industry, 2199, 2201;
        Lough Neagh fishing community, 2167
FIVE YEAR PLAN FOR ULSTER, 1764

FLAX WORKERS, 3116
FLECK, Billy, 2923
FLOODING, 2667
FLUTE BAND, 5355
FOCUS FOR ACTION, 3791
FOLK MEDICINE, 3410, 5399; see unofficial
        healing
FOLK QUEST, 539
FOLKLORE, Ulster, 5285
FOLKWAYS, 5319, 5332
FOREIGN POLICY, of Irish Coalition Government,
        1158
FOREIGN RELATIONS, Irish, 43
FOREIGN SECTOR, 1918; see capital, investment
FOREST PARKS, 5370
FORESTRY, 1824, 2276, 2296, 2315, 2337;
        afforestation, 2328
FORTNIGHT OPINION POLL, 491-493
FOSTERING, 3127
FREEMAN, Thomas Walter, 19, 5523
FREIGHT, transport, 2277; services, 2274
FRONTLINE REPORT, 5655
FUND-RAISING, 3128
FUNERAL COSTS, 2273
FURTHER EDUCATION, 3517, 3853, 3858, 3963,
        4028, 4158

GAA, 5330
GALLAGHER LTD, 2183
GANDHI, 1222
GARDINER COMMITTEE, 5136; Memorandum to,
        4943
GARDINER REPORT, 5066, 5177
GARRETT'S CRUSADE, 1113
GAS, pipeline, 2284; see electricity, oil and
        gas
GAYS, 3499, 4947; see homosexuals
GENERAL ELECTION, 1555, 1560; (1969), 1631;
        (1970), 1614; of 1973 (NI), 1461;
        (1974), 1634; British, 1613, 5656-5657;
        results, 1340; Westminster (1979), 1593
GENERAL MEDICINE, 3391
GENERAL PRACTICE, 3131, 3145, 3235, 3237,
        3338, 3423, 3550; academic career
        structure in, 3907; pharmacy, 3351;
        undergraduate teaching of, 308
GENERAL STRIKE (1926), 2425
GENERATION GAP, 3608
GENOCIDE, psychological, 3611
GEOGRAPHY, 19, 3961, 5750; at Aberystwyth,
        5645; of development, 1935; economic,
        1922, 2075-2076; forty years of, 5446;
        historical, 10, 5424, 5448; human, 54;
        of human fertility, 2628; industrial,
        1871; of Ireland, 5459, 5523; Irish,
        5524; in Irish education, 3859; in
        Irish universities, 3875; local, 3900;
        manufacturing, 2066; and nationality,
        5461; physical, 5447; and political
        problems, 443; regional, 5428, 5447,
        5486; religious, 4398; of sectarianism,
        4541; of settlement systems, 5698;
        systematic, 5451; systematic and
        regional, 5468; teaching of, 3995; of
        of unemployment, 2395; and voting
        behaviour, 1328, 2567
GEOLOGICAL SURVEY, 5567
GERIATRICS, 3072;
        geriatric hospitals, 3246
GIBSON, (N J), 1804
GLOSSARY, of Ulster terms, 5427
GLUE-SNIFFING, 3297, 3660
GOSSIP, 5372-5373
GOVERNMENT OF IRELAND ACT (1920), 1479, 1490
GOVERNMENT TRAINING CENTRES, 2458, 3322
GRAIN, storing, 2231
GRAMMAR SCHOOLS, 3878, 3880, 3917, 4016, 4032,
        4068, 4078, 4113; girls', 3931; see
        schools
GRAND LODGE OF FREE AND ACCEPTED MASONS OF
        IRELAND, 5589
GRANT-AIDED SCHOOLS, 4090, 4301
GRASS, efficient use of, 2179
GRASS ROOTS LEADERS, 5528

GREATER WEST BELFAST COMMUNITY ASSOCIATION, 3452
GRIFFITHS, Hwyel, 3435
GROUP, formation, 572, 1861; identification, 4548; techniques, 5501, 5527; understanding, 5575
GROWTH CENTRES, 1757, 2668
GUIDANCE SCHEME, 3752
GYNAECOLOGICAL ILLNESS, 3423, 3550

H-BLOCK, 1112, 1245, 1251, 2539, 4991, 5047, 5115, 5140, 5151, 5160; conveyor belt, 4863, 5173
HALL REPORT, 1855
HANDICAPPED, 3433; children, 3101, 3108, 3252, 3298, 3396, 3921, 3959; persons, 3141, 3374; handicap, 3456, 3721, 4109; see mentally handicapped, subnormality
HARLAND AND WOLFF, 31, 2111; see shipbuilding
HARMLESS BULLET, 4856; see "less lethal" weapons, plastic/rubber bullet(s)
HARRIS MARRIAN AND CO LTD, 2168
HEALING, unofficial, 5301
HEALTH CENTRES, 3130, 3342
HEALTH EDUCATION, 2458, 3311-3320, 3322, 3978-3983, 3985, 3988-3989
HEARING-IMPAIRED PUPILS, 4156
HECHTER, Michael, 833, 2012
HERITAGE, 5787; of Ireland, 5307; Irish, 5320; Northern, 5324
HETEROSEXUALS, 3543
HIGH SCHOOLS, 4016; see school(s)
HIGHER DEGREES, 24
HIGHER EDUCATION, 3992, 4064, 4077, 4513; future of (Chilver Report), 3790; future structure, 3826; in NI (Lockwood Report), 3932; women in, 3547
HIGHTOWN RULES, 3642
HIGHWAY CONSTRUCTION PROBLEMS, 5567
HIRSCHMAN, 5358
HISTORIOGRAPHY, 151-152, 170, 181, 184, 5753, 5769
HOLYWELL PSYCHIATRIC HOSPITAL, 3177
HOME HELP, Service, 3221
HOME RULE, 290, 393; in NI, 1641; Ulster, 5841
HOME-SCHOOL, contacts, 3797; links, 3827; Links Project, 4139; liaison, 3976
HOMELESSNESS, 2906
HOMICIDE, 5145
HOMOSEXUALS, 3543; see gays
HOODED MEN, 4671
HORSE, disappearance of, 2182
HORTICULTURE, 2150, 2283
HOSPITAL(S), 3255; activity analysis, 3171-3172; district general, 3282; management committees, 1520, 3383; pharmacies, 3387; Plan for NI, 3334, 3337; service(s), 3354, 3379; see Day Hospital, mental hospitals
HOUSE OF COMMONS, (British), 1408; of NI, 1423, 1648, 1721
HOUSEBUILDING, conventional, 2897; productivity, 2899
HOUSEWORK, 5694
HOUSING ACTION AREA(S), progress, Report, 2870, 2886, 2905, 2978
HOUSING ALLOCATIONS INQUIRY, 2932
HOUSING COSTS INQUIRY, 2931
HOUSING MANAGEMENT, training, 2929
HUMAN CURRICULUM, 3804; see curriculum
HUMAN RIGHTS, 4653, 4760, 4948, 4974, 5040, 5079, 5096, 5135, 5138, 5159; abrogation of domestic, 5071; see European Convetion on
HUMAN SEXUALITY, 5689
HUME, John, 1145, 2157
HUNGER STRIKE, 1093, 1117, 1150, 1188, 1191, 4905; hunger strikers, 1092
HUNT (REPORT), 4925, 5019
HYDEBANK, 3648, 5062
HYSTERECTOMY, 3649, 3556

IDB, 2135

IDEOLOGY, 424, 3090, 5510, 5686; of containment, 816; of control, 2451, 3668; Protestant, 770, 1039; social, 5586; and the state, 2000
ILL TREATMENT, 4914, 5076; see torture
IMMIGRATION, 2594
IMPERIALISM, 281, 686, 689, 703, 951; British, 252, 442, 670, 690, 876, 890, 892, 953; social, 687, 1697; anti-imperialist struggle, 466; Anti-imperialists' Guide, 614 imperial relations, 702; workers against, 1698
IMPRISONMENT, politics of, 5030-5031
INCITEMENT, 5202; see anti-incitement legislation
INCOME, 1832; civilian, 1805; distribution, 2063
INDEPENDENCE, economic and feasibility study of, 2080; (Irish), 320, 5739; of NI, 229, 1289; Ulster, 1628; what price?, 1553; independent NI, 1654, 2090; independent Ulster, 1628
INDUSTRIAL, accidents, 2070, 2532; change, 1751, 2068, 2787; city, 5631; dispersal, 1926-1927; diversification, 2033; Handbook, 2083; incentives, 1962, 2021; key centre policy, 2027; linkages, 1872; movement, 1904, 1956; policy, 1876, 1947; specialisation, 1919; strategy, 2083; tribunals, 2356; inter-industry linkages, 2065
INDUSTRIAL DEVELOPMENT, 1752, 1755, 1910, 1964, 1973, 1995, 2030, 2074; facilities, 1965; policy, 1986, 2046
INDUSTRIAL LOCATION, 1900; political imagery of, 1875; locational advantage (of industry), 1904
INDUSTRIAL RELATIONS, 2426, 2438, 2472-2473, 2545, 5792-5793; law, 2519; legislation, 2499; management, 2404; reforms, 2501
INDUSTRIAL RELATIONS (NI) ORDERS (1976), 2355
INDUSTRIAL TRAINING ACT (1964), 2421
INDUSTRIAL TRAINING BOARD, 2537
INEQUALITY, 40, 2580, 4511, 5746; legislative, 3526; regional, 1866
INFANT SCHOOL, 4141
INFANTICIDE, 3265, 3653
INFLATION, of house prices, 2902
INFORMATION, development, 5518
INFORMERS, 4864
INJURIES, of civil disorder, 4848; rubber bullets, 4787; of terrorist bombing, 4786; see harmless bullet, "less lethal" weapons, missile injuries, plastic/rubber bullets
INLA, 4596
INN OF COURT (NI), 5158
INNOVATION(S), 867, 1992; diffusion, 5570; in school(s), 3904, 3946-3947
INPUT-OUTPUT MODEL, of NI economy, 1946
INSTITUTE FOR CONTINUING EDUCATION, 3751
INTEGRATED EDUCATION, 3757, 3811-3812, 4009, 4012, 4030, 4088, 4338, 4381-4382, 4473, 4475, 4488, 4529; see non-sectarian education
INTEGRATED SCHOOL PUPILS, 3871, 4411; integrated schooling, 4087, 4523
INTEGRATION, 4089, 4530, 5364; and Division, 2570, 2376, 5643; northern schools and, 3956, 4456; religious, 4153, 4554
INTELLECTUALS, 5586
INTELLIGENCE, 4612; distribution, 3861; social ecology of, 5563
INTENSIVE-CARE UNIT, 3398
INTER-COMMUNITY BALANCE, 4352
INTER-GROUP CONFLICT, 4366, 4498, 4804; inter-group differences, 4467; inter-group relations, 4406, 4549
INTERDEPENDENCE, 953
INTERIM-ALTERNATIVE-REVISED TRANSFER SYSTEM, 3764
INTERMEDIATE TREATMENT, 3692, 5124
INTERNAL COLONIALISM, 574, 1863; internal colonial thesis, 833, 2012
INTERNAL SECURITY, 5735; operations, 4652, 4720
INTERNATIONAL DIVISION OF LABOUR, 2019-2020
INTERNEES' FAMILIES, 1233

LOW INTENSITY OPERATIONS, 4745
LOW PAY, 5638
LOYALIST(S), 4807; opposition, 1626; strike,
        4775; Ulster, 421; verse texts, 5286;
        violence, 4860; loyalism, 870; see
        Ulster Workers' Council (UWC) Strike
LOYALTY, cultural aspects, 5358-5359
LUNG CANCER, 3137
LYNCH, (Jack), 1057, 1142

MAGEE (UNIVERSITY COLLEGE), 3902, 4047
MAGISTRATES COURTS, domestic proceedings in,
        3521, 4982; see courts
MALADJUSTED SCHOOLCHILDREN, 3097, 3579
MAN-MADE FIBRES, 2189
MANAGEMENT, 1739; availability, 1977;
        centre, 2285; needs, 1740; of NI
        industry, 1741; of schools, 3830;
        see industrial relations
MANPOWER, 2407; policy, 2392; scheduling
        projects, 2486
MANSERGH, 92
MANUAL INSTRUCTION, 3843
MANUFACTURING INDUSTRY, 2055, 2075-2077;
        attraction of, 1957; foreign
        participation in, 1845; stock of
        capital in, 1889;
        manufacturing mix, 2067
MAPPING TASKS, 5604
MARGINAL LABOUR FORCE, 2432, 2602
MARITAL, expectations, 3532; problems, 3423,
        3554
MARRIAGE(S), 2608; breakdown, 2260, 3647,
        5061, 5747; and mental handicap, 3427;
        mixed, 4466; violence in, 3231
MASON, Roy, 5042
MATER INFIRMORUM HOSPITAL, 3118
MATERNAL DEATHS, 3203, 3524
MATHEMATICS, 3898, 4066, 4085, 4159;
        mathematical models, 3913
MARXISM, 631, 758, 874;
        Marxist interpretations, 688
THE MAZE, 1044, 1047, 4970, 5028; see
        detention, internment, Long Kesh
MCALOONE, Paul, 3114
MACBRIDE, SEAN, 1254
MCCRACKEN, J L, 5805
MCCARRITY PAPERS, 4638
MCLACHLAN, Peter, 3437
MCMILLAN, Liam, 1256
MACNEILL, Eoin, 1120, 5761
MCQUADE, John, 1213
MACRORY REPORT, 1482
MEDICAL, ethics, 1093; manpower, 3194; record
        linkage, 2615, 3309; school, 3411, 4084;
        students, 2557, 3082, 3236
MEDICINE, 3162
MEDIUM TERM FORECAST OF NI ECONOMY, 1892
MELCHETT, Lord, 3436
MEMOIRS OF A REVOLUTIONARY (MACSTIOFAIN), 4766
MENS REA OF MURDER, 5048
MENTAL HEALTH, 3272, 3476
MENTAL HEALTH ACT (NI) (1961), 3254
MENTAL HOSPITALS, 3246; see hospitals
MENTALLY HANDICAPPED, 3144, 3251, 5689;
        mental defect, 3217;
        mental handicap, 3134-3135, 3167;
        mentally ill, 3483;
        mentally retarded individuals, 3117;
        see handicapped, subnormality
METAGAME, analysis 210; theory, 213
METHODISM, 2577, 4208; Irish, 4260
METHODIST CHURCH, 4205
METHODIST COLLEGE BELFAST, 3950
MICROCOUNSELLING, 3147, 3833; see counselling
MICROTEACHING, 3219, 3874, 3897; see teaching
MIDWIFE, 3159
MIGRATION, 54, 2593, 2596, 2599, 2611-2612,
        2963; intra-urban, 2625;
        migrants in Belfast, 2610
MILITARY INTERVENTION, legal basis of, 5016
MILITARY OPERATIONS, legal control of, 4690
MILK, 2261; and fresh cream industry, 2303;
        industry, 2108, 2200, 2235; marketing,
        2094; products, 2261
MILLING, 2312

MINIMUM SENTENCES ACT, 4936
MINING, 2250, 2320, 5767; quarrying and
        derelict land, 2344
MINISTRY OF DEVELOPMENT, 2826
MISREPORTING, 5248; Ulster, 5227
        Media Misreport NI, 5277; see news
MISSILE INJURIES, 3110, 3478, 4600, 4900; see
        harmless bullet, injuries, "less lethal"
        weapons, plastic/rubber bullets
MODERATE OPINION LEADERS, 522
MONGOLISM, 3166, 3195
MONOGLOTTISM, 5281
MORAL EDUCATION PROJECT, 3934
MORAL JUDGMENT, 5556
MORBIDITY, 3247; trends, 2424, 3248
MORTALITY, early, 3164; infant, 3329, 3450,
        3686, 3721; occupational, 3399
MOTOR-MAKING, 2259
MOUNTBATTEN, Earl, 1115
MULTICULTURAL SOCIETIES, 580
MULTINATIONAL STATE, 1860
MULTIPLE SCLEROSIS, 3079-3080
MULTIPLIERS, estimation of, 1891;
        internal multiplier of an industrial
        complex (linen), 2323
MUNICIPAL HISTORY, 44
MUSHROOMS, growing, 2128; marketing, 2126;
        prices, 2130; production, 2127
MUSIC, traditional, 5337
MYOCARDIAL INFRACTION, 3398, 3471

NATIONAL ASSOCIATION FOR IRISH FREEDOM, 1203
NATIONAL DEMOCRATIC PARTY, 1701
NATIONAL DEVELOPMENT, 5476
NATIONAL HEALTH SERVICE (NHS), 3384, 3388
NATIONAL INCOME(S), 1781
NATIONAL INSURANCE RECORDS, 3247
NATIONAL INTEGRATION, 577, 1866
NATIONAL LABOUR MOVEMENT, Delegation Report,
        5472
NATIONAL PARKS, 2694
NATIONAL OPINION POLLS, 259, 681
NATIONAL TERRITORIES, 1342
NATIONALISM, 276, 377, 385, 439, 619, 669,
        720, 763, 801, 831, 914, 991, 2009,
        2380, 2382, 5757, 5763; in Anglo-Irish
        poetry, 5366; Catholic, 1415, 4427;
        celtic, 819, 5696; ethnic, 928; Irish,
        119, 148, 162-163, 442, 595, 810, 829,
        876-877, 892, 974; Irish Presbyterianism
        and, 4253; minority, 1700; new, 1384;
        Northern, 638; peripheral, 830;
        revolutionary, 5236; UK, 694; Ulster,
        278; women and, 3511;
        neo-nationalism, 767
NATIONALIST GOVERNMENT, 1418
NATIONALITY, 141
NATIVES, 922
NEAVE, Airey, 983, 4596
NEO-NATAL, care, 3300; death, 3299, 3443, 3662
NEO PENTECOSTALISM, 4297
NERVOUS-SYSTEM MALFORMATIONS, 3161
NEURAL TUBE DEFECTS, 3359
NEUROTICISM, 3567, 4328
NEUTRALITY, 131
NEW CITY, 2653; Craigavon, 2708-2710, 2723;
        survey, 2706
NEW TOWN(S), 2648, 2680, 2694, 2748, 2815;
        Antrim, 2765, 2767; centre, 2649;
        Craigavon, 2838
NEW UNIVERSITY OF ULSTER (NUU), 3874
NEW YORK TIMES, 4822, 5257
NEWS, and current affairs (BBC), 5205; as a
        field dressing, 5227; law-and-order,
        5218; manufacture of, 5670; see
        misreporting
NIASL, 5128
NI COMMUNITY RELATIONS COMMISSION (NICRC),
        1404-1405, 3100, 3208-3209, 3223-3224,
        3413, 3418, 4421-4422
NI CIVIL RIGHTS MOVEMENT, 923, 1265; see civil
        rights, NICRA
NI CIVIL SERVICE, 1309, 1363
NI COUNCIL FOR EDUCATIONAL RESEARCH (NICER),
        3972, 4157
NI COUNCIL FOR NURSES AND MIDWIVES, 3364
NICRA, 5134, 5136; see civil rights, NI Civil
        Rights Movement

SEGREGATION, 2605-2606, 2940, 4440, 4496;
        politics of, 2979; religious, 3923,
        4004, 4357, 4444, 4470; religious
        residential, 4517-4518; of Roman
        Catholics, 4439; in West Belfast,
        4347; urban social, 5790;
        segregating and mixing, 4346;
        segregational ecology, 4443
SELECTIVE EMPLOYMENT TAX, 2143
SELF GOVERNMENT, 199
SELF-HELP, 2222, 3190; projects, 1902, 2087;
        skills, 3962
SENATE OF NI, 1361, 1423, 1513
SEPARATISM, 416
SETTLERS, 922
SEX, 2507, 4521; education, 3463, 4113
SEX DISCRIMINATION LAW, 3514
SEX DISCRIMINATION (NI) ORDER (1976), 3507
SHANKILL DISTURBANCES, 4884
SHELTER (NI), 2890
SHELTERED TENANTS SURVEY, 2928
SHIFT AND SHARE ANALYSIS, 2067
SHIPBUILDING, 2138, 2308, 2316, 2324;
        redundancy, 2305, 2514;
        shipyards, 2306-2307; see Harland
        and Wolff
SHORTS, 2314
SICK, children, 3475, 3730; chronic, 3377,
        3700
SICKNESS BENEFIT COSTS, 3335
SINGLE-PARENT FAMILIES, 3519; see family,
        one-parent families
SINGLE TRANSFERABLE VOTE (STV), 1445, 1447
SINN FEIN, 1677, 1682, 1696, 1718
SIROCCO, 2224
SIXTH-FORM, experiment, 3800; religion, 3887,
        4244-4245
SMALL CLAIMS, 5012, 5014
SMALL FIRMS, 1945; risk capital for, 1522;
        small business, 1744, 2661;
        small manufacturing business, 1742
SMOKING SURVEYS, 3402
SMUGGLING, 2121; cattle, 2208
SMYTH, Douglas, 3434
SOCIAL, accounts, 1781, 2091; areas, 5728;
        cleavages, 1338; control, 5415, 5803;
        indicators, 1504, 4000, 4467;
        movements, 1770; need, 3175;
        organisation, 5357, 5668; pressure,
        5556; priority schools, 3829;
        problems, 59, 367, 3098-3099, 5415,
        5658, 5729; provision, 3175, 3325,
        3520, 3672; research, 5450; sciences,
        58; security, 2327; service
        reorganisation, 1392; space, 2677-
        2679; trends, 2578
SOCIAL ANTHROPOLOGICAL HERITAGE, 5289
SOCIAL DEMOCRATIC AND LABOUR PARTY (SDLP),
        1670, 1689, 1699, 1702, 1714, 1723;
        social democrats, 990
SOCIAL ENTERTAINMENT, Working Party Report,
        5314
SOCIAL HISTORY, 114, 140; economic and, 5516;
        see economic history
SOCIAL MOBILITY, 2619; see occupational
SOCIAL POLICY(IES), 1716, 3090-3091, 3148,
        3325, 3348, 3672, 5113, 5651; and the
        political parties, 3439
SOCIAL RELATIONS, 4420, 5303, 5372;
        ideological, 4362;
        social relationships, 5373
SOCIAL SKILL(S), 3084, 3750; training, 3160,
        3466, 3849, 4115
SOCIAL STUDIES, 4082; Reader, 5473
SOCIAL WORK, 3083-3084, 3188, 3193, 3242-
        3243, 3283, 3342, 3421, 3453, 3750,
        5056, 5627, 5789;
        social workers, 3226, 3473; see CQSW
SOCIALISM, 276, 302, 543, 587, 619, 742, 879,
        914, 970
SOCIALIST, analysis, 354; Republic, 941;
        socialists, 469
SOCIETAL DISINTEGRATION, 584
SOCIOBIOLOGY, 669
SOCIO-ECONOMIC, change, 1859; studies, 55
SOCIOLINGUISTIC, patterns, 5831; study, 5318

SOCIOLOGICAL, analysis, 4252; Association of
        Ireland, 5815-5818; theory, 920;
        Yearbook, 5734
SOCIOLOGY, 5415; of education, 56; of
        journalism and the press, 5665;
        political, 4275, 4674; rural, 54;
        teaching of, 4028; urban, 54
SOCIO-RELIGIOUS RESEARCH, 4318
SPATIAL, equity, 1849; planning, 2006; units,
        1343, 2568
SPECIAL EDUCATION, 3948, 4015; treatment,
        3743
SPECIAL POWERS, 4949, 4977, 5133; Act, 4966,
        5085, 5122
SPIES, 5601
SPINA-BIFIDA, 3163, 3170
SPRINGFIELD RIOT REPORT, 4598
ST. AUGUSTINE'S BOYS, 3837
STABILITY-ANALYSIS, 214
STAGFLATION, 1860
STANDING ADVISORY COMMITTEE ON HUMAN RIGHTS,
        5089
STATE OF EMERGENCY, 1465; see emergency
STATE INDUSTRY, 1983
STATISTICAL AND SOCIAL INQUIRY SOCIETY OF
        IRELAND, 5639
STATISTICAL SOURCES, housing in NI, 2901
STEREOTYPES, 4481, 4505-4506; cultural, 5350;
        of Irish students, 4474;
        stereotypic first names, 3585, 4367;
        stereotyping, 5249
STEWART, (A T Q), 786
STIRLING WORKSHOP, 5495, 5501
STORMONT, 282, 812, 1163, 1352, 1403, 1853,
        4395; post-war debate at, 1412; reform
        of, 1552, 1650; Westminster relations,
        1505; Westminster relationships, 1312;
        Working at, 1568
STREET SONGS, 5394
STRIKE(S), political general, 4770; see
        Ulster Workers' Council (UWC)
STUDENTS, New University of Ulster, 3874;
        performance of, 3770; QUB, 2595, 3220
SUBNORMALITY, intellectual, 3217; mental,
        3071, 3284-3285, 3307;
        educationally sub-normal children, 3321;
        high grade sub-normals, 3306;
        subnormal(s), 3286-3287, 3308, 3962;
        subnormal children, 3994; see
        handicapped, mentally handicapped
SUBVERSION, 4692, 4745
SUICIDE, 1049; attempted, 3270, 3282, 3389-
        3390;
        suicidal behaviour, 3268
SUMMARY TRIALS, 5009; see trials
SUNNINGDALE, 242, 1295, 1444, 1462; and the
        law, 1489, 5090; strategy, 1590
SUPREME COURT (OF NI), 5070
SURVEILLANCE, 4610
SUSPENDED SENTENCE, 5148
SYMBOLIC INTERACTIONISM, 5328

TEACHER(S), 3320; attitudes, 3311, 3978;
        centres, 3840; communication style,
        3773; Curriculum Project, 3905;
        dogmatism, 4001; education, 3899;
        expectations, 3952; innovativeness,
        3968; non-graduate student, 3772;
        participation in school decision
        making, 3970; perceptions of students,
        3858; practices, 4125; probationary,
        3767; recruitment, 4048; and
        religious education, 3888, 4246; and
        research, 4052; shortage/surplus, 3860;
        of Sociology, 4028; student, 3844-3845;
        supply of, 3740; training, 3873, 4039,
        4048, 4117; training colleges, 3836;
        unions, 2462, 4034
TEACHING, 4092; and assessment of science,
        4147; controversial issues, 4002; of
        Economics (A-Level), 3960; of English,
        3795; of Geography, 3995; of History,
        4059; of Irish history, 3942-3943, 4019;
        mathematics, 4085; post-primary science,
        3986; primary school history, 4094;
        reading, 4126; recruits to, 3846;
        religion, 3891, 4248, 5718; of science,
        3920; of senior certificate history,
        4068; structured, 3962; see
        microteaching

TECHNICAL COLLEGES, 3870
TECHNICAL CHANGE, in NI manufacturing, 1846,
        1924-1925
TECHNOLOGY, advanced, 1975; advancing, 2010;
        of political control, 4556; of
        repression, 4593; of riot control, 4846;
        technological change, 2225
TELECOMMUNICATIONS INDUSTRY, 2225, 2444
TELEVISION (TV), 3447, 3587, 5213; coverage,
        5234, 5265; mobilisation of volunteers
        via, 5263; Northern Irish news in, 5226;
        and politics, 5252; state and
        "terrorism" on, 5230; viewing, 3735;
        patterns of leisure viewing, 5275;
        how TV tips the balance, 5239;
        Ulster: a Switch Off, 5241
TENANT(S), action, 5726; Report on
        Unsatisfactory, 2893
TERRITORIALITY, 2561; and class, 4348; on the
        Shankill/Falls divide, 4349-4350
TERRITORIALS, 5538
THATCHER('S), 590, 1142, 1199; Britain, 653;
        initiative, 1143; Irish policy, 1103
THEATRE, 5290, 5352-5353, 5401; subsidised,
        5367
THEOLOGY, 5749
THYROTONICOSIS, 3216
TIME-SERIES ANALYSIS, 1401-1403
TINKERS, 5541; and travellers, 5542; see
        itinerants
TODD, James Eadie, 5678
TORTURE, 4671, 4812, 4870, 4915-4916, 5076,
        5139, 5179; British, 4837;
        secret torturers, 5041; see ill
        treatment
TORIES, 816, 1017; Ulster, 1193;
        Tory cuts, 544
TOTAL INTEGRATION OPTION, 1394, 1833
TOURISM, 2280, 2793;
        tourist industry, 2193, 2355
TOWN AND COUNTRY PLANNING, 1519
TRADE DISPUTES, 2452, 5099; Act, 2348, 2428
TRADE OF NI (1922-1939), 1922
TRADE UNION(S), 2456, 2463, 2509, 2513, 2551;
        beginnings, 2371; centre, 2494; and H-
        Block, 5187; Irish, 377, 2374, 2380,
        2447, 2449-2450, 2520; legal controls
        over, 2481; officials, 2503;
        organisation, 2448, 2500; unity, 2446,
        2495;
        role of union officer, 2504
TRADE UNION MOVEMENT, 2368; Irish, 2482;
        TUC, 2523
TRADE UNION CAMPAIGN AGAINST REPRESSION
        (TUCAR), 1074
TRADE UNIONISM, clerical, 2457; in Ireland,
        2387; limits of, 2508; Ulster, 2549-
        2550;
        trade unionists, 450, 2398
TRADITION(S), 5299; cultural, 5311
TRAINING, 2414, 2420, 2479, 3770, 3962; of
        girls, 2399, 3512; industrial, 2353,
        2421; labour, 2360; school(s), 3663,
        3733, 5050, 5097, 5197; of women, 2419,
        3525; see Youth Training Programme
TRANSFER AT 14, 4003
TRANSNATIONALISM, 1432
TRANSPORT, 2704, 2730, 2734, 2743, 5778;
        policy, 2810; public, 2799; Report of
        Tribunal, 2800;
        transportation, 2701, 2754, 2825
TRANSSEXUALISM, 3544
TRAUMATIC ONSET DISABILITY, 3193
TREATY (1921 ANGLO-IRISH), 118, 837, 1380,
        1390, 1651; negotiations, 838
TRIALS, Ulster, 5023; see summary trials
TRICOLOUR, 371
"TROOPS OUT", 546, 5022
TRUANCY, 3957-3958
TUBERCULOSIS (TB), 3085, 3121, 3140, 3165,
        3326, 3405
TURF WORKING, 2110; see peat
TUZO, General, 4649
TWO NATIONS, 286, 311, 734, 1034; theory, 220
TWOMEY, Seamus, 4705
TYPHUS FEVER, 3356
TYRIE, Andy, 1110

UAOS LTD, 2210; see cooperatives
UDA, 4847
ULSTER BANK, 2213; see banks/banking
ULSTER COLLEGE, 4115
ULSTER DEFENCE REGIMENT (UDR), 4618; violence,
        4860
ULSTER HOSPITAL, Story of (1873-1973), 3292;
        see hospitals
ULSTER MEDICAL SOCIETY, 3458
ULSTER MUSEUM, 5529
ULSTER WOMEN'S UNIONIST COUNCIL (1911-1974),
        1694, 3531
ULSTER UNIONIST ASSOCIATION, 448
ULSTER VOLUNTEER FORCE (UVF), 4584
ULSTER WORKERS' COUNCIL (UWC) STRIKE, 4588,
        4677, 4832, 4888; see loyalist(s)
UNDEREMPLOYMENT, structural, 2400
UNDER-FIVES, 3439, 3716
UNEMPLOYED, boys, 2370; cohort survey of,
        2390; population, 2397; rural, 2420;
        young, 2515, 3714
UNEMPLOYMENT, 1768, 1880, 2352, 2360, 2367,
        2429, 2434, 2442, 2478, 2518, 2521,
        2547, 3248, 3581, 5675; in
        Andersonstown, 2351; denomination and,
        2488, 4507; differential, 2384, 4374;
        distribution, 2511; geography of, 2394;
        patterns, 2396, 2476; problem, 2505;
        recommendations, 2378; religion and,
        2459, 4486; report, 2540; social and
        industrial effects of, 2369; spatial
        aspects, 2466; and wages, 2409-2410;
        among young males, 2534, 3723; and
        young offenders, 5004; and young people,
        2375; youth, 2451, 2479, 3668, 3701;
        young people without work, 2526;
        see offenders
UNEVEN DEVELOPMENT, 2009
UNITY/UNITED IRELAND/UNIFICATION OF IRELAND,
        215, 292, 453, 541, 629, 668, 674, 710,
        753, 836, 918, 964, 1071, 1588, 5564;
        the Republic and the Church of Ireland,
        4309;
        attitudes to reunion, 358;
        reunification, 441
UNIONISM, 847, 1007; Irish, 107-109, 275;
        Ulster, 134, 279, 535, 719, 876, 1248,
        1929, 5419-5420
UNIONIST PARTY, 1673, 1675; Ulster (1882-
        1973), 1687
UNIONIST REGIME (1921-1968), 1647;
        unionist rule, 1250, 1601
UNION JACK, 371
UNITARY STATES, 1389
UNITED NATIONS (UN), 1076, 1125, 1127
UNIVERSITY(IES), 13, 3448, 4076, 4092, 4097;
        courses, 3772; Irish, 3875; at
        Londonderry, 3933; students, 3955, 5562,
        5577-5579; Ulster's new, 4117; see
        students
UNOFFICIAL HEALING, 5301; see folk medicine
URBAN RENEWAL, 2684
US NETWORK NEWS COVERAGE, 5271

VAIZEY, J, 4798
VANDALISM, 2863, 3707; and discipline, 3748;
        and indiscipline, 4168, 5776
VANGUARD, Ulster, 1075
VATICAN COUNCIL (SECOND), 4206
VENEREAL DISEASE, 3319, 3988
VERNACULAR, urban, 5381
VILLAGE STRUCTURE, 2740
VIOLENCE AND CIVIL DISTURBANCE IN NI
        (SCARMAN), 4851
VOCATIONAL, adjustment, 3606; aspirations,
        2467, 3688; education, 3967; guidance,
        2471, 3865, 3867, 3967
VOLUNTARY, associations, 3375; organisations,
        3409, 3440, 3516, 5453; schools, 3778,
        4023
VOTERS, and non-voters, 1499;
        voter preferences, 1369
VOTING BEHAVIOUR, 1364, 1577, 1579, 2567; and
        voting patterns, 1577

WAGE(S), 1832, 5694; patterns, 2440
WAR (SECOND WORLD), 70, 100, 112, 131, 150,
       5596
WATER, 2813; pollution control, 5543; quality,
       5513; resource management, 2346; and
       society, 1786; supply, 1399, 2666; use,
       1784
WEALTH, 1832, 3490; personal, 1793, 1911
WEATHERMEN, 4682
WELFARE SERVICES ACT (NI) (1949), 3154, 3605
WESTLINK, 2830; pensioners' dwellings, 2862
WHISKEY, 2240
WHITE, 795
WHITEFIELD EXPERIMENT, 5064
WHITEHALL, 1651
WHITELAW('S), 4649; tribunals, 4994
WIDGERY, Lord, challenge to, 4968; tribunal,
       4901, 5105
WILLIAMS, Betty, 1087
WILSON REPORT, 1761, 1780
WITCHCRAFT AND DEMONOLOGY, 5405
WIVES, 3545; violence against, 3494, 4935
WOLFE TONE, 5677
WOLFF, Congressman, 1271
WOMANPOWER, 2542-2543, 3559
WOMEN'S AID, 3538
WOMEN'S LIBERATION, 3492, 3538
       women's movement, 3549
WORD-DEFINITION, categories of, 4154
WORK EXPERIENCE PROGRAMME, 2418, 3628
WORKER PARTICIPATION, 2111, 2377, 2531
WORKERS', Party, 1713; Republic, 1704;
       rights, 2547; unity, 543
WORKING CLASS, and adult education, 3262,
       3937; analysis, 1425; in Belfast, 741,
       2461; Catholic, 3190; community, 4148,
       5378; divided, 756, 2465; Irish, 462;
       loyalist, 385; Protestant, 261, 771,
       1673; solution, 1035; suburb, 3532;
       viewpoint, 1665
WORLD CONGRESS OF PEACE FORCES, 1255
WORLD HEALTH ORGANISATION, 3444
WRITING, the course of, 5345; some notes on,
       5347

X-VOTING, 1537

YOUNG FARMERS' CLUBS,   , 5499
YOUTH CLUB MEMBERSHIP, 3731
YOUTH EMPLOYMENT SERVICE, 3644
YOUTH SERVICE, 3442, 3687; Directory, 5736
YOUTH TRAINING PROGRAMME, 2401, 3607; see
       training
YOUTH UNEMPLOYMENT SERVICE, 2433

RATHCOOLE (BELFAST), 2711
RATHLIN ISLAND, 2191, 2589, 5503, 5515
RAVENHILL ROAD (BELFAST), 1202
REPUBLIC OF IRELAND (IRISH REPUBLIC), 154,
        215, 397, 762, 1258, 1358, 1431, 1775,
        1781, 1878, 1907, 1919, 2004, 2042,
        2121, 2205, 2432, 2481, 2517, 2593,
        2606, 2631, 3464, 4309; see Eire
RHODESIA, 922
RIVER LAGAN, 2722, 2749, 3400
RODEN STREET, 2819
ROME, 948

SANDY ROW (BELFAST), 1048, 2766, 2827
SCOTLAND, 69, 457, 503, 1308, 1903, 2623,
        3587, 3641, 3992, 5051, 5213, 5449,
        5522, 5649
SHANKILL (BELFAST), 2663, 2684, 2857-2858,
        3482, 3580, 4349-4350, 4884, 5545,
        5560
SHORT STRAND (BELFAST), 1204
SLIEVE GALLION (CO. DERRY), 5389
SOUTH AFRICA, 348, 438, 4592
SOUTH BELFAST, 2698
SOUTH TYROL, 207
SPERRIN MOUNTAINS, 2139
SPRINGFIELD (BELFAST), 4598; Springfield Road,
        4800
STIRLING (SCOTLAND), 5495, 5501
STRABANE, 2407, 2467-2468, 3688-3689
STRANGFORD LOUGH, 2119, 2289
STRANMILLIS (BELFAST), 2749
STRASBOURG, 4942

TULLYWEST (CO. DOWN), 4755
TWINBROOK (BELFAST), 2924
TYRONE, 2242-2243, 2744, 3356, 5390; East
        Tyrone, 2238, 2717; West Tyrone, 2778-
        2779

UGANDA, 2062, 2481
UNITED STATES (USA), 90, 459, 1509, 1607,
        3176, 4441, 4532, 4831, 5271-5272; see
        America

WALES, 69, 1308, 1903, 2130, 2623, 2917, 2936,
        3229, 5522
WATERSIDE (DERRY), 3253
WEST BELFAST, 2487, 2918, 3385, 3452, 3600,
        3736, 3745, 3976, 4347, 4590, 4964
WEST ULSTER, 2175, 2291, 2406, 5801
WESTERN EUROPE, 5407
WHITEHALL, 1651